W9-AAH-408

Advance Buzz for *Brothers and Sisters in Adoption*

"What a courageous treatment of the issues in adoption. Arleta James dares to talk about the day the family becomes immobilized—that dark secret in child welfare that only the families themselves have, in the past, seemed capable of acknowledging openly. After walking with the reader through those depleting and terrifying days, she takes us to re-mobilization and renewal. She gets us to the place that families want to be, without overlooking the excruciatingly tough middle part."

Michael Trout
DirectorInfant-Parent Institute
Co-author of *The Jonathon Letters*
Champaign, Illinois

Arleta James has captured so much of what actually happens in adoptive families in Brothers and Sisters in Adoption. *Children who are already in the adoptive family often are exposed to difficult situations when parents decide to add a child to their family, and James addresses the issues head-on. This book will become the Bible for those families who choose to bring children into their existing families and for those professionals with whom they work."*

Gregory C. Keck, PhD
Founder and Director of the Attachment and Bonding Center of Ohio,
co-author of *Adopting the Hurt Child* and *Parenting the Hurt Child*, and author of
Parenting Adopted Adolescents: Understanding and Appreciating their Journey
Cleveland, Ohio

"Don't be fooled by the title! Yes, this book is about brothers and sisters but it is also a most comprehensive look at adoption. The title could just as easily be "Realistic Expectations About Adoption," hearing the stories of all members of the family. It explores pre and post-adoption as well as the psychological timeline of moving from immobilization to mobilization, and it includes many resources that would benefit all members of the adoptive family. Being comprehensive, it explores strengths and weaknesses, joys and challenges, moms and dads, brothers and sisters. This book should be an important guide for assisting families in making their ongoing journey of adoption."

Dan Hughes, PhD
Therapist and Speaker, author of *Building the Bonds of Attachment: Awakening Love in Deeply Troubled Children*, *Attachment-focused Family Therapy*, and *Facilitating Developmental Attachment: The Road to Emotional Recovery and Behavioral Change in Foster and Adopted Children*
Pennsylvania

"Arleta James has managed to write an engaging book that is so comprehensive that it may attain the status of a signature text. Arleta skillfully combines a scholarly review of the literature with numerous vignettes or stories which illustrate and educate so that the reader sees the situation or the problem through the eyes of the story teller. The perspective of the child adopted internationally or domestically, resident siblings, fathers, and mothers is so illustrative that an understanding of behavior as a form of communication should be enhanced. In addition, each family member will feel understood and validated as personal feelings and struggles are identified in the stories of others. Relatives, teachers, adoption professionals, social service social workers and mental health professionals will find this book essential if they truly want to understand the perspective of the child and his or her adoptive family. The letting go of the old expectations in the section on grief and the acceptance of a new normal in family relationships provides a fitting resolution to this realistic, insightful book."

Joanne May, PhD
Founder of The Attachment Counseling Center of Minnesota

Kudos to Arleta James, who has filled a gap in the classic adoption literature with this book devoted to the well-being of siblings. Her book is not only thorough, but thoroughly enjoyable. In particular I liked her charts, including her easy-to-follow trajectories of children's needs from placement into the coming years, and her "Mobilization Inventory" to help all family members to stay healthy. Thanks, Arleta, for this excellent resource. I will be referring to it in my practice and trainings.

Deborah Gray, MSW, MPA
Author of *Nurturing Adoptions: Creating Resilience after Neglect and Trauma* (2007)
and *Attaching in Adoption: Practical Tools for Today's* Parents (2002)
Seattle, Washington

Thank you, Arleta, for providing for us an extremely important book that should be required reading for prospective adoptive parents and social workers involved in all facets of adoption. What a fantastic basis for discussion as we design, develop, and implement preparation for post-placement supportive programs!As this book documents so well, noone's needs—parents or children's—can be put "on hold" until healing has occurred. In fact, as many of us doing this type of parenting will acknowledge, total "healing" may never occur. We do know, however, that how we parent our children has a chance of at least making our grandchildren's lives better. In my experience, that has served as a realistic expectation and goal. Thank you for providing some tools for us to ponder and use.

Barbara Tremitiere, MSW, PhD
Author, Consultant, Trainer, Adoptive Parent
www. Barbara_Tremitiere.com
North Carolina

The child welfare field, parent and practitioner, will unquestionably welcome this comprehensive guidebook to the world of adoption. Parents and potential parents, caseworkers, and therapists are given a great deal to ponder. This is ultimately a book about understanding, about communicating, and about normalizing adoptive family life . . . and it gives hope throughout. The "real life" family examples are excellent, as are the resources found at the end of each chapter. Although self-defined as a book about siblings in adoption, it actually goes far beyond sibling issues. Rather, it offers a great deal of valuable information for families who are still without children, or who have no birth children, and who are considering their first adoption. There is a wealth of relevant statistics, and an in-depth realistic approach to adoption. Congratulations to Arleta James, who reaches out personally to each reader!

Maris H. Blechner, MEd, LCSW
Executive Director Family Focus Adoption Services
New York

Don't let the title of this book fool you! Arleta James has written a book not just about Brothers and Sisters in Adoption, but about the dynamics of any family formed by adoption. This approach to how a child's past influences his blending into family dynamics is comprehensive, yet not bogged down with academic details. Examples from Arleta's work as an attachment therapist are interwoven into the narrative to enrich this thorough, yet fast read. If you are working with families as they start the adoption process, put this at the top of the reading list. If you are a family seeking to grow through adoption, read this now, then again and again. If your family was formed through adoption years ago, this book will help you navigate the challenges of growing together as a family. This is an important tool for all who work in adoption to have at the forefront of one's professional and personal library.

Deborah Borchers, MD
Pediatrician Specializing in Adoption Medicine, Adoptive Parent
Cincinnati, Ohio

Brothers and Sisters in Adoption

Helping Children Navigate Relationships When New Kids Join the Family

Arleta M. James

Perspectives Press, Inc.
Indianapolis, Indiana

Perspectives Press, Inc.
P.O. Box 90318
Indianapolis, IN 46290-0318
USA
(317) 872-3055
www.perspectivespress.com

Book and cover design by Bookwrights
Manufactured in the United States of America
Hardcover ISBN-13 978-0-944934-35-7

The family stories sprinkled liberally throughout this book are based on real clients, and these real people wrote their own letters and essays to include in the Kids Talk and Families Talk and Dads Talk vignettes. All names, and, in some cases other identifying details, have been changed to protect privacy. We are grateful to these families for their willingness to share their experiences to make life better for future families.

Library of Congress Cataloging-in-Publication Data
James, Arleta M., 1960-
Brothers and sisters in adoption : helping children navigate relationships when new kids join the family / by Arleta M. James.
p. cm.
Includes bibliographical references and index.
ISBN 978-0-944934-35-7 (hardcover)
1. Adopted children—United States--Psychology. 2. Adopted children—Family relationships—United States. 3. Adoptive parents—Family relationships—United States. 4. Adoptive parents—United States—Psychology. I. Title.
HV875.J36 2009
362.7340973--dc22

2008039280

Dedication

To my family—thank you for giving me my home.

Table of Contents

Introduction

Why was this book written?

This book has been written to fill an oversight in the expression widely utilized by the systems involved in the care and placement of children moving into adoptive families—*in the best interest of the child.* Children waiting to be adopted are not the only children whose best interests need to be served by the child welfare system and international adoption programs. Many families coming forward to adopt are already parenting children—children born to them and/or children they have adopted. The arrival of an adopted sibling alters the lives of these children as well as their parents' lives. This is especially true if the adoptee enters the family with a history of trauma—abuse, neglect and abandonment—as have a large majority of waiting children, infants to adolescents, domestic and intercountry.

Trauma can have long-lasting adverse effects that are inadequately represented by the phrase *special needs*, which is so commonly used to depict the children waiting for a place to call home. *Brothers and Sisters in Adoption* will move quickly from the use of the term *special needs* to using the term *complex trauma. Complex trauma* offers a more realistic portrait of the damage inflicted on and suffered by abused, neglected or abandoned children coming to families via foster, orphanage or kinship care. *Complex trauma* better describes the potential for such a child to develop mental health issues which may not simply fade away with time and love.

Caring for a child with mental health issues—mild to severe—can be equivalent to parenting a child with a serious medical condition. Certainly, mental health issues carry the same threat to a child's well-being as do medical diagnoses.

Which families will benefit from this book?

This book is about integrating traumatized children into families whose composition already includes typically developing children. These typically developing children, whether by birth or adoption, are those children whose development is proceeding on track through predictable stages. Socially, emotionally, cognitively and physically, these typically developing children are flourishing. They are able to learn, explore their environment, make and keep friends, express and accept affection, participate in extracurricular activities and, overall, simply enjoy and happily absorb what life has to offer them. These children already residing in a family which adds a child with complex trauma are also referred to variously in this book as *brothers and sisters, birth and/or previously adopted children, resident children, typical children, healthy children, appropriately developing children* or *children who are on track developmentally*. These children may have been born to the family or they may have been adopted, as certainly there are many adoptees who enjoy appropriate development.

There are two groups of adoptive families which fall outside the above defined scope of this book. They are

- families parenting all typically developing children, whether born or adopted.
- "second families," which are families created when parents adopt in their middle years (ages 50+). These families include adoptees (infants through adolescents) and adult typical children.

The family with typical birth and typical adopted children sometimes expresses concerns that their children won't form solid attachments, or that they somehow won't fit well in their families. As the children are all typically developing, it is not adoption that is causing the problems in these families. The sibling rivalry, diverse interests and talents, personality conflicts, etc., are those "normal" types of issues that would be experienced by any family parenting all typical children. While this book addresses sibling rivalry and information relevant to any adoptee (e.g., talking with an adoptee about his or her past), again this book was specifically created for families integrating traumatized adoptees into their family system.

"Second families" will find this book useful in understanding and alleviating the complex trauma issues with which their younger arrivals present. However, the focus of this book is on facilitating relationships among children during the growing up years—infancy through young adulthood. So difficulties such as adult children fearing the impact of the adoptee's behavior on their own children (the adoptive parents' grandchildren), withdrawal of support, criticisms about child-rearing practices, etc. will be touched upon throughout the book (including an overview in the Appendices), yet not fully addressed.

What does this book address?

Navigating relationships among children who are thriving with those who are struggling presents various challenges. Frequently, parental time and family resources shift to caring for the ailing family member—the adoptee. The needs of the typically developing brothers and sisters, as well as the parents, are often put on hold until the adoptee heals. Once in this pattern of focusing so much of the family's resources on the child with complex trauma, parents find it difficult to rectify the situation by rebalancing. Their needs, and those of their resident children, continue to go unmet. Frustrated, exhausted, overwhelmed and stressed out, many turn to professional help. However, the very systems designed to assist them—child welfare, mental health, the school, etc.—often blame the parents or work individually with the troubled adoptee rather than with the family as a unit. Parents, and especially brothers and sisters, receive little direction, voice or support. So the family becomes immobilized. Progress seems elusive.

Parents begin to question themselves, often asking

"Did we make the right choice by adopting?"

"How is this affecting our typical children?"

"What can we do for them?"

"Will our adopted son or daughter heal?"

"Will our family ever be the same as it was before we adopted this child?"

Brothers and Sisters in Adoption responds to the above questions and related issues in an honest and forthright manner. There has been no attempt to hide or to sugar coat the difficulties that are faced by families working to weave the needs of a child with complex trauma into its fabric. The book covers difficulties from pre-adoption through post-adoption and even into adulthood for the siblings in such a family—each phase of the adoption process receives attention. Sharing the struggles of families who, with inadequate support and professional help, find themselves immobilized is a part of *Brothers and Sisters in Adoption*'s process of helping new and previously formed families discover ways to improve the well-being of each family member. Readers will meet families which, despite great challenges, are navigating improved relationships among family members. These families have mobilized. The parents have found ways to care for themselves, their traumatized adoptee and their birth and/or previously adopted children in a balanced manner, thereby creating a "new and different" family.

Readers will travel the pages of *Brothers and Sisters in Adoption* with experienced guides. Throughout the journey, they will engage with these families as they read and are inspired by their personal stories. These poignant accounts contributed by brothers, sisters, adoptees and parents make the content alive and interactive. This expert assistance will provide validation, comfort, hope, advice and inspiration.

This book, then, offers information reflecting each adoptive family member's perspective. However, as the book's title suggests, the emphasis is on the needs of the typically developing brothers and sisters. These resident children are most often left out of the adoption process. Pre-adoption, they develop—usually on their own and with little input or information from parents or professionals—expectations about what their sibling-to-be will be like. These expectations, however, soon clash with the reality that life with a child who has experienced complex trauma will bring. Post-placement, these children are shocked and stunned, as is reflected in the sentiments of the four typical children ages 6 to 14 who share their thoughts below.

"It's annoying. When my new brother moved in, I didn't think he was going to have any problems. When I figured out he did have problems, I just wished he had been born to my mom and dad. Then he would be okay. I don't like it when we go somewhere and he starts acting bad and then Dad starts yelling."

"Prior to the adoption, I felt having a sister would be great. I felt it would be like having a best friend who lived in the same house as you and who you could trust all your secrets to. I felt that she would love me and I would love her. I thought the sibling would be like my friends' siblings. I thought she would be cute and annoying at the same time. I thought that I would understand them and they wouldn't embarrass me around my friends too much. I expected to have a best friend in the family that I could trust with my life. I thought that having another person in the family would make it so I always had someone to play with outside.

"Prior to the adoption, someone could have told me how attention-needing she was. Someone could have explained to me that having a little sister was not going to be all fun and games. The changes she brought to the family have affected me. I have had the loss of a peaceful household, the loss of parental time and the loss of privacy. She, at age 10, knows much more about 'bad words' and what they mean on TV shows than I did at her age, or anyone at her age should."

"I thought having a brother would be a lot of fun. I thought my brother would be so much fun to play with. Since we adopted my brother, it has been really noisy at our house. Whenever he gets mad, he will scream and cry. Also, when he doesn't get something he wants, he will scream and scream!

"My friends and I have to always go into my room and lock the door so that my brother doesn't keep bothering us. He'll scream and pound on the door until Mom or Dad calm him down. Whenever we offer to have him play with us, he goes crazy. He only wants to play what he wants to play, and he will scream until he gets his way. No one wants to play with him because we always have to play what he wants or else he will throw a big fit and cry and scream. It gets really embarrassing when he throws fits in front of my friends.

"I get really mad at my brother. I also feel like I can't go anywhere without him right behind me breaking something of mine or making fun of me, copying me or touching something of mine that he shouldn't be touching."

"Mom and Dad spend too much time with my brother. I don't have anything to myself anymore. It's been crazy around here and I never get to have friends over because he always messes things up for me."

This book seeks to prevent such dismal reports from future families. This can be accomplished by arming parents and professionals with the information to provide these developmentally on-track children with

- effective pre-adoptive education
- greater inclusion in the home study process
- clarification of the complex trauma issues presented by the particular child chosen to join the family
- enhanced involvement in the actual process of moving the sibling-to-be into the family
- ideas to effectively facilitate parent-child communication
- strategies to cope positively with all of the changes the adoptee may bring to the family
- ways to acknowledge the positive impact adoption can have on their lives.

When educated and included, brothers and sisters do shift their perspective, as is exemplified by the young man below.

"I was excited and even ecstatic. I had bothered my parents all my life to adopt again. This is because I was an only child and very lonely. When I heard that my parents were adopting, I expected the children to act like I did. I thought that I was finally going to have play partners. I thought they would be normal and just want to play with me. I thought having siblings would be fun and we could help kids have a better life at the same time.

"Since we adopted my brother and sister seven years ago, my household has not had many peaceful moments. I've lost a lot of parental attention. This makes me jealous and angry. For a while, I had to share a room with my new brother and I lost a sense of privacy and space in the process. I was angry that I couldn't have my own room. I also had to lock a lot more things up after my brother started stealing from me. I lost a lot of material possessions. I didn't get as much as I used to and the things that I did have were often broken by my siblings. This angered me once again because some of the things had sentimental value to me. I definitely lost a peaceful household and fun activities.

"Eventually, my parents and I started to talk a lot about the situation. I learned to ignore the things that my siblings are doing. I do have to admit that sometimes I still do explode and my parents have to remind me that my siblings do things to push me away because they are scared of being loved.

"To tell the truth, in the beginning, I was mad, sad, jealous and embarrassed. I learned (and am still learning) that feeling and being 'stuck' in those feelings doesn't do any good for you. And now, even though I will never admit this to my siblings or anyone, my feelings have now changed to love and happiness, especially toward my brother. I don't know what I would do if he wasn't in my life.

> "There are so many positive aspects of adoption! Yeah, it's scary as hell to bring a total stranger into your home who doesn't want to be there, but the positive aspects outnumber the negative aspects so greatly. I enjoy playing with, talking to and teaching my younger brother a lot of things. Even though the siblings act like they don't love you, they do and will eventually show you. Also, adopting forces you to look deeper into people and to have a better understanding of why people act the way they do. The greatest of all, though, is that I know that I partook in giving two children a home."

The more education this young man received, the better able he was to cope and to navigate positive relationships with his siblings. It is so unfortunate that this took seven years! Certainly, an intended goal of *Brothers and Sisters in Adoption* is to reduce the amount of time family members spend engaged in negative family interactions. This can be achieved with pre-adoptive planning and with post-placement strategies developed with each member of the adoptive family in mind. Chapters 9 and 10 deliver these very types of solutions. The book is also loaded with resources. These chapter-by-chapter references to other books, websites and articles help family members (and the social service, mental health and education professionals reading over their shoulders) explore any facet of adoption, trauma or family life in great detail.

When each member of the adoptive family—parents, adoptee, brothers and sisters—has his or her needs taken into account, closer, more positive relationships can be navigated. Operating in the "best interest of the *family*" benefits everyone!

CHAPTER ONE

The Development of Realistic Expectations: Myth or Actuality?

Parents come to the adoption process along many avenues. Some consider adoption after a long thought process. Others are thrust into providing permanency for a child via a relative's child in need, or a foster child unexpectedly becoming available for adoption. A single adult comes to adoption out of a desire to become a parent. Many intersect with a child along their career path—a teacher or coach learns that a student or team member needs a "forever" family and so on and so forth. No matter the route, parents arrive at adoption with a set of expectations about what adding a child to their family will mean for them, the child and their typically developing children, in cases in which the family is already parenting one or more children. When their parents make the decision to adopt, the brothers and sisters-to-be also develop a set of expectations about their new sibling. Parents and professionals contribute to the expectations of the typically developing children.

This chapter will provide an overview of initial expectations of parents and children as they enter the adoption process. This is necessary, as pre-adoptive expectations tend to be optimistic and idealistic. A significant goal throughout the adoption process is to assist parents and their children in forming "realistic expectations." Holding realistic expectations increases the family's ability to accept the child, with all of his needs, and to integrate him into the existing family system. The chapter concludes with "The Development of Realistic Expectations: Myth or Actuality." This segment suggests what is feasible regarding expectations prior to the arrival of the new family member.

Parental Motivations and Expectations

If you are reading this book, you are probably already parenting at least one child. That child may have been born to you or adopted by you, or perhaps you have blended some step siblings into one family. Now you have been motivated to consider adoption, you have decided on adoption, or you have already adopted to add to your family.

Motivations for taking action are accompanied by sets of expectations, so the two go hand in hand. The most common types of motivations for adopting are presented below, as are the predominant expectations that flow from these motivations.

As you read this chapter, think about your own motivations for adopting and your expectations about what that would be like. Write down your expectations. In Chapter 9, we will talk about the benefits of revising expectations, so having a list will be helpful in order to prepare for content yet to come in this book. As you read this and subsequent chapters, return to these questions and answer them again. Continue to ask yourself:

What is my motivation to adopt?

What expectations fall out of my motivation?

What experiences have I had in which my expectations were not met? How did I feel in these situations? How did I cope with these situations?

What are my expectations about sibling relationships?

Did I always get along with my brother or sister?

Did I willingly share friends with my close-in-age sister?

Did I willingly babysit my younger brother?

Did I feel resentful or angry when my sibling "got away with" a behavior for which I was certain that I would have received consequences?

How are my sibling relationships at the present time?

What was my role in the family?

Do I have expectations about what roles my typically developing child will assume once I become an adoptive parent?

Do I have expectations as to what role my child by adoption will assume once he or she enters my family?

What are my expectations of my spouse?

Are we united about adopting?

About child-rearing?

About the division of household responsibilities?

Are my expectations about adopting changing as I am provided with information from my agency's pre-adoptive training program, readings, surfing the Internet and networking with families already parenting an adopted child?

Are my expectations in accord with my adopted child's abilities?

What are my typically developing children's expectations of a new sibling?

Have I talked with them?

Are they receiving any information about adding a sibling to the family through adoption?

"I want to help a child in need."

Many parents who proceed with the adoption of a child with special needs do so out of a long-term desire to help a child in need. This may stem from a religious upbringing that instills strong values regarding caring for others, from having grown up alongside foster or adopted children, or from having been raised with a strong sense of community.

Ray and his wife adopted Paul when he was 18 months old. Paul is now 13 years old. Ray expressed that he always wanted to adopt. Throughout his whole life, he had felt that adoption offered a way to help another human being. Ray's family of origin placed great emphasis on lending a helping hand to those in need. Ray thought, "I couldn't fulfill this philosophy better than by taking in a child."

An expectation generated by Ray's motivation to adopt is that helping someone in need should result in gratitude on the part of the person being helped. Instead, Paul is angry that he was adopted. He believes, albeit inaccurately, that he could be with his birthmother if Ray and his wife had not adopted him from Korea. Paul expresses his anger by throwing things and making statements such as, "I never wanted to be adopted anyway." Ray, infuriated due to years of this ongoing issue, states, "You have no idea how much better off you are that we adopted you." While this may be true, Paul is only able to see what he doesn't have: his birthfamily. Paul is not able to see what he does have: a loving adoptive family which provides an assortment of opportunities. Ray feels let down and unappreciated. The two lived at odds until each was helped to see the other's viewpoint.

Ray's expectation of the adoptee being grateful is shared by many.

Toni and Grace adopted two brothers, Ben and Jacob, ages 10 and 4½, respectively. They stated, "Our expectation was that we were providing Ben and Jacob a situation that was a lot better than their previous situation. To some degree, we were rescuing them. Their lives with their birthfamily were replete with domestic violence and drug use. We thought they would be happy to be a part of a healthy family situation. We really thought kids coming from the background that our two boys came from would welcome a loving, caring home where parents were there all the time, genuinely taking an interest in their lives. However, they didn't see it this way at all. Their background prevented them from understanding what it meant to be a part of a family. Five years later, we finally feel we are moving out of the conflict and tension that has been so much a part of our lives since their adoptions. Yet, there are still many difficult days as we continue to help Ben and Jacob fit into our family."

Charles, speaking of Alan, who was adopted in adolescence, said, "My expectation for Alan was to provide him with the same kind of household and give him the same opportunities as my other kids had—opportunities he never had. In return, we expected that he would adapt to that and be gracious and mold himself into part of the family. This didn't happen."

"I am unable to have children."

The pain of infertility cannot be underestimated. It is an experience which involves multiple losses (Johnston, 1992). At least one in six couples will endure the expense and the emotional roller-coaster of infertility procedures. Some will be successful. Later, these families may choose adoption as a means to expand their family. Some will adopt first and then continue to pursue the experience of having a child by birth. Other families will be able to have a birth child but will be unable to conceive additional children. This is referred to as secondary infertility. Many of these families will adopt as a means of enlarging their family.

Mark and Charlotte underwent years of infertility treatment without a positive outcome. Motivated by a desire to become parents, they adopted a sibling group of three. They loved and cared for their children well. Each of their children had special needs as a result of the trauma experienced prior to the adoptions. Mark and Charlotte educated themselves, sought resources and learned to advocate within the school system for special education services. Their children progressed under their care. As new infertility procedures became available that offered them fresh hope to have a child by birth, they resumed treatment. Adoption had made them parents. Adoption did not resolve the losses associated with infertility. Throughout their adoption process, each had retained a strong desire to create a child that was a genetic part of them.

Adopting due to infertility is a valid motivation to adopt. The desire to be parents is imparted in all of us. When I was a case worker assisting families to identify children to become part of their family, I was constantly asked by the children's workers, "Has the family resolved their infertility?" This is a difficult issue to determine. Having a child seems such an inherent right. Does one really come to resolve this loss fully? Even if infertility losses are resolved initially, they can be triggered by adoption, by reaching an age when it will become impossible to have a child, by watching a mother and her children at the park and so on. It is a developmental loss that may be revisited throughout the lifetime of the infertile couple. What is important is whether the family can adequately parent the child who joins their family by adoption in light of the emotions surrounding infertility. Certainly, most families achieve this scenario successfully.

However, as Mark and Charlotte demonstrate, an expectation that sometimes occurs when infertility is a motivation is that becoming parents will alleviate the losses caused by infertility. This is an expectation to re-think.

> Margaret and her son, Bryan, were in therapy. Margaret and her husband adopted Bryan when he was age 8. In a very poignant moment, Bryan looked at Margaret and asked, "How would you have taken care of me if you had me when I was a baby?" Margaret burst into tears. She was sad for him that he didn't have a mother who rocked him and sang lullabies to him. She was also sad for herself. The pain of not having a child by birth came back in that instant.

"I heard an ad on the radio."

Others enter the adoption process in response to advertisements regarding the children available for adoption. These children are often referred to as "waiting children," and they may be described in blurbs such as these.

> "Bobby, 10 years old, has big brown eyes and an adorable smile that draws people to him. Bobby loves to give and receive hugs, listen to music and play on the computer. Bobby enjoys going to church, riding his bike and playing ball. Bobby is fascinated with fire trucks and motorcycles. Bobby's favorite cartoon is 'Scooby Doo.' Bobby is full of energy and loves to have plenty of things to do."

> "This precious baby boy was born ten months ago in Kazakhstan. He is said to be a nice healthy baby and he needs a family of his own."

> "Lydia, age 4, is a very affectionate and friendly little girl. She loves giving and receiving hugs and loves to laugh. She bonds well with adults and gets along very well with other children."

> "This dynamic duo are Tyrone and Tyhesia and they both enjoy being outside! Tyrone is a young man who likes school and is motivated to learn. He enjoys a variety of sports, especially basketball, baseball and swimming. Tyhesia likes winter and enjoys making snow sculptures, igloos and sledding. She excels at about everything she tries."

> "This 5-year-old boy, from Africa, is in need of a family. He is said to be a normal, healthy little boy who should do well in an adoptive family."

> "Jillian is a very sweet young lady who is anxious to find a home. She loves being active and has a lot of different interests. Her favorite hobby is horses. She loves horses, knows how to ride and helps take care of the horses in her current home. Jillian loves all kinds of animals and would like a family who has cats and dogs. Jillian works very hard at her school work. She says she really wants to learn and tries her very best. She does not like math or English, but she does like reading. Jillian also likes to cook (especially desserts) and to go shopping (especially for earrings). Jillian also likes to put puzzles together, color, draw, and watch television. Jillian says that it is very important to her that her family goes to church and believes in God."

Prospective parents responding to such ads begin to create an image of life with the child.

> "My brother-in-law is a fireman. Wouldn't it be great to take Bobby to the fire station?"
>
> "I like to read and cook. We have two cats and a dog. Maybe I should inquire about Jillian. We could have such fun together."

Sadly, the dream child inspired by advertisements like these may not mesh with the actual child being described. Such advertisements attract families based on shared mutual interests. While shared interests are a benefit in developing relationships, they are but one of many reasons for a child to be selected for placement with a particular family. The predominant criterion in family selection is that the family is able to meet the needs of the child, and unless the parents understand that there will be needs, dreamy impressions do a disservice to both child and family.

Think about first impressions for a moment. "Firsts" tend to stay with us. You can most likely quickly recall your first boyfriend or girlfriend. "Firsts" are important. Who doesn't want to make a good initial impression at a job interview? Media presentations suggesting opening your heart and your home to a child in need, however, too often create the first impression that a loving family or a good home is all that is necessary to make a difference in the life of a waiting child.

This philosophy that love is all that is needed is compounded systemically. There are still a number of professionals who believe that all children are, by nature, resilient. This philosophy entails such thinking as, "Once the child is placed in a 'good' family, the child's past will fade." Or, "Take this child and love her. She will be fine. She won't remember anything. She was too young." This philosophy does hold true for some children. However, for other children there will be lifelong issues due to the trauma they experienced in their families of origin or a foreign orphanage.

Parent after parent with whom I've worked has stated, "We thought love would be enough." "We thought we could love the past away." "We attended pre-adoptive training but thought we could overcome all of the problems with love and stability." It is wonderful when a family loves a child. However, love will not be enough. The child who has experienced trauma prior to his or her adoption may require a lot of vigorous work, at much hardship to the adoptive family, in order to become as successful a human being as is possible.

While it is necessary to recruit on behalf of the children who wait for families, advertisements must be balanced and truthful. Some states and agencies, such as Oregon, seem to recruit and place children with balanced ads that provide a description of the child commingled with anticipated difficulties. Hopefully, more organizations will follow suit, offering more realistic descriptions, like the one that follows.

> Andrew, born in October, 2001, is adorable, with short light brown hair and blue/grey eyes. A bundle of energy, he is very bright and on track developmentally. He came into foster care in 2003. Andrew needs to be challenged and directed, though, as he can get into mischief when left to his own devices. Andrew has been making considerable progress working with a child therapist over the past six months and is developing healthy ways to deal with his issues of past trauma.
>
> Andrew, who just finished his second year of Head Start last month, is socially appropriate and has been very successful in his early schooling. He knows all of his letters and sounds and is currently learning how to read. Andrew has developed an extensive imagination and enjoys music and singing.

Andrew does well with a strict routine. He is capable of following through with morning tasks, which include making his bed, brushing his teeth and putting his pajamas in the laundry.

Andrew wants a family to call his own. He'll be a wonderful addition to a loving, caring family that can guide him through childhood. Andrew moved to a new foster home last fall, where he has shown a lot of growth and has established a positive sense of house rules, routines and expectations for behavior.

It will be important for Andrew's adoptive parents to have a good grasp of how early neglect and abuse amidst domestic violence and parental substance abuse can impact a child's sense of well being and safety, and his emotional and behavioral development. It is hoped that Andrew's adoptive parents will be open to some contact with his older brother as Andrew grows up.

"I know what they have been through."

It is not uncommon that prospective adoptive parents' own histories contain such painful experiences as childhood sexual abuse, domestic violence, physical abuse, growing up with an alcoholic parent, the death of a parent or sibling and so on. Thus, upon learning that children with special needs share this common ground, these families feel connected to the waiting children. They feel that in addition to a home, they can offer a parent who sets an example that early adversity can be overcome, and a parent who can empathically assist the child in healing from early heartbreaks.

On one hand, this reasoning is accurate. There is little ability to deny that associating with people who have the same experiences is of benefit. We only have to look at the success of the ever expanding number of support groups to know that human beings gain many positives when they gather with others who share similar life circumstances.

On the other hand, these same families are often unprepared for the impact the adoption of a child with a history of trauma will have on them.

Brenda and Steve adopted two boys from Eastern Europe. Bryce, adopted at age 1½, entered therapy at age 4 due to lengthy temper tantrums during which he could become aggressive. Brenda stated, "Each time that he attempts to hit me, flashes of my abusive father instantly appear in my head."

Brenda is a very intelligent woman in her late thirties. She felt that she had resolved the physical abuse she suffered at the hands of her father. She was blindsided by the flashbacks Bryce's behavior triggered. Because she had not been appropriately prepared, she had no expectation that parenthood would cause her own issues to surface again. Issues such as abuse, the untimely death of a parent or sibling, the impact of alcoholism and the emotional unavailability of a parent during one's childhood are developmental. They are triggered by various life stages such as becoming a parent. Many parents will find that they engage in a parallel process of healing subsequent to an adoption. Parents will need to re-work unpleasant childhood experiences while simultaneously assisting their adopted child to do the same.

The parents' ability to enter the process of recovering from childhood hurts as often as is necessary is critical to the integration of the child into the family. Unfortunately, many families will become immobilized by the collision of the parent's unresolved grief with the child's unresolved grief. Chapters 3 and 8 provide a depth of understanding of the negative emotional climate that results when grief meets grief in this manner. Chapters 9 and 10 will offer suggestions regarding ways to weather blustery emotional storms.

"My spouse or partner wants to adopt."

It is quite typical that one partner is far more the driving force behind the family adopting than the other. Referred to among adoption workers and therapists as "draggee vs. dragger" syndrome, the dragger in the pre-adoptive phase is the one who contacts the adoption agencies, determines when training will be attended, makes the follow-up phone calls and obtains information on prospective children. Post-adoption, the dragger surfs the Internet to obtain resources, has the child evaluated, locates the relevant service providers, transports the child to all of her appointments, works hard to implement the treatment recommendations and continues to carry out the same amount of household responsibilities as before the adoptee moved in. The end result of this situation is the emotional and physical exhaustion of one partner, while the other partner—the draggee—seems to disengage even further from family matters.

Early studies comparing couples at different stages of family life suggest that marital satisfaction declines over the first 15 years of marriage, only to rise again when children start leaving the nest (Hicks and Platt, 1971; Lewis and Spanier, 1979). Below are several of the common contributors to marital dissatisfaction:

- Limits on parents' time and energy make it less possible for the couple to engage in the companionate activities that maintain and build marital intimacy (Glenn and Weaver, 1978; Miller, 1976; and Ward, 1998).
- The perceptions of how household responsibilities will be divided are important. Frequently, the male partner becomes the principal earner. Often, when a child is added to the family, men increase their work hours while women reduce their employment outside of the home. The husband's view is that being a good provider contributes directly to the welfare of the wife and children. The woman's view is that the husband is pulling away from the family at a time when he is vitally needed at home (Cowan, Cowan, Heming, Garrett, Coysh, Curtis-Boles and Boles, 1985). When chores and responsibilities are not divided in a mutually satisfactory way, the wife does not receive adequate physical and emotional support. In turn, the husband does not receive adequate companionship, and his patience and tolerance are continually tested. Then the marriage is likely to be in trouble (Belsky and Kelly, 1994).
- Often, the child with special needs creates conflict between his parents. He is kind and respectful to one parent, usually the father. The mother experiences a child who is callous and uncooperative. The father begins to blame the mother for the problems the family is having with the child. The mother is devastated by this lack of support on from her spouse. This pattern of family dynamics is a result of the child's ability to "split" adults. The adopted child feels very let down and hurt by his birthmother. She was supposed to protect him and keep him safe, and she did neither. These emotions are vented onto the mother who is present—the adoptive mother. Splitting will be re-visited in Chapter 8.
- Changes in the family's support system also occur. It is not uncommon that the negative behaviors of a child with special needs are far more apparent in the home than at school, at church or at family gatherings. This "invisible" component of parenting an adopted child causes great stress for all immediate family members. Additionally, this situation can lead to conflict with extended family and friends. Friends and family offer advice and suggestions that are not useful or that send a message that there is something wrong with the type of parenting being utilized by the adoptive family. Not wanting to be assaulted in this manner, already stressed partners isolate themselves from friends and family. They minimize their

interactions with others so as to offset receiving additional comments. Isolation is a critical issue in the adoption of children with special needs. It will be addressed in more detail in Chapter 8. Chapter 10's section "Finding Oases : Creating Support" will offer solutions to reduce the isolation experienced by parents, brothers, sisters and adoptees.

Kim and Joan, both adoptive mothers, made the following statements at an adoptive parent support group:

> "After a while, the craziness in your home takes away from your friendships with other adults. You have no time to go out or your child is having a temper tantrum so you can't really leave the house. Your friends and family can't relate to what's happening or they don't want to relate to what's happening."

> "In the beginning, I was telling my best friend of twenty years the types of behavioral problems Neil had. She looked at me and said, 'You know Joan, I've known you a long time and I don't know what's wrong with you anymore.' "

The draggee vs. dragger syndrome carries the expectation that one parent can carry the majority of responsibilities. Actually, due to the factors presented above, this phenomenon may serve to heighten marital discord. Marital quality, in turn, affects the quality of parent-child relationships (Cummings and Watson-O'Reilly, 1977). In particular, marital conflict has been associated with the quality of parenting practices and parent-child attachment (Davies and Cummings, 1994). This applies to all of the parent-child relationships in the family—birth and adoptive, whether having arrived at birth or at an older age! Marital relations can be a source of support for or can undermine the parenting role (Belsky, 1984).

Additionally, in a two-parent family, the child should have two parents equally invested in the well-being of the child. He has already lost at least one set of parents. He does not need the further rejection of a parent who spends little time with him or a parent who makes minimal effort on his behalf. Chapters 4 and 8 will expand on partner matters.

"I thought a child would strengthen our marriage."

There are parents who believe that the addition of a child will resolve their marital conflict. The material presented under the previous heading, "My spouse or partner wants to adopt" should dispel this notion. A child may only increase marital discord.

> Anna and Grant had been married for five years. The marriage was difficult from the beginning. Grant frequently changed employment positions. Between jobs, Anna's income provided their financial stability. Grant, when unemployed, did not carry out any extra household responsibilities. The couple was infertile and this was a source of conflict as well. Anna initiated the idea of adoption. She felt that adopting would help Grant become more responsible. Both Anna and Grant believed that a child would help them move beyond the infertility. Because they would have a child to love and care for jointly, they believed that they would be drawn closer together. They would have to communicate and work together.
>
> They opted for an international adoption as it would require spending several weeks in Kazakhstan, and they felt this time together would be similar to a second honeymoon; their sense of romance would be rekindled by this "vacation."
>
> Their arguments started again, however, within a few months of returning home with their new daughter. Neither partner had made lasting changes in his or her style of com-

munication, thoughts on household chores or their ideas as to who should earn money and how it should be spent. A year later, the couple bitterly divorced. Their daughter, now age 6, spends every other weekend and two weeknights with Grant. The remainder of the time she is with Anna. She blames herself for the divorce, as she was old enough to hear their fights, many of which centered on her care. This child, already separated from her birthmother, orphanage friends and culture, now must deal with the additional layer of losses caused by a divorce.

This situation carried the expectation that the child would meet the needs of the parents. A child with special needs is especially ill-equipped to be the emotional support of the parents. Entering adoption with expectations that the child will meet the needs of the parents is unrealistic and inappropriate.

"A relative's child needs my help."

Kinship care is the term used to describe children being parented by relatives of a birthparent. Most children in kinship care (59%, or 1,360,000 children) live with their grandparents, and about a fifth (19%, or 440,000 children) live with aunts and uncles. The remaining 22% live with other relatives.[1]

Kinship care may be arranged in three ways:

- Private Kinship Care: The arrangements are made among family members with no involvement from an adoption agency (though an attorney may handle necessary legal issues.)
- Voluntary Kinship Care: The public agency is involved in placing the child with relatives but without utilizing the court system to take legal custody of the child. The birth parents may be asked to sign a voluntary placement agreement. For example, a public agency may assist a birthparent in placing his child with a brother or parent while he pursues substance abuse treatment.
- Kinship Foster Care: A public agency has court-ordered legal custody of the child, and this agency seeks to place the child with a relative.[2]

Kinship care occurs for the same reasons that lead children to be removed from birth families, placed in foster care and perhaps ultimately adopted from the child welfare system—parental substance abuse, neglect, physical and sexual abuse, incarceration, abandonment, lack of finances or death. Yet, kinship caregivers frequently accept a relative child without preparation for the impact of these traumas on their new kin arrival, themselves and their resident children.

In some cases, family members are aware that a grandchild, niece or nephew is residing in a dangerous or neglectful situation. These relatives may have been providing care on and off to their kin children. The family members may have been actively involved in motivating a public child welfare agency to take custody of the grandchild, niece or nephew. These kinship parents and the siblings living in their household have then been preparing for the possibility of kin children entering their home. But, in many other instances, kinship placements occur with little advance notice. Siblings or an adult child may show up at the door or call and request that the child stay with the relatives. Knowing that the home situation is poor or even deplorable, parents, brothers and sisters feel unable to decline such requests. Some relatives who have been discon-

1. Urban Institute. *Children in Kinship Care.* http://www.urban.org/publications/900661.html

2. Child Welfare Information Gateway. *Kinship Caregivers and the Child Welfare System.* http://www.childwelfare.gov/pubs/f_kinshi/f_kinshia.cfm

nected from their child or sibling may not even be aware that the grandchildren, nieces or nephews exist or that these children were living in woeful conditions until an emergency situation occurs. For example,

> Peggy, 13, and Jeff, 14, arrived at the home of their cousin, 13-year-old Pat Ann and her parents within a matter of days. The two children had been abandoned by their birthmother very early in life. Their birthfather, Pat Ann's paternal uncle, was an alcoholic. He was prone to violent outbursts. Peggy and Jeff had been removed from and returned to his custody several times. However, this cycle ended when he was sentenced to a five-year jail term for assault. Suddenly, her two cousins, with their complex issues, became Pat Ann's close-in-age siblings.

Overall, kin families may need to read, attend seminars and network with veteran kin families after the child moves in, receiving "on the job training," as it were. This book will help kinship caregivers understand the trauma experienced by their grandchild, niece, nephew or cousin. This book will also clarify the types of education that will benefit the kinship parents, their children and their relative child. However, this book may not fully meet the needs of kinship caregivers with regards to establishing boundaries between themselves, birth parents and extended family members. Included in the Resources are a list of books, articles and websites to assist kin with visitation matters as well as legal options, financial assistance, etc.

"I want my children to have more siblings."

> Erick and Marianne adopted Peter as an infant. They were concerned that Peter would be alone at some point in his life. They felt adoption offered him the opportunity to have "company" now and later. When Peter was age 9, they adopted Mark and Mike, ages 10 and 6 respectively.

> Corrine and Tom have four children; two sons by birth and two daughters through adoption. They were introduced to Shawn at a fundraiser conducted at Corrine's company. One of the factors that led to their decision to adopt Shawn was that his age was between that of their two sons. Corrine stated, "I had hoped that he would get along with the boys. He was in the middle of our two sons. He hadn't had siblings to depend on before."

The decision by parents to have more than one child is sometimes rationalized as offsetting loneliness in the first-born, creating opportunities for healthy competition and providing each child with the "gift" of a ready-made playmate or companion. Parents often fantasize that their children will magically become close, affectionate, and mutually responsive and may even remain life-long friends—a parental legacy expressed in the phrase, "After we're gone, you'll always have each other" (Bank and Kahn, 1977).

Parental Expectations about Sibling Relationships

The sibling relationship is taking on greater importance in light of changes in family structure.

- The average number of siblings is currently one.
- The sibling relationship is our longest relationship. Longer lifespan means that we may become dependent on our siblings, rather than our partners, throughout the course of our lives.

- An increase in divorce and geographic mobility may cause us, young and old alike, to cling tightly to the constancy and permanency a brother or sister can provide.
- The absence of parents due to stress, employment obligations, and marital tension and divorce invites siblings to band together as a mutual support system (Goetting, 1986).

These facts make clear that positive sibling relationships are of great value. It is no surprise then that parents expect and want to create intimate bonds between their resident children and the sibling they add by adopting. Referring back to the Introduction, there are children who have joined their families by adoption and who are typically developing. However, as the Introduction pointed out and as Chapter 2 will make clear, a significant portion of children adopted from institutional settings and foster care have various difficulties that will interfere with their capacity to develop the type of relationships envisioned.

The expectation of close sibling ties is created by other factors as well. These factors are explored below. It should be noted that the content of this book focuses on sibling relationships from birth through late adolescence—the time in which siblings are growing up together.

Expectations Inherent in Developmental Tasks

Ann Goetting (1986), in her comprehensive literature review of siblings, identifies three primary developmental tasks of siblings in childhood and adolescence. First, and most important, siblings provide companionship, friendship, comfort and affection for one another. Support for siblings as social agents is abundant.

Second, siblings are a primary means of child care. It is probably true that single-parent families, families in which both parents work, large families, and families overwhelmed with a child with a disability are more likely to delegate care taking responsibilities to siblings.

Lastly, siblings benefit each other by managing relationships in various ways between parents and siblings. A child can protect a sibling from a confrontation with the parent by distracting one of the parties from the potentially destructive or explosive situation. Siblings can join forces with one another against the parent to strengthen resources for negotiation.

> "If you bought us all bikes, you could save a lot of driving time and gas!"

Siblings may also translate a sibling's behavior to the parent.

> Melanie, age 7, was under the care of her 16-year-old sibling, Carol, for the summer. Melanie, adopted after four years in a Belarusian orphanage, has great difficulty comprehending the consequences of her actions. She also has a very limited sense of danger. While Carol was babysitting, several of her friends stopped by. A television commercial regarding drugs caused the older children to make what they thought were some humorous comments about drug addicts. Melanie's interpretation of their remarks was, "I would be cool and likeable if I took drugs." And, indeed she did. She swallowed almost a whole bottle of a prescription medication. Carol, upon realizing that something was very wrong with Melanie, called 911. After eight hours in the hospital, Melanie's vital signs stabilized. Carol accepted responsibility for the situation. She explained to her very upset parents that Melanie's behavior was the result of the conversation with her friends. Carol intervened on Melanie's behalf. She diffused the situation quite well. As a result, Melanie's parents were able to calmly discuss

this situation with each other and Melanie. Since this incident, Carol's friends no longer stop by while she cares for Melanie. All medications have been placed in locked containers. Melanie's grandmother visits more frequently while Melanie's parents are at work.

Expectations abound within these developmental tasks. Visions of siblings playing games, ganging up on mom and dad to obtain privileges and assisting with household responsibilities are the types of experiences families want to facilitate, as well as experience for themselves.

Expectations Derived from Roles

Who were you in the family? Were you the "peacemaker?" Were you the "responsible one?" The sibling relationship can be a major determinant of both identity formation and self-esteem (Cicirelli, 1995). Return to the questions on page 15-16 and think about your role in your family of origin for a moment. Then read on.

Birth Order

Place in the family—oldest, youngest, middle child—figures prominently in adult perceptions of sibling relationships as well. Birth order contributes to role identification and as adults we often carry out the roles learned as children—"the helper," "the baby." Thus, our role becomes a large part of our identity.

There exists a bias within the child welfare system to avoid placements that move a typically developing child out of his role as oldest child (Jewett, 1978).

When Mike and Nancy added Patty and Dave to their family, their birth son, Ryan, age 11, became the second oldest. Patty was 10 months older than Ryan. Ryan's difficulty adjusting to Patty and Dave had nothing to do with the birth order. In fact, Ryan continued to receive all of the privileges usually ascribed to the oldest child as his development was in accord with his chronological age. Patty's development, on the other hand, because of the pre-adoptive trauma she had experienced, resembled a child about 5 or 6 years old. Therefore, her freedoms and the possessions provided to her were doled out based on what she could handle in light of her developmental delays. Ryan's adjustment was related to the behavioral problems Patty and Dave brought into the family. Patty, who had an extensive history of trauma, had experienced eleven placements prior to coming to live in Mike and Nancy's home. Throughout her residences, her place in the family had changed repeatedly. Sometimes she was the oldest. Sometimes she was the youngest. Sometimes she was the middle child.

Ascribed Roles

Roles in the family may also be ascribed due to qualities, for example "the brain" or "the beauty." When parents extend and elaborate these differences over the years, such original trait assignments may even become a person's lifelong and satisfying identity. However, a negative identity such as being a "fool," "the bad seed," or the "black sheep" can become a yoke around a child's neck; it may begin innocently, but once set in motion, it remains fixed and even grows with terrible consequences for a lifetime (Bank and Kahn, 1997).

Referring back to Patty from above, her moves were the result of negative behaviors. Foster family after foster family refused to deal with Patty's aggression, lying and bedwetting. Patty's ascribed role was that she was "bad" and "difficult." Her ascribed role caused her to act poorly. She defined herself as "too bad for anyone to keep." The worse she acted, the more she moved. It was a six year endeavor to assist Patty to see herself in a more positive light.

The roles learned in the family of origin lend themselves to creating expectations of the roles parents believe the adopted child will assume. As Patty makes clear, adopted children may have little experience with roles or they may have taken on a role that is not beneficial to themselves or the adoptive family.

Time as an Expectation

One year seems to be a marker frequently put forth as an adjustment period. It seems that there is a belief that in about a year the newly adopted child will be established in the adoptive family, and the adoptive family will be settled and moving forward. Chapter 2 will explain that the child's traumatic past may take years to overcome. Two other factors which may further exacerbate the time it will take to integrate a child into an adoptive family include psychological fit and shared history.

Psychological Fit

Psychological fit relates to the interplay between parental experiences, expectations, desires and wishes, and the child's capabilities and performance (Trout, 1986). Let's exemplify this concept and then discuss it further.

> Peggy and Cameron had four children by birth. These children ranged in ages from 7 to 14. Two were boys and two were girls. Peggy and Cameron felt very blessed. Their children were all healthy, excelled academically, and had terrific musical and artistic talents. Evenings were spent singing and playing the piano, flute, trombone and cello. Great pleasure also resulted from painting and trips to art museums. The family was fortunate financially. They decided to share their blessings by adopting an orphan. Eight-year-old Owen joined the family from Columbia. Owen struggled academically. He preferred baseball, soccer and swimming to reading and math. He also had no interest in singing, art or playing an instrument. His lack of "fit" affected everyone in the family. The cultural difference between Owen and his family further affected the "fit." Owen's presence in the family led to many questions and overt stares from neighbors, family friends, classmates and strangers.
>
> Peggy stated, "We simply cannot relate to him. He is not like us at all. We certainly expected that he would choose to do well in school. We thought that he would accept our interests as his own. We have attended his sporting events and have disliked every moment spent as spectators. We didn't realize that others would so acknowledge his 'color.' Everywhere we go, we feel people looking."
>
> Peggy and Cameron ultimately made the decision to dissolve their adoption of Owen. A new family was located for Owen. This family enthusiastically enjoys watching Owen score home runs and goals. Owen, scarred from the abandonment by his birthmother and his years in the orphanage, has been further hurt by the loss of his first American parents and his four siblings. He has little capacity to believe that his second adoptive family will "keep" him.

Peggy, Cameron and their children were not able to mesh with Owen. Peggy and Cameron were raised in families that placed great value on education and self-enhancement. They offered these values to their birth children who readily accepted and executed them. Owen's school performance defied their experiences and expectations. They were disillusioned by a child to whom academic success seemed to have no meaning. Peggy, Cameron and their children were always looked at as a wonderful family. The children received many accolades for their accomplishments. In turn, Peggy and Cameron were given compliments for their excellent parenting abilities. Now, they received confused looks, and embarrassing and rude questions because Owen was of a different culture. They did not like being in the spotlight in this manner. Their wishes for him to join the family's creative endeavors were thwarted by his preference for athletics. Ultimately, they felt that trying to blend Owen into their family was comparable to putting a round peg into a square hole—Owen would never "fit."

> Donna is the youngest of three female adolescent birth children. Several years ago, her family adopted Maggie. Maggie is now 9 years old. She has presented various challenges. She is clumsy. It seems that every time she enters a room she breaks something. She has little knowledge of personal boundaries. She enters Donna's bedroom without knocking. If she sees something she likes, she takes it. She constantly interrupts conversations. She is "busy"—she walks or runs around the house constantly. Sitting still is difficult for Maggie.
>
> Donna expected a sister who would enjoy dressing up, painting her nails and having her hair fixed. These were all things she enjoyed with her sisters. Maggie would have none of this. Maggie preferred toy trains and cars. She liked toys she could move around and that made noise. Donna and her sisters were quite compliant children. They wanted to please their parents. Maggie, on the other hand, wanted to do things her way. Donna could not comprehend this type of disobedience. Daily conflict erupted due to Maggie's insolence. Donna wrote the following:
>
> "I found it increasingly hard as the years went on to bond with Maggie. I felt most of my family's arguments and problems were her fault. Everything she did I felt was bothering me and I couldn't stand being around her. I resented her a lot for the problems that began to arise in my family, especially the constant arguments. I developed anxiety because of all of the conflict. It became really hard for me to be nice to her and even to think about getting close to her. I felt all she did was to keep trying to push away from my family and have my family push away farther from each other. I was mean to her. I yelled at her for not doing anything. I hated to be in the same room with her. I blamed everything on her.
>
> "I have had to work hard to overcome my feelings of resentment towards her. I no longer get irritated by her as much or as quick. I am always trying to be nice to her even though I know I slip and will be mean—she can still get on my nerves. I know that I do handle the problem a lot better now and I don't have near as many problems with her as I used to. I try to do fun things with her that I know she will like and that will be fun for her. When I look back at how mean I used to be to her, I feel terrible about it. I never want to act that way towards her again. It made me sad to think how much I could have been hurting her feelings and her views about herself. It also made me angry at myself that I could treat her that way and think it was okay. I realize that the problems in my family are no way near her fault. I now know she isn't the whole reason my family gets into arguments. I know I was being irrational about it. I would say I have mostly overcome the problem. I am able to handle being around her and playing with her without getting frustrated, angry or annoyed by her. I was able to become closer to her and know she was going to be my sister forever if I liked it or not. I would have to make it work without hurting her or myself."

Donna's poignant account helps us understand the personal struggle that she underwent in order to attain a level of "fit" with her sister. Maggie did not live up to Donna's experience of a sister nor her expectations of a sibling. Maggie entered the family with her own unique interests, abilities, temperament, strengths, weaknesses, values, attributes, etc. Initially, Donna focused on all of the things Maggie didn't have. Ultimately, Donna realized that there were some areas the two could share. She went about connecting—"fitting"—with Maggie in those areas. At present, Donna and Maggie can sometimes be found laughing together!

Many adoptive families will have to follow Donna's lead. Experiences, expectations, desires and wishes will have to be tailored to "fit" with the unique characteristics of the adoptee. This will be a process for each member of the adoptive family—parents, the children already in the family, and the child about to move into the family.

Facilitating psychological fit will also mean learning to "nurture a shared family culture" (Johnston, 2002). The gist of this idea is to steep the newly adopted child in the family's rituals and traditions, and to highlight the ways in which the adoptee is similar to the adoptive family.

Shared History

Psychological fit is further complicated as the toddler or older adopted child is someone who is not initially a "true" sibling. He is placed into the sibling role but does not know the rules by which the other children (whether born into the family or adopted into it years before) have grown up (Ward and Lewko, 1988). For that matter, he also does not know the family history, the likes and dislikes of family members, the inside jokes, the holiday traditions, birthdays and so forth.

Almost all of us have had the experience of being the "new person." For example, when you started your job, how long did it take to get to know your co-workers, the workplace dynamics, the formal and informal rules, where supplies were located, etc.? Learning all of this and assimilating into the workplace probably took time. Learning about a family and incorporating into a family will most likely take longer. The formation of parental and sibling relations will occur gradually over a long period of time—perhaps years.

Parents and professionals alike must control their expectations and their internal calendars for when change is expected. Having high expectations that must be achieved within a certain period of time and attempting to fit the child into the family within that time period may only lead to disappointment for all involved (Gill, 1978).

Typically Developing Children's Expectations of the Adoptee

"I will have a playmate!"

Brothers and sisters' expectations generally mirror those of the parents. When asked as part of the home study interview what they think about their parents' plan to adopt, many children perceive that they are getting a playmate with whom they will ride a bike, play football, or share their dolls. Some believe that they will get a younger brother or sister who will benefit from their help with homework or who will be open to absorbing their knowledge. Other children may be excited by the prospect of a sibling who will share in the chores. Such expectations make sense, especially if there is an existing healthy sibling relationship in the family prior to the placement of another sibling.

> "Simply put, siblings are socialization agents. The sibling relationship provides a context for social development. Through ongoing, long-term interactions siblings teach social skills to one another. Siblings are available as long-term playmates and companions. They help each other and teach each other. The relationship provides opportunities for sharing and the expression of feelings. They learn to share. They provide advice to each other. They offer a support system that continues through adulthood (Powell and Gallagher, 1993)."

Given that these children are rarely provided any pre-adoptive information by parents and professionals which would challenge their expectations, it makes even more sense that siblings-to-be enter the adoptive experience from a positive perspective.

Parental and Professional Contributions to Typically Developing Children's Expectations

"I am supposed to have a positive attitude about my new sibling."

Parents and professionals often unknowingly contribute to the resident children's expectations. One common method of preparing brothers and sisters for the arrival of an adopted sibling is to emphasize that the child is unfortunate and needs parents and a permanent home. Brothers and sisters-to-be are admonished to make the adoptee feel at home, and to help atone for the past deprivations experienced by the newcomer (Poland and Groze, 1993; Ward and Lewko, 1988).

Such post-adoption sentiments continue when parents encourage the typically developing children, "Put yourself in his place—he hasn't had what you have had," "We need to be more understanding," "We need to be more sensitive to how she feels." Such statements cause resident children to believe that they must maintain a positive attitude about the adoptive child and thus the experience overall. The typically developing children often believe a positive attitude is expected of them. So resident children keep questions or concerns to themselves.

Expectations of the Child Who Is Moving into the Family

"I won't be staying here."

The state of Ohio's Pre-finalization Adoption Services (Ohio Child Welfare Training Program, 1999) training program for families and professionals points out that children must complete two tasks before they are ready to accept adoptive status:

1. They must understand their history to the degree possible given their developmental level.
2. They must know that reunification with previous caregivers is not possible; they must psychologically separate from previous caregivers.

These ideas are reiterated and expanded by Vera Fahlberg in her book, *A Child's Journey Through Placement* (Indianapolis: Perspectives Press, 1991):

> Children cannot make optimum use of their placements until they have resolved their grief and formed new attachments. Unresolved separations may interfere with the development of new attachments. New attachments are not meant to replace old ones. They are meant to stand side by side with existing relationships. Bowlby (1980) points out that the success of a new relationship isn't dependent on the memory of an earlier one fading; rather the new one is likely to prosper when the two relationships are kept clear and distinct. Interference with the development of new attachments may occur when the child's focus is on the past rather than the present.
>
> Resolution of the grief process for children separated from birthparents means acceptance of having two sets of parents. Many times it is adults who adopt with the expectation,

"I want a child to love me," who have the greatest difficulty accepting that the child has two mothers or two fathers. The attitudes of parents who are threatened by the importance of other caregivers in their child's life may pose the biggest obstacle for him. Although most parents readily accept the fact that they can love more than one child, many have difficulty accepting that children can love more than one mother or father. The child may love each in different ways, but it does not have to be one over the other.

There are a number of children who have received therapy and pre-adoptive preparation. These children may enter the adoptive home with excitement and joy. They have longed for a "forever" family and now their dream is coming true. However, it is important to realize that many children moving into adoptive homes will not have been given the opportunity to resolve the loss of previous caregivers. Many believe that they will be reuniting with their birth families, a foster family or a birth relative. Thus, they may view the adoptive family as a holding tank, an interim place to live until they return to where they feel they most want to be.

Dustin, now age 14, was adopted from Romania at age 1½. Throughout his residence with his adoptive family, he has utilized an array of negative behavior to avoid forming a relationship with his adoptive parents. As a young child, he resisted nurture. He would push away or become stiff when his parents attempted to hug him, yet he was very affectionate with strangers. He would not make eye contact. He preferred to be alone. He was very demanding. He acted as if parents were only necessary to provide him things. He lacked a sense of reciprocity. Even at present, he continues to exhibit negative behaviors. For example, if asked to wash the dishes, he throws the silverware away, or makes sure to "forget" to wash a number of the dishes. Yet, he always remembers to put these dirty dishes in the cupboard. He frequently throws his homework out the bus window or in the trash upon arrival at school. Obviously, this has caused much hostility between school personnel and Dustin's parents. The teachers and principal believed that Dustin's parents were not helping him with his homework. Ultimately, when age 11, Dustin's parents brought him to therapy. The therapist asked Dustin if he ever thought about his birthmother. He was very quick to respond, "I think about her every day. I want to meet her. I would like to give her flowers and take her to lunch." Dustin's parents were stunned. They had no idea that he even thought about his birthmother, let alone that he had a definite plan to meet with her.

Tom joined his adoptive family when he was 10 years old. His history included six years with his birthfamily, almost two years with his birth grandfather, who died of an aneurysm, and then two years in the foster home of Jane and Lincoln. The plan for Tom was to be adopted by Jane and Lincoln. Several days before the adoption, these parents changed their minds. They decided they really could not manage Tom's sporadic temper outbursts. Tom was moved to the home of Elliot and Ruby. Subsequently, he was adopted by this family. However, when asked in therapy about Jane and Lincoln, Tom stated, "I really think I will go back there. They just couldn't mean it that they didn't want me." At the time of this statement, Tom had been at Elliot and Ruby's for four years.

Sarah, age 7, was removed from her birthmother as an infant. She was then placed in a foster home with a single mother, Mary. She resided in this home until age 4½, at which time she was moved to the home of Susan and Frank. The move occurred as Sarah's birthmother had a second child. This infant was taken into custody at the hospital by social services workers as the child tested positive for cocaine. The workers had arranged with Susan and Frank to take the infant. Subsequently, the agency realized they had two siblings residing in two separate homes. The agency decided to remedy the situation by moving Sarah to

Susan and Frank's home. The move happened after only three pre-placement visits between Sarah and her new family. Sarah was shocked. Mary was the only mother she had known. She actually thought Mary was her birthmother. So she believed that Susan and Frank had "stolen" her from her birthmother. Between the ages of 4½ and 7, Sarah stole constantly. She stole from family members, stores, neighbors and the church. To date, with much professional intervention, Sarah is coming to understand that her perceptions of Susan, Frank and Mary are inaccurate. As such, improvements are occurring.

"I think you will abuse me."

Monica was removed from her birth home at age 3 due to substance abuse and physical abuse. She spent two years in a foster home from which she was subsequently removed because of sexual abuse. She entered her adoptive family at age 5. Monica presented many challenges to her adoptive mother, Helen. The greatest difficulty occurred at bedtime. She would not go to sleep until she exhausted herself. This did not occur until 1:00 or 2:00 a.m., and only after she had screamed, pounded on her walls and ran up and down the stairs repeatedly. Helen had two older adopted children, so this situation was a cause of much stress for all family members. No one could get any sleep. Helen, a very astute woman, recognized that her young daughter was plagued with anxiety because nighttime was when her sexual abuse had occurred. She began discussing with her, daily, that she was not leaving her nor was anyone in her home going to hit her or have sex with her. She also put an alarm on Monica's door and informed her that the alarm would go off if anyone tried to come into her room. "The alarm is to help you feel safe." Over the next 18 months, her excellent solutions paid off. The bedtime problems were gradually reduced.

Monica's only experience of a family prior to her adoption by Helen was that, "Parents are people who hurt you." She had moved to Helen's house fully expecting that abuse would occur. Her behaviors were her irrational way of attempting to protect herself. Her illogical behaviors were also her way of letting her new mom know that she needed help to comprehend what had happened to her in her previous homes.

"I think you are another orphanage."

Institutional settings have a "culture" as do families. Culture is a system of values, beliefs, attitudes, traditions and standards of behavior that govern the organization of people. The chart on page 33 highlights several key differences between the "culture" of an orphanage and that of a family.

Institutionalized children spend a bulk of time with other children. They reside in a group environment wherein interaction with peers is dominant. Prospective adoptive families must understand that the child adopted internationally has learned about group living, not about family life. Children learn this group philosophy at very early ages. Certainly, it is not uncommon to see children adopted at 12 months old (and in some cases younger) and up operating in a family as if the parents only exist to provide food, clothing and toys. These children seek little adult interaction beyond that which is essential. In essence, the child feels as if he has been moved to a different orphanage. Your family may have more food, better quality food, a softer bed, nicer clothing and an abundance of toys, yet the adults are looked at as caregivers rather than parents. Sibling relationships are skewed as well. In some cases, the adoptee attempts to use siblings to meet his needs. The adoptee is more comfortable with children. It is the sibling who approaches the parents for snacks, drinks, new toys and privileges on behalf of the

ORPHANAGE CULTURE VS. FAMILY CULTURE	
Survival/Self Reliance Poverty, governmental policies, lack of staff education, lack of medical care, etc. may cause an atmosphere in which the meeting of physical needs prevails. Meeting psychological needs not a priority.	**Reciprocity/Trust** Parents desire to have and raise a child within an environment of caring and sharing. This meets the child's physical and psychological needs.
Uncertainty Caregivers may not provide nurturing. They change shifts, leave to pursue other employment or may be a source of abuse. Peers leave as a result of adoption, a move to a different orphanage, illness or death. The child learns that people go away. Those who should provide me affection do not. Those who should protect me do not always do so. Often, there is little or no focus on the child's future due to the demands of meeting the day-to-day basic needs. The child internalizes a one-day-at-a-time attitude as tomorrow everything may be different.	**Predictability** Parents instill trust and safety by consistently meeting the child's needs. The child learns that parents behave in predictable ways. "I can rely on my parents." The child transfers this knowledge to other spheres of life such as, "I can rely on my teacher." There is emphasis on the child's future. Parents provide education and experiences essential to carry out career goals, marriage, family life, friendships, etc. The child internalizes the family's values. The child views investment in the future as valuable and worthwhile.
Routine Orphanages utilize a regimented routine to provide for children. Children eat on a schedule, go to the bathroom on a schedule, sleep on a schedule and so on. This schedule is based on a timeline created by the staff. The child may not learn to regulate bodily functions. The child does not learn to express his needs. The child may determine that he meets his own needs. For example, "I hold my own bottle. I provide my own food."	**Internal Regulation** Families also utilize routines to carry out daily tasks. However, the routines are more flexible and take into account individual needs. For example, an infant is fed as the infant expresses a cry of hunger. An older child may be provided three meals per day and snacks on request. The family accommodates its members, rather than the members totally accommodating the routine. The child learns many valuable life skills from this—reliance on parents, delaying gratification if parents are involved in meeting the needs of another family member, internal regulation of bodily functions, interdependence, cooperation, etc.

adoptee. In other instances, the adoptee may avoid forming relationships with siblings if he is uncertain as to whether or not the siblings will remain in the family. After all, he thinks, many orphanage friends left the orphanage to be adopted, to move to another orphanage or because they were ill.

This situation may be compounded by the use of professional child care soon after the adoptee has arrived in his new family. A room full of children and staff resembles an orphanage to the formerly institutionalized child. Depending on the number of hours the child is in a child care program, the child's integration into the family may be inhibited.

Additional Prominent Expectations

"I want to adopt a young child. A young child will be easier to integrate into the family."

Once motivated to adopt, a majority of adoptive families have a preference to adopt as young a child as possible. The expectation is that younger children will be easier to integrate into the family. The expectation is also that younger children will have few to no problems.

Chris and Jenny adopted two children from Eastern Europe. Their son, Don, was adopted at 6 months old. He is currently 12 years old. He exhibits periods of raging, during which he becomes aggressive and uses profanity in his interactions with his parents. At other times, he is depressed and screams that he wants to kill himself. He has been evaluated and treated by various professionals. Eight years of services have effected little change. Jenny continues to have a hard time believing that six months could have caused so much damage. She has stated many times, "We adopted so young. I was certain that we wouldn't have problems."

Their daughter, Danielle, on the other hand arrived at age 2. She does well in school and loves to play basketball. She helps around the house and enjoys spending time with her mom reading. Danielle spent two years in an institutional setting, yet was minimally impacted by this experience.

There are currently schools of thought as to why traumatic events impact some more than others. However, at this time, it is difficult to say with any certainty why one person is more affected by traumatic experiences than another.

Both Bill and Natalee came from large families. They dreamed of having a large family of their own. They had three beautiful birth daughters. A fourth child was not possible due to secondary infertility. Age was considered the source of the infertility problems. They became foster parents and through fostering they adopted two sons and another daughter. Each of their children was adopted young; under the age of 16 months old. Currently, these adoptees are ages 9, 7 and 5. As a group they are involved in special education, psychiatric services, mental health therapy, occupational therapy and speech therapy. Natalee often comments, "I wish I had better understood that adopting younger wasn't a guarantee that the children would be problem-free. I thought that because we got the children so young, we wouldn't have the types of problems I heard other foster and adoptive parents describe." Neither Bill nor Natalee regrets the addition of their three adopted children to their family. They do, however, wish they had been more assertive regarding the depth of information they received about each of their adopted children before the adoptions were finalized. They also wish they had been more open-minded during their pre-adoptive education training program. They entered the pre-adoptive education classes feeling as if their parenting experience and their love would be enough to overcome anything a foster child had encountered. Now, years later, they realize these expectations were erroneous. Their children are slowly recovering from their past. However, this is occurring due to much professional assistance and because Bill and Natalee continuously strive to develop and implement new parenting tools.

Chapter 2 will provide information regarding the impact of various traumas experienced by children prior to adoption. The content makes clear that most damage occurs in the first two years of life. ***Therefore, the belief that younger children will present fewer problems is unfounded.***

In addition, families involved in the adoption of children through foster care often indicate a desire to adopt a child age infant to age 5. Currently, the average age of the children available through the foster care system is 8 years 6 months. Of the 114,000 children available for adoption in 2006, 62% were age 6 and older (AFCARS, 2006). The expectation of getting a very young child is a mismatch with the population of waiting children.

"I don't want to deal with birthparents."

The media has unfortunately sensationalized those rare instances in which birthparents returned for a child that had been adopted. Prime time movies, newspapers and television news have given the false impression that adoptions are reversed, via court proceedings, on a frequent basis! In fact, only 1% to 2% of all adoptions end in such a manner (Pertman, 2007). The vast majority of adoptions are never challenged. The domestic or international adoptee, once adopted, remains with his or her adoptive parents.

Frightened parents report that a major factor in deciding to adopt internationally is they feel that intercountry adoptions are immune from birthparents tracking them down to reclaim their adopted son or daughter. So they escape the physical appearance of the birthfamily.

However, no form of adoption evades the psychological presence of the birthparents. As we learned under the heading, "I won't be staying here," adoptees, even those adopted as infants, fantasize about their birthparents. As soon as the adoptee comprehends that he was not born to his adoptive parents, he becomes aware that another mother "gave him away." From that point on, he is susceptible to feeling the loss of this other mother. Chapter 8 will explain that this loss is developmental. The adoptee will grieve this loss throughout childhood, adolescence and well into adulthood.

Recognition of the adoptive status also sets in motion thoughts about what life would be like if the adoptee had remained in his or her birth home. Depending on the child's age at the time of the adoption and the circumstances surrounding the adoption, children will ask various questions among which may be,

"What do my birthparents look like?"

"What are their names?"

"Do I look like them?"

"Do they have any other children?"

"Do I have any aunts or uncles or grandparents?"

"What are they doing?"

"What would I be doing if I were with them?"

"What is my medical history?"

"Why did they place me for adoption?"

Questions such as these lead 50% of all adopted persons to search for their birth relatives at some point in their lives (Child Welfare Information Gateway, 2004; Muller and Perry, 2001).

The child's knowledge that he was adopted, and his natural curiosity about his birthfamily, makes adoptive parents vulnerable to "dealing with" birthparents.

"My agency will provide me with all the information I need."

Prospective adoptive families rely on the expertise of agency staff to help select a child who will best fit into their family. Professionals have an obligation to portray a potential placement as accurately as possible. Yet as Chapter 5 will explain, the placing of children is not an exact science. There are many factors which confound the placement process.

The child is served by numerous workers throughout her stay in foster care. There are workers who remove the child from her birthfamily. There are workers who know the child as they conducted the birthfamily reunification efforts. There are professionals who supervise the child's life in the foster home. Then, when the child is legally free for adoption, the child may be assigned a worker from the adoption unit. There are also workers who guide the family through the adoption process. These social workers for the family are learning about the child simultaneous to the family. Each worker knows the child at different time periods, so each worker's experience of the child is diverse. Professionals may have a different knowledge base as a result of the length of time they have been in their positions. Developing competency regarding the wide array of special needs presented by the waiting children takes time. So the abilities of agency staff to present children to prospective adoptive families will vary due to their experiences with the child and due to their knowledge of the issues the children available for adoption present.

The child may be coming to the adoptive family after a lengthy stay with one foster family or the child may have moved through a series of foster homes. The child may be coming from a treatment facility. Many caregivers may be or may have been involved with the child. Information coming from multiple foster parents or numerous treatment staff varies as children's responses to individual caregivers differs. Thus, the child's reaction to the adoptive parents may be hard to predict.

There are wide variations in the information provided to the adoptive family prior to the adoption. The history of international adoptees is often quite sketchy. Usually the summary given to the parents includes some medical information plus a few details about the birthparents and the circumstances which caused the child to come into institutional or foster care. Many families are not allowed to tour the orphanage in which their child has resided. Parents often cannot gain a sense of what the child experienced while in residence there.

There is an assumption that when foster parents adopt, they already know everything about the child. A tendency exists to minimize the need to review all information available about the child.

> William and Robin became foster parents in response to radio advertisements. Their birth children were both in college. Fostering seemed a good way to help the community as well as take away the feelings about their empty nest. Shortly after they completed their paperwork, 3½-year-old Eddie arrived. They fostered Eddie from age 3½ to age 6 when they were asked if they would like to adopt Eddie. William and Robin, like many foster parents,

never expected to become adoptive parents. However, Eddie had lived with them almost three years. How could they abandon him after all this time?

Even though he had behavioral difficulties, they believed that once he was adopted, he would recognize his permanent status in their home, and so he would "settle down." Their social workers had agreed with this view. Three years later, his negative behaviors had escalated. They sought a variety of mental health and special education services. Their current mental health provider asked at intake what they knew about Eddie's history prior to his placement in their home. Robin recollected that there seemed to have been "some" neglect, and that he was also separated from a younger female sibling. The intake professional inquired as to whether they had any written documentation of his pre-adoptive life. Indeed, Robin and William stated that they had been given a packet of information at the court house just before the finalization ceremony. She knew she had the packet "somewhere." At their next appointment, Robin had located the packet from the "back of the closet." She and William acknowledged that they had never even looked at the documents.

A review of the materials revealed that Eddie had been exposed to cocaine prenatally, that domestic violence prevailed in the birth home, and that the neglect included that Eddie spent a large majority of his time locked in a small bedroom alone. His younger sibling was so malnourished at the time the children were removed from the birthmother, that she was life-flighted to the local hospital. There was not "some" neglect. There had been "profound" neglect. His birth sister had been placed in a foster home and this foster family eventually adopted her. The packet contained a letter written by her adoptive mother. She provided her contact information so that Eddie could be a part of his sister's life.

William and Robin were quite surprised by the additional facts they learned about their son. They truly had not grasped the extent of the trauma he had experienced prior to residence in their home. This new information caused them to realize that Eddie's needs were greater than they had anticipated. This family entered a state of crisis. For several months they considered attempting to dissolve the adoption. They had not bargained for a child whose issues would take so much time and energy to resolve.

Robin reported, "I never expected that we would adopt once we became foster parents. Once faced with the choice to move Eddie on or keep him we just couldn't believe that moving him to another family was fair to him. Now, we are faced with the long-term prospect of doing our best to help him heal. We never anticipated fostering would change our lives to this degree."

Actually, 60% of foster children are adopted by their foster parents (AFCARS, 2006). Foster parents may want to consider that they, like Robin and William, may become adoptive parents. This calls to light the need to approach fostering as if the child will be yours permanently. Gathering information throughout the entire time you foster a child may be of great benefit to each member of your family.

Overall, Eddie's agency had provided a wealth of pertinent information about Eddie's pre-adoptive history. The manner of delivery did not allow William and Robin time to review the paperwork and make an informed decision about their capacity to manage Eddie's needs over the long-term. Eddie's case calls to light the need for foster parents and workers to review the child's history, in its entirety, before the foster family consents to an adoption.

Domestic adoption may offer a greater amount of information about a child, especially if the child has resided in foster care for a period of time. These written materials and/or verbal presentations provided to acquaint a family with a child are full of broad terms or diagnoses—sexual abuse, Bi-polar Disorder, AD/HD, neglect, domestic violence and so on. Without adequate assistance parents are not always able to interpret the meaning of the descriptors commonly utilized throughout the child welfare and mental health systems. The language of professionals is a new and unfamiliar language to the family. Parents may hesitate to ask questions as well. They may fear that too many inquiries will jeopardize their chances of being selected for a particular placement. Chapter 5 will offer suggestions as to how to interpret the information a family receives about a child. Expectations may also prevent families from reviewing the child's history adequately.

Ellen and Don were foster parents to Kevin when he was 3 and 4 years old. Kevin was then reunified with his birthmother with whom he remained until he was age 7. One day, Kevin went to school and a teacher noticed that he had numerous bruises. Social Services was contacted. The social services worker decided that it was not safe for Kevin to return to his birthmother's home. Kevin entered foster care again. His behavior was difficult and as such he entered a cycle of moving. He passed through eight homes in a four-year period; six were foster homes and two were potential pre-adoptive homes. His social worker, searching for another prospective adoptive home for Kevin, decided to contact Ellen and Don. Ellen and Don were immediately interested. They had fond memories of Kevin as a pre-school age youngster. The social worker provided Ellen and Don an extensive summary of Kevin's life. The social worker arranged for Ellen and Don to meet with all of the professionals involved with Kevin. Kevin's therapist asked if they had had time to review the reports and if so, what questions did they have. Ellen replied that she had no need to read the assessments and she had no questions. She stated that the reason Kevin had not been adopted was that the previous families had "not really loved him." Ellen was convinced that the love that she and Don had to offer Kevin would resolve Kevin's problems. Kevin was placed with Ellen and Don. The placement quickly entered a state of crisis. The placement remains unstable to date. Ellen's expectation that love would be enough did not match with the reality of parenting Kevin. Additionally, Kevin was no longer a cute and fun young child. He was a pre-adolescent with many serious mental health issues. Ellen's expectations and her image of Kevin prevented her from making an informed decision about the types of parenting challenges Kevin would present post-placement.

There are cases in which trauma experienced by the child comes to light post-placement.

Hannah resided with her birthmother until age 6. A neighbor notified the county social services agency that Hannah was not being cared for adequately. Upon investigation, Hannah was found alone and bruises covered her face, arms and back. There was no food or running water. Hannah was placed in foster care. Subsequently, she became legally free for adoption. She was adopted by Peter and Rachel when she was 10 years old. During fifth grade, she attended a presentation on puberty. A few days after this lecture, Hannah and Rachel were running errands. Hannah blurted out that her birthmom let men touch her "private parts." Peter and Rachel made arrangements for Hannah to enter therapy. During her course of therapy, Hannah revealed sexual abuse including intercourse and oral sex. The acts occurred with many men, all of whom were known to Hannah as "boyfriends" of her birthmom.

Peter and Rachel had been told, pre-placement, that it was suspected that Hannah was sexually abused as she exhibited behaviors associated with sexual abuse. The placing agency had no knowledge of the extent of the abuse. Hannah stated that she finally told Rachel about the abuse since she felt comfortable with her and she "couldn't stop thinking about it" after the discussion of puberty occurred.

Prospective adoptive families have the right to full disclosure prior to accepting a child into their home. Full disclosure is complicated by the factors described above. Chapter 5 will offer suggestions to improve the dissemination of information to adoptive parents.

"I can return to my agency if I need help."

"Yes" and "no" is perhaps a good way to address this statement. "Yes," the adoptive family may certainly call their placing agency or their local home study agency for assistance post-placement. However, a placing agency may be just that: an agency who specializes in the placement of a child with a family. Such agencies, public or private, may be able to offer referrals to community services, resources to expand parental knowledge of the child's needs, brief respite or simply a voice on the other end of the phone to listen. Beyond that, the family will need to look elsewhere—the mental health system or adoption medical clinics—to obtain more intensive services. So "no," the adoptive family may not return to their agency to have all of their issues resolved long-term.

Families, once they realize the extent of the problems presented by an adoptee, may develop anger toward the agencies involved in the placement of the child in their home. Many parents state that they feel they were "lied to" or "no one told us it could be like this." At times, the family feels as if the agency "owes" them services and the funding to acquire the necessary interventions. The parents' perception is that they took a child who was damaged through no fault of their own. Therefore, it is up to agencies to cover expenses relevant to helping the child achieve a state of well-being.

Agencies, on the other hand, may have a very different perspective. They may feel that the family adopted of their own free will. They often feel that the family made a commitment to the child. Agencies feel that fulfilling that commitment means that the parents are responsible to facilitate acquisition and implementation of needed services. Further, local, state and federal budgetary guidelines do not always allow monies for post-adoption services.

From a child-centered perspective, services should be made available. The child did not ask to be abused, neglected, institutionalized or abandoned. The child did not ask to have pre-natal drug exposure or learning disabilities. Unfortunately, there are gaps in the systems that serve adoptees and their family members. Adoption subsidy is essential and helpful. It may not cover all expenses and it may not cover adoption-competent professionals. International adoptees are not eligible for adoption subsidy monies. As such, families need to ask—prior to adopting—as to the availability of services in their community. Several chapters, especially Chapter 10, will present content regarding the types of services commonly utilized post-placement. Parents need to investigate whether or not funding, exclusive of subsidy, is available post-adoption. Parents need to factor this information into their decision to adopt. Parents who proceed with adoption may expect to have to advocate, travel and put forth out-of-pocket expenses in order to adequately meet the needs of the child who experienced trauma prior to his adoption.

In-depth food for thought regarding this topic is available in *Strengthening Families and Communities: An Approach to Post-Adoption Services*. This White Paper is put forth by Casey Family Services and is available online at www.caseyfamilyservices.org/pdfs/casey_pawhitepaper.pdf.

The Clash of Expectations with Reality

The content and the vignettes thus far should have helped to clarify that parents, brothers and sisters come to adoption with expectations that may be both unrealistic and contrary to those of the adoptee. The post-placement result of such dissonance is a clash between expectations and reality. The family is expecting a new family member who is thrilled to join their family. The adoptee is often expecting to go someplace else, to suffer more abuse or to continue to live as if in an institutional setting.

Chapter 2 will make clear that children with special needs are not always capable of being good playmates nor do they always readily accept help with their homework. They may have a preference to attempt to manage their own needs rather than seek assistance from a parent or sibling. Their traumatic pre-placement experiences have left them with fragmented development and as such their actual skills are in discord with their chronological ages.

The following statements made by typically developing children, ages 6 to 15, will offer a precursor as to what happens when expectations do not match with reality. These sentiments were expressed in interviews I conducted with resident children several years after an adoption had taken place in their family.

> "I expected children who were like my sister and me. I thought I could teach them the fun things I did when I was younger, like dolls, sidewalk chalk and sewing. At first, there was a nice period. And then, they basically started terrorizing the house—running around, breaking things, fighting. So it turned into a mess. I expected a lot different from what we got."

> "When he came to our house, everything changed. He screamed, he copied me, he pinched me and he broke my toys."

> "Well, I wasn't really prepared for the big change. I had two sisters and a brother before he came. We got along and played a lot. I thought he would be the same. I didn't think that he would be the way that he was. I thought he was going to be like us, more civilized."

> "I thought I was going to get a fun little brother. Everything really changed after he came. I was disappointed. He just seemed to run around and be all crazy and wild."

> "I wanted a sister who would like to play games and use her imagination with me. I thought it would be pretty fun having her here. Her behavior has not been very good. We have to do a lot more work helping her than we used to. My dad has more gray hair now. Our house isn't as much fun because she takes up most of our time. It kinda upsets me. I thought we were going to get a baby. It does make me happy that I can see what she does that's wrong so I can keep from doing that myself."

> "When they first came, we played like regular brothers and sisters. Later, that period ended. I expected to have some fun brothers and sisters to play with. It's not fun at all. Sometimes my brother plays with me, but my sister and I don't even talk most of the time. I expected a happier family. I ended up with a family that isn't so happy. I am mad about that. I am mad at my brother and sister, but mostly I am mad at my parents because they made a decision that changed my life."

> "He was staying with one of our friends. I met him for like two minutes at a fair. I figured it wouldn't matter; just someone to hang around the house and play with and stuff. I was wrong. I am eight months older and I expected to just have another brother to hang out with. He's a pain. He isn't as bad as he used to be, but he's still so annoying."

The Development of Realistic Expectations: Myth or Actuality?

It would be wonderful if every adoptive family could go into their adoption expecting a specific array of problems for which they were well prepared. The parents would patiently assist their adoptive child to heal from past hurts. They would be calm in light of managing various behavioral difficulties. They would not fret over calls from the teacher recanting Johnny's latest insolence at school. Adoption-competent mental health services would be easily accessible and affordable. Agencies would have a system in place to advise families in crisis. Is this possible? Most likely, the answer is currently "no." The child welfare system and public mental health system are under-funded and fraught with staff turnover. This statement is not offered as an excuse. It is put forth as a fact. Families need to be aware that systems operate as they do, not always as they should.

So what is feasible? Following are some ideas about what might be realistic to achieve in the pre-adoptive phase. The common thread of these suggestions is that they lead to the family obtaining early intervention. Help attained at the onset of trouble is likely to minimize the duration and intensity of the family's struggles.

- The prospective adoptive family should be provided with a thorough pre-adoptive training. An overriding theme of pre-adoptive education must be to expect problems. As a result, even if the family does not believe the material, they will gain trust in the agency. As such, when post-placement difficulties do crop up, the family recalls that the agency informed them that problems could occur. So the family does not hesitate to call the agency for assistance. The family is aware that the agency will not think they are "bad" parents who should not have the child. The family who calls and states, "You told us things wouldn't always go well, but we didn't believe you" is in a much better position than the family who feels the agency left them ill-informed or misinformed. This family is not likely to call the agency to ask for referrals to qualified adoption-competent professionals. Critical time is lost in accessing help.
- It must be recognized that any pre-adoptive training is virtually a drop in the bucket of knowledge. We go to college for two, four or more years to prepare for a career. We go to pre-adoptive education classes for 20, 24, or 36 hours to prepare for parenting a child who has experienced many insults to his development and beliefs about the world. In essence, we receive less training to carry out the most important job undertaken by adults—parenting! Further, the prospective family is frequently receiving information in light of having no experience with children who have been neglected, abused, abandoned, institutionalized, etc. There is a big difference between what is learned in college and starting a first job. There is a big difference in understanding that a heart attack can occur and actually having a heart attack. Real experiences often cause us to understand information we have received. Overall, parents and professionals alike must develop appropriate expectations of what pre-adoptive training can accomplish. It is a starting place. It must be looked at as one means—an important means—of helping the adoptive family understand the journey on which they are about to embark. Much learning will occur "on the job" after the child has arrived in the family.
- During the training process, the adoptive family should have the opportunity to form a support system consisting of the agency staff, the other families comprising their pre-adoptive training classes and one or more veteran adoptive families. An array of supports means that the family is likely to get hold of someone, with

experience, to talk to quickly. Families who enter a crisis need help fast! They need to talk to someone who can "normalize" what is happening in their home. They need to converse with someone who can offer solutions—immediate and long-term.

- A component of the pre-adoptive phase should include identifying adoption-competent professionals within the family's community. In some cases, such resources might be geographically situated a distance from the family's home. However, it is often better to seek the help of an adoption specialist, even if there is travel time involved. Pre-adoptive trauma creates a mental health threat to the child and family akin to the physical threat posed by cancer, diabetes, cystic-fibrosis or other terminal and chronic medical conditions. Armed with this list of resources, the family is swiftly able to arrange for relevant services.

Parents must recognize that they need to be pro-active. Seek out other adoptive families prior to the child's arrival in your home. Determine whether there is local, state or federal funding available for post-adoptive services. Learn the guidelines for such monies and the types of services these programs cover. Talk to your health insurance company. Gain an understanding of your mental health coverage. Learn what types of services are covered and what your co-pay responsibility is. Contact mental health professionals in your area. Chapter 5 offers a list of questions to ask these providers. In this manner, you will have services in mind prior to your need. Lastly, read, read and read some more! Over the past ten years there has been an explosion of information in the areas of attachment, adoption and trauma. Utilize the chapter by chapter resources in this book to assist you in obtaining information. Ultimately, you will be responsible to help yourselves, the children you already parent and your adoptee navigate the relationships necessary to become a family.

Conclusions

Parents, typically developing children and prospective adoptees enter the adoption process with expectations. In Chapters 8 and 9, we will return to and expand upon this topic of expectations. It is important to revise these expectations in order to integrate the adoptee into the family unit. Trauma causes a further clash with parental and typically developing siblings' expectations. The adopted child does not simply "forget" his past or "leave it behind" once in a new family. Chapter 2 moves to the pre-adoptive training phase of the adoption process. This chapter will make clear that the child's trauma may greatly impact the ability of the adopted child to blend into a new family system. The expectation that an adoptive family will heal all of the child's past hurts is an expectation that needs to be shed by all members of the adoptive family and the adoption community at large.

Resources

Books for All Families

Bank, Stephen P. and Michael D. Kahn. *The Sibling Bond*. (New York: Basic Books, 1997.)

Barret, Robert and Bryan Robinson. *Gay Fathers: Encouraging the Hearts of Gay Dads and Their Families*. (Hoboken: Jossey-Bass, 2000.)

Blomquist, Barbara Taylor. *Insight Into Adoption: What Adoptive Parents Need to Know About the Fundamental Differences Between a Biological and an Adopted Child and its Effect on Parenting.* (Springfield: Charles C. Thomas Publisher, 2001.)

Clunis, D. Merilee and G. Dorsey Green. *The Lesbian Parenting Book: A Guide to Creating Families and Raising Children.* (Seattle: Seal Press, 1995.)

Davenport, Dawn. *The Complete Book of International Adoption: A Step by Step Guide to Finding Your Child.* (New York: Broadway, 2006.)

Eldridge, Sherrie. *Twenty Things Adopted Kids Wish Their Adoptive Parents Knew.* (Colorado Springs: NavPress, 1999.)

Eldridge, Sherrie. *Twenty Life Transforming Choices Adoptees Need to Make.* (Colorado Springs: NavPress, 2003.)

Gray, Deborah D. *Attaching in Adoption.* (Indianapolis: Perspectives Press, Inc., 2002.)

Hughes, Daniel A. *Facilitating Developmental Attachment.* (Dunmore, Pennsylvania: Jason Aronson/Inghram Book Company, 2000.)

Johnston, Patricia Irwin. *Adoption Is a Family Affair! What Relatives and Friends Must Know.* (Indianapolis: Perspectives Press, Inc., 2001.)

Keck, Gregory C. and Regina M. Kupecky. *Adopting the Hurt Child: Hope for Families with Special-Needs Kids: A Guide for Parents and Professionals.* (Colorado Springs: NavPress, 1995.)

Register, Cheri. *A Mother Reflects on Raising Internationally Adopted Children.* (St. Paul, MN: Yeong and Yeong Book Co., 2005.)

Schooler, Jayne E. and Thomas C. Atwood. *Whole Life Adoption Book.* (Colorado Springs: NavPress, 1993, revised 2008.)

Varon, Lee. *Adopting on Your Own: The Complete Guide to Adopting as a Single Parent.* (New York: Farrer, Straus and Giroux, 2000.)

Verrier, Nancy Newton. *The Primal Wound: Understanding the Adopted Child.* (Verrier, 1993.)

Websites for All Families

AdoptUsKids
www.adoptuskids.org

Adopt Us Kids provides a national photo listing service of available children throughout the United States. The website offers an overview of "getting started" with the adoption of children from the foster care system. Parents can request to be contacted regarding questions about foster care or the adoption process. The site also hosts a prospective parent blog. Adopt Us Kids is a valuable resource for professionals as well. Training and technical assistance are available in the areas of recruitment, retention and placement practices.

Child Welfare Information Gateway
www.childwelfare.gov

The Child Welfare Information Gateway is a comprehensive resource on all aspects of adoption and is a service of the Children's Bureau; Administration for Children and Families; and the Department of Health and Human Services. Services include technical assistance to professionals and policy makers, a library collection, publications, searchable databases on adoption resources, and information on federal and state legislation. This website is packed with articles on all aspects of adoption and trauma. Parents and professionals will find this organization of utmost assistance pre- and post-adoption.

Child Welfare League of America
www.cwla.org

The Child Welfare League of America (CWLA) program spans adoption, adolescent pregnancy prevention and teen parenting, child day care, child protection, children affected by incarceration, family foster care, group residential care, housing and homelessness, kinship care, juvenile justice, mental health, positive youth development, substance abuse prevention and treatment, and a range of community services that strengthen and support parents and families. As the nationally recognized standard-setter for child welfare services, CWLA provides direct support to agencies that serve children and families, improving the quality of the services they provide to more than nine million children every year. This website includes an online store that offers a large selection of books and gifts for both adults and children.

Evan B. Donaldson Adoption Institute
www.adoptioninstitute.org

The Evan B. Donaldson Adoption Institute's mission is to provide leadership that improves adoption law, policies and practices—through sound research, education and advocacy—in order to better the lives of everyone touched by adoption. All adoption professionals should review this website periodically to stay abreast of cutting edge research and recommendations pertaining to all facets of adoptees and the adoption process.

Joint Council on International Children's Services
www.jcics.org

The Joint Council on International Children's Services (JCICS) is the lead voice on intercountry children's services. Its mission is to advocate on behalf of children in need of permanent, safe and loving families. Joint Council promotes ethical child welfare practices, strengthens professional standards and educates adoptive families, social service professionals and government representatives throughout the world. This website contains a parent section which provides useful information to guide families through the international adoption process. Joint Council also puts forth country specific information for over 50 countries. The website includes information about the JCICS annual conference.

Perspectives Press
www.perspectivespress.com

Perspectives Press has specialized in publishing books about adoption and infertility for 25 years. The website provides an overview of each of the books available. Purchases can be made directly through the website. Perspectives Press also features an array of articles written by its authors as well as the authors' speaking schedules.

Tapestry Books
www.tapestrybooks.com

Tapestry Books offers more than 300 adult and children's books on adoption, infertility and parenting adopted children. The children, pre-teen and teen topics include understanding adoption, thinking about birthparents, celebrating differences and being in foster care. For adults, topics include international adoption, transcultural adoption, pre-adoption preparation, talking about adoption, adopting older children/children with special needs, attachment, search and reunion, foster parenting and infertility. The bookstore may be browsed by topic, author or title.

The Sibling Support Project
www.siblingsupport.org

The Sibling Support Project is a national effort dedicated to the life-long concerns of brothers and sisters of people who have special health, developmental or mental health concerns. The Sibling Support Project believes that disabilities, illness, and mental health issues affect the lives of *all* family members. Consequently, they work to increase the peer support and information opportunities for brothers and sisters of people with special needs and to increase parents' and providers' understanding of sibling issues. Their list serves connect siblings of all ages.

Magazines for All Families

***Adoption Today* Magazine**
www.adoptinfo.net

This is the only magazine dedicated to international and transracial adoption.

***Adoptive Families* Magazine**
www.adoptivefamilies.com

Adoptive Families magazine is a national award winning adoption magazine providing information for families before, during and after adoption. The *Adoptive Families* website offers a wealth of adoption related articles!

***Fostering Families Today* Magazine**
www.fosteringfamiliestoday.com

This magazine is packed with honest and poignant articles related to foster care and adoption. This magazine is a must read for anyone involved with children from the child welfare system.

Resources Especially for Kinship Caregivers

Books

Crumbley, Joseph. *Kinship Care: Relatives Raising Children.* (Washington, D.C.: Child Welfare League of America, 1997.)

Melina, Lois Ruskai and Sharon Kaplan Roszia. *The Open Adoption Experience: A Complete Guide for Adoptive and Birth Families—from Making the Decision through the Child's Growing Years.* (New York: HarperCollins Publishers, 1993.)

Takas, Marianne. *Grandparents Raising Grandchildren: A Guide to Finding Help and Hope.* (New York: The Brookdale Foundation, 1995.)

Articles

Beltran, Ana. "Kinship Care Providers: Some Permanency Options." North American Council on Adoptable Children. http://www.nacac.or/adoptalk/kniship.html

Child Welfare Information Gateway. "Kinship Caregivers and the Child Welfare System." http://www.childwelfare.gov/pubs/f_kinshi/f_kinshia.cfm

Conway, Tiffany and Rutledge Hutson. "Is Kinship Care Good for Children?" Center for Law and Social Policy. http://www.clasp.org/publications/is_kinship_care_good.pdf

Financial Support

Child Welfare Information Gateway. "Adoption Assistance for Children Adopted from Foster Care." http://www.childwelfare.gov/pubs/f_subsid.cfm

North American Council on Adoptable Children. Adoption Subsidy Resource Center. http://www.nacac.org/adoptionsubsidy/adoptionsubsidy.html

US Department of Health and Human Services. "Children in Temporary Assistance for Needy Families (TANF) Child-Only Cases with Relative Caregivers." http://aspe.hhs.gov/HSP/child-only04/report.pdf

Websites

American Association of Retired Persons (AARP)
www.aarp.org

AARP is the leading nonprofit, nonpartisan membership organization for people age 50 and over in the United States. The group is known for providing a host of services to this ever-growing segment of the population. Among these services is their Grandparent Information Center which offers an array of information to relatives raising relatives.

The Brookdale Foundation
www.brookdalefoundation.org/index.htm

The Brookdale Foundation Group focuses on the needs and challenges of America's elderly.

Their mission is to enhance the quality of life for America's senior citizens and to further the fields of gerontology and geriatrics. The Relatives as Parents Program (RAPP) encourages and promotes the creation or expansion of services for grandparents and other relatives who have taken on the responsibility of kinship care giving. This organization offers a number of publications related to kinship parenting, and the organization offers grants to establish kinship services.

Generations United
http://www.gu.org//index.asp

Since its beginning in 1986, Generations United has been the leading intergenerational membership organization in the United States. In a unique national partnership, AARP, Child Welfare League of America, Children's Defense Fund and Generations United have created fact sheets containing the most up-to-date state information related to grandfamilies, including:

- Census data on the number of grandparent caregivers
- A comprehensive list of kinship care family resources and services
- State foster care policies for kinship caregivers
- Information about key public benefits programs
- State kinship care laws

The Kinship Center
www.kinshipcenter.org

The Kinship Center is dedicated to the creation, preservation and support of foster, adoptive and relative families for children who need them. Sign up for their online class, Relative Caregiving: Strategies for Kinship Caregiving.

Kinship Navigator

Kinship Navigator programs are state initiatives that provide information, referral and follow-up services to grandparents and other relatives raising children to link them to the benefits and services that they or the children need. Navigators help relatives access services and programs like Temporary Assistance for Needy Families (TANF) grants, Medicaid, the Children's Health Insurance Program, other public benefits like food stamps, and legal assistance through partnerships with local law schools and legal aid clinics. Kinship navigator programs also sensitize agencies and providers to the needs of relative-headed families. Check your state's website to see if there is a Kinship Navigator program in your area.

CHAPTER TWO

Pre-placement Preparation: The Child's Past Is Important

Pre-adoptive preparation is a means of helping prospective parents understand the types of issues that have caused children to be available for adoption. The content, format and length of pre-adoptive preparation vary per state regulations, the Hague Convention on Protection of Children and Co-operation in Respect of Intercountry Adoption, and/or individual agency preferences.

At this stage of the adoption process, excitement, optimism, and thoughts of hope and love abound. Prospective parents are focused on the goal: the arrival of the child. Frequently, pre-adoptive preparation is viewed as a means to that end.

However, as adoption professional Ken Watson has noted, "Adoption is not just a legal act that transfers parental rights but an event that profoundly changes all of the participants for the rest of their lives. The bottom line is that adoption, no matter how early or how successful, means that the child always experiences a painful loss of the birthfamily. When families fall apart and their children move to foster homes, the children do not leave their trauma behind. Such a loss can be a serious blow to an adopted person's self-esteem. They were 'given up' or 'given away.'"[1] This quote emphasizes the abandonment experienced by the child. Sexual abuse, physical abuse, domestic violence, institutionalization, neglect, separation from siblings, pre-natal drug/alcohol exposure, failed reunification efforts and multiple moves within foster care or orphanage care are additional traumas that the child will not leave behind.

The Importance of Preparation

Pre-adoption preparation is the first opportunity to lay groundwork for all members of the adoptive family that the child's history may present lifelong challenges. The information shared during pre-adoptive preparation is critical to the post-placement well-being of each family member. Agencies and professionals have an obligation to deliver a quality educational program. Prospective parents have a responsibility to listen attentively, ask questions and request additional resources. Parents and professionals need to provide the children already in the family age-appropriate information so that they too are prepared for the arrival of their new sibling.

1. Lutz, Lorrie. Strengthening Families and Communities: An Approach to Post-Adoption Services. *Casey Center for Effective Child Welfare Practice White Paper*. Casey Family Services, http://www.caseyfamilyservices.org/p_ccenter_publications.html

Agencies Need to Set the Tone for the Importance of Preparation

As an author of a pre-adoptive preparation program for international adoptive families and as a professional who served in a placement position, I understand the costs, staff time constraints, family time constraints and the competition that exists among agencies to recruit adoptive families. These factors are not a license to take short cuts, nor do they permit tailoring a program designed more for the *convenience* of the family than for the thorough *preparation* of the family. For example, myths seem to exist that if we burden the family with training-related fees, or if we do not offer the training on a flexible schedule, families will take their business elsewhere. Overall, this perspective warrants thought.

> A family arrived for a placement consultation excited that they were able to complete their required 24 hours of pre-adoptive training over the course of one weekend. The prospective father commented, "Thank goodness, that's over with!" The topics included sexual abuse, neglect, attachment, separation, discipline, cultural issues, an overview of the child welfare system, team building and the effects of care giving on the family. The quality of the information was above average. Yet, the manner of delivery allowed limited time to develop relationships with the other participants or the agency's staff. This format certainly did not allow the family time to absorb the depth of the topics covered. This program sent a very clear message that education is a task to be completed rather than an opportunity for gaining information and insight.

The negative post-placement outcomes due to inadequate preparation are many. Families feel as if they have been lied to. Agencies are often blindsided by a family in crisis requesting the removal of a child. Many mental health professionals as well as school personnel lack knowledge of adoptive families. So, the child with special needs and his family languish in inappropriate services, sometimes for years. The toll of these scenarios, on the family and society, is immeasurable.

Families, who have not developed positive feelings about an agency and its staff's knowledge, approachability, patience and supportiveness, are unlikely to refer other prospective families to the agency. Perhaps the win-win situation is the agency who maintains strong standards regarding preparation for parents open to receiving it. This is the agency whose families call quickly upon having post-placement difficulties. Thus, the agency is not driven by a crisis mode and the family is connected to the help needed.

Overall, agencies must set the tone for the importance of pre-adoptive preparation. Families will follow the lead.

Families Need to Make Preparation a Main Criterion in Selecting an Agency

It is common to research a major financial purchase such as a car or home. Thus, it should be obvious that the addition of a person to the family should be subject to even more careful research. In selecting an adoption agency, prospective families need to inquire about the pre-adoption information provided. Request an outline of the content of the pre-adoptive classes. Ask questions.

What topics are included?

What format is utilized? Group? Online?

Who conducts the training?

Will the family have the opportunity to meet other prospective adoptive families?

Will experienced families make presentations?

Will the training include an overview of available community resources? In cases in which the agency is geographically distant from the family, what provisions will be made to help the family locate assistance? Will the family be connected with a local agency?

Is additional training available post-placement?

Is training available for my typically developing children? If not, will suggestions be offered to assist my resident children?

Families whose composition include birth and/or previously adopted children are in essence opening their homes to children who have experienced some of the worst atrocities that exist in our society.

Ryan was adopted at birth. When he was 11 years old his parents adopted a sibling group of two children. Kiana was also 11 years old, while Terrell was age 8. Ryan said, "My mother would go to Kiana's room to talk to her about something and the next thing I knew, my new sister was on top of my mother hitting her!"

Nathan and Erin, the parents of two adolescents by birth, adopted Richard and his infant brother, Thomas. Richard, age 3, when he came to live with the family, entered therapy at age 6. Erin described his lengthy temper tantrums and his continual public urination. For example, she recalled an incident at a soccer game in which Richard dropped his pants and urinated on the soccer field. On another occasion at a playground, he climbed the slide and then stopped and urinated from the top of the slide. A variety of parenting techniques had been utilized to end such behaviors to no avail.

Julie and Robert, the adoptive parents of two typically developing adolescents, decided to adopt 5-year-old Lori as a result of strong religious convictions to give to someone less fortunate. The family received little information regarding Lori's pre-adoptive history. However, they felt little concern. They believed their experience as parents would ensure that Lori would do fine in their home. They thought that love would conquer her early years of living in a dysfunctional birthfamily. Lori's arrival was met with several welcoming parties attended by supportive extended family members as well as friends from their church and community. At one point in therapy Julie stated, "She received 16 Barbie dolls, two Ken dolls and a Barbie Dream House. We were trying to teach our older children that sex outside of marriage was not acceptable. Yet, in Lori's play, Ken was always in the hot tub with five naked Barbies. Everything became sexual with Lori."

On a tragic evening, 4-year-old Kelly witnessed the murder, by physical abuse, of her younger sibling at the hands of her birthfather. Once the birthfather and birthmother realized the injuries, they placed both Kelly and her sibling in the car and drove to the hospital. En route, they concocted a story of innocence. Kelly, scared, was unable to speak to the police. However, the event was ingrained in her memory as was her last moment with her sibling, connected to life support. Eventually police arrested the murderer. Kelly was placed in foster care. Subsequently, at age 5½, she was adopted. Once in her adoptive home, Kelly relayed the details of the murder verbally and through play. All of her dolls were named after her sibling. The adoptive family's birth children were stunned by Kelly's portrayal of her life prior to her placement with the adoptive family. Certainly, the doll play and the drawings

Kelly created were shocking to the resident children who had lived a life enveloped by safe and loving parents.

As the above stories demonstrate, adoption may mean that the adoptee's new brothers and sisters will be directly exposed to children who have had very disparate life experiences as well as to children who exhibit difficult behaviors. Therefore, parents must acquire information in advance of placement in order to develop their capacity to handle the adopted child's needs, and parents must ensure that their resident children have the information and tools needed to cope with the changes adoption could bring to the family.

The Topics of Preparation: The Tough Stuff

Certainly, there is an endless amount of information that could be included in a preparatory program. The content needs to include an introduction to the adoption process, an overview of how children arrive in out-of-home placements, and the demographics of the children available for adoption. Transcultural adoption issues are also critical. Information about the types of parental skills and strengths that lead to a successful adoption is well worth covering. Most importantly, the content of the preparation program needs to emphasize the issues that cause the vast majority of children to enter foster care or orphanage settings. These traumas include abandonment, sexual abuse, physical abuse, domestic violence, pre-natal exposure to drugs and alcohol, and neglect. Once in out-of-home placement, there is also the impact of being separated from siblings, deprivation as a result of institutional care giving, and the effects of multiple moves. It is important that parents have knowledge of each of these traumas. However, it is most important that they gain an understanding of what importing a traumatized child into a healthy family means to each member of the family.

Abandonment

Whether the birthparents made a plan to place the child for adoption or termination of parental rights occurred through protective agencies in conjunction with the court system, the message frequently received by the child is that the people who were supposed to be his parents decided not to be his parents. The child does not always recognize the safety risks that were involved in his day-to-day living situation with abusive or neglectful parents or the birthmother's decision that the child would have more opportunities with an adoptive family. The child's perception is that he was somehow defective or that she made her birthmother angry and thus the abandonment occurred.

Carl, adopted from a Kazakhstan orphanage at the age of 3, is certain that his birthmother left him, as a newborn infant, at the hospital due to his being born with Cerebral Palsy. He genuinely believes that if his legs were like those of "other kids" she would have "kept me." Carl's condition was diagnosed when he was 2 by a team of American doctors who were visiting his orphanage. His birthmother had no idea he had Cerebral Palsy when she abandoned him.

Susan's birthmother became angry with her due to Susan's mishandling of a glass doll, a birthday gift from the birth grandmother. As a result of Susan's inability to handle the doll correctly, it shattered. The birthmother subsequently dragged Susan up a flight of stairs and dropped her over the railing. This resulted in Susan sustaining several broken ribs. Susan and her older siblings were quickly removed from their birthmother's care. The children never returned to their birth home despite a significant family reunification effort. Susan stated, "If I hadn't made her mad, we would still be with her."

Kenneth, age 9, resided in a Russian orphanage for six months after his birth. He is very angry that his birthmother did not "keep me." Additionally, he questions why there was "no one in the whole country who wanted me," and he inquires, "Why didn't the orphanage ladies take me home?"

Kenneth's story makes clear that international adoptees have an additional layer of abandonment issues. They feel unwanted by an entire country.

In most instances, the child loves the birthparents no matter what the circumstances. This is often difficult for adults to understand.

Kathryn, the adoptive parent of a 15-year-old son, was quite saddened when her son stated that he continued to have strong feelings for his birthmother. His sentiments were articulated in therapy four years after being adopted by Kathryn and her husband. He expressed that his birthmother would change if she knew how her actions had affected him. He believed that if only he could talk to her she would be "sorry." Thus, she would make the changes necessary for him to live with her. Kathryn struggled with this information for quite some time. She felt that all of her efforts as a "good mom" had been in vain. She stated, "I have been the mom helping him with his homework, taking him to his baseball games and virtually just doing everything to give him a good life. After years in our family, he still wants her. He wants the mom who beat him and sold him sexually in order to support the family. What have all my efforts really meant?"

In conclusion, children who have been abandoned enter the family with negative self-perceptions and/or with reunification fantasies. They lack trust that the adoptive placement is permanent. After all, if my birthparents did not want me, why do strangers want me? Families—parents and children—need careful and detailed preparation for such challenging differences in expectation versus experience.

Sexual Abuse

Sexual abuse is defined as activity with or interaction between a child and an older person where the intent is to sexually arouse one or both of the parties or to control the juvenile (Duehn and Anderson, 2004). The older person may be an adult or a juvenile. There is an array of sexual behaviors that occur with children—fondling the child, the child fondling the adult, exposing the child to pornography, having the child participate in pornography, prostitution, intercourse, oral sex, masturbating the adult, kissing, etc. Approximately 10% of sexual abuse victims are between the ages of 0 and 3. Between ages 4 and 7 years, the percentage almost triples to 28.4%. Ages 8 to 11 account for a quarter, 25.5%, of cases, with children 12 years and older accounting for the remaining 35.9% of cases (Putnam, 2003; U.S. Department of Health and Human Services, 1998). Some authorities believe that, as a risk factor, age operates differently for girls than for boys, with high risk starting earlier and lasting longer for girls (Putnam, 2003). Social workers believe that at least 75% of children who enter foster care have experienced sexual abuse (Child Welfare Information Gateway, 1990). Clinical experience with children adopted from institutional settings in foreign countries makes clear that such settings are not immune to sexual abuse either.

Margaret is currently 6 years old. She was adopted at age 1½. Throughout these years, she has masturbated excessively. Therapy was initiated as Margaret continued her habit of

Characteristics Associated with Greater Trauma in Child Sexual Abuse Cases

- Frequency (of the sexual abuse)
- Duration (of the sexual abuse)
- Penetration or Intercourse
- Onset at early age
- Significant age difference between perpetrator and victim
- Physical abuse at same time
- Victim's strong feelings of responsibility for abuse
- Victim's strong feelings of powerlessness/betrayal

Briere, John. *Child Abuse Trauma: Theory and Treatment of the Lasting Effects* (Interpersonal Violence: The Practice Series). (Thousand Oaks: Sage Publications, 1992.)

masturbating upon entering school. Margaret's history includes digital vaginal penetration by her birthmother.

Sally and Maureen, birth sisters, were adopted by a single foster mother. Already in the home were two younger foster children. One evening, the foster mother entered the younger children's bedroom and found Sally fondling one of the children's genitals. Subsequently, both Sally and Maureen revealed that their birthfather orchestrated a sexual relationship between them. He would direct them in acts of kissing and fondling each other's vaginas and breasts. Maureen reported that he smiled and laughed while he watched the girls act out sexually with one another.

Rose reported that her birthfather and his brothers frequently "got together to watch television." During these times, Rose was made to take off all her clothes and walk about so these men could touch her as they chose to. Rose also reported that her birthmother was present. A perpetrator by omission, the birthmother never opted to stop this sexual abuse.

Five-year-old Jeffrey arrived from Bolivia. Present in the family were two parents and their two children by birth, ages 10 and 12. Motivated to adopt by a desire to provide a child a loving home, the family was surprised by Jeffrey's perpetual stealing, hoarding food and destruction of household items. However, the family was devastated when Jeffrey sneaked into their female birth child's bedroom during the middle of the night and attempted to "get on top of her." In therapy, Jeffrey talked of the chronic sexual activity between children in the orphanage. The institutionalized children, lacking adult nurture, utilized sexual gratification as a means to offset their fears and loneliness.

The above examples are unfortunately a few of the scores of examples that could be presented. Sexual abuse leaves the child with irrational thinking like the following about himself and adults.

- "I should have been able to stop the abuse from happening to me." This belief may be intensified for boys due to the socialization process which instills in boys thoughts regarding their physical strength and a capacity to take care of themselves.

- "I am damaged goods. Who will want to date me as a result of what happened to me? Who could possibly love me after what happened to me?"
- "I am very different than other kids my age." Imagine sitting with peers during lunch or being on the playground for recess and listening to other children discuss the latest style, the movie they went to see over the weekend, Girl Scouts, etc. Such normalcy is in stark contrast to the experiences of the child who has been sexually abused.
- "Am I homosexual or heterosexual?" Same-sex sexual abuse sometimes causes sexual confusion as the child has experienced sex with a person of the same sex.
- "If you love me, you will have sex with me." There is a confusion regarding sex and love. The child may believe that if the new parents love him, they will be sexual with him.
- "At times, I was happy that my sister was picked instead of me." Siblings are often aware that their brothers and sisters are also being abused. Fear and their young age prevent them from stopping this abuse. Children in such situations struggle with feeling relieved that, at times, the abuse was occurring to their brother or sister rather than to themselves. They worry that their siblings are mad at them for not helping them more. They feel guilty that they did not do more to stop the abuse from occurring to their siblings.

There is a component of sex that feels good at any age. Physically, the body is primed to enjoy sex. At some point, the child becomes guilty because he or she may have experienced some pleasure during acts of sexual abuse.

Cultural beliefs create another dynamic, in that maleness is purported to advance when sexual interactions occur with an older woman.

It is important to point out that the child may not disclose sexual abuse until the child perceives that her placement is safe. Therefore, many children enter adoptive families with no known history of sexual abuse.

Emotional Abuse

Emotional abuse is the constant bombardment of one person by another with negative words or behavior. Criticizing, blaming, isolating, belittling, rejecting, corrupting, harassing and terrorizing a child are all examples of emotional abuse. Withdrawing affection or exposing a child to a violent or sexually inappropriate environment also constitutes emotional abuse. Low self-esteem and feelings of worthlessness that often last into adulthood typify the outcomes of such abuse.[2]

Brendan entered therapy with his single adoptive mom, Jocelyn. Brendan had come to live with Jocelyn when he was age 11. Prior to that, he had several foster care placements, and he had experienced physical and sexual abuse while in residence with his birthmother and her paramour. He was guarded about discussing the sexual abuse. Finally, in an emotional frenzy, he blurted out, "He said he would kill me or my birthmom if I ever told anyone." While the abuse had ended five years before, Brendan still perceived his abuser as having the power to cause harm.

Lisa, Kendra and Leslie, ages 5, 6 and 7½, resided with their birthmom and dad. A neighbor called 911 one evening to report the following. "I can hear an argument. I can hear a lot

2. American Medical Association. "Child Abuse." http://www.medem.com/search/article_display.cfm?path=n:&mstr=/ZZZBRKNPVAC.html&soc=AMA&srch_typ=NAV_SERCH

of swearing like 'f------ lazy b----. Kids you need to say good-bye. Your mother can find you another father. I don't need to live with such a pathetic b----.' " When the police arrived, the birthfather was waving a gun. He was threatening to "kill everyone" if the police tried to arrest him. Needless to say, he was arrested. Lisa, Kendra and Leslie entered foster care.

Children's thoughts become quite distorted as a result of such profanity and threats, as the following examples make clear.

"I could die or someone I love could die at any given moment."

"I need to comply with adults in order to stay alive or to keep my family members alive."

"I worry about my birthmom and my brothers and sisters to this day. I don't know who they are living with or how they are being treated."

"If my birthmom had just left her boyfriend or my birthfather, we would still be together." "If she leaves him now, I can go back." Some children do not understand that the non-offending parent was supposed to stop all forms of abuse occurring in the birth home. The child believes he can return to the birth home if the perpetrating parent is no longer in residence.

"She picked him (her boyfriend or the birthfather) instead of me. I guess she loved him more than me." Other children realize that their birthmother could have removed herself and her children from a harmful situation. These children feel doubly rejected. They ask, "Not only didn't she pick me, she chose to stay with someone who was so mean to her. Why?"

"I am bad, dumb and stupid. My birthparents told me so." Children believe they are what adults tell them they are.

Domestic Violence and Physical Abuse

Physical abuse means causing or attempting to cause physical pain or injury. It can result from punching, beating, kicking, cutting or burning a child. *Domestic violence* refers to a full range of assaultive and coercive conduct between intimate partners including marital partners, cohabitating partners, and former partners, as well as non-cohabitating dating partners. In homes in which domestic violence occurs, even children who are not abused themselves may witness or be exposed to the full range of domestic violence (i.e., hear shouting in another part of the house, see the aftermath in injuries to their parents, try to interrupt the violence or be in their mother's arms when she is physically attacked, etc.)[3]

George came into foster care at age 4½ and was placed with a family who subsequently adopted him. In therapy, at age 8, he clearly described an incident in which his birthfather became angry with him and hit him over the head with a wine bottle. He recalled the bottle shattering upon impact.

Diane and Donald were removed from their birthfamily at ages 6 and 1 due to a physical altercation between their birthmother and her paramour. This incident involved the paramour stabbing the mother. As a result, she was hospitalized. Diane stated, "I tried to get between them but he pushed me away."

---

3. National Child Traumatic Stress Network. "Types of Traumatic Stress." http://www.nctsn.org/nccts/nav.do?pid=typ_main

Dustin and Kristen entered their pre-adoptive family at ages 5 and 4. Shortly upon their arrival into this family, Dustin became angry with a neighbor child and immediately located a plastic bag. He then attempted to place the bag over the child's head. Fortunately, adult intervention occurred. When asked why he had done it, he was quite clear that his birthfather often "beat me with a belt" and "tied bags over my head" when he was angry. It was certainly a long time before Dustin was able to play without adult supervision.

Mark, a 4-year-old, arrived into his adoptive family after a four-year stay in a Ukrainian orphanage. Early in his placement he presented an array of behavioral difficulties. Attempts to consequence Mark were often met with his running to cower in a corner or a closet. Frequently, he would cover his face and shout, "No, please don't hurt me!" Bewildered by this behavior, the family entered mental health services. Over time, Mark described that some members of the orphanage staff would hit the children with sticks for behavioral infractions. He assumed the adoptive family would do the same.

The child who has experienced violence presents with distorted assumptions, like those that follow, about the appropriate use of violence and aggression.

- She may think that aggression is a means to solve problems. In homes replete with domestic violence and physical abuse, it is the strongest member of the family who gets what he wants (Perry, 1997).
- He may wonder, "What is happening to my birthmom now?" Many children are preoccupied with the status of their birthmother who lived as victim of domestic violence. They question her safety. They question if she is alive or dead. They feel guilty that they are not present to protect her. Frequently, children will comment, "I am older now and I could help take better care of her."
- She may think, "I was not behaving and this is why I was abused." or "I made my birthmom mad and this is why she hit me." As with sexual abuse, children who have experienced physical abuse believe that they were the cause of the abuse.

A child who has been a victim of unpredictable sexual or physical abuse learns that if this abuse is going to happen, it is far preferable to control when it happens. As a result, children who have been physically assaulted will frequently engage in provocative, aggressive behavior in an attempt to elicit a predictable response from their environment (Perry, 1997).

Also as was presented within the sexual abuse segment, the child believes that he should have been able to stop the abuse from occurring to himself, his birthmother or his siblings. Lastly, the child experiences a mixture of emotions including relief, guilt, anger and sadness when a family member other than himself is the recipient of the violence.

Pre-Natal Exposure to Drugs and Alcohol[4]

The content in this section is taken from *Risk and Promise: A Handbook for Parents Adopting a Child from Overseas* by Ira Chasnoff, MD, Linda Schwartz, PhD, Cheryl Pratt, PhD and Gwendolyn Neuberger, MD. *Risk and Promise* helps clarify the risk and protective factors presented by the children coming into their families via intercountry adoptions. It provides content on the array of challenges the children may present as well as checklists that parents may utilize to immediately begin assessing their child's develop-

4. Chasnoff, Ira, Linda Schwartz, Cheryl Pratt, and Gwendolyn Neuberger. *Risk and Promise: A Handbook for Parents Adopting a Child from Overseas.* (Chicago: NTI Upstream, 2006.)

ment. Please see the Resource section at the end of this chapter for more information about this book and its authors.

Alcohol, cocaine, opiates, marijuana and tobacco are substances that may pose long-term issues for the child and thus the adoptive family. It may be difficult for the adoptive family to know the specific types of substances utilized by the birthmother during her pregnancy. This is because obtaining such information is often via self-report rather than by toxicology screening upon the birth of the child.

Prenatal drug and alcohol exposure, as with the other traumas presented in this chapter, is not just a phenomenon present in domestic adoption. Studies estimate that at least 13%–45% of the children from the former Soviet bloc nations and Romania have Fetal Alcohol Syndrome (FAS) and another 60% were exposed prenatally to alcohol. There appears to be a growing trend of heroin use by women from Asian countries and Central and South America. In addition, cocaine, heroin and marijuana use in the South American countries continues at high levels, including among women of child bearing age.

Alcohol

Many prospective adoptive families express concern and reluctance regarding adopting a child with a diagnosis of FAS. Many families adopting internationally utilize the assistance of professionals to review video of the intended adoptee for the purpose of ruling out that the child may have FAS. FAS includes three main diagnostic features: growth deficiencies, central nervous system involvement and facial dysmorphology. The last, meaning that there are actual facial characteristics causing an overall flattening of the middle portion of the face (see www.nofas.org). However, it is important to point out that alcohol exposure at any point in gestation can cause significant problems for the child. In fact, children who lack facial features display problems in intellectual, behavioral or emotional development with significant impact on learning and long-term development.

Fetal Alcohol Spectrum Disorders (FASD) is an umbrella term describing the range of effects that can occur in an individual whose mother drank alcohol during pregnancy. These effects may include physical, mental, behavioral, and/or learning disabilities with possible lifelong implications. The term FASD is not intended for use as a clinical diagnosis. Rather it is a spectrum of disorders and can include Fetal Alcohol Syndrome (FAS), Alcohol Related Neurodevelopmental Disorder (ARND) and Alcohol Related Birth Defects (ARBD).[5]

Tobacco, Cocaine and Opiates

Tobacco is one of the most harmful common substances a woman can use during pregnancy. It produces a very high rate of low birth weight, prematurity and health problems in the newborn and child. In addition, a woman who admits to using tobacco during pregnancy is more likely to have used alcohol or illegal drugs.

Cocaine use during pregnancy leads to an array of difficulties. It can cause poor growth in the womb and premature labor. Cocaine exposure has long-term effects on the function of the central nervous system in general and on behavioral regulation. Infants develop poor muscle tone and have difficulties interacting with their environment. Parents may see shaking, arching of the back, clenching of the fists, curling of

5. National Organization on Fetal Alcohol Syndrome, online.

the toes, trouble feeding, sleep disturbances and frequent startle reactions. For a new parent, these issues may feel rejecting or create guilt in that the parent is unable to console and enjoy their long-awaited child. Overall, the opiates result in similar issues. A difference between cocaine exposure and opiate exposure is that opiates result in the physical addiction of both the mother and the fetus, while cocaine use in the mother does not addict the child. The newborn infant exposed to opiates is born addicted and goes through withdrawal.

Marijuana does not have a direct effect on the pregnancy, yet there is an impact on fetal brain development. Children whose mothers have used marijuana during pregnancy have a higher rate of learning and behavioral problems, especially related to planning and follow through with a task. Like tobacco, a woman who uses marijuana is more likely to have used other substances including alcohol, tobacco and other illegal drugs.

MOST COMMON PROBLEMS IN CHILDREN PRENATALLY EXPOSED TO ALCOHOL OR OTHER DRUGS

Poor Executive Functioning

Gets lost in conversations with others
Cannot follow sequence instructions
Difficulties making decisions

Delinquent Behaviors

Exhibits little or no guilt after misbehaving
Lies, cheats, or steals

Anxiety and Depression

Feels the need to be perfect
Feels unloved
Feels that others are out to get her
Feels worthless and inferior
Feels nervous, anxious, tense
Feels sad and unhappy
Worries excessively

Thought Problems

Can't get his mind off of certain thoughts
Repeats particular acts over and over
Stares
Has strange ideas

Aggressive Behavior

Argues a lot
Demands attention
Destroys his own things or those of others
Is disobedient and stubborn
Has sudden changes in mood
Talks too much and is unusually loud
Has temper tantrums

Attention Problems

Can't concentrate for long
Can't sit still and is restless
Daydreams more than usual
Has impulsive behavior
Has difficulty staying on task

Social Problems

Acts younger than her age
Is clingy
Doesn't get along with others
Gets teased a lot
Is not well liked by other children

Source: Chasnoff, Ira; Linda; Schwartz; Cheryl Pratt, and Gwendolyn Neuberger. *Risk and Promise: A Handbook for Parents Adopting a Child from Overseas.* (Chicago: NTI Upstream, 2006).

Above is a table which provides an overview of the most common problems seen in children who have been prenatally exposed to alcohol or other drugs. It is important for prospective parents to realize that no one substance can be associated with any one particular problem. This is because substance abusing mothers are more likely to utilize a combination of drugs and alcohol during a pregnancy. Therefore, it is difficult to sort out the effect of any individual substance. Studies of the long-term effects are still on-going.

The irrational thinking that stems from removal from a substance-abusing family includes

- "Why didn't my birthmother give up her drugs instead of me?" "Why wasn't I more important than her drugs or drinking?" These children struggle to understand why their birthparents chose this lifestyle.
- "I should have stopped my birthmom from doing drugs." Many children do make attempts to pour alcohol down the drain or flush drugs down the toilet, even though such actions put them at risk of harm if discovered.
- These children continue to worry about the health of their birthparents long after their removal from the birth home. They question, "Will my birthmother go to jail for having drugs?" or "Will my birthparents overdose and die?"

Children who are older at the time of their removal are able to connect the substance abuse problems to the other traumas they experienced.

Donna was placed in foster care at age 7. In therapy, seven years later, she stated, "Everything was about the drugs. The free food was sold to buy drugs. Any presents my birth aunt gave me for Christmas were sold for drugs. The men she sold herself to were because of the drugs. When we had no heat, it was because of the drugs. The beatings were because she was high and so were her boyfriends. Everything that happened was because of the drugs. The social workers said they took me because of the hitting. Really, it was because of the drugs."

Neglect

"The true potential of the human brain is rarely, if ever, realized. The major expresser of that potential is experience. The most critical and formative experiences are those provided to the developing child in the incubator of the family and, optimally, by a vital invested community (Perry, 1997)."

Neglect is a <u>lack</u> of experience. In fact, neglect means that the child lives in a chronic state of hunger, filth, and loneliness. The neglected child is not provided the food, clothing and shelter needed. Neglect may also include lack of medical care and/or mental health services as well as poor supervision, no supervision, or leaving the child in the care of someone not capable.

The police removed 4-year-old Robert and his birth siblings from their birthparents due to reports of physical abuse. Upon entering the home, police saw cockroaches scatter. There were piles of dirty clothing which served as the beds for Robert and his sisters. The cupboards were empty. There was no running water. A bucket, located behind the house, was being used as a toilet.

Brittney arrived in America after 13 months in a Chinese orphanage. She uttered no sounds. She was unable to crawl or walk. She did not reciprocate facial expressions or smiles. She rarely cried as a means of informing her adoptive parents of her needs. She was used to a life of lying in a crib, waiting for a bottle, waiting for potty time, waiting to fall asleep, etc. She was accustomed to a change in caregivers with each eight hours that passed. She was not used to having two loving caregivers who would respond to her cues. She was certainly not familiar with adults who desired to play with her and nurture her.

Malnutrition

Malnutrition, both before birth and during the first few years after birth, has been shown to result in stunted brain growth (Pollitt and Gorman, 1994; Shonkoff and Phillips, 2000). These effects on the brain are linked to cognitive, social, and behavioral deficits with possible long-term consequences (Karr-Morse and Wiley, 1997).

For example, iron deficiency (the most common form of malnutrition in the United States) can result in cognitive and motor delays, anxiety, depression, social problems and problems with attention (Shonkoff and Phillips, 2000).

Protein deficiency can result in motor and cognitive delays and impulsive behavior (Pollitt and Gorman, 1994). The social and behavioral impairments may be more difficult to "repair" than the cognitive impairments, even if the nutritional problems are corrected (Karr-Morse and Wiley, 1997).

Child Welfare Information Gateway. "Understanding the Effects of Maltreatment on Early Brain Development." http://www.childwelfare.gov/pubs/focus/earlybrain/earlybrain.pdf

Karr-Morse, R. and M.S Wiley (1997). *Ghosts from the nursery. Tracing the roots of violence*. New York: The Atlantic Monthly Press.

Pollitt, E. and K.S. Gorman (1994). "Nutritional deficiencies as developmental risk factors." In Nelson, C.A. (Ed.) *Threats to Optimal Development: Integrating biological, psychological and social risk factors*. Hillsdale, NJ: Lawrence Erlbaum Associates, 121–144.

Shonkoff, J.P. and D.A. Phillips (2000). *From neurons to neighborhoods. The science of early childhood development*. Washington, D.C.: National Academy Press.

The child who has been neglected experiences all caregivers as unreliable. That is, one time the child may cry and someone may come; however at other times, the child's cries are dismissed or go unheard because no one is there. In fact, many children who are neglected are left alone for hours and in frequent instances for days. There is no one talking, playing peek-a-boo, rocking him or just spending time gazing into his eyes telling him what a beautiful boy he is. Neglect, therefore, contributes to a lack of trust that adults can meet the child's needs. The neglected child believes, "I must take care of myself. You big people can't be counted on."

Further, responsive, sensitive caretaking and positive early life experiences allow children to develop a model of self as generally worthy and competent (Cook, Blaustein, Spinazzola and van der Kolk, 2003). In contrast, repetitive experiences of harm and/or rejection by significant others, and the associated failure to develop age-appropriate competencies, are likely to lead to a sense of self as ineffective, helpless, deficient and unlovable (Cook, Blaustein, Spinazzola and van der Kolk, 2003). Thus, the child of neglect has poor or very limited positive sense of self. The end result of multiple attempts to be acknowledged and cared for, only to be disregarded, confirms to the child that she is not worthy of her birthparents' or caregivers' time and attention.

Separation from Siblings

Don, Betty and Mary were removed from their birthparents early one morning. By evening, each was placed in a separate foster home. In one day, they lost the only parents they had ever known as well as each other. Can you imagine losing your entire family in one day?

Sergei came to America at the age of 9. During his years in Russia, he moved through three orphanages. His older brothers continue to reside in institutional care in Russia.

Kierra was sitting in our waiting room while her birthsister completed her therapy session. She noticed an *Adopt Ohio* magazine and began leafing through it, only to come across a photo and description of her birthsibling from whom she had been separated for eight years. She was overwhelmed with excitement! A call to the sibling's case worker confirmed it was her birthbrother. The two were able to initiate exchanges of letters and photos.

Pam resided with her three brothers in their birth home, and then the four siblings resided in a foster home for several years. Unfortunately, the foster mother was diagnosed with multiple sclerosis. She decided not to proceed with her plans to adopt the children. The news of her medical condition and the need to move to a new home caused the children's mental health to deteriorate. The end result is that all four children were placed separately. Pam, now age 11, has come to terms with the loss of her birthparents. She was able to process their acts of neglect, abuse and abandonment and conclude that she is "better off" being adopted. However, the loss of her siblings is an ongoing struggle. She continues to create fantasies of the four children reuniting and living together again. This is not possible as two of her brothers were adopted while the other aged out of foster care. This brother's whereabouts are unknown.

Luis resided in an orphanage in Mexico for almost six years. He developed a close tie to another boy who was in the orphanage. He refers to this boy as his brother to this day. Luis has ongoing guilt regarding the fact that he now has a rich life full of food, toys and family members while this brother remains in residence in grim conditions. Luis has a profound sense of sadness over the loss of this brother.

Harry and Julia, birth siblings, have been adopted by separate families. They resided together in their birthfamily until ages 7 and 6 respectively. Upon entering foster care, Julia presented an array of behavioral difficulties. As such, foster family after foster family requested her removal. The agency, who believed siblings should be kept together, was put in a quandary when eight placements failed in short succession. Was it fair to keep moving Harry because of Julia? Eventually, the decision was made to separate the children. Harry's adoptive family made numerous efforts to arrange sibling visits. However, Julia's family, for reasons unknown, never responded to these requests. To date, Harry strives to come to terms with the fact that he may never see his birthsibling again. He continually questions, "Why won't Julia's family return our calls?" "Are her problems my fault? I was older and should have taken better care of her. If I did, maybe we would be together."

Harry's questions and thoughts are common. Harry's case highlights a situation in which the agency had to weigh the deleterious effects of repeatedly moving a child against the sibling relationship. Frequently, the needs of one sibling prevent the placement of brothers and sisters in the same home as does the space readily available in foster homes when children are brought into care. Siblings are separated due to age differences. One family may take the younger of the siblings while another family has a preference for older children. It is currently estimated that 70% of children in foster care who have siblings in care are not placed with those siblings (Child Welfare Information Gateway, 2006). Certainly, clinical experiences with international adoptees would support that many of these children are separated from their brothers and sisters as well.

Pam's case demonstrates that the loss of siblings often outweighs the abandonment by the birthparents. That is, children may lament the loss of their brothers and sisters longer than they grieve the loss of the birthmother and birthfather.

Pam's case also highlights another possible scenario that may occur upon placement in an adoptive family. Pam resides in an adoptive family in which she has two brothers and three sisters. She has been reluctant to form any type of relationship with any of these children. In fact, she regularly plays by herself. She resents the fact that these children have had the opportunity to grow up together. She wants to know, "Why didn't I get to grow up with my brothers and sisters? They get to."

Luis' case alerts us to an issue posed in international adoption. Children who reside together for long periods of time develop ties to each other. They think about the children left behind at the orphanage. They have difficulty comprehending that they can be happy while these children reside in conditions far less plentiful than what their adoptive family has to offer. Such survivor guilt is difficult for these children to overcome.

Multiple Moves

The longer a child remains in care, the more placements he is likely to have (Barbell and Freundlich, 2001). Thirty-seven percent of foster children in 1998 were reported to have three or more placements (Barbell and Freundlich). This means that the child has lost at least three sets of parents, siblings, friends, school mates, pets, communities, toys, clothing and holiday rituals. Each new family has a unique set of values, beliefs, and ways of celebrating.

These losses are overwhelming, and to the child, he has lost everything that is most important—time and time again. As a result of these multiple, repetitive losses, people and things begin to lack meaning.

Toys can be removed for behavioral infractions and the child is not fazed.

Things are often lost or broken. There will be more at the next house.

Living is based on today because tomorrow could mean another move, on to new people and new experiences.

There is no point getting settled and making plans. There is no point getting attached.

As stated in Chapter 1, the child who has had multiple moves enters the adoptive family with the belief that "you too will give me back." "I am too bad for any family." This child may exhibit various negative behaviors in order to create emotional distance between himself, his parents and his siblings. After all, there is less emotional pain if "I push you away before you push me away." These types of behavioral difficulties often cause the placement to disrupt.

> Donna, currently 18, was adopted at age 10 after three failed reunification efforts and 11 foster care placements, states, "It was hard for me to move from foster home to foster home and settle down to a family that cares. Trying to trust them and love them back is really hard because it got messed up somewhere in between all the homes I've been in. My adoptive family has bent over backwards to show their love for me, but it is still hard for me. I know in my head that they won't do the things to me that my birthfamily did but there is still that side of me that says, be careful someone might leave you or you might get hurt."

Jane was 15 and in her eleventh family since being placed in foster care. However, in residence with her birthfamily, her birthmother had left her with numerous relatives on a frequent basis. She stated, "My birthmom passed me around like a dish at Thanksgiving dinner. She didn't want me and neither did my grandmother nor my aunts. I am too bad for anyone to keep me." Jane was used to moving, and upon entering foster care she utilized negative behaviors such as running away, property destruction and temper outbursts to perpetuate the familiar pattern of going from home to home.

Children who have moved numerous times may be struggling with a reunification fantasy. The child may falsely believe that if he can leave the current family he will return to his birthfamily, to a residence with a sibling, to his orphanage or to a foster family who has meaning to the child.

Jason was 9 when he entered therapy with his potential adoptive family. This was his seventh placement. His previous placements included his birth home, a foster home, and five pre-adoptive placements. His foster placement with "Grandma Rachel and Grandpa Jim" had lasted two years. When Jason became available for adoption, Grandma Rachel and Grandpa Jim determined, due to their age, that they did not want to provide Jason permanency. In therapy, Jason was asked where he most wanted to live. He was quick to reply that he wanted to live with Grandma Rachel. The pre-adoptive family was empathic and established contact with Grandma Rachel immediately. She was happy to hear from Jason, and she was able to reiterate her reasons for her decision not to adopt him. She gave him permission to love his new family. Subsequently, Jason's behavior improved. His adoption was finalized with Grandma Rachel and Grandpa Jim present.

Children who move multiple times are at great risk. Repeated moves jeopardize their opportunity to develop secure attachments with caregivers and trusting relations with adults. A large body of evidence links multiple placements with behavioral and mental health problems, educational difficulties, and juvenile delinquency (Barber, Delfabbro and Cooper, 2001; Children and Family Research Center, 2004; Cooper, Peterson and Meier, 1987; Dore and Eisner, 1993; Hartnett, Falconnier, Leathers and Testa, 1999; Palmer, 1996; Pardeck, 1984; Proch and Taber, 1985, 1987; Smith, Stormshak, Chamberlain and Whaley, 2001; Stone and Stone, 1983).

The Meaning of Preparation: The Impact of Trauma on the Adoptive Family

It is imperative to gain a basic understanding of what the impact of a child's trauma means for the day-to-day life of an adoptive family. As should be becoming clear, the content of pre-adoptive training is important. The *application* of the content is what will help each family member function and flourish.

As you read this section, think about the expectations surrounding adoption which were laid out in Chapter 1. Professionals and parents alike need to come to some conclusions that initiate the very important process of adjusting those expectations. In turn, this will create the ripple effect needed to help the children already in the family to do the same. The traumatized child may not simply blend into the adoptive family. The adoptive family does not have the magic wand that will erase the abuse and neglect suffered by the child. However, the adoptive family can, over time, mitigate the child's traumatic scars. This starts with all involved in the adoption process understanding the impact of trauma on each member of the adoptive family.

Complex Trauma

The term *complex trauma* describes the dual problem of children's exposure to traumatic events and the impact of this exposure on their immediate and long-term well-being. *Complex traumatic exposure* refers to children's experiences of multiple traumatic events that occur within the care-giving system—the social environment that is supposed to be the source of safety and stability in a child's life. Typically, complex traumatic exposure involves simultaneous or sequential occurrences of child maltreatment—including emotional abuse and neglect, sexual abuse, physical abuse and witnessing domestic violence—that are chronic and begin in early childhood (Cook, Blaustein, Spinazzola and van der Kolk, 2003).

Many children available for adoption, internationally and domestically, come with histories of complex trauma. The prospective child's history includes a combination of the traumas presented in this chapter. That is, it would be very rare to adopt a child who has been removed from her birthfamily solely because of neglect, or exclusively due to sexual abuse. The institutionalized child has experienced neglect and abandonment, a move to an orphanage and a move to the adoptive family, along with loss of culture, loss of friends and possible loss of siblings. Chapter 5 will offer suggestions as to how to review a child's history in order to glean from that information the types of traumas the child has experienced.

Complex trauma causes impairment in seven primary areas as represented and described in the table on the next page.

Following is a discussion of selected areas of this chart. The elected topics allow for salient points to be made with regards to the application of adoptive preparation material. That is, the following information provides clarity as to how the child with special needs—complex trauma—impacts the adoptive family.

Attachment

If you are one of the majority of infants born to a loving home, a consistent, nurturing caregiver—a mother or father—will be present and repeatedly meet your needs. Time and again, one or both parents will come when you cry and soothe you when you are hungry, cold or scared. As your brain develops, these loving caregivers provide the template that you use for human relationships. This template is profoundly influenced by whether you experience kind, attuned parenting or whether you receive inconsistent, frequently disrupted, abusive, or neglectful "care" (Perry and Szalavitz, 2006).

Attachment is the process by which infants develop a model of human interaction. It sets the tone for the infant's sense of self as a good, worthwhile, important human being.

Children who enter adoptive families frequently arrive with a continuum of attachment problems. Their experiences have distorted their thinking about themselves and adult caregivers. This is why the irrational thoughts were presented earlier in this chapter. Many potential adoptees will enter the adoptive family with misperceptions. These thoughts will steer their day-to-day interactions. For example, if the child is guided by a belief that he is unlovable, he will strive to make this belief a reality.

Clay was adopted from India at age 2½. Due to deprivation and abandonment, he entered his adoptive home with a view of adults as uncaring. In turn, he felt as if there was something wrong with him. He believed that he was somehow inherently defective and that this situation caused the lack of nurture he received in the orphanage. He also thought this caused his birthmother's abandonment of him. So, he sought to make himself unlovable

COMPLEX TRAUMA IN CHILDREN AND ADOLESCENTS

Attachment

Uncertainty about the reliability and predictability of the world
Problems with boundaries
Distrust and suspiciousness
Social isolation
Interpersonal difficulties
Difficulty attuning to other people's emotional states
Difficulty with perspective taking
Difficulty enlisting other people as allies

Biology

Sensorimotor developmental problems
Hypersensitivity to physical touch
Analgesia
Problems with coordination, balance, body tone
Difficulties localizing skin contact
Somatization
Increased medical problems across a wide span, e.g., pelvic pain, asthma, skin problems, autoimmune disorders, pseudoseizures

Affect Regulation

Difficulty with emotional self-regulation
Difficulty describing feelings and internal experience
Problems knowing and describing internal states
Difficulty communicating wishes and desires

Dissociation

Distinct alterations in states of consciousness
Amnesia
Depersonalization and derealization
Two or more distinct states of consciousness, with impaired memory for state-based events

Behavioral Control

Poor modulation of impulses
Self-destructive behavior
Aggression against others
Pathological self-soothing behaviors
Sleep disturbances
Eating disorders
Substance abuse
Excessive compliance
Oppositional behavior
Difficulty understanding and complying with rules
Communication of traumatic past by reenactment in day-to-day behavior or play *(sexual, aggressive, etc.)*

Cognition

Difficulties in attention regulation and executive functioning
Lack of sustained curiosity
Problems with processing novel information
Problems with focusing on and completing tasks
Problems with object constancy
Difficulty planning and anticipating
Problems understanding own contribution to what happens to them
Learning difficulties
Problems with orientation in time and space
Acoustic and visual perceptual problems
Impaired comprehension of complex visual-spatial patterns

Self-Concept

Lack of a continuous, predictable sense of self
Poor sense of separateness
Disturbances of body image
Low self-esteem
Shame and guilt

> to his new family. In particular, he lacked any sense of self-care. He refused to shower. He hoarded food that would spoil in his bedroom. If his parents did not help him clean the room, foul odors would permeate the home. He would often wear the same clothes day after day. He spent long periods of time in his room away from the family. He refused to participate in family fun such as watching movies or playing cards.
>
> Clay's parents sought years of professional services to help Clay integrate into the family and form meaningful relationships with them, their birth son and peers. Finally, when he was age 13, a successful course of therapy was implemented. Today, Clay seeks interaction with the family. His sense of self has improved significantly. He no longer keeps bologna under his bed and he bathes daily! Board games are becoming a weekly event for Clay and his little brother.

This example illustrates that attachment difficulties impact each member of the family. Clay's parents were sad that he could not enjoy being with the family. They lamented the child they had hoped for when they traveled to India. There was anger as well for the negative behaviors that daily affected the running of the family. He was unable to reciprocate affection. He cringed each time he was hugged by his mother, father or brother. Overall, he paid very little attention to his younger brother, who desperately wanted Clay to play with him. Clay and his family lived under these circumstances for approximately 10 years before finding an effective treatment. In essence, they worked for ten years to develop a relationship with their son!

The early care-giving relationship provides a relational context in which children develop their earliest models of self, other and self in relation to others. This attachment relationship also provides the scaffolding for the growth of many developmental competencies, including the capacity for self-regulation, the safety with which to explore the environment, early knowledge of agency (i.e. the capacity to exert an influence on the world), and early capacity for receptive and expressive communication (Cook, Blaustein, Spinazzola and van der Kolk, 2003).

Most professionals who work with and study the process of bonding and attachment agree that a child's first 18 to 36 months are critical. It is during this period that the infant is exposed—in a healthy situation—to love, nurturing and life-sustaining care. The child learns that if he has a need, someone will gratify that need, and the gratification leads to the development of his trust in others. This cycle of needs is repeated thousands of times in the first two years of an infant's life, forming the foundation of every other developmental task of human life (Keck and Kupecky, 1995). Attachment not only shapes the child's world view, it is the context in which development—neurological, social, emotional, cognitive, behavioral and physical—is put into motion.

Cognitive Development

A part of *intellectual* or *mental development*, cognitive activities include thinking, perception, memory, reasoning, concept development, problem-solving ability and abstract thinking. Language, with its requirements of symbolism and memory, is one of the most important and complicated cognitive activities.

In her book, *Toddler Adoption: The Weaver's Craft* (Indianapolis: Perspectives Press, 1998), Mary Hopkins-Best describes rudimentary cause-and-effect thinking and problem-solving skills as developing between 12 and 18 months of age.

It is quite common when a family enters our agency for services that they proclaim, "He is so smart!" And indeed, it is usually true. Intelligence tests confirm that many traumatized children who are being adopted today have a good level of overall intelligence, which is often translated into being bright. However, without the capacity to reason or generate solutions, the smart child is impaired.

> Alice is age 9. She was adopted when age 4. One evening, at age 1½, social workers had arrived at her birth home and removed her. Her birthmother did not participate in reunification efforts and so she never saw her birthmother again. Her perception of her removal is that she was "stolen." This is certainly understandable. What else would a toddler think when women come into your home, take you, and then give you to another family? Alice has stolen on a regular basis since coming to reside with her adoptive family. Jewelry, video games, pens and pencils disappear routinely despite consequences much to Alice's dissatisfaction.

Alice lacks basic cause-and-effect thinking. She repeats the same behavior over and over. She does not learn from her mistakes or consequences. She is deficient in creating solutions to solve her problem of feeling stolen. The only way she is able to demonstrate her confusion for the loss of her birthmother is to reenact the event of stealing.

Imagine the problems this poses for this family. It is difficult to instill morals and values into the older birthson while Alice continues to steal. He questions, "Why can't my parents make her stop stealing?" He becomes angry when she steals from him. Then he feels guilty for the constant conflict in their relationship. Different times Alice has stolen from relatives' homes. This is a cause of much embarrassment.

Another area of cognitive development that poses difficulty for adoptive families is that of concrete thinking. The concrete thinker sees the world as black or white. There is no gray. There is limited or no abstract thinking. The concrete-thinking child often appears defiant.

> Cody, age 11, has been stealing since he was placed with Dan and Rita six years ago. Dan stated, "Cody, you have sticky fingers and it needs to stop!" Cody, puzzled, began to feel his fingers. He replied, "Dad, I washed my hands a few minutes ago. My fingers aren't sticky." Dan, annoyed, said, "Cody, you know what I mean." Cody replied, "No really. I washed my hands just a few minutes ago." Dan then stated, "Enough. I don't want to hear anymore."

Actually, Cody had no idea what his father was talking about. His immature thought processes only allow for literal interpretations. Because of this, arguments frequently occur due to the child's exacting manner. A once peaceful household may become teeming with anger and frustration. Exasperation permeates the home. The family's ability to relax and have fun gradually diminishes.

Lastly, many traumatized children, due to their cognitive delays, receive labels as being learning disabled (Perry, 1997). Tutoring and special education services require time to locate, negotiate with a school district, monitor, as well as time if travel is involved or meetings need to occur. The child with special needs begins to dominate the family's time.

Social Development

This domain of development includes the child's interactions with other people, and the child's development in social groups. The development of relationships with adults and peers, the assumption of social roles, the adoption of group values and norms, adoption of a moral system and eventually assuming a productive role in society are all social tasks.

The development of social skills is emphasized in today's society. Parents spend much time involving their children in a variety of organized sports. There are also the martial arts, dance classes, camps and play dates. It is with good reason that we strive to teach children social skills:

- Unless children achieve minimal social competence by about age six, they have a high probability of being at risk throughout life (McClellan and Katz, 1993).
- Indeed, the single best childhood predictor of adult adaptation is not school grades and not classroom behavior, but rather the adequacy with which the child gets along with other children. Children who are generally disliked, who are aggressive and disruptive, who are unable to sustain close relationships with other children and who cannot establish a place for themselves in the peer culture are seriously at risk (Hartup, 1992).
- The risks of inadequate social skills are many; poor mental health, dropping out of school, low achievement, other school difficulties and poor employment history (Peth-Pierce, 2000; Katz and McClellan, 1991).

According to the Centers for Disease Control and Prevention[6], social skills begin to advance in early infancy. For example, infants only months old watch and imitate others, are sensitive to social approval and disapproval, are interested in getting attention and creating social effects, and enjoy simple games like peek-a-boo and bye-bye. The 12- to 23-month old likes to lug, dump, push, pull, pile and knock down. He also likes to climb and kick. During this time period, there is pleasure in stringing beads, learning to catch a large ball, looking at pictures in books, nursery rhymes and interactive games such as tag. By 24 to 35 months, there is lots of physical play such as jumping, climbing, rolling, throwing and retrieving objects, and pushing self on wheeled objects. This is also the age of developing first counting skills, as well as the time children begin to draw and mold with clay. Children of this age enjoy matching objects, sorting objects by size and playing with patterns. Imaginative play increases. The main interest is still in parents, however there is the beginning of cooperative play with others.

This last sentence—that the main interest is still in parents—is a key concept to understand. Social skills develop early and they develop within the parent-child relationship.

- Social competence is rooted in the relationships that infants and toddlers experience in the early years of their life. Everyday experiences in relationships with their parents are fundamental to children's developing social skills (Peth-Pierce, 2000).
- In particular, parental responsiveness and nurturance are considered to be key factors in the development of children's social competence (Casas, 2001). Children who have close relationships with responsive parents early in life are able to develop healthy relationships with peers as they get older (Peth-Pierce, 2000).

The child who has resided in a home wherein he was neglected and abused was consumed with his own survival. Toys there were minimal as was quality adult interaction. This child enters an adoptive family with limited ability to play. The expectation that the adoptee will make a playmate for the children already in the family is quickly shattered. In fact, it is not uncommon that neglected children 8, 10 or 12 years old are still parallel playing. They have not developed the skills to know how to enter a group.

---

6. Centers for Disease Control and Prevention. *Child Development* and *Learn the Signs: Act Early*. http://www.cdc.gov/ncbddd/child/infants.htm and http://www.cdc.gov/ncbddd/autism/ActEarly/

Failure to Thrive

Failure to thrive is a medical diagnosis given to children who don't gain weight or are consistently underweight in comparison to children of the same age. Most diagnoses of failure to thrive are made in infants and toddlers.

Failure to thrive can be caused by any of the following factors:

- Neglect
- Poverty
- Parental depression, history of abuse as a child or substance abuse problems
- Gastoresophageal reflux, chronic diarrhea, cystic fibrosis, chronic liver disease and celiac disease (these conditions limit the body's ability to absorb nutrients)
- Cleft palate or pre-mature birth (these conditions can prevent calorie intake)
- Parasites, urinary tract infections, tuberculosis (these conditions consume energy; nutrients are utilized rapidly)
- HIV/AIDS
- Cerebral Palsy
- Down Syndrome

Failure to thrive can lead to serious long-term issues. The child's brain grows more in the first year of life than at any other time. Poor nutrition, during this critical window, impacts subsequent development. Children with a history of failure to thrive are at risk for impairments in intellect and verbal skills. Attachment may be disturbed thus, social and emotional development may not keep pace with peers.

Failure to thrive usually occurs within the context of a high-risk environment. So, it is often one factor combining with many others to inhibit the child's health and well-being.

Krugman, Scott, D. and Dubowitz, Howard. "Failure to Thrive." American Family Physician. http://www.aafp.org/afp/20030901/879.html

KidsHealth. Reviewed by, Barbara Homeier, M.D. "Failure to Thrive." http://kidshealth.org/parent/nutrition_fit/nutrition/failure_thrive.html

Block, Robert; Nancy Krebs, and the Committee on Child Abuse and Neglect, and the Committee on Nutrition. "Failure to Thrive as a Manifestation of Child Neglect." *Pediatrics* 2005; 116; 1234–1237 or online, http://aappolicy.aappublications.org/cgi/reprint/pediatrics;116/5/1234.pdf

They are unable to take turns, lose graciously or play a game according to the rules. Their physical development is delayed and so, they want to play and ignore the wants and needs of other children. Frequently, they flit from toy to toy. They are unable to choose an item and sit for a period of time to enjoy the item. Other children simply sit among their toys not knowing exactly what to do with the toys. Their play is often filled with themes of their life experiences.

> Tammy is currently age 6. She joined her adoptive family three years ago. She enjoys playing house. However, Jean, her mother, states, "When she plays house, the Daddy doll is always yelling and hitting the Mommy doll. The baby doll is off in the corner. The end result is that the police are called to rescue the Mommy and the baby dolls."

> Paula, the adoptive mother of two female siblings described that doll after doll had been purchased. "One by one, their clothes disappeared, and their arms and legs were removed.

It was as if they were breaking the dolls in the same manner they felt broken by the sexual abuse they had sustained at the hands of their birthfather."

Such social lags create a variety of difficulties in the adoptive family. The resident children lose interest in playing with their new brother or sister, as do children in the neighborhood. Invitations to parties and play dates, for the adoptee, may be rare. This area often leads typically developing children to make statements such as, "I don't want to play with him. He's no fun." "I want to go to my friend's house alone. He is embarrassing to have around my friends." "Do we have to adopt him?" Frequently, the brothers and sisters will begin spending more time at the neighbor's house than at home.

Delayed moral development also impacts adoptive family interactions. *Moral development* is the capacity to control one's own behavior internally (Santrock, 1995). It is a process which involves acquiring and assimilating the rules about what people should do in their interactions with other people. The process requires reasoning skills and the ability to feel a wide range of emotions—empathy, sympathy, anxiety, admiration, self-esteem, anger, outrage, shame and guilt. We can all most likely recall a childhood situation in which our peers wanted us to do something that would definitely lead to parental disapproval and consequences. Immediately the following thought popped into our heads, "My mother would kill me if I did that!" Our moral system went into effect, and we were able to make a decision about how to best handle the situation.

When models who behave morally are provided, children are likely to adopt their actions (Santrock, 1995). Many adoptees lacked moral models while in residence with their birth families or in institutions. They witnessed violation after violation of principled behavior while experiencing and witnessing abuse, neglect and drug use. Therefore, they enter the adoptive family with a system of morals and values that is in direct contrast to that of the family.

Moral development consists of three stages. In pre-conventional reasoning, moral thinking is based on rewards and self-interest. Children obey when they want to and when it is in their best interest to obey. What is right is what feels good and what is rewarding. Conventional reasoning sees children adopting their parents' moral standards, seeking to be thought of by their parents as a "good girl or boy." Post-conventional reasoning is the highest stage at which the person recognizes alternative moral courses, explores the options and then decides on a personal moral code (Santrock, 1995). Adoptive parents may find that the child they adopt displays pre-conventional reasoning well into adolescence or beyond. They may not internalize the parent's moral standards, or at least not quickly.

Grant, age 16, removed a chocolate cream pie from the refrigerator and sat down at the kitchen table. He ate almost the entire dessert. Made earlier for the church bake sale, the pie was not for consumption by the family. This had been made quite clear by Sarah, Grant's mother. Sarah was livid when she came into the kitchen. Grant, adopted by Sarah and her husband at age 6, violated rules and boundaries daily. If he wanted to use a tool, he simply took it, never returning it. If he wanted money, he took it from Sarah's purse. If he wanted his brother's stereo, he took it. If he wanted his sister's CD player, he took it. The list could go on and on. Locks had not worked. He would find ways to remove them. Door alarms offered no solution either. He dismantled them.

The end result of Grant's lack of morals was a family in emotional turmoil. On one hand, each family member was angry with Grant for ravaging through their personal possessions for years. On the other hand, each had concerns for his future. If he did not stop this behavior, what kind of a life would he have? Would he be able to work? Would he go to jail?

Emotional Development

This realm of development includes the ability to identify, express and regulate feelings. These skills allow the capacity to enter into reciprocal emotional relationships.

There is currently much information available regarding traumatized children and emotional development. Much of this information refers to *hyperarousal* or *dissociation* more commonly known as *fight or flight behaviors* presented by children who have resided in situations during which they were under chronic threat.

The following information is summarized from "Maltreatment and the Developing Child: How Early Childhood Experience Shapes Child and Culture"[7], *The Boy Who was Raised as a Dog and other Stories from a Child Psychiatrist's Notebook: What Traumatized Children can Teach Us about Loss, Love and Healing* (New York: Basic Books, 2006)[8] and "Understanding the Effects of Maltreatment on Early Brain Development."[9]

In utero and during the first four years of life, a child's rapidly developing brain organizes to reflect the child's environment. So, what this means is that early life experiences have disproportionate importance in organizing the mature brain. The brain organizes in a sequential manner, meaning that the lower more regulatory parts of the brain develop first and then the higher parts of the brain become more organized and more functionally capable. The first areas to develop are the brainstem and the midbrain; they govern the bodily functions necessary for life. The last regions to develop are the limbic system, involved in regulating emotions, and the cortex, involved in abstract thought.

The brain also develops in a user-dependent way. The repetition of experience strengthens neural pathways. Chronic stress sensitizes neural pathways and over-develops certain regions of the brain involved in anxiety and fear responses. Children who experience the stress of physical or sexual abuse will focus their brains' resources on survival and responding to the threats in their environment.

When a child is exposed to any threat, his brain will activate a set of adaptive responses designed to help him survive. Hyperarousal is one response. A child adopting a hyperarousal response may display defiance, aggression, anxiety or panic. A second response is dissociation. This involves withdrawing from the outside world and focusing on the inner world. A dissociative child is often compliant or may self-stimulate (i.e., rocking, chew on fingers, play with hands, etc.). Parents often describe the child who is dissociative as "appearing to be in a fog" or "acting like she just isn't there." When an adult asks them to do something, they do not respond. If the adult becomes angry, the child becomes more anxious and moves further into dissociation.

A child with a brain adapted for an environment of chaos, unpredictability, threat and distress is ill-suited to the modern classroom or playground. When children experience repetitive threats, there is over-activation of the stress response system. Their brains are always in a higher state of activation, always ready to go into flight or fight.

7. Perry, Bruce. (2004). "Maltreatment and the Developing Child: How Early Childhood Experiences Shapes Child and Culture." http://www.lfcc.on.ca/macain/perry1.html

8. Perry, Bruce and Maia Szalavitz, *The Boy who was Raised as a Dog and Other Stories from a Child Psychiatrist's notebook: What Traumatized Children can teach Us about Loss, Love and Healing.* (New York: Basic Books, 2006.)

9. Child Welfare Information Gateway. (2001). "Understanding the Effects of Maltreatment on Early Brain Development: A Bulletin for Professionals." Washington, DC: US Department of Health and Human Services. http://www.childwelfare.gov/pubs/focus/earlybrain/earlybrain.pdf

Those of you familiar with deer know that they flee in an instant when frightened. Deer are hypervigilent—always wary of their environment. Traumatized children operate in a similar fashion. They are physiologically in a state of alarm, of "fight" or "flight," even when there is no external threat or demand. So, a stressor arises. Perhaps there is an argument with a peer or a demanding school task. The child escalates into a state of fear very quickly; a temper tantrum occurs, an argument ensues, an object gets thrown. Parents, siblings or peers are left wondering what has happened.

In a state of calm, we use the higher, more complex parts of our brains to process and act on information. In a state of fear, we use the lower, more primitive parts of our brain. As the perceived threat level goes up, the less thoughtful and the more reactive responses become. Actions in this state may therefore be governed by emotional and reactive thinking styles. There is little ability to think about the consequences of actions taken.

> In describing Gina, their now 13-year-old daughter whom they adopted, John and Nancy stated, "We never know what is going to set her off. Everything can be calm and off she goes—shouting, swearing, running up and down the stairs. This can go on for several hours. Just the other night, we decided to play board games. We popped popcorn and made hot chocolate. The whole family sat down and she started screaming. We tried to ignore it. However, it was hard to ignore someone screaming while we were trying to have fun."
>
> Nancy went on to say that incidents like this are particularly disruptive to the whole family, which is also comprised of their two birth children, Joshua, age 9 and Carol, age 11. She continued by discussing that she expected that their lives would be more hectic with three children. She expected there would be more transportation issues, more homework to help with, more laundry, etc. To Nancy, what the adoption of Gina brought to the family was chaos. Plans often had to change based on her hyperarousal, or plans had to be cancelled. Promises of activities or one-on-one time to Joshua and Carol were broken.

While chronic abuse and neglect can result in the overactivation of the stress response system, neglect alone can result in other problems. As described earlier in this chapter, neglect means that the child's physical and psychological needs go unmet. In order for the child to develop, he needs stimulation and acknowledgement. If these elements are not provided, the basic neural pathways that were ready to grow through experiences with caregivers, wither and die.

- If babies are ignored, if their caregivers do not provide verbal interaction, language is delayed.
- If a child does not receive kindness, he may not know how to show kindness.
- If a child's cries go unheard, he may not know how to interact positively with others.

These capacities may not fully develop because the required neural pathways were not activated. Again, the brain is use-dependent. It needs repetition of experiences to develop the skills necessary for the individual to function.

This additional information related to neglect is especially important for the family adopting internationally. The ratio of caregivers to babies and toddlers in institutional settings is often poor. Review of countless hours of orphanage video clearly demonstrates five or more infants with one caregiver. This would be the same as a family having quintuplets! Although, in an institutionalized setting, a mother, mother-in-law, sisters, church members and neighbors aren't available to help out.

Subsequent chapters explore and significantly expand on this area of emotional development and its post-placement impact on the adoptive family.

Grief and Loss

The content thus far has alluded to the loss issues the children available for adoption sustain due to the circumstances which caused them to enter out-of-home care. Sharon Kaplan-Roszia, MS and Deborah N. Silverstein, MSW, LCSW, in their article "Adoptees and Seven Core Issues of Adoption," have created an organized seven-part system in which to view loss and its related facets from the adoptee's perspective. They see the seven core issues as Loss, Rejection, Guilt and Shame, Grief, Identity, Intimacy and Relationships and Control.

Core Issue 1: Loss

"Without loss, there would be no adoption. Adopted persons suffer their first loss at their initial separation from their birthfamily, often when they are young and most vulnerable. Current research is validating what adopted persons have felt for a long time. Awareness of the adoptive status is inevitable. Even if the loss is beyond conscious awareness, recognition or vocabulary, it affects the adopted person on a very profound level. Any subsequent loss, or even the perceived threat of separation, becomes more formidable for adopted persons than their non-adopted peers.

"Loss, for the adopted person, is not a single event, but rather a series of ongoing losses. Triggers such as birthdays, Mother's Day, Father's Day, the anniversary of the adoption, transitions from one school grade to another, high school graduation, engagement or marriage, death or divorce of adoptive parents, etc. can be experienced as both a reminder of the original loss and the ongoing nature of that loss.

"In addition to the primary loss—birthfamily—secondary losses abound: loss of culture; other caregivers (i.e., orphanage staff, foster families, relatives, etc.); religion; medical information; birth history; siblings; orphanage friends; language; familiar sounds, tastes and smells; pets; school mates; somebody with a physical resemblance; the chance to be just like friends who are growing up with the families they were born to, and on and on. As children move again and again, this list gets longer and longer. Even after the adoption is complete, there are possible additional losses as adoptive families change through moves, deaths, illnesses, and other adoptions or births.

"Whenever possible, families must work to minimize the loss for their children. This may include keeping connections to important people, places and events. Parents must be assertive in acquiring information about their children's lives before they came into the family."

Core Issue 2: Rejection

"Adopted persons often view the placement by the birthfamily as a personal rejection regardless of the circumstances. Feelings of fears of rejection can chip away at a person's self-esteem."

Self-esteem is the collection of beliefs or feelings that we have about ourselves, or our self-perceptions. How we define ourselves influences our motivations, attitudes and behaviors, and affects our emotional adjustment. We have a mental picture of who we are, how we look, what we're good at and what our weaknesses might be. Self-esteem is about how much we feel valued, loved, accepted and thought of by others—and how much we value, love and accept ourselves.[10] Patterns of self-esteem start very early in life. For example, when a baby or toddler reaches a milestone he experiences a sense of accomplishment that bolsters self-esteem. Simultaneously, the child receives praise and

10. Homeier, Barbara. "How Can I Improve My Self-Esteem?" TeensHealth. http://kidshealth.org/teen/question/emotions/self_esteem.html

support from his parents. The child experiences feelings of parental love. In fact, parents are the most important influence on self-esteem.[11] Among the most damaging things parents can do to thwart the development of self-esteem is to abuse their children. The breakdown of the family is likewise a source of harm to self-concept.[12]

Clearly, the child who experiences rejection lacks the foundation for self-esteem. Abuse and neglect compound the damage. For children with negative self-concept, challenges become a major source of frustration and anxiety, they have a hard time finding solutions to problems and they are plagued with negative self-thoughts—"I am stupid," "I can't do anything right" or "I don't deserve a family." Faced with a new and immediate challenge, their immediate response is "I can't." They frequently become passive, withdrawn or depressed. Poor self-perceptions are also linked to teenage pregnancy, eating disorders, suicide attempts and suicidal thoughts.

Core Issue 3: Guilt and Shame

The sense of deserving abuse and abandonment that has been portrayed throughout this chapter "may lead adoptees to experience accompanying feelings of guilt and shame. Again, these children may believe that there is something intrinsically wrong with them, or that their actions caused the trauma. It is often very difficult to dissuade adoptees from these beliefs. It takes children time to understand that adults, not the children, were responsible for what happened."

Core Issue 4: Grief

"Every loss must be grieved. Adoption-related losses are no different. The losses in adoption, however, are sometimes difficult to mourn in a society where adoption is seen as a joyful event. For example, children arriving from other countries may be expected to be happy and grateful, rather than suffering from culture shock and grief. Children removed from abusive homes may be expected to feel only relief and gratitude, not grief."

Grief includes shock, denial, anger, depression, bargaining and ultimately acceptance (Kübler-Ross, 1969; Kübler-Ross and Kessler, 2005). As described previously, traumatized children present with difficulties identifying, expressing and regulating emotions. Further, their delayed cognitive processes hinder their ability to figure out what has happened to them. Therefore, they lack the skills to grieve. So, the grieving process is delayed. Acceptance may take years to accomplish. Rather than verbalizing feelings and visibly demonstrating feelings through perhaps crying, children express grief through physical symptoms such as stomach aches, headaches, regression to an earlier stage of development, explosive acting out behaviors, or they may prefer to isolate themselves or withdraw from activities. Overall, "the grieving child looks very different from a grieving adult."

> Isabella was adopted at the age of 6. She is currently age 14. Each February, she withdraws from family activities, friends and extra curricular activities. Her preference is to spend extended time periods in her room, listening to music. February is a month of past reminders for Isabella. Her birth aunt, who was in the process of adopting her, died very unexpectedly in February. Therefore, February is the month Isabella entered foster care. February is also

---

11. Sheslow, David and Colleen Taylor Lukens,. "Developing Your Child's Self-Esteem. KidsHealth. http://kidshealth.org/parent/positive/talk/self_esteem.html

12. Emler, Nicholas. "The Costs and Causes of Low Self-Esteem." Joseph Rowntree Foundation. http://www.jrf.org.uk/knowledge/findings/socialpolicy/n71.asp

her birth month, and her birthmother's birthday is in February. February triggers Isabella's ongoing grief for her birthfamily.

Core Issue 5: Identity

"Adoption may also threaten an adopted person's sense of identity. Identity is defined both by what one is and what one is not. Adopted children frequently wonder who they really are and where they belong—Are they more like their birthfamily or their adopted family? What have they inherited and what have they acquired? Are they a 'bad seed' destined to become like their birthparents? Why were they born? Were they an accident or mistake? For male and female adoptees, the problems associated with the development of a full identity may be compounded by the lack of information about birthfathers. Therefore, for some adopted persons, adoption complicates the development of a complete or integrated sense of self. Adopted persons may experience themselves as incomplete, deficient or unfinished.

"A lack of identity may lead adoptees, particularly in the adolescent years during which development of identity is a major developmental task, to seek out ways to create a feeling of belonging. Sometimes they devise extreme measures such as running away, drug and alcohol usage, becoming pregnant, or rejection of the adoptive family." It is also important to consider that many adoptees will not have the developmental complexity necessary to navigate the process of identity formation (Keck, 1999). That is, development is cumulative. Early development is the basis for later development. The better the child masters tasks at earlier stages, the easier it is to master the more complex tasks of later stages. Many of the developmental delays presented in this chapter carry over into adolescence, impairing or immobilizing the adopted adolescent from completing the steps involved in answering the question necessary for identity formation—"Who am I?"

Core Issue 6: Intimacy and Relationships

"Adopted persons have reported that they are aware of holding back a part of themselves in relationships, always cautious and watchful. Some state that they never truly felt close to anyone. Others report a lifetime of feelings of emptiness. Adoptive parents find themselves challenged to move past their children's barriers and to create close, secure attachments. The attachment process may take years and may have to be reworked again and again as adopted children grow, change, and struggle to incorporate their pre-adoptive trauma and their adoption experience into who they are and who they will become."

Core Issue 7: Control

Children who have histories of institutionalization and foster care are well aware that they were "not party to the actions and decisions that led up to the adoption. They had no control over the loss of their birthfamily, the choice of adoptive family," the choice of being institutionalized, the choice of being abused, the choices of professionals, etc. As such, their perceptions that adults cannot be trusted cause them to find ways to meet their own needs and to take control in order to survive. Therefore, asking them to give up control is difficult, because to them, it is what kept them alive (Keck and Kupecky, 2002). Additionally, children who are prevented from discussing their histories freely feel a lack of control over information that pertains to them. Such, they may attempt to take control of the family through negative means—power struggles, lying, chronic behavioral problems, running away and so on. (Keefer and Schooler, 2000).

The major recommendation that falls out of these seven core issues revolves around parents being open and honest with the adoptee about the facts of her life. Certainly, this information is replete with difficult material. It is also filled with topics which the typically developing children may have little awareness of, unless older, and which parents seek to protect their children from realizing until they are adolescents or young adults. Adoption will change this situation. The child who has experienced trauma needs her history in order to recover and become a productive member of the adoptive family. Brothers and sisters require information to make sense of their new sibling's behavior, developmental delays, academic challenges as well as the types of experiences described by the adoptee. Parents will need to have candid conversations with the traumatized child and their resident children about sex, drug use, mental health issues, violence and so forth. Chapter 5 will provide sample discussions. In essence, the family's timeline for allowing their typically developing children to discover the world's social problems is advanced.

At times, the resident children express disappointment that the adoptee remains invested in his birthfamily.

> Ellen is the 14-year-old birth child of Sharon and Todd. She is one of three birth children and three children by adoption. Ellen attended therapy with her mother and one of her brothers by adoption, Kenny. During therapy, Kenny described how he continued to miss his birthmother. He also discussed how the loss of his birthfamily created a disconnect between himself and his adoptive family. Kenny's birthfamily is Mexican and his adoptive family is Caucasian. Daily, when he compares his skin color to theirs, he is reminded of his losses. Ellen was saddened. She stated, "I thought we were his family now." Once Ellen was provided with information about the seven core issues of adoption, she recovered from this experience. She came to understand that his feelings were normal rather than indicative of a rejection of "her" family.

Thus, information is necessary to normalize the experience of adoption for all members of the family.

Behavioral Difficulties

Interwoven into the content of this chapter are the types of behavior difficulties presented by children adopted from the child welfare system and through intercountry programs. Each area discussed lends to the manifestation of behavioral problems within the adoptive family.

Because what causes the behavior difficulties is intricate and comprised of many factors, alleviating negative behaviors is a process that occurs over months and, in many cases, years. The vignettes were designed to provide an overview of the types of more common behaviors the family may experience.

The negative behaviors of the child joining a family through adoption often become a major source of frustration, anger, and despair for parents and, typically developing children. In fact, the child-by-adoption becomes the identified problem in the family. His temper tantrums, stealing, lying, inability to enjoy outings, poor table manners, poor hygiene, destruction and so on are blamed for the entire state of the family. Life begins to revolve around "fixing" the problem—the adoptee—so the family can resume life in the same manner as prior to the adoption. Time, energy and financial resources are devoted to the child with complex trauma issues.

The fallout of this scenario has many facets. Valuable time with the birth and/or previously adopted children is lost. The resident children perceive that the way to get attention is to act out or overachieve. Or, observing the stress their parents are already under, they harbor their thoughts and feelings. Anger and resentment build. The children in the family prior to the adoption, begin to dislike the adoptee. Then they feel guilty for having these feelings about their sibling.

Traditional parenting techniques may fail. Parents struggle to devise new ways to manage the child with a traumatic history. Parents seek professional assistance. Parents begin to argue over the best ways to cope. Family fun occurs less frequently. Again, time is consumed by the child with a history of trauma.

Brothers and sisters begin to question their parents' decisions and love—"What were they thinking when they decided to adopt?" "Why wasn't I enough?" "Why did they go get more kids?" "I would never get away with the things he does. Why do they let him act that way?"

In essence, the arrival of the child with complex trauma may create a complex family system. Chapter 8 will elaborate on this phenomenon in detail. Chapters 9 and 10 will offer an array of solutions to offset the long-term impact of importing a traumatized child into a healthy family system, so that each member of the family—adoptee, parents and the children already in the family—can flourish and thrive.

Preparing the Typically Developing Children: Considerations

While formal research studies regarding the impact of a placement on the typically developing children in families which adopt children with difficult backgrounds are limited, those that do exist conclude that the stability and satisfaction with foster care and adoptive placements are impacted by the children—birth and/or adopted children—residing in the home at the time another child enters the family system (Gilman, 1992; Holtan, McCarrgher and James, unpublished; Kaplan, 1988; Lemieux, 1984; Mullin and Johnson 1999; Murphy, 1964; Poland and Groze, 1993; and Ward and Lewko, 1987 and 1988). The majority of these studies suggest that preparation and support for the family's existing children may be the necessary keys to reducing disruption rates; retaining foster and adoptive families; maintaining the emotional well-being, security and stability for the appropriately developing children; and easing the transition for everyone concerned, thereby enhancing the success of a foster care placement or an adoption (Holtan, McCarrgher and James; Kaplan; Mullin and Johnson; Poland and Groze; and Ward and Lewko).

Further, sibling experts Meyer and Vadasy (1994) and Lobato (1990), write that throughout their lives, brothers and sisters have a need for information about their sibling's condition. Their need will closely parallel their parents' informational needs. So, providing typically developing children with information is important in offsetting disruption, and it gives reassurance, answers questions and helps resident children prepare for the future (Meyer and Vadasy, 1994).

Information Dissemination: Influence on Adjustment

How a family handles the dissemination of information about special needs will greatly influence the adjustment of the children already in the family (Meyer and Vadasy, 1994). Some parents seek to protect their children from the reasons for their adopted siblings' actions and issues. This is not a good idea. Without information, children tend to make up their own stories; and often their version of the situation is worse than the actual circumstances.

Traditional information—books, articles, community trainings, videos—is usually geared toward parents. Siblings are usually excluded from another traditional source of information—the teachers, physicians, therapists, social workers, and others providing services to their traumatized brother or sister (Meyer and Vadasy).

The isolation, loneliness and loss some siblings experience will be complicated by a lack of information about their sibling's special needs. In some families, siblings receive a clear signal that the problems are not to be discussed, leaving siblings to feel alone with their concerns and questions. However, even when parents are happy to answer questions, some siblings will keep their questions and concerns to themselves. These resident children feel their parent is too stressed or saddened by the adopted child's needs. So, they keep quiet in order to try to be helpful to their parents. Some parents are unaware that their children actually desire information. On the parent's part, they assume everything is fine if their typically developing children do not present with their issues.

"Experienced" sisters and brothers tell us that parents must be proactive in offering information (Meyer and Vadasy). In their book, *Sibshops: Workshops for Children with Siblings with Special Needs*, Meyer and Vadasy make the following recommendations for sharing of information:

- Keep the sibling's special needs an open topic
- Answer siblings' questions about the condition in a forthright manner
- Provide siblings with written materials
- Include siblings in visits with service providers
- Determine the sibling's knowledge of the adoptees' difficulties (i.e., What do you know about why your brother came to live with us? Why do you think your sister has such problems learning? Why do you think we take your brother to therapy?). Provide the information necessary to fill in gaps or misperceptions.

Information Dissemination: Based on Age

Pre-schoolers

- Very young children often do not even refer to their brother's or sister's special needs when they describe them to others. Rather, at a young age, siblings focus on the actions, appearance and their own gut emotional reactions. This is not to suggest that pre-schoolers are unaware of or insensitive to their brother's or sister's problems. In fact, they usually recognize that the child has special problems and acknowledge that there are more disruptions in their family plans and routines (Lobato).
- Young children who have been exposed to pre-school, play dates, organized activities, Sunday school, etc., have most likely had positive peer interactions as well as negative peer interactions. As such, they have more experiences than we think. So, they can comprehend some of the difficulties a traumatized sibling may have.
- Common misconceptions about the cause of the problem reflect a youngster's self-centered and concrete thinking. They often believe that something they did caused the problem (Lobato).

  It is quite a common practice for parents to compare their children to one another. It is also common for siblings to do the same. The young child looks for similarities and differences between himself and the child with special needs in order to determine whether they are well and able themselves (Lobato).
- Young children ages 2 to 6 are very concrete thinkers. Explanations of complex trauma should therefore be as clear as possible. Children as young as 3 can recognize some of their brothers' and sisters' problems, especially when they have

had contact with other children and when their siblings are older than they are. Three years old is not too early to share comments about an adoptee's difficulties (Lobato).

Cora is 2 years old. She was adopted after her brother, Steven. Steven exhibits very difficult behavioral issues. The most serious negative behavior is his frequent aggressive temper outbursts. Cora's parents have taught Cora to go to a "safe spot" when Steven escalates. One day, while reading *One Fish, Two Fish, Red Fish, Blue Fish* by Dr. Seuss, Cora associated her brother with the "very, very BAD fish" which is depicted as hitting and slapping another meek fish. Cora's mom reported being speechless that Cora was so intuitive at such a young age.

School-Aged Children

- During their grade-school years, siblings need information to answer their own questions about their sibling's problems as well as questions posed by classmates, friends or even strangers. More so than pre-schoolers, school-aged children may have more specific questions (Meyer and Vadasy). They may ask, "Why does he take medication?" "Why does she go to therapy?" "Why can't he act right?" "When will he act right?" "When will he be able to play?"
- School-aged children most likely have peers who reside in families where there has been a divorce. They may have experience with death, and therefore grief and loss. They have been presented the Drug Abuse Resistance Program (D.A.R.E.). They may be assisted to apply this knowledge to the thoughts and feelings of the child with complex trauma issues.
- School-aged children may hold beliefs about the cause of the difficulties that places blame on the child with special needs (Meyer and Vadasy).
- Information needs to be relayed to school-aged children in short segments, perhaps 20–30 minutes in length.
- In lieu of accurate information, school-aged children may harbor their own private, albeit inaccurate, theories to explain their sibling's problems (Meyer and Vadasy).
- School-aged children may have experience with other children who have been adopted.

Adolescents

- Even adolescents may have misconceptions about their siblings' problems. Some may assign a psychological or metaphysical (i.e., God brought my brother in to bring the family closer) reason for the issues that present from the adoptee's background of complex trauma (Meyer and Vadasy).
- Like school-aged children, adolescents have specific questions about their brother's or sister's special needs (Meyer and Vadasy).
- Adolescents have more exposure to the issues which bring children into foster care and adoption, or at least to similar issues. They have witnessed peers involved with drugs or alcohol. They may have personal knowledge of suicide or suicidal ideation. It is likely they have experience with death. Certainly, they have familiarity with sex and sexual behaviors. Thus, they have the capacity to handle an array of topics with a depth of content.

- Adolescents have the capacity to attend informational presentations of a length similar to adults.
- Adolescents may also have experience with children who have been adopted.

Information Dissemination: Potential Models and Content

The primary audience of this book is parents. However, parents and professionals frequently read the same materials. This segment is written with both groups in mind. The content includes the types of information the children already in the family need in order to have a more successful adoption experience. The division into potential models, that could be utilized to deliver information to these brothers and sisters-to-be, will be helpful to agencies interested in implementing pre-adoptive education for these prospective siblings.

Inclusive

Older children may be provided pre-adoptive preparation in an inclusive format: they could attend preparatory classes with their parents. This model has various advantages. The parents and their child are privy to identical information. Once home, they can have ongoing discussions as to what the particular content of a training session may mean to the family. The family, as a unit, could complete small group exercises. As such, family members begin to learn to communicate about difficult topics. Families would also be provided the opportunity to begin to devise ways to solve various problems that may occur. For example, below is a sample training exercise utilized after content is delivered pertaining to sexual abuse. Participants are asked to read each brief scenario and answer the following questions about each:

How do you feel?
How might you react?
What do you say to the adoptive child?
What do you recommend for the children you already parent?
Who could you talk to about this?
What services may the adopted child need?
Are there future safety issues?

Your family is watching television when your newly adopted 5-year-old daughter straddles the arm of the couch next to you and starts rubbing herself in a sexual way.

Your child-by-adoption gives you a "French" kiss.

Your birth son walks into the garage and sees your two prospective adoptees kissing.

Your new child is engrossed in a television program and suddenly starts masturbating.

You and your sister-by-adoption are sitting on the couch after supper. Your dad comes in and gives both of you a friendly hug or pat on the shoulder. Your sister looks extremely upset and pulls away.

You are informed that your new child has unzipped his pants on the playground at school and has shown everyone his "wiener." He is in the same school building as your birth daughter.

Two children from one family have come into your home. You hear unusual noises from the bedroom. When you open the door, you see one child rubbing or sucking the penis of the other child.

Your birth child is in bed sleeping. Your newly adopted child slips into his or her room and attempts to get in bed with your birth child.

By the time the family works through these various training situations, they have gained clarity as to the needs and issues that adopting a child with a history of sexual abuse may present. Parents have been able to witness the reaction of their typically developing child to these descriptions of behavior. Parents have been able to think about their reactions and feelings. Parents and resident children alike gain a depth of information as to the possible impact of adoption on each member of the family.

While the family may still be shocked when such behavior occurs in their home, they can reflect back to such exercises and implement the strategies developed. Lastly, tools created under the guidance of a trained professional have an added advantage. The facilitator can guide the family to effective solutions as a result of her knowledge and experience. As a result, family members gain trust in the agency. Such exercises, conducted with the family as a whole, set the tone that the agency expects there may be problems after placement, and that the agency can be relied upon to assist.

Disadvantages to this model are primarily for the agency. Inclusion of more participants obviously creates larger group size. Therefore, the agency may have to make provisions or adjustments to their training schedule. Or, the agency may have to increase the number of facilitators conducting pre-adoptive training.

Parallel

A parallel model may offer a means to train young and school-aged children whose attention span requires more frequent breaks or more hands-on oriented activities. This model would offer training to parents, as a group, and simultaneous training to children in a separate group. A review of literature of psycho-educational groups run for children who have a sibling with cancer, developmental disabilities or a parent with a mental illness suggests that the topics children need include concrete information as to the issues, coping skills, expression of feelings and communication with parents regarding their needs. In the case of adoption, children also need an overview of how children come into out-of-home care as well as information regarding the roles and responsibilities of the professionals who will be involved in their lives.

An overview of a potential pre-adoptive training program for the children already in the family is included in the Appendices. In summary, the training model includes the seven sessions that follow:

Session 1: Overview

This educational period would provide content and group activities that would answer the following questions:

Where is your new brother or sister coming from?

How did he or she get there?

What has to happen before he or she will actually move in?

Who will be helping your family adopt a brother or sister, or a sibling group?

Session 2: The Cycle of Needs

A presentation of the Cycle of Needs lends to helping school-aged children understand why a child needs a new family.

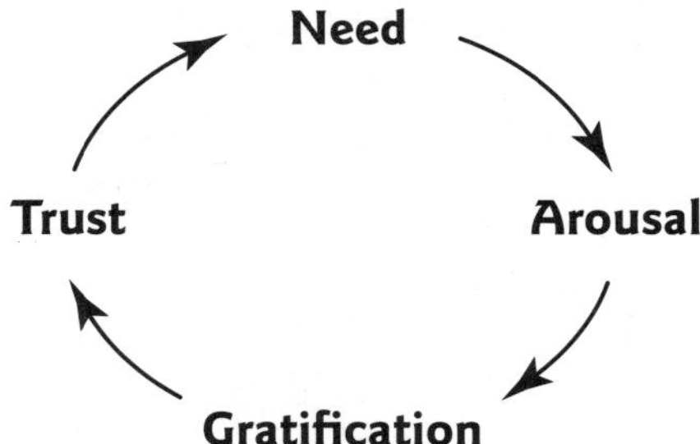

The cycle demonstrates that when the resident child was a baby, his mom and dad met his needs. He cried and Mom or Dad brought him a bottle, changed his diaper or just gave him attention. As a result, he learned the world was safe and that Mom and Dad could be trusted.

Discussion in this session would define a "need" versus a "want." Children can then list the various needs provided by their parents. Children will use this knowledge of needs to compare and contrast their life to the life of the sibling they are anxiously awaiting. The conclusion drawn would be something similar to "Children who enter orphanages (or foster care) have not always received such attention. He may have cried and the orphanage caregivers were too busy with other babies to come and feed him or to pick him up and hold him. So, your new brother or sister didn't learn that adults take good care of children. He or she will have different ways of thinking and acting than you do, because his or her needs were not met. It may take some time before your brother or sister settles into the family."

Session 3: Coping Skills

The purpose of this session would be to help children understand what coping skills are and why they are important. Overall, children will need help coping with the new sibling's behavior, immature social skills, and with the questions that will be posed by friends and others. They also need specific instructions regarding situations that cause safety issues, such as temper tantrums, pushing, shoving, hitting or again, sexual behavior.

Session 4: Talking about Feelings

As presented earlier in this chapter, the typically developing children avoid conversation with their parents as they do not want to burden the family with what they perceive to be additional stress. Some resident children harbor their feelings as they feel guilty for having negative emotions toward their new brother or sister. Children need to know that the expression of feelings is important, and that any feeling they have is acceptable.

Session 5: Transcultural Adoption

This segment is necessary if the parents, brothers, sisters and the sibling-to-be will be of different cultures. In such cases, children need to have an understanding of the cultural background of their new brother or sister. It may be fun for children to read about various countries or the history of African Americans.

On a more serious note, however, when parents make the decision to adopt transculturally, the entire family becomes "different" as pointed out in Chapter 1. Some friends, extended family members, neighbors and strangers will embrace transcultural adoption while others may be more inclined to stare and perhaps make negative comments. Children need preparation for this latter situation.

Session 6: Panel of Typically developing Siblings

It is common practice to provide a panel of experienced adoptive parents during pre-adoptive preparation. So, it makes sense that a panel of experienced siblings would be beneficial to children in families who are moving toward adoption as a means to add to their family.

Children, especially if an only brother or sister, should be encouraged to maintain contact with their group members via email, phone and play dates. In this manner, the children begin to develop a peer support system similar to the one always recommended for parents. Post-placement there will be great value in having a friend who understands the experiences of a resident child within an adoptive family.

Session 7: Positives, Final Questions and Closure

Chapter 10 will cover the positives of adopting a child with a history of trauma for the parents, the brothers and sisters, and the adoptee. Parents and siblings alike need to know that in light of various difficulties, typically developing children can emerge from the adoption experience with maturity, advanced coping skills, career goals, an awareness of consequences of such things as substance abuse during pregnancy, lack of care giving provided to a child, an appreciation that they were born into a healthy family and a depth of understanding of what it takes to be parents.

A parallel model of pre-adoptive training places demands on agencies to develop and implement the content. Ethically, there is a responsibility to make sure that all members of the family are informed. This ensures a better outcome for parents, the children in the family at the time of the adoption and the child with a history of complex trauma. This supports the systemic philosophy of operating in the best interests of the children on behalf of whom we have the responsibility to help find and keep a permanent home.

Parent-to-Child Dissemination

A third model of conveying information to typically developing children is via transfer of learning from parent to child. This parent-to-child dissemination model has pros and cons.

Parents are often overwhelmed with the content of pre-adoptive training themselves. Asking them to provide education to their children simultaneous to their own learning process would be cumbersome. At the pre-adoption stage, parents need to absorb information themselves. Professionals have a depth of knowledge not yet internalized by prospective parents. If this model were utilized, it would make sense that professionals would provide guidelines and specific types of written materials and exercises to direct parents appropriately. The workbooks by Barbara Jordan, *Living with the Sexually Abused Child* and *Preparing Foster Parents' Own Children for the Fostering Experience* (see Resources) cover many of the topics presented in the parallel model. In a parent-to-child dissemination model brothers and sisters are not offered the opportunity to meet veteran siblings. So, they lack the ability to develop a support system.

Utilizing the Jordan workbooks or activities prepared by agency staff makes parent-to-child dissemination of information more feasible. In this manner, parents are transferring the relevant knowledge to their children. Parents thus have the opportunity to practice communication skills. And, parents will learn the thoughts and feelings of their resident children with regards to what they are thinking about the family adopting.

This model is certainly an advantage in the area of intercountry adoption. Frequently in this form of adoption the placing agency may be geographically distant from the adoptive family. As such, the group format may not be practical. Agencies that provide services to a smaller number of clients may not always have enough typically developing children to conduct group training. So, this is another situation in which the parent-to-child dissemination model may need to occur.

Conclusions

This chapter emphasized the need for thorough pre-adoptive training for all members of the family. Pre-adoptive training is a means of helping parents and the children already in the family understand the types of issues which cause the need for children to be adopted, as well as helping family members gain the insight as to the ways they may be impacted by adoption.

Again, as Chapter 1 stated, pre-adoptive preparation is but a beginning. It should be viewed as a jump-start to the ongoing education that will be needed to have a successful adoption experience. Each member of the adoptive family is encouraged to continue to read, and to talk with veteran adoptive parents, brothers and sisters and each other throughout the entire adoption process. Integrating the adoptee into the existing family system may be an extensive process lasting a lengthy period of time. The child's past is important. The child's past does not simply fade once placed in an adoptive home. The family more able to see this prior to adoption will certainly fare better once the child with a history of trauma arrives.

Resources

Books

Borba, Michele. *Building Moral Intelligence: The Seven Essential Virtues that Teach Kids to do the Right Thing.* (Hoboken, New Jersey: Jossey-Bass, 2002.)

Buxton, Bonnie. *Damaged Angels: An Adoptive Mother's Struggle to Understand the Tragic Toll of Alcohol in Pregnancy.* (Jackson, Tennessee: Carroll and Graf, 2005.)

Chasnoff, Ira; Linda Schwartz; Cheryl Pratt and Gwendolyn Neuberger. *Risk and Promise: A Handbook for Parents Adopting a Child from Overseas.* (Chicago: NTI Upstream, 2006.)

Greenspan Stanley I. and Jacqueline Salmon. *The Challenging Child: Understanding, Raising, and Enjoying the Five "Difficult" Types of Children.* (New York: Pereus Books, 1995.)

Greenspan, Stanley I. and Nancy Breslau Lewis. *Building Healthy Minds: The Six Experiences that Create Intelligence and Emotional Growth in Babies and Young Children.* (New York: Perseus Publishing, 2000.)

Greenspan, Stanley I.; Serena Weider and Robin Simons. *The Child with Special Needs: Encouraging Intellectual and Emotional Growth.* (New York: Perseus Books, 1998.)

Hopkins-Best, Mary. *Toddler Adoption: The Weaver's Craft.* (Indianapolis: Perspectives Press, 1998.)

Hughes, Daniel A. *Building the Bonds of Attachment: Awakening Love in Deeply Troubled Children.* (Dunmore, Pennsylvania: Jason Aronson/Inghram Book Company; 2nd edition, 2006.)

Johnson, Toni Cavanagh. *Helping Children with Sexual Behavior Problems: A Guidebook for Professionals and Caregivers.* (San Diego: Institute on Violence, Abuse and Trauma, 2007.)

Johnson, Toni Cavanagh. *Understanding Children's Sexual Behaviors: What's Natural and Healthy.* (San Diego: Institute on Violence, Abuse and Trauma, 2007.)

Jordan, Barbara. *Living with the Sexually Abused Child: A Handbook for the Foster Parents' Own Children.* (King George, Virginia: American Foster Care Resources, www.afcr.com, 1997.)

Jordan, Barbara. *Preparing Foster Parents' Own Children for the Fostering Experience.* (King George, Virginia: American Foster Care Resources, www.afcr.com, 1997.)

Kleinfield, Judith. *Fantastic Antone Grows Up: Adolescents and Adults with Fetal Alcohol Syndrome*. (Fairbanks: University of Alaska Press, 2000.)

Miller, Margi and Nancy Ward. *With Eyes Wide Open: A Workbook for Parents Adopting International Children over Age One*. (St. Paul: Children's Home Society of Minnesota, 2001.)

Perry, Bruce and Maia Szalavitz. *The Boy Who was Raised as a Dog and Other Stories from a Child Psychiatrist's Notebook: What Traumatized Children Can Teach Us about Loss, Love and Healing*. (New York: Basic Books, 2006.)

Siegel, Daniel J. *The Developing Mind: How Relationships and the Brain Interact to Shape Who We Are*. New York: The Guilford Press, 2001.)

Streissguth, Ann. *Fetal Alcohol Syndrome: A Guide for Families and Communities*. (Baltimore: Brookes Publishing Co., 1997.)

Verny, Thomas and John Kelly. *The Secret Life of the Unborn Child*. (New York: Dell Publishing, 1981.)

Verrier Nancy. *The Adopted Child Grows Up: Coming Home to Self*. (Baltimore: Gateway Press, 2003.)

Books for Professionals

Stern, Daniel N. *The Interpersonal World of the Infant*. (London: Karnac Books, 1998.)

Brodzinsky, David and Marshall Schechter (editors). *The Psychology of Adoption*. (New York: Oxford University Press USA, 1993.)

Schore. Allan N. *Affect Regulation and the Origin of the Self: The Neurobiology of Emotional Development* (Philadelphia: Lawrence Erlbaum Associates, 1999.)

Websites

Adoption Learning Partners
www.adoptionlearning partners.org

Adoption Learning Partners, founded by The Cradle, seeks to improve adoption outcomes for all members of the adoption circle by providing a vibrant, innovative, educational resource on the Internet. Adoption Learning Partners offers highly valuable, timely, web-based educational resources for adoptive parents, adopted individuals, birthparents and the families that love them.

Association for Treatment and Training in the Attachment of Children (ATTACh)
www.attach.org

ATTACh is an international coalition of professionals and families dedicated to helping those with attachment difficulties by sharing their knowledge, talents and resources. The ATTACh vision is to be an international leader in creating public awareness and education regarding attachment and the critical role it plays in human development. They provide a quarterly newsletter, an annual conference, membership directory and other benefits to members and the public. CDs of workshops from their annual conferences are available. The topics cover all aspects of the attachment between child and parent as well as various aspects of adoptive family life.

Child Trauma Academy (CTA)
www.childtrauma.org

CTA recognizes the crucial importance of childhood experiences in shaping the health of the individual and, ultimately, society. A major activity of the CTA is to translate emerging findings about the human brain and child development into practical implications for the ways we nurture, protect, enrich, educate and heal children. This site contains many valuable articles related to attachment, trauma, and grief and loss. There are also free online courses pertaining to attachment, brain development and the impact of trauma on children development.

Children's Research Triangle
www.childstudy.org

The Children's Research Triangle works extensively with children who are adopted or in the foster care system and who have experienced abuse, neglect, and prenatal alcohol and drug exposure. Prenatal or postnatal counseling is available for families considering a domestic or international adoption of a high risk child, especially children prenatally exposed to alcohol, cocaine, methamphetamines or other drugs.

National Child Traumatic Stress Network
www.nctsn.org

NCTSN is a unique collaboration of academic and community-based service centers whose mission is to raise the standard of care, and increase access to services for traumatized children and their families across the United States. Combining knowledge of child development, expertise in the full range of child traumatic experiences and attention to cultural perspectives, the NCTSN serves as a national resource for developing and disseminating evidence-based interventions, trauma-informed services, and public and professional education. This website is a must read for parents and professionals. It covers the impact of all types of trauma on the child's development. There are articles and videos viewable online. This website is the home of information related to the complex trauma described in this chapter.

The Infant-Parent Institute
www.infant-parent.com

The Infant-Parent Institute specializes in clinical services, professional training and research related to the optimal development of infants and their families. Michael Trout is the founder and director. The Infant-Parent Institute works with the foster care and adoption systems. They also treat adults whose depression, marital problems or parenting struggles have risen out of conflicted experiences in the first few years of life. They offer wonderful videos related to attachment, infant development, adoption and foster care.

The National Organization on Fetal Alcohol Syndrome
www.nofas.org

NOFAS is the leading voice and resource of the Fetal Alcohol Spectrum Disorders (FASD) community. This website provides articles and additional resources for those parenting or working with children with FASD. The "Living with FASD" section offers great strategies for helping children with FASD. The tips are organized according to the child's developmental stage.

NTI Upstream
www.ntiupstream.com

NTI Upstream, formerly the National Training Institute, is an educational multimedia production company and community solutions training center. NTI Upstream specializes in providing resources focusing on the healthy development of children and their families. The "Upstream" in their name refers to the importance of addressing a problem at its source, rather than merely trying to manage its effects. The book, *Risk and Promise: A Handbook for Parents Adopting a Child from Overseas* by Ira Chasnoff, MD, Linda Schwartz, PhD, Cheryl Pratt, PhD and Gwendolyn Neuberger, MD, may be purchased through this website. *The Listening Heart*, a 37-minute video portraying life with children with FASD, and the book, *The Nature of Nurture* are two other resources adoptive families and agencies may want to consider adding to their libraries.

The Trauma Center
www.traumacenter.org

The Trauma Center provides comprehensive services to traumatized children and adults, and their families. The Executive Director is Joseph Spinazzola, PhD and the Medical Director and Founder is Bessel van der Kolk, MD—these two prominent professionals are part of the group responsible for the creation of complex trauma as presented in this chapter. In addition to clinical services, the Trauma Center offers training, consultation and educational programming for post-graduate mental health professionals. Their Certificate Program in Traumatic Stress Studies has state-of-the art seminars, lectures and supervision groups. Their Weekly Lecture Series is open to all mental health professionals.

CHAPTER THREE

Taking Stock: Are We a Family for a Child?

After a careful reading of Chapters 1 and 2, and further education using the resources listed so far in this book, prospective adoptive parents should be coming to recognize that the adoptive family will be providing an environment in which the adoptee can heal, to the degree possible, from past hurts. Within this healing environment for the newly adopted child, parents must maintain the well-being of the children who were already living in the home as well as themselves. Various strengths are beneficial in achieving this quality of life for each member of the adoptive family.

After initial legally required screening processes such as financial and criminal background checking are completed, one main purpose of what has always been called a home study is that it is a matching tool. It is sent to workers who have children in need of families. It is also used by courts to finalize an adoption.

However, another primary purpose of the home study is for the family and the agency to mutually assess the family's strengths in relation to the needs presented by the waiting children and to prepare them for the specialized way of looking at things and the unique skills that adoption requires. A pertinent question to be answered is, "Are we a family who has or can develop the skills necessary to parent a child with special needs?" The implication of this question is two-fold. First, the adoptive family must think in terms of the child who is joining the family. Just as establishing a career, maintaining a marriage or parenting typically developing children require sets of skills, parenting a child with special needs entails abilities as well. Second, it is likely that competency in a job, as a marital partner or in parenting was developed over a period of time. For example, to achieve career goals, one seeks co-worker support, a mentor relationship with a supervisor and additional training. Time and experience also lend to facilitating expertise in the career field of choice. Adoptive parenting is similar. It is a developmental process that begins when the family first considers adoption. It continues through pre-adoptive training, the home study and post-placement, and well into the adulthood of the adoptee. Therefore, the second implication of a home study is that families may not demonstrate all of the strengths necessary at the time of the home study. An additional purpose of the home study, then, is to identify the areas in which the family may want to consider additional skill enhancement.

This chapter looks at parental strengths believed to underlie successful adoptive families. In addition, this chapter will present ways to include the siblings-to-be in the home study process. Most often, little time is devoted to them during the home study process and little space is utilized to portray them in the final written home study report. I believe that including them in the family expansion preparation process can be an important element in helping the expanding family to assimilate new group members.

As you read this content, think in terms of the fact that parents will be helping the adoptee, themselves and their resident children form relationships. The child who has experienced trauma displays difficulties in intimate relationships because of past negative experiences. Thus, many of the skills presented are those utilized daily to form and nurture relationships. So, there will be some familiar territory in this chapter. However, forming a successful family which includes a child who joins it by adoption will require implementing these skills with greater frequency and over a long period of time. Adoptive parenting will also require learning new skills. As you read, use current relationships as a context. Ask yourself questions about your relationships with your siblings, parents, spouse or partner, the children you parent now, friends, co-workers, etc.

Assess the quality of each of your life's important relationships—marital, parent-child, friend-to-friend, with extended family and so on. How is each satisfying or dissatisfying?

Overall, are your relationships satisfying? Why are they satisfying?

Have you experienced relationships that were not fulfilling? What was missing? What did you contribute to this situation?

How often do you see your parents and siblings?

Do you harbor unresolved feelings for past events that occurred in your family of origin? If so, how do these issues impact your current relationships? How does this impact your parenting?

How often do you get together with friends?

Who can you depend on? How has this person demonstrated this?

How many long-term relationships do you have? If there are few, what are the reasons for this situation?

What do you enjoy most about parenting? What do you enjoy least?

Have you been disappointed by a child you are currently parenting? What was this like?

When have you been proud of your resident children? What was this like?

Are you currently a step-parent? If so, what types of issues has this presented? What difficulties emerged in blending children from two families? How long was the transition process or is it still ongoing?

How easily do you build new relationships?

Are you able to ask for help?

Strengths for Successful Adoptive Parenting

The Strength of Time-Management

Work, grocery shopping, yard work, laundry, driving the kids to soccer, arranging play dates, meeting friends for dinner, completing homework, spending time alone with your partner, birthday parties, visiting extended family—where does the list end! Add to the already long list therapy, psychiatric appointments, tutoring, school meetings, and occupational, physical and/or speech therapy. All children need time. The child with special needs may require extensive time. Below are comments made by typically developing children, ages 11 through 19, after their families adopted children with special needs.

"I lost a lot of attention because I was the only child until they came. My parents told me I would lose attention, but I never thought it would be as much as it has been."

"We lost a peaceful family. When they came, we had to spend so much time with them. Attention to me was lost."

"Since the adoption, things have changed a lot in our household. After my adopted sibling was brought into our lives, Mom and Dad switched to focusing more on my adopted sibling. They started seeing signs of irregular behavior around the age of 3 or 4 and took my adopted sister to multiple doctors' offices to try to understand what was going on.

That was only the beginning. As my sibling grew older and older, the problems got worse. She would have a fit when she couldn't get one of the many things she wanted. She also started lashing out for the simplest of things, such as making noise in her play area, asking her to get off of the computer, etc.

My parents started paying a lot more attention to her, and therefore, less on my brother and me. It has gotten to a point where they spend almost 100% of their time on her. This has really discouraged me, because it makes me feel like I'm not really important."

"We lose time with our parents because they are always with him."

"I've lost a lot of time with my parents. I remember my mom, me and my sisters could just go out shopping like every weekend. Now, I don't want to be in the house. I go out and find things to do. I do anything to get out of the chaos of the house."

"Our time with our parents was taken. My brother and my dad used to go golfing and every Sunday I used to go shopping or out to eat with my mom. We can't do this anymore because they take up so much time."

"We lost shopping time. It seems like we are always worried about money. It seems like we can never get anything done. As soon as something is finished, it seems like there is a problem with Gabe and we all have to stop and wait for that to end."

Prospective families often recognize that adding another child to the family will increase the grocery list, the pile of laundry and the transportation duties to and from extra curricular activities. Prospective families do not always recognize that time will also be diverted to the newly adopted child due to the parental attention and professional services this child may need to improve his physical, emotional, cognitive and social well-being. Gabe's sister is quoted last. Let's use her family as an example:

Cole and Becky, a Caucasian couple, adopted Gabe from Guatemala at age 16 months. He is now 6 years old. Already present in the family were Jennifer, Jessica and Mary. These three children were adopted from China, and currently they range in ages from 8 to 14. They were ages 3 to 9 when Gabe entered the family. Mary has various learning disabilities, a residual effect of her history of institutionalization. She receives special education services which Becky negotiates each school year. She requires assistance with her homework. Jessica and Jennifer are typically developing children. They all play on a travel soccer league, and among the three of them, their other activities include horse-back riding, science club, basketball, track, photography class, sewing class and volleyball. Cole and Becky each work full-time outside of the home. Cole's position requires at least two out-of-state business trips per month. These trips are several days in length.

Gabe's birthfamily decided to place him for adoption due to financial circumstances. He moved through two foster homes prior to his adoption. Cole and Becky were also informed that he had experienced failure to thrive. Since placement in their home, Gabe has been

> diagnosed with Sensory Integration Dysfunction and pre-natal drug and alcohol exposure. He attends a first grade special education class as he has ongoing struggles learning how to read. He receives occupational therapy twice weekly and meets with a psychiatrist monthly because medication is necessary to manage his difficulties with attention and impulsivity.
>
> Gabe also attends therapy twice per month. He recognized early the cultural difference between himself, Cole, and Becky and his sisters. As such, he has had many questions about how he came to live with this family. His questions have persisted in spite of Becky's many efforts to explain why his birthparents had chosen to relinquish their rights, and why he had resided in foster care. Professional services became needed to help Gabe accept the abandonment he experienced.
>
> Behaviorally, Gabe steals, lies and has lengthy temper tantrums. His problems with attention make it difficult for him to sit and play for more than a few minutes at a time. This same issue makes it quite problematic to take Gabe places such as sporting events, where he must sit and watch a game in its entirety.
>
> Prior to Gabe, the family's lifestyle was busy. Since Gabe, the family has been stretched beyond what one family can manage. Jennifer, the oldest, is frequently left to supervise her younger siblings while Becky and Gabe attend appointments. Jennifer understands the situation, yet she is often frustrated by the additional responsibilities. Jennifer, Mary and Jessica must depend on friends' parents for transportation and for congratulations after sporting victories that Cole and Becky now attend "sometimes" rather than regularly. Gone are home-cooked meals. These have been replaced by take-out food. All of the children yearn for the time they used to have with their mom and dad. Cole and Becky miss the time they used to spend with their children and each other. Friday evening had been "movie night" while Saturday was "game night." Gabe's behaviors disrupt this family fun to a point that the family now opts not to attempt to even try to play a game. Cole and Becky are guilt ridden regarding the status of their family.
>
> Cole stated,"I feel I have lost spending more time with the other kids and my wife—it's sad to say that she is on the bottom of the list. You know, you take care of the kids first and whatever is left, which is very little with my job and stuff, goes to her. If you had 100% of time, with four kids, everyone should get a fair share of that time. Gabe eats up 60% or 70% of the time. The other kids have to share the little bit that is left. If I am not directly taking care of Gabe, I am worried about where he is, what he is doing and what he is capable of doing where he is. It is just hard."

In Chapter 9 we will return to Gabe and his family. We will learn how Becky and Cole utilized time management skills as well as their other strengths to implement changes that enhanced the quality of life for each family member.

Prospective adoptive families may benefit from examining how their time is utilized. For example, determine the areas in which time is spent over a one week period. This may be accomplished by using an Activity Log such as is available at www.mindtools.com or by using the pie graph below. Each of the 24 sections represents 1 hour. Using different colored markers, color in how many hours are devoted to sleep, exercise/sports, work, school-related matters, personal care/grooming, transportation, meal preparation/eating/clean-up, relaxation, socializing, family commitments and medical appointments.

Then ask yourself the following questions.

How will we make time to accommodate another person and his needs, interests and talents into the family?

What areas of time can decrease if necessary?

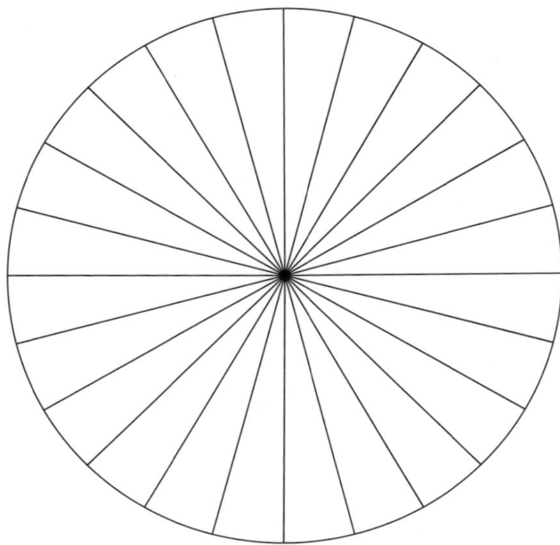

How flexible is my job? If I need to attend school meetings or mental health appointments during the day, will I need to use sick time or vacation days? What is the impact on other family members of consuming vacation days to meet the new child's needs? Can I use Family Medical Leave Act time?

What sacrifices might I have to make to ensure that all of my children benefit from my time and attention? Am I willing to make these sacrifices?

What time do I need for myself so that I can maintain the emotional health needed to parent effectively?

Again, reflect on your relationships. Who can you rely on for help?

Stress Management: Maintaining a Healthy Emotional Climate

Stress is a condition or feeling experienced when a person perceives that demands exceed the personal and social resources the individual is able to mobilize. In short, it is what we feel when we think we have lost control of events. People feel little stress when they have the time, experience and resources to manage a situation. They feel great stress when they think that they cannot handle the demands put upon them. Stress is therefore a negative experience. And it is not an inevitable consequence of an event. It depends a lot on people's perceptions of a situation and their real ability to cope with it.[1]

Some of the early research on stress established the existence of the well-known "fight-or-flight" response. This work showed that when a person experiences a shock or perceives a threat, hormones are released that help the person to survive. Unfortunately, this mobilization of the body for survival also has negative consequences. In this state, we are excitable, anxious, jumpy and irritable. This actually reduces our ability to interact effectively with other people. With trembling hands and a pounding heart,

1. MindTools. *Stress Management.* http://www.mindtools.com/pages/article/newTCS_00.htm

we can find it difficult to execute precise, controlled skills. The intensity of our focus on survival interferes with our ability to make fine judgments by drawing information from many sources. We find ourselves more accident-prone and less able to make good decisions.

There are very few situations in healthy family life in which the fight-or-flight response is useful. Most situations benefit from a calm, rational, controlled and socially sensitive approach.

The sources of stress are many, and may include things such as work overload, conflicting priorities, inconsistent values, conflict with others, unpleasant environments, and perceived threats to our social standing or to other people's opinions of us, or to our own deeply held values. An adoptee's negative behaviors can create these very sources of stress.

> Jack and Leah adopted Nathan from the foster care system when he was 2 years old. He is currently age 10. Jack is a member of the school board. Leah volunteers for many activities at their church. Nathan exhibits various negative behaviors such as temper outbursts, lying and being destructive of personal possessions. These behaviors occur at home, at school and at church. During second grade, Nathan rummaged through his classmates' lunches, eating their snacks. He stole an array of pens and pencils. He threw a book at a teacher, and he used profanity when speaking to the teacher and principal. Shortly after the start of third grade, Nathan wrote profanity on the wall of the boys' bathroom. It was up to the school board to determine if this was a violation of the school's policy regarding defacing school property. If so, Nathan's consequence would be to attend an alternative school for ten days.

> Rachel and Greg adopted Amber when she was 8 years old. Amber was originally from Kazakhstan. Amber was placed with Greg and Rachel after the dissolution of her first adoption. The first adoptive family brought her to America when she was age 6. Greg and Rachel reside in a small town. Greg is well-respected for his work as a carpenter. One evening, the family was outside working on landscaping. Rachel realized that she hadn't touched base with Amber for several minutes. She began looking for Amber. She located Amber etching a penis, with a key, on the side of Greg's work van.

Imagine the embarrassment of your child searching for food in other children's lunches! Imagine being a member of the school board which is now meeting about your own son! Think about how you would go to work at a client's home with a penis drawn on the side of your work vehicle! What type of reaction might this cause when taking the van to have the paint repaired? What will other people think of you? How do these behaviors cause conflict with your own values? What type of home environment do such behaviors create? Typically, parents respond with anger and frustration. Parents also become worried about what will happen to their son or daughter if they cannot influence behavioral change. How do you explain such behaviors to your typically developing child? How do others' opinions of your family impact those children? How are the brothers and sisters affected by a home environment sated with conflict?

The child who has experienced trauma creates stress which in turn may cause a ***negative emotional climate*** within the family. The family that was going through life experiencing sprinkles of difficult times now finds themselves in frequent full blown thunder storms! On a smaller scale, many of us have been involved in this type of change in our emotional climate:

> Pat, husband to Marian and parent to one typically developing adolescent and two adolescents with complex trauma issues whom he adopted, has been under stress at work. His

company was sold and the new management is restructuring the manner in which Pat's department operates. Pat must attend meetings and learn new ways to conduct business. Many of his co-workers have sought new employment, so Pat must also learn to work with a new team of colleagues. He arrives home each evening grumpy. He complains about his job, the clutter of the home, the dinner selection and so on and so forth. Shortly after his arrival home, each family member feels down in the dumps. Pat is transferring his feelings of anger about his work situation to his wife and children.

A transfer of emotions may occur non-verbally.

Kim and Tony are the parents to their birth son, Tony, Jr., age 14. Feeling very blessed, they have opted to adopt. A set of twins, age 12, was placed in their home. Madeline and Mackenzie have had a long history of abuse and neglect. While in foster care, they experienced 11 moves. Their needs turned out to be considerable. Tony would often arrive home from work to find Kim cleaning. He knew this meant that it had been a bad day. As such, he immediately made himself busy, leaving his wife alone. However, he also knew that she was sad that their daughters struggled to learn to be a part of their family. Each day it took great effort just to get the girls off to school. Once at school it was likely the teacher or principal would call regarding a behavioral incident for which there would be a detention or suspension. His wife's "cleaning" made him feel sorrow as well.

A child who has experienced trauma alters the emotional climate of the home on a frequent or a long-term basis as we will see in Chapter 8. Negative behaviors are the main way in which these children communicate. There are several reasons for this.

- The child who has been beaten, raped, abandoned, institutionalized, separated from siblings and/or moved from foster home to foster home has internalized intense feelings as a result of these traumas. Inside, she feels rage, sorrow, hopelessness, helplessness, profound sadness, frustration, loneliness and lost. Who wouldn't?
- The adoptee's traumatic experiences often occur when he or she has little or no language development. Their traumas are also so extensive that it is difficult for them to find words to describe their sufferings. Overall, there is an inability to verbalize the events and the emotions.
- Their world is riddled with cognitive dissonance. They look around and feel out-of-sync. For example, the international adoptee arrives at the airport. Grandparents, aunts, uncles and siblings are holding signs and balloons. They are excited, smiling and crying tears of joy. The adoptee, on the other hand, is scared, sad and lonely. He is thinking; "Where am I? Who are these people? They don't smell or sound familiar. What happened to all of the other babies I was living with? What is this place called America? What is this place called home?" His experience does not match with those around him. As he ages, he realizes that his life in the orphanage was a different beginning from that of the other children in his neighborhood, his pre-school, kindergarten and so on. Feelings continue to develop. Inadvertently, among the adults in the adoption community, the act of being adopted is frequently portrayed in a positive light. "Your birthmother was so poor, she couldn't keep you. She wanted you to be adopted because she loved you so much." The adoptee is again in a situation that may be inconsistent with his thoughts and emotions. He feels sad and angry that he was given away, no matter what the circumstances. He feels the loss of the life that was supposed to be. Yet, he is not sure how to convey these feelings, because those around him

are not demonstrating that they understand his perspective, which seems to be so different from theirs.

- Foster children frequently lack the opportunity to convey their thoughts and feelings. They are uncertain as to how long they may be in residence with a particular family. They may feel that there is no point starting a process of healing that they may not be able to finish. They often languish in therapeutic services that wait for them to build a trusting relationship resultant from which they will reveal their past hurts. These revelations may not occur because the child does not have the words to express his trauma. Interventions are interrupted because they must move. Services are not provided due to lengthy waiting lists. Or, services are not initiated due to a philosophy that promotes that time and love will make the problems disappear. These children will begin the process of emotional healing only after placement with the adoptive family. Then they will wait until they feel safe and secure in the new family.

The traumatized child's negative behaviors create stress and heightened emotions in those around them, especially in their parents and siblings. This is their way of determining how to express feelings. That is, they are watching to see how the family members handle their own feelings. They are looking for models to resolve their emotions in order to feel whole. *They do this with frequency.* As their feelings are so intense, the family can become overwhelmed. At times, the family feels as if it is losing control:

> The early years of Luke and Molly's marriage had been rocky. Luke spent a bulk of time pursuing career goals. He had a vision of early retirement. The couple attempted to remedy their time apart by creating a business together. During this endeavor, their time together consisted of driving to business meetings, presenting at trade shows and working together at their office. There was little time for relaxation and simply enjoying each others' company. In the midst of this period, their infertility was diagnosed and treated. Infertility treatment was ineffective.
>
> In their mid-thirties, dissatisfied with life, Luke and Molly determined to make some major changes. Both had been raised in families of origin that valued religious participation. Luke attended seminary and then obtained employment at a local church. This position entailed evening work three weekdays as well as being available each Sunday morning and evening. Molly accepted a position as an administrative assistant at a nearby factory. After ten years of marriage, the couple finally felt settled and this contributed to their decision to adopt Brett and Derrick.
>
> Brett and Derrick, ages 7 and 9 respectively, were in foster care. Luke and Molly had known Brett and Derrick for 18 months through a family in their church which had been fostering the boys. When it became obvious that Brett and Derrick would not return to their birth home, Luke and Molly prayed and came to believe that adopting these siblings was the path chosen for them. In very short order, Brett and Derrick moved to Luke and Molly's home. Eight months later, the adoptions were finalized.
>
> Katelyn arrived as a toddler two years later. Shortly after Katelyn's adoption, Brett deteriorated. While he had always had various behavioral difficulties, such as writing on his clothes with pens, cutting holes in his clothing, losing personal possessions and stealing, he now became prone to temper outbursts, name-calling and arguing at any time he was asked to carry out a routine task. He yelled when Katelyn cried, "Make her shut up. Just make her shut up!" He would cover his ears, run upstairs, slam his bedroom door and begin throwing things or kicking the walls.

On the evenings when Luke was working, Molly had great difficulty managing the three children. She began calling Luke at work for ideas. This made it difficult for Luke to concentrate on his responsibilities to his parishioners. Once Luke arrived home, Molly then relayed to him the entire evening's events.

Molly began to dread the nights when she would have to parent alone. Luke began dreading his arrival home from work. The couple engaged in numerous fights. Molly felt *alone* in her marriage and she was *scared*. She was afraid of what Brett might be capable of doing during his outbursts. Luke felt *inadequate*. He was not able to console his wife. He could not find ways to end Brett's behaviors nor reduce his wife's stress. He felt *out of control* of his own home. He found ways to arrive home even later from work. In essence, because he could not find ways to resolve the situation, he began *avoiding the problem*.

Brett and Derrick's early years in residence with their birthfamily had been replete with domestic violence, physical abuse and neglect. Brett had suffered two broken bones by the time he was 18 months old. His birthmother, a substance abuser, beat Brett and Derrick when they cried. The birthfather and birthmother fought to the extent that each sustained various injuries. Brett and Derrick can both recall "picking up glass because they threw dishes and beer bottles." They can also describe telling their birthparents to "shut up" to try and stop their fights. Each child clearly tried to help their birthparents become better parents in the only ways they could think of as young children. Brett's thought pattern upon entering therapy was one of *feeling alone, being scared, feeling inadequate* to cause changes and thus *lacking the control* to prevent the actions and the eventual loss of his birthparents. The arrival of Katelyn acted as a trigger for remembering the trauma Brett had endured in the first 5½ years of his life.

The issues that were apparent early in Luke and Molly's marriage were heightened as Brett escalated. Molly's feelings of loneliness that had arisen because of her husband's passion for work rose again with his church work schedule. She felt as if she was a single parent in a two-parent family. She felt trapped with Brett four evenings per week. Again, she was *fearful* that Brett would *lose such control of himself* that she would not be able to prevent him from injuring Katelyn, Derrick or herself. She longed for a husband who worked a 9 to 5 job. At one point in therapy she stated, "I thought once we had children he would be home." When asked why she thought this in spite of the fact that each was supportive of the decision for Luke to work in the ministry, she said, "I just always wanted a family. My father was a weekend alcoholic. I spent most of the weekend sitting in my room listening to my parents argue about my dad's drinking. Their fights were always full of threats. My mom would threaten to leave my father and my father would tell her to go if she didn't like the way he was. I never felt like I could talk to either of them about the problem. I was always worried that my parents would separate." In other words, Molly had spent a sizable portion of her childhood alone and scared. Now, she was in a similar position within her own home. The longer the situation went on, the more unavailable Luke became. Just prior to their decision to enter therapy, Molly had called Luke on numerous occasions threatening to leave the marriage if Luke could not alter his work schedule to be home more evenings.

Luke was quite startled by Molly's revelation. As he reflected, his early childhood had been ideal. He had two loving parents. However, his father's social drinking became alcoholism by the time Luke was 11. His parents argued frequently as well. Luke's solution to this situation was to become involved in various extra-curricular activities: sports, the church youth group, student council, the yearbook committee and the school newspaper. He withdrew from the home environment because he had no capacity to alter it. His father joined Alcoholics Anonymous when Luke entered college. Today, the two have repaired their relationship. Yet, the pattern of avoiding difficult situations remains Luke's primary coping skill. Once Luke finished explaining, Molly felt as if she was finally able to understand why he had been "pulling away" from the family.

Luke and Molly are a representative example of the types of issues that arise in response to a traumatized adoptee. A family who had some troubles prior to adoption finds themselves in a full-scale state of crisis several years into their adoption. Brett entered the family feeling scared and alone. He transferred his thoughts and feelings to Luke and Molly because each had a foundation for these same beliefs and emotions. In essence, Brett triggered Luke and Molly's past histories. Prior to Brett, their relationship skills were adequate. However, tipped out of balance by the stress of parenting Brett, each engaged in ineffective patterns of communication, problem-solving, time management, patience and so forth. Each lost their sense of humor. Each lost the ability to have empathy. They arrived at therapy angry and depressed. Molly reported that she was "bursting into tears" at work and home. Luke had become so angry on one occasion that he punched a hole in a wall.

Neither had ever believed that they could have such intense feelings! The intensity of their feelings was a mirror of the intensity of emotions Brett felt for his abuse and abandonment. Each expressed concerns about their emotional state on their jobs and in their marriage. Each had stopped participation in activities they once enjoyed. Each had let friendships go by the wayside. Each worried about the impact of their condition on Derrick and Katelyn. What kind of a life was this for Derrick and Katelyn?

The Impact of Stress on the Family

This segment presents the core of what can happen in families after the placement of a traumatized child. A family that had previously been functioning adequately becomes overwhelmed. Their capacity to manage their stress declines. A myriad of problems falls out of this—marital discord, parent-child conflict, loss of interest in pleasurable activities, isolation from support systems, work stress and/or conflict and so on. Luke and Molly and this concept of negative emotional climate will be re-visited in Chapters 8, 9, and 10. Chapter 8 will expand this concept further. Chapters 9 and 10 will offer ways to weather the storm successfully. Stress management skills that include communication skills, the capacity to express feelings in positive ways and the ability to maintain emotional regulation are key skills that contribute to the well-being of each member of the family. Learning to maintain emotional regulation is essential to the well-being of each member of the family.

Think about how you deal with stress by asking yourself the following questions:

How do I manage stress? Do I become frustrated? Do I become angry? Do I become physically ill? Do I calm myself down and prioritize? Do I take breaks to relax?

How do I express my emotions? Do I withdraw? Do I let things build up and then explode? Am I able to walk away and then return when I have calmed down? Have I learned to deal with my feelings in productive or unhealthy ways?

How well do I communicate? Do I offer solutions before I have actually heard what the other person is saying? Do I interrupt? Do I think before I respond? Do I provide reassuring clichés? Do I have to have the last word? Am I able to listen with empathy and see the other's point of view? Do I actually face the person who is talking, or do I continue reading the paper or surfing the Internet?

How Stress Builds in a New Adoptive Family

Child arrives with unresolved emotions

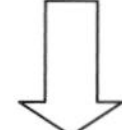

Child acts out behaviorally

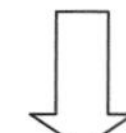

Parents' own unresolved issues are triggered

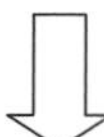

Child and parent engage in negative emotional interactions

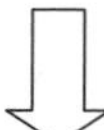

A Negative Emotional Climate is Created

Taking a Proactive Approach to Sex and Sexuality

Colleen and Roy have two sons and a daughter by birth; Tori, Glenn and Nathan are ages 11, 9 and 8. Colleen and Roy felt very blessed. They had three great children, thriving careers, a lovely home, and wonderful friends and relatives. Rather than having a fourth birth child, they opted to share their good fortune with a child in need of a home. They flew to Belarus and arrived back in America with 22-month-old Aimee.

Aimee presented immediate difficulties. She was unable to sleep for longer than two hours at a time. When awake, she cried constantly. She also masturbated chronically. It was not uncommon to find Aimee in the living room masturbating. It is not known if Aimee was sexually abused during her stay in Belarus or if she learned to stimulate herself by masturbating in order to survive the deprivation of the orphanage environment. In any event, Aimee's sexualized behavior was initially shocking to Colleen, Roy, Tori, Glenn and Nathan. Colleen and Roy have made significant efforts to stop Aimee's masturbation. However, Aimee, now age 9, continues to masturbate when under stress.

Shelia and Wendell have one child by birth. Staci is 14. She is attractive and smart. Their second child, Yvonne, joined the family via adoption. She is 12 years old. Recently, condoms have been turning up in her back pack, purse, jeans' pockets and her bedroom. The family's home is located within walking distance of the school. When Yvonne was late in arriving home from school one day, Shelia began canvassing the neighborhood looking for her. When she could not spot Yvonne, Shelia began knocking on neighbors' doors asking if anyone had seen Yvonne. Indeed, one mother reported that Yvonne had come home with her 13-year-old son. The two were "upstairs listening to music." This parent went upstairs to let Yvonne know that Shelia was waiting for her. There was quite a rustle on the other side of the boy's bedroom door. So, the mother opened the door to see what the commotion was about. The two were attempting to put their clothes on. Upon being questioned by both mothers, the two told conflicting stories as to how far the sexual interactions had gone. Shelia's suspicions as to why Yvonne had condoms had been validated.

Subsequently, Wendell and Shelia presented this situation to their family physician. After much discussion, Yvonne was placed on birth control. The family has increased their supervision of Yvonne. Shelia and Wendell have also engaged in extra conversations about sex with Staci, age 14. They were working with her on this issue anyway, but they became fearful that Staci would be influenced by Yvonne's behavior, so they stepped up their discussions with Staci.

Karl and his wife Helen adopted siblings, Teri and Drew. Karl had grown up in a dysfunctional family of origin. His father was obsessed with pornography and he sexually abused Karl's younger sister. Karl had spent years in therapy overcoming his guilt for not being able to stop the abuse, and his rage toward both parents—his father for perpetrating the abuse and his mother for ignoring the abuse. Drew and Teri had been sexually abused in their birthfamily. Their birthmother prostituted the children as a means of financial support after the birthfather abandoned the family.

Shortly after Drew and Teri moved in with Karl and Helen, Karl realized that he was having a hard time showing Teri any affection. He was uncomfortable when the two of them were alone in the same room. He avoided taking Teri on outings if Helen or Drew were not available to go along. At age twelve, Teri was already well into puberty. Boys were finding her quite attractive. Over the next few years, Karl found himself monitoring Teri's wardrobe. Anything that he perceived as too "tight or revealing" was immediately thrown in the trash. He also found himself prohibiting Teri from participating in school dances, trips to the mall with friends, parties, sleepovers and any other activity that he could not personally supervise.

On one hand, Helen and Teri understood his desire to protect Teri. On the other hand, Teri was missing experiences important for a girl her age. Conflicts began occurring. Teri was angry. She wanted to be a "normal kid." Teri was also disappointed and confused. She was responsible with her chores and diligent with her school work. Yet, she felt that all of her efforts had not helped her earn her father's trust. Worst of all, she interpreted Karl's inability to hug her or kiss her good night as a sign that she was unlovable due to the fact that she had been sexually abused.

Helen suggested that Karl resume therapy to discern why he was unable to balance his need to protect Teri with Teri's need to engage in age-appropriate peer-related events. Once in therapy, Karl realized that his desire to shield Teri was really reflective of his inability to protect his younger sister. Unconsciously, he was working to keep Teri safe from any possibility of additional sexual abuse. Further, Karl revealed that deep inside he was fearful that he might sexually abuse Teri. He had thoughts that he would turn out like his own father even though he had never engaged in any type of inappropriate sexual behavior with girls or women. Eventually, Karl worked through these issues and his relationship with Teri improved. However, in the meantime, he and Teri missed many opportunities for intimate and enjoyable father and daughter moments.

A social worker called Ilene and Leo late one afternoon to inquire about whether they would accept placement of their two great nieces and their great nephew. The children had been in custody for several years and it had finally been determined that the children would be adopted. Ilene and Leo were ecstatic! Over the years, Ilene and Leo had made significant efforts to help the children and their birthmother. However, the birthmother moved frequently and for the past few years, Ilene and Leo had been unable to locate the children. The state agency with custody had only recently learned that Ilene and Leo were relatives. Otherwise, the social worker explained, they would have contacted them sooner.

Three weeks later, the children arrived: Claire, age 15, Bret, age 13 and Nora, age 12. Within several months, Claire began talking about her friend, Fran. Everything was "Fran this . . ." or "Fran that . . ." Then, the school principal called to inform Leo and Ilene that Claire and Fran had been observed walking through the halls holding hands. There were also reports the two had been seen kissing. A discussion with Claire confirmed that indeed Fran and Claire were "dating." Claire explained that she lacked any desire to involve herself romantically with boys. She was disgusted by boys and men due to the sexual abuse she sustained by her birthmother's boyfriends. In a subsequent conversation with Nora and Bret, they indicated they had known about the relationship between Claire and Fran for "quite some time." Nora stated, "Of course we knew. Everyone in the school knows that my sister is gay! Kids ask me questions or make comments a lot."

Ken and Robin had several children by birth and one child by adoption. The oldest had completed college. He was employed, and he resided in his own apartment. One was in college. She lived in the dormitories and so was only home on breaks. Their third birth child, Taeisha, was 14, while their son-by-adoption, Devon, was age 15. Devon had entered the family as a toddler. So, he and Taeisha had grown up together.

At age 13, Devon apparently began making many attempts to have sexual intercourse with Taeisha. Taeisha endured this situation for about ten months before she told Robin about Devon's efforts to rape her.

Robin had been sexually abused as a child by a relative. She had worked hard to move beyond this abuse. As a parent, she prided herself on open communication. She talked to her children about everything, including sex. She spoke to them, time and time again, about speaking up for themselves in the event someone did attempt to sexually abuse them. When Taeisha informed her of Devon's activities, Robin immediately informed Ken. She made arrangements for Devon to stay with her sister and she contacted the appropriate authorities. These steps were excellent. She set a great example for Taeisha of a mother protecting her children. Subsequently, she made arrangements for each teen, Devon and Taeisha, to attend counseling.

As the dust settled, Robin became guilt ridden. She could not believe that this had happened in her own home. She questioned how she could have "missed" this. She wondered why Taeisha had not told her sooner. She had worked diligently to be a good parent. She felt like she had failed in what was, to her, her most important job in life.

Nolan and Rosemary, American teachers working in El Salvador, volunteered to help repair the roof on a nearby orphanage. During this process, they became aware of four siblings living in the orphanage. The brother and sisters were available for adoption. Nolan and Rosemary had married while in their late 40s, and so having birth children was not a viable option. The couple prayed and eventually decided that it was their path to adopt the four children.

Within one year, Maggie, Ashley, Christian and Linda had moved in. The children ranged in ages from 6 to 11. The adjustment period was significant, as would be expected when going from a family of two to a family of six!

One day while delivering clean laundry to Christian's room, Rosemary found Christian and Linda engaging in sexual intercourse. She was shocked, angry and distraught! She immediately informed Nolan. Subsequently, Rosemary and Nolan discussed the situation with Christian and Linda. Christian was quite confused at first. He did not understand why Nolan and Rosemary were having such difficulties with his sexual relationship with his sister. He revealed that he was simply acting as he had been taught by his birth uncle and birthfather. The four children had been removed from their birth home by the police for reports of physical abuse and neglect. Before going to the orphanage, they had lived with their birthmother, birth uncle and birthfather. The uncle and father sexually abused Maggie and Ashley. They also initiated sexual activity between Christian and these siblings. To Christian, having sex with your sisters was a way of life. Ashley and Maggie verified Christian's story and added many more examples of the sexual abuse they had sustained while in their birth home.

John is 14 years old. He was adopted by Marcy and Dan when he was age 10. The couple also has two birth children, presently ages 11 and 8. They made the decision to adopt after hearing radio advertisements.

Marcy and Dan have made great efforts to monitor their children's use of the Internet as well as the music they listen to and the movies they watch. However, John always seems to find ways around their parental controls. Each time he obtains access to the Internet, he downloads pornography. Pornography turns up in the bedroom he shares with his younger brother, in the bathroom, in his backpack, and once it was left, in plain sight, on the dining room table!

Prior to adopting John, the family was made aware that he had been born with drugs and alcohol in his system. His birthfather had been incarcerated on numerous occasions for theft and selling narcotics. His birthmother was prone to homelessness. She and John often lived in cars or abandoned buildings. She had been arrested several times for prostitution. Dan and Marcy were also informed that John had engaged in some sexual acts with children while in foster care. However, the incidents were vague and the social workers were convinced that they were really the result of "natural curiosity." So, Marcy and Dan had had little concern in bringing John into their home.

As time went on, however, and they ran out of ways to attempt to alleviate this behavior, they became concerned as to how their birth children were being impacted as a result of finding and seeing the pornography John strew around their home. They began to wonder if John had the capacity to sexually abuse their young son or daughter.

Eventually, the couple sought professional assistance. Over time, John described sexual abuse by several men and his birth grandfather. It became clear that the pornography was his way of attempting to let Dan and Marcy know that he had been sexually abused. He was also verifying that seeing men having sex with women made him feel heterosexual. That is, as long as he was "excited" by what he considered "normal" sex, he did not feel as if his sexual experiences with men had "caused him to be gay."

The above examples begin to make clear that adoptive parenting frequently means addressing various sexual issues with the adoptee and the typically developing children. Such discussions may need to be initiated when the children are at younger ages than the parents had anticipated. For parents who have experienced sexual abuse themselves, adoption may mean re-visiting painful memories in order to be an effective parent. For parents raised in homes where sex was not discussed, or in which children were shielded from the realities of the world, open and honest dialogue about sexual matters may be uncomfortable or foreign. In addition to the tips that conclude this segment,

Chapter 10 will offer some additional advice regarding parenting the sexually abused child. Prospective parents need to examine their thoughts and feelings regarding sex and sexuality.

Certainly, all parents need to address sexual matters with their children. However, as the following facts about sexual abuse make clear, there is a greater urgency to do so in families who adopt a child with a history of sexual abuse.

- Physical problems that have been associated with child sexual abuse histories include headaches, stomach pain, asthma, bladder infections and chronic pelvic pain. Some proportion of medical complaints presented to physicians and other health care practitioners may less reflect inherent bodily dysfunction than anxiety.
- Sexual abuse victims tend to perceive themselves as different from others and tend to be less trusting of those in their immediate environment. They are less socially competent, more aggressive and more socially withdrawn. They have fewer friends during childhood, less satisfaction in relationships and report less closeness with their parents than do nonvictims.
- Sexual abuse negatively impacts overall academic performance.
- A history of sexual abuse contributes to poor self-esteem. This translates into a continuing inability to define one's own boundaries or reasonable rights when faced with the needs or demands of others in the interpersonal environment. Such problems, in turn, are associated with a greater likelihood of being victimized or exploited by others.
- Child victims are more than four times as likely to receive a diagnosis of major depression as nonabused children. Adults with a history of sexual abuse may have as much as a four-time greater lifetime risk for major depression than do individuals with no such history.
- The rate of teen pregnancy among sexually abused girls is approximately four times higher than non-abused girls. In addition, sexually abused girls are significantly likely to have another (i.e., a second) pregnancy than are non-abused girls.
- At ages when sexual activity is appropriate, sexual aversion may develop. Unpleasant memories and feelings connected with traumatic sexualization become associated with subsequent sexual arousal. There may be a specific aversion to sexual thoughts, feelings and situations reminiscent of the abusive experience. This negative association with sex may interfere with sexual pleasure and may even result in sexual dysfunction.
- Those sexually abused in childhood are more likely to experience sexual preoccupation expressed in the form of pornography consumption, excessive masturbation and an overactive sexual fantasy life. Unexpressed or internalized sexual compulsions can also be expressed through compulsive spending, gambling, overeating or binging.
- Sexually abused adolescents are 18 to 21 times more likely to become substance abusers.
- A history of childhood sexual abuse is highly correlated with an increased number of sexual partners and consequently much higher rates of sexually transmitted diseases, including HIV.
- Overall, sexual abuse survivors have up to five times greater likelihood of being diagnosed with at least one anxiety disorder than their nonabused peers.

- Adults who were molested as children document more frequent suicidal behavior and/or greater suicidal ideation. (Briere and Elliott, 1994; Kendall-Tackett, Williams and Finkelhor, 1993; Putnam, 2003; Putnam, 2006; Trickett, McBride-Chang and Putnam, 1994 and Trickett and Putnam, 2003)

The types of issues parents need to think about and discuss in advance of adopting are exemplified in the vignettes and the statements presented above.

Aimee's story, for example, calls into light masturbation. Masturbation is considered a "normal" activity in adolescence. Do you agree or disagree with this statement? Parents need to think about how they feel about masturbation. How would you react to a child masturbating? Colleen and Roy were faced with their birth children asking, "What is she doing?" How might you respond to such a question?

Overall, masturbation can often prove to be a difficult behavior to end. Once the body experiences sex, it seeks sexual gratification no matter what one's age. Many families find themselves in a value crisis as a result of this sexual behavior. This may be especially true for parents with religious convictions that view masturbation as a moral failing or sin. Frequently, the resolution to masturbation issues is to teach the child to carry out the behavior in his or her bedroom with the door closed. In this way, the behavior is at least private from the other family members. However, knowing that your child is engaging in a sexual activity, in your own home is uncomfortable and may go against the grain of your belief system.

Yvonne's case highlights parental attitudes toward birth control. Parents should ask themselves these questions:

Does placing an adolescent on birth control provide a license to be sexually active?

What would happen if our adolescent experienced an unplanned pregnancy? Could the baby be placed for adoption? Would we want to help raise our grandchild?

How do our plans to teach abstinence fit with the child's desires to engage in sexual behaviors?

How does birth control mesh with our religious convictions?

How do we balance supervising the sexually promiscuous child with the child's need to experience age-appropriate activities?

How do we help a child who has experienced sexual activity understand that such activity should occur within a loving and kind relationship? That is, the child who has experienced sexual abuse is often quite knowledgeable of the mechanics of sexual activity. Yet, unfortunately, this child is unaware of the beauty of sex within a relationship wherein sex is a special and mutually satisfying part of that relationship.

What is the impact of a sexually active child on the birth and/or previously adopted children? Will younger children use the adoptee as a model? Will resident adolescents think they can act as they see the adoptee acting?

How do we teach our typically developing children values and morals when we have a child who acts in ways that are incongruent with our belief system?

Yvonne's story further brings to the forefront coming to terms with your thoughts on pre-marital sex, as well as how the parents will help the child reduce exposure to AIDS and sexually transmitted diseases.

Claire's sexual preference is homosexual. Certainly, this is an issue that brings forth strong feelings for many.

John's case forces us to examine pornography.

What will your reaction be if faced with these matters?

Overall, gaining clarification about your sexual beliefs prior to accepting a new child into your home will be of benefit. In addition to the questions raised in preceding content, consider the following as well:

What were you told about sex?

How were you told about sex?

When were you told about sex?

Did you get enough accurate information about sex while you were growing up?

Is whatever two consenting adults do sexually their business? How about two consenting adolescents?

What were your early childhood, adolescent and young adult sexual experiences?

How much of your past sexual behavior would you change? How much of your past sexual behavior would you share with your child?

In your family of origin, what was the family message regarding sex?

In what ways have your sexual attitudes changed since age 18?

How did you feel about the rate of your sexual physiological development?

In what ways did your parents respond to your developing sexuality (wet dreams, masturbation, birth control, sex education, etc.)?

Again, what are your thoughts on AIDS and sexually transmitted diseases, homosexuality, masturbation, pre-marital sex, birth control and pornography? How comfortable are you discussing these issues with your children? How comfortable are you discussing with your children the effects of puberty and sex?

Have you ever had a negative sexual experience? If so, how have you dealt with it?

Does your negative sexual experience impact your parenting? Does it impact other relationships?

Are you willing to re-work this trauma again if need be?

The last five questions bring us to instances in which the prospective adoptive parents have themselves experienced sexual abuse. The anecdote of Karl and Teri offers the situation of a parent's history of abuse interfering with the parent-child relationship. This type of scenario occurs frequently. As was put forth earlier in this chapter and in Chapter 1, sexual abuse, as well as various other traumas that parents have experienced in their own childhood may be triggered during the adoption process. If not resolved again, the family becomes immobilized. We'll be providing solutions to this matter in Chapters 9 and 10. Hopefully, you will work with an agency who will request that you write an autobiography as a part of your home study requirements and you will share such childhood traumas with your worker in that autobiography. If you are not asked about past traumas, examine your history. Identify potential issues that may surface. Generate solutions so you are prepared to take action when the need arises.

Robin, Ken, Rosemary and Nolan bring us to another facet of this topic of sex and sexuality. Their families include children sexually acting out (or attempting do so) with other children in the family. A first point that needs to be made is that most children who have been sexually abused do ***not*** go on to be life-long sexual perpetrators. The large majority of children who have experienced sexual abuse will never engage in or will learn to stop sexual interactions with other children. Once they move into a healthy family, they frequently conclude, or they are taught by healthy adults, that engaging in sexual activity with one's siblings, other children or adults is improper.

A thorough pre-adoption training program covers the types of precautions parents are able to implement in order to prevent an occurrence of sexual acting out in their family. Such a program should include the following practical suggestions

- A home with adequate bedroom space is preferable. If resident children and adopted children must share a room, then it is essential that the typically developing children be old enough to comprehend what would be considered a sexual touch. Brothers and sisters need to understand clearly that sexual advances should be immediately reported to the parent.
- Door alarms offer the ability to offset opportunities for sexual acting out. An alarm on each child's bedroom door ensures that everyone is in his respective bedroom. The child who has experienced trauma often feels a sense of safety as a result of a door alarm. He knows that no one has access to him. Thus, he can sleep soundly without fear of re-victimization.
- Periodically ask your children if sexual advances have been made. Children are more likely to tell when adults make clear that they are open to such disclosures. However, as the case of Robin and Ken illustrates, even in families who have created an atmosphere of open communication, children may still opt not to tell. Children are fearful of what will happen as a result of divulging such information. They worry that they or their sibling will "get in trouble." They are frequently fearful of repercussions from the perpetrator.
- Implement an Adoptive Family Safety Contract. This type of contract is designed to keep everyone in the family safe. It lists the rules for living together safely, for respecting the rights of others, and for ensuring the personal safety for everyone in the family. A sample contract is included in the Appendices.
- Also explain the types of touch that are acceptable in your family (e.g., hugs, bedtime kisses, snuggling on the couch while watching a movie, etc). Clarify rules regarding privacy. More specific suggestions are included in Chapter 10 and the Appendices.
- If you do discover sexual activity, attempt to react as calmly as possible. Make clear your expectations that the behavior you witnessed or were informed of needs to cease permanently. Be clear, direct and use anatomically correct language. Contact the appropriate authorities if need be. Seek professional help.
- Be vigilant! Do not allow yourself to believe that sexual interactions cannot happen in your home.

Being proactive about sex and sexuality may not come easily to some pre-adoptive parents, but, as these stories indicate, proactivity is an invaluable tool for families adopting children coming from traumatic backgrounds.

The Ability to Set Goals

Goal-setting helps clarify what is important. Concentrating on accomplishing specific goals enhances the capacity to manage stress, while having a focus helps us make more effective use of our time. Goal-setting requires having patience, being flexible and prioritizing. Goals must also be periodically reviewed and revised.

Most parents want their children to achieve academically, have friends, participate in extracurricular activities and form close ties within the family. Families also want their children to develop values and morals, honesty, the ability to be responsible, industriousness, trustworthiness and trust in others, generosity, compassion, optimism, self-discipline and mutual respect for others—including their siblings. In young adulthood, parents hope that each of their children completes high school and perhaps attends college, develops a career, marries and has children. There is a desire to provide children every opportunity to achieve a satisfying and meaningful life.

As described in Chapter 2, the child who has experienced trauma arrives in the adoptive family with an array of difficulties. Parents must spend time discerning the child's strengths as well as the child's problem areas. Only then can the family determine the best ways to approach mending the injuries caused by the trauma.

Clyde and Lillian were parents to four beautiful birth daughters. Clyde and Lillian valued what would be considered a traditional family. Lillian was a stay-at-home parent. Clyde worked his way up the corporate ladder. The family was financially comfortable as a result. Their daughters made good grades. They were popular. All four girls, ages 9–15, had interests: sports, student government, chorus, band, cheerleading, Girl Scouts, youth group and other activities.

One Sunday, after the service, their church hosted a presentation by a local foster care agency. Feeling that they had much to offer children, they proceeded with the process to become foster parents.

Tami arrived within a year. She was 16 months old. She had been removed from her birthmother's care due to domestic violence, neglect and substance abuse. The agency with custody attempted to reunify Tami with her birthmother. However, after almost two years of providing the birthmother with multiple services, the birthmother had demonstrated no progress. The parental rights were terminated, and Clyde and Lillian adopted Tami.

Sleeping had been a major source of stress throughout the two years that Tami resided with this family prior to her adoption. Tami simply did not sleep well. Once in her crib, she screamed for several hours. She would kick and thrash about. It seemed that only after she wore herself out could she finally fall asleep. However, about four hours later, she would awaken the entire house with a new bout of screaming. Lillian tried everything suggested, and when the adoption was finalized, Tami, age 4, was sleeping almost seven hours each night. However, getting her to fall asleep was still a task.

Over the next three years, Tami did not seem to move past the "terrible twos." Temper tantrums continued. Mostly, the outbursts occurred when she was denied something she wanted. As she grew physically, the fits intensified. She kicked, hit, bit and threw things. Her social skills were delayed in comparison to her peers. Alone, she enjoyed drawing, coloring, building with Legos and helping Lillian bake or do chores. In fact, chores were perhaps her greatest strength. She enjoyed vacuuming and folding laundry. She was quite helpful putting away groceries and making beds. But, among children her own age or when her older sisters attempted to play with her, she refused to share, was a poor loser, cheated and was very bossy. She struggled to learn how to read as she moved through kindergarten and first grade. She had consistent difficulties pronouncing consonants. The teachers were concerned about her inability to focus and to transition from one subject to the next.

Tami's siblings grew weary of her fits and the bedtime struggles. In addition, the family continued to foster. Numerous children came and went from the home. So, the family composition varied from a minimum of seven members to a maximum of ten members. This affected the quality and quantity of parent-to-child time. With each foster child's departure, the family's losses compounded, and each time Tami seemed to regress. She wondered why she stayed while the others were able to return to their birth families. She asked, over and over, "When I am going back?" She could not seem to grasp the permanency of adoption.

Tami is currently age 8. Clyde and Lillian's two oldest daughters are in college. Leann and Betsy remain in the home. Leann readily admits that her involvement in after school activities is a means to prevent spending time at home. Betsy, a very sensitive young woman, started showing signs of depression. She has lost weight, withdrawn from friends and activities she once enjoyed, and she would sleep away the entire weekend if allowed. She reported, "I am so sad about all of the conflict and chaos. I just want to be alone."

Clyde and Lillian were shocked that their older daughters had not readily accepted their younger sibling. Certainly, Tami's behavior interrupted family time. However, they had expected their daughters to be forgiving and patient. Instead, it seemed their three children were alienated from them and from each other. Clyde and Lillian questioned, "How did our family get to this place?" "Why didn't Betsy or Leann speak to us about their feelings?" "What are we going to do to recapture the unity the family once had?" "How long will it be before our family resumes a sense of balance?"

If this was your family, what would you do? Where would you start? There are three children now presenting with issues: Betsy, Tami and Leann. Would you continue fostering or would it be time to take a break? Tami's needs are multiple. Which take priority—academic, social or behavioral? What can be worked on simultaneously and what can be deferred? Will you seek help at the first sign of problems or will it take a crisis for you to recognize the need for help?

Chapter 9 will offer suggestions as to how prioritize these layers of issues that confront adoptive families and set goals for change. Chapters 9 and 10 will also present ways to ensure that typically developing children and parents maintain communication.

Providing a Nurturing Environment

It might seem that it should go without saying that nurture would lead to a successful outcome. Children want and need hugs, kisses and snuggling. Parents are happy to give this affection. Providing nurture to a child with special needs goes beyond typical ways of expressing love. Nurturing the adoptee who has experienced abuse or neglect involves maintaining empathy and being tolerant in light of difficult and demanding behaviors and other trauma residue (Buehler, Rhodes, Orme and Cuddeback, 2006).

The vignettes have highlighted various negative behaviors presented by children with special needs. Chapter 2 explained the causes of these behaviors. It is time now to start thinking about living with these behaviors, as a traumatized adoptee frequently enters the adoptive family with a lengthy list of behavioral difficulties (See Chapter 5). Lying, stealing, aggression, destroying household objects and toys, bedroom floors cluttered with candy wrappers, hoarding food under mattresses or in a closet, name calling, profanity, repetitive incomplete homework assignments, lack of personal hygiene, bedwetting, smearing feces and so on are all behaviors that collide with the value systems of healthy, "normal" families.

But behavioral change takes time. We have all had the experience of making New Year's resolutions. We pledge to diet, to exercise, to stop smoking, to eat healthier, to spend more time with family and friends, to develop a hobby, to give up drinking, and the list goes on. Some are able to accomplish their resolution. Many are not. February arrives and the resolution has already gone by the wayside.

It is no easier for children than for adults to change their habitual negative behavior. In fact, many of these children's behaviors were developed to survive the abuse and neglect they experienced. So, the child who suffered trauma believes that his behaviors have kept him alive. Giving up the behaviors is thus perceived as giving up the very things that saved his life.

Yesenia and Tania resided with their birthmother and their three older birth brothers. Their birthmother would leave the children alone, sometimes for several days. The children became adept at rummaging through garbage cans in order to eat. The garbage also contained broken toys and tattered clothing. These items were treasures to these five children. Upon being adopted, Yesenia, age 6, continued to pick through the neighbors' trash. On the neighborhood's assigned garbage pick-up day, she would delight in going from home to home digging through each trash can. She would excitedly arrive back at her own home with pictures, small pieces of furniture, toys, clothes, cardboard boxes and so on. She thought these items were valuable contributions to the household.

Yesenia continued to believe that she needed to provide for the family.

Toby's birthmother had serious mental health issues. When angry with her children, she withheld food. Toby reported that his birthmother was angry "a lot." When food was provided, there was little, and it was thrown on the floor. Toby and his brother had been forced to scavenge around on the floor to retrieve the food. Food was plentiful in his adoptive home. So abundant in fact, that Toby would eat until he vomited. He always made sure to awaken in the middle of the night to raid the pantry. On his way back to his bedroom, he carried as many snacks as he could.

Toby was determined never to be hungry again.

Kurtis was placed in foster care at birth as his birthmother had been incarcerated for theft and possession of narcotics. Kurtis was shuffled through five foster homes and then, at age 10, he moved to his adoptive family. It seemed that each time he moved few of his clothes and toys followed him. In fact, he usually reached his new destination with one garbage bag of items. Vivian, his adoptive mom, was shocked with Kurtis' never-ending carelessness. New mittens were lost. Jeans were riddled with doodling in magic marker. Brand new toys were broken within minutes. School books disappeared. Dishes shattered if he was asked to clear the table.

Objects had little meaning to Kurtis. There would be more at the next house.

It is fairly easy to appreciate the development of various behaviors when we connect the behavior to its origin. However, living day-to-day with children who lie, steal, cheat, destroy property, swear, and so on is demanding, grueling and challenging for parents, brothers and sisters.

Prospective adoptive parents may expect that the child they are adopting will have similarities and dissimilarities from the other family members. However, the family often anticipates that the differences will be more in the areas of food preferences, clothing and hair style, or hobbies. We all have relationships in which these differences exist. How often at the mall do we see the men sitting outside of the store waiting for their wives? Women want to look through the sales racks and men often do not. Or, during a shopping trip, the family splits up. Mom and the daughters proceed to the shoe stores. Dad and the sons go directly to power tools. Most families have more than one television. Everyone gets to watch his or her favorite shows.

Adoption brings with it such disparities. However, adoption may also mean attempting to form a relationship, obtaining a "psychological fit," with a person who has a very different value system. Over time, the child's behavior can be perceived as a direct affront to the mother's and father's good parenting and their efforts to help the child become a successful human being. Parents begin to make statements such as,

"He steals instead of asking."

"He hoards when we provide more than enough to eat. For Pete's sake, we aren't going to run out of food. We aren't his birthfamily!"

"I work hard and he breaks everything he gets his hands on. Who does he think is going to replace this stuff? Money doesn't grow on trees!"

"I can't believe the things he says to me. I would never have talked to my parents that way!"

It is also not uncommon to hear,

"I love him, but I really don't like him anymore."

"There are days I simply don't want to live with him any longer."

Empathy has turned to anger. Tolerance has vanished as well. Feeling that all of their good intentions have been rejected, the parents begin to withdraw from the child. What is the point in giving when it does not seem that it is received? Guilt heaps higher—"What example is being set for our resident children?"

Think for a moment about this value discord. Have you served on a committee or in a community organization in which there have been value conflicts? Perhaps you have a co-worker with whom you find it difficult to engage for this reason. Perhaps you have an extended family member with whom you don't share beliefs. What is this like? How do you manage interactions in these instances? Chapters 9 and 10 will contain ways to help parents maintain their capacity to nurture themselves, their adoptee and their typically developing children. Chapters 9 and 10 will also offer guidance regarding altering negative behaviors.

Dealing Openly with the Adoptee's Past

It seems that each time email is checked, there is an advertisement to find a classmate. Family gatherings are replete with siblings kidding each other about childhood events. Memories of deceased relatives permeate such get-togethers as well. How many times do we review photo albums? Or, for those old enough, how many times did you watch slides of the family vacation to Yellowstone or Niagara Falls? Our past is important to us.

The past is as important to the child who has been abandoned, abused or neglected as it is to a member of an intact family. She has memories, thoughts and/or feelings about her experiences just as we all do. Still, reflecting on her past is often painful and dismal, so families tend to avoid it for a number of reasons:

Parents are frequently encouraged by various types of professionals to wait—wait until the child can handle it, wait until the child is old enough or wait for the "right time."

Families may hold on to the mistaken belief that children are resilient and will simply recover from their trauma.

Realizing that discussing the adoptee's past is likely to generate grief for both child and parents, the desire to avoid this grief is often a reason that the child's history remains unspoken.

In reality, these situations force children to repress their normal curiosity about their roots. Lacking answers impairs their sense of security and self-esteem, and thwarts their expressions of their feelings of different-ness. This scenario leaves the adoptee no room to express fears about loss, abandonment and rejection. The adoptee cannot determine how past events influence present behavior. He is not able to work through his doubts about the adequacy of his bonds to his adoptive family (Kaye, 1990).

Marge contacted our office to request an assessment for her two daughters, Paulette and Kati, ages 15 and 16. The girls had been placed with Marge and her husband, Peter, when they were 5 and 6 years old. The children's history contained a vast amount of sexual abuse. It seems that their birthmother had prostituted them in order to support her drug habit.

Marge reported that Paulette and Kati had brought the sexual abuse up over and over. Marge stated, "Each time they talk about it, I tell them that it ended a long time ago and there is no need to think about it anymore. Daddy and I love them, and we make sure that nothing like that happens to them."

Marge asks, "Why have I responded to my daughters that way? Why didn't I realize they were trying to talk to me seriously? Perhaps if I had listened all of these years, they would be better."

Her reason for requesting services was that the girls had started running away several months ago. They were gone for hours. Marge and Peter had no idea where they were or who they were with. Their attempts to ask their daughters what was going on were met with shouting and profanity. Paulette was failing school and Kati's grades had declined significantly. Boys—lots of boys—were calling their home at all hours of the late evening and early morning. Clothing, make-up and jewelry that Marge and Peter did not approve of were turning up in their book bags, school lockers and bedrooms.

The case of Marge, Peter, Paulette and Kati is unfortunate but not unusual. Certainly, Kati and Paulette's inability to sort out their past is contributing to, if not totally responsible for, their current decline in functioning.

The truth is essential. As discussed in Chapter 2, without the truth, children blame themselves for their abandonment and abuse. Lacking an ability to determine that the separation from the birthfamily was not their fault, they develop reunification fantasies which inhibit them from forming attachments to the adoptive family.

They may believe that they are "too bad" to be loved.

They may assume that they will be returning to the birthfamily, so there is no need to form relationships with the adoptive parents, siblings and peers.

They resist forming friendships as they feel "different." "If the other kids knew what happened to me, they wouldn't want to be my friend so why bother?"

They fear future abandonment based on the separation from their birthfamily.

The concept of permanency or a "forever" family defies their experiences.

They develop fears regarding whether they will develop medical or mental health issues.

Each member of the adoptive family benefits when the adoptee is able to integrate the past and the present. This process, which includes asking questions and receiving hard answers, struggling with painful facts, awful memories and expressing intense grief, allows the adoptee to move beyond her past, and thus join the adoptive family.

Assessing Parents' Capacity to Handle Grief and Loss

How were losses handled in your family of origin?

What is your experience of grief and loss?

How do you respond to a loss?

How do you include your children in the grieving process?

How do you help your children grieve?

This section also raises the matter of discussing sensitive and painful topics with children.

What are your views on telling children the truth about their past?

Can you picture yourself discussing abuse, neglect and abandonment?

What might you need to do to prepare yourself for such conversations?

What potential losses may such discussions trigger for you?

What will be the impact of such discussions on your typically developing children?

If you do not have well thought out responses to these questions, ample materials exist to help you formulate answers and develop this strength. Chapter 8 will cover the stages of grief. Suggestions for coping with the grief of each family member will be shared in Chapter 10.

Awareness of Transcultural Issues

We live in a society that remains plagued by prejudices, discrimination and the stereotyping of various groups of peoples based on their race, religion, sexual preference, citizenship and their socio-economic status. Even the fact that some families are not related by genes and birth, rather "only" by adoption is something that numerous individuals cannot accept without negative assumptions about the people it touches, and that some religions actually ban. It shouldn't be surprising, then, that adopting transculturally adds another complex layer to the experience of adoption.

What do we mean by the word *transcultural*? An adoption is considered to be transcultural when any of the family members are of a different race than the others. This is often referred to as *transracial* or *interracial* adoption. Adoptions are also considered transcultural if older children and their adoptive parents and/or siblings come from different countries but are of the same race. For example, if a white American couple adopts a white toddler from Eastern Europe or an African American family adopts an Ethiopian child, these adoptions are not transracial, but they are transcultural. Nearly all international adoptions are transcultural, while it is estimated that about 15% of domestic U.S. adoptions are transcultural because they are transracial.[2]

Identity formation is a difficult process for all of us. Race, ethnicity, and culture can make identity formation even more complicated, and as Chapter 2 pointed out, identity formation is even more complicated for adoptees. The transnationally or transracially adopted child must learn what it means to be bi-racial, or to be a Black-, Asian-, Latino-, Korean-, Chinese-, Peruvian-, Mexican-American or to be a member of a multi-racial family—an even more complex process yet! In addition to adjusting to the cultural climate and values of yet another family, adoptees may need to adjust to a new socio-economic climate, and perhaps an entirely different language and/or religion.

The identity development of transcultural adoptees is influenced by the environment in which the child lives. Those of us in the dominant culture—the group that has power over the distribution of goods, services, rights, privileges, entitlements and status, and those with access to education—develop confidence, self-esteem and goals because we see others like us achieving in virtually any chosen endeavor (Crumbley, 1999).

Children who are members of groups our society deems as minorities—groups subject to the power, control, discretion and distribution of goods and privileges by another group—frequently observe others who are not like them. They observe or experience prejudice, discrimination and stereotypical remarks, and thus may learn that they have more limited options and that their groups are somehow "not as good" as the prevailing cultural group. Thus a child's confidence, self-view, worth, self-respect and goals may be negatively affected (Crumbley, 1999).

---

2. http://www.adoptioninformation.com/Transracial_adoption

White families adopting transracially most often need special preparation for issues such as these. Because they have lived (often subconsciously) in a climate of "white privilege" as the dominant culture in the U.S., they may not fully understand how biases and discrimination impact people of color on a daily basis.

In addition to the parenting task of facilitating a positive cultural identity in their adoptee, these parents must also realize that they and their same-race resident children will be impacted by a transcultural adoption. They, too, will frequently find themselves the brunt of comments, questions, and criticisms as well as being spotlighted by the stares of curious strangers.

Rick is currently 15 years old and a sophomore in high school. He was adopted as an infant. He is bi-cultural: his birthmother is Caucasian and his birthfather is of Middle Eastern decent. He has dark brown, almost black, hair and dark brown eyes. His skin is olive. He has resided with his adoptive parents in the same community his whole life. His appearance, in comparison to his European-American parents, has caused some issues over time. Strangers stare when the family is out. Kids have asked him why he looks different than his parents. However, overall, Rick has had little difficulty.

Rick's life changed when our country declared war on Iraq. An American soldier from his home town died in Iraq. Classmates that he had known his whole life began implying that the death was due to "people like him." Rick was stunned. He had no idea how to respond to these remarks. It seemed the less he replied, the more the comments flowed. Rick's two Caucasian brothers, ages 12 and 13, attend the same school as Rick. They overheard these prejudiced statements. In their efforts to aide their brother, a fist fight broke out. Shortly thereafter, the parents were called to meet with the principal. The end result of the meeting was a school assembly designed to raise awareness of the value of cultural differences. At home, Rick and his parents and siblings began a series of discussions regarding how each family member could more effectively handle prejudice and discrimination in the future.

Danielle's birthparents were Latino and African American, but her adoptive family consisted of white parents and a white sibling who had also been adopted. The family lived in a small, mostly white town in Northern California. Danielle and her sister DeeAnne were well accepted at school, at synagogue and were active in scouting and sports during their elementary and middle school years.

When their father was transferred to a large city, the family moved to an integrated middle class suburb and put the girls into public middle school and high school. Suddenly the earth shifted under Danielle's feet. Perfectly comfortable with white kids like those she had grown up with, she suddenly found herself the target of black and Hispanic kids—especially the girls, who accused her of "talking white," "dressing white," and "acting white" as she drew the attention of boys of all races. After a year or so she made a conscious decision to claim her Black heritage and worked hard to model her dress, her behavior and her talk on those of the group she wanted so much to be a part of. At the same time DeeAnne began to complain loudly to their parents that Danielle's new behavior was an embarrassment to her.

Where did Danielle belong?

Before adopting transculturally, parents are encouraged to review materials pertaining to transcultural adoption. Parents must be aware that "isms" exist. They must prepare themselves and ***all*** of their children to handle this matter. Parents must ensure that their adoptee has access to role-models from minority cultures.

Linh's family "got" this need from the beginning. They had chosen to adopt from Korea partly because they lived in an upper Midwestern city with a large Korean community made up of first through third generation families who had arrived in the U.S. by immigration, as well as a large number of grown and still growing Korean adoptees. From the beginning, they chose to immerse their family in the city's Korean community—attending a Korean Presbyterian Church and enrolling all of their kids (including two born to them) in Korean culture camp and language classes.

Each family must embrace the culture of the adoptee by incorporating foods, holidays, traditions, music and art reflective of the child's culture into their daily life. The adoptee must be able to answer the question, "Who am I?" and she must "see" that her culture is important by her family members' actions and example. The Resource section at the end of this chapter lists an array of books, movies and websites to assist families in accomplishing this task. Subsequent chapters will contribute to expanding family's knowledge in this vital area.

The Capacity to Identify, Access and Utilize Resources

Hopefully, the reading you have completed, or will do, and the pre-adoptive classes in which you have participated, or will participate, help you to understand that helping each member of your family adjust to the adoption experience may require seeking various types of support and services. Exploring this area prior to placement demonstrates that you are already experiencing the growth necessary to make your adoption journey as successful as possible. You are acknowledging that adoption will bring challenges, and you are preparing for these challenges.

Overall, the acquisition of resources as early as possible has proven benefits:

- Learning and development are most rapid in the pre-school years. Timing of an intervention becomes particularly important when a child runs the risk of missing an opportunity to learn during a state of maximum readiness. If the most teachable moments or stages of greatest readiness are not taken advantage of, a child may have difficulty learning a particular skill at a later time. However, this is not to say that children adopted at older ages cannot learn new skills or make progress. Fortunately, the brain has a quality known as "plasticity." This is the capacity of the brain to remodel itself and learn new skills at later ages.
- Earlier intervention has a significant impact on the parents and siblings of children with special needs. Early intervention can result in parents having improved attitudes about themselves and their child, improved information and skills for teaching their child, and more time for leisure and employment.
- Society reaps maximum benefits. The child's increased developmental and educational gains and the family's increased ability to cope provide economic as well as social gains.[3]

Chapters 5 and 10 contain information about the types of services and supports most relevant to the adoptive family. As shown in the list above, help—especially early help—makes a significant difference in the life of the child, the parents, the siblings and society at large. It is important, at this point, to examine your attitudes about accepting help.

The introduction to this book established that many families will be adopting children diagnosed with various mental health disorders. Mental Health America,

3. KidSource. *What is Early Intervention?* http://www.kidsource.com/kidsource/content/early.intervention.html

the nation's leading nonprofit organization dedicated to helping people live mentally healthier lives, has concluded that Americans are more likely to view mental illnesses as personal or emotional weaknesses rather than real health problems.[4] Certainly, how an illness is viewed affects how the condition will be treated.

This is also the time to begin taking stock of the informal and formal supports available to you. Further, it is important to recognize that there is a trend to decrease support to the adoptive family once a placement has been made and the adoption has been finalized. That is, the placing agency too often views their task as complete at this point: the child has a home and the family has a child. The agency moves on to facilitate matches for other children and families. So, the task of identifying, locating and implementing services often falls on the family. Think about the following:

What are your views on individuals with mental health issues? Do you see a mental health disorder as a "health problem" or an "emotional or personal weakness?"

Do you know anyone with a mental health issue (i.e., depression, anxiety, alcoholism, etc.)? If so, what have you learned from this experience that would be applicable to parenting a child with special needs?

Are you aware that children receive medication for various mental health issues (i.e., depression, anxiety, impulsivity, attentional difficulties, etc.)? Do you have a perspective on this?

Are you willing to seek professional mental health services?

What type of mental health coverage do you have through your health insurance policy?

Do you know other adoptive families with children with special needs?

Have you ever utilized therapy or support groups? Do you know if adoptive parent support groups exist in your area?

Do adoption-focused services exist in your community? Where does the funding come from for these services?

Do you have any experience with special education?

Do you have the capacity to be assertive? Do you mind being persistent? Acquiring services is best described as being the "squeaky wheel getting the grease." That is, parents often have to advocate for services.

Who comprises your personal support system? Are they learning about adoption along with you?

Are you involved in any organizations, such as a church, from which you may be able to obtain support?

How well do you acquire information?

How much effort have you made to seek out information specific to adoption and trauma at this point in time?

If married, is your spouse participating in this learning process? Or, is this endeavor one-sided?

4. Mental Health America. "10-Year Retrospective Study Shows Progress in American Attitudes about Depression and Other Mental Health Issues." http://www.nmha.org/index.cfm?objectid=FD502854-1372-4D20-C89C30F0DEE68035

In adoptive families, early intervention should start the moment the parents decide to proceed with the adoption process. As Gregory Keck and Regina Kupecky make clear in both *Parenting the Hurt Child* and *Adopting the Hurt Child*, "Most adoptive parents are **not** responsible for creating the difficulties their children have, but they **are** responsible for helping to correct them."

Maintaining a Sense of Humor

Humor allows us to experience joy even when faced with adversity (Wooten, 1996). The benefits of humor are amazing. Humor.

- reduces stress
- lowers blood pressure
- elevates mood
- boosts the immune system
- improves brain functioning
- protects the heart
- results in a respiratory cleansing, leading to muscle relaxation similar to deep breathing
- increases energy
- gives us a sense of perspective on our problem
- is free.

Some events are clearly not occasions for laughter. However, most situations do not carry that type of gravity. Learning not to take ourselves and daily events too seriously is important. In other words, there will be times when lightening up is important. At these times, take a step back and put the situation in context and find the humor within the event.

Adoptive families would benefit from creating a "humor kit"—a collection of their favorite funny movies, books, CDs of their favorite comedians, comic books—anything that is guaranteed to generate a chuckle! As subsequent content will demonstrate, adoptive parents will be responsible for setting a positive and nurturing mood in their home. There will be days when this is difficult—very, very difficult! Humor will be a most important tool for carrying this out because when we laugh together, it can bind us closer together instead of pulling us apart (Lindeman, Kemp and Segal, 2007).

To laugh or not to laugh will be your choice!

Identifying Strengths through the Home Study Interview

As has been stated previously, this book is written with famiiles foremost in mind. However, it is likely that professionals will read the book as well. Thus, it would be remiss to overlook the opportunity to offer some professional best practice suggestions regarding the content of the home study—especially in the area of siblings-to-be. So, the remainder of this chapter puts forth some food for thought for those writing these most important documents. Throughout this segment, we are focusing on the "cutting edge" work of Dr. Wayne Duehn. Dr. Duehn is a Professor of Social Work, University of Texas at Arlington. He created and trains, "*Let's Get It Right: Interactional Methods in Assessing in Home Studies and Post-Adoption Services*."

Overall, the home study is frequently viewed as another task to complete along the way to getting a child. Families rarely ask to see the contents of their completed home study. Many agencies see no need for, or no value in, having prospective families review their home study. Families trust that the outcome of their interviews and home tour is a document that adequately reflects them and their lives. Professionals and parents view the home study as a document that meets various legal and agency requirements necessary to move a child into the family. As long as these requirements are met, the document is satisfactory. Families are hesitant to ask too many questions about their home study. Eager to expand their family, they tolerate agency policies.

It would certainly be beneficial if we eradicated the above beliefs. The family assessment process needs to be looked at as an opportunity for the family and the worker to mutually assess the qualities possessed by each family member. In this reciprocal process, there is an emphasis on exploring the family's experiences—life lessons that contribute to the family's ability to envelope and integrate a child with a traumatic past into their family system. We also need to learn about the ways the family behaves. The manner in which a family acts—positive and negative—impacts those already in the family and those who will be joining the family. Let's look at how we can accomplish these two goals.

What's in a Question?

Gathering information for a home study is traditionally accomplished in a question and answer format. The family is asked such questions as, "How do you resolve marital discord?" "What is your neighborhood like?" "What were your relationships like with your siblings?" As Dr. Duehn points out, this format has some limitations:

- Research concludes that self-reports, like the traditional question and answer process of the home study, are subject to omissions, subjective bias and massive distortions.
- A question and answer format requires good verbal skills. A question and answer method is thus biased against certain minorities or those from lower socioeconomic status. For example, for some, the interview may not be conducted in their first language. Or, for others, sharing highly personal information with someone not well known or a person outside of their family is against their cultural values and beliefs.
- Adoption workers often fall back on their own very subjective perspectives of what constitutes a healthy family. Often these subjective appraisals are based on their own life experiences—both positive and negative—and are rooted primarily in their own family of origin experiences.
- A question and answer process is not a format that works well with children. Depending on a child's developmental stage, he or she may not have the verbal and cognitive skills to respond to the questions. Remember the adage, "Out of the mouth of babes . . .?" Children often share interesting and honest perceptions of the family when we tap into approaches that make it feasible for them to share their insights.

In part the limitations of the Q and A format are reflective of the types of questions asked. Frequently, when conducting home study interviews, social workers utilize predictive questions. For example, the family is asked, "What will you do if the child lies, steals, wets the bed, etc.?" Predictive questions require that the family determine, usually without actual knowledge, what action they will take in the event something occurs. Even a question like, "What is your school district like?" is predictive. There may be a significant difference between the standards achieved in a school district's regular education services and the level of adequacy of that same school district's special education services. If the family is unfamiliar with the special education services, their response is moot. What do we really learn about the family when we ask them to respond to "what if?" Wouldn't it be better to ask them, "What is?" Open-ended questions are designed to encourage a full, meaningful answer using the individuals' own knowledge and/or feelings. Open-ended questions also tend to be more focused on the objective.

Let's look at an example and then discuss this matter of questions further. Below are *actual* excerpts taken from the written home study of Frank and Penny, who parent Scott, whom they adopted as an infant. Scott was 9 years old at the time this home study was written. We will read and then critique the selected portions of this home study. Then, we will see some of the updated version of the document. Lastly, we will draw conclusions.

> Frank was born 11-21-59. His mother was a homemaker and his father worked for a newspaper. He has four siblings, three male and one female. When Frank was 7 years old, his mother passed away as a result of cancer. Two years later, his father re-married. Frank felt fine with the marriage and at first had a good relationship with his step-mom. However, his father and step-mother were alcoholics, and after a few years of marriage, the family was traumatically affected by their alcoholism. The family split up.
>
> When Frank was in the 10th grade, he came home from school to find that the family had been evicted from their home. That night he stayed with friends and ended up staying with them for some time. On occasion he would see his father and step-mother. Frank's step-mother died in 1988, and his father died in 1997. Prior to his death, Frank's father lived with Penny and Frank at their home in Florida.
>
> Penny was born 8-30-61. She has three brothers and one sister. Her relationship with her family was not very good growing up. She was an unruly teen. She was not bad, but gave her parents a hard time. She didn't follow rules or respect authority. Now, as an adult, she gets along well with her family.
>
> Penny identifies the most significant events in Penny's life as adopting Scott, marrying Frank, her father's heart attack and her mother's surgery.
>
> When asked about their infertility, Penny stated that it was no big deal. It really doesn't matter how children come into the family. They were just as happy to adopt.
>
> Penny and Frank feel it is important for children to know that they were adopted. When they adopted their son, Scott, they never hid the fact that he was adopted. When he was 2 or 3, he would ask Penny if he grew in her tummy, and she answered him truthfully. In regards to an open adoption, they will not completely close the door to the past. Their philosophy is to take the situation one day at a time.
>
> Frank and Penny do have an understanding of the various needs and issues that are present in biological families that lead to the removal of children.
>
> Scott has brown hair and brown eyes. He is of average height and weight. He is in fourth grade. He has fun in school and states that math is his favorite subject. Scott stated that he would like to have a sibling to play with, preferably a boy who is a little bit younger than he is. He likes to ride his bike and play soccer and basketball. He doesn't anticipate having any problems with the new child, and feels that he/she will fit in fine with the family.

This family languished for two years with no placement as their home study raised more questions than it answered:

How has Frank come to terms with loss of two parents and a step-parent?

What is meant by, "His step-mother and father were alcoholics . . . and the family was affected traumatically?" What was the nature of the trauma? How did Frank cope with this trauma?

Why was Penny an "unruly" child? How did she get from being "unruly" to "having a good relationship with her family now?"

How could infertility not matter?

What was significant, to Penny, about her father's heart attack and her mother's surgery?

What "various needs and issues that are present in biological families" are they familiar with?

Has Scott received any preparation? It does not seem so, as he "doesn't anticipate having any problems with the new child."

Scott has been an only child for nine years. Has any discussion occurred about what information he has been provided about becoming a brother?

Frank and Penny indicated a preference to adopt a sibling group. If there is a male child in this group, he and Scott would most likely need to share a bedroom. Have safety issues been addressed with Scott?

Most importantly, what did Frank, Penny, Scott or their worker learn during this home study phase of the adoption process? Did the worker discover any specific skills or lack of them that might impact the way that Frank and Penny would parent a hurt child? Did the family gain any insight as to the skills they would need to help a troubled child navigate a difficult childhood? Did they learn how these skills might help them form relationships with their new children? Was Frank offered any information as to how helping a child with a traumatic past might trigger his own childhood issues?

Frustrated by the amount of time they were waiting to become parents again, Frank and Penny transferred their case to a different agency. Their new worker conducted interviews rich in open-ended questions that tapped the experiences of this family. A selection from their second home study reads like this:

> When asked, "What loss issues have you experienced?" Frank immediately began talking about his father. Frank felt that he had lost his father in childhood emotionally and then he lost his father in adulthood physically. He discussed that grieving has been a lengthy process. When his family was first evicted from their home, Frank and his siblings each went to live with a family friend or a relative. Initially, Frank decided to try to help his family so that the family could all live together again. At 16, he obtained odd jobs, thinking that money would help. He also visited his family, thinking that talking to them would help. He thought that they wanted to be a family again as much as he did. As time passed, he realized that his efforts were having no impact. This was devastating to him.
>
> He graduated from high school and began working for Penny's father. Ultimately, he began living with Penny's family. At this time, Penny had yet to resolve matters between herself and her parents. Joined in their grief over their poor relationships with their parents, the two married and moved to South Carolina. Both now agree that they were really "running away." They believed that South Carolina would allow them to start over—they could put the past behind them and move on with life. However, the distance really only served to make matters worse. Neither could stop thinking about their families and how things seemed to be hanging in mid-air.
>
> When Frank's father, ill with cancer, came to live with Frank and Penny, this brought the father and son's past trauma right back into the present. Frank found himself constantly re-living his childhood. His father's physical presence triggered him to think about his past.

He would often burst into tears while driving to the grocery store. He found himself preoccupied, unable to concentrate on simple tasks.

Overwhelmed with emotions and thoughts, he realized that he had tried to reunify his family, he had tried to run away from his past, and now the time had come to move beyond his past. He began talking to Penny and to another close friend about this. Frank was motivated to talk to his father as his father's illness was progressing. Frank's father was not able to provide many answers to explain why he hadn't been able to stop drinking so that he could parent his children. However, having this talk with his father helped Frank to allow himself to be sad about the relationship they had never had and could never have.

Once he allowed this grieving, he reports that he began to feel like a "different person." He was able to start to look at the future and the life he and Penny could have. Simultaneously, the couple had selected a faith. Frank reports that this spiritual connection furthered his ability to grieve his past. He realized that there are not always apparent reasons for what happens to a person in life. It is up to the person to move on and determine how to live his life.

Frank stated that his life experiences helped to prepare him to parent a child with special needs in several ways. He acknowledged that it took talking to friends and family members to move beyond his many losses. He realized that he and Penny would need to learn to talk honestly about their children's birthparents, abuse, multiple moving and any other trauma. Frank was able to talk, and chuckle, about the many behaviors he had used to reject his step-mother. So, he expects some behavior!

This review of Frank's experience caused Penny to think about how hard it will be for children to accept a new mother. She now has an expectation that she may be the recipient of acting-out behavior as well.

Frank was also able to discuss how the losses in his family affected each of his siblings differently. Therefore, he has the ability to recognize that individual children may require different approaches to achieve resolution of their past trauma. He also acknowledged that children who are adopted cannot move into a new home and simply "start over." Their past is a part of them, and somehow he and Penny must find ways to help their children "merge" their pasts and their present.

Wow! What a difference! The second worker gained abundant information about this family. It is clear that the family has many qualities that will lend to a successful adoptive placement: a wealth of experience with and knowledge of grief, the ability to generate coping skills, communication skills, and empathy and experience in dealing with trauma and adoption. The fact that the family persisted in the adoption journey in light of having had no placement for two years in and of itself demonstrates their capacity to set and pursue a goal, and to be patient and tenacious.

The new worker was able to discuss with Frank and Penny that helping a child heal from loss may, in turn, trigger the need to re-think one's past in the same manner that occurred when Frank's father, ill with cancer, moved into their home. Triggers result in grief. Grief, if left unresolved, contributes to the negative emotional climate described earlier in this chapter. It is important to identify potential triggers. The home study process offers a wonderful means to accomplish this task. Chapter 8 will expand adoptive parent's knowledge of the post-placement role of triggers. Chapter 10 will offer a trigger management plan.

The entire interview process also identified some areas of concern for Frank and Penny. It was noted that while the family had a support system in their church, they were geographically separated from the majority of their extended family members. Frank's work as a landscaper required long hours, especially during the summer months. Penny would have the responsibility for managing the home at these times. Additionally, they resided in a very rural area with limited mental health resources. It would be a 90 minute drive to specialized adoption services. It was discerned that Scott had received no preparation. The worker discussed transcultural adoptive issues with the family. Scott is bi-racial. His birthmother was from South America while his birthfather was Caucasian. Scott's cultural difference from Frank and Penny had raised questions and stares from time to time. Frank and Penny reported to the worker that they handled situations as they occurred. They had not received any training or done any reading pertaining to transcultural adoption. Frank and Penny were open to adopting transculturally again.

The worker made recommendations based on all of the information she pulled from her interview with Frank and Penny:

- Scott should participate in the agency's pre-adoptive training program. This required that Frank and Penny would attend education classes a second time as the agency utilized a parallel model. This included interactive exercises between the parents and the typically developing children who are like Scott, and their families.
- Frank and Penny would expand their support system prior to placement. Such support would help both Frank and Penny. It would be particularly beneficial to Penny when Frank was working overtime. They would search their area for other adoptive families. They would determine if there were any parents they could network with or any support groups Penny and Frank could join. They would investigate in person as well as online groups.
- Frank and Penny would educate themselves in the area of transcultural adoption. They would read books and review websites suggested by the worker. They were also required to attend a workshop on this topic sponsored by the agency.
- Frank and Penny had well thought out attitudes about sex and sexuality. However, they were unprepared, and thus so was Scott, for the types of sexual behavior a child with a history of sexual abuse might present. This concern would be alleviated as Frank, Penny and Scott would be participating in a pre-adoptive class on sexual abuse. The worker suggested additional websites and books for further investigation. She also recommended that Frank, Penny and Scott complete the workbook, *Living with the Sexually Abused Child* (see Resources Chapter 2).

Frank and Penny could begin to carry out these recommendations at the conclusion of the home study interviews. There is nearly always a time lapse between this stage of the adoption process and the point at which a child is placed with the family. Parents have the opportunity to participate in ongoing training during this interlude. An effective worker can direct the family to those areas of adoption issues, trauma information or skill development that will bolster the family's ability to have a successful post-placement experience. The home study provides an excellent means to identify the types of continuing educational topics that will benefit the parents, the already present children in the family and the child yet to arrive.

Scott: An In-Depth Look at a Typically Developing Child

The paragraph that appears on page (115), is all that was written about Scott in the original home study. The second home study minimally expanded on this content. This is a common occurrence. This does quite a disservice to such resident children in families considering adoption. Children such as Scott need help in identifying their skills and their experiences in order to assist them in forming relationships with their new siblings.

There was much information that could have been learned about Scott, who was 11½ at the time the second agency became involved in this case:

- Scott was involved in Cub Scouts, and played basketball and soccer. He was an honor roll student. He managed all of his activities and his homework with little help. He had learned to prioritize. Scouting and sports taught him to work with others.
- Scott had experienced loss. His grandfather, Penny's father, had passed away only a year before. He and his grandfather had spent much time together. The two particularly enjoyed fishing. Scott misses his grandfather greatly. He tears up when his grandfather is mentioned. He has empathy for those who lose family members dear to them.
- Scott was also adopted. He will readily admit that he thinks about his birthmother regularly. He especially thinks about her on his birthday and throughout the holidays. There are times, such as when his team won a basketball tournament, that he wonders what it would be like if she were by his side in the winners' circle. He does hope to meet her someday. He has very little information about his birthparents, which frustrates him. He has many unanswered questions. At times, he gets angry about this. As a result of his pre-adoptive classes, he felt fortunate. His birthmother placed him for adoption right away. He did not suffer abuse or neglect. He shows a capacity to view circumstances from more than one perspective.
- Scott has difficulty expressing anger. He stores his anger and then reaches a point at which he becomes argumentative. This issue has manifested more recently. It may be connected to the death of his grandfather and/or his approaching adolescence. Frank and Penny are actively working with Scott on this unhealthy manner of dealing with feelings. They purchased a workbook and spend time with Scott practicing the techniques contained in this guide. Scott likes to write. He has been journaling a few minutes each day. He feels this is helping him manage his anger more effectively. Scott can recognize a problem and seek parental assistance to resolve his difficulty.
- Scott is small in stature in comparison to his male peers. He has been the brunt of many jokes. His South American heritage earned him the nickname "Speedy Gonzalez." He has not always been fond of this teasing. He has learned various coping strategies. Sometimes he walks away. Sometimes he asks kids to stop. Sometimes he joins in. He made a tee-shirt in art class with "runt" stenciled on the back. He found that this "teasing" himself greatly reduced his classmates' name calling. He has the capacity to generate solutions as problems appear.

All of the above combine to show that Scott has many qualities which will help him navigate the new family that is about to come together in his home. Scott's story affirms that more time needs to be spent with the family's typically developing children during the home study interviews. We need to understand their expectations. If the home study reveals that they are still expecting a playmate, we need to determine ways to help them adjust these expectations prior to the sibling-to-be moving in. We need to see what types of age-appropriate skills they have developed. We need to inform the parents of any concerns so that these may be worked on in the pre-placement phase. In essence, we need to mirror the home study process of the parents for the siblings-to-be.

Dr. Duehn also suggests the following types of questions:

- *Circular questions* provide a structure for eliciting information from various family members about the operations and transactions embedded in the family. This type of question is nonthreatening because the circular questions generally ask family members to comment on the family structure from the view of an outside observer. For example,

A child may be asked, "How do your mom and dad solve disagreements?"

A father may be asked, "Why does your older son pick on his younger brother?"

"What does Mom do when your sister 'mouths' off?" might be posed to a sibling.

"How were things different for you a year ago?"

"Who is most strict, your mother or father?"

"Pretend for a moment that I have magic powers to send you on a vacation to an adventurous island. Who in your family would you take with you?"

"If you are sick in bed, who in the family would you want to take care of you?"

- *Conversational/Therapeutic questions* help the interviewer become like an anthropologist, seeking more and more understanding about the family from the insider's view. Processes and patterns become apparent. Dr. Duehn offers the following example of dialogue between a brother and a sister:

Interviewer: Mary, you sound very concerned about Billy punching others.

Mary: Yes, he has a real temper and a mouth of his own. I've been the target of it myself. (Billy rolls his eyes.)

Interviewer: Billy, I noticed you rolled your eyes when Mary was talking about your bad temper. What did that mean?

Billy: I don't know. I guess I'm not the only one with lip. (He frowns)

Interviewer: Ah! You're saying Mary gives lip, too?

Billy: Yeah, and she is always griping at me about school and to dad. He gets mad at me because of her.

Mary: I am the one who has to go to school and face those people when you're in trouble.

- *Tracking Problems, Attempted Solutions, and/or Exceptions to the Problems* looks at ways the family has tried to solve problems. A problem is identified and then questions are asked:

"How have you tried to solve a problem?"

"What does each family member do before and after the problem to try to keep it from happening?"

"Who does what to make it better?"

"Does it work?"

Exceptions are then tracked:

"Tell me when the problem doesn't occur."

"What did you do differently?"

"What activities prevent the problem?"

"What activities are prevented because of the problem?"

Linda parents an adolescent son, Rob, and a middle-school age daughter, Marian, whom she adopted. Linda is preparing to adopt another child. The adoption worker arrived for the home study assessment. During the interview the worker asked the family to identify a problem. Linda was quick to point out that she loves to take her kids to special places. She reports that prior to leaving for the trip both kids start to argue. Often she has cancelled the event as a consequence for this behavior. However, this solution only leaves the whole—now angry—family stuck at home with one another. The social worker asked Rob and Marian, "What activities are prevented because of the problem?" They responded, "Well, recently we missed a trip to a museum, seeing Christmas lights, having hot cocoa out at a restaurant and ice skating." The worker's next question was, "What does each family member do before and after the problem to try to keep it from happening again?" Rob said, "Well, I don't know if I try to make it better. But after the fight, I go to my room and am quiet. I feel bad about yelling at my mom." The worker empathically sighed, "Hmm." Rob then quietly said, "Going out some place special reminds me of the times when the whole family was together and we did fun things. I miss my dad. I want to spend more time with him." Linda and Rob's dad had divorced four years before. Linda's ex-husband claimed he was "not cut out" to parent Marian, who had arrived in the family with several mental health diagnoses. He opted to leave the family. Rob sees him only every other Saturday.

This manner of tracking problems often leads to surprising outcomes. Clearly, patterns of behavior as well as other pertinent issues can be discerned and discussed. As for this family, Linda planned another trip. This time the family proceeded, in spite of the conflict. Once at the baseball game, everybody settled in and had a great time! Rob is currently in therapy to help him address his issues surrounding his parent's divorce. Linda has opted to wait until Rob is better before adopting another child.

Questions that discern what is going on in the family and what is transferable from their life experiences to the parenting of an adopted child glean a wealth of information. What if adoption professionals changed their home study interview process to include the types of questions we just learned about?

Interactional Family Assessment Tools

The limitations of the question and answer format can also be overcome when we utilize Dr. Duehn's interactional assessment tools. A main theoretical rationale for Dr. Duehn's work is that of David Olson and colleagues.[5] [6] The Olson model suggests that family health or dysfunction can be determined by assessing *cohesion* or *adaptability*.

Cohesion is the amount of emotional bonding members have with one another and the degree of autonomy a family member has within the family system. Families with extremely high cohesion are referred to as enmeshed—members are so closely knit that there is little autonomy or fulfillment of personal needs and goals. At the opposite end of the continuum are disengaged families. These families experience very little closeness or solidarity. However, there is much autonomy and individuality.

Adaptability is the ability of a family system, or a marital system, to change its power structure, role relationships and rules in response to needs and stress. Changes may occur because of a specific situation or at various developmental stages. *Chaotic* and *rigid* are the two extremes of adaptability. Chaotic families have few to no rules. They are constantly in flux. Roles are not well-defined. Role reversal may occur—children are parenting the parents. Rigid families are characterized by a significant number of rules,

5. Olson, D.H. and Ryder, R. G. (1970). "Inventory of marital conflict: An experimental interaction procedure." *Journal of Marriage and the Family*, 32, 443–448.

6. Olson, D.H., Russell, C.S. and Sprenkle, D.H. (1989). *Circumplex model: Systemic assessment and treatment of families*. (New York: Haworth).

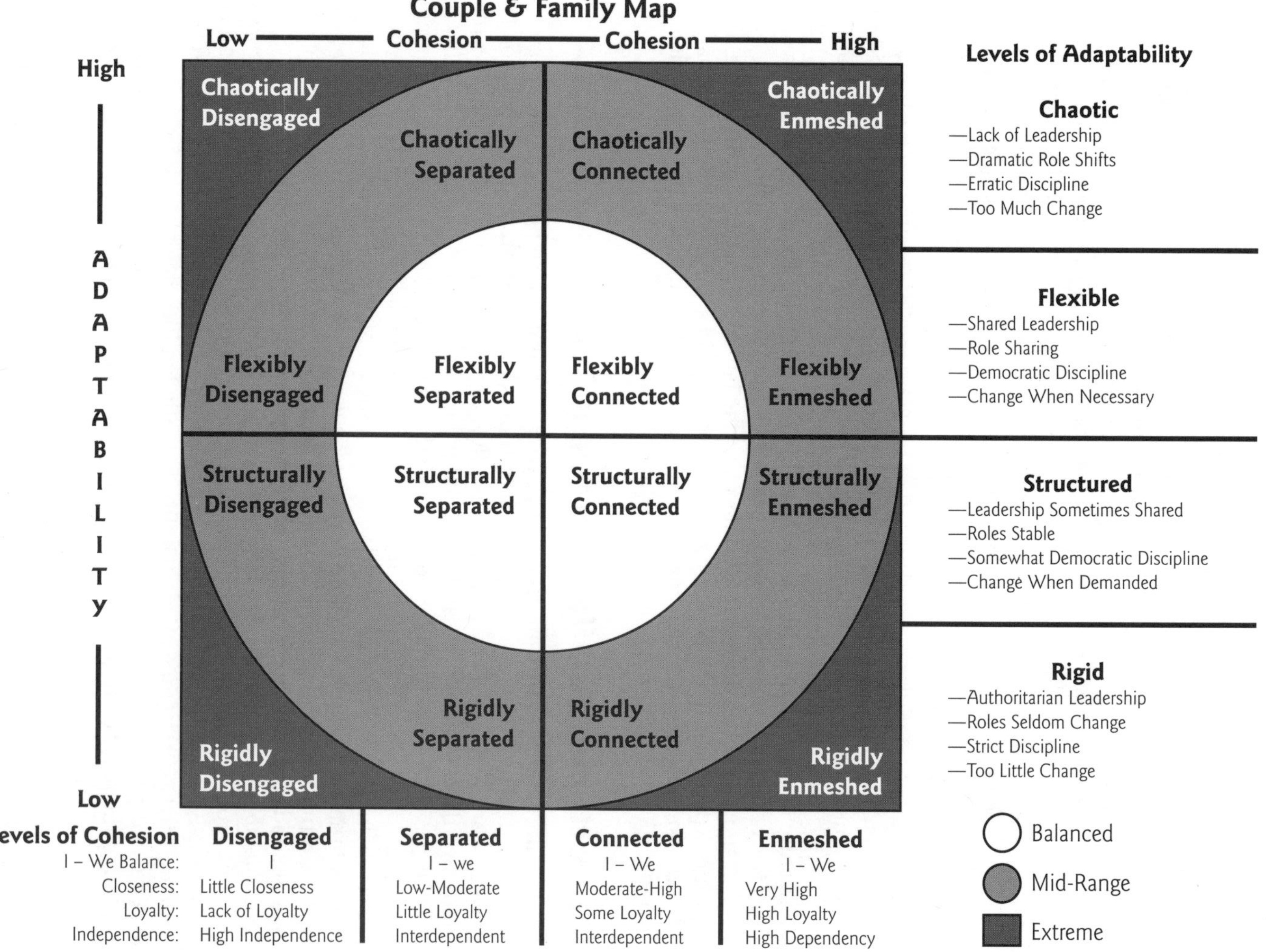
Couple & Family Map
Low — Cohesion — Cohesion — High
High
ADAPTABILITY
Low
Chaotically Disengaged
Chaotically Separated
Chaotically Connected
Chaotically Enmeshed
Flexibly Disengaged
Flexibly Separated
Flexibly Connected
Flexibly Enmeshed
Structurally Disengaged
Structurally Separated
Structurally Connected
Structurally Enmeshed
Rigidly Disengaged
Rigidly Separated
Rigidly Connected
Rigidly Enmeshed
Levels of Cohesion
I – We Balance:
Closeness:
Loyalty:
Independence:
Disengaged
I
Little Closeness
Lack of Loyalty
High Independence
Separated
I – we
Low-Moderate
Little Loyalty
Interdependent
Connected
I – We
Moderate-High
Some Loyalty
Interdependent
Enmeshed
I – We
Very High
High Loyalty
High Dependency
Levels of Adaptability
Chaotic
—Lack of Leadership
—Dramatic Role Shifts
—Erratic Discipline
—Too Much Change
Flexible
—Shared Leadership
—Role Sharing
—Democratic Discipline
—Change When Necessary
Structured
—Leadership Sometimes Shared
—Roles Stable
—Somewhat Democratic Discipline
—Change When Demanded
Rigid
—Authoritarian Leadership
—Roles Seldom Change
—Strict Discipline
—Too Little Change
Balanced
Mid-Range
Extreme

and these rules are fixed—nonflexible. Family roles are often traditionally defined, perhaps by age and gender.

Olson's model would find nurturing, safe and committed families in the middle of the continuums of cohesion and flexibility:

Utilizing interactive activities, social workers can determine where in the quadrants a family lies. The worker can then identify a family's strengths as well as areas of concern. The worker and the family can predict the impact of how these positives and negatives may play out post-placement. Mothers, fathers, sisters and brothers are better prepared to accept the placement of their new son, daughter or siblings.

An example of an exercise that Duehn suggests to help discern a family's place in the Olson model is *Build a Dream House*. The family is asked to work together to build their idyllic "dream house." The family is given a budget, precut construction paper rooms of varying sizes (each with a price tag) scissors and a pen. The family is to come to an agreement, make decisions and create a floor plan with these materials. A 30-minute timeframe is provided. Family interactions are observed in terms of cohesion and adaptability. At the end of the time period, the worker tours the home. Going from room to room, he asks the following questions:

How is each room furnished?

Who spends time here and what do they do?

What are the rules for this room?

Responses from family members are assessed in terms of who responds. The family roles and rules which emerge both during the task observation and the debriefing are interpreted in terms of adaptability. Similarly, patterns of communication, where individuals spend time together and apart, and individual and generational boundaries are evaluated in terms of cohesion.

The "Family Log" requires that the family, together or separately, track each family member's activities throughout a typical day at half hour intervals beginning with the family member who is first to arise in the morning and ending with the family member who is the last to go to bed. Using a spread sheet format, the worker fills in the entries by asking very specific, concrete questions related to time, place, activity, etc. For example, parents may be asked of their son, Jim, 10 years old, "Where is Jim at this time?" "What is Jim doing?" "Who is Jim with?" "What class is he in?" "Who is his teacher?". Disengaged family members will not be able to answer these detailed questions or be able only to give vague and the most general responses while enmeshed family members will be able to offer minute details of the most insignificant activity.

Additional activities include "Plan a Meal Together" and "Duehn's Family Sculpting." Dr. Duehn also teaches social workers how to make better use of genograms and ecomaps and much, much more.

It should be obvious that these interactional assessment tools have untold potential to enhance the home study process, and the best part is that these exercises include each member of the family—parents and kids! What if your agency started using them?

Should you like to arrange a workshop, Dr. Duehn's contact information is duehnl @airmail.com, or http:www2.uta.edu/ssw/duehn, or 2200 Wilson Drive, Arlington, TX 76011-32276.

Conclusions

The home study process—evaluation, interview, and family assessment—is another step in developing the family to prepare for the arrival of a child with special needs. It is not simply a "task" to be completed or a "hoop to jump through." It is not just a means to an end. It is a time in which the family and the worker should mutually assess the qualities and the behaviors of each family member—parent, and previously adopted and/or birth children.

It is a time to accurately reflect on the life experiences of each family member. Adverse experiences should be viewed as having contributed to the strengths the family has developed rather than as warts or blemishes that make them less than a "perfect" family. Yet, post-placement, childhood hurts can be triggered when parents must help the adoptee heal from similar events. The home study offers a time to identify these potential areas of difficulty. A plan may be developed to offset the negative impact of such matters on the parent, the adoptee, and the brothers and sisters living in the family before the placement.

While experience is one of life's greatest teachers, there is no substitute for knowledge. The two go hand in hand. Areas of concern need to be identified during the home study process. What did the family "hear" during pre-adoptive preparation classes? What did they miss? Recommendations need to be made in order that the family continues educating themselves pre-placement. Ongoing education may be in the areas of personal skill development, trauma or adoption issues, etc. Prospective parents and their resident children may attend additional workshops, read books, surf the Internet, network with other adoptive families or opt to participate in therapy in order to be as prepared as possible for the arrival of the new child.

The siblings-to-be are often limitedly involved in the home study process. This leaves these children very vulnerable. They are open to profound shock, disappointment, anger and sorrow when their new brother or sister does not turn out to be the playmate they expected. Their safety is jeopardized when we do not inform parents and children already in the family of the needs their new sibling may present. There is no need to damage healthy children because of heartfelt desires to expand families or give a waiting child permanency.

Chapter 5 will look at the process of matching the family with a child. As Chapter 1 explained, the matching process is not an exact science. However, there are ways to gain helpful insights from information provided about a waiting child so that a family may anticipate potential challenges.

As for Frank, Penny and Scott, eight months after their home study was re-written, their family expanded! Marcus and Celeste, siblings, arrived at the ages of 8 and 12 respectively.

Resources

The resources listed focus on transcultural adoption.

Books

Alperson, Myra. *Dim Sum, Bagels, and Grits: A Sourcebook for Multicultural Families.* (New York: Farrar, Strauss, Giroux, 2001.)

Coughlin, Amy and Caryn Abramowitz. *Cross Cultural Adoption: How to Answer Questions from Family, Friends, and Community*. (Washington: Lifeline Press, 2004.)

Cox, Susan Soon Keum, ed. *Voices from Another Place: A Collection of Works from a Generation Born in Korea and Adopted to Other Countries.* (St. Paul: Yeong and Yeong Book Company, 1999.)

Crumbley, Joseph. *Transracial Adoption and Foster Care: Practice Issues for Professionals.* (Washington: Child Welfare League of America, 1999.)

John, Jaiya. *Black Baby, White Hands: A View from the Crib.* (Silver Spring: Soul Water Rising, 2005.)

Johnson, Kay Ann and Amy Klatzkin. *Wanting a Daughter, Needing a Son: Abandonment, Adoption and Orphanage Care in China.* (St. Paul: Yeong and Yeong Book Company, 2004.)

Mathias, Barbara and Mary Ann French. *40 Ways to Raise a Nonracist Child.* (New York: Harper Perennial, 1996.)

Nakazawa, Donna Jackson. *Does Anybody Else Look Like Me?: A Parent's Guide to Raising Multiracial Children.* (Cambridge: Da Capo Lifelong, 2003.)

Register, Cheri. *Are Those Kids Yours: American Families with Children Adopted from Other Countries.* (New York: Free Press, 1990.)

Register, Cheri. *Beyond Good Intentions: A Mother Reflects on Raising Internationally Adopted Children.* (St. Paul: Yeong and Yeong Book Company, 2005.)

Simon, Rita and Rhonda Roorda. *In Their Own Voices: Transracial Adoptees Tell Their Stories.* (New York: Columbia University Press, 2000.)

Steinberg,Gail and Beth Hall. *Inside Transracial Adoption.* (Indianapolis: Perspectives Press, 2000.)

Tatum, Beverly Daniel. *Why Are All the Black Kids Sitting Together in the Cafeteria?* (New York: Basic Books, 1997.)

Tranka, Jane Jeong, Julia Chinyere Oparah and Sun Yung Shin. *Outsiders Within: Writing on Transracial Adoption.* (Cambridge: South End Press, 2006.)

Wright, Marguerite. *I'm Chocolate, You're Vanilla: Raising Healthy Black and Biracial Children in a Race-Conscious World.* (New York: Jossey-Bass, 1998.)

Wu, Frank. *Yellow: Race in America Beyond Black and White.* (New York: Basic Books, 2003.)

Websites

Dr. Joseph Crumbley
www.drcrumbley.com

Author of *Transracial Adoption and Foster Care: Practice Issues for Professionals* (see above) and *Kinship Care: Relatives Raising Children*, Dr. Crumbley has also produced a series of videos:

- Special Needs of Minority Children Adopted Transracially
- The Impact of Transracial Adoption on the Adopted Child and Adoptive Family
- Parenting Tasks in Transracial Adoptions
- Assessing a Family's Ability to Adopt Transracially.

Dr. Crumbley provides training and consultation in the areas of transracial adoption and kinship care.

North American Council on Adoptable Children (NACAC)
www.nacac.org

NACAC promotes and supports permanent families for children and youth in the U.S. and Canada who have been in care—especially those in foster care and those with special needs. NACAC offers a quarterly newsletter—*Adoptalk*—replete with cutting edge articles pertaining to all aspects of adoption. Their annual conference is always exciting and informative. Child care is available at this parent-friendly conference. Tapes of conference workshop sessions may be purchased at www.adoptiontapes.com. The NACAC website contains articles covering all facets of transcultural adoption. Subsidy information and a nationwide listing of adoptive parent support groups can also be found at NACAC.

Pact—An Adoption Alliance
www.pactadopt.org

Pact is a non-profit organization with a primary mission to serve children of color in need of adoption or who are growing up in adoptive families. In every case, the child is their primary client. They believe that to serve the child we must support and serve his or her adoptive parents by offering the very best resources to help them cope with a world whose attitudes too often reflect "adoptism" and racism. If you are looking for information related to any transcultural adoption issue, you are sure to find it on the Pact website! Pact makes available *Below the Surface*, a self-assessment guide for parents considering transcultural or transracial adoptions. Pact also has an online book store—all books are reviewed by Pact prior to selection for this store.

RainbowKids.com
www.rainbowkids.com

This online magazine is a great source of adoption-related information. You can search their database for articles written on any topic related to adoption. RainbowKids makes obtaining information quick and easy!

Videos

"I Wonder . . ." Teenagers Talk about Adoption. A diverse group of adolescent adoptees share their thoughts on various aspects of adoption. This video is available at www.fairfamilies.org—Families Adopting in Response.

First Person Plural. The blurb states, "In 1966, Deann Borshay Liem was adopted by an American family and was sent from Korea to her new home. Growing up in California, the memory of her birthfamily was nearly obliterated until recurring dreams lead Borshay Liem to discover the truth: her Korean mother was very much alive. Bravely uniting her biological and adoptive families, Borshay Liem's heartfelt journey makes *First Person Plural* a poignant essay on family, loss, and the reconciling of two identities." The video is available through PBS—www.pbs.org.

Struggle for Identity: Issues in Transracial Adoption. Transracial adoptees and their families discuss the difficult issues of racism, identity and sense of place. This video is available at www.nysccc.org—New York State Citizen's Coalition for Children.

CHAPTER FOUR

"Getting to Know Him": Dads in Adoption

By Neil Tift

Adoption services tend to be dominated by women. The professional designation *social worker* most likely conjures up a stereotypical image of a female even in today's changing society where occupational selection has become more a matter of choice than gender. This typecasting holds true in a majority of instances. Additionally, adoptive mothers are most often the driving force in initiating the adoption process. Overall, the adoption journey will include only a sprinkling of male presence.

Even adoptees themselves, as we learned in Chapter 2, are typically consumed with the female-related questions, "Why did my birthmother give me away?" "I wonder what my birthmother looks like?" "Why didn't my birthmother want me?" These questions tend to reflect biases about the essential importance of a mother's love for her child. It's not nearly as frequent that we hear a child ask "Why didn't my birthfather want me?" "Where is my birthdad?"

Yet, both fathers and mothers possess the capacity to significantly influence the healthy growth and development of their children with special needs, and to impact their potential as successful and well-adjusted adults. Often, the unique strengths (and weaknesses), viewpoints and needs of male parents in the lives of their children-by-adoption are not addressed. Likely, the gender imbalance in the adoption process and in the adoption community at large contributes to this situation. This leads to many questions:

Is the adoptive father's perspective understood as well as possible?

What are his expectations? What are our expectations of him? Are the expectations realistic?

How does he cope? How can we help him cope?

Do fathers feel important as parents? Are they truly given the opportunity to parent their children?

Do they make an effort to assume parenting responsibilities? Do we support them in these efforts?

How do they view fathering—"the breadwinner," "the playmate," "mother's helper," an "emotional caregiver?" How can we help them achieve a style of parenting that effectively meets their children's needs?

Are fathers inadvertently excluded from fully utilizing services? Do they feel invited and welcome to participate in the adoption process?

Are there ways to be more inclusive of these critical male parents—in all phases of the adoption process?

This chapter is designed to focus on the father—"getting to know him." This chapter will attempt to help identify some of the unique contributions that fathers make, and how essential it is for them to work in cooperation with mothers to achieve the desired results for all of the children in families impacted by the adoptee with complex trauma issues. Throughout this chapter adoptive fathers share their experiences which are highlighted in the "Fathers Talk" boxes.

This knowledge will allow us to further expand the process of helping families identify their strengths and areas of concern initiated in Chapter 3. This chapter provides preparation for the types of post-adoption dynamics that Chapter 8 will cover and the solutions to come in Chapters 9 and 10.

Neil Tift was invited to write this important chapter. Neil is an adoptive father of two daughters with special needs. He is the founder of the Father's Resource Center in Minneapolis, Minnesota. Neil has worked with literally thousands of fathers in many types of situations since becoming a father himself in 1975.

Gender Differences in Parenting Styles: Complements Abound

Clear differences in maternal and paternal parenting styles are exhibited from the minute the child first enters her or his new home—whether the child arrives by birth or by adoption.

Research conducted over two decades by Dr. Kyle Pruett, Clinical Professor of Psychiatry, Yale University Child Study Center, yields the rich nuances of how mothers and fathers parent in different, yet complementary, ways. While this research did not specifically study adoptive parents, the findings are certainly relevant to mothers and fathers across many cultures.

The chart on the next two pages depicts some of the father's contributions to infants and toddlers. During the grade school years, the father's influence is important for self-concept and academic achievement (Biller and Kimpton, 1997). In adolescence, closeness to fathers is related to the postponement of sexual activity among adolescent daughters—this is critical for all daughters but even more essential for the daughter who experienced sexual abuse prior to her adoption. Adolescents' attitudes about alcohol are more like those of their father. Fathers may be the primary role models for adolescents because drinking is more prevalent among males. Fathers may have a greater impact on their adolescents in areas where they are more involved than mothers or where they serve as the primary role models (Hosley and Montemayor, 1997).

The parenting styles of the mother and father, when operating in harmony, guide the child's development nicely, whether the child is typically developing or has been

Fathers Talk

I don't ever remember anyone saying that parenting could be this hard. I remember hearing that marriage could be hard and that two parents make the job easier, but never that you'd have days you just wanted to quit. Sure I remember my mom saying that there were days she would have gladly given me away to willing church people, but I didn't expect that I'd have days that I really regretted bringing them (two sons) home (or at least I've come close).

MOTHERS' AND FATHERS' DIFFERING INTERACTIVE STYLES WITH THEIR CHILDREN	
A mother typically picks up her infant to tend to his care. This indicates that a mother sees her primary role as meeting the physical and emotional needs of her child.	About 50% of the time that fathers pick up their infants, it is to "make something happen." This indicates that the father sees his role is to take care of his child in stimulating and playful ways.
By one month of age, a mother has a distinctive way of holding her baby, and she holds him that way nine times out of ten.	A father on the other hand will pick up his infant nine different ways out of ten.
A mother is likely to hold her infant facing her breast, offering a sense of comfort, warmth and security.	A father is more likely to hold his infant facing outward, tucked in his arm, allowing her a sense of exploration and freedom.
At six weeks, infants can distinguish their father's voice from their mother's voice.	
A quiet and alert 6-week-old infant will attend more quickly to a mother's voice.	An upset or fretting infant will calm more readily to a father's voice.
In a split screen study of 8-week-old infants seated comfortably, researchers noted significant differences in the infant's response to an approaching parent in order to test what is called anticipatory behavior. *The results . . .*	
When the 8-week-old infant sees her mother approaching, her eyes narrow, her shoulders relax, and her heartbeat and respiration decrease. The infant becomes calm in the presence of her mother. Even at this early age, her experience has taught her that when her mother approaches, her pattern is to gently pick her up, cradle her softly, maybe sing to her, rock her smoothly back and forth, kiss her lightly and perhaps breastfeed her. Mom's interactions are quite different than Dad's and the baby enjoys both.	When an 8-week-old infant sees her father approaching, her eyes widen, her shoulders rise, and her heartbeat and respiration increase. The infant becomes stimulated in the presence of her father. She has learned that when her father shows up, his voice is deep and his movements are more stimulating. He might toss her in the air, blow on her belly, place her on his knees or bounce her on his feet, and his whiskers tickle when he kisses her or blows on her neck. Dad's interactions are quite different than Mom's and the baby enjoys both. Dad excites and explores, while Mom calms and soothes.

MOTHERS' AND FATHERS' DIFFERING INTERACTIVE STYLES WITH THEIR CHILDREN (*Continued*)	
Infants who have time alone with their father show richer social and exploratory behavior than children that are not exposed to such experiences. Fathers help children individuate. That is, Dad is typically more willing to let a child out of his sight than will Mom. A father will let the child crawl twice as far as Mom will before retrieving the infant. One of the most critical roles that a dad plays in the life of his child in the toddler years (18 months to 42 months) is helping the child safely and securely separate from the intense maternal dependency of infancy.	
Mothers tend to simplify and slow their speech to get and hold their toddler's attention.	Fathers use bigger words and longer sentences spoken in less rhythmic sequences, perhaps showing a reluctance to "baby" his child.
Mothers help toddlers learn what words to use when he is mad, sad, scared , tired, jealous, angry, etc.	Fathers often see their responsibility to help the toddler learn when and how to express those emotions. For example, fathers typically remove a child from a public place when he is having a temper tantrum, screaming or otherwise acting out. In so doing, fathers are taking on the task of helping his child stay in control, watch his language, to fit in with peers and to keep other people safe from his rage. The mother teaches the child to say "anger" and the father teaches the child how to show that anger appropriately.
Mothers are less likely to restrict children to stereotypical gender-typed play.	Fathers have a slight proclivity to encourage preschool children of both genders to play with sex-typed toys. That is, dads tend to encourage boys to stick to playing with toys that are traditionally for boys and girls to play with girl toys.
When mothers engage in play with their children, they tend to use traditional games, stories and songs that they learned as a child.	Fathers are apt to be less predictable, and are more likely to make up stories and songs, promoting a tendency for exploration themes.
When a child confronts a novel situation—a dog, a stranger, a new toy—mothers instinctively move closer, offering the reassurance of her familiar presence.	In the same situation, fathers tend to stay back and allow the child to explore the situation for herself. He typically stands three times the distance that Mom will, thus encouraging a sense of freedom, exploration and confidence.
Adapted to chart form from Pruett, Kyle. *Fatherneed: Why Father Care is as Essential as Mother Care for Your Child.* (New York: Broadway Books, 2000.)	

impacted by complex trauma. In fact, the child who has two psychologically active parents is

- exposed to a diverse array of interests and activities
- more socially flexible
- more successful in his or her academic endeavors
- more successful in athletic endeavors
- higher in self-esteem
- better able to problem solve
- less impulsive
- stronger in moral development/empathic concern for others
- less stereotypical with people regarding gender issues
- more resilient at times of maximum stress
- less likely to engage in various types of risk-taking behaviors
- more satisfied with family life and sibling relationships (Lamb, 1997; Biller and Trotter, 1994 and Pruett, 1987 and 2000).

The Impact of Socialization: Boys Become Fathers

"Messages" about Masculinity: Growing Up

Unfortunately, fathers spend less time than do mothers interacting with their preschool, school-age, adolescent and college-age children (Lamb, 1997 and 2003). This may be due to genuine employment demands such as long hours and traveling. This may also be due to how a father defines his role in the family. If he perceives himself as the breadwinner, he may not see the need to contribute to his family in other ways. He may not have experienced an involved, close relationship with his own father. So, he lacks a blueprint for fathering. He may have antiquated perceptions of masculinity—thinking, for example, that intimate, caring, nurturing interactions are counter to being a man. Wives' attitudes toward the fathering role and experiences with their own fathers have been found to strongly predict the behavior of their husbands. Men are more likely to be highly involved caregivers if their wives view their own fathers as having been nurturing (Lamb, 1997; Radin, 1981 and 1986).

Male socialization clearly impacts fathering. In general, many men were taught as young boys that they need to act tough in order to be seen as strong, never ask for help so as to be considered independent, give orders to be in control at all times and stuff emotions except for anger to be perceived as a real man. Such qualities obviously do not contribute to the development of a healthy father.

A capable father needs to understand the "messages" about masculinity that he received as a boy growing up and consciously select those qualities that he knows will help make him be a good man and a connected father. All children benefit from the

Fathers Talk

I really don't know. By nature I think that dads are prone to drift toward a Lone Ranger or John Wayne sort of parenting model. We're supposed to be tough. We're supposed to have all the answers. Kids with mental health issues put us so far out of our element that we don't even begin to know how to deal with it. Somehow dads need to know that they're not alone and that it's okay to ask for help. One of the biggest hurdles dads face is in reaching a point where they are willing to ask for help. Dads need to understand that they risk losing too much if they try to go it alone.

Fathers Talk

I didn't receive any advice from anyone about being a father. Not having a father myself, I was at an even greater disadvantage. I knew I wanted to be there for my kids because when I was growing up I always felt left out. Other boys had their fathers at baseball and cub scouts. I felt embarrassed. Although my mother tried to take his place, I didn't appreciate her being there. Fortunately, for me, in my early teens we had very special neighbors move in a few doors down. They had four children and in no time we became close friends. Jack, their father, sort of took me under his wing and became a father figure for me.

active engagement of men who are open to connecting, teaching and modeling appropriate ways to interact.

"Messages" about Masculinity: Media Influence

Media portrayals of what it means to be a man are plagued with stereotypes. The organization, Children Now, released the report, *Boys to Men: Entertainment Media Messages about Masculinity*.[1] The report contains the survey results of 1,200 young people, ages 10 to 17, and information from focus groups in which boys offered their own insights into the media they consume. Some of the results include

- While male characters in the media display a range of emotional behavior—fear, anger, grief—they are rarely observed crying.
- Males on television were described as violent and angry by the majority of the survey respondents.
- Across boys' favorite media, men are closely identified with the working world and high prestige positions. Women continue to be identified with domestic life. Overall, men are defined by their careers and not by their relationships.
- White male characters are consistently more motivated than minorities by succeeding in work. Minority males are consistently more motivated than Whites by pro-social behavior (i.e., offering advice, talking about feelings, helping others, providing affection).
- Men of color are more likely than white men to engage in physical aggression with weapons.
- Male (and female) characters are largely heterosexual—1% are homosexual or bisexual.

According to the Media Awareness Network, professional sports is an area that continues to be male dominated—from the players to the coaches to the commentators. This organization states that sports commentary reinforces perceptions of violent masculinity by praising athletes who continue to play while injured, and by the language utilized to describe the action occurring during games.[2] Certainly, the poor conduct of

1. Heintz-Knowles, Katharine and Li-Vollmer, Meredith, MA (writers). Chen, Perry, Harris, Tamara, Haufler, Adrienne, Lapp, Joan and Miller, Patti (researchers). *Boys to Men: Entertainment Media Messages about Masculinity*. Children Now (1999). http://publications.childrennow.org/assets/pdf/cmp/boys/boystomen-media.pdf 1999

2. *Masculinity and Sports Media*. Media Awareness Network. http://www.media-awareness.ca/english/issues/stereotyping/men_and_masculinity/masculinity_sports.cfm

many major league stars combined with the publicity that accompanies such behavior contributes to skew the male image further. This situation overshadows those players who live and play by high moral standards—features about such athletes are rare.

Susan Bordo, author and Professor of English and Gender and Women's Studies, University of Kentucky, has analyzed gender in advertising, and concludes that men are usually portrayed as virile, muscular and powerful. The emphasis is on being fit and having well-sculpted muscles.

On a different scale:

> For my daughter's second Christmas, I had ordered a child's audiotape that was called "Songs for Hannah." The company weaves the name of your child into each of the six songs on the tape. When Hannah opened our gift on Christmas Eve, she immediately wanted me to find the tape player so we could play the songs for her.
>
> The second song on the tape was called "The Alphabet Song." As we listened to it together, we heard the musician sing A is for apple, B is for birdie and so on. We heard G is for gramma and M is for mommie. Unfortunately, we also heard her sing D is for doggie and F is for froggie. As we went through the tape, we heard no letters symbolizing her dad.
>
> In the entire 26 letters of the alphabet that my 20-month old daughter was learning, this major toy company was selling products that offered NO reference to a father figure.

Overall, regarding sports, television, Internet, music CDs, radio, video and computer games, advertisements and movies, we must ask, "What messages do dads and boys—future fathers—receive about their roles as men, fathers, partners, etc.?" "How do these messages influence the way they carry out their roles?"

"Messages" about Nurture

Men also need to explore the "messages" they received about nurture as boys and adolescents. The message about nurturing has been corrupted by our society, to be a feminine only quality. It is true that maternal nurturing is a female quality, but paternal nurturing is a masculine quality. Fathers nurture children in ways that are different than, but not better or worse than, how mothers nurture. Let's explore some important examples.

Across all studied cultures, one of the primary ways that fathers engage with their children is through play. Many times it is through the "rough and tumble" play that fathers and young children appear to truly enjoy a method of relating to one another. This is shaped by cultural messages around play, but it typically takes the form of tossing the child in the air, roughhousing, tickling, pillow fights, tug-of-wars, wrestling, interactive sports—especially contact sports—and other types of hands-on father/child interaction. As this is considered an innate expression of their paternal instincts, adoptive fathers would also share the tendency to play with their children in this manner.

Some contend that this yearning for interactive physical contact on the part of fathers is their attempt to provide balance for the time that a birthmother has to connect with the child. The mother experiences the child growing in her womb for forty weeks, and she has the capacity to breast feed the infant.

An important contribution of paternal involvement is the predisposition of fathers to activate their children in order to engage with them. Children from a very young age express the tendency to anticipate their father's energy level and playfulness that is different from the mother's. Healthy play teaches children important lessons of life, such as impulse control, team work, considering others' feelings, following and applying rules, swift judgment calls and attention to task—more positive influences to add to the list of father's contributions to child development

Fathers Talk

Because my parents were divorced and I lived with my mother as a child, I think that my initial inclination towards parenting was that it ought to involve nurturing. For my mother though, nurturing usually meant something artificial and unproductive like pampering or coddling. Personally, I felt as though I never received the message that I could do things myself; things were usually done for me and the unspoken message was that "I wasn't competent." So when we brought our three adopted children home, my first instinct was pity; I felt as though I should be coddling them. And that seemed to be what most people speculated that they needed. It's a pretty natural conclusion; they've had a hard life, so we should feel bad for them and make things easy.

I think one of the things that I feel most proud of is that my wife and I decided from early on that there was no time to lose, and that our children would not be coddled. A professional explained to us that indulging in sympathy and pity, if overdone and not balanced, could not look like strength and stability to a child in need. For most people, pity focuses too much on the past while giving up structure in the present. Whether they showed it or not, and our children showed it in strange and bizarre ways, they were scared, and what our children desperately needed was safety. For them, structure was safety. What they had lacked for all of their young lives was stability. My wife and I both caught this concept very early on, and I'm proud of that because I think our children could have lost years if we had done it any differently.

I should mention, though, that because my parents had such an affected style of nurturing, it is a constant struggle for me not to rely on structure to the exclusion of any identification with them as individuals. Even six years down the road, they still fight our structure. It's different than I'd have to imagine that it is with most children, because they're not exploring their limitations of independence. They simply don't trust our ability to be in charge. Sometimes it feels as though we spend so much time setting up rules and communicating those rules to each other, that we don't have a lot of time left for much else. So I'm still finding my balance as the "parent who's in charge" and the "parent who relates." This seems like a continual process.

When fathers rough house, tickle and wrestle with their children, kids become emotionally stimulated—their little bodies are responding to a caring adult in a way that is seen most often as different from how mothers tend to interact with their children. A father's presence offers a significant difference to the child than the mother's presence.

An example of the benefit of play for children is a father playing "monster." When a pre-schooler asks her father to join her little friends to be the monster, she unknowingly is inviting him to teach them survival skills and coping strategies. If the children run and hide from the monster and Daddy eventually finds them, they each must decide how they are going to respond to this perceived threat. One child might scream and laugh, another run away, a third might hug him, a fourth child might cry and cower, while a fifth might try to hit or kick the monster. Each of these children is deciding, in a relatively safe environment, how they must respond to a scary, silly, uncertain situation.

Studies show that mothers tend to use objects from their environment such as books, puzzles, games, crayons, and toys and dolls when she is engaging with her young child. A father will typically make use of his body when interacting with his infant. He becomes the jungle gym, monkey bars, rocking horse or he gives piggy back rides, gator bites or "noogies."

Thus, children begin observing that when they are with Mom, they feel a sense of comfort, warmth, calm and support. When they are with Dad, they feel a sense of excitement, action, and adventure. A mother tends to be more predictable and consistent in her one-to-one interactions with her child, while a father tends to be less predictable and more exploratory and stimulating with his child.

It is important to interject into this the premise that parents, especially fathers, are frequently discouraged from touching, playing and showing affection to daughters who have experienced sexual abuse prior to their adoption. The rationale is that "rough and tumble" play may remind her of her abuse and thus cause her further trauma. This recommendation stifles "father nurture" and it denies the daughter the opportunity to gain valuable father-child development interactions. Chapter 10 is going to return to this issue. A case will be made for a "middle ground" between no touch and re-traumatizing this new daughter. In this manner, fathers and daughters can reap the benefits of father nurture.

In light of the above information it is important to strengthen the role of the father in the lives of *all* of his children. The child that experienced trauma, as Chapter 2 explained, has an array of cognitive, emotional and social delays. This child will especially benefit from a joint parenting approach. Some considerations to assist fathers and mothers in enhancing their parental roles throughout the adoption process include

- Incorporate content pertaining to parental influences on child development as a component of pre-adoptive education classes. Provide resources for ongoing learning. Doing this early in forming relationships with prospective parents sends a clear message that fathers are valued as equal partners in the adoption process.
- Facilitate parental exploration of their views regarding their respective and complementary parenting roles:

    How do they view parenting responsibilities?

    How did their views develop?

    How might they consider changing their roles in light of gaining a greater depth of understanding about the value of each parent's contributions to the healthy development of their children?

An exercise that is useful with fathers is to ask each man what his blueprint for masculinity is and how he wants to instill that in his son or daughter. What will he tell his son about how he should act, talk and believe in order to grow up to be a healthy man and to treat girls and women in respectful ways? What will he tell his daughter about how to act and talk to grow up to be a healthy woman and how to relate to boys and men in her life in respectful ways?

- Assess parental strengths and areas of concerns with knowledge of gender differences in mind. For example, when looking at the *Strength of Time Management* (Chapter 3), it is helpful to have parents look not only at the *quantity* of time spent with their children but the *quality* as well.

    How do parents and children spend their time—chores, television, homework, playing, talking, hobbies, eating dinner together, rushing from one activity to the next?

    What type of parent-child communication occurs during time together—lecture/discipline, sharing of opinions and ideas, ethical decision making, compliments, praise, sharing of each other's day, problem-solving related discussion, exploration of feelings?

What happens in the morning? Are both parents available? Is it a frenzy of activity? Does the family eat together or separately?

What happens when the children arrive home from school? Is a parent home? Is there time for connecting and discussing the day? Which parent is more involved in homework? In meal prep?

What happens at bedtime? Is there a routine? Who participates?

- Or, in looking at *Providing a Nurturing Environment* (Chapter 3) and *Maintaining a Healthy Emotional Environment* (Chapter 3) considerations could include:

  Is affection given to boys and girls by fathers and mothers?

  How are children helped to express feelings? Are feelings facilitated by both parents?

  Do parents display affection to each other in front of the children?

  How is affection displayed by fathers and mothers? Do children perceive both parents as warm and caring?

  Examining day-to-day interactions helps to identify the intimacy exhibited between children, fathers and mothers. Parents and professionals can brainstorm suggestions to increase the closeness of family members. Thus, time spent between fathers and daughters, fathers and sons, mothers and daughters, mothers and sons or the whole family together will truly define and model quality time.
- Follow up with fathers and mothers post-placement. In studying fathers of children with mental challenges, it was found that meetings conducted during the day led to no father presence, meetings held both day and night yielded a response of 2.6 fathers per 10 mothers, and programs that consistently offered evening hours allowed attendance by 5.3 fathers to 10 mothers (Meyer, 1986). Adoption professionals cannot be expected to accommodate the schedules of each client. However, it must be recognized that not all clients have employment positions that allow flexible scheduling. Financially, lost work time may undermine the father's self-identity as provider. Supporting a child with special needs may require attending work regularly.

Accepting "Complements": Parents as Allies

My six-year-old daughter Hannah and I walked out of our home to run some errands, with my wife Denise to follow in a minute. Hannah tried to open the door to a van that we had just purchased and was having difficulty. I was standing a few feet away encouraging her to push the door button with both hands and to firmly plant her feet.

When Denise walked out the door, she saw that Hannah was struggling and said that she would help her open the door. I politely asked Denise to wait and let Hannah try to open the door herself. After a couple of tries, Hannah figured out how to open and close the door to our van. As we backed out of the driveway, Hannah stated, "Daddy, thanks for letting me do that myself."

In daily events in which a child confronts a frustrating situation, mothers generally are much more likely to intervene quickly, while a father is less likely to fix the situation, thus encouraging and strengthening the child's problem-solving skills.

So, Denise's response to the situation was not a bad or inappropriate one, but merely her maternal instinct kicking in. My response was not better or worse than hers, rather was my paternal instinct kicking in.

Fathers Talk

Although obvious on the surface, it is incredibly important to find out what works for each individual child. We have twins who couldn't be more difficult. Both exhibit varying degrees of mental health issues and both can exhibit behaviors that can be completely maddening. Even then, both boys are dramatically different and what worked a year ago doesn't always work now. One of the boys is softer spoken and is immediately responsive to even a marginal rise in volume, the other is the child we had to stop spanking when he was 3 because the only response we would get was laughter. We were genuinely afraid that we'd have to hurt him to get any attention so we had to find something else. The same child today shuts down if I raise my voice and although he excels at pushing my buttons and making me crazy, I am learning, thanks to the wonderful perception and advice of my wife, that we do much better if I lower my voice and speak calmly rather than yelling and ranting at him like a madman. Sometimes parenting is a moving target, so you need to be adaptable.

But, how often do these types of occurrences create parenting adversaries rather than parenting allies? One parent feels contradicted or undermined. One parent scolds the other, "Why didn't you help her?" "Why don't you let her do more on her own?" It is as if mothers and fathers engage in a pseudo competition to demonstrate that their parenting approach is superior to their partner's.

A final point needs to be made about the differences between male and female parenting styles—they are often a source of conflict! As preceding chapters have pointed out, the child entering the family comes with various deficits and many challenging behaviors. So, the adoptee's needs give rise to increased conflict as parents attempt to heal and manage the new child effectively.

Pre-adoption is the time to investigate how fathers and mothers resolve such conflict that stems from gender differences:

Do such differences create conflict immediately?

Are fathers and mothers able to step back and look at the outcome of a particular parenting intervention, and then decide that the child benefited and that is what counts?

How similar are parental goals for their children? Is each parent working on their own "agenda?" Is there one unified "agenda?"

Is the child receiving a cohesive message about the values and expectations of the family? Is the child receiving "mixed messages?"

Fathers Talk

Don't be afraid to be tag team parents. On any given day, your children can make you crazy. Take turns. Recognize when your spouse has had enough and give them a break. Be willing to send them out of the house for the day or the afternoon without the kids to go to the mall or go for a walk. Give your partner a break to do what they want.

Fathers Talk

My wife and I adopted a 7½ year old boy from Romania in 1996. At that time, she had a Master's degree in special education and was working at a school for behaviorally handicapped children (aka: children out of control). I was working in the business world with an MBA in finance. On many occasions, she tried to inform me of the challenges that lay ahead with our son. While I understood the word "challenging," I had no idea that it would become an all-consuming set of circumstances. I wrongly assumed that because she was an expert in the field that she would be able to handle any issue that came our way.

Little did I know that working with other kids would be so different than working with your own child. Initially, it led to many feelings ranging from frustration to defeat to mistrust. I really felt that she had not conveyed the seriousness of what we were facing in taking on this child. I began to look at work as an escape from the day to day (hour to hour) strain of dealing with our son. Even there at the workplace, however, I still never knew what the next phone call would bring.

When we would go to visit child psychologists to discuss our child, the two of us were often grouped together as the source of our son's issues. While this was infuriating at times, it also helped bring us back together. It became an "us vs. the world" attitude, and we were determined not only to change this perception but also to help our son to understand that we loved him and wanted him to be a member of the community, a society that he certainly did not understand at the time.

When we finally found the right people who could help our son deal with his adoption and attachment issues, there were still many long and frustrating days. I learned the importance of exercise and a healthy diet. Getting together with friends and family once in awhile, having a beer and watching a sporting event, all became key components of coping with the stress of a child with mental health issues. I often recall a conversation with my father-in-law in which he stated that no matter how bad things had gotten, one day our son would make me proud. It might not be for five or ten years or even longer, but one day the frustration would be worth it. Keeping that in the back of my mind always seemed to help.

But most importantly, my relationship with my spouse was the key. Even when I was completely overwhelmed, just having someone there to listen and say, "I understand" meant everything. The ability to vent (sometimes loudly!) and still have your partner love and care for you really is the best coping mechanism of all. When we started to work as a team without the feelings of frustration towards one another, then the progress of our child moved at a steadier but still slow pace. Even now, while he is doing better at age 19, we still have to work on having a team approach. It's just easier when things are moving in the right direction.

Does the mother consider the father a "baby-sitter" or a full parenting partner? Does she allow the father to make his own mistakes thereby navigating his own relationships with his children?

Do fathers and mothers check with each other before assigning consequences and approving privileges?

Is the father authoritarian or controlling, superseding decisions made by his wife and thereby reducing the autonomy of, and respect for, his partner?

Parents who can learn to accept the complements of a two-parent approach benefit their marital relationships, the children they already parent and the child about to enter the family.

Dads and Adoption

Let's now turn our attention to the father's reactions, positive or negative, to the child entering the family. There are at least four factors that appear to influence an adoptive dad's manner of understanding and coping with the news that his child has special needs. They are

- Timing: Learning that the adoptee is affected by past experiences
- Reactions: Involvement and coping styles
- Reactions: Grief and trauma
- The strength of his support network

The following sections will address each of the four influencing factors listed above.

Timing: Learning That the Adoptee Is Affected by Past Experiences

One factor that impacts the adjustment level of parents, including fathers, is whether the child's diagnosis is known in advance of the adoption, is obvious at an early age or if there is the dawning of a gradual awareness that their child is living with a disability (Wikler, 1981).

Later identified issues may result in fathers responding by denial. There may be an especially prolonged period of denial among fathers who have minimal interactions with their children (Lamb and Billings, 1997). Again, time spent with children and the quality of that time, as discussed above, may be a critical component in the father's capacity to accept the adoptee that arrives affected by complex trauma.

Across cultures, men are reluctant to accept that such a situation has occurred to them and their family. Their response is, "This isn't really happening." "This happens to other families, but not to us." It may take considerable time to finally acknowledge the situation and begin taking steps to seek targeted assistance for the child and the family.

Jeff and Paulette adopted Mary Beth domestically. She arrived when she was 3 years old. She was always an impulsive child, yet in the home setting she was manageable. However, once she entered kindergarten and was in a larger group, the full extent of her impulsivity became quite clear. She would blurt out answers. She constantly interrupted the other children and the teacher. If another child was playing with a toy she wanted, she would simply grab the toy. Frequently, the other child was not willing to part with the item and in such instances, Mary Beth would push or shove the child if need be to get the toy.

The teacher relayed Mary Beth's behaviors to Jeff and Paulette. Jeff's response was always the same, "Why isn't the teacher watching the kids more closely?" "What is going on in that classroom?" "Maybe we need to meet with the teacher and find out why she can't manage Mary Beth better?" "I'm sure other kids act the same way." "I think she is just bored. She's too smart for the work they are giving her."

Jeff did not want to accept the fact that Mary Beth had problems. His denial continued through Mary Beth's first and second grades. Paulette provided him articles, websites,

Fathers Talk

I don't feel as though I ever doubted that my children had problems. My wife and I were somewhat educated about the problems of adoptees from the beginning. There are some things, however, that make the process difficult for a man in particular. As the man, I feel as though it is my responsibility to protect my wife and to protect my family. As much as that means protection from danger (i.e., protecting the children from strangers and traffic, etc.) it also frequently means protecting both my wife and my children from people who might exploit them for their innocence or ignorance. The marketplace is full of exploitation and whether it's meant to be aggressive or not, people have to make a living. When your family has needs, there can be seemingly no end to the options available for treatment. Some are very legitimate, while others seem questionable to me. So, I guess that if I've had any difficulty in learning that my children have problems, it has been in the ways that it has been provided to me, and in the ways that I've received it. When I have therapists trying to explain, "cognitive this" and "behavioral that" to me, my first instinct is that I'm being buffaloed. It all sounds like big words that in turn mean big dollars, and my role when that happens, as I see it, is to protect my family from manipulation. But later, when I see that my son is acting so strangely, making noises and jumping around when he's nervous; when my youngest daughter beats her head against the wall in a crazed fit; or when my oldest daughter looks at me like she thinks I'm going to kill her, then it all makes a little more sense. When it's simplified and I can see these things happening, then I don't feel as though I have that much trouble accepting my children's problems. It's the medical system that's made me nervous in the past, and that's what I felt like I've been fighting.

books, etc. She attempted to engage him in discussions. Only after Mary Beth injured another child did he realize that he must confront his denial and cooperate with Paulette in obtaining services.

Denial is a stage in the grieving process. In Chapter 8 we will come to learn that grief is a powerful dynamic in adoptive families. Chapters 9 and 10 will provide suggestions to help move parents through the grieving process.

As Jeff, Paulette and Mary Beth exemplify, grief can contribute to the timing of the family obtaining services. Paulette was seeking answers and implementing techniques from her readings. Jeff continued to believe that Mary Beth was "fine" and that she

Fathers Talk

When we first discussed the idea of adopting an older child my two concerns were he cannot be a molester because we have young girls in the house and I can't live with a thief. Those were my two basic concerns. I said I could pretty much deal with anything else. During the honeymoon stage of the fostering for the year before we actually adopted him, he seemed to be a very good kid. After the adoption was finalized, he became comfortable with the situation and he started stealing everything that wasn't nailed down.

Fathers Talk

Knowing that they had a problem wasn't that hard—after a while it simply became obvious our kids weren't like other kids. After awhile I could no longer ignore the fact that they were getting farther and farther away from the boundaries of what most people would consider normal. The hard part was finding someone who could do something about it or who even understood what the problem was.

would "grow out of this." Mary Beth suffered the consequences of this lack of a cohesive parenting approach. After several years of poor peer interactions, she was identified, by her classmates, as a child to avoid.

Certainly, acknowledging that your child may require therapy, medication, special education, medical care and so on is heartbreaking for any parent. Fathers report that such news is exacerbated by the insensitivity of professionals who treat them like second class parents. Some fathers also convey that it is difficult to obtain information from doctors, and other fathers only find out about their child's difficulties after their wives have been informed (Erickson, 1974).

In conclusion, most adoptive families will receive information about prospective adoptive children in advance. Chapter 1 explained various factors that affect the quality and accuracy of that information. Chapter 2 covered complex trauma and concluded that the child's past experiences can impact her functioning. Chapter 5 will explore—in-depth—how to interpret a particular child's history. These chapters, plus reading, attending pre-adoptive training and connecting to veteran families will help parents arm themselves for potential problems. This is important for all members of the adoptive family, but perhaps especially essential for the father's adjustment. The earlier the father can recognize his adoptee's reaction to her traumatized past the greater the potential for his acceptance. The manner in which professionals interact with fathers can also play an important role in his adjustment.

Fathers Talk

When we finally found a counselor who really understood what we were up against and who genuinely understood the problems that our children faced, we filled out an application form and underwent an assessment. Somewhere we were asked, point blank, what our expectations were for our child. At that point I realized my aspirations for having a college educated child with a well-respected professional career wasn't going to happen. What came out of my mouth was realistic but represented a major adjustment in my thinking. What I said, and I remind myself of today, is that I would be pleased if the outcome of counseling was to give my son a chance to have a life that approached "normal" but didn't involve felonies and ending up in prison. With counseling, we are making progress but the hopes and dreams of "normal" parents for their children will likely never be realized. Whether I like it or not, this is a significant loss and we have to allow ourselves to grieve.

Fathers Talk

The first signs of problems I dismissed as high energy. She has been on the go since we brought her home from Russia. I did not understand the aggressiveness toward peers and family pets. I hoped some socialization at church, family outings and get-togethers with friends would correct that. However, even with counseling, the problem still exists today although with less intensity. I did not fully accept that my daughter had problems until our family entered counseling. To accept, I had to admit defeat, failure. It still saddens me today. I have always thought of her as my daughter, not my adopted daughter. I love her as much as I feel I would love a birth child. I guess I have expected the same love in return from her, but she can't. I do believe she loves both my wife and me from a safe distance.

Reactions: Involvement and Coping Styles

Once informed that the adoptee has mental health issues, educational needs, physical disabilities or other conditions, fathers and mothers respond differently. Fathers often become especially concerned about the costs of providing for their children, whether their children will fit in and develop successfully, and whether their children will be able to support themselves in adulthood. Mothers are concerned about the emotional strain of caring for children with special needs and about the child's ability to get along and be happy.

Fathers are also more concerned about whether or not their child—especially sons—interact in socially acceptable ways. They are concerned about the level of social and occupational status their child achieves. Overall, fathers tend to be more concerned with the long-term implications of their children's difficulties (Lamb, 1997).

These responses contribute to the ways in which parents involve themselves in caring for their children with special needs just as timing contributed to *denial*. Jill and Mitchell adopted Ivan and Svetelina, ages 3 and 6 respectively, from Eastern Europe. They offer an example of *withdrawal* as a male coping style. Jill writes,

> "I'm the one who's most affected by their mental health issues and at times I feel very alone. Although my husband is supportive, there are times that he just doesn't get why I am so depressed. I don't think he really understands just how hard it is for me. He's been gone all day. It's easy for him to forget what it's like to be with the children all day. I think he would like to forget and just think everything is normal. When I'm in a bad mood or he sees that things have not been done around the house, he's annoyed.

Fathers Talk

At first, I played down the severity of the issues, relating them to my own childhood experiences. As I began to grasp the nature of her issues, I tried to help my wife cope with the rejection issues she was having with our daughter. I became a buffer between my wife and child. I wanted peace in the household. I also look for escape by immersing myself in projects around the house. I don't go out much or stay late at work. I come home each day hoping things will have gotten better—hoping my daughter finally understands what she has to do to fit in.

"I'm frustrated, angry and depressed. Why can't he see that I'm so spent and a hug would go a lot farther? I feel very overwhelmed and I feel he's insensitive to the trauma that is my life. It would be nice if he would just understand and appreciate what I've been through all day. I try so hard to do the things that will cause change in our children. It's not easy or convenient, but for some reason I just can't quit even for a day. I want to make it better! Sometimes I wish I could just relax and let it go because it seems I'm just spinning my wheels. The saddest thing of all is, I really do want to love them! I want them to be mine. They just make it so hard. They resist any kind of connection to me and seem to repel with force, it's like when you put two magnets together. Having unhealthy children is extremely depressing. Before this, I had never been depressed in my life. I hate the way it changed who I am. I'm not the same person. I'm nervous all the time and angry often. I used to be happy!"

Mitchell frequently states:

"I now work a 60-hour work week to support my family. My income allowed for the addition of two children to the family. Clothing, food, toys, extra utility costs, a van, the adoption costs were all affordable. However, the insurance co-pays for occupational therapy, physical therapy, speech therapy, mental health services, the gas to travel to all of these services, childproof locks, and repairing the damage Ivan and Svetelina do to walls, cupboards, furniture, etc., require that I work overtime on a regular basis. When I get home, I am tired. Why can't she understand that I want to relax? Why can't she understand that everything I do is to support her efforts to help our children? If I didn't work so much, we couldn't pay for all of their services."

Mitchell's response to his children's mental health issues is to focus on family finances—he is the "bread winner"—while Jill's reaction is much more focused on emotional well-being. The different ways in which they involve themselves in meeting their children's special needs is causing marital strain. Jill would like more nurture. Mitchell wants time to relax. Neither feels supported nor understood by the other regarding the contributions each makes toward healing their children. Jill works directly with the children to alleviate their mental health issues. Mitchell works extra hours to support

Fathers Talk

It is terrible to learn that your children have incredibly horrible problems. For us, this was our oldest son sexually abusing our youngest daughter, and she also abusing our youngest son. The emotional pain and sorrow was incredible, as was our anger at our oldest son and youngest daughter. The stress at knowing that sexual abuse could occur at any time, including the dog being abused, is constant. While the pain is incredible, the joy is also great at seeing four of our children (we adopted a sibling group of six) make major changes. Our four oldest have wonderful possibilities of normal lives. Few things are as exciting as seeing them change.

My grief has to do with how well our two youngest will turn out unless they change. Their lives will be a nightmare. My youngest daughter, now 10½, could very easily become pregnant as an adolescent. My youngest son, age 8, could very well end up in prison or in an abusive relationship. Grief also has to do with how this has affected so negatively our marriage. We have stayed together, and always will, but, unless we both make major changes, we will never have an intimate marriage.

Fathers Talk

Whether you like it or not, there are significant pressures brought to bear on your marriage when children arrive and even more so when you discover that they do not fit the mold of "normal" children. If your kids exhibit behavioral problems, your marriage will feel the strain. You will need to be deliberate about spending time, energy and money to build up your marriage so that you can have the emotional resources to spend on your children. It will not help your children if you and your wife end up in divorce court. Be pro-active! Take the time to be alone together without the children. Go out to dinner. Go out to the movies. If your problems are becoming severe then do not hesitate to seek out a good marriage counselor while there remains a chance to fix what's broken. A good counselor is your friend and can help to provide the tools that can pull you together instead of pushing you apart.

the professional services that help heal the children. Mitchell becomes upset when he arrives home and "things around the house aren't done." This instantly puts Jill on edge. She feels that he truly does not understand the energy needed to parent the children. She feels he does not see the children's mental health issues accurately. Over time, Mitchell has continued to increase his work hours in an effort to avoid the marital tension, and the strain of parenting two children with histories of complex trauma.

The most common response pattern of fathers in this type of situation is withdrawal from child-care and childrearing responsibilities (Lamb, 1997). Many men increase their work obligations or their participation in activities outside of the home. As in Jill and Mitchell's case, spousal conflict occurs. The wife states, "You need to be home more!" or asks, "How can you (husband) leave me (wife) to deal with so much?" The husband says, "I'm working so much. How much more can you *expect*?"(There is that issue of *expectations* again. It crops up over and over in adoptive families!) Jill and Mitchell offer us a pre-cursor of content yet to come in Chapter 8—expectations—differing, unmet, too high, too low—which can lead to conflict and grief. Chapter 8 will also examine coping styles further. Coping styles, such as withdrawal, contribute to immobilizing the family. Chapters 9 and 10 will offer solutions necessary for parents to operate as a team—complementing each other and meeting the needs of each member of their family—themselves included.

Overall, a disengaged dad is frequently a grieving dad. His marriage is in conflict and diminished marital satisfaction often leads to a decrease in male self-esteem (Cummings, 1976). His role as financial provider for the family is compromised. The future of his newly adopted child is unknown. Time with birth and/or previously adopted children has been reduced. These are all losses.

We must help men understand the consequences of pulling away from the family. Rather than remind fathers of their responsibilities to their wives and children, we need to increase our capacity to help men acknowledge and resolve their grief and loss. Such recommendations are put forth at the end of this chapter and in Chapters 9 and 10.

Restricted attachment to the adoptee may occur if a father perceives his special needs child as consistently presenting major disruptions to treasured family activities. He may have trouble integrating this child fully into the home and daily activities.

Chuck and Tara parent their birth son, Evan, age 6. They opted to adopt in response to advertisements regarding Ethiopian orphans in need of homes. Six-month-old Millie, named after Tara's grandmother, arrived when Evan was 7½.

Chuck, Tara and Evan were an active family. They enjoyed many types of activities—antique shopping, concerts, hiking, boating, museum exhibits, professional football games and so on.

Millie didn't tolerate many of these outings well. Crowds, bright lights and noise sent her on lengthy scream-filled rages. As time passed, the family's outings dwindled. Or, Tara would leave the event with Millie while Chuck and Evan stayed until the excursion's end.

Tara eventually realized that her "fun" time with Evan had become quite limited. She discussed this matter with Chuck who would say, "Next time, I'll take Millie home." However, when it came time to follow through, Chuck resisted. Tara, not wanting to cause a scene in front of Evan, would give in.

Fathers Talk

Family vacations have been very helpful. I think that one of the things that people really don't appreciate about adoption is how awkward and forced it can be. I remember going to pre-adoptive parenting classes and listening to a couple explain how strange it was that they drove to their destination with no children, and suddenly returned with two little people in their backseat. I can look back on that now and say, "That's not strange; that's terrifying, and mostly for the children!" Our 1½-year-old screamed like a banshee on the plane ride back. At the time I didn't know any better. I figured she was a baby and babies cry. Now I look back and realize that we were turning her world upside down. It makes me very sad when I think about that; how scary it must have been and how terrified she probably was. Even at that age, I think she knew something was wrong.

When you're adopting, what the services don't tell you is that if you don't already have children, adoption doesn't create an instant family. And if you do already have children, your adopted children don't instantly become new family members. Adoption of these children is the awkward process of inviting a stranger to spend the night, someone you don't know and have never met. With the exception, of course, that instead of spending the night, they stay forever. And in some cases, against their will. Just like having a stranger over, there's a steady, subtle mood of tension and anxiety. I can feel that even when my parents visit, and I've known them all my life. My children, on the other hand, are still trying to figure out—four years later—if they trust us. My 9-year-old is convinced we stole her.

Anyhow, my point is that it seems we get stuck in our ruts—my doubts about how I'm handling things and how we're perceived, and my children's fear and loneliness. Even though it might sound trivial, family vacations seem to be a good thing for us. Everyone likes a vacation because it gets you away from your worries about work, and commitments and shortcomings. But I think newly adopted families need this all the more because their homes tend to become battlegrounds, and each familiar room tends to become associated with the negative feelings that they have of distrust and fear and resentment. Getting out of that environment for a short period of time gives everyone the opportunity to regroup, and it allows everyone the opportunity and the energy to work on bonding. I think that we all desperately want to bond; it's the elemental thing that's just naturally missing for all of us. But when you're mired down in the distrust that seems to saturate your home, it becomes nearly impossible until you shake things up.

Fathers Talk

Greg Keck, PhD is the founder of the Attachment and Bonding Center of Ohio, co-author of the books, *Adopting the Hurt Child*, and *Parenting the Hurt Child*, author of *Parenting Adopted Adolescents* and single adoptive father of two sons. He connected to his sons through their interests in athletics and by being a parent his children enjoyed being with. He writes,

Becoming a father through adoption has many facets. It was a new role for me, and to have NEW children who are really OLD, ages 13 and 17 at the time of their adoptions, was, at once, fun, challenging, exciting, frustrating, energizing, draining, perplexing, fulfilling, and this list could go on and on. I think what helped me most do what I did was my sense of humor and my capacity to parent in a friendly and fun manner. Adolescents typically like adults—they just don't appear to like their parents. This is different for kids who have not had fathers or, at least, good fathers. Both of my sons seemed to be very happy at having a father . . . of being able to say 'my dad' frequently. That phrase, almost alone, allowed them to level the social playing field when talking with both peers and other adults in their lives, such as coaches, teachers, etc.

Both of my kids were always able to be affectionate openly in public; they never seemed to have to disconnect in social situations where there were both their peers and other parents present. Adopting children or adolescents who have had trauma requires that parents are friendly—not by being just a friend, but by being friendly and fun to be with. I never understand how people adopting older children or adolescents think that they can just step into the parental role by directing, assigning, correcting, and consequencing. There has to be a reason for the adolescent to begin to feel close to the parent, and the initial reason needs to be that the parent is likeable.

I sat through more athletic events and tournaments than I had in my entire life. I enjoyed seeing them wrestle, play football, and basketball. On more than one occasion, after a team or individual loss, they would say, 'Oh well, I wish we'd have won, but at least I have a family!'

The great times provided some immunity from the trauma of the challenging times. Living with hurt children or adolescents guarantees that the parent will share the hurt and pain—it's unavoidable and should be expected. I think that seeing so many severe issues in my practice also served to mitigate some of the frustrations I faced. Since I have seen so many adolescents, adopted and not adopted, that had serious mental health issues, I could keep our issues in perspective.

"Brian and James shared their journeys with me, and for that, I am grateful. As with all journeys, there were detours, chuck holes, and bumps, but reaching the destination made everything worthwhile."

Millie was age 3 when Tara learned about Sensory Integration Dysfunction. Treatment alleviated Millie's symptoms, but not the marital strain. Chuck's relationship with Millie didn't automatically improve either. His commitment to Evan remained strong, but he only paid attention to Millie when necessary. His early perceptions of Millie as an interruption to the family impaired his capacity to form an attachment to her and integrate her into the family.

As for Evan, the family division left him quite confounded. He stated, "I just want Mom and Dad to get along again."

Overall, dads look for *similarities* between themselves and their newly adopted children, just as a birthfather looks for common interests between himself and his birth child. He knows that his transculturally adopted daughter may not have his eyes or complexion, but with his early and consistent influence, she may develop his sense of humor or his enjoyment for blues music. This enlightened coping response offers another avenue for a father to assimilate this child into his family. Let's look at an example that presents two sides of this coin.

> Candice and Eugene adopted Danny from the foster care system when he was 8 years old. At this young age, he was already displaying great skill in baseball and hockey. Eugene had been quite an athlete in high school and college. He and Danny connected immediately due to their shared interest in sports. Their relationship flourished.
>
> Early in adolescence, Danny became quite depressed. He became preoccupied with his birthfamily. In his effort to determine, "Who am I?" he developed behaviors similar to his birth parents. His grades plummeted—A's and B's quickly became D's and F's. He became so argumentative with his teachers that the school ultimately requested his removal from regular education. This academic downturn resulted in a suspension, per school policy, from all sports. Eugene was devastated. Danny, now with no area of success, became more depressed. This made Danny very irritable and thus very difficult to get along with in any environment. Eugene, Candice and Danny arrived at therapy in a state of utter exasperation.
>
> Eugene stated, "We simply have no way to relate anymore. Our lives revolved around his sports. We so enjoyed attending his games. We met his friends. We got to talk to their parents. We'd go out after games and recap his home runs or goals. We'd talk—I knew so much about him. Now, I feel like I don't know him at all."

The attachment between Danny, Eugene and Candice contributed to Danny's successful treatment. During therapy, Danny talked in detail about the physical abuse he had experienced at the hands of his birthfather. The abuse was accompanied by a strong message that "Boys don't cry. They take it like a man." Thus, his depression was caused, in part, by his inability to convey his feelings for the loss of his birthparents. Eugene realized that he must make more effort to talk with his son about matters of the heart. Danny needed a male to model emotional expression in order to reverse the birthfather's negative impact. As a result of Eugene's lead in this area, Danny was able to integrate his past and his present. This father and son attachment grew through the sharing of Danny's grief—an emotional connection developed.

Despite the varied responses fathers may have to their children's needs, families are likely to be strengthened when fathers are emotionally (as with Danny's grief) and concretely (as with Danny's athletics) involved with their wives and children (Lamb, 1997).

By age 15, Danny resumed the good level of functioning he enjoyed prior to his identity crisis. Eugene and Candice, once again, proudly cheer him to victory in his

Fathers Talk

For me golfing is one of the most relaxing things I can personally do. And it's neat because now I'm enjoying it with my kids. This includes my son-by-adoption as well as my birth son. Although my son-by-adoption is not quite as relaxed on the golf course, and gets frustrated and is not always the most pleasant kid to be on the golf course with, I'm hoping that over time it will become a place where we can be together and enjoy each other's company.

numerous athletic endeavors. This family's experience demonstrates the need to forge multiple connections between fathers and their children. This story puts forth the advantage of post-placement services that include the entire family. This is a point that will be emphasized in Chapters 8, 9 and 10.

In conclusion, fathers and mothers possess myriad ways of coping and involving themselves with the needs of children who join their families by adoption. Some coping and involvement styles are clearly more beneficial than others. Some, such as denial and withdrawal, are often clearly misunderstood. It is important that fathers have opportunities to express and enhance their coping skills in ways that support their family members. Positive coping strategies can strengthen a family's relational bonds and enhance their chances of healing.

Reactions: Grief and Trauma

As we have learned, fathers and mothers express a wide range of responses to the fact that their child has complex trauma issues. Earlier we reviewed coping and involvement styles that result from parental perceptions and experiences with their child with special needs. In this section we will look closer at emotional responses.

Emotional reactions include that some fathers will feel a sense of grief, while others will experience trauma. A grieving response does not necessarily attack one's sense of identity. A father who grieves experiences sadness and anger, or denial such as Jeff in the example provided earlier in this chapter. Typically, anger associated with grief is not destructive. Feelings that occur as part of grief are associated with loss.

A father who is traumatized responds with a sense of terror and panic: "What will I do? How will I handle this? Can I handle this?" Thus, in a traumatic response pattern, one's identity may become distorted as it impacts an individual's sense of capabilities, worth and dignity. When men experience trauma, their anger response is more likely to be verbally or physically destructive. Often times, fathers exhibit their anger in ways that are different from, and more aggressive and harmful than, how women express theirs. This is one reason that men are incarcerated at seventeen times the rate that women are in the U.S.

Fathers Talk

More generally, dads need to realize that adoption is not the same as natural childbirth. While this may seem obvious on the surface, there are significant differences even if dads don't experience this for themselves. There is a good chance your wife will experience significant grief over this. Yes, you finally have the child that you always wanted and yes, you will both experience great joy as parents, but none of that will eliminate your need to grieve the loss of not being able to have children in the usual way. Many paths lead to this place because there are many reasons that people decide to adopt, but many arrive here because for one reason or another they are unable to have children through childbirth. Your wife may have dreamt her entire life of having children and that dream probably included having them in the customary way. Even though you now have a child, which may go a long way toward healing that pain, the grief over losing the dream doesn't go away as if by magic. Your wife may still need the space, and your understanding, to grieve the loss of the children you couldn't have even as the children you are adopted are held in your arms.

Fathers Talk

For myself, as a man who has never had a naturally born child, my grief often seems very clear. I can't have something that I very much want to have, and something that I have wanted to have for a very long time. It's something very basic and elemental that the majority of my friends and family have been allowed to enjoy. And, without getting too dramatic, it's a need and a right that extends back as far as any written religion, so I don't assume that I'm going to get over it any time soon. Seriously, childbirth is a major theme for all three major religions. How could I not be devastated?

Part of my grief is that, in all my life, I will never know what it is like to have a naturally born child. With my children-by-adoption, half of the time I think I am crazy. The majority of feedback that we receive is bad enough, since so many friends and family members seem to think that we will somehow find comfort in hearing that all of the problems are simply child-rearing problems which any family would face. We'd like to feel that isn't the case. But, it's so much worse, because we have no way of defining our opinions, we have no experience raising a birth child. How would we know the difference?

Part of my grief is that I will never know what it is like to see part of me or my wife in my child's face. I imagine that there must be a piece of immortality in seeing yourself "reborn" that way. It makes me a little choked up just to think about it. My neighbors just seem to take it for granted. To me, it feels like a handicap; like I've been amputated. I'll never know what it feels like to be whole in that way.

As men know, they become very uncomfortable when they feel they have no control over something that they expect to be able to handle, and they struggle with figuring out how to move beyond this. Throughout the adoption process, and in parenting birth and/or previously adopted children, as well as the adoptee with a traumatic past, there will be many areas that challenge men's sense of control. Many of the items listed hold true for women as well. Yet, again, loss of control seems to challenge men's self perceptions to a greater degree.

- Infertility—The ability to have a child by birth is not possible. Infertility treatments are a constant reminder of this loss of control over one's capacity to become

Fathers Talk

Adoption has been one of the greatest challenges to our marriage, and we've seen our share. I say that for one simple reason. Every time that my wife and I have faced a problem, it has been sad and painful, but we've always taken pride in the fact that it's made us stronger. At this point, when it comes to adoption, I don't feel as though I can say the same because we haven't yet found an "endpoint," and there doesn't seem to be one coming any time soon. I feel good about what we've done, and what we're doing, and I know that there have been dramatic changes in our family along the way. But stabilizing our family is a constant, preoccupying struggle every day, and even when we do find time as a couple, it's hard not to feel distracted. Maybe all of the growth that my wife and I experienced before we started our family was meant to prepare us for adoption. But for now, our focus is constantly split, and I honestly have to say that I miss the simple, undistracted union that I used to feel with my wife.

Fathers Talk

My biggest grief is that they (son and daughter) may never fit into mainstream society. If the problems continue, then we'll have more problems as they get older. Then there is much sadness because everything I missed growing up without a father I thought I'd be doing with my children. This is just passing us by. They are not able to have the kind of relationship I'd hoped for.

a parent in this "normal" manner. Sexual relations become scheduled and regimented. Spontaneity is lost. Sexual pleasure is diminished—"I am no longer in control of my sexual interactions with my wife."

- Sterility—The inability of the man to procreate may have a significant impact upon his sense of masculinity, of being a whole or real man.
- The home study—"I have to be 'approved' to be a parent." "I have to wait until the agency can schedule my home study." "I resent the extent to which our financial and family privacy is invaded in this process."
- Matching and pre-placement—"I have to wait on a bunch of social workers." "I am passed over for children with no explanation." "I don't hear back on children I am interested in." "I have little input as to when the child will arrive. Travel, pre-placement visits—mostly determined by others—usually women who don't understand me."
- Post-placement—"My newly adopted child does not respond to my discipline." "My wife is calling me at work for ideas. I hear him screaming in the background. I am helpless to offer solutions or to be there to stop him from treating my wife badly." "He hurts my other children, and often I cannot stop this. I am often at a loss to decide what to do." "I cannot take the time off from work to attend meetings and appointments. I must rely on my wife for information."

Obviously, after placement discipline becomes quite problematic. It affects the father's ability to operate a smoothly running household. It interferes with his interactions between his wife and children. He feels guilty for the impact of the adoptee on the brothers and sisters. He is uncertain how to parent a mix of healthy and traumatized children.

Roger, the adoptive father of two boys, one by birth and one by adoption, writes the following in which it is apparent his issues involving grief and the areas in which he is struggling to regain a sense of control.

Fathers Talk

The grief feelings I have center around what I envisioned our family would be and what it is. I dearly love my wife and daughter, but I still hold onto the desire for a happy, loving family. At times, I am sad, angry, emotionally withdrawn and depressed. I cling to the belief that with love our family will help our daughter through to adulthood and someday she will understand what my wife and I have done for her.

Fathers Talk

We adopted a son and daughter four years ago and completely put our life on hold, both growing with Dave (whom we adopted first) and together as a couple. Things have been really difficult. I think that the calmness is gone. The caring that I thought I had for children has been lost to some extent.

"I honestly thought that since we were adopting and 'giving a child a life he would not have in Russia' that this would be an extremely easy transition, much like with our natural child. I thought he would be a 'normal' child in every way. I thought he would adapt to our family and act like we taught him.

"I expected our birth child and our new child to be the best of friends. We adopted our son, Ray, at 8 months of age. At that time our birth child, Vince, was only 18 months older. Both were very young, so I thought they would act like 'twins' often do. They are now ages 6 (Ray) and 8 (Vince).

"The problems of attachment were barely mentioned to us. They were mentioned, but the agency gave us 'tips' on how to make attachment successful. Tips given included not letting anyone else hold the baby (not realistic) and staying at home totally for the first month (also not realistic). The impression I got from our agency was that the chances of not bonding were extremely slim, and if it did happen, doing the above tips would eliminate the problem.

"Prior to the adoption, we were not told anything about the effect a newly adopted child could have on a birth child. The only time our son Vince was mentioned was when we were told that he could not accompany us to Russia.

"Our marriage has been severely impacted. Ray has kept the stress level so high in our household and has managed to prohibit my wife and me from spending time together. I would say if it was not for our strong faith in God, our marriage would not have survived.

"I love Ray with all my heart and soul. But, if I had it to do all over again. . . . I would like to know exactly what to be prepared for. I only hope that no father goes through international adoption without being fully aware of the potential consequences—good AND bad. I consider myself fairly intelligent, and I certainly was blindsided by this entire situation. Without my wife's instincts, I would probably still be trying to parent my son-by-adoption just like I do my birth son. That would be a disaster! It's ironic that one reason (in fact, the main reason) we chose international adoption was the fact that it is so hard to adopt an infant in the United States, and we didn't want an older child because we thought they would have extreme emotional problems. And here we are!

Fathers Talk

I think my wife and I lost a lot with our older kids. We had two teenage daughters and then we adopted two younger daughters, ages 2½ and 5. We used to do a lot of things with our teens, and we used to sit and listen to them. We helped them with things. And, then it seemed like we just didn't have the time anymore for it. We couldn't give them the attention that we needed to. I think we maybe lost some of their trust to a large extent. I think the losses we have had so far—I don't think we'll ever get back.

Fathers Talk

Sometimes I don't cope very well. The personal effects of raising children with mental health issues can be difficult. I have sometimes disliked the person that I saw in the mirror or the person that I thought I was becoming. I have said and done things that I never thought I would say or do, and although I don't think I have crossed the line, legally or morally, I have come far closer to that line than I ever thought I would. This is no time to think that you are the dad from the 1950's sitcoms; the dad who can do anything and who knows all the answers, real life with these kids is not like "Father Knows Best" or "My Three Sons." In order to raise these children, and stay sane while you are doing it, you need to recognize that you will probably need help. Talk to somebody who knows what it's like to raise these kids. ***Most therapists have no idea***. I have spent time talking individually with a therapist to work through my anger and help me discover why a 9 or 10 year old (adopted at 1 year of age) could turn me into raving lunatic as well as discussing parenting strategies with a counselor who specializes in adoption of children with mental health issues.

"It is difficult for me to parent Ray and Vince. This has been my greatest task, and I struggle with it daily. When we first came home with Ray, we expected him to 'fit' right in with the family. We knew he might have slight developmental delays, but with all the research I had done regarding international adoption, I was convinced that Ray would quickly catch up developmentally—in a few months. And, in fact, physically he did. What I was not prepared for were the emotional delays he suffered from. It is this emotional growing process that has taken so much more time than I ever possibly imagined. I was depending on the old adage 'love conquers all,' and felt that with extra tender loving care it would soon be difficult to tell which child was adopted and which was biological.

"Initially, when we brought Ray home, I had a tendency to protect and nurture him more than my biological child. I had deeply rooted feelings that he had been 'wronged' by his biological parents, through no fault of his own. I was determined to make up for this by giving him special attention. I soon found that this began to cause jealousy with Vince. I honestly thought that Vince would understand *why* his adopted brother needed extra attention. I now see this was an impossible concept to expect Vince, now age 8, to understand.

"Ray creates havoc within our family by hurting or attempting to hurt Vince. It is very hard to tell Vince not to defend himself when he is repeatedly under attack by his younger brother. To make matters worse, we could not apply the same rules of discipline for both children. Vince would be reprimanded for the slightest infractions, while it seemed to him that Ray could get away with much worse infractions without being punished. We have come to realize that although Ray may have a 'big boy' body, emotionally he is, in fact, a very small child. I had to learn that our two children were distinctly different, and as such, they needed to be disciplined distinctly differently. 'One size' certainly does not fit all in this situation. It is a day-to-day struggle for me because it truly is not fair to Vince. Vince did not ask for this upheaval in his life; it was forced upon him by our desire for another child, coupled with our decision to adopt internationally. It is difficult to grasp the fact that when we unselfishly remove a child from a life with no future by bringing him into our family, then help to provide him with the endless possibilities he now has awaiting him, that he would not accept these options.

"The upside to this story is that our family continues to heal. As Ray continues to receive therapy, he continues to develop emotionally. Likewise, as Vince receives his own therapy, he continues to heal. He now seems to understand that each person is uniquely different, and that his brother, through no fault of his own, sometimes cannot stop the way he acts. I struggle to overcome feelings of guilt from putting Vince through this, and I sometimes struggle to overcome feelings of anger towards Ray for creating such turmoil with our family. It helps tremendously to understand that Ray cannot help a lot of his behavior, and he is (finally) making efforts to overcome burdens placed upon him by his biological parents."

As a second example of a father's emotional reactions to his children, Doug writes an account of his adoption experience. Overall, Doug's story exemplifies many of the points made throughout this chapter.

"When we decided to become foster parents, we did not expect to adopt any children. The family fell in love with our foster son, Brandon. I had five birth daughters, ages pre-adolescent and adolescent, and thought having a son around the house was a great idea. I had very few expectations going in. I assumed it would be just like having one of my birth kids in the house. I had significant reservations about the next three children we adopted. I am very concerned about the financial burden, the impact on the other children and our age (50s). My five birth children and my wife felt very strongly about the adoptions. While I disagreed with the decision, I felt that the larger burden would fall on my wife. I have a demanding job and work long hours.

"One very important mistake we made is underestimating the needs of foster children. We had kids previously that were very easy to raise—good grades, excellent behavior and didn't require a great deal of discipline. We assumed this would continue to be the case with foster and adopted children. Since the family felt so strongly about adoption, we felt that the kids would get along well. Again, a naïve opinion.

"I thought the county did a poor job of preparing us for adoption. The entire process is cumbersome, bureaucratic and isn't focused on the right things. Specifically, the focus could be on moving fast, getting the child placed in the right environment and preparing you for the children you are taking on. I believe the one thing we could have done was engage an adoption professional to assess our current situation, assess the child we planned on taking on and provide guidance. I would have gladly paid for this service. I think the county should offer it. I think the down side is that fewer children would be placed. I would have welcomed a third party expert opinion. I feel that we took this on because we loved

Fathers Talk

Marriage wise, I do believe in the past few years that has suffered. I believe that we were so caught up with arguing with Joy (adopted daughter) that I harbored much resentment against Joy and my wife because she wanted to adopt. I never expressed this to my wife until recently. Our lives were a constant fight and I resented the fact that even when I was not involved with the issues I was dragged into it as the enforcer. Phone calls in the middle of work from school or home often left me in a bad mood. I would walk in the door from work and enter the middle of a homework battle or worse. I couldn't go to the basement or yard without worrying about a fight erupting elsewhere. Joy knew how to push all of my wife's buttons to get her pissed off and I would jump in to defend my wife only to have my wife turn on me as part of the problem. I was exhausted. We had no idea why Joy did what she did.

the children and didn't want them to suffer through getting re-attached to another family. I didn't understand what I was really agreeing to take on.

"At times I feel angry and trapped. Many of my peers, at my income level, have things I could afford if I didn't have such a large family to support. It would be nice to have a vacation home, belong to a country club, travel more and have a maid. I enjoy getting away with my wife. That rarely happens; and when it does it feels like it may not have been worth the effort, particularly for my wife, who has to make all of the arrangements. I am very concerned about our mounting debt and inability to pay for my children's college educations. I like the Frank Sinatra line—'Regrets I have a few but then again too few to mention.' I used to always feel that way. Now I feel like I have enough to mention, particularly around my wife. I did underestimate how hard this would be on our marriage. I have lost individual time. The house is loud and when I come home from work I would like to have quiet.

"On the other hand, I do feel incredibly fortunate with how my life has turned out. We haven't faced serious medical issues, bad accidents, and we're too busy and we can't afford an affair. I feel loved and hopefully so does everyone in our family. I am a firm believer that what doesn't kill you makes you stronger and God only gives you as much as he thinks you can handle. My life is different than I planned. At times, I feel burnt out at work and would like to retire in five or so years but know that won't happen. But, all in all, I really don't have a lot of significant problems to complain about.

"There's a lot of anger in our house. I never thought I had the capacity to physically hurt a child because I was angry. Yet, my children-by-adoption can make me feel that way. After about the age of 5, my father never hit me or my siblings. My mom gave us occasional spankings. We had our share of yelling. I am able to control my anger only because I know, at times, our children we adopted don't have the capacity to control theirs. It's not something they are doing intentionally. But, their behavior, at times, requires me to walk away and count to ten. We also laugh a lot in our house. I strongly recommend that. It's easier when the kids burn off energy outside all day.

"I have the closest relationship with my oldest daughter. We think alike. I spent more time with her in the earlier years. I don't feel like I have a close relationship with the next four. There's a variety of reasons for this. Foster care and adoption had an impact. I could have made a better effort. My work hours certainly have had an impact. Betty, our daughter-by-adoption, is particularly attached to me and, one on one, she is absolutely delightful to be around. She wants to visit my mother every Saturday. She wants to go with me anytime I leave the house. When I take her, I enjoy the company.

"I consider all my kids mentally healthy. To some degree, I may have my head in the sand. The children we adopted have challenges, but it's becoming very manageable. I do think the techniques we learned in therapy have made a difference. I do think therapy is working.

Fathers Talk

Just finding someone to talk to, other than your spouse, can be a huge relief. The challenge is finding someone who won't just spout platitudes about how patience and love will win the day. Find an understanding person who is willing to listen or maybe an electronic support group over the Internet. I belong to an online hobby forum where I can chat daily with other adults and sometimes we share parenting frustrations as well as other off-topic discussions.

Fathers Talk

Parenting our children has been a real test of patience. You're constantly on high alert. Every minute is a constant battle of wills that tries your patience to the point of madness. Even the simplest of things that most take for granted is a huge ordeal. For instance, trying to have a conversation with my wife—there's almost never a time when we are not interrupted.

I have found it best not to set any expectation too high with the kids, or my wife for that matter. What doesn't work is coming home complaining to my wife about the normal things that just don't get done—dinner, keeping the house clean, or complaining that she's in a bad mood or depressed and telling her to snap out of it.

What works is coming home, giving my wife a big hug and then pitching in and having a united front where the children are concerned.

There really is no support for dads and that's probably our fault. We just don't talk about these things. The guys don't want to hear it. The best thing you could do for fathers is respite for him and his wife. We miss our wives. She is so drained she has no time or energy left for us by the end of the day. Respite gives us time to have some peace and quality time with our wife. It's rejuvenating. Without a very strong marriage, there's no way any couple could make it.

My children-by-adoption are yelling and hitting less. Bed time has improved dramatically. Sometimes they voluntarily go to bed the first time they are asked."

In conclusion, fathers need to develop an array of methods to react to difficult and highly stressful situations so that they can re-gain a feeling of being in control of their home. Professionals need to make efforts to assist fathers in developing and implementing new skills. Their losses need to be acknowledged and their grief facilitated. Chapter 8 is going to cover grief and the traumatic impact of the traumatized adoptee on each member of the adoptive family in significant detail. Chapters 9 and 10 will offer solutions to cope with grief and trauma.

Chapters 9 and 10 are also going to provide explanations about parenting roadblocks—new parenting tools will be offered. For example, men often begin to rely on instilling fear in the newly adopted child as a means to control the adoptee's negative behavior, and as a way to restore their control of their home. Instead, men want to develop trust. Trust entails respect and increased responsibility on the part of the adoptee as well as the birth and/or previously adopted children.

Men also tend to view the child's problems as the mother's fault as we learned when we discussed splitting in Chapter 1. In review, the child is often delightful with one parent—usually the father and difficult for the other—usually the mother. This will occur in heterosexual and homosexual relationships as well. The child projects his anger onto

Fathers Talk

I honestly have no idea how one copes without the help of Jesus Christ. The pressure is so intense and the grief so deep that I don't know how it can be supported without the help of Jesus.

Fathers Talk

Hobbies are good. Whether your hobby is in computers, stamp collecting, model building, bird watching or whatever, don't be afraid to stay involved in your hobby. Use it as a place to be in the company of other adults. Hobbies can be a place to get your head on straight or just be an emotional release where you can relax.

Likewise, don't be afraid to find a new hobby that you and your kids can do together. Working together building a Pinewood Derby car or model rocket can provide an invaluable opportunity to relate to your kids on a different level than what occurs in the normal day-to-day school/homework/piano lesson/soccer practice/bedtime routine.

the mother or onto the partner that he perceives as the mother figure. He is mad at his birthmother's lack of care and concern, and he is angry with her because she abandoned him. The adoptive mother figure receives this anger, as she is the mother available. The father figure dismisses the mother's concerns and experiences. He has not educated himself to understand this concept of splitting, and he spends less time with the child who has experienced trauma so he sees, and is the recipient of, less of the adoptee's negative behavior. Obviously, this lends to marital tension. It also causes discipline problems. The father feels as if the mother is "too hard on the child" so he becomes more lenient. Marital arguments increase affecting all of the children. The adoptee also suffers because he has two parents who are not providing consistent discipline and structure.

Chapters 9 and 10 will promote building trust, resolving splitting and suggestions as to how to parent a combination of typically developing children and traumatized children. This may mean parenting each child *differently* in order to parent *effectively*. Fathers are encouraged to read on to Chapters 9 and 10.

The Strength of His Support Network

Humans have developed a wide range of methods to adapt, to heal and to flourish. One of the most common and effective means, is to seek the understanding and emotional support of other people. In many cultures, women appear to be more open to establishing and maintaining a broad, healthy and long-lasting system of friendships than are men.

Men tend to have higher levels of emotional and social isolation than do women. Many men establish a very limited group of friends and neighbors with whom they can share their stories, dreams and problems. A man might have an old high school buddy that he can call from time to time to talk about sports, work or politics, but when he is in need of a trusted friend to share his personal fears about his capacity to be a good dad

Fathers Talk

I think as a Christian family, my wife and I, we knew that God was on our side. We did a lot of prayer, maintained our faith and had a lot of hope. We just never gave up. We do have a very strong marriage. We do love each other. We're not going to let things come between us. Things are going to chap us once in a while but we get over it. We spend time in prayer. Our church has been very supportive of us.

Fathers Talk

I personally think it is extremely difficult to get support from others. No one can truly understand, unless they're going through it. That means it needs to be through the wife, but she is naturally so overwhelmed that that is very hard. Support is helped by information. I've gotten a lot of information from our counselor and my research. I think the counselor needs to also help both the mom and the dad to understand that, while the role of the mom is primordial for attachment, the role of the father both in supporting and serving is essential, and becomes extremely influential as the children age.

to a traumatized child or to support the mother of their child in a skilled way, that isn't really on many men's horizons. He never really thought about or sought to establish that type of long-term, gut-sharing, tell-all friendship with another man. Indeed, up to now, it may have been only his wife with whom he shared intimacies like this, if he shared them with anyone at all!

Other men have been raised to recognize the benefit of such a support system. This dad might have a few friends from his work world, a couple of guys from his church or temple, several high school or college buddies and one funny guy from down the street that comprise his social network. He doesn't necessarily gather them all together on a regular basis, but he knows that if he needs to try to figure out a safe response to a challenging situation, he is not alone.

Women generally develop relationships and establish closeness with other women through conversation. It is quite common for a mother to call another mother and ask, "Can we get together to talk?" As they share their concerns and tell their stories, they are building the trust and closeness that are essential for a healthy and solid relationship. Women accomplish tasks by building relationships first.

Men, on the other hand, tend to gather around tasks in order to establish strong, trusting relationships and spend guy time together. For example, fathers might gather to watch a baseball game, NASCAR or Monday Night Football. They might play golf or poker, or go bowling, hunting or fishing. They might take a trip to the track or the casino, shoot some pool or buckets, or tinker under the hood of a car. While they are attending to a shared task, men are also engaging in conversation, involved in the give-and-take that helps men build trusting, healthy male-to-male friendships.

It is in these situations, these shared tasks, that fathers may feel free to discuss their fears, shift their gears, share some beers, shed their tears, and calm their rage about

Fathers Talk

The support I get mostly comes from myself. Next would be from my wife. I try not to burden my wife with too much. She has much worse issues with our daughter than I do. Having a child with attachment issues has proven to be a strain on our marriage. We differ at times in how to handle situations that arise at school, home and social settings. My wife and I don't go out as a couple very much at all now. Babysitters are burnt out quickly, and are hard to replace. Our work schedules have been altered to accommodate childcare. We don't vacation as much as we did before adopting. Our lifestyle has been altered, however, each night we still roll over to kiss each other goodnight.

concerns that are important for their mental health and the long-term survival of their families.

Unfortunately, too many social service professionals make this worse by ignoring fathers. Adoption support programs typically offer a range of resources for mothers, staffed by female service providers in a mother-friendly climate. These same agencies rarely employ any staffers who have real experience working effectively with fathers, nor do they often have any full-time male staff providing direct—face-to-face—services to fathers.

Yet, programs that include men or are designed for men demonstrate promise. Programs that included the below three criteria concluded that fathers reported less sadness, fatigue, pessimism, guilt and stress, as well as greater feelings of success, enhanced self-satisfaction and better decision-making abilities (Vadasy, Fewell, Meyer and Greenberg, 1985).

- peer support
- involvement with their children
- information relevant to their child's special needs and child development.

Regarding the latter point, men specifically seek information relevant to diagnosis and prognosis. A man's learning style is to gather and understand the data available so that he can address the condition with a focus on shaping his children's lives.

In conclusion, allowing men opportunities to gather may contribute to the well-being of each member of the adoptive family. Chapters 9 and 10 will demonstrate the need for fathers and mothers to prioritize taking care of themselves and each other. Self care and partner care is one of the most important points of this book—it is essential for the well-being of the parents and all of the children. There are also solutions in the resources section which follows.

Ten Suggestions for Adoptive Fathers of Children with Special Needs

1. Give yourself plenty of time, space and opportunities to process your reactions to the unfolding information about your child's condition and/or challenging behavior. Initial reactions of fear, anger, retreat, denial and sadness are normal, but may be over the edge or initially difficult to handle. *Take your time and pace yourself, but don't retreat from your parental responsibilities.*
2. Develop a plan to collect lots of relevant data, informational statistics or diagnostic materials about the specific condition of your child. Rarely is there a need to make any immediate decisions about your child's future. Speak with professionals and service providers with expertise who will help clarify your concerns in a calm and clear manner.
3. After discussion with your child's mother and other helpful family members, begin figuring out what your options are likely to be for your child, now and in the future. Give serious consideration to how you will support your other children's transitions. Focus upon avoiding the displacement pattern that many siblings experience when a child with a history of complex trauma takes so much time away from their family time.
4. Make it a priority to maintain and strengthen your relationship with your child's mother. Too many fathers place the primary focus on their children's needs, to the exclusion of their couple connection. Build in time for the two of you and respect that needed time.

5. Never give up your dreams for your child, but be open to adapting them as time progresses. Dreams don't die, they grow and shift and thrive.
6. Be open to meeting and talking with other fathers who have dealt with similar situations. Find a local father's program, a parent organization, your adoption agency or a family support group that encourages fathers to share insights and assist with problem-solving.
7. Get immersed in the daily routine of your child and family and learn to enjoy the journey. Enhance your knowledge of the ages and stages of child development, especially how her/his diagnosis will impact those stages. Pay attention to the details so you can anticipate and address situations that may add significant stress to your family dynamics. Most importantly—be there, be there, be there.
8. Tune in to your own needs and take care of yourself. Schedule your couple time, father/child time with each child you parent, mother/child time and alone time. Be especially open to feelings of grief and loss. Most men ignore or minimize these emotions and tend to express them through anger and control.
9. Become an advocate for your child. Learn how to positively navigate the systems that should and will be providing services for your child. Research and understand the laws that will affect your child—IDEA, IEP's, ADA, Section 504 and others (see Chapter 5).
10. Develop a list of targeted resources that are available to families of children with similar special conditions—medical, psychological, financial, social, educational, spiritual, cultural, legal, recreational, vocational and family supports.

Suggestions to Help Adoption Agencies Become More Father-Friendly

1. Expect staff to offer balanced contact with both parents.
2. Schedule home visits when both parents are home.
3. Avoid basing parenting responsibilities and preferences on gender stereotypes. One adoption staff person sat down only with Mom to show the preferred method to mix baby formula, and Dad was righteously upset that he was not expected to learn such a skill.
4. Sponsor occasional activities for dads and children: Be creative and offer a variety of activities, such as gym night, baking holiday goodies, kids' Olympics, Lego building, Saturday afternoon at the movies, planting a garden, arts and crafts fair or a fishing clinic. Try to avoid limiting your calendar to just building birdhouses before the third Sunday in June.
5. Occasionally break adoption training into separate groups for men and for women.
6. Invite birth and adoptive fathers to present on adjustments to the adoption process.
7. Recruit and hire male instructors and group facilitators to augment female staff.

Assessment Sheet for Agency Service Delivery: Fathers of Children with Special Needs

Use the following questions as a means for assessing your agency or organization's effectiveness in providing services for fathers of children with special needs. If you are the parent of a child with special needs, are the following ideas being implemented?

Yes No Service Delivery—Questions for Active Consideration:

☐ ☐ Do you have staff in-service programs about improving the quality of service delivery to fathers/males? Is some of the training provided by fathers themselves?

☐ ☐ Do you incorporate what has been learned from fathers into curriculum and in-service programs for staff and professionals?

☐ ☐ Do you actively recruit and employ male staff members?

☐ ☐ Do you have fathers on the agency's/organization's board and standing committees?

☐ ☐ Do you involve men/fathers in all aspects of program development, from policy making to implementation?

☐ ☐ When family/child intake is being completed, do you make an effort to have the father or a key male figure in attendance?

☐ ☐ At intake, if the father is not in attendance, do you inquire about him or other important male figures in the child's life? Do you make it clear that the father or other male figures are important and necessary in the delivery of services to the child and family?

☐ ☐ When a father/male attends a meeting with his wife or significant other, do you direct ideas and questions towards him? Do you let him know his input is valued and needed?

☐ ☐ When you telephone a family at home to discuss the child, do you talk with the father as well as the mother?

☐ ☐ If the mother is the custodial parent, do you also mail all materials regarding the child to the father (if approved and legally appropriate)? Do you give him adequate notice regarding upcoming meetings?

☐ ☐ When scheduling an I.E.P. or I.F.S.P. meeting, do you make every effort to have the father or important male in the life of the child in attendance?

☐ ☐ When scheduling an I.E.P. or I.F.S.P. meeting, do you give the family adequate lead time (at least two weeks) so all parental figures may arrange their work or personal schedule to attend?

☐ ☐ Does your agency/organization schedule the I.E.P./I.F.S.P. meetings at hours conducive to father attendance (i.e., lunch, early morning, late afternoon, periodic Saturday mornings)?

☐ ☐ Do you have fathers routinely involved in agency and organization services and programs (therapy, the classroom)?

☐ ☐ Does your agency/organization newsletter and printed material reflect the valuable concerns and roles men play in the lives of their children (i.e., a column written by a father, an article aimed at fathers); do your printed materials and hallways have pictures of men actively engaged with their children?

☐ ☐ Do you have programs aimed specifically at fathers (i.e., father panels, Pops 'n Tots nights, social occasions)?

☐ ☐ Do you have a father support program available in the agency or the local area? Do you give families information about such programs? Do you ask mothers if you can make a referral of the father to this program?

☐ ☐ Do you have fathers of children with special needs available on a one-to-one support basis for discussion, information and sharing?

☐ ☐ Do you have a quality resource library available (written, audio, video) so a father may gain necessary information about the special needs of the child? Are your materials available in a variety of languages?

Contact Information for the Author: Neil Tift, Native American Fatherhood and Families Association, Mesa Arizona, 480.833.5007, ntift@yahoo.com

Resources

The resources included reflect fathers' needs as well as books and websites related to couple's issues.

Books

Anderson, Kevin. *The 7 Spiritual Practices of Marriage: Your Guide to Creating a Deep and Lasting Love.* (Monclova, Ohio: CLB Press, 2005.)

Brott, A.A. and J. Ash. *The Expectant Father: Facts, Tips, and Advice for Dads-To-Be* (2nd Edition). (New York: Abbeville Press, 2001.)

Chapman, Gary. *The Five Languages of Love: How to Express Heartfelt Commitment to Your Mate* (Men's Edition). (Grand Rapids: Zondervan Publishing House, 2004.)

Cowan, Carolyn Pape and Philip A. Cowan. *When Parents become Partners: The Big Life Change for Couples.* (Philadelphia: Lawrence Erlbaum Associates, 2000.)

Gerrold, David. *The Martian Child.* (New York: Tom Doherty Associates, 2002.) This book is based on a true story of a single father adopting a son. The movie version is wonderful for the whole family.

Golden, Thomas R and James E. Miller. *When a Man Faces Grief: 12 Practical Ideas to Help You Heal from Loss.* (Fort Wayne, Indiana: Willowgreen Publishing, 1998.)

Golden, Thomas R. *Swallowed by a Snake: The Masculine Side of Healing.* (Gaithersburg, Maryland: Golden Healing Publishing, 2000.)

Gurian, Michael. *Love's Journey: The Seasons and Stages of a Relationship.* (Boston: Shambhala, 2001.)

Gurian, Michael. *The Good Son: Shaping the Moral Development of Our Boys and Young Men.* (New York: Penguin Group, 2000.)

Gurian, Michael. *The Wonder of Boys.* (New York: Penguin Group, 2006.)

Gurian, Michael. *The Wonder of Girls: Understanding the Hidden Nature of Our Daughters.* (New York: Simon and Schuster, 2002.)

Gurian, Michael. *The Minds of Boys: Saving Our Sons from Falling Behind in School.* (Hoboken: Jossey-Bass, 2007.)

Meyer, Donald J. *Uncommon Fathers: Reflections on Raising a Child with Special Needs.* (Bethesda: Woodbine House, 1995.)

Pruett, Kyle D. *Fatherneed: Why Father Care IS as Essential as Mother Care for Your Child.* (New York: Broadway Books, 2000.)

Pruett, Kyle D. *The Nurturing Father: Journey toward the Complete Man.* (Clayton, VIC: Warner Books, 1987.)

Tannen, Debra. *You Just Don't Understand: Women and Men in Conversation.* (New York: Harper Paperbacks, 2001.)

Books for Professionals

Lamb, Michael ed. *The Role of the Father in Child Development.* (New York: John Wiley and Sons, 1997, 3rd edition.)

Lamb, Michael, ed. *The Role of the Father in Child Development.* (New York: John Wiley and Sons, 2003, 4th edition.)

Websites

Children Now
www.childrennow.org

Children Now is a national organization for people who care about children and want to ensure that they are the top public policy priority. Children Now combines research and advocacy. They investigate media influences on children, children's health and healthcare, and education, and they promote ways of "Talking with Kids" about tough issues—sex, AIDS, violence, drugs and alcohol. This website is the home to the *Boys to Men* report quoted in this chapter. Fathers and mothers might also want to look at the Children Now report, *Reflections of Girls in the Media.*

Dads and Daughters
www.dadsanddaughters.org

This organization believes that all families benefit from active, engaged father/daughter relationships and that these relationships help girls grow and overcome obstacles. The content on the website is meant to maximize the power and potential of father/daughter relationships. The website is nicely organized with information for expectant fathers, and fathers of school-aged, middle school-aged, teenage and adult daughters.

The Fathers Network
www.fathersnetwork.org

The Fathers Network provides current information and resources to assist all families and care providers involved in the lives of children with special needs. This information is up-to-date, helpful and designed to promote the resilience of all family members. They have award-winning monographs, videos, newsletters and curricula available upon request. Visit their links about families, fathers, disabilities, health care and legal issues. Learn about their work in Washington state and their 15 statewide programs which provide powerful, positive support and fellowship.

MenWeb
www.menweb.org

This is a website with information for men regarding fathering, anger, grief and depression. MenWeb recognizes that men's issues are not *just* men's issues but issues for men and women. So, there is much information relating to marriage and relationships. MenWeb keeps men up to date with the latest books written with men in mind.

National Center for Fathering
www.fathers.com

The mission of the National Center for Fathering is to improve the well-being of children by inspiring and equipping men to be more effectively involved in the lives of children. The center was founded by Dr. Ken Canfield to conduct research on fathers and fathering, and to develop practical resources to prepare dads for nearly every fathering situation. This website has certainly accomplished this latter goal! There is information on any topic a father may want to explore. Additionally, there is an area for adoptive dads to post messages to each other.

National Child Care Information and Technical Assistance Center (NCCIC)
http://nccic.org/poptopics/fatherinvolvement.html

The link takes you directly to the "Fathers Involvement in the Lives of their Children" section of this organization. Fathers will find information about being involved in the care, education and support of their children. NCCIC is a service of the Child Care Bureau and it provides comprehensive child care information.

CHAPTER FIVE

Joining "Waiting" Families and "Waiting" Children: Matching Is Not an Exact Science

In 2005, 51,278 children were adopted from the public child welfare system and 22,170 children were adopted internationally (AFCARS, 2006; U. S Department of State, 2006). Thousands of adoptive families were created! Families who remain invested in the adoption process will likely find a child to join their family.

Matching is about joining a child with a family that can best meet the needs of the child. The information known about the child is shared with the prospective adoptive family. Subsequently, the adoptive family, typically in conjunction with a social worker, determines whether or not the family will accept placement of the child.

As Chapter 1 pointed out, the matching of children and families is not an exact science. The experience and knowledge of social workers, the perspectives of multiple caregivers, the availability of information, the depth and quality of information, the manner in which the information is presented, parental expectations, parents' willingness to listen critically and to ask for clarifications or expansions, and parents' level of education regarding trauma may combine to make the child's needs appear less than the child's actual issues. As the child's difficulties unfold post-placement, the family frequently feels that the child's history was misrepresented.

A main purpose of this chapter is to provide suggestions for interpreting a child's history so the family can make as informed a decision as is possible. The content of this chapter allows integration of material covered in the previous pages. Additionally, this chapter will expand the family's knowledge of special needs.

Throughout the chapter, we will begin to create a Prediction Path. The Prediction Path, developed by adoption expert Kay Donley Ziegler, is a valuable pre- and post-adoption tool. It will help us identify the potential needs of the child who has experienced trauma prior to the adoption. We can then identify the types of services the adoptive family may expect to utilize. We can determine strategies to promote the well-being of each member of the family. Overall, the Prediction Path helps prospective adoptive parents clarify what it will mean—for themselves and their resident children—to add a specific child to the family.

This chapter will cover points regarding inclusion of the siblings-to-be in the decision-making phase of the adoption process. A family will frequently receive little information regarding the potential of an older adoptee's capacity to form sibling relationships, even when the child has resided in numerous foster homes where there has been opportunity to interact with brothers and sisters.

Additionally, the exchange of information regarding specific waiting children is usually a process conducted among the adults: the parents and social workers. Unless parents take the initiative to conduct family meetings putting forth particulars about the new child, it is likely that the children already in the family will receive only bits and pieces of information about their potential new sibling. Chapter 1 pointed out that it is common to focus on the positive aspects ("I hear John likes to play baseball." "We were told that Sally enjoys crafts."). The cursory nature of the information given to the children already living in the family prevents them from anticipating potential difficulties. As Chapter 2 suggested, the family's manner of disseminating information directly influences the adjustment of the prospective brothers and sisters.

Guidelines for talking to your resident children about the potential new sibling were covered in Chapter 2's section "Preparing the Typically developing Children: Considerations." In this chapter, examples of talking with your resident children about the new child will be offered intermittently in "Family Talk" boxes throughout this chapter. As you come across these Family Talk blurbs, think about actually having such conversations with the children you already parent.

Sources of Information about a Referred Child

The sources of information about a child may include birth records, medical records, historical information regarding the issues that caused the child to come into care, birthfamily history, psychological/psychiatric evaluations, observations about current level of functioning, areas of progress, therapist's reports, school records, and input from previous and current caregivers.

The manner in which the child's history is delivered to the adoptive family varies. Some families will receive a packet of information in the mail. Some families will be invited to attend a meeting during which the history is presented verbally. Some families will be allowed to review the child's entire record. Some families will learn about their prospective child only when they arrive at an orphanage across the world! Some families will receive information in a combination of ways.

Following are descriptions of six waiting children—Eric, Renee, Marie, Christopher, Ava and Katie—and portions of their histories as provided to prospective adoptive parents. The type of information presented about each child is reflective of the kinds of specifics you will actually receive when you enter this matching phase of the adoption process. We are going to use these children and their referral information throughout the rest of this chapter. We are going to look at their history as presented, and we are then going to interpret the information. Ready?

> ***Eric*** is currently age 9. He is a Caucasian male in need of a home with his younger sister. He was born at 37 weeks gestation via a Cesarean section. His APGAR scores were 8 at one minute and 9 at five minutes. Eric was 5 pounds and 11 ounces at the time of birth. He was 19 inches in length. Eric was described as a normal newborn in the birth record. Eric was released into the care of his birthmother from the hospital. The birth records indicate that the birthmother denied any substance abuse during her pregnancy. However, his birthmother has a history of substance abuse issues (i.e., alcohol dependence, cocaine dependence, and marijuana use).
>
> Eric's birthmother was diagnosed with Dysthymic Disorder, Cocaine Dependence, Alcohol Dependence and Personality Disorder with Anti-Social traits. Eric's maternal grandmother has a history of depression and reportedly attempted suicide on at least one occasion. Eric's birth brother has been diagnosed with ADHD and Bi-Polar Disorder. Eric himself is

diagnosed with Nocturnal Enuresis, ADHD, Major Depressive Disorder, Adjustment Disorder with Mixed Disturbance of Mood with Conduct and Emotion, Mood Disorder, NOS, and R/O Bi-Polar Disorder. Eric has been prescribed several medications, over time, to help with these issues. The medications include Concerta™, Zoloft™, Ritalin™, Adderall™ and DDAVP.

The agency received numerous referrals about Eric and his siblings between 1997 and 2001. There were concerns that the utilities had been cut off because the birthmother had not paid them. The home was reported to be "deplorable." The children were urinating in a sink, causing a horrible smell in the home. Eric's oldest brother appeared to be caring for Eric and the younger sister. It was also alleged that the children had bruises on them all the time and that when asked, the children reported that their daddy or mommy hit them in the head. The children were reported to be dirty and unwashed. The birthmother seemed to have a new boyfriend every couple of months. The trailer was roach-infested. The birthmother was heard, by neighbors, screaming that she would break the children's "f------ necks." The neighbors reported that this went on "all the time." There were reports of drug use, and the neighbors indicated that the birthmother used monies given to her for food to buy drugs. The children finally came into care as a result of being left with a neighbor for several days. The neighbor called the police and stated that she could not care for the children, and that she did not know the whereabouts of their birthmother. The police were not able to locate the birthmother and as such, the children were placed in foster care. Eric was age 6. His sister was age 5. His older brother was age 10. The older brother eventually went to live with his birthfather.

Between 2001 and 2005, Eric and his sister moved through five foster homes. The first foster home was determined to be using inappropriate discipline. The next two foster homes requested removal of the children due to an inability to manage the children's behaviors. Eric and his sibling moved from their fourth foster home to an adoptive family. This placement disrupted and the children moved to another foster home where they have resided for the past nine months.

Eric has struggled with managing his behavior in the home and school setting. He has had problems with noncompliance, lying, stealing, tantrums and other disruptive behaviors. Many efforts have been made to stop the Nocturnal Enuresis. He has made improvements regarding this behavior and has been able to go for extended periods of time without wetting. During periods when he does wet, he often hides the evidence. Previous caregivers report that they feel that Eric and his sister are getting used to moving when they start to have problems or if they feel that they can get something better or less demanding elsewhere. Eric reportedly gets along well with others. He is very active and enjoys group sports.

The birthmother reported kidney stones and a hysterectomy. She stated that her mother had kidney problems and Diabetes. She also reported that Diabetes was present in her maternal grandfather and a maternal aunt. Paternity was never established.

Renee is a 7-year-old Caucasian female. She is pleasant and likeable. She is friendly and has a happy demeanor. She is playful and active. She does like to get her way and does tantrum, throw things and have strong outbursts when she doesn't get her way. She has anxieties and can become easily frustrated. She does like to play games. She enjoys showing you things that she has learned. She likes to sing and dance. She enjoys going to school. Reading is a particular strength. She enjoys playing with toys, doing arts and crafts, and watching television. Renee loves animals, especially dogs.

Renee is diagnosed with Sensory Integration Disorder, ADHD, PTSD, and Generalized Anxiety Disorder. She is currently taking Risperdal™ twice daily for her anxiety. Without the medication, she was biting her nails until her fingers would bleed. She was a crack-exposed baby. Upon entering foster care, a blood test revealed a high level of lead.

Renee came into care in 2002, at age 2½. She was first placed at the home of the maternal grandmother along with her older sister. Subsequently, the birthmother moved into this home. As such, the children were moved to a foster home. Six months later, Renee was moved to another foster home upon the request of the foster parents. They felt they were not able to deal with all of her needs and the needs of the other children in the home. Renee's sibling remained in the home. Renee continues to reside in her second foster home. This foster family is not interested in becoming adoptive parents due to their age.

The relationship between Renee's birthparents was violent, and Renee witnessed a lot of domestic violence. The family moved several times as they did not pay their bills. They utilized their money to buy drugs. Eventually the parents split up.

Renee's maternal grandmother and grandfather are married. They both work and have good jobs. They own their own home and take care of Renee's half-brother (i.e., both children have the same birthmother) who is mentally retarded.

The agency provided the birthparents with a case plan and referred them to services. They were provided with family preservation, drug assessment, random drug screens, drug treatment, domestic violence education, employment resources, safe and stable housing resources, day care assistance, psychological assessment and therapy. The birthmother failed to comply with the case plan. The birthfather did complete the case plan. However, he realized he was unable to care for his children. As such, he voluntarily agreed to allow both children to be adopted. A maternal aunt adopted Renee's sister.

Renee's birth was reported to be normal. She was born at 8 pounds and 4 ounces. She was 21 inches long. The hospital performed a toxicology screen and it came back negative. Renee has always had some delays with motor ability. She started school in a specialized pre-school program. Renee receives special education services. She has an individualized education plan (IEP) at school.

In Russia ***Marie*** resided with her birthmother for just six weeks. She was found, alone, in an apartment building. It is not known who found her. It is also not known who took her to the orphanage. The one-page summary provided to her now-adoptive parents explains that the birthmother was informed as to her child's place of residence. She knew that she was supposed to keep in touch with her daughter. However, for the whole period of Marie's ten month stay in an orphanage, her birthmother didn't get interested in her life.

Information about the birthmother shows that she had negative circumstances. She is alcohol abusive and hasn't been working for a long period of time. The birthmother was informed that a court hearing would be held to determine whether or not she would remain Marie's parent. She did not attend the hearing, so her parental rights were terminated.

Attached to this summary were a birth certificate and a list of immunizations Marie had received with minimal medical information. Marie was born at 36 weeks gestation. She weighed 2400 g, had a height of 48 cm and a head circumference of 31cm. There was also a note on the immunization report that the child presented with mixed disorders of "psychical" development.

Christopher was placed in an orphanage in Peru when he was one week old. His birthmother expressed an interest in terminating her parental rights. Fifteen months later, his adoptive family flew to Peru. They were provided with the birthmother's name, and they were told that she had placed her son in the orphanage due to poverty. The family was also informed that Christopher had spent the previous month in a hospital for a breathing problem. Apparently, he has been prone to these breathing difficulties, and he has needed medical care on several occasions. When sick, he eats little. As a result, he is malnourished.

Ava is a beautiful 12-year-old girl. She has a charming personality and a good sense of humor. She can be warm, affectionate and generous. She is very artistic. She is very bright; however, she does not live up to her academic potential.

Ava came to the attention of the agency when she was age 6. She and her siblings had been placed with a maternal aunt. This placement did not work out. The aunt became overwhelmed with the care of the children. She returned all but one child to the birthmother. At present, the aunt is the legal guardian of the sibling she kept.

Ava remained with her birthmother for three years. Then, her birthmother voluntarily placed all of the children in foster care. While in foster care, Ava alleged that her step-father had sexually abused her and her siblings. The step-father was charged and convicted of sexual abuse-related offenses.

The birthmother was unable to make any progress on her case plan goals. She abruptly signed over her parental rights. She then left the state without saying good-bye to any of her children.

Following is Ava's placement history:

Birth–November 1994	Birthmother and step-father
November 1994–June 1997	Maternal aunt
June 1997–October 1997	Birthmother and step-father
October 1997–March 2000	Foster home #1
March 2000	Psychiatric hospitalization
March 2000–May 2000	Residential treatment facility #1
May 2000–September 2000	Foster home #2
September 2000–March 2001	Foster home #3
March 2001–present	Residential treatment facility #2

Ava exhibits various difficult behaviors. She often refuses to complete her homework. She is argumentative. She is mouthy. She, at times, has tantrums during which she throws things. There was one occasion that Ava attempted suicide, but it was felt that this was more of an attempt to cry out for help rather than an actual desire to end her life. Placements in homes with other children caused Ava to be very jealous. She would compete for attention. This was one of the main reasons that the foster parents requested that Ava be removed from their home. Ava tests rules, boundaries and authority.

Ava has had extensive therapy. She has had individual therapy, group therapy, sexual abuse therapy, specialized adoption therapy, and she is prescribed medication to help stabilize her moods.

Ava has five birth siblings. As stated above, one resides with a maternal aunt. One is beyond the age of 18. He entered the military after foster care. The remaining three siblings remain in foster care. Separate adoptive placements are being sought for Ava and her siblings.

Ava has routine physical and dental examinations. Her general health is good.

Katie was abandoned in a hospital in Kazakhstan. At six months, she moved to an orphanage for children ages birth to 3. She was approximately 3 when she moved to an orphanage for children ages 3 to 8.

She came to America, at 6 years old, for six weeks. She was to stay with a host family who was also interested in adopting a child.

Within 24 hours, they requested her removal. She was moved to another host family for 24 hours. She was then placed with a family who had just completed a home study. She arrived with a leg injury sustained in a fall that occurred on an escalator at the airport. This third host family decided they were interested in adopting Katie. The adoption required that Katie return to Kazakhstan while the family completed additional paperwork. Nine months later the family arrived in Kazakhstan. Each day for three weeks, they visited Katie at the orphanage or took Katie on outings to a playground. The visits at the orphanage were all conducted in the same room. The family was prohibited from touring the orphanage, so they were only able to obtain photos of the visiting room and the outside of the orphanage. Other than learning the name of Katie's birthmother, the family was provided little information about Katie or her birthmother's decision to abandon her.

Interpreting the Information

Interpreting information means looking at what has been provided, as well as identifying additional sources of information. It also means, for the family, attempting to put emotions aside and to maintain a focus on the facts. This will be difficult for the family who is eager to provide a child a home.

Right now, I want you to take out some paper or get a highlighter. Review the cases for Eric, Renee, Marie, Christopher, Ava and Katie. If you have already adopted a child, consider using the history provided to you for your own child rather than the case examples. It is likely that you will learn something new. Outline the areas about these children and your family that you feel will contribute to post-adoption difficulties and then those that might contribute to post-adoption success. Then, read on. Throughout this chapter, keep asking

What does this information mean to us as parents?

What does this information mean for the children we are already parenting?

Are we the family for this waiting child?

Identify the Pre-adoptive Traumas

First, let's identify the types of traumas that occurred to each child. Each of our sample cases has experienced several of the pre-adoptive traumas covered in Chapter 2. Therefore, each may exhibit many of the issues presented in that chapter's discussion of complex trauma. Once you have completed your list, review the complex trauma portion of Chapter 2 and think about the types of issues each of our example children may present.

Chart out your findings in a fashion similar to the chart on page 69. After each major heading in this chapter, there will be a chart. Combined, the charts will become the foundation of our Prediction Path.

Now let's make some key points. Such key points will be made throughout the remainder of this discussion of interpreting a child's history:

Key Point—*Information received may contain conflicting facts.* In Renee's written summary, it is reported that, "She was a crack-exposed infant." It was also stated that, "The hospital performed a toxicology screen and it came back negative." Further, when the prospective adoptive family was provided copies of her psychological evaluations, two of the five evaluations described Renee as having Fetal Alcohol Effect. Agency staff were unable to provide definitive clarification as to whether or not Renee was exposed to substances prenatally. Such discrepancies present additional risks for the adoptive family.

TYPES OF TRAUMAS EXPERIENCED BY EACH CHILD		
Eric Neglect Physical Abuse Emotional Abuse Separation from a Sibling Abandonment Multiple Moves Suspected Pre-natal Substance Exposure Suspected Sexual Abuse	**Renee** Neglect Suspected Pre-natal Drug Exposure Domestic Violence Emotional Abuse Multiple Moves Separation from Siblings Abandonment	**Marie** Abandonment Multiple Moves Institutionalization Suspected Pre-natal Alcohol Exposure
Christopher Abandonment Institutionalization Hospitalization Multiple Moves	**Ava** Abandonment Separation from Siblings Sexual Abuse Domestic Violence Multiple Moves	**Katie** Abandonment Multiple Moves Institutionalization Suspected Sexual Abuse

Family Talk about Trauma

The typically developing child who receives pre-adoptive training will have familiarity with the types of trauma experienced by his new brother or sister. So, parents may initiate a conversation by referring back to the educational sessions, such as the following, for example.

"Do you remember when we went to the classes at the adoption agency? Good. We received some information about a girl named Renee. She is 7. It seems that her birthparents hurt her in several ways. She was often hungry and left alone. Her birthparents fought so bad the police were called to her birth home. She must have been so scared.

"She enjoys some of the same things we do like singing and reading. She also has some problems. She has temper tantrums and she throws things.

"We do have some ideas about how to help Renee with these tantrums. We will also be getting some help from a therapist, a person who helps kids like Renee, and from the social worker whom you already met.

"Do you have any thoughts about having a sister who yells and throws things?

"When we go to the meeting, we would be happy to ask any questions you may have. Write them down and give them to us."

This introductory conversation would work well with school-age and pre-adolescents. If the resident child is young, emphasize the potential safety issues involved with Renee and let the child know that you will be teaching him to go to a "safe spot" during Renee's tantrums in the event that Renee turns out to be the child the family adopts.

If the prospective brother or sister is a teen, it might make sense to include him in the information sharing meeting at the adoption agency. He needs to know as much about his new sibling as is possible in order to prepare for the changes in the family. He especially needs information about his new sibling if he will be providing any child care.

Key Point—*International children's histories are most often less informative than those of domestic children.* In the cases of Eric, Renee and Ava, we can capture some of the essence of their stark and terrifying lives. We have snapshots of their experiences due to the reports of neighbors and professionals who had contact with these children and their birth families. We have access to mental health records, school records, previous caregivers, professionals who have worked with the children and so on. For the international adoptees, on the other hand, much of the information we would like to have is not present. Frequently absent are maternal medical history; details on the pregnancy, labor and delivery; gestational age at delivery, whether or not the mother used drugs or alcohol; birthfamily mental health and medical history; developmental milestones; and information about personality, etc.[1]

Key Point—*International adoptees and domestic adoptees experience the same types of pre-adoptive traumas.* In the 2002 National Adoption Attitudes Survey, 53% and 63% of respondents respectively noted that medical problems and mental health issues were major worries when adopting from foster care. Excluding domestic adoption in hopes of avoiding medical or behavioral problems is flawed reasoning because the children currently available from abroad share many of the same risk factors and medical and behavioral problems as children in domestic foster care (Johnson, 2005). Overall, the outcome three years+ after arrival of children who spent eight months or more in institutional care looks like this.

- Thirty percent have several serious problems (e.g. IQ is less than or equal to 85, atypical insecure attachment, severe behavior problems, ongoing stereotyped behavior)
- Thirty-five percent have a few serious problems but are making progress
- Thirty-five percent have made wonderful progress.[2]

These outcomes are very similar to the rates of difficulties identified for children in U.S. foster care.

- A 1994 study by the U.S. Department of Health and Human Services found that 27 percent of the children in foster care were emotionally disturbed.
- And more recently, the American Academy of Pediatrics estimated that 30 percent of children in foster care have severe emotional, behavioral or developmental problems (The Casey Center for Effective Child Welfare Practice, 2000).

Identify Medical Needs

International Adoptees

Following are selected quotes from the University of Minnesota's, International Adoption Medicine Program. Their website is http://www.med.umn.edu/peds/iac/. The

1. University of Minnesota, International Adoption Medicine Program. "On Choosing a Child." [online]. http://www.med.umn.edu/peds/iac/choosing/home.html

2. University of Minnesota, International Adoption Medicine Program. "New Kids, New Challenges." [online]. http://www.med.umn.edu/peds/iac/topics/challanges/home.html

Family Talk about the Orphanage

"Your new brother is coming home from Peru. He has been living in the orphanage. What do you remember from the classes we went to?

"That's right. There are a lot of babies and only a few ladies to take care of all of the babies. So, your new brother may not know much about a mom, a dad, or a brother or sister. We will have a lot to teach him. He may not know how to play or how to eat correctly. We will have to be patient. He will be scared. He will be moving to a new country and a house with a family. This will all be new. We will have to understand that while we are all happy to be getting him, he will have feelings of sad, mad and scared. We will have to be patient.

"Let's review some of the books about adoption and the ones about having a new brother or sister that we have read. Would you like to start with *A Pocket Full of Kisses* (see Resources)?

"There will be times when we get very busy with your new brother. Let's talk about ways you can let us know when you need more of our time."

Chapters 6 and 9 will offer solutions for meeting the time needs of each child in the family. If your resident child has already experienced the arrival of a new child by birth or adoption, review those experiences. What went well about those additions to the family? What problems were there in those transitions? Talk about what may be different this time. Explain the unknowns presented in this chapter.

website contains a wealth of information. Please make sure to review the website prior to your adoption. The implications of this information will follow the passages below.

> "Kids aren't in orphanages because they come from loving, intact families with a good standard of living and ready access to good health care and nutrition. Abandonment by a destitute single parent with poor prenatal care and inadequate diet is the most common reason why a child is available for adoption. The second most common reason is termination of parental rights because of neglect and/or physical/sexual abuse (often alcohol-related). Over 50% of institutionalized children in Eastern Europe are low birth weight infants, many were born prematurely, and some have been exposed to alcohol while still in the womb. Finally, children with major medical problems or physical handicaps may be placed in orphanages by their parents due to limited access to corrective treatment and rehabilitation services. These kids are a high-risk group by any standard.[3] Although most children appear healthy and well nourished when they arrive in the United States, studies have shown that more than 50 percent have an undiagnosed medical condition at the time of initial evaluation in the United States, regardless of age, gender or country of origin" (Johnson, 1997).

> "An orphanage is a terrible place to raise an infant or young child. Lack of stimulation and consistent caregivers, suboptimal nutrition and abuse all conspire to delay and sometimes preclude normal development, speech acquisition and attainment of necessary social skills. Physical growth is impaired. Children lose one month of linear growth for every three months in an orphanage. Weight gain and head growth are also depressed. Finally, congregate living conditions foster the spread of multiple infectious agents. Intestinal parasites,

3. University of Minnesota, International Adoption Medicine Program. "A Letter from Dr. Dana Johnson." [online]. http://www.med.umn.edu/peds/iac/topics/letter/home.html

tuberculosis, hepatitis B, measles, chickenpox, middle ear infections, etc. are all found more commonly in institutional care settings".[4]

"Head growth has been used by generations of healthcare providers as a marker of brain well-being. Plotting head growth is a ritual in the offices of child healthcare providers world-wide, and children whose heads measure too small or too large for their age are viewed with great concern. However, problems may be encountered with obtaining and interpreting this measurement. These problems are magnified when the child's head is being measured by another individual and interpreted in the absence of complete medical and social information about the mother and child. Nevertheless, head circumference is one of the few pieces of objective information usually included in the referral document."[5]

"It is our observation that a number of Chinese children arrive with bone fractures. Rickets is a common diagnosis on Chinese medical forms. Our studies have confirmed that the older a Chinese child is on arrival, the greater the risk of rickets. Thus, fractures may be due to this nutritional disorder as well as abuse. Any child who arrives with bone deformities, swelling or tenderness should be evaluated for fractures and rickets. Not only is this important in terms of the child's well-being, it is important for the adoptive family's safety to document that these fractures occurred prior to the child's arrival in their home."[6]

"We have recently found that approximately 60% of children who were reported to have received three or more Diphtheria, Pertussis, Tetanus (DPT)/oral polio (OPV) vaccines in China, Russia or Eastern Europe have no antibodies for these diseases. This means that the vaccines used were outdated or improperly stored, the child lacked an appropriate immunologic response after vaccination, or the vaccination certificate is fraudulent."[7]

"Children in Korea and Guatemala are carried as infants and young children. China has a practice of swaddling children in multiple layers of clothing. This restricts movement. These cultural practices inhibit the development of gross motor skills."

"Ninety percent of the information received by prospective international adoptive families lists specific medical diagnoses. However, many of these diagnoses are obscure, utilize arcane terminology, or have terrifying prognoses. The use of medical terminology differs among countries. Complicating this matter is that a diagnosis may also be applied in situations in which the orphanage director does not want to appear to be placing too many 'normal' children abroad or if the institution wants to be eligible for additional funding. The indiscriminate and non-medical use of these and other terms has led many adoption professionals to advise their clients to ignore the medical diagnoses listed in their child's medical history."[8]

---

4. University of Minnesota, International Adoption Medicine Program. "A Letter from Dr. Dana Johnson." [online]. http://www.med.umn.edu/peds/iac/topics/letter/home.html

5. University of Minnesota, International Adoption Medicine Program. "How to Measure Head Circumference." [online]. http://www.med.umn.edu/peds/iac/topics/headgrowth/home.html

6. University of Minnesota, International Adoption Medicine Program. "Bony Fractures, Physical Abuse and Rickets." [online]. http://www.med.umn.edu/peds/iac/topics/bonphysrick/home.html

7. University of Minnesota, International Adoption Medicine Program. "Immunizations." [online]. http://www.med.umn.edu/peds/iac/topics/immunizations/home.html

8. University of Minnesota, International Adoption Medicine Program. "Understanding Medical Information." [online]. http://www.med.umn.edu/peds/iac/topics/medinfo/home.html

"If the pre-adoptive parents received a videotape of the child available for adoption, the video only captures a tiny fraction of the child's life. The bright lights, additional attention and conflicting commands from caregivers often confuse a child—portraying them as either immobile, non-communicative zombies, or as performing puppets with little sense of self-direction or awareness. Time of day and relationship to mealtimes make a tremendous difference in how a child responds. A video is rarely well enough made or of sufficient technical quality to confirm a specific medical diagnosis; it is another piece of information. While all pieces of information are valuable, remember to interpret it in the context of all other information available on your child."[9]

"Learn about the country from which you are adopting. There is a direct relationship between a nation's economic status and its health care delivery system. Therefore, children from a country where economic standards are high will receive good health care, immunizations will be up to date, medical information will be accurate, and the possibility of getting follow-up information will be quite good. The opposite is true in destitute countries—children are at increased risk for a variety of infectious diseases, immunizations will be incomplete or non-existent and information may be inaccurate, with little likelihood that additional information will follow."[10]

Domestic Foster Care Adoptees

Children who enter foster care in the U.S. are often in poor health. What's more, the healthcare these children receive while in placement is often compromised by insufficient funding, poor planning, lack of access, prolonged waits for community services, and lack of coordination among health and child welfare professionals (*Pediatrics*, 2002).

Information about health care services children received prior to placement in foster care is often hard to obtain. For example, Ava resided with her birthmother and birth aunt for 8½ years, during which the family moved back and forth between two counties. When the children were sick, the birthmother utilized the nearest emergency room. There was no family physician. Gathering Ava's medical history was an arduous task. This undertaking was made more complicated because Ava moved six additional times once in foster care. Each of these residences was in a different city, and so a new physician was utilized with each move.

Foster care parents often have been given limited training in health care issues or in accessing the health care system. Social workers frequently lack information about the type of health care services that children in foster care receive and are, therefore, unable to effectively oversee the amount or quality of care delivered (*Pediatrics*, 2002). Renee's case serves as a good example.

It was obvious to Renee's current foster family that Renee's speech was poor. She was very difficult to understand. The social worker felt that she simply needed time to "catch up" and so would not authorize approval for a speech and language evaluation. The foster mom, persistent, spoke to the physician. His office located early medical records at a hospital near where the birthfamily had resided. The records confirmed chronic otitis media (i.e.,

9. University of Minnesota, International Adoption Medicine Program. "Understanding Medical Information." [online]. http://www.med.umn.edu/peds/iac/topics/medinfo/home.html

10. University of Minnesota, International Adoption Medicine program. "Planning for Health Needs." [online]. http://www.med.umn.edu/peds/iac/topics/planning/home.html

ear infections). Due to this history, he ordered a hearing test which confirmed a hearing loss. Subsequently, Renee was referred for the necessary services.

In the midst of this, Renee was presented to a potential adoptive family. This new information was not included in referral documents, as the worker was unaware of the foster mom's activities. The adoptive family learned of Renee's history of speech and hearing difficulties at their first pre-placement visit with Renee.

Stories such as this are not rare. In placing children in adoptive families, it is not uncommon to learn of their asthma, allergies, dental needs, hearing problems, vision problems, and physical, occupational and speech therapy needs after placement in the adoptive family.

Additionally, children entering foster care are likely to be incompletely immunized, and determining the types and number of immunizations that a particular child has received in the past may be difficult. Young children entering foster care come from settings in which substance abuse and sexual promiscuity are common. They should be considered at high risk for HIV infection, hepatitis, and other sexually transmitted diseases (*Pediatrics*, 2002).

Key Point—*Many medical needs will be identified after the adoption.* The preceding content identifies numerous reasons that cause families to receive sketchy medical information. Clearly, many medical needs may become apparent after the child is placed with the family, no matter if he is a domestic or intercountry adoptee.

Key Point—*Adoptive families must determine who will provide medical care to their adoptee.* Neither international nor domestic adoption is well-addressed during medical training (Johnson, 2005). The family physician may not be the best qualified care provider for a child born in another country. There are now approximately 50 adoption medical clinics in the United States. These clinics, even if they require a lengthy trip, may prove an invaluable resource. Their broad knowledge of the health concerns of international adoptees as well as their country-specific familiarity will ensure early identification of any health related matters. Many of these clinics provide services to domestic adoptees as well. Most offer pre- and post-adoption services to families, and are ready and willing to assist local care providers as requested.

Now, let's return to our example children and fill in information that we would associate with medical care. This will allow us to make another key point.

Key Point—*Pre-adoptive preparation and books such as this one focus on the broad picture in terms of the needs presented by waiting children.* The content puts forth areas of concern common to the population of waiting children. A formal presentation of a particular child will often reveal child-specific needs. For example, Renee's history mentions that there was a high level of lead in her system upon her entering foster care. It is also stated that she has a Sensory Integration Dysfunction. Christopher suffered from malnutrition (see Chapter 2). These issues compound those posed by complex trauma. Let's use lead as an example.

Babies and young children are especially susceptible to lead exposure because they have a tendency to put objects in their mouths. They may eat or chew paint chips, or their hands or other objects placed in their mouths may

MEDICAL NEEDS OF EXAMPLE CHILDREN		
Eric Nocturnal Enuresis Stated to have a "normal" birth history Maternal history of diabetes and kidney problems	**Renee** Stated to have a "normal" birth history History of chronic otitis media Hearing loss (identified at pre-placement visit) Sensory Integration Dysfunction Lead exposure Gross motor delays	**Marie** Mixed disorders of "psychical" development Head circumference 31cm Birth weight 2400g Birth length 48 cm
Christopher Breathing problems—(no specific diagnosis provided) Malnutrition	**Ava** Ava has routine physical exams and dental examinations. Her general health is described as "good."	**Katie** Hepatitis B (identified after the adoption)

be contaminated with lead dust. Lead poisoning is more dangerous to fetuses, babies and children than to adults because lead is more easily absorbed into growing bodies. The tissue of children also is more sensitive to lead's damaging effects.

Lead poisoning is still a problem, especially in low-income children, urban children, and those living in older housing. It is estimated that 2.2% of children in the United States (about 434,000 children) aged 1–5 years have a blood lead level greater than or equal to 10 mcg/dL, the level at which lead is thought to cause harmful health effects.

Concerning new reports show that there may be no safe lead levels. Some recent reports have shown small declines in IQ points for children even if their lead level was less than 10 mcg/dL. Another report showed a delay in when puberty begins in girls with lead levels less than 3 mcg/dL.

Each year more than 100,000 children are adopted in the United States. Almost 22,000 of these children are from overseas. The number of international adoptees has been consistently increasing (though there was a downward trend in 2007). In many of the foreign countries from which families adopt most often, the documented risk for lead exposure is much higher than in the United States.

Exposure to even low levels of lead may cause brain damage, nervous system damage, kidney damage, learning disabilities, speech and language problems, behavioral difficulties, poor muscle coordination, decreased muscle and bone growth, and hearing damage.[11]

11. Mayo Clinic. "Lead Poisoning." [online]. http://www.mayoclinic.com/health/lead-poisoning/FL 00068

Key Point—*Today's adoptive family has a wealth of opportunity to investigate the needs presented by the child about to enter the family*. For that matter, so do professionals. These facts about lead presented above were gathered in a few minutes using Google. Certainly a more thorough search would uncover a greater depth of data. The point is that adoptive families are at an advantage in this day and age of the Internet. It is easy to locate information. Subsequently, the family can review their findings with a qualified professional. Give it a try. I did not search Sensory Integration Dysfunction (SI). See what you find and think about what SI may mean to the adoptee, the siblings-to-be and yourselves.

Identify Mental Health Needs

AD/HD, ODD, PTSD, RAD—what is all of this alphabet soup anyway? All of these are mental health disorders as identified by the *Diagnostic and Statistical Manual of Mental Disorders* (DSM-IV-TR) compiled by the American Psychiatric Association. Diagnosing mental health disorders is similar to the manner in which physicians diagnose the

Family Talk about Mental Health Disorders

Children of all ages can most likely equate a mental health disorder with a medical problem. You might talk to your children about mental health issues like this.

"Do you remember when you were sick and we took you to the doctor? He gave you some medicine. You stayed home for a few days and felt better. Well, your new sister has some mental health problems. Her birthparents hurt her and so she doesn't feel very good about herself. She is all mixed up about parents and living in a family. She needs medicine to help her think better. We will be going to therapy with her. She will talk with the therapist and this will help her realize that we are a good family who won't hurt her. This is going to take time. Let's see, you are 9 now. She may be better when you are 10 or 11. It may even be longer.

"The actual names of her problems are Bi-polar Disorder and AD/HD. These are some of the ways she may act. She may get really sad and then really happy. Sometimes she will be cranky. She may forget things. She may sleep a lot. Sometimes, she won't want to play with you. This has nothing to do with you. She may also have a hard time sitting still. She may not be very good at sharing or taking her turn. This may make watching a movie, getting homework done or playing a game difficult.

"We are reading and going to a support group for parents who have children with AD/HD. So, we will be learning ways to handle this. We will be passing on what we learn to you.

"Do you have any questions? What do you think? If you think of any other questions, let us know. Let's talk about this again in a couple of days after you have had time to think about this."

Search the Internet and find age-appropriate information for your children regarding their new sibling's mental health issues. If you have adolescents who are bilingual—English and computer—have them assist you in finding information regarding the potential adoptee's mental health disorders. Make sure you or your teen visit the Channing Bete website (see Resources). This company makes booklets about mental health disorders (and medical illnesses). They are written in a style great for kids.

flu, diabetes, cancer, high blood pressure, etc. The client provides the mental health professional—psychiatrist, psychologist, social worker, counselor, therapist (see Chapter 10)—with symptoms, information about the onset of the problem, relevant history, reports of previous treatments, reports of previous means the client attempted to solve the problem and so on. The mental health professional then determines the correct diagnosis or name of the problem. Subsequently, a treatment plan is formed. That is, goals for what is to be accomplished are set, and the specific interventions or ways of accomplishing the goals are listed.

It will be quite common to see a list of mental health disorders[12] in the content of history documents of domestic adoptees such as we see in Eric's history. Among those commonly seen are

Adjustment Disorder
Asperger's Disorder
Attention-Deficit / Hyperactivity Disorder (AD/HD)
Bi-polar Disorder
Conduct Disorder
Dysthymic Disorder (i.e., depression)
Generalized Anxiety Disorder
Obsessive-Compulsive Disorder (OCD)
Oppositional Defiant Disorder (ODD)
Pervasive Developmental Disorder (PDD) / Autistic Spectrum Disorders
Posttraumatic Stress Disorder (PTSD)
Reactive Attachment Disorder (RAD)

It will be routine to see that medication is being utilized to help reduce the symptoms of the child's mental health disorders. Again, in Eric's case, he has been prescribed such medications as Concerta™, Zoloft™, Ritalin™, Adderall™ and DDAVP. Parents have many questions and concerns about the use of medications. Adoptive parents may want to consider having a conversation with their family physician or a psychiatrist (see Chapter 10) prior to adopting a child who will arrive with medications in his baggage. Questions parents may want to ask include

How does the medication help?
What are the side effects that commonly occur with the medication?
Is the medication addictive? Can it be abused?
How often is the medication typically taken? In what dosage?
Are there any laboratory tests which need to be done while my child is taking the medication?
How often will there be a medication check?
Are there any other medications or foods which my child should avoid while taking the medication?
Are there any activities my child should avoid while taking this medication?

---

12. In this book, the term *mental health disorders* is being used to describe actual mental health diagnoses as well as terms used in other sources such as *emotional problems*, *behavioral problems*, *serious-emotional disturbance*, etc. It is believed that the term *mental health disorders* is less confusing to the reader.

How long will my child need this medication? How will the decision be made to stop the medication?

What do I do if a problem develops?

Does my child's school nurse need to be informed about the medication?[13]

The National Institute of Mental Health's (NIHM) website offers an in-depth look at mental health disorders. It is certainly suggested that an adoptive family review each diagnosis listed in the information given to them about any specific child. For example, if we look at the NIHM website for AD/HD,[14] some of the symptoms include:

- *Impulsiveness:* Impulsive children seem unable to curb their immediate reactions or think before they act. They will often blurt out inappropriate comments, display their emotions without restraint and act without regard for the later consequences of their conduct. Their impulsivity may make it hard for them to wait for things they want or to take their turn in games. They may grab a toy from another child or hit when they're upset. Even as teenagers or adults, they may impulsively choose to do things that have an immediate but small payoff rather than engage in activities that may take more effort, yet provide much greater but delayed rewards.
- *Hyperactivity:* Hyperactive children always seem to be "on the go" or constantly in motion. They dash around touching or playing with whatever is in sight, or talk incessantly. Sitting still at dinner or during a school lesson or story can be a difficult task. They squirm and fidget in their seats or roam around the room. Or they may wiggle their feet, touch everything, or noisily tap their pencil. Hyperactive teenagers or adults may feel internally restless. They often report needing to stay busy and may try to do several things at once.
- *Inattentive:* Inattentive children have a hard time keeping their minds on any one thing and may get bored with a task after only a few minutes. If they are doing something they really enjoy, they have no trouble paying attention. But focusing deliberate, conscious attention to organizing and completing a task or learning something new is difficult. Homework is particularly hard for these children. They will forget to write down an assignment, or leave it at school. They will forget to bring a book home, or bring the wrong one. The homework, if finally finished, is full of errors and erasures. Homework is often accompanied by frustration for both parent and child.

Bi-polar Disorder[15] symptoms are described on the NIHM website like this.

> Children and young adolescents with Bi-polar Disorder often experience very fast mood swings between depression and mania many times within a day. Children with mania are more likely to be irritable and prone to destructive tantrums than to be overly happy and elated. Mixed symptoms also are common in youths with bipolar disorder. Older adolescents who develop the illness may have more classic, adult-type episodes and symptoms such as those listed on the chart on page 179.

13. American Academy of Child and Adolescent Psychiatrists. "Psychiatric Medication For Children And Adolescents Part III: Questions To Ask." [online]. http://www.aacap.org/cs/root/facts_for_families/psychiatric_medication_for_children_and_adolescents_part_iii_questions_to_ask

14. National Institute of Mental Health. "Attention Deficit Hyperactivity Disorder." [online]. http://www.nimh.nih.gov/health/topics/attention-deficit-hyperactivity-disorder-adhd/index.shtml

15. National Institute of Mental Health. "What are the Symptoms of Bi-polar Disorder." [online]. http://www.nimh.nih.gov/health/publications/bipolar-disorder/symptoms.shtml

BI-POLAR DISORDER SYMPTOMS	
Symptoms of Manic Episode	**Symptoms of Depressive Episode**
Increased energy, activity and restlessness	Lasting sad, anxious or empty mood
Excessively "high," overly good, euphoric mood	Feelings of hopelessness or pessimism
Extreme irritability	Feelings of guilt, worthlessness or helplessness
Racing thoughts and talking very fast, jumping from one idea to another	Loss of interest or pleasure in activities once enjoyed
Distractibility, can't concentrate well	Decreased energy, a feeling of fatigue or of being "slowed down"
Little sleep needed	Difficulty concentrating, remembering, making decisions
Unrealistic beliefs in one's abilities and powers	Restlessness or irritability
Poor judgment	Sleeping too much, or can't sleep
Spending sprees	Change in appetite and/or unintended weight loss or gain
A lasting period of behavior that is different from usual	Chronic pain or other persistent bodily symptoms that are not caused by physical illness or injury
Increased sexual drive	Thoughts of death or suicide, or suicide attempts
Abuse of drugs, particularly cocaine, alcohol and sleeping medications	
Provocative, intrusive or aggressive behavior	
Denial that anything is wrong	

It should be obvious that such a review of listed diagnoses gives the family greater insight into the types of challenges the child they are proposing to bring into the family may present. On the other hand, diagnosis, like many other areas covered, is not an exact science. For example,

- If we look at the symptoms listed for AD/HD and Bi-polar Disorder we can see that many of the symptoms are the same. In fact, in children and adolescents it can be hard to tell one problem apart from another. While irritability and aggressiveness can indicate Bi-polar Disorder, they also can be symptoms of Attention-Deficit/ Hyperactivity Disorder, Conduct Disorder, Oppositional Defiant Disorder, or other types of mental health disorders more common among adults such as major depression. Drug abuse may cause a similar set of symptoms as well.[16]
- Diagnosis is limited by the DSM-IV-TR. The complex trauma symptoms presented in Chapter 2 are a systematic means to describe trauma. Complex trauma is not a diagnosis.[17] In fact, the DSM-IV-TR has limited diagnoses that adequately portray children who have experienced trauma. So, a child must often be assigned several diagnoses to encompass the symptoms presented. Can you imagine if you had

16. National Institute of Mental Health. "Can Children and Adolescents have Bi-polar Disorder?" [online]. http://www.nimh.nih.gov/health/publications/bipolar-disorder/can-children-and-adolescents-have-bipolar-disorder.shtml

17. Complex trauma has been submitted as a diagnosis to be called, Developmental Trauma Disorder, for the next version of the DSM-IV-TR.

to go to your medical doctor and receive four diagnoses instead of one? What would you think? However, this is currently the way the mental health system operates. There are professionals attempting to correct this situation and indeed a new version of the DSM is underway. However, resolution of this matter is many years away.

- Diagnosis implies a course of treatment. In the same way that diabetes, high blood pressure or cancer lead to a course of therapy, a mental health diagnosis does as well. Unfortunately, many families pursue a course of treatment exclusive of the other issues with which their child presents. It is not uncommon that families receive a diagnosis of AD/HD, Bi-polar Disorder or Dysthymic Disorder and then pursue interventions relevant to those disorders. Certainly, the child may indeed have the particular mental health disorder. However, as time goes on, only some of the child's problems dissipate. This is often because there was a failure to look broadly enough at the child's presenting symptoms. We must make more effort to look at the child as a puzzle with each of the pieces of complex trauma. Each of the pieces needs treatment to bring the child to an optimal picture of well-being.
- Maintaining accurate diagnoses requires re-evaluating the child over time. As Chapter 8 will describe, issues are developmental. That is, what a child thinks about her abandonment at ages 5–7, 9–11 and in adolescence is different. The same may be said for abuse issues. Some mental health disorders are more prone to onset at later ages. Schizophrenia, for example, is most likely to manifest in men in their late teens or early twenties, and women in the twenties and thirties.[18] The child who may have had a successful course of therapy at age 9 may require another course of therapy, or may develop additional mental health diagnoses in adolescence or young adulthood.
- Diagnosis is complicated when the family history is unknown. Of our six example children, there is limited to no history of mental health disorders presented regarding the maternal or paternal side of the birthfamily. The family doctor uses medical conditions that are common to the family to aid in diagnosis. Mental health professionals do the same. This lends to more accuracy in making a diagnosis. Most often in adoption, we lack sufficient family history. This renders assigning a diagnosis more difficult.
- Diagnosis is affected by the experience and knowledge of the professional.

"All families seeking mental health services for their children confront a patchwork of underfunded services and supports, guided by an often-bewildering mix of theories, philosophies, and treatment interventions. The vast majority of families—adoptive or otherwise—inevitably rely on publicly funded services or services available through private health insurance programs. Thus, they routinely face limitations in the availability, intensity, and duration of mental health services. The challenge of finding competent mental health services is even more complex when adoption-related issues are a component of the mental health services (Casey Center for Effective Child Welfare Practice, 2000)."

"Although adopted children and adolescents comprise only a small minority of the population in the United States, Canada and other countries, they have been reported to account for a significant number of young patients treated in mental health settings. Adopted children are three to six times more likely than non-adopted peers to be referred for mental health services (Ingersoll, 1997)."

18. National Institute of Mental Health. "Schizophrenia." [online]. http://www.nimh.nih.gov/health/topics/schizophrenia/index.shtml

Key Point—*Many families will adopt children with mental health disorders.* In some cases, these needs will be identified prior to the adoption. In other cases, the mental health needs will be identified as the family becomes familiar with the child or as the child matures.

Key Point—*There is a mismatch between the population of adoptive families needing services and mental health providers who understand the needs of each member of the adoptive family.* Locating a competent adoption-literate and trained mental health provider may prove challenging.

Key Point—*Most families obtaining mental health services should see progress within one year.* If no progress is occurring, this warrants a discussion with the mental health provider. ***Progress does not mean "fixed" or "cured."*** Progress means there should be improvements in the way the adoptee, parents, brothers and sisters act and interact. There are cases where the mental health issues are severe and progress may take longer. These are usually the exception rather than the rule. If there do not seem to be valid reasons for the lack of positive growth, it may be time to consider seeking a new mental health professional.

Parents can call prospective mental health providers or schedule an initial interview to find out basic information. Some therapists will offer an initial brief consultation that is free of charge. Even if you must pay for this, ensuring that the mental health professional is adoption competent can save much time and money in the long run. The following are some questions to discuss:.What is your experience with adoption and adoption issues?

How long have you been in practice, and what degrees, licenses or certificates do you have?

What continuing clinical training have you had on adoption issues?

Do you include parents and siblings in the therapeutic process?

Do you prefer to work with the entire family or only with the children?

Do you give parents regular reports on a child's progress?

Can you estimate a timeframe for the course of therapy?

What approach to therapy do you use? Why do you think this is effective?

What changes in the daily life of the child and family might we expect to see as a result of the therapy?

Do you work with teachers, juvenile justice personnel, daycare providers and other adults in the child's life when appropriate?

Do you offer emergency coverage outside of your regular office hours?

What are your appointment times and availability?

What type of payment options do you offer (e.g., private insurance, sliding-scale fees, Medicaid, adoption subsidy monies, etc.) (Child Welfare Information Gateway, 2005).

A chart for our example children appears on page 182.

Identify Cultural Needs

Long-term Cultural Needs

Christopher, Marie and Katie's adoptive placements will be transcultural based on the definition of a transcultural adoption offered in Chapter 3. Renee, Ava and Eric

MENTAL HEALTH DISORDERS OF EXAMPLE CHILDREN		
Eric AD/HD Major Depressive Disorder Adjustment Disorder Mood Disorder, NOS R/O Bi-polar Disorder	**Renee** AD/HD PTSD Generalized Anxiety Disorder	**Marie** Unknown
Christopher Unknown	**Ava** Bi-polar Disorder PTSD RAD ODD These were ascertained by talking with Ava's therapists.	**Katie** PTSD ODD AD/HD These mental health disorders were identified after the adoption.

may or may not be transcultural placements depending on the composition of their adoptive families. As suggested in previous chapters, the adoptive parents must prepare themselves, the children already in the family, and the adoptee for potential issues with cultural or racial prejudice. The adoptive family must facilitate the adoptee's identity development. This means embracing the culture of the adoptee.

Mental Health Services Needed by Adoptive Families

Adoptive families identify the need for a number of clinical services to meet their needs. Where will you get these services?

- Counseling for families, including assistance with the child's attachment issues
- Guidance in responding to children's emotional, behavioral and developmental issues
- Crisis intervention services
- Counseling for children, including groups for older child
- Specialized children's treatment services, including psychiatric services and drug and alcohol treatment

Freundlich, Madelyn, and North American Council on Adoptable Children staff members. (2007). "Post-Adoption Services: Meeting the Mental Health Needs of Children Adopted from Foster Care." North American Council on Adoptable Children. http://www.nacac.org/adoptalk/postadoptpaper.pdf

The North American Council on Adoptable Children offers some questions to help parents think about how they may fulfill the child's cultural needs. Think about how you may respond to their queries using the example of Christopher, who is arriving from Peru in the table which follows.

WHAT ARE YOU WILLING TO DO?	
Child's Challenges	**How Are You Willing to Change?**
Transplanted from his birth country and placed with your family—a new country, a new home, a new family, a new neighborhood, etc.	Are you willing to move to a neighborhood that reflects the child's background? This would mean relocating to an area with access to Peruvian Americans or others of South American heritage. The majority of Peruvian Americans reside in New Jersey, New York and Florida.
Expected to make friends with the children of your friends.	Are you willing to develop close positive relationships with persons of Christopher's culture?
Expected to attend your place of worship.	Are you willing to attend a religious institution of Christopher's country of origin? The predominant religion in Peru is Roman Catholic. Or, are you willing to join a religious institution with a culturally diverse population?
Attend school, daycare or a community center in your neighborhood.	Are you willing to participate in activities at a community center in a neighborhood that reflects cultural diversity? Are you willing to find child care and/or educational facilities in which there will be others who look like Christopher?
Asked to eat food common to your culture.	Are you willing to incorporate Peruvian favorites into your menu? What about Peruvian holiday traditions, history, art, music, etc.?
Endures prejudiced comments from neighbors, classmates and relatives.	Are you willing to respond constructively when you hear prejudiced comments from colleagues, acquaintances and loved ones?
Asked to take vacations with your immediate family.	Plan trips to places that reflect the child's heritage? Are you willing to invest in culture camps or a homeland tour? (See Chapter 10)
From Transracial Parenting Self-Awareness Tool, by Jeanette Wiedemeier Bower, published by the North American Council on Adoptable Children in February 1998. Accessed (2008) from www.nacac.org.postadopt/transracialWilling.html.	

Key Point—*Adoptive families cannot be culture blind.* There is an abundance of research that concludes that children adopted transculturally need families invested in fostering their cultural connections as well as role models who can "tutor"[19] them about how to be Peruvian-, Chinese-, Latino-, Black-, Korean-American, etc.

19. Reisner, Deb. (2007). "Transracial adoption: Love is just the beginning." http://www.nacac.org/adoptalk/TransAdoption.html

Family Talk about Culture

"Dad and I have been reading up on adopting a child of a different culture. We are realizing that we must look at our family and our community. We thought we could make this a family activity. We thought you could start checking out your school. Your older brother is going to do the same. Are there any children or teachers from Peru? How many are of a different culture? What about your after-school program?

"I thought you and I could go to the library and start doing some reading about Peruvian culture. We can learn about the religion, food, holidays and customs. All of these things will be important to your brother and our family as he grows up.

"I found a great book for you, *If the World were Blind* (see Resources). Dad and I are going to help you learn more about prejudice and discrimination—you learned some at your pre-adoptive training.

"We'll have more of these talks before and after your brother arrives. What questions do you have so far?"

Immediate Cultural Needs

The international adoptee arriving at the airport will be exposed to new sounds, sights, smells, language and climate. Going to bed might mean sleeping for the first time alone in a room or with only one or two new siblings rather than a group of infants, toddlers or young children. The foster child may move from a rural foster home to an adoptive family in a suburb or a city. The socio-economic status of the family in which the child resides may have increased or decreased. The religion could shift from Protestant to Catholic or Jewish. The child may move from a family who does not attend religious services regularly to a family who attends multiple church functions per week. Daily routines vary among families. Some shower in the morning, others bathe in the evening. Some families complete homework immediately upon arrival home from school. Other families allow some play time and then homework is completed. Actually, this list is probably endless. Each foster family, orphanage, neighborhood, residential treatment facility, etc., has a culture unique to itself. Moving to a new family with its distinctive culture will require an adjustment period.

Pre-placement is a time for the family to ask lots of questions regarding the child's current lifestyle. International adoptive families may spend several weeks in their child's

LONG-TERM CULTURAL NEEDS OF EXAMPLE CHILDREN		
Eric Contingent on the composition of the adoptive family.	**Renee** Contingent on the composition of the adoptive family.	**Marie** Transcultural placement—What will Marie's family be willing to do?
Christopher Transcultural placement—What will Christopher's family be willing to do?	**Ava** Contingent on the composition of the adoptive family.	**Katie** Transcultural placement—What will Katie's family be willing to do?

country of origin. There is opportunity to glean much about the child's surroundings. Some families will visit their child's orphanage. These parents can gain a sense of what their child has experienced on a daily basis. Parents adopting domestically will have access to the child's current caregivers. Compare your life style to that of the child you plan to adopt. Think about what is similar and what is different. Think about transitions in your life—moving, starting a new job, becoming a parent for the first time, getting married—what was difficult about these changes? What helped you cope with these changes?

Overall, the adoptee must acclimate and accommodate to the new family. However, as will be presented in Chapter 6, there are ways to ease these immediate cultural needs for everyone—parents, siblings-to-be and the child joining the family.

The Culture of Behavior

Behavior mirrors values. Those who value working hard, for example, tend to take good care of their home and possessions. Values are a part of culture. Children entering your home will behave in ways that directly conflict with the value system of your family. Behaviors are hard to change.

Each family must identify the behavioral challenges a child moving into their home could present. Each family must think about living with a child who acts in ways that will be frustrating, and to an extent even bizarre, to parents and siblings with traditional morals and values.

For example, Eric is reported to lie, steal, have tantrums during which he is destructive and he wets the bed. Subsequently, he hides his urine-stained clothing and bedding. Renee has tantrums during which she throws things. She is easily frustrated. Without medication, she bites her fingers until they bleed. Ava refuses to complete homework. She is argumentative, mouthy and has temper outbursts. She tests rules, boundaries and authority.

Family Talk about Behaviors

"Your new brother, Eric, may act very different from you. Remember from the classes at the adoption agency, he didn't have a mom and dad who were there to teach him all the right things.

"We learned from his social worker that he has temper tantrums. Sometimes, when he is mad, he uses bad words. Sometimes he throws things.

"He wets the bed—do you know what that means? Sometimes, he hides the wet clothes in the closet. This may make his room smell and even the hallway. We will be checking his room and helping him remove any wet clothes or sheets. This will help with the odor.

"In the other homes he lived in, he blamed other children for the mistakes he made. We are expecting this to happen here too. We know you and how you act. We will be able to decide who is telling the truth.

"We also want you to know that all the rules are staying the same. We expect that you will follow the rules even when he doesn't. We know that doesn't seem fair. We will certainly be working to change the way he acts. In the meantime, you still need to act correctly.

"What do you think about these things? Keep asking us questions as you think of them. We'll be talking more about this before he moves in and after he moves in."

- Hoarding food
- Rummaging through classmates' lunches for snacks
- Overeating
- Picky eater
- Acting in sexual ways
- Throwing temper tantrums
- Screaming and yelling
- Throwing things
- Being aggressive
- Being argumentative
- Refusing to shower
- Wearing the same clothing for several days
- Running away
- Lying
- Stealing
- Being overly friendly with strangers
- Completing homework and then throwing it out the school bus window or in the trash
- Asking questions, over and over, to which they already know the answer
- Talking loudly
- Constantly interrupting conversations
- Breaking toys
- Refusing to get out of bed in the morning
- Refusing to go to bed
- Carrying out chores sloppily
- Constantly losing possessions
- Cutting holes in clothing
- Writing or drawing on clothing
- Making poor eye contact
- Mumbling
- Using the possessions of others without permission
- Swearing
- Urinating in public
- Enuresis
- Encopresis (i.e., fecal soiling)
- Smearing feces
- Cutting themselves
- Pulling out eyelashes and eye-brows
- Pulling out teeth
- Picking off toe nails
- Head banging
- Suicidal ideation
- Suicidal threats
- Suicidal attempts
- Behaving in a superficially charming manner
- Not asking for help

The list above, which is by no means exhaustive, allows us to see how the traumatized child's behavior clashes with the family's values. The family values honesty; the child may lie and steal. The family values education; the child may refuse to complete homework. The family values privacy; the adoptee enters anybody's room at any time, taking whatever he or she wants. The parents value a clean house; the child hoards food and hides clothing full of feces.

Prospective adoptive parents often say things such as:

"That won't happen in my house!"

"All kids do that."

"Our love will fix these problems."

"We're getting her so young we won't have these problems."

"He just needs good parents. There must be something wrong with his foster family."

If you are thinking these kinds of things, you might want to consider waiting to adopt until your expectations are a bit more realistic. Even very young children exhibit behaviors that can be causes for concern and distressing to parents.

Infant through pre-school age international and domestic adoptees can exhibit any of the following behaviors

Cries, miserable all of the time, chronically fussy
Resists comforting or nurture
Resists or dislikes being held
Exhibits poor eye contact
Displays a flat, lifeless affect
Likes playpen or crib more than being held
Rarely cries (overly good baby)
Cries ragefully
Is exceedingly demanding
Looks sad or empty-eyed
Experiences delays in developmental milestones (crawling, walking, talking, etc.)
Stiffens or becomes rigid when held
Likes to be in control
Does not hold on when held (no reciprocal holding)
When held chest to chest, faces away
Doesn't like head touched
Is generally unresponsive to parent
Cries or rages when held beyond his wishes
Demonstrates overly independent play or makes no demands
Reaches for others to hold him rather than parent
Shows little or reduced verbal responsiveness
Does not return smiles
Shows very little imitative behavior[20]

Key Point—*Adoptive parents need to expect behavioral difficulties*. These unwelcome behaviors will occur with a frequency and intensity well beyond that of a "normal" child. Adoptive parents need to understand that changing these negative behaviors may be a difficult process. Behavioral change will occur gradually over a long period of time.

Key Point—*As Chapter 3 made clear, the child's behaviors are his way of attempting to resolve his past hurts*. Once accomplished, he can form an attachment to the family. Isn't this what we all really want? There is virtually no birth of a child without labor pains. There are likely few adoptions that will occur without behavioral pains.

20. Walter Buenning, PhD "Infant Attachment Checklist." http://www.reactiveattachmentdisorder treatment.com/infantattachchecklist.pdf;
Hopkins-Best, Mary,.*Toddler Adoption: The Weaver's Craft*. (Indianapolis: Perspectives Press, Inc., 1997);
Institute for Attachment and Child Development,"What you should know before you adopt a child." [online]. http://www.instituteforattachment.org/articles/article_43.htm

PROBLEMATIC BEHAVIORS IN EXAMPLE CHILDREN		
Eric Lies Steals Enuresis—hiding wet bedding and clothing Temper tantrums Swears Disruptive behavior Does not accept responsibility for his actions Hoards food	**Renee** Temper tantrums Throws things Easily frustrated Impulsive Hyperactive Talks loudly Asks persistent questions Overeats Refuses to go to bed	**Marie** Unknown
Christopher Unknown	**Ava** Refuses to complete homework Argumentative Mouthy Temper tantrums Yells Throws things Overeats Mumbles Does not ask for help Cuts holes in clothing	**Katie** Unknown

Are you feeling overwhelmed at this point in your reading? Good! You are taking the addition of a child to your family seriously! You are among those who will do well after the adoption.

> "It is very apparent that families who make an informed decision and are prepared beforehand do better once the child arrives and feel more positive about the adoption." (Iverson and Johnson, 2005).

"No, a defibrillator doesn't make someone tell the truth."

Do you remember that in Chapter 3 we talked about the value of humor? Well, here is something to start the humor kit recommended in that chapter. A little humor will help us get through the rest of this chapter. Don't forget . . . solutions and positives are coming!

Identify Educational Needs

How does moving numerous times affect academic performance? How does having a mental health disorder affect learning? Many international children struggle with speech and language delays as a result of learning English at later ages. How does this affect their ability to keep pace with peers? These are but a few of the questions that could be asked when considering the educational needs of both domestic and international adoptees. Ava's history notes that she is "very bright," yet she "does not live up to her academic potential." Renee's summary mentions that she has an IEP. What do these types of things mean when included in information about a waiting child?

The Individuals with Disabilities Education Act (IDEA) aims to ensure that all children receive a free and appropriate education and special services to assist in meeting their educational needs. Children who have difficulty learning adequately may qualify for special education services. Under IDEA, once a child is deemed eligible for special education services, the child is entitled to have an Individualized Education Plan (IEP). The IEP includes annual goals and short-term objectives, and is developed with the participation of the parents. Once an IEP is completed, parents or the school can request changes to it, but no changes can be made without the parents being informed. The IEP is reviewed annually, but may be reviewed as often as needed with any needed changes made (National Resource Center on AD/HD, online).

A Section 504 plan is typically faster, more flexible and a less stigmatizing procedure for obtaining some accommodations and services. Less information about the child is needed to obtain eligibility. However, regulations do not dictate the frequency of review of the 504 plan, and do not specify the right of the parents to participate in its development (National Resource Center on AD/HD, online).

The family interested in adopting Renee needs to request a copy of her IEP. They should also consider meeting with her teacher and any other relevant school professionals. They want to familiarize themselves with the process of negotiating an IEP. Overall, Renee's IEP was developed as a result of her speech and language delays resultant from her hearing loss. She receives speech therapy, two times per week, and she receives two hours of one-on-one help, weekly, to improve her reading level. She has some classroom accommodations as well. She sits near the teacher. Verbal instructions are supplemented by visual instructions. Her teacher ensures that any homework assignments are written in a passport—a notebook passed back and forth between the teacher and the parents.

Family Talk about Education

"Dad and I want to talk to you about your new sister. She may not be able to learn as well as you. She will have to learn a new language when she moves here and she may have learning disabilities. These are problems that make it hard for her to understand what the teacher is saying.

"She may get very frustrated. Sometimes, we will have to put her homework away and work on it another day even though our rule for you will be to finish your homework before you go out with your friends.

"We may have to give her a lot of extra help with her homework. We may have to take her to tutoring. Sometimes, you may have to find rides to football practice. We may not be able to play as much as we do now.

"If there are specific ways you can help us, we'll let you know. Mostly, this is our problem. Your job is to be a kid.

"What do you think about the changes that may happen? Let's sit down and figure out the things we do as a family. Which of these are most important to you? We want to continue the ones most important, to you, even if your sister takes up a lot of our time."

Renee offers a domestic example of a child with speech and language delays. International adoptees are prone to speech and language delays as well. The most intensive period of speech and language development for humans is during their first three years of life. These skills appear to develop best in a world that is rich with sounds, sights and consistent exposure to the speech and language of others. There is increasing evidence that there are "critical periods" for speech and language development in infants and young children. This means that the developing brain is best able to absorb a language, any language, during this period.[21] So, children residing in orphanages often do not develop proficient speech and language skills in their native language due to the lack of stimulation provided in the institutional environment (Glennen, 2005; Glennen, online). Early speech and language also leads to the development of our literacy skills—the ability to read and write. In school, children with communication disorders are more likely to struggle with literacy skills. They often perform poorly in school, have reading problems and have difficulty understanding and expressing language.

Sharon Glennen, PhD is a Certified Speech Language Pathologist and Assistant Professor, Department of Audiology, Speech Language Pathology and Deaf Studies at Tow-

21. National Institute on Deafness and Other Communication Disorders. "Speech and Language Developmental Milestones." [online]. http://www.nidcd.nih.gov/health/voice/speechandlanguage.asp

son University. She is also an adoptive parent. Dr. Glennen combines research, personal experience and professional knowledge to inform us about the speech development of international adoptees. The following four paragraphs are taken from her website—http://pages.towson.edu/sglennen/index.htm.[22] This content is also summarized in her article "Speech and language in children adopted internationally at older ages" which is quoted below and can be located in the *American Speech Language Hearing Association Division 14 Newsletter*.[23]

> "One issue that clouds the language learning process for older children is the notion of bilingualism. Internationally adopted children are often considered to be bilingual when in reality they are not. Bilingual language learners are learning to speak two languages. Some children are exposed to both languages from birth. Others learn one language at home and are later exposed to a second language when they reach school-age. In both cases, proficiency in the first language is used as a scaffold to help learn the second language.
>
> "The process of prematurely halting language development in the birth language before it fully develops is known as *arrested language development*. This is what internationally adopted children experience. They are not bilingual. Prior to adoption they learn a first language, the birth language, which is prematurely and suddenly stopped when the child is adopted because most adoptive parents do not speak the child's original language. The child, having been put in a 'language limbo,' then begins learning a new first language. Loss of birth language occurs quickly after adoption even in older children. Russian children adopted at ages 4 to 8 lost expressive use of their language within three–six months of adoption and all functional use of the language within a year (Gindis, 2004). International adoptees are only bilingual for a very short window of time after the adoption.
>
> "The loss of the first language before the new language develops leaves the internationally adopted child in a linguistic and educational limbo. Unlike the bilingual child who has a strong first language to fall back on, the internationally adopted child suddenly has no communicative language until English develops. This is a significant issue for older adopted children, who need to begin school right away. Because the children are not proficient in English, cognitive and linguistic development is often negatively affected.
>
> "Consider these facts. The typical 6-year-old understands over 20,000 English words. A 5-year-old adopted from another country would need to learn an average of 54 new words every day in order to fully catch up in language comprehension abilities by age 6. However, while this child has been playing catch-up, his 6-year-old friends have also added an average of 5,000 words to their vocabulary. In summary, expecting older children to develop proficient English language skills within one or two years of adoption is unrealistic. Learning a new language to proficiency takes years. This will have educational impact."

Poor language skills can be the basis for later learning disabilities. There are four areas of learning disabilities:

- Recording information in the brain—Learning depends on the brain correctly perceiving what is seen or heard.

---

22. Glennen, Sharon. (2002). "Orphanage care and language." http://pages.towson.edu/sglennen/index.htm

23. Glennen, Sharon. (2007). Speech and language in children adopted internationally at older age. *Perspectives on Communication Disorders and Sciences in Culturally and Linguistically Diverse Populations: American Speech Language Hearing Association Division 14 Newsletter*, 14(3), 17–20.

- Understanding information—Once recorded, information must be put in the right order (sequencing), and understood in context and integrated with other information (organization).
- Storage and retrieval (memory)—Information must be stored so that it can be retrieved, either quickly (short-term memory) or later (long-term memory). So, a child may either have a short-term memory disability or a long-term memory disability.
- Communicating or taking action—You communicate information by using words (language output) or by actions such as writing, drawing and gesturing. A child may have an output disability.[24]

What does all of the above mean for the family who is interested in adopting Katie? Because Katie was institutionalized for six years, Katie's prospective parents need to address Katie's potential issues with their local school district. What resources can the district put in place to assist Katie? With school system services in place, will she need additional tutoring? How will this expense be covered? Most likely, Katie will need the services of a speech pathologist. Is such a professional accessible near the family's home? What are the family's expectations of Katie regarding education? Do they expect her to be a high achiever? Is this realistic?

Discrepancies among your child's apparent intellect and effort and her academic performance may be reflective of a learning disability. Could this be Ava's problem? Ava has not lived any place long enough for a school or family to fully investigate why her intelligence and actual school performance are at a discord. The family who adopts Ava will want to get to the bottom of this matter.

It may be that Ava has a learning disability. Yet, we also know that anxieties about abandonment and abuse preoccupy children. Thus, school work suffers because such children are not able to attend to the degree necessary to grasp information put forth by the teacher. This issue is reflected in Ava's journaling. Ava learned to journal as part of her various therapies. Her writings, below, are left unedited. Her entries—these three were made at separate times over a several month period—are poignant and moving.

> "All the people who were here before are nomore. My hopes getting small. I feel there is no love at all. The blue sky is fading gray. The hand of help say go away. As I cry for help I get no replie. I sit alone in the dark with no family. No love. Asking why? Why?"

> "You left on corner. You said I'll see you soon. I was so young and inasent. It's like you put vinger in my wound. You were sappost to be a mother. We were sappost to love each other. You were sappost to comfort me and now your gone forever."

> "It's not fair. You weren't there. It's not. You didn't care. It's not fair you hated me so much when all I need was a mothers love touch. It's not fair you took my childhood. It's not fair all the thing I never understood. It's not fair you let guys rape me. It's not fair. It wasn't the way it was sappost to be. It's all the pain you put on me. It's not fair I have no family. It's not fair I couldn't be like other kids. It's not fair all the things I've missed. That not the way a father was sappost to kiss a daughter. It's not fair you don't care that he hurt me as long as he was here for you. But were you here for me. It's not fair I had to cry when he touched me. Or how I feel be the way he love me. It's not fair I'm all alone. It's not fair the way he wanted me. This isn't how it sappost to be. It's not fair. I was so young. It's not fair.

---

24. Adoption Resources Center, Family Helper. "Learning Disabilities." [online]. http://www.familyhelper.net/arc/lng.html

EDUCATION NEEDS OF THE EXAMPLE CHILDREN		
Eric Regular education performing average to above average	**Renee** IEP	**Marie** Unknown
Christopher Unknown	**Ava** Regular education "Very bright" "Does not live up to academic potential"	**Katie** Extensive educational needs due to lengthy period of institutionalization

You were my mother. We sappost to help and love each other. I have to work through it. I thought it was my fault. I have to get over you."

Ava helps us clearly understand how trauma can impair academic achievement. At the time of these writings, she had been separated from her birthmother for almost four years. Yet, daily, thoughts of her pre-adoptive experiences were on her mind. How can we expect her to learn with the issues with which she is grappling? What future does she see for herself? So, what value does she place on education? Is education the priority for Ava at age 12? Or, should we be more concerned about helping her resolve her abuse and abandonment?

Key Point—*Many educational needs will be identified after the adoption.* As with medical problems and mental health disorders, many of the child's academic needs will become clear after the adoption, rather than before placement. The factors contributing to academic performance are vast. Many are contingent upon the child's course of development. In addition to those factors already discussed, other barriers to academic success for children who are adopted include the following:

- Anxieties due to being from a different culture or simply having a different physical appearance.
- Neurological impairments due to pre-natal drug and alcohol exposure.
- Attachment difficulties. The pathways that create the components of a secure attachment are the same ones that regulate communication and organization of memory. Thus, interruptions in the attachment process inhibit the brain's capacity to develop in these areas.[25]
- Genetics. For example, the incidence of AD/HD is increased five-fold among first degree relatives. Based on the information already presented regarding AD/HD it is quite easy to see how this mental health disorder interferes with classroom performance. There is also a genetic disposition for learning disabilities. People who relinquish children are more prone to have a genetic basis that includes learning disabilities.

25. Stuart, Annie. "Identifying Learning Problems in Adopted Children." [online]. http://www.schwablearning.org/articles.aspx?r=689

Finally, extracting from Chapter 2:

"Indeed, the single best childhood predictor of adult adaptation is not school grades and not classroom behavior, but rather the adequacy with which the child gets along with other children."

Key Point—*Expectations for educational success may need to be adjusted.* When children have deficits in multiple areas, we must prioritize alleviating those most necessary for long-term healthy functioning. This will be a struggle for many parents as it may mean letting go of some of their hopes and dreams. Chapter 9 will offer advice regarding establishing priorities.

Identify Strengths and Areas of Progress

In the midst of clarifying the potential problems a child being considered for adoption has, it is important to remember that each child has strengths. In essence, we want to identify what is going well in the child's life. Are there areas in which the child excels? Are there areas in which the child has made improvement? What activities does the child enjoy? These factors lay the foundation for the family's relationship with the child. In the difficult times, these positive traits and the positive experiences they create act as a savings account. That is, as the child makes "withdrawals" in terms of the resources the family utilizes to alleviate the child's needs, the "deposits," positive memories, lend to balancing the child's account with the family. As such, the child's strengths and progress, even if small, can prevent the family from becoming totally drained. So, it is critical that we obtain information about

- areas in which the child is competent
- characteristics that create a sense of personal accomplishment
- coping skills
- qualities that promote the child's personal, social and academic development
- factors that contribute to satisfying relationships with family members, peers and adults.

Family Talk about Play

"The social worker said your new brother loves to play baseball and soccer. You two seem to have some things in common.

"The social worker also said he can be really competitive. He is known to push and shove other kids to get the ball. We want to talk about some of the ways you could handle this. We know how important your friends are to you. So, we want to help keep your friendships going okay."

OR

"We learned today that your new sister sometimes likes to play house. Isn't that great! You know, sometimes kids who didn't have good parents play house differently. They play that there is no food or water. They play that the mommy isn't home and so the baby dolls are alone. They may also want the dolls to fight and hit each other. If this happens, we want you to come and get one of us right away. Your new sister isn't doing anything bad. We just want to be able to come and teach her the right way to play so you two can have fun. How does this sound?"

Renee, for example, enjoys reading. In fact, as her speech has improved, her teacher finds that Renee beams when she is selected to read aloud to the class. She is playful, active, and loves animals, singing, dancing and crafts. Renee recently participated in a school concert. She received great pleasure from this event. She is often pleasant and quite likeable.

Eric functions quite well in the school environment. Academically, he excels in social studies. He participates quite successfully in soccer, swimming, football and karate.

Katie's orphanage experience included that a music teacher provided instruction to the children two days per week. The teacher taught piano and dance. Katie performed for her adoptive family when they were in Kazakhstan. Katie continues with dance lessons in America. Her recitals are well attended by family members. Katie's ability to shine in dance helps offset her feelings of inferiority in the academic arena.

Ava possesses a wonderful sense of humor. She can be warm and affectionate. Ava's journaling demonstrates a significant triumph for Ava. She is learning to express her thoughts and feelings through words rather than via negative behaviors. She has developed a positive coping skill. Ava's journaling further reveals a child who is willing to explore her past trauma. She is coming to understand that her abuse and abandonment were not her fault. She is willing to experience the pain of her losses. Ava is a child well on the way to healing from her past hurts. As Ava continues to recover, she will be able to improve academically and socially. Ava and those around her will enjoy mutually satisfying relationships.

Overall, most of our example children have areas in which they are competent and through which they can gain a sense of personal accomplishment.

Previous Relationships with Brothers and Sisters

Interestingly, the last bullet point in our strengths and progress model—factors that contribute to satisfying relationships with family members, peers and adults—is an area addressed briefly or not at all for our example children. This area would include how well a prospective adoptee functions in relationships with siblings. All we know is that Eric "gets along well with others" and Ava "would compete for attention and become jealous when placed in homes with other children. This was one of the main reasons for the foster parent request that Ava be removed from their home."

As pointed out in Chapter 1, many parents and professionals assume that children will simply develop positive sibling relationships. In fact, parents need to investigate this matter during the process of reviewing a child's pre-placement history.

For example, Ava has lived in three foster homes and two residential treatment facilities. Regarding the statement, "This was one of the main reasons for the foster parent request that Ava be removed from the home," *foster parent* is singular. *One* foster family requested her removal for this reason. The other four placements did not report this problem. Actually, interviews with all of her previous foster parents, one of her foster homes described Ava's interactions with the other children in the home as "excellent." The foster mother pointed out that Ava was a "big help" with the younger children. "She would play with them for long periods of time." The ages of the children in this home were 9 (Ava), 5 and 4. The younger children were a brother and a sister. Ava became very depressed during her residence with this family. This period of mood instability occurred after Ava attended the adoption of her youngest birthsibling. Ava threatened to commit suicide. The agency with custody placed Ava in a psychiatric hospital. This hospital in turn recommended that Ava be placed in residential treatment. The disruption of Ava's placement with this family had nothing to do with her actual one-on-one interactions with the resident children.

The composition of the family who requested Ava's removal included four other children. In this home, Ava had three older sisters and one younger brother. The ages of the children were 15, 14, 12, 11 (Ava) and 8. Ava had conflicts with the older siblings. She wanted to wear their clothing and use their hair care products and make-up. If they had friends over, she would not leave them alone. She did this with great frequency. As such, the family felt that she was causing "too much conflict."

Katie's family obtained a glimpse of her interactions with other children when they visited her at her orphanage. Each day, when they arrived for their meeting with Katie, many children were sitting in a circle. Katie was often sitting next to children. However, she was talking little to the child on either side of her. The day that Katie was to leave the orphanage, Katie's new mom arranged a small party. The mom purchased balloons. She blew up a balloon for each of the children. None of the children had any idea what to do with the balloons. So, the mom and dad started tapping a balloon back and forth to each other. Soon, all of the children were tapping their balloons. But, each was tapping his own balloon, by himself, up and down, rather than tapping back and forth to another child or with a group of children. In essence, Katie was 6 years old and was still in the stage of parallel play. This is the type of play expected of a child 2 to 3 years old. Leaving the orphanage to go to the airport, Katie simply turned and walked away. She barely said good-bye to any of the children. Numerous of the orphanage staff hugged her and were tearful. Yet, Katie did not reciprocate their gestures or emotions.

Eric's reported ability to "get along well with others" is true when describing his participation in team sports. He is able to interact well when engaged in athletic activities. Eric has had five foster placements. Each of these five homes had other children. Whether Eric was among the younger or the older, each family reported that Eric had difficulty in sibling interactions. One family reported that "Eric fought with the other children over everything." Another family said, "Our son had to share a room with Eric. The smell of urine became so strong in their room, we couldn't leave our son in there. It was like being in a port-a-potty. We didn't have any other space for Eric." A third family commented that "Eric accepted no responsibility for his actions. He blamed the other kids for things he had done. He created so much chaos that we felt Eric would be better off someplace else."

This type of information is vital to prospective families comprised of typically developing children. Such information needs to be made routinely available during the matching phase of the adoption process. Families need to prepare themselves and their resident children for the positive and negative types of interactions that may occur between the existing brothers and sisters and the sibling entering the family.

Questions that could be asked in relation to sibling interactions include the following:

What was the composition of the child's previous and current homes?

What have been the ages of the children in the previous homes?

What has been the age of the prospective child in relation to the other children in the homes?

What are the child's strengths in sibling interactions?

What are the child's problems in sibling interactions?

What types of activities have posed the most problems?

What types of activities went well?

Are there are any safety concerns?

KeyPoint—*Ask for clarification and examples when something is not clear or when depth is lacking.* We acquired a much different picture of Ava and Eric's interactions with other children when we gathered more facts from those who had lived with these children.

KeyPoint—*Adoptive families need to identify the types of additional information relevant to their making an informed decision.* Once the family has thoroughly reviewed the information provided, they can discern the gaps. Additional information can then be requested. Such supplemental information may include the following:

For Domestic Adoptees

- Psychological or psychiatric evaluations
- Birth records
- Medical records
- IEP or 504 Plan
- Written statements from mental health providers or teachers
- In-person or phone conversations with the child's past and previous caregivers
- In-person meeting with relevant school professionals
- In-person meeting with the child's mental health provider
- Conversations with other adoptive families
- Attending adoptive parent support groups as well as needs-based support groups such as Children and Adults with Attention-Deficit/Hyperactivity Disorder (CHADD) or National Alliance on Mental Illness (NAMI). There are many types of support groups that are useful in understanding the special needs that waiting children present.
- Photos or video of the child
- A meeting (if possible) with the staff who removed the child from the birth home, or who were part of the effort to reunify the child with the birthfamily. These professionals often have a wealth of information.
- Reading, reading and reading some more!

For International Adoptees

- Pre-adoptive consultation at an international adoption medical clinic
- Asking questions of the orphanage staff
- Orphanage photos and videos—there are websites that contain video and photos of orphanages in many countries. Review these. They will certainly help you understand what your child is experiencing pre-adoption. You may also obtain video and photos of your child's orphanage from other families who have traveled there.
- Participation in adoptive parent support groups in person and online
- Reading, reading and reading some more!

Our charts for how each of our sample children's sibling interactions follows:

Continuing to Build the Prediction Path

We have now completed Step 1—identification of the child's needs—in creating a Prediction Path. We are ready to put all of those needs—complex trauma, medical, mental health, education, culture/behavioral difficulties, strengths/progress, sibling relationships—together. It is important to note that the Prediction Path is set up to

SIBLING RELATIONSHIPS OF EXAMPLE CHILDREN		
Eric Sibling Relationships: Three families report difficulties in sibling interactions	**Renee** Sibling interactions: Unknown. Renee lives in a foster family with no other children.	**Marie** Unknown
Christopher Unknown	**Ava** Sibling Relationships: Ava did well in a family with younger children. Ava had difficulty in a family with older female siblings.	**Katie** Sibling Relationships: Katie appears to have social delays as evidenced by parallel play. Katie easily left the orphanage. She exhibited no emotion leaving and barely said good-bye.

follow the premise used throughout this book: the child's past is important. The child's special needs stem from the trauma. The Prediction Path offers a visual means of seeing this flow. Selecting one each (domestic and international) of our example children, let's proceed with the completion of the Prediction Path. This includes accomplishing the following three steps:

- Step 1: Clarification of the child's needs. Again, this step is completed.
- Step 2: Identification of the "formal and informal supports" the family may need in order to alleviate the adoptee's needs, and to insure the emotional well-being of each member of the adoptive family. Much of the information in this column is yet to come in Chapters 6, 8, 9 and 10.
- Step 3: Identification of "additional solutions" essential to maintaining a balance between healing the adoptee and meeting the needs of the parents, brothers and sisters. Again, much of this information is to follow in Chapters 6, 8, 9 and 10.

In conclusion, pre-adoption the prediction path helps parents determine if a potential child is a "match" for their family. If so, the family has a visual picture of the type of issues the family may expect. Post-adoption, when experiencing difficulties, the family can return to their prediction path for solutions.

 **Final Key Point—***Adoption involves risks!* Marie's Prediction Path is a virtual array of unknowns. There is no way of predicting the types of needs or the level of needs Marie will present. Even with Renee, for whom we have much more information, her Prediction Path is a picture of Renee at this moment in time. There is no way to determine if Renee's issues will resolve or compound over time.

Empathy: Seeing the Whole Child

We have spent this chapter dissecting the potential adoptee's problems and needs. Overall, interpreting the information received regarding a waiting child means identifying pieces of medical information, slices of educational needs, chunks of mental health disorders, wedges of trauma, smatterings of strengths and sections of child-specific

PREDICTION PATH FOR MARIE (AGE 13 MONTHS, INTERNATIONAL ADOPTEE)

Problems	**What's Known**	**Formal and Informal Supports** (Inclusive of ea. family member)	**Additional Solutions** (Inclusive of ea. family member)
Complex Trauma Issues Mental Health Needs	Abandonment Multiple Moves Institutionalization Suspected pre-natal drug and alcohol exposure *The above issues create* • possible impairments in forming healthy attachments • cognitive, Social and Emotional Delays • grief and Loss Issues • irrational thought processes about adults and family as a whole *All of the above, in turn, may create mental health issues:* Unknown—Marie is at risk for mental health issues based on the above factors, and genetics can also play a role in mental health issues.	Marie's family will want to gain knowledge of "normal" child development. They will be looking for any signs of delays in the cognitive, social and emotional domains of development. If Marie exhibits delays she may require various evaluations. • Neurological • Neuropsychological • Psychological • Psychiatric Marie's family will want to understand the developmental nature of adoption issues (Chapter 8). They should educate themselves about the value of honesty regarding sharing the adoptee's history, and about how to create a narrative and lifebook (See Chapter 8).	This would include moving Marie with sensitivity as described in Chapter 6. This would also include acknowledging the potential unhealthy dynamics that may result post-placement. This information is covered in Chapter 8. Additionally, this would include implementing relevant solutions provided in Chapters 8 and 9 under the headings: • Developing Realistic Expectations: Achieving Cognitive Consonance • Acquiring New and Effective Coping Skills • Weathering the Storm: Creating and Maintaining a Healthy Emotional Climate • Coming Ashore: Letting Grief Flow • On a Positive Note: (Yes, There Are Positives!) • Finding Oases: Creating Support—Renee will especially require a high level of nurture This would also include avoiding the "roadblocks" identified throughout these chapters.
Medical Needs	Mixed disorders of "psychical" development Birth Statistics: • Head Circumference 31 cm • Birth Weight 2400 g • Birth Length 48 cm	Marie's family should visit an International Medical Clinic within a few weeks of arrival home and at regular intervals as established by the clinic. Marie should be given an immediate speech and language evaluation (Chapter 6).	

PREDICTION PATH FOR MARIE (AGE 13 MONTHS, INTERNATIONAL ADOPTEE) (*Continued*)

Problems	**What's Known**	**Formal and Informal Supports** (Inclusive of each member of the family)	**Additional Solutions** (Inclusive of each member of the family)
Cultural Needs	Marie will be a Russian-American.	Marie and her family should participate in the following types of activities: Heritage Camp Heritage Tour Support Group	Refer to "*What are you willing to do?*" (Chapter 5). In general, Marie's family should be willing and able to • respond to questions from strangers and others. • incorporate Marie's culture into daily life. • network and associate with others of Marie's culture.
Educational Needs	Unknown	There is a potential for academic problems. Again, the family needs to monitor Marie and her academic progress closely.	
Behavioral Challenges	Unknown		
Strengths and Areas of Progress	Unknown		
Competence in Sibling Relationships	Unknown		

RENEE'S PREDICTION PATH (AGE 7, DOMESTIC ADOPTEE)

Problems	**What's Known**	**Formal and Informal Supports** (Inclusive of each family member)	**Additional Solutions** (Inclusive of each member of the family)
Complex Trauma Issues ⇨ Mental Health Needs ⇨	Neglect Suspected pre-natal drug and alcohol exposure Domestic Violence Multiple Moves Separation from Birth Siblings Abandonment *The above issues create* possible impairments in forming healthy attachments cognitive, Social and Emotional Delays grief and Loss Issues Irrational thought processes about adults and family as a whole *All of the above, in turn, contribute to Renee's mental health issues.* AD/HD PTSD Generalized Anxiety Disorder	Various types of evaluations to determine the impact of the trauma: • Neurological • Neuropsychological • Psychological Psychiatric • Evaluation • Medication Therapy • Individual/Family Psycho Education • Materials to help each member of the family understand the mental health issues and to realize that many issues are developmental (Chapter 8). Support Groups Respite	This would include moving Renee with sensitivity as described in Chapter 6. This would also include acknowledging the potential unhealthy family dynamics that may result post-placement as covered in Chapter 8. Additionally, this would include implementing relevant solutions provided in Chapters 9 and 10 under the headings: • Developing Realistic Expectations: Achieving Cognitive Consonance • Acquiring New and Effective Coping Skills • Weathering the Storm: Creating and Maintaining a Healthy Emotional Climate • Coming Ashore: Letting Grief Flow • On a Positive Note: Yes, There Are Positives! • Finding Oases: Creating Support—Renee will especially require a high level of nurture This would also include avoiding the "roadblocks" identified throughout these chapters.

RENEE'S PREDICTION PATH (AGE 7, DOMESTIC ADOPTEE) (*Continued*)

Problems	**What's Known**	**Formal and Informal Supports** (Inclusive of each family member)	**Additional Solutions** (Inclusive of each member of the family)
Medical Needs	Stated to have a "normal" birth history History of chronic Otitis Media which caused partial hearing loss Sensory Integration Dysfunction Lead exposure Gross motor delays	Renee should have Occupational Therapy for Sensory Integration Dysfunction Routine follow-ups should be conducted by an Adoption Medical Clinic.	
Cultural Needs	Contingent upon the composition of the adoptive family.		
Educational Needs	IEP	The IEP includes speech therapy and physical therapy for the gross motor delays.	
Behavioral Challenges	Impulsive Hyperactive Temper tantrums Throws things Steals	Due to her complex trauma issues, Renee's family should anticipate that there are bound to be some challenges that await them. To prepare ahead of time, they should have pre-identified a family therapist who is also an adoption specialist.	Renee's family will want to understand the concept, "Parenting at the Social and Emotional Age." The family will want to learn many behavioral interventions designed to reduce negative behaviors while facilitating developmental growth. Both of the above are explained and illustrated in Chapters 9 and 10.

Strengths and Areas of Progress	Reading Is playful Active Loves animals, singing, dancing, crafts Pleasant Quite likeable	Renee has ample interests to participate in various extra curricular activities.	
Competence in Sibling Relationships	Unknown (Renee resides in a foster home with no other children.)	Renee may or may not relate well to her new siblings and this will certainly provide relationship challenges for the entire family. As above, an adoption specialist who can provide the family with therapy as needed should be identified ahead of time.	Renee's family should make time for family fun as it works for them! Play is a great way to get to know each other and forge family bonds.

issues. At some point, you must step back and think about the child as a whole. In doing so, you absolutely must take the time to imagine the child's life to date. This will help you develop empathy for the child and what she experienced prior to arrival in your family. Empathy is the understanding of another person's feelings by remembering or imagining being in a similar situation. Without empathy, we will see the child as simply an ongoing array of problems and needs. We will lose sight of the person.

Empathy will also help you, as parents, through the hard times. When you are overwhelmed with the behavior, when you become frustrated at how hard you have to advocate for services, when you are angry and exhausted due to the child's transfer of emotions to you, when you wish you could have a break and there is no one available to provide respite, when your typically developing children want to send her back, when you feel guilty for how you believe the brothers and sisters are being impacted, it is empathy that will help keep you going. It is saying to yourself, "She didn't ask to be beaten, raped, moved, abandoned and separated from her siblings. Yes, she needs to learn to function in a manner acceptable to society. However, becoming whole is difficult when you missed the early pieces so necessary for healthy development."

Empathy is also a component critical to your child's healing process. If you cannot think about what happened to her or talk about her experiences, how will you be able to assist her in her efforts to recover? For those of you adopting young children, you will be the person who has memories of her orphanage. You may have been present during the birthfamily reunification efforts. So, you may remember what her birthmother looked like. You need to provide this information. The fewer missing pieces she has, the more clear her image of herself becomes. This will generate progress. The traumatized child's progress has a direct positive impact on the well-being of each member of the family.

This task will be emotionally painful. It is difficult to think about a child lying in an orphanage with no one to soothe her crying. It is heartbreaking to think about a child being sexually abused, bruised, hungry, cold, dirty and alone. Yet, at some point you must think about these things—for yourself, the children you already parent and the child you adopt.

If you are ready to experience some empathy right now, ponder the lyrics to the song, "The Eleventh Commandment" by Lisa Aschmann and Karen Taylor-Good (recorded by Collin Raye)[26]

She hears his heavy breathing in the dark
His footsteps coming closer down the hall
She's so ashamed, she's Daddy's secret love
She wants to cry, she wants to die, but he can't get enough

The bruises on his face will go away
Mom keeps him home from school till they fade
She's sorry he was born and tells him so
He takes it in, he hangs his chin, he ducks another blow

Did God overlook it
What ought have been written
The eleventh commandment

26. Permission to reprint these lyrics was granted by the writers, Lisa Aschmann and Karen Taylor-Good, Nashville Geographic. 4869 Torbay Drive, Nashville, TN, 37211. The Eleventh Commandment was performed by Collin Raye and recorded by SONY/EPIC records.

Honor thy children

He cries for hours, cries and never stops
He shakes so hard his little cradle rocks
He'll never have the chance to be brand new
He'll never walk, he'll never talk, he's addicted too

Did God overlook it
What ought have been written
The eleventh commandment
Honor thy children

Thou shalt not kill
Thou shalt not steal
Thou shalt not take the Lord's name in vain
Thou shalt not cause thy children pain

God does not overlook it
What ought have been written
The eleventh commandment
Honor thy children
Honor thy children

Resources

These resources relate to mental health issues, speech and language acquisition, academic issues and medical needs. There is an also an extensive collection of children's books so parents can talk to kids about anything!

Books

Barkley, Russell and Christine Benton. *Your Defiant Child: 8 Steps to Better Behavior*. (New York: Guilford Press, 1998.)

Barkley, Russell. *Taking Charge of ADHD: The Complete, Authoritative Guide for Parents*. (New York: Guilford Press, 2000.)

Bell, Teri James. *When the Brain Can't Hear: Unraveling the Mystery of Auditory Processing Disorder*. (New York: Atria, 2003.)

Geddes, Heather. *Attachment in the Classroom: The Links between Children's Early Experience, Emotional Well-Being and Performance in Schools*. (London: Worth Publishing, 2006.)

Gurian, Michael. *The Boys and Girls Learn Differently Action Guide for Teachers*. (Hoboken: Jossey-Bass, 2003.)

Koegel, Lynn Kern and Clair LaZebnik. *Overcoming Autism: Finding the Answers, Strategies, and Hope that Can Transform a Child's Life*. (New York: Penguin, 2005.)

Kranowitz, Carol Stock. *The Out-of-Sync Child Has Fun: Activities for Kids with Sensory Integration Dysfunction*. (New York: The Berkley Publishing Group, 2003.)

Meese, Ruth Lyn. *Children of Intercountry Adoption in School: A Primer for Parents and Professionals*. (Westport: Bergin and Garvey, 2002.)

Miller, Lucy Jane. *Sensational Kids: Hope and Help for Children with Sensory Processing Disorder*. (New York: Penguin Books, 2006.)

Papolos, Demitri and Janice Papolos. *The Bipolar Child: The Definitive and Reassuring Guide to Childhood's Most Misunderstood Disorder*. (New York: Broadway Books, 2002.)

Reiff, Michael and Sherrill Tippins, eds. *ADHD: A Complete and Authoritative Guide*. American Academy of Pediatrics. (Elk Grove, Illinois: American Academy of Pediatrics, 2004.)

Whitten, Kathleen. *Labor of the Heart: A Parent's Guide to the Decisions and Emotions in Adoption*. (New York: M. Evans and Company, 2008.)

Wilens, Timothy. *Straight Talk about Psychiatric Medications for Kids*. (Third Edition). (New York: Guildford Press, 2008.)

Wood, Lansing and Nancy Ng. *Adoption and the Schools: Resources for Parents and Teachers*. (Palo Alto, California: Families Adopting in Response, 2001.)

Websites

American Academy of Pediatrics (AAP)
www.aap.org

The American Academy of Pediatrics is an organization of 60,000 pediatricians committed to the attainment of optimal physical, mental, and social health and well-being for all infants, children, adolescents and young adults. Browse any health topic you can think of! Parents can use their database to find a pediatrician experienced with the population of adopted children.

American Academy of Child and Adolescent Psychiatry (AACAP)
www.aacap.org/

The AACAP is the leading national professional medical association dedicated to treating and improving the quality of life for children, adolescents and families affected by mental health disorders. The website provides descriptions of child and adolescent mental health disorders and treatment options. Their fact sheets for families are published in numerous languages. Families will find great information regarding when to seek help and what type of professional help to obtain.

Children and Adults with Attention-Deficit/Hyperactivity Disorder (CHADD)
www.chadd.org

CHADD is a national non-profit organization providing education, advocacy and support for individuals with AD/HD. This website contains abundant information pertaining to this mental health disorder. However, the website is also quite a valuable resource for those obtaining or in the process of negotiating special education services. Detailed descriptions of a 504 plan and an IEP are provided, as is a sample IEP.

Channing Bete Company
www.channing-bete.com

This company produces booklets and workbooks for parents to use with children of all ages. Topics range from abuse, neglect, mental health disorders, dating, peer relationships, feelings, prejudice, discrimination, life skills and etc. Their resources are a great way to discuss an array of difficult issues with children.

International Adoption Medicine Program, University of Minnesota
www.med.umn.edu/peds/iac/

This clinic was the first clinic in the United States to provide for the health needs of internationally adopted children. Anyone interested in international adoption should review the assortment of articles contained on this website. The articles offer a wealth of information about the medical needs of children adopted intercountry as well as the types of long-term developmental issues parents may expect to face. There are also recommendations for pre- and post-placement evaluations.

Mayo Clinic
www.mayoclinic.com

Are you looking for information about any health condition? This website is the place to find it! Their A-Z links make finding any medical illness fast and easy. If you are interested in healthy living, this is covered in-depth as well.

National Institute on Deafness and Other Communication Disorders (NIDCD)
www.nidcd.nih.gov/

The National Institute on Deafness and Other Communication Disorders (NIDCD) is one of the Institutes that comprise the National Institutes of Health (NIH). Established in 1988, NIDCD is mandated to conduct and support biomedical and behavioral research and training in the normal and disordered processes of hearing, balance, smell, taste, voice, speech and language. The website offers information regarding the process of speech development as well as content pertaining to acquiring a second language. There is also an array of articles pertaining to speech and language disorders.

National Institute of Mental Health (NIMH)
www.nihm.nih.gov/

NIMH is the largest scientific organization in the world dedicated to research focused on the understanding, treatment, and prevention of mental disorders and the promotion of mental health. The website provides thorough coverage of any mental health disorder listed in the DSM-IV-TR. Along with each disorder treatment recommendations are included. There is also much information about the use of medications in the treatment of mental health disorders.

Post-Adoption Learning Center (PAL Center, Inc.)
http://www.bgcenterschool.org/index.shtml

This online school offers courses, CDs, publications, presentations, workshops and group consultations that help to raise awareness and prepare parents and professionals for addressing language, developmental and educational needs of internationally adopted older children. All information comes from professionals, who work with internationally adopted children on a daily basis. This website is also the home to the International Adoption Article Directory—www.adoptionarticles-directory.com/. Adoptive parents will find over 500 articles on all aspects of international adoption. A number of these articles are devoted to the academic needs of intercountry adoptees.

Sharon Glennen
http://pages.towson.edu/sglennen/index.htm

Sharon Glennen, PhD, is a Certified Speech Language Pathologist and Assistant Professor, Department of Audiology, Speech Language Pathology and Deaf Studies at Towson University, as well as an adoptive parent. Her work in the area of international adoptee language acquisition was cited earlier in this chapter. Visit her website to read her work in its entirety.

U.S. Department of Education
www.ed.gov

The U.S. Department of Education's website offers content about a 504 plan and the IEP process. Parents will find a wonderful question/answer section pertaining to obtaining services for children with special needs. There are also informative articles/brochures regarding helping children learn and develop.

Books for Children and Adolescents

Bernstein, Sharon Chesler. *A Family that Fights*. (Morton Grove, Illinois: Albert Whitman and Company, 1991.)

Blomquist, Geraldine and Paul Blomquist. *Zachary's New Home: A Story for Foster and Adopted Children*. (Washington: Magination Press, 1990.)

Brodzinsky, Anne Braff. *The Mulberry Bird: An Adoption Story*. (Indianapolis: Perspectives Press, 1996.)

Brown, Margaret Wise. *The Runaway Bunny*. (New York: Harper Trophy, 1977.)
Burnett, Karen Gedig. *If the World Were Blind: A Book About Judgment and Prejudice*. (Felton, California: GR Publishing, 2001.)
Cole, Joanna. *I'm a Big Brother*. (New York: Harper Collins Children's Books, 1997.)
Cole, Joanna. *I'm a Big Sister*. (New York: Harper Collins Children's Books, 1997.)
Collodi, Carlo. *Pinocchio: A Classic Illustrated Edition*. (San Francisco: Chronical Books, 2001.)
Coville, Bruce. *The Lapsnatcher*. (East Sussex: Bridge Water Books, 1997.)
Fisher, Antwone Q. and Mim E. Rivas. *Finding Fish: A Memoir*. (New York: Harper Torch, 2002.)
Girard, Linda Walvoord. *My Body is Private*. (Morton Grove, Illinois: Albert Whitman and Co., 1984.)
Grossnickle, Mary. *A Place in My Heart*. (Speaking of Adoption, www.speakingofadoption.com, 2004.)
Hale, Natalie. *Oh Brother! Growing Up with a Special Needs Sibling*. (Washington: Magination Press, 2004.)
Harris, Robie. *It's So Amazing: A Book about Eggs, Sperm, Birth, Babies and Families*. (Somerville, Massachusetts: Candlewick, 2004.)
Huebner, Dawn. *What to Do When You Dread Your Bed: A Kid's Guide to Overcoming Problems with Sleep*. (Washington: Magination Press, 2008.)
Johnson, Julie Tallard. *Understanding Mental Illness: For Teens Who Care about Someone with Mental Illness*. (Minneapolis: Lerner Publications Company, 1989.)
Kasza, Keiko. *A Mother for Choco*. (New York: Puffin Books, 1992.)
Kearney, Meg. *The Secret of Me: A Novel in Verse*. (New York: Persea, 2007.)
Kennedy, Pamela. *A Sister for Matthew: A Story about Adoption*. (Nashville: GPKids, 2006.)
Koehler, Phoebe. *The Day We Met You*. (New York: Aladdin Paperbacks, 1990.)
Krementz, Jill. *How It Feels to be Adopted*. (New York: Knoph, 1988.)
Krishnaswami, Uma. *Bringing Asha Home*. (New York: Lee and Low Books, 2006.)
Lance, Judith. *It's Not Your Fault: A Guide for Children to Tell if They're Abused*. (Indianapolis: Kidsrights, 1997.)
Little, Jean. *Emma's Yucky Brother*. (New York: Harper Trophy, 2001.)
Loftis, Chris. *The Words Hurt: Helping Children Cope with Verbal Abuse*. (Far Hills, New Jersey: New Horizon Press, 2006.)
Lovell, Cynthia Miller. *The Star: A Story to Help Young Children Understand Foster Care*. (Self-Published, 1999.)
MacLeod, Jean. *At Home in this World: A China Adoption Story*. (Warren, New Jersey: EMK Press, 2003.)
McLain, Paula. *Like Family: Growing up in Other People's Houses, a Memoir*. (New York: Back Bay Books, 2004.)
McMahon, Patricia and Conor Clarke McCarthy. *Just Add One Chinese Sister: An Adoption Story*. (Honesdale, Pennsylvania: Boyds Mills Press, 2005.)
McNamara, Joan. *Borya and the Burps: An Eastern European Adoption Story*. (Indianapolis: Perspectives Press, 2005.)
Meyer, Don ed. *The Sibling Slam Book: What's It Really Like to Have a Brother or Sister with Special Needs*. (Bethesda: Woodbine House, Inc., 2005.)
Miller, Faith. *Jo Jo, A Tiny Story of Faith: A Journey through Adoption*. (Nashville: Abingdon Press, 2002.)
Mitchell, Christine. *Welcome Home Forever Child: A Celebration of Children Adopted as Toddlers and Preschoolers and Beyond*. (Bloomington, Indiana: Author House, 2006.)
Munsch, Robert. *Love You Forever*. (Richmond Hill, Ontario: Firefly Books, 1986.)
Nelson, Julie. *Families Change: A Book for Children Experiencing Termination of Parental Rights*. (Minneapolis: Free Spirit Publishing, 2007.)

Nemiroff, Marc and Jane Annunziata. *All About Adoption: How Families Are Made and How Kids Feels about It.* (Washington: Magination Press, 2004.)
Parr, Todd. *The Family Book.* (New York: Little, Brown and Co., 2003.)
Payne, Lauren Murphy. *We Can Get Along.* (Minneapolis: Free Spirit Publishing, 1997.)
Peacock, Carol Antoinette. *Mommy Far, Mommy Near: An Adoption Story.* (Morton Grove, Indiana: Albert Whitman and Co., 2000.)
Pellegrino, Marjorie White. *My Grandma's the Mayor.* (Washington: Magination Press, 1999.)
Penn, Audrey. *A Pocket Full of Kisses.* (Terre Haute, Indiana: Tanglewood Press, 2004.)
Petertyl, Mary E. *Seeds of Love: For Brothers and Sisters of International Adoption.* (Grand Rapids: Folio One Publishing, 1997.)
Rashkin, Rachel. *Feeling Better: A Kid's Book about Therapy.* (Washington: Magination Press, 2005.)
Rogers, Fred. *Let's Talk about It: Adoption.* (New York: G.P. Putnam's Sons, 1994.)
Sanford, Doris. *I Can't Talk about It: A Child's Book about Sexual Abuse.* (Portland: Multnomah Press, 1986.)
Sheldon, Annette. *Big Sister Now: A Story about Me and Our New Baby.* (Washington: Magination Press, 2006.)
Sheppard, Caroline. *Brave Bart: A Story for Traumatized and Grieving Children.* (Grosse Point Woods, Michigan: 1998.)
Slade, Suzanne. *Adopted: The Ultimate Teen Guide.* (Lanham: Scarecrow Press, 2007.)
Small, David. *Imogene's Antlers.* (New York: Crown Publishers, 1985.)
Snow, Judith E. *How it Feels to Have a Gay or Lesbian Parent: A Book for Kids of All Ages.* (New York: Routledge, 2004.)
Spelman, Cornelia Maude. *When I Feel Angry.* (Morton Grove, Illinois: Albert Whitman and Co., 2002.)
Spelman, Cornelia Maude. *When I Feel Good about Myself.* (Morton Grove, Illinois: Albert Whitman and Co., 2003.)
Spelman, Cornelia Maude. *When I Feel Jealous.* (Morton Grove, Illinois: Albert Whitman and Co., 2003.)
Spelman, Cornelia Maude. *When I Feel Sad.* (Morton Grove, Illinois: Albert Whitman and Co., 2002.)
Spelman, Cornelia Maude. *When I Feel Scared.* (Morton Grove, Illinois: Albert Whitman and Co., 2002.)
Spelman, Cornelia Maude. *Your Body Belongs to You.* (Morton Grove, Illinois: Albert Whitman and Co., 1997.)
Stoeke, Janet Morgan. *Waiting for May.* (New York: Dutton Children's Books, 2005.)
Sugarman, Brynn Olenberg. *Rebecca's Journey Home.* (Minneapolis: Kar-Ben Publishing, 2006.)
Taylor, Clark. *The House that Crack Built.* (San Francisco: Chronicle Books, 1992.)
Wilgocki, Jennifer and Marcia Kahn Wright. *Maybe Days: A Book for Children in Foster Care.* (Washington: Magination Press, 2002.)

Websites for Children and Adolescents

Adoption Clubhouse
http://www.adoptionclubhouse.org

The Adoption Clubhouse is a program of the National Adoption Center, whose mission it is to expand adoption opportunities throughout the United States, particularly for children with special needs and those from minority cultures. The Adoption Clubhouse was designed for children's adoption needs. Through the activities and information on this site children can experience a sense of belonging to a wider adoption community of peers. The site includes a library of books and movies, response to questions kids get asked about being adopted, advice on completing school projects and topics—family tree, bringing in a baby picture, genetics—and a lot more. This is a great website!

The Sibling Support Project
www.siblingsupport.org

The Sibling Support Project is a national effort dedicated to the life-long concerns of brothers and sisters of people who have special health, developmental or mental health concerns. The Sibling Support Project believes that disabilities, illness and mental health issues affect the lives of *all* family members. Consequently, they work to increase the peer support and information opportunities for brothers and sisters of people with special needs and to increase parents' and providers' understanding of sibling issues. Their list servs connect siblings of all ages.

CHAPTER SIX

Moving to the Adoptive Family: Through the Eyes of the Child

Learning that you have been selected as a family for a child causes instant joy and excitement. The air simply crackles with delight! Your long wait is over. Your child is coming home. You have all kinds of questions: When will we meet her? Will we hit it off? What gift should we take on the first visit? What color should we paint the bedroom? When can she meet our children? How many preplacement visits will there be?

However, the adoptee may have a different perspective. The exercise below is designed to help adults see moving through the eyes of the child.

> You are sitting in your apartment's living room on a warm summer evening. Your spouse is dozing peacefully on the sofa. You're curled up with a good book, and your feeling is one of contentment.
>
> Suddenly, there is a knock at the door. You rise to open it. Standing there is a tall woman you have never seen before. She gently takes you by the arm, and ushers you into her car. She tells you there is no need to take any of your possessions as everything will be provided for you. Before you can comprehend what is happening, she's driving you away from your home.
>
> Soon you stop in front of a beautiful house with a broad, manicured lawn. The woman leads you inside, where she introduces you to the people there. They are warm and pleasant, and smile sweetly at you. The tall woman tells you that this is your new family. The new home is much bigger and more nicely furnished than your previous home. You are shown to your room. All of your new belongings are pointed out, and you are told to make yourself at home. The new people keep smiling at you. You look over your shoulder at the tall woman, who's smiling too. She assures you that this new family will love you forever. And all they expect in return is for you to love them back.
>
> You slowly look at your new surroundings. Your emotions are swirling out of control. You feel as if you are moving through a dream. This new family may be wonderful—superior to your old family in every way—but they're not your family. You don't even know them, how can you be expected to love them?
>
> The tall woman prepares to leave amidst your protests. You have lots of questions about your old family. She assures you that you do not have to worry about the past. You have a new family now and everything will be okay. She drives away.[1]

1. Versions of this exercise are widely used in adoption training programs. The creator of this exercise is unknown and thus proper credit cannot be provided.

Think about the ensuing questions. As you do, keep in mind that you are an adult. You have well-developed coping skills. The child you are moving into your home is still in the process of developing the proficiency needed to deal with major life transitions. If from a foreign country or if a very young child, she will not even have the language skills to tell you her thoughts or feelings.

What were your thoughts and feelings about leaving your home?

What were your thoughts and feelings about your new home?

Were you comfortable with your new family?

How did you feel when you were protesting and were told that everything was okay as you have a new family?

What do you suppose is happening in your old home?

How long would it take you to adjust?

Would you always have questions or thoughts and feelings about your previous family, friends and co-workers?

Would you need help to adjust? If so, what type of help might you need?

Hopefully, this exercise has helped you realize that the adoptive family and the prospective adoptive child may have diverging points of view about the pending move. The prospective adoptive child may have a mix of feelings. He may be happy that the move means a final residence, yet he may also be sad to leave behind those who have been caring for him and were currently involved in his life. He may also be anxious about whether or not this home will work out. He may be angry that his life is interrupted again. All this, while dealing with his past traumas and abandonments.

The children already in the family may also have a mix of thoughts and feelings which might be reflected in questions and statements such as: "What happened to his old family?" "Why did he have to move?" "Who was that lady who brought him here?" "I am so excited. I'll teach her all kinds of things." "She seems sad and scared. I'll show her around and cheer her up." "I hope she likes to play house." "I hope she likes my family and me."

Additionally, moving is a very stressful event even when it is for a positive reason. In fact, moving is among the factors listed as a main source of stress on the Social Readjustment Scale[2] (see Appendices). This scale allows you to determine the total amount of stress you are experiencing for various life events by adding up the relative stress values known as Life Change Units.

The purpose of this chapter is to look at the actual transition of the child into the family. This chapter is divided into "domestic considerations" and "international considerations," as there are differences in how children are moved in each of these types of adoption. However, each section is designed to be complementary of the other rather than to contain redundant information. So the reader is encouraged to review the chapter in its entirety. Both the domestic considerations and the international considerations include

- overviews of the people involved in moving a child to an adoptive family
- overviews of the pre-placement visitation period
- responses to the questions we must ask ourselves in order to plan a sensitive move

2. Thomas Holmes and Richard Rahe. "Social Readjustment Rating Scale." This scale was first published in the *Journal of Psychosomatic Research*. 1967, vol. II p. 214.

- potential types of *turbulence* which, in spite of planning, may arise and inhibit the smooth arrival of the child into the adoptive family
- suggestions to increase the sensitivity of the transition—smooth or abrupt. These recommendations allow the family to be excited while simultaneously acknowledging the adoptee's feelings to the contrary.

This chapter also includes "Adoptees Talk" boxes. The insight of these adoptees is quite interesting. The information comes from the report *About Adoption.*[3] The purpose of this report was to find out what adopted children thought about adoption—about the way they got adopted, about being an adopted person and whether or not that makes a difference at home or at school, and about what might be special about being adopted. The information was gathered by sending the adoptees question cards. Each card contained a question and a space for a response. The Adoptees Talk boxes contain the cumulative responses to these questions. The survey includes responses from 208 adopted children.

- The average age of the adoptees who responded was 11.
- The age range of the respondents was 6 to 22.
- The average age at which the children had been adopted was 4.
- Just over one in ten, 11%, had been adopted when less than one year old.
- Nearly a quarter had been adopted before they were 2 years old.
- Nearly one-half had been adopted under the age of 4.
- A quarter had been adopted when they were age 7 or older.
- Only 6% of children had been adopted after they reached "double figures" in age at 10 or older.
- The average time since being adopted was seven years.

It should be stated that while this book does put forth suggestions to enhance the way in which children are moved into adoptive families, *Brothers and Sisters in Adoption* is written primarily for parents. Consequently, the recommendations here may not thoroughly meet the needs of professionals reviewing this book. This audience is directed to *A Child's Journey through Placement*, by Vera Falhberg, and *Nurturing Adoptions*, by Deborah Gray (see Resources). These books are designed with the professional in mind, and both of these valuable resources offer discussions about moving children with sensitivity.

Moving Children with Sensitivity: Domestic Considerations

Who will we meet along the way?

Obviously, the prospective adoptive family and the waiting child are involved in the move. However, there may also be an array of other people involved in transitioning children to adoptive families.

3. Morgan, Roger. *About Adoption: A Children's Views Report*. (November 2006). Office of Children's Rights. http://www.rights4me.org/content/beheardreports/105/about_adoption_report.pdf

Adoptees Talk

Adoptees were asked, "What are the most important things that social workers should look for in a family?" Their responses were

- that they are kind and caring.
- that the child is likely to get along with them and be happy.
- that they like children and really do want another one.
- that they have the same background as the child they are adopting.
- that they will be able to look after the child properly.
- that they have things in common with the child.
- that they understand the child's needs.
- that their police check is OK.
- that they live in the right surroundings for the child.
- that they will go on loving the child forever.

Public Agency Staff

Typically, the child is in the custody of a public agency—a county agency regulated by a state and funded with public monies. The public agency is given the legal right to investigate abuse and neglect, remove a child from a home when necessary, and plan for the reunion of the child with the birthfamily or the severing of parental rights in cases wherein it is deemed unsafe for the child to return to the birthfamily. Once parental rights are terminated, the child is legally free for adoption. Thus, this agency then proceeds with determining by whom the child will be adopted.

A professional from this agency is assigned to manage the tasks associated with getting the child adopted. This would include recruitment efforts on behalf of the child, reviewing home studies of families being considered, interviewing prospective adoptive families, scheduling pre-placement visits, ensuring that a placement is supervised, preparing court paperwork, preparing a subsidy agreement, and granting consent for the finalization of the adoption.

The potential adoptive family may or may not be involved with the same agency. For example, the family may be a foster family who is adopting a child who has been in their care. Their foster care worker may handle the adoption, or another worker may be designated to complete the adoption. The public agency is also referred to as the custodial agency, the legal guardian or the legal parent.

Private Agency Staff

Often, public agencies work jointly with private agencies to locate an adoption resource for the child. A private agency may be established through a charitable group, by a religious community or as a community organization that offers services to children. Private agencies may recruit potential adoptive families, provide pre-adoption education classes and complete the home study. A professional from this agency will then submit the family's home study to the public agency in order to facilitate a match between a family and a waiting child.

This private agency then oversees the post-placement tasks as well—required post-placement visits to the adoptive home, referrals to needed services, crisis intervention, helping the family obtain an attorney to finalize the adoption, and post-placement adjustment matters to name a few.

Adoptees Talk

Adoptees were asked, "What did you want to know about when you were being adopted?" Their responses included these:

- About the process.
- When you would be allowed to see your birthfamily.
- What your adoptive parents are like.
- Why you have to be adopted.
- What happens if your adoption goes wrong?
- Does it have to be forever?
- How long will it take to be adopted?
- Where are you going to live?
- What will being adopted feel like?
- Will you be safe?

Eleven percent of children said there was nothing they wanted to know that they didn't already know when they were being adopted.

Foster Family

The foster family's role is to provide care to the child until the child either returns to the birth home or is adopted. As Chapter 1 noted, the foster family often becomes the child's permanent family. In the event the foster family is not the adoption resource, an adoptive family is located.

The foster family can play a vital role in transitioning a child to an adoptive family. The longer the child has resided with the foster family, the better this family knows the child. Foster parents can provide the adoptive parents with a wealth of information about the child—his likes and dislikes, personality "quirks," physical and emotional needs, effective parenting strategies, his routine, clothing sizes and much more. A foster family who is supportive of the adoptive family is often integral to a smooth transition.

Other Professionals

Frequently, the child's therapist is asked to assist in moving the child to the adoptive home. The types of tasks a therapist may carry out include hosting the initial meeting between the child, foster family and adoptive family. The therapist may meet with the prospective adoptive family to share information about the needs of the child and the types of interventions the child will require post-placement. In various instances, the therapist is asked to gather feedback after pre-placement visits in order to inform the public agency worker about how the placement seems to be proceeding. Some agencies use therapists to assist the family immediately upon post-placement. In this manner, each member of the adoptive family has a sounding board, and when problems arise, the family is already connected to support.

If the child is moving from a residential treatment facility or a group home (such as Ava whom we met in Chapter 5) then there may be numerous professionals involved in the child's life. Children living in facilities receive education and therapeutic intervention on site. Psychologists and psychiatrists are available to provide assessments and medication. There are staff members who oversee the living quarters. In essence, these professionals are the child's quasi caregivers. Most often, there is one particular professional who assists in scheduling and processing the pre-placement visits, and offers observations to the other parties involved in the transition of the child. Together, this team of professionals can provide the adoptive family valuable insight as to the child's needs and they can give the child "permission" to move on to adoption.

A Court Appointed Special Advocate (CASA) may be another person involved in the child's life. The mission of the National CASA Association is to support and promote court-appointed volunteer advocacy for abused and neglected children, so that they can thrive in safe, permanent homes.[4] CASA workers are community volunteers, appointed by the court, to speak up for the best interests of the children. A CASA volunteer is asked to work with a child until his or her case is closed, so a CASA worker may know a child for a long period of time.

The Court System

The public agency presents information to the court system on behalf of the child. It is a judge who makes the final decisions regarding the child's life. It is the judge who ultimately must decide if there is evidence to return a child to a birth home or if there is cause to move a child to an adoptive home. It is the judge who will also finalize the child's adoption.

Each child has a Guardian ad Litem as well. A Guardian ad Litem is most often an attorney appointed to represent the child. However, many Guardian ad Litems are volunteers from all walks of life. A Guardian ad Litem may carry out such responsibilities as:

- informing the child about court proceedings
- gathering and reviewing information about the child in order to recommend a resolution that is in the child's best interest
- determining whether a permanent plan has been created for the child in accordance with federal and state laws, and whether appropriate services are being provided to the child and family
- submitting written reports with recommendations to the court on what placement, visitation plan, services and permanent plan are in the best interest of the child
- attending and participating in court hearings, and other related meetings, to advocate for a permanent plan which serves the child's best interests.[5]

In addition to all of those above, there are other children and adults involved in the child's life at the time of a move. These other people may include church members, friends, school teachers, birthfamily relatives, neighbors, coaches, and foster family members.

The graphic on the next page depicts the many people who will help the child move to the adoptive home, as well as the children and adults with whom the child may have relationships. It is meant to illustrate that although moving to the adoptive home means gaining a permanent family, it also means leaving the comfort and security of many good friends and helpful, loving adults.

---

4. National Court Appointed Special Advocate Association. "Mission Statement." http://www.nationalcasa.org/about_us/mission.html

5. Florida Guardian ad Litem Program. "Frequently Asked Questions." http://www.guardianadlitem.org/vol_faq.asp

Considerations for Moving a Child Domestically: People Factors

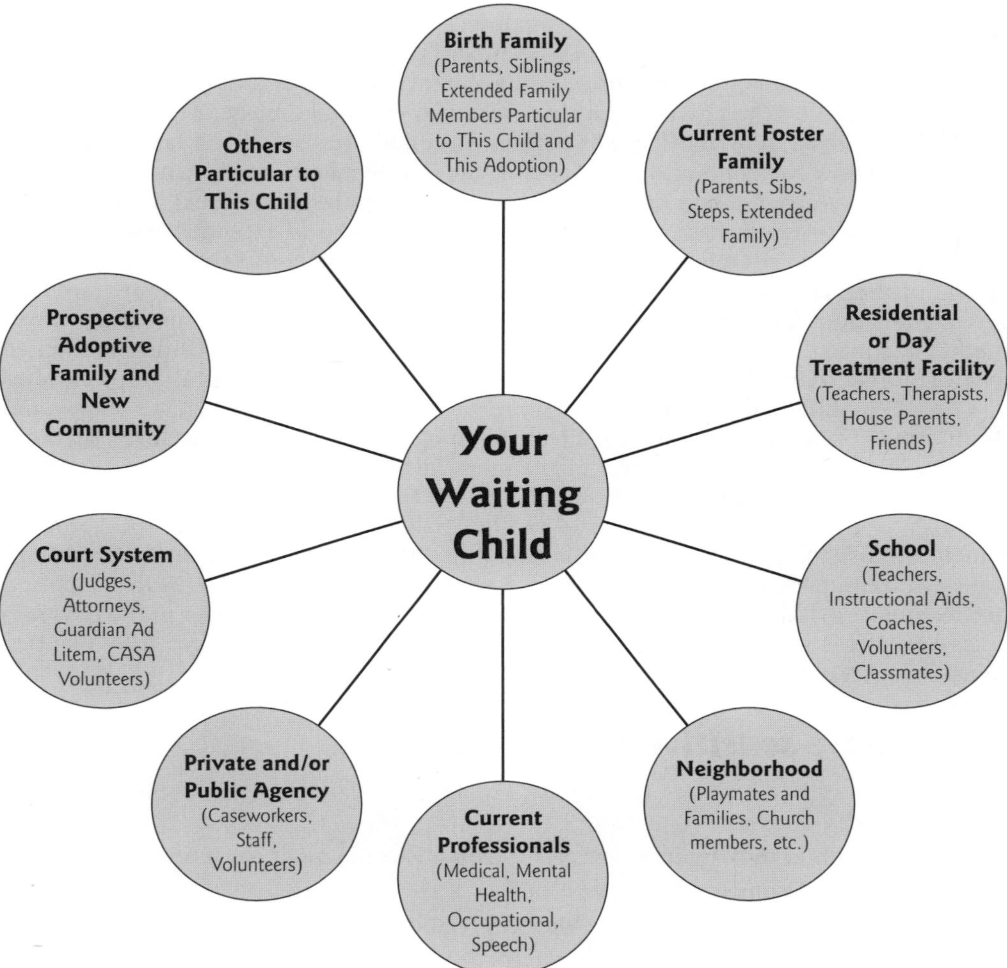

What are pre-placement visits and what will they be like?

Pre-placement visitation should occur prior to the placement of the child in your home. In general, there will be a series of visits during which the family and the child can become acquainted. If the family and the child reside within driving distance of each other, the first visit may be brief. It may consist of a few hours with the child at the foster home, group home, residential treatment facility or a neutral location that provides for a family activity. Subsequently, the family may take the child for an outing. Gradually, the child comes to the adoptive home for some overnight visits. Then the child moves in.

When the child is moving a significant distance that requires air travel, the overall visitation period may not involve as much transition time. The getting-to-know-each-other process may be carried out with a hotel or the child's current residence as a base. The child may or may not become acquainted with the adoptive family's home and neighborhood. Depending on expenses, there are cases in which the adoptee does not even get to meet his new siblings prior to placement. The family and the child's interactions are limited by the environment in which the visits take place. That is, the child does not get to see how the family operates on a daily basis and the family gains no insight as to how the child may interact with the family members. Transitions like this, almost always restricted due to financial constraints, are less than ideal. Families who can should make every effort to lobby for a more sensitive and extended transition.

In general, the pre-placement visitation period will be complete within a month or two of the first pre-placement visit (Fahlberg, 1991). Adolescents may require longer to transition. Overall, the probability of a placement disrupting—ending prior to the finalization of the adoption—increases with the age of the child. Children adopted when younger than 12 have about a 7% to 10% chance of disruption. Disruption rates of 47%, 24%, 22% and 13.5% have been reported for children over age 12 (Berry and Barth, 1990) (also see Chapter 7). Ensuring successful adoptive placement for adolescents often requires a high level of planning and preparation. Infants and toddlers can be transitioned within a few weeks (Fahlberg, 1991). This briefer transition period for younger children, however, should not be attributed to them being "too young to remember" or "too young to know what is going on." Actually, these common assumptions are completely inaccurate. Rather, the several week timetable refers to the period needed to adequately transfer an existing attachment from one caregiver to the new parents. Again, it is in a family's long-term best interest to insist upon a carefully planned transition period for the child, no matter what their age.

Is the move sensitive?

There are some questions we can ask ourselves to determine if the move is sensitively planned:

Is the child moving in a manner in which I would want to be moved?
Are the reasons for the move clear?
What is needed to help the child feel comfortable about the move?
What is the process to be followed?

Let's take each of these questions and explore them in more depth.

What is the process to be followed?

Children have many questions about the adoption process:

How long will it take?
How did my adoptive family find me?
How was my adoptive family "picked" for me?
How will I get to know the family?
Who will my social worker be?
Who will be checking to see if I am safe?
Who will talk to me about how I like the family?
What happens if I am not getting along with my adoptive family?
What happens once I am adopted?

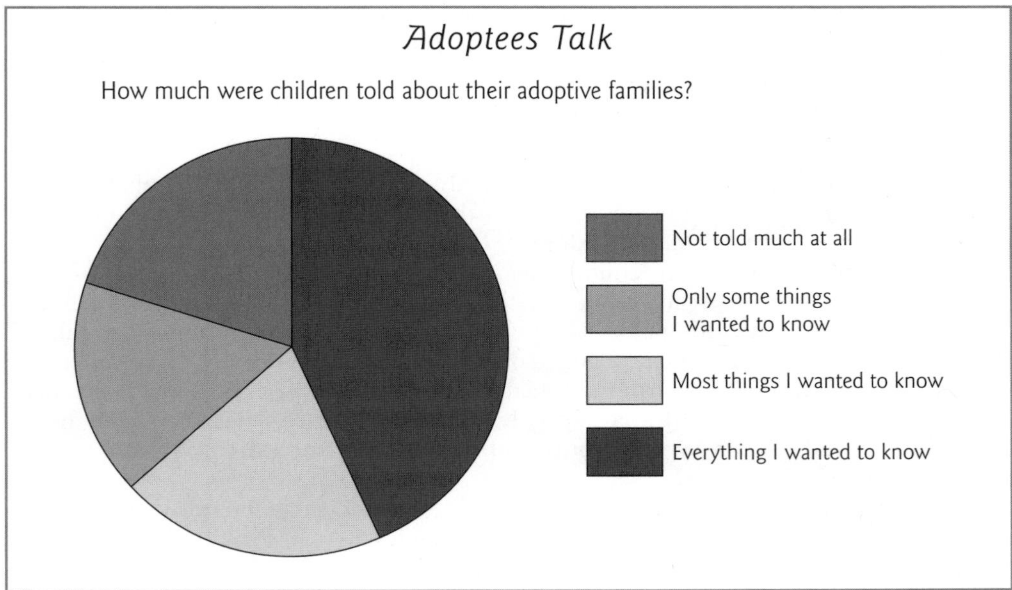

Children experience a profound loss of control once in the foster care system. They have no voice as to when they can see their birth parents or birth siblings. They reside in a foster home selected by a social worker. The therapist they see, their academic endeavors, whether or they can go on vacation with the foster family and even in some instances the style of their haircut is decided by someone else. Virtually all areas of their life are managed for them.

Responding to their questions about the adoption process restores some individual dignity and helps children become invested in the process. Older school-age children and adolescents in particular are more likely to have successful adoptive placements if they have input into decision making about their future (Fahlberg, 1991). Think about endeavors in which you were invested; you most likely worked hard to ensure that the venture turned out well. You probably tried different approaches as needed. Perhaps you asked others for input. Involving the child in the adoption process, responding to his questions, seeking his perspective and, when he is old enough, obtaining a commitment from him about his willingness to make the placement work are factors which enhance the outcome of the adoptive placement.

 **Key Point**—*Children need honest and clear responses regarding their concerns, fears and general questions about the process of adoption.* Children deserve to know what is going on in their life. Older children are more likely to join their adoptive families willingly if they are invited to invest in the process.

Are the reasons for the move clear?

Austin, age 8, boarded the bus to go home from school. In each hand, he proudly held a small flowering plant. The bus driver commented on the plants. Austin stated, "We grew them in class for Mother's Day. One is for the mom I live with now. The other is for my 'real' mom. I'll give it to her when I go live with her again." The bus driver was left speechless. The driver thought he remembered a day when Austin was absent from school because he was being adopted. After mulling over the conversation, the bus driver decided to inform

> Austin's parents. Austin's mom, Jamie, was shocked. Austin had been placed in their home when he was 6 years old. His adoption had been finalized one year ago. Jamie and her husband, Matt, decided to seek professional assistance. Shortly into the course of therapy, it became clear that Austin truly did not understand that he would not be returning to his 'real' mom's home.

Austin's story is actually fairly common. Unlike the structured programs that exist to provide parents preparation for adoption, there are limited formal procedures for preparing children for placement in adoptive families. Certainly, social workers explain adoption to children. However, children learn best by repetition. Think about helping your son or daughter learn his or her math facts. How many times did you need to go through those flash cards before your child could recite the multiplication tables? Often, we tell children complicated things only a few times and usually we are not clear. We say things such as, "Your birth mom really loved you. She just had some problems." In reality, "problems" are day-to-day struggles we all experience—flat tires, being in the checkout lane and realizing you forgot to stop at the bank, and missing a deadline on a big project at work.

The "problems" of birth families are much greater. They may include drug use, sexual assault, physical abuse, domestic violence, homelessness or leaving the child alone for extended periods of time. Social workers should be saying, "Your birth mom used drugs. These were not drugs the doctor gave her because she was sick. These were drugs people are not supposed to use. I don't know why she made this choice, but because of the drugs she wasn't safe for you to live with. She didn't always have a house, food or clothes. Sometimes she left you alone. You were too little to be by yourself. Sometimes she left you with people she didn't really know. It is okay if you want to be sad and mad about all of these things. You need a family to grow up in. All kids need families. I am going to help you find a new family called an adoptive family. Let's talk about some of the things you might like in a new family. Is it scary to think about moving to a new family? Would you like to tell me how you are feeling?"

Children benefit from honest discussions of the facts and their feelings. They must be able to answer the question, "Why can't I return to my birthfamily?" Children who have had several foster families must also know the reasons for each of these placements. Such conversations allow the child to grieve. Children who move through the grieving process begin to psychologically separate from their previous caregivers. Thus, they develop more capacity to attach to their new family.

Key Point—*Pre-placement is the time to ask the professionals and the caregivers involved in the transition the specifics regarding what the child has been told about his need to be adopted.* Who prepared the child and over what period of time? Did the child have access to group preparation or was it individual? What specifically has the child been told about his past and about adoption? Children who have only recently been informed about adoption may experience difficulties transitioning. Children who have had little preparation or less time to prepare for a move may require immediate connection to an adoption-competent mental health professional upon moving to the adoptive family. Overall, adoptive families can discern the child's level of preparation. Families need to realize that a lack of preparation inhibits the integration of the child into the family. Families should be aware that they can obtain services post-placement to assist the child in understanding his placement in the adoptive family. Chapter 9 will offer ways to talk to the child about his past. Parents will find that these suggested activities will also aid in integrating the adoptee into the family.

Is the child moving in a manner in which I would want to be moved?

Janine was 3 years old when the police arrived at her birth home. They had come to arrest her birth parents for the manufacturing and selling of drugs. The birthfather attempted to flee the scene. He was caught while trying to escape out a bathroom window. The birthmother was physically removed from the home, handcuffed on the front lawn and placed in a police car. Janine was picked up by a social worker, placed in a van and transported to the hospital for a physical exam to determine if she required any medical treatment because of exposure to the chemicals being utilized to manufacture the drugs. Once discharged from the hospital, she was transported to a foster home. The birthmother was pregnant at the time of her arrest. Her son, Jimmy, was born in prison. He was placed in a separate foster home. Jimmy and Janine remained in their respective foster homes for almost three years and then parental rights were terminated, legally freeing the children to be adopted. During this time, Jimmy and Janine had sporadic sibling visits.

The agency with custody felt strongly that the two children should be placed together in an adoptive family. Janine's family did not want to adopt due to their age and the fact that they had already adopted a number of their foster children. Jimmy's family wanted to adopt Jimmy but not Janine. They felt her behavioral issues were more than they could handle. Consequently, the custodial agency went about the process of locating an adoptive family.

Randy and May were selected. They were ecstatic. Between them, from earlier relationships, they had four children by birth. However, for reasons that could not be determined medically, they had been unable to conceive a child together. Randy's son and daughter resided with his first wife. They visited Randy and May every other weekend. May's two sons were in a shared parenting arrangement. Her sons spent Wednesday evenings and Saturdays at their dad's home. They also lived with their father for extended periods over holidays and summer vacation.

Randy and May flew to the state in which the children lived. They spent one week in a hotel. Janine was transported to the hotel daily for visits. Jimmy's foster mother was so distraught about his moving that she was unable to participate in this process. In fact, Jimmy was transported to the hotel by his social worker and, at the request of the foster mother, he never returned to her home. Seven days later, Randy, May, Jimmy and Janine flew home. Within another two weeks, Janine was attending her first grade class in her new school.

Let's think about this example for a moment. Jimmy abruptly left his mother of three years! She was the only mother he had ever known. He got on a plane with virtual strangers. He flew to a new home not knowing if he would ever see his previous home or neighborhood again. He met new parents, four new siblings and new pre-school classmates—all within a three-week period! Janine, age 6 when this move occurred, had only seven days to say good-bye to her foster family, neighbors and friends. The shock and confusion to these children was overwhelming!

Compare Jimmy and Janine's move to the transition of Ava.

Ava, age 12, was residing in a residential treatment facility when she met the woman who would eventually become her adoptive mom. Given Ava's age, it was difficult to find an adoptive family who would consider adopting her. So her custodial agency decided to seek a family who would take Ava on weekends and holidays. The agency believed that if someone would get to know Ava, they might decide to become her family.

Candice, a foster parent, expressed that she would be willing to respite Ava in this manner. Gradually, over a six month period, Ava enjoyed weekends with Candice. Candice loved

Adoptees Talk

Adoptees were asked, "What did you want to know about your adoptive family before you moved in?" Their concerns were

- what sort of people they are.
- the number of children and young people in the family.
- where they live.
- their personality and beliefs.
- reassurance that they want you and are friendly toward children.
- their family background.
- why they want to adopt you.
- if they have pets.
- if they have a story book or DVD about the family.
- if they will have contact with my birthfamily.

to cook and bake, and Ava also found this pleasurable. Candice had a college-age birth son, Todd. Todd's girlfriend Holly was studying cosmetology. Todd, Holly and Ava hit it off quite well. Ava especially liked it when Holly practiced various hair styles on her. Ava was able to participate in this family's traditions throughout the Thanksgiving, Christmas and New Year holiday season. She met Candice's parents, brothers, sisters, nieces and nephews. She had time to learn the neighborhood, the layout of the house and the routine of the family.

Candice also had time to learn about Ava's history. She spoke with the staff at the residential treatment facility, Ava's social worker and Ava's previous foster parents. Although she experienced Ava's defiance first hand, she experimented with various discipline techniques and learned that Ava could make changes. Candice broached the subject of Ava permanently moving to her home with Ava's social worker. The worker was thrilled. When Ava was informed, she was also excited. Approximately ten months later, Ava's adoption by Candice was finalized.

Would you rather be moved like Ava, or like Jimmy and Janine? As parents, how would you like your own children transitioned in the event something happened to you? While Ava flourished after her move to Candice's home, Jimmy and Janine struggled. Jimmy had terrible night terrors. He followed May everywhere she went. She could barely go to the bathroom without Jimmy knocking on the door to assure himself of her presence. He was inconsolable when May needed to go out without him. Janine could barely manage at school. She repeatedly asked her teacher when it would be time to go home. Her preoccupation with when the school day would end greatly interfered with her capacity to learn. Certainly, a considerable portion of these difficulties were a direct result of the traumatic manner in which Jimmy and Janine had been moved. Their experience of moving to Randy and May's house taught them that adults might simply disappear one day. In fact, everything familiar may vanish. Their trust in caregivers was shattered.

Key Point—*The adoptive family typically carries out pre-placement visits in the manner designed by the agency professionals. Yet, the adoptive family has the capacity to recognize when their adoptee is being moved in an abrupt fashion and should speak out.* Parents can look at the transition period and empathize with the child. They can put themselves in the child's place, and they can draw on experiences of their own life transitions to make determinations about whether the move seems planned or abrupt. Adoptive parents have the capacity to understand that abrupt moves are more injurious than planned transitions (Fahlberg, 1991). Traumatic moves can inhibit the formation of attachment post-placement. Adoptive parents can utilize care, compassion, concern and professional assistance to change or offset the impact of a traumatic transition.

What is needed to help the child feel comfortable about the move?

Think about a time when you were a "new" person—perhaps at a job, in joining a gym, when attending a new church or meeting your in-laws for the first time. Being the "new person" is often unsettling.

Listed below are the issues that should be addressed in order to reduce a child's awkward feelings of being the newcomer. These bullet points are for children ages 3 and older. Infants and toddlers have additional transitional needs that will be discussed later.

- Ensure closure with those being left behind.
- Make concrete plans for post-placement contact with those persons of significance to the child.
- Introduce the child to the people with whom the adoptive family spends time on a regular basis.
- Transfer belongings which are important to the child.
- Give a basic idea of the new family's routine.
- Provide advance opportunities to explore the new neighborhood.
- Review the rules of the new family and the types of discipline utilized for rule violations.
- Identify some of the interests the child and the family have in common.
- Identify the ways the family shows affection.
- Provide an opportunity for the child to meet the social worker who will be handling the post-placement visits.

Blemishes and warts: You mean you still wanted me?

It is important that the child, the adoptive parents, the foster family and the social worker review the information that has been provided to the adoptive family.

Danny entered foster care at age 7 because his older birth brother alleged that his birthmother's paramour was sexually abusing both boys. The sexual abuse included viewing pornographic movies and oral sex. Upon entering foster care, Danny began to engage in various sexual behaviors. Danny had been caught in a closet with a younger male child. The younger child reported that Danny had made the child "rub his private part." On the school bus, Danny was reported to be masturbating in front of several students. As a result of these behaviors, several foster families had requested Danny's removal from their homes. Danny was moved to a group home at age 11. He was still residing in this facility when William and Cindy applied to adopt him. William and Cindy lived near the group home. So during pre-placement visits they were included in his therapy. His therapist conducted a session during which he asked the family to tell Danny what they had learned about him to date. William and Cindy said, "Well, we know that Danny likes Mexican food. We were also told that he enjoys football, music and video games. We know when Danny came into foster care, and we know that he can't go back to his birthfamily because of the sexual abuse. We also know that Danny is sometimes sexual with other children." At that moment, Danny sat up and said, "You mean you know all that and you still want me?"

We initiate services, at the Attachment and Bonding Center of Ohio, by going over any documents the family received prior to the adoption of the child. This is necessary because, and contrary to the advice in this book, in most instances, the information has been kept from the child. Most children react as did Danny. They are surprised and relieved that their adoptive families chose them in light of knowing about their trauma and the types of challenging behaviors displayed. Actually, if we ponder this for a moment, it becomes clear that we all want to be accepted for our positive qualities *and* our blemishes and warts. The adoptee is no different. Unfortunately, many children live with chronic fears: "If you really knew what happened to me, you wouldn't want me." "If you knew the things I did, you couldn't love me." How can a child attach to a family if she is constantly worried that the family "wouldn't want her" or "couldn't love her?" Neglecting to let the child know the extent of the information given to adopting parents inhibits the quality of the attachment between the child and adoptive family members.

 **Key Point—***Adoptive parents can ease the re-location of the adoptee by acknowledging the types of information a "newcomer" needs to make him feel comfortable.*

 **Key Point—***Attachment is enhanced when the child knows she was selected in light of all that she thinks makes her unacceptable and unlovable.*

All of the preceding key points combine accepting that the child has a past while simultaneously inviting the child to join your family. In this manner the adoptive family makes clear to the adoptee, "We know you have a past. We know that past is important to you. We will be helping you with that as you need us to. We also want to tell you about ourselves. We will be important in your life as well." The dual acknowledgement will allow the child to grieve his past and thus, he can accept your invitation to join your family!

Adoptees Talk

Below are children's top ten ideas for improving the adoption process.

- Make it quicker.
- Involve and support the child more.
- Keep the child in touch with what is happening—in their birthfamily as well as in the adoption itself.
- Give more information about adoption.
- Don't change social workers in the middle of being adopted.
- Don't separate brothers and sisters.
- Go to only one foster home before getting adopted.
- Make the process more fun and enjoyable.
- Have more trial days with the new family.
- Let children themselves make the final decision on their new parents.

Turbulence in the Transition

Grief Reactions

Complicated placements may result in a child's rocky arrival. Grief reactions are one such difficulty. Grief reactions occur frequently, and while we should anticipate them and be prepared to offset them, we most typically respond by rushing the child to the adoptive home. A grief reaction is a behavioral response to a pending change. The child who is moving has many feelings about joining a new family. As explained previously, children who have experienced trauma often lack the capacity to express their feelings. Consequently, their emotions may spill out through negative behavior. With each pre-placement visit, the grieving child's behavior may deteriorate. The child may return to the foster home and unleash an array of difficult behaviors. In response, it is not unusual for the foster family to request that the placement be moved along more swiftly. This request is typically accommodated. The prospective adoptive family is called, and within short order the child is packed up and moved to the adoptive home. Do you remember Frank and Penny from Chapter 3? They adopted Marcus, age 8, and Celeste, age 12.

> Frank and Penny first met Marcus and Celeste at a fast food restaurant located halfway between their home and the foster home. The following weekend, Frank, Penny and Scott drove to the foster home and picked up Marcus and Celeste for an overnight visit. There were to be three more visits—two full weekend visits and then a one-week stay with Frank, Penny and Scott. However, the social worker called and asked if the children could move in right away. The worker explained that the foster mother had contacted her to report that the children's misbehavior had escalated since the visits were initiated. The foster parents wanted Marcus and Celeste removed from their home as soon as possible. Frank and Penny were in a quandary. They did not feel that they had had much of an opportunity to become acquainted with the children, but they had waited so long for children that they feared losing the opportunity to have the children at all if they said no. Early the following Saturday morning they drove to the foster home, filled their van with the children's belongings and drove home with Celeste and Marcus. By Thursday, the children had started school.

As might be expected, this placement was in a state of crisis for well over a year. There were many times when the placement was on the verge of disruption. Fortunately, the custodial agency was willing to invest in adoption-competent services and eventually, with this support, Frank and Penny proceeded with their adoptions of Celeste and Marcus.

As Valerie's example will highlight, grief reactions can occur for foster families as well.

Adoptees Talk

How should social workers check to see that children are happy in their new homes?

- Ask the child—but listen to the answers.
- Make visits to see the child.
- Speak to both the parents and the child—both alone and together.
- Spend time talking to the child away from the family home.
- Check how the child is fitting in both at home and at school.

Brad and Courtney were matched with 9-year-old Valerie. Their first visit occurred at a park. The foster family arrived with Valerie. Brad and Courtney were already there. They had brought a picnic basket and as they ate they shared photos of themselves, their two birth children, their home, pets and school. The visit seemed to go well. They were eager to get home and tell their children what they had learned about Valerie.

However, during the week, the foster mother expressed concerns to Valerie's worker about Brad and Courtney. The foster mother felt that Valerie needed a family with more experience with special needs. She did not feel that this was a good match. Valerie's worker spoke with the foster mother at length. He believed that he had handled the matter effectively.

The following weekend when Brad and Courtney arrived at the foster home to visit Valerie with their two birth children, no one was at home. They waited two hours and then drove home. They were disappointed as were their children. Subsequent visits had to be chaperoned by social workers. This certainly inhibited Valerie and her prospective family being able to interact in a casual style. The social worker was a constant reminder of the tension between the two families.

Due to the level of animosity expressed by the foster family, fewer visits occurred than had initially been planned. The placement was rushed. Valerie left her foster home of several years without the blessing of her foster mother. Later, Brad and Courtney learned that the foster mother wanted to adopt Valerie very much. Her husband would not agree. The foster mother's reaction to Brad and Courtney was that of her own grief for the pending loss of a child she loved dearly.

For the benefit of everyone involved, social workers must learn to be more sensitive to the loss issues that occur for the foster family when a child is leaving their home. They are letting go of a child whom they have nurtured and made a member of their family. While cautioned by professionals not to "get too attached" to the children in their homes, this philosophy is certainly difficult, if not impossible, to implement. We know that children need attachments to develop appropriately. This type of advice benefits no one. Valerie's foster mother needed assistance to process the loss of Valerie. She needed support throughout the transition of Valerie to her adoptive home. Valerie needed the foster mother's validation that the move to Brad and Courtney's was a positive move that would be of benefit to her. Everyone "lost" in this less than optimal move.

Valerie's case is a frequently seen scenario—one foster parent wants to adopt while the other does not. A heart-broken foster parent must come to terms with the loss of the child. In Jimmy's case, the decision to move him was made by the public agency. Thus, the foster family lacked control over the decision. Some foster parents desire to provide the child a home, but they do not want the legal responsibility that adoption brings with it. They are not given education about the benefits of adoption for the child. Consequently, they are often surprised when the custodial agency is able to locate an adoptive resource for the child. In other instances, the foster parents' decision not to adopt the child is voluntary. They may feel their age is prohibitive. They may have already adopted a number of children and so feel they are at their limit as to how many children they can parent over the long term. They may simply be a family who wants to foster. That is, they feel equipped to be an interim resource for children but not a permanent one. They may feel they cannot adequately meet the needs of the child. Whether voluntary or involuntary, a child leaving a home is an emotional event. Better education and support for all involved will benefit everyone—most importantly, the children.

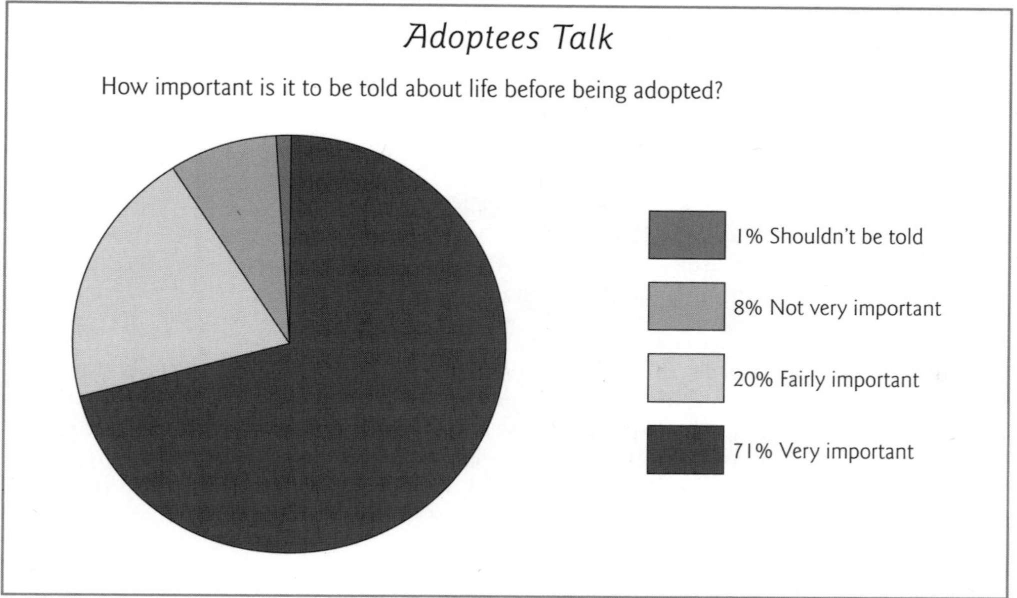

Adverse Reactions: Lack of Fit between the Foster and Adoptive Family

At times, foster parents and adoptive families react adversely to each other.

Richard and Claire parent seven adopted children ranging in age from 20 to 2. Their two oldest children are employed. The oldest is making plans to attend community college. Of their younger children, two are birth siblings ages 12 and 10, and three are birth siblings ages 7, 5 and 2. Within their younger sibling group, Donald, age 7, came to their home as a foster child; Patty, the now 5-year-old, had originally been placed in a separate foster home. Subsequently, this family decided that Patty's needs were too much for them to handle, so they requested her removal. The custodial agency contacted Richard and Claire and they agreed to accept Patty at age 3½. The youngest of the sibling group, Rose, was removed from the birth parents at birth, so she came to Richard and Claire's home at three days old.

The transitions of these seven adopted children were well planned and well executed. There were ample pre-placement visits carried out over an adequate period of time. There was wonderful cooperation between the foster families, the social workers and Richard and Claire.

However, the move of Nicole, age 8, the fourth and the oldest of Richard and Claire's younger sibling group was a very turbulent transition.

Nicole resided in a foster home. After three years, her foster family determined that they would not adopt her. Marital issues and Nicole's behavior were cited as the reasons for this decision. Upon hearing of this news, Richard and Claire immediately contacted the public agency and expressed their interest in Nicole. Nicole's worker promptly began the process necessary to facilitate the move. A first pre-placement visit was arranged. Two days before the visit was to occur, Nicole's foster family called the agency and reported that they had changed their minds; they now wanted to adopt Nicole. They further stated that they did not feel that Richard and Claire were an appropriate adoptive family. They felt that Richard and Claire "already had enough kids."

Ultimately, the agency held firm to their decision to move Nicole to Richard and Claire's home. Nicole's foster parents were very adversarial toward Richard and Claire during the course of the pre-placement visits. Nicole's placement was rushed, as everyone felt this was an emotionally harmful situation for Nicole.

It has now been two years since Nicole's placement with Richard and Claire. While she is flourishing, she still grieves the loss of her previous foster parents. She especially questions why they have never called, visited or even sent a birthday card. Richard and Claire have hard feelings toward the foster family as well. They resent the manner in which this family treated them and Nicole.

The underlying factors that led to this antagonistic situation actually revolved around feelings of guilt and anger on the part of the foster family. They thought they had failed with Nicole. She had spent three years in their home and made little progress. They were actually angry with the agency because they felt the agency had not done enough to support Nicole's placement in their home. Their dream of having a daughter had been shattered. They were grieving this loss by lashing out at Richard and Claire.

Jerry and Paula were motivated to adopt because of secondary infertility. They longed for a sibling for their birth son, Jason, age 6. They were matched with 9-year-old David. Jerry and Paula would be considered a fairly typical middle class family. They were both employed. Jerry was in management and Paula in computer programming. They attended church services on Sunday. Jason attended a private school. They enjoyed golf, reading, swimming, hosting cook outs and going on day trips. Paula enjoyed having the neighborhood kids over to play. They had a lovely finished basement complete with computer game equipment.

David's foster family attended church services several times per week. In fact, their lives revolved around church activities. David's foster mother was a stay-at-home mom. This situation required sacrificing financially. However, the family strongly believed that children needed a parent available.

The value differences between the two families were apparent at the first pre-placement visit. David's foster family questioned the selection of Jerry and Paula as the family for David. They made their position clear to the public agency worker and to Jerry and Paula. Jerry and Paula were stunned. The manner in which they carried out their values might differ from that of the foster family, but certainly their core values were appropriate and similar. They valued hard work, honesty, integrity, commitment and being responsible. They felt certain they were good parents with much to offer David. They were also angry. They had waited a long time for a second child. Now, their excitement was being ruined; a joyous occasion was quickly eroding into an upsetting experience.

This type of scenario happens when foster parents feel that they have been left out of the process of selecting the adoptive family. They believe that they know the child best, and, due to the contributions they have made to the child's life, they should have a say in the home chosen for the child. These may also be families who have had poor interactions with their agency so they are skeptical of agency decisions.

Placements plagued with such negativity become an emotional roller-coaster for all persons involved. Social workers feel as if a placement is jeopardized, and again the first reaction is often to move the child abruptly. Sometimes there are cases in which the entire placement is called into question. The custodial agency may second guess their decision-making process and the adoptive parents become quite distraught. After

Adoptees Talk

What do children most want to be told about their pasts?

- Why they couldn't stay with their birthfamily and so were adopted.
- Details about their birthfamily.
- Whatever they ask about.
- About their own life before they were adopted.
- Where they were born.
- If they have any brothers or sisters living someplace else, and why they were split up.
- Whether they can make contact with their birthfamily.

mounds of paperwork and scrutiny, plus the waiting period to find the "right" child, they feel as if they are being evaluated all over again. They become fearful that the placement will not happen. Well-meaning foster parents are angry at their lack of inclusion in the selection process of the adoptive family. Often the child is privy to the concerns of the foster parent. He develops anxiety about his move to his new family. Overall, feelings are flowing from all parties involved.

Toxic Environments: Lack of Fit between the Foster Family and the Child

A toxic environment is one in which a child and a foster family are not getting along. There simply is not a good fit between the foster family and the child. This type of environment creates a dilemma for the professionals involved with the child. The question becomes, "How long can we leave a child in a toxic environment?"

Olivia and Susan, ages 9 and 7 respectively, had been in foster care for about five years. They had resided in six different foster homes since their placement in foster care. Several of the moves were unrelated to the children. For example, in one foster home the foster mother had become seriously ill. So this family felt it better that the children move to another home. In a second home, Susan was discovered to have several bruises. The foster father was suspected of physically abusing her. Olivia and Susan were moved pending the results of an investigation. The current foster parents adored Olivia. However, they had a very difficult time finding anything positive about Susan. They frequently threatened to send her back to the agency. They often referred to her behavior as monstrous, an idea which they reinforced by having her dress as a monster for Halloween. The public agency had recently obtained the termination of parental rights for these children, so the process of finding an adoptive family was in the early stages.

The present family expressed an interest in adopting Olivia. They were adamant, however, that they would not adopt Susan. They expressed this view to the workers and to the children directly. The worker was in a quandary. She knew that Susan was being emotionally damaged by the negative comments directed at her by the foster family. Certainly, there was damage being done to the sibling relationship as well. Olivia wanted to stay with the foster family and she began blaming Susan for the fact that she had to lose yet another family.

The worker had two options. She could move the children to a temporary foster home and then move them again when she located an adoptive home. Or, she could expedite the search for an adoptive home, move them there, and hope the placement would work out. She opted for the latter choice. She contacted private agencies who faxed and emailed home studies to her office. She and her supervisor read the home studies and scheduled an information-sharing meeting with the family they felt best suited to adopt the girls. This meeting occurred on a Tuesday. The worker then arranged to go to Olivia and Susan's school to inform them of her decision to place them with a different family.

By Friday, the prospective adoptive family responded favorably to the prospect of accepting Olivia and Susan into their home and Saturday they met the children. On Monday, however, Olivia and Susan's foster family called the agency and informed the worker that they wanted the children moved immediately. The worker contacted the prospective adoptive family who, although feeling uncertain, decided to say yes to Olivia and Susan moving in. Two social workers picked up Olivia and Susan and their belongings, and drove the children to their new family. The move occurred within one week of the children being informed that adoption was being considered and the adoptive family being provided the children's history.

Some readers may find this particular story appalling. Yet, situations such as this one do occur with some frequency. While I certainly do not agree with the manner in which Susan was treated, I do know that grief over some past loss issues in the foster parents' histories played a role in the actions of this foster family. These past losses were creating a wave of grief.

Let's return for a moment to the content of Chapter 3, in a section called "Stress Management: Maintaining a Healthy Emotional Climate." These foster parents were extremely angry with Susan's behavior and exhibited their anger through punitive actions toward Susan. On one hand, this is reflective of the family's lack of understanding of a child's traumatic past. On the other hand, if we delve a bit deeper into the parents' histories, it is actually likely that something about Susan was triggering issues from their past. Unaware that this anger was unresolved grief for a past relationship, loss or trauma of their own, the anger was displaced onto Susan. Chapters 8, 9 and 10 will help us understand this phenomenon in greater detail.

It is important to point out that our example cases help illustrate that prospective adoptive families often feel pressured to accept placements. The family often perceives a power differential between themselves and the agency. The family views the agency as having the power to give them a child or not give them a child. They fear that a "no" from them may mean the loss of a child. This needs some reflection. The family is going to be doing the parenting—this means hard work, and hard work over a long period of time. As parents, if you feel you need a longer pre-placement period, I encourage you to say so. Agencies utilizing pressure tactics need to stop these unethical practices.

In conclusion, grief is often the common denominator in troubled transitions. Chapter 10 will offer ideas about facilitating the grief of adults and children.

Moving Children with Sensitivity: A Menu of Suggestions

This section provides some ideas that can be implemented during the pre-placement visitation process. Recognizing that each child and family are unique, and taking into account that the actual placement will vary along a continuum from smooth to abrupt to turbulent, an assortment of suggestions are put forth. The recommendations invite the child into the adoptive family while simultaneously acknowledging that the child has a past. As the *key points* presented earlier in this chapter explain this past-present manner of welcoming a child into the family establishes the groundwork needed post-placement to facilitate attachment among all members of the adoptive family. Parents and workers, individually or jointly, can select those suggestions which most seem to satisfy the needs of all involved in a particular placement. These strategies offer ample opportunity for the children already in the family to participate in the transition of their new brother and sister.

Photos: Yours and Theirs

"Our Family" Album

Prior to the start of visits, you might forward photos and information about your family. Many families opt to make a photo album of "Our Family" for the child. This allows each member of your family an opportunity to participate in pre-placement activities. Let your children select favorite photos of themselves and add some fun captions. Include photos of each family member, your home, extended family members, the school the new child will be attending, your community and family pets. Other families decide to make a video or DVD containing this information. Allowing the adoptee the opportunity to "meet" you before you arrive is a great way to reduce his anxiety about what you look like, how many people are in the family, what type of home you have and what kind of neighborhood he will be moving to.

"Their Past" Photos

It never ceases to amaze me how few photos children have of their life prior to their adoption. Despite the fact that the creation and maintenance of a life book for each child who enters care has been considered a "best practices" standard in North American social work for many years, only a minority of children have photos of their birth parents and siblings, themselves, and previous foster families, schools and neighborhoods. Even smaller numbers of children adopted from outside North America have such photos. It is very difficult to put your life together when you have so little information. The analogy we often use in therapy is that these children are like a 500 piece puzzle missing 400 of the pieces. Photos are an integral part of healing the traumatized child.

Throughout my years in adoption, I have helped many families go back and obtain pictures. However, once the adoption is complete the task becomes complicated—foster families have moved, are no longer with the agency, or have become ill or died. Professionals take different jobs or retire, siblings have moved and so on. Additionally, once an adoption is finalized, many states' laws require sealing the child's earlier child welfare file. This means that the contents cannot be accessed without a court order. Let me urge you to ask for photos and materials such as report cards and school awards during the pre-placement process. Janine, for example, had lived with her foster family for three years. They had taken an abundance of photos. Actually, sorting through the photos

> *Adoptees Talk*
>
> What are the best ways of getting to know your adoptive family?
>
> - Visiting and staying a few days before moving in.
> - Going on days out with the family.
> - Spending time talking with your future adoptive parents.
> - Being given a video or book about the family.
> - Having fun and playing games with the family.

turned into a great way to get to know Janine. She was eager to talk about the places she had been and the people who accompanied her.

Make it a priority to obtain as many photos as you can. If the foster family has any video, gather that up as well. Copies are easy to make if the foster family does not want to part with their originals.

If the child was in more than one foster home, gathering photos can be initiated pre-placement and then completed post-placement. Work with the social worker to identify these families, pressing if you must. The custodial agency has a record of where the children were in placement. Celeste's story provides a good example of how to go about this.

> In helping Celeste piece together her life after her adoption, we knew that she and Marcus had been in eight previous homes. We had the starting dates and ending dates of each placement. Although Celeste remembered some of the families' names, she did not know their addresses. Her adoptive mother and I composed a letter to each of the families on our office stationary.[6] We explained who we were and when Celeste and Marcus had resided in their home. We explained that we were seeking photos or any other information they would be willing to share. We enclosed a return envelope addressed to our office with each of the letters. Marcus and Celeste's public agency worker kindly completed the mailing as all she had to do was address the envelopes. Several of the families responded. Celeste and Marcus were thrilled to see pictures of themselves and their previous caregivers! One foster mother took the time to write the children a letter about herself and their time with her. She closed the letter by telling them how happy she was that they had been adopted. This was the first time that Celeste felt as if any of her previous families had cared about her!

The Lifebook

The lifebook provides a chronology of the child's life, helping the young person understand and remember what has happened to him in the past (Fahlberg, 1991). As mentioned above, lifebooks have been widely used for years as a tool to help children heal from past traumas. Many children adopted from the child welfare system will have a lifebook, or at least a lifebook may have been initiated. Ask if the child has a lifebook. If so, review it with the prospective adoptive child and the children you already parent. Again, this lets your prospective adoptee know you are interested in all parts of his life. This will help your resident children as well since it will likely generate questions. These questions may be repetitive of those asked during pre-adoptive training:

"What happened to her birth mom?"

"Why do some kids need new families?"

"Where would we live if something happened to you and Dad?"

"Why has she been in so many homes?"

"Why do people use drugs?"

"Why do people hurt each other?"

Remember—children learn best by repetition. It is important to continue to provide the children you already parent opportunities to ask questions. The better the brothers and sisters understand the adoptee's troubled beginnings, the better context they have for the problems that may set in post-placement. This understanding contributes to

6. We always suggest using an intermediary such as a therapist or social worker when making first contact with any person from the child's past. This ensures confidentiality, should that be important to you or to any foster family.

coping. We all cope best when we have information. This is true for parents as well. Chapter 5 offered some examples of how to talk with the children already in the family. Chapter 9 will give more of these illustrations, and Chapter 9 will discuss the lifebook in more detail.

In return, when the adoptee visits your home, share your family photos albums and scrapbooks. These are, to a large extent, your already-resident children's lifebooks. This gives the adoptee a sense of the types of family fun she may expect. It also begins to give the adoptee a sense of your family history.

A Photo-Taking Adventure

If the child has few photos, you can go on a photo-taking adventure. This would include taking photos of the child's current family and residence. This type of photo-taking adventure is a great pre-placement visit activity for you, the children you already parent and the child joining your family. Make sure the child has several pictures of the foster family and foster home, as well as the child's bedroom, school, favorite places in the neighborhood, pets and anything else that seems important.

While you have the camera, take photos of the "new" family—parents and all of the children. Display several of the photos during pre-placement visits and send the new child a couple via regular mail or email. The brothers and sisters need to see the family as it will be, and the son or daughter-to-be needs to see himself or herself as a member of your family. You can also use this visual to re-visit discussions with the children you already parent regarding any pending role changes or changes in birth order. "When Jean moves in, you are going to be the big brother. Have you thought about what being a big brother means? Let's sit down and talk about your new responsibilities."

Jim and Andrea combined photo taking with a closure event.

> Jim and Andrea were in the process of pre-placement visits with 10-year-old Grace. They felt it important that Grace be able to say good-bye to her classmates and her teacher. Andrea worked with Grace's foster mother and teacher to plan a social event that was held in Grace's classroom. The social included snacks, games and a brief presentation about adoption. Throughout the social, Andrea helped Grace collect phone numbers and emails. Jim spent his time taking lots of photos. Andrea had also purchased a new journal for Grace. She invited each of Grace's classmates to write something they would miss about Grace in the journal and then sign their name. The principal and Grace's soccer coach were able to attend the gathering as well. Grace received the support of many peers and adults as she transitioned to her adoptive family. After her move to Jim and Andrea's home, the journal and the photos proved a source of comfort for Grace.

Overall, photos offer a means to get acquainted with your child while simultaneously acknowledging that the child's past and current relationships are valued by the new family.

Contact between Visits

Time between visits or the lead time prior to the start of visits can be maximized. This may be a particularly beneficial solution when the placement involves distance.

> Logan and Sophie parented two children by birth, Zack, age 11 and Paige, age 9. Seven-year-old Faith was soon to join the family. As Faith lived in a different state, two pre-placement visits were planned. On the first visit, Logan and Sophie would spend a period of four days. It is often best if the parents only meet the child on the first pre-placement visit. This sets the tone for the importance of the parent-child relationship (Fahlberg, 1991).

Adoptees Talk

How can an adoptive family help a new child settle into their home?

- Spend time with the child.
- Love and care for them.
- Make them feel welcome and comfortable.
- Give them treats.
- Give them reassurance and support.
- Decorate their room with them.
- Show them around everywhere they need to know.
- Provide for the child's needs.
- Understand the child's feelings.
- Give them personal space.

> The second visit would occur three weeks later and would include Zack and Paige. Sophie explained to Faith's foster mom that each night before going to bed, the family shared the "best" and "worst" part of their day. Sophie wanted to include Faith in this ritual. She thought it would help all of them get acquainted. The foster mom agreed. They altered the tradition just a bit. Sometimes, they did the best and worst part of their day. Other times, they utilized questions about bests and worst to learn about Faith's likes and dislikes and vice versa. They created a series of questions about likes and dislikes. For example, what is the "best" and "worst" food for dinner? What is the best and worst rule? What is the best and worst chore? What is the most fun game? What games do you like the least? They learned that Faith's foster mom made chocolate chip pancakes on her birthday and that Faith just thought this was great. They also learned that Faith enjoyed playing the game, Trouble as did Paige. Faith was used to going to sporting events as she had two older foster brothers. Zack participated in athletics year-round. Faith's least favorite chore was cleaning her room. Her favorite dinner was macaroni and cheese and hot dogs. Her least favorite dinner was meatloaf. Paige agreed with the latter!

Learning likes and dislikes is a great way to begin to form relationships. Email, snail mail, cell phones, the capacity to download photos and Instant Messaging make connecting with the child between visits or prior to the start of visits much easier than it was in years past.

Keep to Your Routine

When the adoptive family and their prospective child live in the same area, pre-placement visits do not always have to be an outing. In fact, sticking to your normal routine may be beneficial. It gives your adoptee the chance to truly see how the family operates. It allows the adoptee to view himself as a family member rather than as a guest. Outing after outing gives the child a false sense of the family. If Saturday morning is designated for chores, then assign the adoptee a chore. If Thursday evening is grocery shopping, take the child along. Errands offer the new child a chance to check out the neighborhood. Have your soon-to-be daughter help unload the car when you arrive home.

As you are completing your tasks, provide the child an overview of your expectations. For example, "When we go to the grocery store, I expect you to stay with me." Or, "We are going for videos. Today, it is Tommy's turn to select the movie. Your turn will be the next time you visit with us." Or, "When we all have our chores done, we'll play a game."

Certainly, there will be times when keeping to your routine may not be possible. For example, many families utilize pre-placement visits to decorate the new child's bedroom. This is certainly a great way to welcome the child and to make the child feel comfortable and special. There may be instances when you want to introduce the new arrival to extended family. Or, some of your pre-placement time may be spent in closure activities with the people the child is leaving behind. Overall, incorporate as much "reality" about the family as is possible into your pre-placement period. Additionally, keep in mind that your resident children will be watching to see how you will be treating their new sibling. They need to see you establishing boundaries while simultaneously welcoming the adoptee. They want assurance that they will not be forgotten and they want to know that rules will apply to each child in the family.

Transitioning the Child's Possessions

Once there is an agreement that the child will be moving to the adoptive family, the family should begin to move the child's belongings. A gradual moving of toys, clothing and sentimental items is recommended. First, it is simply easier to move a small amount of things in steps, over time than it is to move a large amount of possessions. Those of you who have moved certainly know this to be true! Second, a slower transfer of belongings allows less chance of forgetting items of importance to the child. It also gives the adoptive family time to look things over and decide what the child has and what the child needs. Third, the child will have familiar items around them during the pre-placement visits. Most of us like to travel with some of our own special toiletries or our favorite pillow. Likewise, a child likes to have his belongings on hand. Fourth, it contributes to the child's understanding that the move is definitely occurring. Lastly, moving day itself is not so shocking to the child nor consumed with a frenzy of packing. There will be adequate time for the foster parents and foster siblings to have closure.

Infants and young children require some special considerations in this area. These youngest children are very sensory. That is, the familiar smells, sounds and "feels" of their environment are their way of knowing their world. Their crib, sheets, toys and clothing should be moved with them whenever possible. They smell familiar, and the child is accustomed to how these items feel and sound. Ask the foster parents about detergents and softeners, and soaps and lotions they use so that you can consider using them for a while as your child transitions. Look around at the lighting of the child's bedroom—as well as whether it is brightly colored or rather plain—and consider using similar lighting and colors. Perhaps the foster mother sings a particular lullaby. A recording of her voice may be comforting to the toddler or infant post-placement. There may be the "white noise" of a radio or CD player constantly playing in the background of this home. Maybe you could play some soothing music throughout the day as well.

An abrupt removal that separates the young child from everything familiar is injurious to his well-being. As it is likely the foster family will go on to accept other children into their family, the adoptive parents can offer to give the foster family the replacement value of the belongings that move with the infant. You can expand the child's wardrobe and other belongings as the child becomes familiar with you. So you do not necessarily have to sacrifice the entire joy that comes along with decorating a nursery or a young child's bedroom. If an exchange is not possible, an alternative would be that the infant or young child is provided items, from you, in advance of the move. These stuffed animals, clothes, linens, pacifiers, rattles, bottles and so on would then accompany the child back to your home.

The infant or toddler also benefits when routines are maintained immediately post-placement. Ensure that you learn the infant's or toddler's routine during your pre-placement visits. The adoptive family should have the opportunity to carry out the tasks of the child's routine as the visits are conducted. As the child becomes acquainted with you, you should begin to feed and bathe the child as well as change her diapers, play with her, help put her to sleep and be there to help wake her up. Even if their routine does not flow with your family's schedule initially upon her arrival in your home, it is important to make the changes necessary to accommodate the schedule to which she is accustomed. Allow the infant or toddler to gradually adjust to your family's everyday life, with its own unique routine and sensory stimulants.

The toddler is in a particularly precarious position during the pre-placement period. He is too young to totally understand what is going on but old enough to know something major is happening in his life (Hopkins-Best, 1997). It is the wise adoptive parent who recognizes this. It is the sensitive adoptive parent who sits with this child and reviews an "Our Family" album. The responsive parent also introduces adoption books such as *A Mother for Choco*, *The Day We Met You* or *Zachary's New Home* (see Chapters Resources). This helps the toddler begin the essential process of understanding how he came to live in your home, and have the opportunity to grow into his adoption story. Being adopted will become a part of who he is. All children—infants through adolescents—benefit from understanding the circumstances that led to their adoption.

Adolescents also like to move with as many belongings as possible. Think about this. Would you even consider moving without your bed, furniture, clothes, favorite CDs, treasured knick-knacks or sentimental possessions? Whenever possible, arrange exchanges of new items for the favorite items of the older child entering your home. This demonstrates respect and dignity to these oldest children who have experienced too many losses. Move their belongings in suit cases. Garbage bags tend to be the luggage of the foster child. The negative connotation is obvious.

Orient the Child to Your Routine

An active family, Jenna and Ben, made a calendar of the family's typical week. For example, Tuesday evening is karate and Thursday is after-school bowling league for their 10-year-old birth daughter, Diana. Using clip art, they put a picture of karate on each Tuesday and a picture of bowling on each Thursday. Wednesday night is choir practice for the entire family. Friday night, the family goes out for pizza and then home to watch a movie. Saturday morning is set aside for chores, and Saturday afternoon is free time. Sunday is church and then a visit to Grandma at the nursing home. Pictures for each of these activities were attached to the calendar as well. They presented the calendar to their new son, Kenny, age 8. This helped Kenny learn the routine of his adoptive family. They also reviewed Kenny's current routine with Kenny and his foster family. They pointed out what would be different for Kenny and what would be the same and added pictures demonstrating the activities he enjoyed—such as Cub Scouts and soccer team—on the days they would occur in his new family.

A Blessing Party

A long-standing adoption tradition is that of good-bye visits or good-bye parties. The blessing party is simply re-framing this tradition (Villanueva, 2005.) Blessings are preferable because they carry the connotation of permission or sanction. Blessings say to the child, "Go ahead, join your new family. This is a good thing." Blessings are more upbeat than good-byes and carry less baggage for the child who has already experienced them in abundance.

A blessing party can be held at the adoptive family's home, the foster home or at a location convenient to those attending. Invite as many people from the child's past as is possible. Decorate a basket or a cardboard box in a manner suitable for the event. Place your basket or box on a table. Surround it with note cards. Ask each person attending to write the child a blessing—a positive statement about the transition to the adoptive family. Read them with the child. Afterwards, create a scrap book. A Blessing Party allows the child to enter the adoptive family on a wave of support.

Assign "Getting to Know Us and You" Activities

Typical siblings-to-be want to be helpful as the adoptee joins the family. Parents can assign specific tasks to help direct this caring energy in productive ways. Being in charge of an important undertaking also helps the children you already parent feel significant in the transition. For example, "When Johnny comes this weekend I was hoping you could give him a tour of the house. Any time he needs anything this weekend, could you be in charge of helping him find it?" Or, "Sally is going to need to know the rules of the house. I thought we could all sit down and go over the rules. Would you like to lead the conversation? I think you could do such a good job. You could also let her know what kinds of consequences we use." Assignments could also be used to identify different family characteristics. For example, who tends to be grumpy in the morning, the ages of each child in the family or which parent to go to for different types of needs (i.e., "Go to Mom when you want a snack. Go to Dad when you need help with math.").

Let's return to Nicole, Richard and Claire for another type of assignment.

> Nicole was the eighth child to join their family. This is a lot of people to get to know! Claire sat the children—young and older—around the kitchen table. Each child had tape, glue and construction paper. Claire and Richard were ready with the scissors. In the middle of the table, Claire put a stack of old magazines. Each child was assigned the task of locating pictures that reflected their interests. By the time they were finished, each child had a collage of, "All about Me." The collages were displayed on the kitchen bulletin board until Nicole became familiar with her new siblings and vice versa.

Arrange Ongoing Contact with Persons of Significance to the Child

Planning contact with those the child is leaving behind is important. It decreases the adoptee's anxiety and emphasizes that relationships are valuable. If we want the child to form healthy new relationships, then we must model good relationship skills ourselves. His past experiences of relationships may be of the abrupt fashion. He may be concerned that once again he will be cut off from everyone familiar.

Pre-placement offers the opportunity to determine who is important to the child. Discuss their importance with these people and the adoptee. "You know, Mrs. Smith, you have been very important in Bobby's life. I know that he has shared a bedroom with your son for two years. I think after he moves, he should continue to have contact with you and your son. I was thinking that phone calls once a week would work at first and then gradually we could go to once a month. This is about how often my other children have contact with their aunt who lives out of town and that seems to work out nicely. I also thought you and your son might like to come to visit. Would a call once a week work for you? Is there a best time to call you? What do you think about a visit?" Then post-placement follow through with this plan for contact.

The child moving on to adoption may be moving with his siblings, or his siblings may be in foster homes or with other adoptive families. In Chapter 2 it was pointed out that 70% of children in foster care who have siblings in care are not placed with those siblings. The loss of siblings is very painful for the traumatized child. Overall, most children benefit from staying in contact with their siblings. However there are cases in which this contact creates additional stress for the adoptee. For example, the sibling may be living in residential treatment (Chapter 10), the brother or sister may still not be adopted or the sibling may be incarcerated. These types of living arrangements cause grief because the implication is, "My sibling isn't doing well." or "My sibling doesn't have a family." There are also instances in which the sibling was sexually or physically abusive to the adoptive child. In these cases, we need to weigh the benefits of contact versus the emotional strain and determine what is best.

Contact with brothers and sisters often occurs along a continuum. Many children are satisfied knowing where their siblings live and how they are doing. This information can be obtained through the parents and passed on to the adoptee. Others want letters, email, current photos and phone calls. Still others want in-person visits. During the pre-placement phase, obtain as much information as possible about where the child's siblings reside. Determine if the foster or adoptive families are open to contact. As you get to know your child, ascertain what type of sibling contact best meets his or her emotional and safety needs regarding continuing connections with brothers and sisters.

Children in foster care may remain in contact with various birthfamily members. Certainly, when the child is adopted by birth relatives—a kinship adoption—it is likely there will be contact with various birth relatives. As a system we have a "blood is thicker" mentality. We tend to support ongoing visitation with the birthfamily. In reality, it may be better to decide this on a case-by-case basis. There are birth parents who have committed serious crimes against their children. If an adult woman is raped, do we suggest that she visit her rapist for the rest of her life? The answer is "no." Yet, in many instances contact means this exact situation for the child with a traumatic past. On the other hand, there are birth grandparents who have greatly contributed to the removal of their grandchildren from neglectful and abusive homes. Due to their age, health or finances, they have opted not to become the long-term caretakers for the child. These relatives prove valuable connections for the child. They can validate that the removal of the child from the birth home was necessary. They can provide the child with family history and medical information.

Overall, we need to conduct visits with birthfamily members based on what makes sense and who is safe. In some cases, a schedule of contact may be needed to help the child put previous relationships in a healthy context. Samantha's situation is a good example.

> Jacob and Rosemary entered therapy with 8-year-old Samantha. She had been adopted about 18 months before. Prior to her arrival in their family, she resided with an elderly single foster mom whom she called, "Grandma." To date, she calls Grandma on the phone daily. On weekends, she wants to call Grandma several times per day. It is Grandma with whom she wants to share the events of the school day. It is Grandma she tells about her class trip or a family outing to the zoo. It is Grandma she wanted to speak to about every aspect of her life.
>
> Samantha was not separating from Grandma. The therapist spoke with Grandma and explained the situation. The therapist helped Samantha, Grandma, Jacob and Rosemary create a schedule of contact. Samantha would initially call Grandma every other day, then once

a week, then once per month, etc. As contact with Grandma decreased, Samantha began talking more to Jacob and Rosemary. Her relationship with Grandma remained important, yet it became secondary to her relationships with Mom and Dad.

Usually in any move, a process occurs wherein as we integrate into our new communities, we meet new people and establish fresh relationships. Simultaneously, we lose contacts with former friends. The same process should occur for adopted children. Initially, they may call friends, foster parents, a social worker or other significant persons frequently. This is normal and should not be taken personally by the adoptive family. When this contact remains so regular that it is inhibiting healthy new attachments between the adoptee and the adoptive family members, however, then we can help the child put previous relationships in an appropriate context by creating a schedule of contact.

Meeting the Foster Parents

All too frequently, foster and adoptive families criticize the parenting methods and lifestyle of one another. It is almost as if a competition develops between the two families as to who is truly the best family for the child. Yes, your new child's foster parents may parent differently than you do. Yes, you and the foster parents may have different interests, professions, religious beliefs or sexual orientations. You may be of a different race or culture. There may be an age difference. "Different," however, does not necessarily mean that inadequate care giving has been provided to the child. Seek points of connection with one another rather than points of contention.

Examples of the types of adversarial relationships that can occur were shared earlier in this chapter. The child does not benefit from these situations because the most frequent end result of adult conflict is the severing of contact with persons the child cared about. The child loses people that he has known, often for years. If the situation becomes adversarial, stay focused on your efforts to transition your child as well as you can and monitor your own responses. Remember, your child's healthy transition and her reaction to new people in her life is what is most important.

Post-placement, recognize that a child who has been rushed into your home will need extra attention. Connect with an adoption-competent mental health professional who can assist you and your son or daughter in putting the circumstances of the hasty move in the proper context.

Rely on your social worker to help you with all transitions, but especially troubled transitions.

Richard, Claire and Nicole's pre-placement visits were fraught with negative interactions. However, they worked with Claire to help her make a list of possessions she wanted from her previous foster home. She also wanted a photo of Natalie, a sibling with whom she had shared a bedroom for three years. Claire made no promise that the items would be obtained. However, she felt it was important that Nicole know that she had made the effort on her behalf. Claire passed this information on to the social worker. The social worker negotiated for these items. Nicole was ecstatic when the social worker arrived with several photos of Natalie and her blue stuffed bear!

Indeed it is important in abrupt or turbulent transitions that the child knows that you have made an effort to obtain possessions of importance, meaningful photos or arranged for a visit. Even if the outcome is contrary to Nicole's outcome, the child learns that you are a parent he can rely on. You are a parent who cares about what is important to him.

Go Back after the Placement

When a placement is rushed, there is still the option of returning post-placement to obtain closure with significant people in the child's life. The case of Jimmy and Janine, whom we met earlier in this chapter, exemplifies this suggestion.

> Several months post-placement, Randy and May realized that Jimmy was not overcoming the loss of his foster mother. After numerous phone calls to the custodial agency, May was able to arrange to speak with the foster mother. Slowly, she had been recovering from the loss of Jimmy so she was now in a position to resume some contact with him. The contact was initiated with a series of cards and then phone calls. The foster mother sent photos, and eventually Randy and May purchased her a plane ticket. She spent a week visiting with the family. Although his road to recovery will still be a long one, having his foster mother's presence and her validation of his placement in his new home helped Jimmy perk up.

Grief often subsides with the passage of time. Previous caregivers, initially overwhelmed with emotions, later become open to the idea of resuming a connection with the child.

> Jimmy has now lived with Randy and May for three years. Since the foster mother's initial trip to their home, Randy and May have continued contact with her via email and telephone. Currently, they are planning a vacation to her state. Jimmy will get to visit her, and they plan to utilize some of this time to gather photos of the hospital where he was born and his former neighborhood. They are also looking forward to having dinner with Janine's previous foster family.

Consider the Feelings of the People Being Left Behind

Actually, Jimmy's transition, if it needed to occur at all, should have been delayed until the foster mother was in a position to provide this closure for him. However, in cases where this is not possible as it was not for Jimmy, Valerie and Nicole, it is suggested that the adoptive family make efforts to contact the previous caregivers, either directly or through a social worker. A letter or a phone call validating their grief and their importance to the child may allow them to feel that they can begin again in their relationship with the child. This is of benefit to everyone.

The child welfare system as a whole purports that part of foster parenting is letting go. In essence, the belief is that letting go is part of the job description of foster parents. The expectation that they knew a move could happen prevents us as a system from offering the foster parents greater assistance with their grief. Certainly, this is an area that could stand significant improvement. However, you as adoptive parents can extend your empathy. You can understand and acknowledge their grief. You can assure them of your desire to care for the child whom they hold dearly in their hearts.

Please keep in mind that the foster family may have children too—birth, foster and/or adopted. Their "brother or sister" is moving. They have feelings about this experience: "I am going to miss him." "I have been in conflict with him. Is he moving because we didn't get along?" "I am mad that my parents aren't keeping her. I really like her and I wanted her to stay." They have concerns: "Where is my brother going? Will I ever see him again?" "Are you going to take good care of my sister?" Acknowledge these children during pre-placement. Make an effort to assure them that you plan to take good care of their sibling. Thank them for contributions they have made in the life of the child who is leaving their home to join your family.

Moving Children with Sensitivity: Considerations in Situations of Kinship Care

As Chapter 1 pointed out, a kinship placement may occur after a pre-placement period or the niece, nephew, grandchild, or cousin may arrive abruptly. Especially if the latter scenario applies, the preceding content can be applied to help the newly arrived relative transition into his new home.

However, kinship placements that continue long-term have an additional consideration. Caregivers with no public agency involvement—private or voluntary kinship care—may have limited access to services and programs. They may have difficulty enrolling the child in school. They may not be able to consent for medical treatment or place the child on their health care plan. The child will also be excluded from federal types of health insurance such as Medicaid.

These limitations often prompt voluntary kinship caregivers to seek a legal living arrangement. This means involving a court system and actually taking a relative to court to obtain the legal right to parent the child. Legal options include traditional adoption, open adoption, guardianship and legal custody. A brief overview of each of these

Questions for the New Kin-Caregivers to Ask Social Workers

Who has custody of the children?

What rights and responsibilities does legal custody have in this state? Physical custody?

May I receive a copy of the signed voluntary placement agreement?

May I be involved in developing the service plan (for reunification efforts) and receive a copy of the plan?

Will I or the children have to go to court?

Who is responsible for enrolling the children in school, obtaining health insurance, granting permission for medical care and obtaining it, signing school permission forms, etc.?

Will someone from child welfare services visit my home on a regular basis?

What are the requirements for me and my home if I want the children to live with me?

Are the requirements different if the children are with me just temporarily?

What services are available for my children and me, and how do I apply?

Are there restrictions on the discipline I can use with the children?

What subsidies or financial assistance is available? What do I need to do to apply?

Am I eligible to become a licensed foster parent and receive a foster care subsidy?

Child Welfare Information Gateway. 'Kinship Caregivers and the Child Welfare System.' http://www.childwelfare.gov/pubs/f_kinshi/f_kinshia.cfm

LEGAL OPTIONS FOR KINSHIP CAREGIVERS

Adoption

- Severs all of the birthparents' rights.
- Relative caregiver becomes the legal parent.
- Birthparents cannot reclaim parental rights.
- Allows access to services and programs.
- May prohibit access to some forms of financial assistance such as Temporary Assistance for Needy Families (TANF) and "child-only" grants (see Chapter 1 Resources).
- May open access to adoption subsidies which include a monthly stipend and health insurance (see Resources). Payments vary state to state.

Guardianship

- Does not sever the birthparent's parental rights.
- Guardian has legal and physical custody. The guardian can act as the child's parent and make decisions about the child. The birthparent often retains some visitation or other rights.
- Birthparents can sue guardians to regain custody, and guardianships typically end at age 18.
- Some states have created "permanent" guardianships that are difficult to terminate.
- Some states have created "subsidized" guardianship so that a kinship caregiver can receive a payment similar to that received via a kinship foster care placement. These subsidized arrangements are typically provided in cases in which the child has been in state custody.
- Guardianship may be especially appropriate if the children are older and want to maintain ties to birthparents or the relatives do not want to terminate the parents' rights.

Open Adoption

- Twelve states have developed legally enforceable tenets for open adoptions that can work well for relative families.
- The kinship caregivers, birthparents and child develop an enforceable plan that sets forth terms (type, frequency and duration) for post-adoption contact.

Legal Custody

- The kin become the legal custodian of the child. The legal custodian can enroll the child in school and sign medical consents.
- Granted by probate rather than family courts.
- Does not facilitate access to as many services or supports as does legal guardianship.
- Custodians often do not have as many rights as do guardians. This varies by state.
- Legal custody can be challenged.
- Birthparent visitation may be a part of a legal custody agreement.

types of living arrangements is in the table on the previous page.[7] [8] Kinship relatives are encouraged to explore their options carefully, and to know their rights and benefits within their state of residence.

Managing Family Relationships

The Center for Law and Social Policy recently summarized existing literature regarding kinship placements and put forth the following conclusions about children in kinship placements versus those in other types of out-of-home placements. Their search demonstrated that children in kinship care:[9]

- experience fewer moves and fewer school changes
- are more likely to live with their siblings
- are less likely to re-enter foster care after reunifying with their birthparents
- are more likely to report liking those with whom they live and to feel loved
- try to leave or run away less frequently
- are rated by teachers and caregivers as having fewer behavioral problems
- are provided access to their ethnic, racial and cultural traditions.

As was discussed earlier in this chapter, and as we will learn in Chapter 7, problems in setting boundaries with birthparents can lead kinship placements to disrupt. So the benefits listed above do not come without struggles. Birthparents are family members. As such, they are likely to have contact with the kinship caregivers and other relatives. They are probably invited to holidays and special occasions. They may want to visit the child. They want to offer parenting input.

All of these situations will require careful thought on the part of the kin parent.

Miriam is just turning 8. She has resided with her Aunt Beth and Uncle Chad since infancy. Her birthmother, Renee, is Chad's sister. Renee is diagnosed with schizophrenia and she has used cocaine on and off since adolescence. The decision to make Beth and Chad Miriam's legal guardians was a decision made by Renee in conjunction with many family members.

Miriam's parents, Beth and Chad, are the hub of the family. Holidays, special occasions, Sunday dinner, cook outs—all occur at their home. Miriam, Chad, Beth and Renee see each other frequently.

Renee insists that Miriam call her "Mom." She also attempts to keep Miriam at her side as much as possible. She states to Miriam, "When we live together again, we'll play all sorts of games. I'll be such a good mom someday." Other relatives reinforce this. The result is that Chad and Beth feel like pseudo-parents. Their two birth children, Angelique and Donna, ages 12 and 14, feel very uncomfortable at these get-togethers. It is as if somehow their family isn't a real family.

At age 8, Miriam is beginning to ask a lot of questions:

"Why does Aunt Renee want me to call her 'Mom?' "

---

7. Child Welfare Information Gateway. "Kinship Caregivers and the Child Welfare System." http://www.childwelfare.gov/pubs/f_kinshi/f_kinshia.cfm

8. Beltran, Ana. Kinship Care Providers: "Some Permanency Options." North American Council on Adoptable Children. http://www.nacac.or/adoptalk/kniship.html

9. Conway, Tiffany and Hutson, Rutledge. "Is Kinship Care Good for Children?" Center for Law and Social Policy. http://www.clasp.org/publications/is_kinship_care_good.pdf

"Why don't I live with her?"
"How come I have to sit with her at Grandma's house?"
"When am I going to live with her?"
"When I live with her, will I get to visit you?"
"Will Angelique and Donna be my sisters?"

At times, Renee is absent from family events due to being in a drug rehabilitation center or a psychiatric hospital. Miriam notices these absences and asks, "Where is Aunt Mommy Renee?"

If you were Chad and Beth, what limits would you set? How would you answer Miriam's questions? Kinship caregivers will have to provide explanations, and they will need to establish boundaries with birthparents and extended family members. At times, these boundaries will be due to safety concerns. A mentally ill or substance-abusing birthparent may exhibit violence. At other times, limits on visits will be for the emotional well-being of the kin child, themselves and their other children. Such limits, though appropriate, have the capacity to cause rifts in relationships among family members.

Due to the increased use of kinship placements, kinship services are cropping up in many communities. Kinship families considering changing their custodial arrangement or having difficulties determining appropriate boundaries want to utilize the "Resources Especially for Kinship Caregivers" located in Chapter 1 to help review their options and make decisions that best meet the needs of each member of their family. These resources also help connect kinship caregivers with other relative care giving families. Veteran families have a wealth of valuable "expertise." Combined, personal and professional knowledge lend to helping relatives achieve the delicate balance needed to manage their nuclear and extended family relations.

Moving Children with Sensitivity: International Considerations

Who will we meet along the way?

In international adoption, we can identify two primary types of agencies involved in the activities necessary to join a child and family.

Placing Agency

A placing agency works with the sending country—countries that allow children to be adopted internationally—which has custody of the child. The placing agency identifies the child who is free for adoption and makes referrals to eligible families. A placing agency is licensed by state regulations to provide adoption services. These agencies have facilitated relationships or received accreditation from countries abroad to place children with adoptive families. These agencies are often referred to as international or intercountry adoption agencies.

In selecting a placing agency, families may want to ask the agency the following questions:

In what state(s) is this agency licensed? Is the license in good standing? (Families may want to contact the Better Business Bureau in the agency's region as well as the state licensing office to make sure that the license is current.)

Adoptees Talk

Best things about being an adopted person are
- being part of an adoptive family.
- having new things to do.
- being loved/cared for.
- feeling special.
- having great adoptive parents.
- feeling safe.
- being different.
- being someone your family chose.
- having two families.
- having fun.
- making friends.

Is this business organized as a not-for-profit or a for-profit organization? Are you governed by a board of directors? Do you carry business liability insurance?

How long has the agency been involved in international adoption? How long has the agency been involved with our preferred sending country?

Does the agency have its own directly supervised staff and an office in its own name overseas? If so, is the staff bilingual? If not, how are legal, translation and transportation services provided?

How many children has the agency placed from the country in which we are interested?

Do you provide a contract that spells out the family's responsibilities and the agency's responsibilities? (Review these contracts carefully—possibly having it reviewed by an attorney specializing in contract law—and think about the commitments, financial and otherwise, outlined for both your family and the agency.)

What are the agency's fees and how, specifically, are those fees broken down? What expenses outside of those charged by this agency should we plan and prepare for? (Although there are almost always unexpected fee expenses, there are many standard fees which the agency should be able to explain or estimate for you.)

What services do you provide? (If the agency you selected is not in your state, you will need to find someone near you who can conduct your home study and assist you in completing post-placement reports.)

Does the country in which we hope to adopt hold this agency entirely responsible for our preparation process, home study and post-adoption supervision, or does the country allow for a two-tier process of referring/placing agency and direct service agency? (You do not want to find yourself in a position where you are instructed not to mention the existence of a second agency in your process to foreign courts or officials.)

How does the agency prepare prospective adoptive family members for intercountry adoption? Will there be opportunities to meet families who have completed the process?

Do you help prepare clients for the adoption trip? Do you help make travel arrangements?

How do you provide updates regarding the status of the adoption program in the country we selected? (The agency should be upfront with you regarding the current status of adoptions from each country which you are considering.)

Can we switch our application to another country if regulations change or a moratorium is declared? Is there a refund policy? (This is critical information in case anything changes in the course of your adoption. There may be changes in circumstances for your family as well as changes in country policies.)

How long will it take from the completion of the home study to the referral of a child?

How will we receive referrals of available children? Will there be videos? Will we receive written information? Will we select or be referred a child before or after traveling to our country of choice? What happens if I don't feel I can accept the child referred?[10][11]

Direct Service Agency

If the family resides within geographic proximity of the placing agency, then that agency may also serve as the direct service agency—the agency that provides education, completes the home study and conducts post-placement services. The family who is geographically distant from its placing agency will require a direct service agency. These agencies are also licensed by the states in which they are located. The direct service agency is sometimes called the *home study agency* or the *local agency*.

There are questions that families will want to ask this agency

Is this business organized as a not-for-profit or a for-profit entity?

Are you licensed as an adoption agency in my home state?

Do you carry business liability insurance?

What is its relationship with our placing agency—formal or informal? Are you legally connected (e.g. the direct service agency is a branch of a larger national organization) or do you operate under the direction of the placing agency? Are you "supervised" by the placing agency?

How much experience does our assigned professional have with international adoption?

What type of education has the professional had in preparation for this position? What type of ongoing education is the professional required to attend?

How long does it take to conduct the home study/parent preparation process once we have submitted the necessary documents?

What are the steps to complete the preparation process? How many interviews? Where and when are interviews conducted? Will we also attend classes with other prospective parents? How many, where and when?

Do you offer opportunities to meet families who have already adopted internationally?

---

10. Joint Council on International Children's Services. "General Steps in International Adoption." http://www.jcics.org/International_Adoption.htm#3.%20%20Selecting%20an%20Agency

11. Child Welfare Information Gateway. "Intercountry adoption: Where do I start?" (2007). http://www.childwelfare.gov/pubs/f_inter/f_inter.pdf

What are the fees involved in the home study/preparation process as well as post-placement services?

What do post-placement visits involve? How often and over what period of time will these visits be conducted? If the country from which we are adopting requires post-placement reports, will you be assisting us with these, or is that the responsibility of the placing agency?

Can we contact you between visits if we are having difficulties?

Do you offer families a list of professionals such as mental health providers, occupational therapists, speech therapists, early childhood intervention specialists, etc. in our area who have been vetted by you as adoption-competent?

Sometimes families opt to utilize a "facilitator" or an "adoption consultant" rather than an adoption agency. These services are mostly unregulated and unlicensed. Still other families adopt independently (in countries where this is legal)—they learn a country's process to the degree they can complete the adoption on their own. Please evaluate your motives when selecting the means through which you will complete your adoption. If you are bypassing pre-adoption preparation or seeking to sidestep legitimate costs, think again. Go back and re-read Chapters 2 and 5. These chapters make clear my bias as a therapist who has significant experience with children adopted with special needs that effective preparation is essential.

It may be true that an ethical adoption service provider who offers quality services may prove more expensive than a facilitator or an independent adoption. Yet, a lack of preparation and guidance can leave the family shocked and confounded post-placement when the adoptee displays issues. Savings on the front end will then result in significant costs post-placement. These costs will not just be financial. They will include the emotional well-being of the entire family. Prospective adoptive parents are advised to ask themselves questions, and families should investigate with great care the licensing and credentials of adoption service providers prior to making a final decision about which provider they select. All families are encouraged to read the book, *Adopting: Sound*

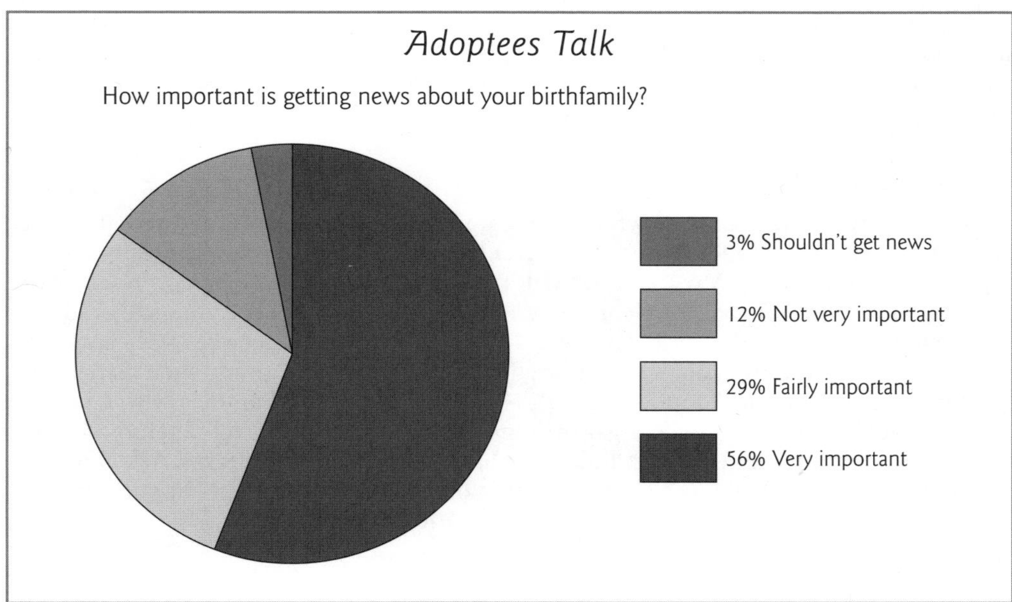

Choices, Strong Families by Patricia Irwin Johnston (Indianapolis: Perspectives Press, 2008). This book thoroughly reviews the various types of adoption service providers that exist, as well as ethical considerations pertaining to adoption service providers and becoming an adoptive family.

Caregivers

In 2003, nearly 23,000 children were adopted internationally in the United States, and it is estimated that prior to adoption perhaps as many as 85% of these children spent time in an institutional setting including baby homes, hospitals and orphanages (Johnson, 2000).

In some instances, parents will not see the child's residence and meet their child's caregivers. For example, Korean adoptees are often escorted to America, and Chinese and Indian children are brought to a designated location where they are handed over to their new parents. The family's opportunity to gather information from those who have directly cared for the child will not occur in those situations.

A large majority of families adopting intercountry, however, will come in contact with the institutional staff—orphanage director, doctor, direct caregivers, etc. These caregivers are paid employees assigned to carry out various duties associated with the daily care of the child. Certainly, there are many stories provided by adoptive families of the staff's concern for the children in their care. There are also many stories to the contrary provided by children adopted at older ages from orphanage settings. As Chapters 2 and 5 have presented, orphanage care is not a substitute for parental love and affection. A busy direct caregiver or a director consumed with the management tasks of an under-funded and under-staffed facility may not know the child you have selected very well. Yet, it may be part of this person's job description to appear to be very familiar with each child. So the quality and quantity and veracity of information you may obtain on-site will vary.

If you do have the opportunity to visit your child's former home and meet his caregivers, take this opportunity as an important way in which information-seeking can help your new child adjust to his family. As mentioned before, with very young children (babies and toddlers) sensory experiences should be well understood. Look closely at the sensory environment in which your child has lived—visual, auditory, olfactory, taste, motion and routine—and look for ways that you can if not replicate it, at least not change it so entirely as to over-stimulate your child.

Other Professionals

There may be professionals who drive you places and coordinate the activities necessary to meet your child and finalize your adoption. The legal process means a judge and perhaps an attorney. Most families will require the services of an interpreter. Many agencies staff offices in various countries. Other agencies connect you with individual persons who provide these services. The quality of these services will vary. The resources provided in this book will link you to several organizations, such as Families for Russian and Ukraine Adoption (FRUA)—www.frua.org and Families with Children from China (FCC)—www.fwcc.org—through which you can contact veteran adoptive families. Spend time chatting with folks who have completed the process. Ask about the potential difficulties that may arise in conjunction with these essential support services. These parents are also a good resource for travel information.

Orphanage Mates

As Chapter 2's section "Separation from Siblings" discussed, children who reside together in institutional settings often establish close ties. They may feel as if these fellow orphanage mates are friends or they may think of them as siblings. Children may spend extensive periods of time in close quarters to another child. In China, for example, children often sleep two to a crib and are referred to as crib mates. Separation from these orphanage companions can be a painful experience. These losses need to be acknowledged. Certainly, the child moving on to adoption may need some closure with fellow orphanage mates.

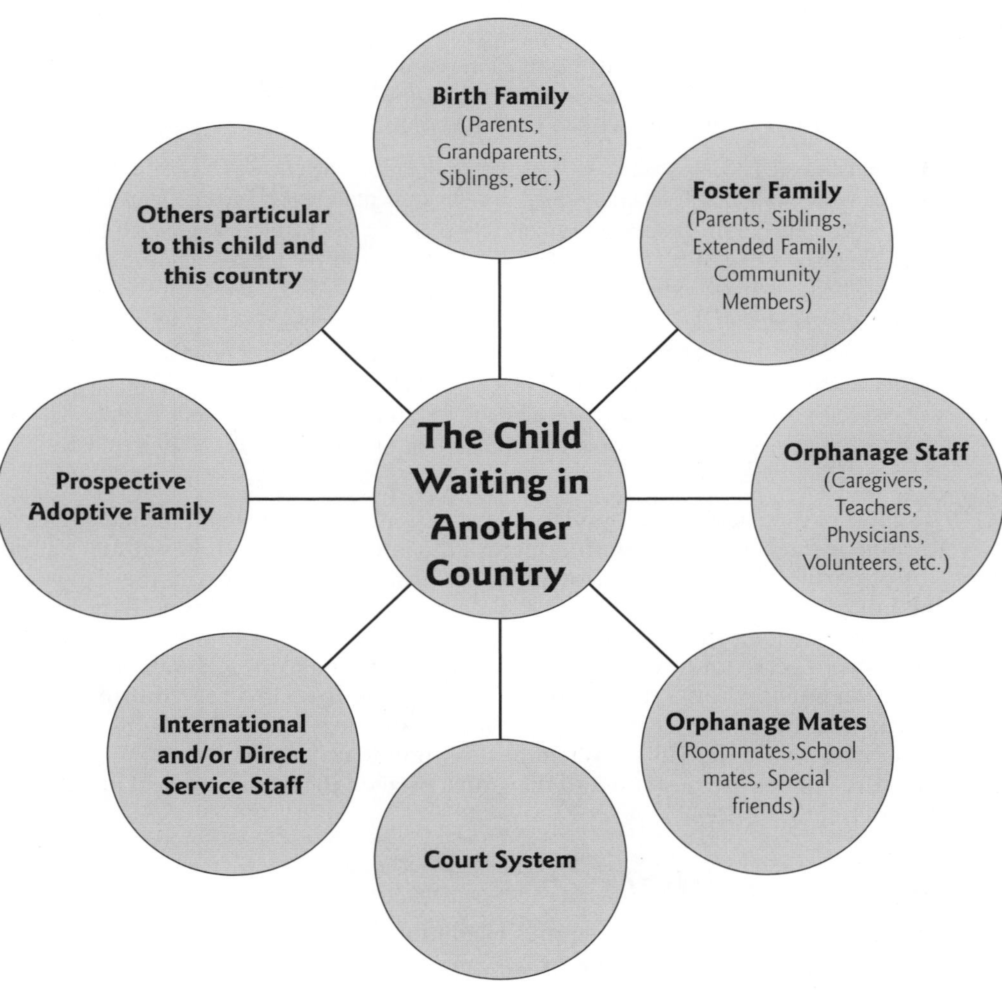

What are pre-placement visits and what will they be like?

The purpose of pre-placement visits in domestic adoption is to learn whether or not the family and the child feel a connection. If so, the child moves to the family's home. There is also a desire to help the child transfer her attachment from the current caregivers to her new parents. This reduces the shock of moving to a different family. The intention is to cause the child as little distress as is possible. There will then be at least an additional six months of getting acquainted before the child, parents, and brothers and sisters need to decide to legalize their living arrangement.

In intercountry adoption this decision-making time is condensed. The pre-placement visitation process typically referred to as *travel* or *travel time* culminates in the legalization of the adoption. In a quick period of time—over the course of only a couple of weeks to a month, the family meets a child, spends some time with her, finalizes the adoption and arrives home! There are now some countries requiring two trips. Trip one is to select and/or meet the child. Trip two is to complete the legal requirements to move the child from his homeland to your home. This timing is considered by these countries to be advantageous in that the time between trips may be utilized by the family to determine whether or not to proceed with the adoption.

> Eric and Kathleen adopted their son, Eduardo, from Brazil when he was 3 years old. They spent six weeks in Brazil. The family stayed in an apartment in which Eduardo joined them shortly after their arrival. They were given his schedule. Eric and Kathleen assumed the day-to-day parenting of Eduardo. Eduardo, Eric and Kathleen had the opportunity to become acquainted prior to making the trip home.
>
> Three years later, the couple went to China to adopt their daughter. Eduardo accompanied them on this trip. Their daughter, 10 months old, was brought to their hotel along with a number of other babies. Families were gathered in a meeting room. Each family was given their respective baby. Each family kept their baby with them at the hotel while completing the adoption process. The paperwork was complete in fourteen days. Eric, Kathleen, Eduardo and "Mia" came home.

The child of international adoption will transition per country and orphanage policies. In some instances, such as with Eduardo, the family and the child will have some depth of opportunity to become acquainted before making the trip home. However, even for Eduardo, in the course of one day he was given to his "parents"—people he had never met! Policies in other countries will vary. The family and the child will have very little time to get to know each other before boarding the plane. Overall, many, if not most, children moving from one country to another will do so in a very abrupt manner. As we learned earlier in this chapter, abrupt moves are more harmful to a child than are planned moves (Fahlberg, 1991). When abrupt moves are required, however, families can do little to change them, so instead they must prepare themselves to deal proactively with the aftermath.

Is the move sensitive?

The response to this question requires examining a series of questions.

What is the process to be followed?

Explaining the process by which the intercountry adoptee came to join your family will occur, for the most part, as the child ages and as the child gains language skills.

Adoptees Talk

Best things about getting adopted:

- joining a new or real family.
- first time being picked up by your adoptive parents.
- the judge.
- being able to stay with birth brothers and sisters.
- knowing that people care about you.
- adoption was quick and smooth.
- being told what was happening.

Sharing the details of the child's pre-adoptive experiences promotes the overall well-being of the child, even when the circumstances of the adoption contain painful material. The long-term transition of the child in the family hinges on the child gaining understanding of how he came to reside with the adoptive family. Again, Chapter 9 will present suggestions about how to talk to children about difficult information.

Pre-placement is the time to gather anything you can about the child's history. You may only make one trip to the child's homeland. You need to make the most of this opportunity. Later in this chapter, I'll share suggestions for capturing your child's history while you bring him home.

Are the reasons for the move clear?

It is interesting to ask older internationally adopted children what they were told about the move to their adoptive family. Children I have worked with have shared these kinds of assumptions:

- "I was told that my mom and dad were coming. When my mom and dad came to the orphanage, I was surprised. I thought that the orphanage ladies meant that my birthparents were coming. I knew right away that Mom and Dad weren't my birthparents."
- "I was told I was going to America. I didn't know what this meant. I knew other kids left the orphanage and didn't come back. I thought maybe they had died."
- "Other kids got picked before me. I wondered what took my mom and dad so long to get me."
- "I thought Mom and Dad were going to be the people who took me back to my birthparents."
- "I really don't remember being told anything. I just remember being scared of the car, the plane, and Mom and Dad. I didn't know what was going on."
- "I didn't want to go. I wanted to wait for my birthmom."
- "I thought my birthmom was one of the ladies who took care of me at the orphanage. I thought Mom and Dad took me away from my birthmom."

One child recently stated, "At the orphanage they didn't let us eat if we were bad. I was so happy that Mom and Dad had food. I was happier when they gave me some. The whole time they were taking me away from the orphanage, I was worried about having food."

Key Point—*Children of international adoption receive little to no preparation for the move to an adoptive family.* Adoptive families can consider offering preparation prior to leaving the child's homeland. For example, the children's book, *Borya and the Burps* by Joan McNamara (Indianapolis: Perspectives Press, 2005), utilizes vibrant illustrations to demonstrate the child's journey from an orphanage to the adoptive home. Translated to the child's native language, reviewing this book several times would at least help the toddler or older child being adopted from any country anticipate what is about to happen in his or her life. Finger puppets, role-playing with dolls, drawing pictures of the events to occur, creating a booklet of clip art combined with family photos or having the translator explain the activities about to take place would be quite beneficial for the child who is about to move. Repetition of the story before departure and after coming home is essential to assist toddlers and children in comprehending what has taken place in their life. Talking to infants is addressed shortly under the heading, "What is needed to help the child feel comfortable about the move?"

Is the child moving in a manner in which I would want to move?

How many of you would like to be moved to a different country in a matter of days or a month? How many of you would like to leave behind everything familiar—people, culture, language, etc.? Certainly, the child receives many benefits from adoption—a family, a higher standard of living, a future filled with endless possibilities. Yet, initially, such understanding is beyond the awareness of most children being adopted intercountry. Overall, the young child perceives with his senses. He is able to *sense* the loss of a voice, a touch, a sound. When you meet him, his impressions are

- "You don't look like anyone I know."
- "You don't smell like my orphanage or my foster mom."
- "You talk differently. You don't sound like any of the people I know."
- "Your clothes feel different." "Your body is shaped differently from my caregivers."
- "This bottle isn't the same." "What am I eating?"
- "Why are you smiling?"
- "What is going on?"

Key Point—*The adoptive family must recognize that their feelings of joy in meeting their long-awaited child may not be matched by the child.* Travel or travel time is really the period to begin to transition your child into the family as sensitively as possible. In addition to deciding what to pack and where to stay, parents should spend some time contemplating what the move is going to be like through the eyes of the child and planning for that.

What is needed to help the child feel comfortable about the move?

Forty-six percent of children adopted internationally enter America under one year old, 43% arrive at ages 1-4, and 46% arrive under five years old.[12] Overall, we are talking about providing comfort to young children who are making a major transition. We must keep in mind several *key points*.

12. Evan B. Donaldson Adoption Institute. "International Adoption Facts." http://www.adoptioninstitute.org/FactOverview/international.html

Children who have spent time in institutional settings typically lose one month of development for each three or four months spent in orphanage care.[13] *So the developmental level of a 3-year-old who has spent two years in an orphanage is similar to that of a child just over 2 years of age who has been raised in a family setting. An infant of 9 months, placed in the orphanage at birth, is developmentally more similar to the six-month-old child of your friend at home. Many children, then, are younger than their chronological age.* The 4-year-old who is really socially and emotionally age 2½ will have different transitional needs than will a 4-year-old who is developmentally on track. Parents are encouraged to develop expectations in accord with the child's developmental skills rather than the child's actual age (see Chapters 8 and 9).

Infants and toddlers do grieve (Bowlby, 1980). Young children often regress developmentally when grieving. Parents must adjust expectations when the child is grief stricken. A 12-month-old may act like a 9-month-old. A 2-year-old may act like a much younger toddler, so he will not exhibit the skills or the types of interaction the parents might be anticipating. As the grief passes, the child's skills will move forward.

The young child's grief reaction may include distress and despair (Bowlby, 1980). Anticipate that your child may react strongly to you. Many families describe loud and rageful crying, rocking, shaking the crib, head banging, arching of the back, pulling or pushing away from the new caregivers, etc. Other parents describe a new child as listless, sleeping a majority of the time and appearing unaware of what is going on around him.

Many parents feel rejected by such behaviors. As such, they begin to withdraw from the child. Parents report such things as, "She wouldn't take a bottle from me. So I let her feed herself." "He didn't like to be held so I stopped holding him." Of course it is painful to feel that you have been rejected by a child you have worked so very hard to bring home! But rather than viewing these behaviors as a personal rejection, try to see them as reflec-

Adoptees Talk

Worst things about getting adopted

- leaving your old family.
- it took too long/too much waiting.
- not knowing enough about the family.
- the social worker.
- not having any say in what was happening.
- how I felt about meeting my new family and getting adopted.
- moving.
- not feeling things were stable.
- being separated from birth brothers and sisters.
- the court.
- being fostered before getting adopted.
- missing my own (i.e., birth) family.

13. University of Minnesota, International Adoption Medicine Program. "Growth: Initial Considerations." http://www.med.umn.edu/peds/iac/topics/growth/home.html

tive of the youngster's capacity to *sense* that a major change is taking place. Thus, the child is reacting due to grief. The child's transition is enhanced when parents can accept the child into their arms with an expectation of "We may need to help her grieve" rather than "We will experience a reciprocal love at first sight."

If you feel that your young child is grieving, a good course of action is to keep yourself calm. Young children attempt to attune to their caregivers. This means that they strive to match your emotional state. If you become anxious or agitated, then the problem will be perpetuated. Once calm, start talking to the infant or toddler in an empathic tone of voice. Discuss the events that are occurring, "Oh my, you are so scared and sad. I don't look familiar. I don't feel or sound right. You are missing your orphanage friends and the ladies that took care of you there. Yes, it is sad. Go ahead and cry. I'll be here to comfort you." You may be surprised at how helpful empathy and calmness are in any language and at any age!

You may be building an attachment rather than transferring an attachment. A secure attachment between a caregiver and an infant develops over the first 12 months of life. As Chapter 2 noted, an attachment develops due to responsive and consistent care giving. Such a scenario has not occurred for the child in residence in an institutional setting. The child's negative behavioral reaction, then, may be due to the fact that the infant has not yet formed an attachment to a caregiver. In fact, children spending the first nine to twelve months in institutional care may not have developed an attachment to a caregiver.

At the Attachment and Bonding Center of Ohio where I work, we frequently receive phone calls from distressed new parents stating, "We don't feel our child has attached to us." When asked how long they have had the child, the response is often a few weeks to a few months. So these parents are correct. The child has not attached. He has not known his new mom and dad long enough to decide that they are safe and reliable, and that they are persons to whom he wants an emotional connection. Building an attachment takes time—sometimes a long time! Patience is the essential component of a successful and sensitive transition.

Turbulence in the Transition

Most families will arrive in their country of choice and be smoothly connected with their adoptee. However, for others, obstacles—turbulence—may impede a sensitive transition. Turbulence refers to difficulties that may inhibit a planned and sensitive arrival of the child into the adoptive family. There are a number of scenarios that may create turbulence in families transitioning to adoption.

Something is terribly wrong!

We have already looked at one type of turbulence above in describing that the child and parents may not fall in love at first sight. Parents have been encouraged to resist taking such an initial encounter as a personal rejection. Instead, grief and attachment issues are likely the root cause. Time and patience are necessary for the child to transition. Difficulties that persist may require professional intervention.

However, this is not to imply that all of the child's problems will disappear post-placement. In a study of 27 families who dissolved (legally terminated) their adoptions, all of the families reported that they had serious misgivings about the child soon after meeting with the child and after receiving additional information from caregivers in the child's homeland. Twenty-six of the twenty-seven proceeded with their adoption in spite of feeling that the child was not a good placement for their family.

> One parent said, "We were concerned about our new daughter's behavior—hyper, defiant of adults, and aggressive—but thought maybe she would adjust as she became used to us. In retrospect, we should have paid attention to our concerns and either passed on the placement or identified another child for adoption."[14]

Further, the majority of families contacted their international adoption agency or their in-country coordinator for advice. These families reported that they were generally told, "It will get better when back in the United States," and that "everything was normal" about what they were experiencing.

> One parent wrote, "We spoke with our coordinator in-country who characterized our daughter's behaviors as typical of a child who was used to the orphanage and she should settle down once she became used to us."[15]

In reality, the problems of these children persisted and eventually proved too great for these families. These children now reside in various living situations outside of these families. These families are dealing with the painful aftermath that accompanies the loss of a child. Their suggestions for prospective adoptive families include:

- Educate yourselves on the consequences of orphanage living, and the influences of neglect and abuse.
- Insist on full disclosure, including the child's medical and psychological information as well as historical information pertaining to the birthfamily.
- Obtain an independent evaluation from an international adoption medical clinic.
- *Walk away* if the match does not seem right or you feel you are being pressured to accept the child.[16]

This study of adoption dissolution is currently being replicated with a larger group of families who are also choosing to dissolve their adoptions. Families do have the choice to say "no." Do not succumb to pressure if you truly feel the child offered is not a good match for you and your family. It is better for your already-resident children that you choose not to proceed rather than to proceed and then dissolve the adoption. You and your typically developing children will suffer from the end result of such a decision. Chapter 7 will cover this issue of dissolution in more detail.

The child we selected was gone!

Jill, an adoptive mother, shares the experience she and her husband had of bringing home their children.

> "We were so excited about adopting; we spent months preparing. First the home study, a huge paper chase, and then preparing the baby's room. It was so exciting when we were finally paper ready. We wasted no time. We mailed our documents via overnight delivery. We were told the wait would be two to five months. The next day, to our surprise, our agency called and asked us, "Would you accept 15-month-old twin girls?" This potential

14. Holtan, McCarrgher and James, unpublished
15. Ibid
16. Ibid

Adoptees Talk

Worst things about being an adopted person

- not having contact with my birthfamily.
- being teased or bullied.
- losing contact with my birth brothers and sisters.
- being different.
- feeling left out.
- knowing you are adopted.
- other people talking about you being adopted.
- complex emotions about it.
- not knowing your heritage.
- losing old friends.
- being asked questions about being adopted.
- feeling frustrated.
- not being believed when you say you are adopted.

18% the respondents said there was no "worst thing" for them about being an adopted person.

match was not according to the specifications on our application or the home study. The agency had insisted that we be very specific when filling out what we wanted, as it would be what they used to match couples to referrals. We asked for a boy and a girl. We asked for one or both children to be less than 12 months old, or one child less than 12 months and one child 2 years old or younger. We made it very clear that we wanted mentally and physically healthy children and as young as possible.

"Twin girls—this was not what we were expecting! But the thought of twins was exciting. It took about half a second to make up my mind. We had to let the agency know that day or lose the referral. I hurried to call my husband at work. He was excited too, and we accepted. All we had to do now was wait for an invitation (i.e.,visa) from Russia). Our agency told us we should prepare to travel in about a month.

"Three weeks later, we had not heard anything. I had a feeling that something was wrong, and then we got the call. We had lost our referral. I was so sad. These two baby girls were in my heart and thoughts for three weeks. I had hopes and dreams for them, and it felt like a death. About a month later we had an invitation to travel and a choice of two different sets of siblings. The first was 5-month-old twins, a boy and a girl. If we were not happy with the twins, they had a sibling group of two boys, 8 months and 19 months. We were very excited and of course we wanted the twins! They were exactly what we'd hoped for; both under 12 months and one of each—a boy and a girl! It couldn't get any better!

"In Russia, we were met by our translator, Natalia. She is the one who basically ran the entire adoption process. She took us to our hotel. She gave us a few minutes to get settled and then she came to talk to us. The first thing she said was, 'I've got some bad news.' The twins were gone and so were the two brothers. However, they wanted to offer us another set of siblings, ages 6 and 3.

"This was just too much! We were 5,000 miles from home, again losing another referral and on top of that, now we're being offered a 3-year-old and a 6-year-old. We thought we would be meeting our babies. There's a huge difference between 5 months old and 3 and

> 6 years old. We never expected this. I was devastated, couldn't speak and burst into tears. There was nothing we could trust, everything kept changing and so far from home, we were completely at their mercy.
>
> "When I could finally speak, I let Natalia know our home study specifications. I explained, 'We have a nursery all ready to go.' Why were we told to be so specific when filling out our paperwork? Why did we fill out the papers at all? It didn't seem to matter what we checked on our application.
>
> "Realizing that we were both upset, Natalia said, 'Okay, get some rest. Tomorrow I will come and take you to the baby house. I will show you babies.' Well, that wasn't very comforting. Once again, we were experiencing what felt like a death. We felt completely helpless, and we were half way around the world in a foreign country alone where very few spoke English.
>
> "After a sleepless night, we were up early and waiting to go. Natalia talked with us before we left for the orphanage. She said they would like to offer us a boy who must be adopted with his sister. They were 2½ and 3½. She would answer any questions we had once we were at the orphanage. We would also get their records. I felt very uncomfortable. We were expecting to have medical records and video before traveling to Russia. We wanted to be able to share this information with our international medical adoption specialists. There was to be a consultation before travel and accepting our referral. This was not going to be an option. All we could do now was hope for the best.
>
> "We met the children in the music room of the orphanage. Ivan was frightened and wouldn't come near us at first. Svetelina was shy but warmed up right away and really seemed to favor my husband. They were beautiful children, although they were a mess. They were very thin, and had cuts and bruises all over. We visited with them for about an hour, and during that time Natalia shared with us some of their history. I took notes, hoping to share anything I learned with the doctors at home. At the end of our visit, Natalia asked if we would accept the children. If we didn't accept, she would show us more babies. However, she also told us that it was Svetelina's last chance. Svetelina was now 3 and soon she would be sent to another orphanage that wouldn't be so nice. This was hard to believe, as the orphanage we were in didn't seem that nice! Once in this new orphanage, her chances of being adopted would be slim. She told us we could have overnight to think about it and then we would need to make a decision.
>
> "I managed to contact the doctors back home to report the limited medical information we had. It was mostly height, weight, and head circumference. The doctors couldn't tell us much, only that the information indicated the children were 'failure to thrive' and basically it was a crap shoot.
>
> "We were under tremendous pressure, especially after meeting the children; our hearts really went out to them. We knew they needed us. We decided that maybe these were the children we were meant to have. Although I really wanted to adopt babies, we could not turn them away, and so we accepted. We signed to move forward with the adoption and were sent home the next day until a court date could be obtained."

Jill and Mitchell returned to Russia two months later to legalize their adoptions of Svetelina and Ivan. Jill and Mitchell's experiences call into light the issue of losing a selected child—an experience Jill compares to a death. Certainly, this loss is even more complicated when there are children already in the family

> Evelyn and Charles were parenting their birth daughter, Kiera, age 13. Motivated by strong religious convictions, they opted to adopt. They selected a country in which their church carried out mission work. They really wanted a son, and this was wonderful news for Kiera.

She truly longed for a little brother. She loved sports and thought a boy would be great! She could teach him to play basketball and soccer. The family selected an agency and completed their paperwork. Then, Charles' mother died very unexpectedly. This event was a profound loss for the family, and they decided some time was needed before bringing a child into the family.

About a year later, the family once again felt ready to proceed. In the meantime, they talked about "Logan" (the name they had selected for their prospective adoptive son), regularly. "When Logan comes, we'll go to Disney World. Won't it be fun to have a younger child on vacation!" Even when out shopping, they discussed outfits they thought Logan would like. Logan's homeland's policy was that the child was selected upon arrival. But once in the country, the family was informed that the only child available was a girl. The other children, they were told by the orphanage director, were all taken. Like Jill and Mitchell, they determined this was "meant to be" and so they proceeded to bring Katrina home. Katrina proved very problematic from the start. Three years in an institutional setting had taken its toll on her capacity to form an attachment. The family kept wondering, "What would our family be like if we had Logan?" Kiera especially wondered, "What happened? I thought I was going to get a fun little brother. Instead, I have a sister who steals my stuff, hits my friends and calls me names." Kiera was so disappointed.

The loss of the child the family believes they will be bringing home is difficult for all members of the family. The family must mourn this loss. Most families, afraid to come home empty-handed, accept placement of another child. Now they are grieving the expected child while attempting to form a relationship with another child.

The cases of Jill and Mitchell, and Evelyn, Charles and Kiera are presented so that families can prepare for this possibility. Each family must decide if they will stay in the sending country and select another child, or if it is better for their family to return home, re-group and make another trip.

Delays, Delays, Delays!

As this book is being written, Guatemala is processing referrals on only a limited basis and Russian adoptions are held up due to the time it is taking agencies to receive accreditation. The wait for a Chinese daughter is long. The processing of a backlog of families' dossiers prompted new requirements. These new criteria are expected to reduce the number of Chinese adoptions. Russia, Guatemala and China are three of the largest sending countries. Countless parents and siblings will be greatly disappointed by the longer waits for a new son or daughter, or brother or sister.

Shannon and Ed adopted Taylor as an infant. The family felt it time to pursue a second adoption when Taylor was about a year away from entering kindergarten. They believed that their second child would arrive just as Taylor began kindergarten so Shannon would have days free to care for the baby. Guatemala was particularly appealing. The family liked that the children were in foster homes rather than in institutional settings.

Their application was delayed when Guatemala had issues becoming compliant with the Hague Convention on Protection of Children and Co-operation in Respect of Intercountry Adoption. The family waited almost an extra year for baby Amelia to arrive. During that year, Taylor kept asking, "Why can't we just go get her?" "Why is this taking so long?" "Who is taking care of her?" "What if I never get a sister?" Additionally, thinking about the pending adoption caused Taylor to begin to ponder his own adoption. Now almost 5 years old, he had more ability to ask questions, "Why don't some moms keep their babies?" "Where is my birth mom?" "Why didn't she keep me?" Shannon and Ed did their best to console

Taylor regarding his questions and confusion about the arrival of the new baby. They felt confounded and overwhelmed by his emerging interest in his own adoption. They had not expected so many questions at age 5. Yet, the pre-school years are the time of "why" about everything. "Why is the grass green?" "Why is the sky blue?" Veteran parents of pre-school age children most likely remember this developmental stage. Shannon and Ed had to struggle with whether or not a second child would arrive, and they had to decide how best to help Taylor with his questions about his adoption.

Delays will be difficult for everyone, yet delays will occur pre-and post-placement. One family described paperwork errors that resulted in an eight month lapse between their first and second trips to Kazakhstan. Can you imagine waiting eight months, especially knowing that your child is receiving inadequate care? This type of situation is an emotional nightmare. Another family discussed that the judge in their chosen country decided to take a week-long fishing trip while they were in country! They had to wait for his return in order to legalize their adoption.

Adoptive families, and even more so international adopting families, need to expect the unexpected! Families already parenting an adopted child need to anticipate that a second adoption may act as a trigger for the previously adopted child. He may need to review his adoption story throughout the process of getting a new brother or sister.

Moving Children with Sensitivity: A Menu of Suggestions

The suggestions that follow recognize that each family is unique. Family members may select those ideas—traveling together or not, and pre-trip, during-trip and post-trip activities—which seem best suited to the particular needs of the family. The recommendations offer ways for each member of the family to participate in the process. The information put forth is designed to help parents, the prospective adoptee and the children already in the family begin to facilitate positive interactions.

Considering Family Travel

Suggestions for moving a child via intercountry adoption need to take into account whether or not the family is traveling to the child's homeland, and whether or not they will be traveling with the children already present in the family. In some instances, country policies may prohibit taking resident children. In cases where the siblings may go, parents must decide who will go on the trip based on their resources and their knowledge of their typically developing children. Pros and cons that may be weighed in this decision-making process include these:

Pros for Parents and Siblings Traveling to the Homeland

- Experiencing the country gives a deeper understanding of what the adoptee's life was like prior to the adoption. In particular, visiting the child's orphanage makes clear the day-to-day living differences between such group life and family life. You can all begin to see the type of work you have ahead of you in teaching the newcomer how to learn to be a family member.
- Experiencing the child's culture contributes to raising the child in a culturally competent manner as explained in Chapters 3 and 5. As your family will be different from those around you, you can all experience first-hand the type of cultural issues you and all of your children may experience once you become a transcultural family.

- If you are traveling as part of a group, you and your resident children have the opportunity to form relationships with other families. These relationships may become a source of support post-placement.
- You will have the opportunity to take photos and video that will prove invaluable to your prospective adoptee as he or she matures.
- You will be more involved in the adoption process.
- You may experience culture shock. You may begin to feel uncomfortable or out of place in a country where nothing is familiar. This is positive, as it will evolve into empathy for the new arrival. He will likely have similar feelings once you bring him home to his new country.
- Older siblings may benefit from the travel to a foreign country. Certainly, there is learning value in experiencing the rich diversities the world has to offer.
- Older siblings may prove helpful. They can carry luggage, get diapers, fix bottles and keep you company. Your children are also good reminders of the fact that you can parent in the event that your new child's interactions are initially less than positive.
- Younger children, who lack a sense of time, may experience less separation anxiety if they accompany you on the trip. At our office, we offer a two-week program of therapy. Frequently, families come from out-of-state for this service. Many times, the younger children left at home become distressed as each day passes and their parents are still in Ohio with a sibling. Two weeks seems like an eternity to toddlers and pre-school aged children.
- If your family already includes a child from overseas, depending on his age, the experience of returning to his homeland or visiting the country you have opted to adopt from this time around may be of great benefit. This is especially true if the child was too young at the time of the adoption to have memories of his own adoption process. Seeing another adoption take place fills in many of the blanks explaining how he joined the family. Again, this may also raise many questions or lead to an expression of grief for the loss of his country of origin, his birthfamily or his orphanage mates. While comforting a grieving child is difficult for parents, active, healing grieving leads to healthy emotional well-being. Chapter 10 offers ways to facilitate grief.

Cons for Parents and Siblings Traveling to the Homeland

- Completing an international adoption may be quite expensive. The family's resources may prohibit taking the children already in the family.
- Travel advisories for your chosen country may prove unfavorable. The U.S. Department of State posts travel advisories (see Resources).
- Parents and children alike may be affected by jet lag and time changes. If you are taking your birth and/or previously adopted children, especially those that are younger, you may want to arrive in the country a day or two early. This will provide some opportunity to adjust prior to initiating the steps necessary to bring your child home.
- The flight is long and the trip may be long—longer if delays occur—and children may become affected by culture shock and by having access to limited activities.
- There are children who will have adverse reactions to an orphanage setting. The reality of children living without parents may be overwhelming to children with more sensitive temperaments. Parents need to think about the entirety of the trip. Depending on the adequacy and availability of child care, children who may

suffer emotionally in seeing an orphanage may be best left at home with a caring relative or family friend.

- If the process is demanding or the prospective adoptee experiences difficulties, families must determine if adequate time can be made available for the children along on the trip.

In Chapter 3, we met Gabe's family. His parents, Cole and Becky, parent a total of four children, three they adopted from China and one they adopted from Guatemala. On each of their trips abroad, they have taken one child while the others stay with relatives and family friends. Becky arranged the travel so that the family had several days together before being joined by the new child. This allowed for sight-seeing of the previously adopted child's homeland. It also allowed for some special one-on-one time for each of the children they already parent.

Overall, families have many different options when making plans for their travel abroad. Families who are planning to travel to the child's homeland may want to consider the positive aspects of this travel and at least plan for a trip to the child's country of origin at some point in time.

Pre-Trip Suggestions

Considerations in this area need to include preparing siblings for the addition of a child—younger or older—to the family, preparing for the trip abroad or preparing for the separation from the parents. Here are some pre-trip activity ideas from which to choose.

Borrow a Child the Age of the Child You Plan to Adopt

Anyone who has parented an infant or toddler is aware of the amount of time required! Typically developing children who have not had the experience of sharing their parents with a young child are often blind-sided by the parental time consumed by a little one. Parents can offer some preparation for the changes about to occur because of the addition of a baby or toddler.

If you know someone who is parenting a child a bit younger or the same age as the child you plan to adopt, offer to babysit. This will be helpful only if you do so on several occasions. As you care for this youngster, point out the tasks it involves. "Oh my, it's time to the change the baby again." Or, "The baby needs another bottle." Each time the baby or toddler returns to his or her parents have discussions with the children you already parent. Of course, caring for a young child who has resided in a healthy family environment will be different from caring for the institutionalized infant. Yet, your resident children will at least gain an understanding that their new brother or sister will require sharing Mom and Dad's time—perhaps much time!

A number of wonderful children's books exist to help present the changes incurred when a family adds a younger sibling. Two excellent titles are *A Pocket Full of Kisses* by Audrey Penn and *The Lap snatcher* by Bruce Coville. Both portray the negative and positive aspects of a young child joining the family from the perspective of an older sibling. Both convey that parents have enough love for all of the children they parent. Many children fear that, "Mom and Dad spend more time with my little brother because they love him more." We want to convey, "We spend more time with your sister because we have to do things for her that you can do by yourself." We want to give the children already in the family this message in as many ways as is possible. Spending time babysitting young children, reading books together, planning family discussions, making lists as to what the older child can do versus what the younger child needs help with and volunteering at the church nursery are all ways to prepare the siblings for pending changes.

Preparing for the New Brother or Sister

Once you have an idea of the age of the child or children who will be joining your family there will be tasks to do such as shopping and setting up a bedroom. Include the children you already parent in these activities to the maximum degree possible. That is, do not carry out all of the preparations while they are at school. Brothers and sisters want to help, and involvement in the process makes them more invested in the arrival of their new sibling. While shopping, let your resident children pick out a few items for their sibling-to-be. Help them sort through packed away clothing and toys that they have outgrown and select items that will be useful for the new child. If old enough, let your children help assemble the crib or bed and other furniture.

If the addition of a new child to the family means that one of your typically developing children will have to share his bedroom, help him make a space just for himself or herself. This should be a space that is off limits to the new sibling. It could be a foot locker for items of special importance or it could mean cleaning out a corner of the den. Assure the child that he will be able to maintain some of the privacy he is accustomed to.

The above recommendation is especially important if the new arrival is a school-age or older child. The prospective adoptee who has resided in an orphanage setting long-term may have no idea about boundaries. The concept of asking permission prior to using or taking things belonging to others is likely a concept with which the older institutionalized child is unfamiliar. Parents are encouraged to review Chapter 3's section "Taking a Proactive Approach to Sex and Sexuality" as well. Chapter 8's section "Social and Emotional Age vs. Chronological Age" and Chapter 9's "Facilitating the Development of Social Skills" will help parents understand that many adoptees do not possess skills in accord with their chronological age. The school-age sibling-to-be may not have the social skills to engage with toys and games designed for his actual age. Parents may want to keep purchases in this area to a minimum until the social and emotional age of the son-or daughter-to-be can be determined.

Daily Reminders

Parents who will be away can leave the siblings left at home a daily gesture to ensure that these children do not feel that they are forgotten. These daily reminders can include cards, notes or small gifts. Provide a memento for each day you anticipate being gone. Leave a few extra in case of delays. Hallmark makes a lovely series of post-it note books. The titles all start with the phrase "Stuck on You." There is *Stuck on You Love Notes*, *Stuck on You Laugh Notes* and *Stuck on You—Warm, Witty, Wonderful You*! Each book contains 100 notes. Kids just love these!

Another suggestion comes from the children's book, *Seeds of Love: For Brothers and Sisters of International Adoption* by Mary Eberjer Petertyl and Jill Chambers (see Resources Chapter 5). In this book, a mom and her daughter plant seeds. Mom tells her daughter that she and Dad will return home when the seeds begin to sprout. Their resident daughter places a daily sticker on the calendar to count down the days until her parents' and new sister's homecoming. This is a lovely story to read with children over and over.

Children also benefit when parents leave them in charge of an item with sentimental value. One mom gave her 12-year-old daughter a quilt to use for the duration of Mom's trip abroad. The quilt had been handmade by the mother's mother. It helped this young adolescent feel as if her mother was with her every day. Whatever you select—a locket with your photo or a key ring with the family photo that is attached to the child's backpack, etc.—mementos and daily reminders lessen the impact of your absence.

Where Will I Stay?

Children of all ages want to know where they will be staying during the time you will be away. Preferably, the child can remain at home and Grandma and Grandpa, an aunt or a trusted family friend can come to your home for the duration of your trip away from your children. In this manner, they can continue school and their extra curricular activities with little to no interruption. Maintaining a routine lessens the impact of the life-altering transition for your resident children.

Of course this may not be possible and alternative arrangements will have to suffice. In these cases, go over what the children may expect in their temporary quarters. For example, "I talked to Janie's mom and she is going to be able to get you to your soccer games while we are away. So if there are any changes in your soccer schedule, you'll be talking to Janie's mom. I wrote her phone number down for you." Lay out all areas that are covered and by whom they are to be covered. Larger families may need to separate their typically developing children among more than one temporary caregiver. Make arrangements for them to communicate in your absence.

Older adolescents and young adult children might be able to stay at home with a trusted adult on call or looking in on them from time to time. Even they will miss you! Freeze some of their favorite meals and leave the cooking instructions. They will appreciate this thoughtfulness.

Leave a camera with the children at home. Encourage them to take photos of all the things they do while you are away. Reviewing these photos will make a great way to re-connect when you return home.

Plans to Prevent "I'm Bored" Syndrome

All parents have heard, "I'm bored" at one time or another. (Actually, parents have probably heard this more times than they want to think about!) If you are taking siblings-to-be with you, it will be particularly important to investigate your accommodations abroad. What amenities are available? What activities can your children take with them for on the plane and while in the country? It is also important to think about how much you can pack. Again, veteran parents who have traveled abroad with their children are a great resource when it comes to helping you decide what to take and what will be available in the adoptee's homeland. Especially search out parents who have traveled in the six months prior to your own trip. These families will have the most up-to-date information for the area and facilities in which you will be staying. The Resources provide several online connections to these "expert" families.

Make Plans to Establish a Post-Placement Routine

Pre-placement is the time to realize that the institutionalized child—of any age—is used to operating on a routine. Likely, these children are also used to a smaller world. They aren't leaving the orphanage on a frequent basis.

Prior to your trip abroad, consider the dynamics of establishing a routine for the newly-arrived child. In what ways can you eliminate some responsibilities for a few weeks or months post-placement? Who can you count on to take the children you already parent to their after school activities? Do not be afraid to ask for what you need from friends and family members. If you know that your friends or family are planning a shower, speak up. Let them know that gift cards to restaurants that deliver would be appreciated. A gift certificate for a cleaning service over the first months with your new adoptee would be of great benefit. Alleviating yourself of duties that others can carry out and making arrangements to take as lengthy an absence from work (or providing a stay-at-home parent) will allow you time to get acquainted with your new son or daughter. It will also give you time to re-connect with the children already in the family. In any event, one-on-one time with each of your children is more important than a few dust bunnies under the bed!

Suggestions for During the Trip

Recommendations in this area focus on gathering the child's history, reducing the abruptness of the transition for the child who is moving and taking care of the siblings, whether they are with you or at home.

Photos, Videotape and Audiotape

I have had the opportunity to review a lot of photos and video taken on trips to the child's homeland. Interestingly, there are usually abundant photos of the main tourist attractions as well as the McDonald's. Actually, in one case, the family had so many pictures of the McDonald's that I actually commented on it. The parents' response was, "It gave us comfort to see something familiar so far away from home." Yet, when it comes to actual photos of the child's orphanage, orphanage mates, orphanage caregivers, the child's birth town and so on, the number of these photos is often few.

Photos and video of the child's actual living quarters, caregivers and friends are important! The child needs to know where he came from and who was there. Photos of Red Square and St. Basil Cathedral, The Great Wall and Forbidden City, or a Mayan temple are nice, but they are not accurate representations of the child's experience in his homeland. The child needs as many (or more) photos of the orphanage as he does the well-known places of his country of origin.

There are cases in which the family is unable to tour the orphanage. In these cases, take photos of what is available—the outside of the orphanage, the grounds, the room in which you spend time with the child, the other children, the staff, the director, your interpreter and so on. Take ample pictures! As children mature, they will want to know where they lived, who took care of them and who helped you adopt them. If you are close to the child's birth home town, make the drive! The child's birth parents are not going to recognize you. If you remain worried that they will identify the child, one parent can make the trip while the other cares for the child in the city where you are staying. Take photos of yourselves and your family at the orphanage. If you are not in the photos, young children often have difficulty connecting to the fact that you were actually at the orphanage. Children forget names over time. This often causes sad feelings. Gather the names of the children and adults you are photographing. This is especially important if the child had a special connection to a particular caregiver or an orphanage mate. Photograph the airports, the people who meet you at the airport, your hotel or apartment—take ample photos of each aspect of the trip!

The lifebook was mentioned earlier in this chapter. The adoptive family will want to organize the photos into a lifebook and Chapter 9 will cover how to put one together in more detail. If your child is a toddler or older, frame some of the photos and display them in her bedroom after you get home. Just as familiar sites will be comforting to you while abroad, photos of familiar people will be comforting to your child as she adjusts to her new home.

Video is wonderful as well, and it records the sounds. I know that this should go without saying, but since I have seen as much video of orphanage caregivers' feet as I have seen photos of McDonald's, ensure that you are aiming the camera appropriately. If the excitement of meeting the new child and simultaneously videotaping the event are too much, then see if someone else is available who can carry out this task. Make it a priority to keep the video and photos safe during the trip and after arriving home. Again, there are many sad stories about what happened to these precious keepsakes.

Video serves another purpose. Video footage can help your adoption medical professionals assess the child's motor skills, obvious medical/congenital problems, severe malnutrition and other risk factors. The University of Minnesota International Adoption Medicine Program's website offers the article, "How to Make a Good Video" (see Resources in Chapter 5).

Audio taping is another consideration. One family recorded an orphanage caregiver singing a lullaby to their son while they were at the orphanage. This, combined with about 30 minutes of the normal sounds of the orphanage, allowed this child to fall asleep more easily in his new home.

Once home, photograph the "new" family. The visual depiction of the change that has occurred in the family helps everyone begin to adjust. Oh, just in case I did not say it enough times, here it is again—take ample photos!

Stay in Touch with Those at Home

Using email wherever you can find capabilities, send as many photos and videos home as you can. The brothers and sisters are eagerly waiting to see their new sibling!

Likely, those at home will want to talk to their mom and dad as well. Call as often as possible. Investigate the cost of international phone calls in advance. Budget this expense into your journey to your child's homeland. The children at home want and need to talk to you as frequently as possible.

Keep a Journal

Children love to hear the story of how you got them; they love to hear it over and over! Keep a journal of the sights, sounds, people, food, your reaction to being in a different country, what it was like meeting your child the first time—simply everything you can think to include. A journal in any medium—written, audio or video—will do. This will be a gift to the adoptee of immeasurable value. In the event you experience culture shock, this will be a good exercise for you to process the thoughts and feelings of this experience.

Accommodate the Sensory Needs of the Child Who Is Moving

It has already been established that infants and young children are very sensitive to sensory experiences, so when their possessions and their world change dramatically they can be harmed emotionally. The family has options to offset the impact of moving young children. Make special efforts to carry out this suggestion. It is so important to the transition of the child into your family.

The family could ask ahead of time if the orphanage is amenable to an exchange of sheets and/or clothing. If so, the family would provide new sheets and outfits for those currently being utilized by the child who is moving to your family. They may not smell good to you, but they will certainly comfort your newcomer. Resist washing them for several days. Wait until the child has had a chance to become accustomed to your scent and then you can go ahead and begin to remove these orphanage items. Keep them! Kids love having these belongings.

If it is not possible to keep some clothing and linens from your child's orphanage or foster home, investigate sending ahead, or at least bring with you some type of transitional object—a blanket, a stuffed animal, a small toy. See if you can leave it in the child's crib. Be aware that sometimes such gifts disappear; however, it is important to make the effort. Let the child keep this object throughout the trip and at home.

Keep in mind that older children will also be experiencing sensory changes. Many school-age adoptees report that the first car ride they remember was with the adoptive family. The toilet flushing, a hair dryer, the flash of a camera, the smell of new foods, the taste of juice, soda pop and water—all of these will be stimulating to a child who has had limited experiences outside of the orphanage.

If feasible, families may want to consider staying in a family setting rather than in a hotel. This provides a realistic glance at what any child, but particularly an older child, will experience upon changing countries. In a family setting, you would have to attempt to communicate, determine what you are eating, learn the family customs and routine, and try to understand social cues and emotional expression. Parents, brothers and sisters would gain a depth of understanding of what the sibling-to-be will feel like upon moving to their home.

Closure with Significant Adults and Orphanage Mates

The feelings of the institutional staff regarding children being adopted varies along a continuum. I have seen video of orphanage staff providing a good-bye party for children leaving with their new families. I have seen video of the staff being indifferent to the child departing. In other snippets, the staff is tearful and hugging the children. The same seems to hold true for orphanage mates. Parents who have the opportunity to visit the orphanage may size up their child's connections to peers and adults. If a closing ceremony seems to be necessary, see what arrangements can be made. If there are any willing adults, have them share stories of their experiences with the child. Record these memories. Children love to hear stories about themselves.

Additionally, if the adults are approving of the move, write down these positive sentiments (see Blessing Party earlier in this chapter). It is of great benefit to children to know they were cared about and that their move to the adoptive family was supported. Share photos of the event with the orphanage friends and the adults. The child can be provided with parting gifts to give to friends and caregivers. Allow time for final hugs and good-byes. Hopefully, your interpreter can attend the event in case anyone—peers or adults—have questions about what is happening. It would be great for you to know what is being said to the child in the process of leaving the orphanage. You are now the child's historian.

Plan Time with the Child Who Came Along

The day-to-day activities may make for a busy trip, although some families report that there was much down time. In any event, ensure that you devote time each day to the child or children making the trip with you. Even if you are busy, a few minutes goes a long way towards validating the typically developing child's feelings about being in a foreign country and sharing his or her parents with a new sibling.

Expect Regression

The children you already parent may regress while traveling with you or post-placement. This is completely normal, especially if they are young. A parent's first instinct is to respond by stating, "Honey, act your age!" Regression is a way for children to express the stress of a change in life. So allow the regression. Usually this passes on its own. However, it is always a good idea to increase parental time with the child who has regressed.

Post-Trip Suggestions

The suggestions in this section are the most important post-placement considerations. These will lay the foundation for the parent-child attachment. Ultimately, this attachment transfers to the siblings. The quality of attachments among family members contributes to the emotional health of each family member.

Arrival Home: Keep Things Low-Key

Certainly, extended family and friends may be excited to meet the new addition to the family. As stated previously, children moving intercountry are sensorily-oriented. Moving may be particularly overwhelming. Many new experiences—the noise of the airport, the popping of their ears on the plane, new people, riding in a car, etc.—occur in a very short period of time. Urge relatives to wait to meet their new grandchild or nephew no matter what the age of the new family member. You can actually schedule such meetings prior to traveling to the child's homeland, which will help these important people understand that everyone will be getting a turn to come and see your new son or daughter (so their needs will be satisfied) as well as why it is important that this be done slowly and carefully (so that the child's needs are satisfied). This protects the child from further sensory overload.

Plan to spend time at home and gradually introduce the child to his surroundings. Put off a trip to the mall or a welcome home party for a few weeks. Limit toys, trips to the park and restaurants.

If the child is older, plan to focus on setting limits, establishing boundaries and safety issues. Recognize that this school-ager or adolescent needs to learn basic daily activities like crossing a street, table manners, how to act in a store, sitting with the family and watching a movie, getting up and getting dressed, etc. Prioritize the most important rules and begin to enforce them immediately. This will help facilitate the child's internal ability to monitor his own behavior. The orphanage environment operated via adults enforcing external structure.

Parents Are Primarily Responsible for Meeting the New Child's Needs

Attachment first needs to form between the parents and the new child. Then, it forms with siblings, extended family and the rest of the world. This is not to imply that siblings cannot interact with their new brother or sister. However, this is to say that parents need to carry out all primary care giving over the first six to twelve months. Parents need to feed the child or provide the food, parents need to change the baby, bathe the newcomer or teach appropriate hygiene, and be the ones there when the child awakens and when the child goes to sleep. Parents need to provide comfort. Parents need to rock the child or teach the child about giving and receiving affection. If an infant, parents need to be the ones holding the baby most of the time. In fact, a sling is strongly recommended for young children. *Wearing* your newcomer is a great way to enhance attachment. It will certainly be tempting to let your older children assume many care giving tasks, however this would delay the attachment between you and your adoptee, further inhibiting developmental growth.

Adolescents, especially females, often rush to carry out the care giving. Parents must find ways to curtail this eagerness. This can be accomplished through a discussion of attachment and how it forms (see Chapters 2 and 10). After that conversation, you can sit with your children and list ways that they can be helpful which will not interfere with your care giving of the new child. Your resident children can heat up bottles, get diapers, carry the diaper bag, change the sheets on the toddler bed, sing lullabies or nursery rhymes along with you and so on. The children you already parent may be especially helpful with the language development of the new child and reinforcing rules. In fact, there are most likely a hundred ways they could help you without directly providing the care to the new child. It could be fun to make a list of these 100 things! Overall, we certainly want to encourage strong sibling relationships. However, there are times when we must direct the manner in which the siblings interact with the adoptee.

Establish a Routine

As stated under "Pre-Trip Suggestions" the previously institutionalized child is used to a routine. There is a time to go potty, a time to eat and a time to sleep. Orphanage life is highly structured. Establish a routine as quickly as possible upon arriving home. The adoptee will function best when his day has predictability. This will contribute to the well-being of each member of the family.

Schedule an Appointment with Your International Adoption Medical Clinic

If you have not scheduled a first appointment with your international adoption medical clinic or adoption-competent mental health professional, do so quickly after arriving home. It is important to begin monitoring your adoptee's health and growth. Early-intervention is a main key in maintaining the emotional well-being of your entire family. Letting problems continue, year after year, with the hope the child will "grow out of it" is one of the primary reasons the family gets stuck in unproductive interactions as Chapter 8 will explain.

As part of this process or in addition to it, have your child (no matter what her age at arrival) undergo cognitive developmental testing in her native language as early as possible after she arrives home. For all children younger than age 7 the assessment should be done within the first few weeks, and for those who are literate in their native language the time-frame is the first few months.[17] Since immigrant children and those adopted internationally immediately begin losing expressive and receptive language in their native tongues (a process known as language attrition), letting such testing wait may mean that meaningful educational testing must be delayed for several years, until the child has fully acquired expressive and receptive language skills in English.[18]

School-readiness is an area that requires consultation with those professionals knowledgeable about older international adoptees. Schools tend to want to place children according to their chronological age. This manner of assigning children a grade ignores language development, social skills, self-regulation abilities, the willingness to participate in a group activity, and cognitive skills and/or neurological problems. A timely psycho-educational evaluation will reveal individual differences and educational needs of your child and lead to proper school placement. This is important for overall adjustment, emotional well-being and future academic success.[19]

Regarding language and school readiness, parents are encouraged to review the articles and services available at the Center for Cognitive-Developmental Assessment and Remediation. The information for this agency is contained in the Resources.

---

17. Gindis, Boris, PhD "Initial Developmental Evaluation of an Internationally Adopted Child: Is it Important?" http://www.adoptionarticlesdirectory.com/Article/Initial-developmental-evaluation-of-an-internationally-adopted-child--is-it-important-/4

18. Gindis, Boris, PhD "What Adoptive Parents Should Know about Language-Based School Difficulties of Their Children," *The Family Focus* (newsletter from FRUA.) Spring, 2008, pp. 4–5.

19. Gindis, Boris, PhD "Initial Developmental Evaluation of an Internationally Adopted Child: Is it Important?" http://www.adoptionarticlesdirectory.com/Article/Initial-developmental-evaluation-of-an-internationally-adopted-child--is-it-important-/4

Post a Large Calendar in a Conspicuous Place in the House

It has been mentioned several times in this book that the addition of a child to the home creates an array of new appointments. Shortly after coming home, there will be your medical clinic visits and there will be your social worker arriving for post-placement visits. The list will probably grow very quickly. Older children need to know when you will be available and when they may need to find rides. They need to know when you will be home and when they will be arriving to an empty house. Or, they need to be informed of when to go to a friend's house until you come and pick them up. Everyone will benefit from hearing this information and seeing it posted on the calendar. The adoptee is not the only one who benefits from structure and routine. All children function better when they know what to expect.

Conclusion: Start a Habit

I am going to close this chapter with one final suggestion (before we get to Chapters 9 and 10, which will be packed with post-placement ways that families can facilitate attachment between all family members). This last suggestion is to start a habit. The habit is spending regular time with the children who were already in the family prior to the adoptee's arrival. I have rarely encountered a typically developing child—of any age—who does not mourn the loss of the parental time and attention that has been diverted to improve the mental health issues of the adoptee. Resident children are often sacrificed as parents think, "We can make up the time once John is better." Or, "The other children are more capable. They can do without as much time."

These thoughts are misperceptions. All children need time—in quality and quantity. Schedule "appointments" with your children. Work together with your spouse, partner, friends or relatives to keep the appointments. This is one habit I hope you never break.

Chapters 9 and 10 will put forth numerous concrete ways parents can make time for all of their children and themselves.

Resources

Books

Beauvais-Godwin and Raymond Godwin. *The Complete Adoption Book: Everything You Need to Know to Adopt a Child.* (Avon, Massachusetts: Adams Media, 2005.)

Cogen, Patty. *Parenting your Internationally Adopted Child: From Your First Hours Together through the Teen Years.* (Boston: Harvard Common Press, 2008.)

Evans, Karin. *The Lost Daughters of China.* (New York: Jeremy P. Tarcher/Putnam, 2000.)

Fahlberg, Vera. *A Child's Journey through Placement.* (Indianapolis: Perspectives Press, 1994.)

Foli, Karen and John R. Thompson. *The Post-Adoption Blues: Overcoming the Unforseen Challenges of Adoption.* (Emmaus, PA: Rodale Books, 2004.)

Gammage, Jeff. *China Ghosts: My Daughter's Journey to America, My Passage to Fatherhood.* (New York: Harper Collins, 2007.)

Gilman, Lois. *The Adoption Resource Book.* (fourth edition). (New York: Harper Collins, 1998.)

Gray, Deborah. *Nurturing Adoptions: Creating Resilience after Neglect and Trauma.* (Indianapolis: Perspectives Press, 2007.)

Johnston, Patricia Irwin. *Perspectives on a Grafted Tree: Thoughts for those Touched by Adoption.* (Indianapolis: Perspectives Press, 1983.)

Johnston, Patricia Irwin. *Adopting: Sound Choices, Strong Families.* (Indianapolis: Perspectives Press, 2008.)

Lieberman, Cheryl and Rhea Bufferd. *Creating Ceremonies: Innovative Ways to Meet Adoption Challenges*. (Phoenix: Zeig, Tucker and Co., 1999.)

MacLeod, Jean and Sheena Macrae (editors). *Adoption Parenting: Creating a Toolbox, Building Connections*. (Warren: EMK Press, 2006-7.)

Mason, Mary Martin. *Designing Rituals of Adoption: For the Religious and Secular Community*. (Minneapolis: Resources for Adoptive Parents, 1995.)

Pertman, Adam. *Adoption Nation: How the Adoption Revolution is Transforming America*. (New York: Basic Books, 2000.)

Uekert, Brenda. *10 Steps to Successful International Adoption: A Guided Workbook for Prospective Parents*. (Williamsburg, VA: Third Avenue Press, 2007.)

Websites

adoption.com
www.adoption.com

This is an extremely comprehensive website covering all aspects of adoption. You will find travel tips, advice about interacting with your newly adopted child, caring for yourself and other children throughout the process and more. The content is a balanced mix of stories from adoptive parents and material provided from professional sources. There are ample venues to connect with other adoptive families. Check out their CDs of adoption songs—they are just wonderful! Adoption.com is the mall of adoption resources—you can browse through its different departments for hours!

Adoption Policy Resource Center
www.fpsol.com/adoption/whoadv.html

This website is a service of Adoption Subsidy Advocates. It covers the guidelines necessary to negotiate a subsidy agreement for those families adopting from the child welfare system. In addition, families may obtain consultation regarding subsidy matters. The website is operated by Tim O'Hanlon.

American Academy of Adoption Attorneys (AAAA)
www.adoptionattorneys.org

AAAA is a national association of approximately 330 attorneys who practice, or have otherwise distinguished themselves, in the field of adoption law. The Academy's work includes promoting the reform of adoption laws and disseminating information on ethical adoption practices. The Academy publishes a newsletter, holds annual meetings and hosts educational seminars. The website offers a national directory, information as to why you may want to consider obtaining an attorney and tips to select your attorney.

Attachment Disorder Site
www.attachmentdisorder.net

The Attachment Disorder Site is an extremely comprehensive place to find any information about parent and child attachment as well as adult attachment issues. The site pulls together a vast array of articles, book titles and other resources pertaining to adoption, Sensory Integration Dysfunction, trauma, finding help, school issues and much, much more! The site offers a place for parents of children with attachment difficulties to communicate with one another.

Center for Cognitive-Developmental Assessment and Remediation
www.bgcenter.com

Dr. Gindis is the principal instructor at the BGCenter Online School, where he teaches courses for parents of internationally adopted children, and school and adoption agency professionals. Parents will also find over 500 articles here pertaining to all aspects of pre- and post-adoption concerns for internationally adopted children of all ages. Dr. Gindis is the author of over 40 scientific articles and book chapters, has served as a guest-editor for psychology journals, and has been a keynote speaker at national and international conferences. He is a Full Professor (retired) and former Director of Bilingual Program at Touro College Graduate School of Education and Psychology. This agency provides an array of assessments to help parents evaluate all of the needs of their son or daughter who joined their family from abroad.

Ethica: An Independent Voice for Ethical Adoption
www.ethicanet.org

Ethica is a nonprofit corporation that seeks to be an impartial voice for ethical adoption practices worldwide, and provides education, assistance, and advocacy to the adoption and foster care communities.

Families with Children from China (FCC)
www.fwcc.org

FCC is a nondenominational organization of families who have adopted children from China. The purpose of FCC is to provide a network of support for families who have adopted in China and to provide information to prospective parents. The purpose of this site is to consolidate the information that has been put together by the families of FCC, in order to make it easier for future parents to consider adopting from China. We also try to provide pointers to other adoption and China related resources available on the Web. FCC has chapters around the country—visit their site and find a support group near you.

Families for Russian and Ukrainian Adoptions (FRUA)
www.frua.org

FRUA exists to support adoptive families who are considering adoption, in the process of adopting and those who have returned home with their precious children. FRUA is an organization that is for everyone; whether you are just beginning to travel the road to adoption or you've been a forever family for a while. FRUA has local chapters across the country and FRUA chat where you can talk online with other pre- and post-adoptive families.

Guatemala-Adopt List / The "BigList
http://home.earthlink.net/~gadopt/gaown.htm

The Guatemala-Adopt List also known as the "Biglist" is the largest list on Guatemalan adoption. With several thousand members, this is a heavily-trafficked list, and it permits open negative or positive discussion about agencies, attorneys or facilitators. This list also talks about Guatemalan politics and culture, international adoption policies, and post-adoption life raising a child of Guatemalan origin. The Guatemala-Adopt list maintains years of detailed archives, featuring every post. This is a wealth of information on agencies, attorneys and facilitators. You need to login to get a free password to review the archives.

Rights4me
www.rights4me.org

Roger Morgan, Children's Rights Director, London, England and his team carefully listen to what young people tell them about the way they are being looked after, and the services they receive while in out-of-home care. Some really important messages have been passed on and have helped to make a difference. This site is home to the report, *About Adoption*, used to create the Adoptee Talk boxes in this chapter. However, other reports of interest include *Children on Bullying*, *Children on Care Standards*, *Care Matters*, *Children and Safeguarding*, *Rights and Responsibilities* and *Views on Standards*.

U.S. Department of Labor
www.dol.gov

Families may find information regarding the Family Medical Leave Act (FMLA) at the Department of Labor website. Under FMLA, covered employers must grant eligible employees up to a total of 12 work weeks of unpaid leave during any 12-month period for one or more of the following reasons: birth and care of a newborn child; placement of a son or daughter through adoption or foster care; to care for an immediate family member (spouse, child or parent) with a serious medical or mental health condition.

U.S. Department of State
www.state.gov

Utilize this website to keep track of potential travel hazards. Travel Warnings are issued to describe long-term conditions that make a country dangerous or unstable, or when the U.S. Government's ability to assist American citizens is constrained due to the closure of an embassy or consulate.

CHAPTER SEVEN

When a Child Leaves the Family: Displacement, Disruption and Dissolution

Most chapters in this book present many families successfully navigating their adoptions in spite of an array of challenges. Tragically, this will not be the case with all adoptions.

- Some children will leave the home in which they have been placed in expectation of adoption and go to another pre-adoptive or foster home prior to the finalization of the intended adoption. This is referred to as *disruption*.
- Some children may require a treatment option that means living outside of the family temporarily—a *displacement* (see Chapter 10). There are instances in which displacement becomes a permanent living arrangement. The child may reside in residential treatment until the age of emancipation. In these cases, the family retains legal parental rights and responsibilities—the child still has a family.
- In other instances, adoptive parents will legally terminate their already finalized adoption and forfeit all parental rights and responsibilities. Chapter 6 pointed out that this is the *dissolution* of an adoption. The custody of the child transfers to a public agency for purposes of finding another placement or a new family may be privately located for the child.

Disruption and dissolution are emotionally charged situations for all involved—parents, children and professionals. The child with a history of trauma is once again without a place to call home. The adoptive parents and brothers and sisters have their dreams shattered and experience a loss akin to the death of a child and sibling. Parents also feel a sense of failure, as do the professionals involved in the case.

Sometimes there is anger and outrage toward the family from their own friends and family, from some other adoptive families, and even from some adoption professionals. There is a moral outlook that the commitment made is to be honored, no matter what the circumstances. There are others who take the perspective that the only placement that failed is the one we didn't try. There is no callousness intended in this view. Rather, it reflects a philosophy that, in spite of the best efforts, a disruption or dissolution can occur.

In addition to the mixed feelings and varied ethical perspectives that surround unsuccessful placements, the research literature in this area includes some conflicting results. The studies that do exist focus primarily on the parents and the adoptee. There is little information regarding the impact of losing a brother or sister on the typically developing children. So, the purpose of this chapter is not to take a "stand" vis a vis adoptions that don't work out, but to

- report on the known statistics regarding rates of displacement, disruption and dissolution
- review reasons that cause disruption, dissolution and displacement
- describe the types of issues, via examples, experienced by typically developing children during and in the aftermath of an adoptee leaving the family.

The Rates of Adoption Disruption, Displacement and Dissolution

The Evan B. Donaldson Institute report *What's Working for Children: A Policy Study of Adoption Stability*[1] provides an extensive summary of the studies conducted to date which pertain to disruption, displacement and dissolution. This summary cites the research of those long recognized for their work in the field of adoption: Richard Barth, Marianne Berry, Trudy Festinger, Robert George, Ruth McRoy, James Rosenthal, John Triselotis, Victor Groze, Susan Smith, Jeanne Howard, and their teams. The research presented pertains almost exclusively to child welfare system adoptions.

The same type of research does not exist for intercountry adoptions or for domestic adoptions (mostly of infants) through private agencies or independent of agencies (mostly through attorneys). However, international adoptions in particular are not immune to the adoptee leaving the home temporarily or permanently, as a growing body of anecdotal reporting, writing and blogging makes clear. The reader may want to review the article, "Specialists Report Rise in Adoptions that Fail" for more information about international adoption dissolutions (see Resources).

The statistical material cited throughout this chapter has been taken from the Donaldson report, and page numbers cited below refer to that document.

Disruption Rates

Taken together, social science research studies on disruption (placements ended before finalization) during the 1980s and 1990s have estimated rates of disruption of U.S. adoptions between 5% and 27%, with rates generally declining through the 1990s. The research that reports higher disruption rates was reporting on smaller numbers of children referred to as "hard to place." This may mean placed at much older ages (p. 9). Anecdotally (no national statistics are kept), during the same period, professionals watching international adoption have noted an increase in disruptions and dissolutions since the mid-1990s.

Disruption is believed to occur most often within 12 to 18 months of the placement of the child in the family. The timeframe from the point when parents discuss their concerns with workers to the actual disruption is almost always relatively brief, with most children being removed within one to two months of the time the parents first report a problem to the worker (p. 9).

1. Evan B. Donaldson Institute. (2004). *What's Working for Children: A Policy Study of Adoption Stability and Termination*. [online]. http://www.adoptioninstitute.org/publications/Disruption_Report.pdf, pp. 1–25.

Displacement Rates

Displacement (placement in a therapeutic setting or with a foster family without ending the legal ties of adoption) rates in U.S. domestic adoption occur in a range from 1% to 8% of placements. It is difficult to gather more precise findings due to the manner in which out-of-home placements are tracked (p. 10).

Dissolution Rates

Comprehensive information on dissolution rates (reversal of a completed adoption, with parental rights of the adopters terminated) is not readily available. It is hard to obtain because children's names change after dissolution, and the court system does not report dissolutions to a state or national tracking system. Overall, dissolution rates of U.S. domestic placements of child welfare system adoptions are estimated at 1% to 2% (p. 11).

Factors Contributing to Disruption, Displacement and Dissolution

The issues that contribute to disruption, displacement and dissolution are grouped into three areas: factors related to the child, factors related to the parent(s) and systemic factors. It is important to point out that a combination of parent, child and agency issues contribute to any instance in which a child leaves a family prematurely. It is also essential to understand that the better we know the types of dynamics that cause placements to end, the more the risk of making poor matches in the future decreases—and more children will have a place to call "home" permanently, after having made fewer moves.

Child Factors

- *The child's age at the time of placement* (p. 12): Older age is believed to be a contributing issue because the child may have had more adverse experiences, may have formed stronger attachments to a prior family (birth or fostering), and the child is reaching an age in which autonomy—seeking independence—rather than connecting to parents, is the normal and predictable developmental task.
- *Behavioral problems* (p. 13): Aggressive and/or "acting out behaviors" which could include stealing, defiance, cruelty, sexual acting out, vandalism and threats of suicide are especially linked to a child leaving a family. In some instances, these behaviors present safety risks to the adoptee, the family and/or the community. The best interest of each member of the family must be weighed to determine the best solution for everyone. In a qualitative exploratory study of 27 Eastern European adoption dissolutions, the families reported that violence/aggression, sexual acting out, a lack of conscience, cruelty to animals, lying and stealing were behaviors that contributed to the decision to end these adoptions. Certainly, this study requires replication with a larger group. However, the survey does provide preliminary evidence that international adoptions dissolve due to factors similar to domestic adoptions.[2]

2. Holtan, McCarrgher and James (unpublished).

- *Prior history of sexual abuse* (p. 14): In addition to aggression and acting out behaviors, sexual abuse is associated with more moves in care, greater behavioral difficulties and attachment problems. Failure to resolve sexual abuse issues intensifies behavior problems or creates increased resistance to attach to the adoptive family, since trust is difficult for the child with a history of sexual abuse. As Chapter 1 pointed out, a history of sexual abuse is often unknown at the time of placement in an adoptive family.
- *Prior disruption history* (p. 14): As Chapter 2 pointed out, children who move multiple times are at great risk. Repeated moves jeopardize the child's capacity to develop secure attachments and trusting relationships with adults. Multiple placements are linked to behavioral and mental health problems, educational difficulties and juvenile delinquency; these are the types of issues mentioned above that decrease the child's chance of a permanent home.
- *Child's capacity to psychologically separate from birthfamily* (p. 16): As Chapter 1 made clear, interference with the development of new attachments may occur when the child's focus is on the past rather than the present. Unresolved separations, then, may hinder the development of new attachments. Adoptive parents desire a child who can connect and form intimate relationships with adoptive family members. A child who expects to return to a previous caregiver is in no position to move away from his past and toward a new family.

Parental Factors

- *Unrealistic expectations* (p. 17): Chapters 1 and 8 cover a multitude of the expectations that parents often harbor when entering the adoption process. Many of these expectations are designed to meet parental needs. Others simply don't make sense, given the trauma the adoptee has experienced. Those families who cannot adjust these expectations often move to terminate an adoption before or after legalization.
- *A rigid family system* (p. 18): There are parents who are simply not flexible. The mindset is that rules are meant to be followed. In response to the adoptee's negative behaviors, structure and rules are increased. This only serves to worsen the situation. Conflict becomes so frequent that the family opts to move the adoptee out of the family.
- *Partners who are not equally invested in the adoption* (pp. 17–18): Chapter 1 covered the "dragger/draggee syndrome." This scenario, in which one parent is the driving force while the other tags along through the adoption process, can have a devastating end result—a child moves from a family in which he was not entirely wanted to begin with. Further, the breadwinning parent's support of the primary caregiver has been determined to be a critical factor in sustaining a placement.
- *Limited or little social support* (p. 21): The initial enthusiastic support of family, friends and the religious community often wanes after adoption (Chapter 8). Isolated and overwhelmed by unexpected behaviors, many families see no other option than to disrupt or dissolve their adoption.
- *Lead time prior to adoption legalization* (pp. 17–19): Foster parent adoptions tend to be more stable, possibly indicating that lead time prior to finalization of an adoption contributes to this stability. The child and family know each other well; there has been plenty of time to comprehend the ramifications of finalizing the adoption. This factor may be especially important to consider in forming international adoptions of children at high risk for mental health issues. Intercoun-

Kids Talk

John Robert is a 20-year-old child living in his family of origin. His parents adopted two sisters. One is currently 17 years old and resides in a treatment setting (displacement), and the other sister, 16, was eventually placed with a different family (disruption). John Robert was 16 when the girls arrived, and has this to say about his experience:

"Prior to the adoption, I was not so keen on the thought of bringing another child or children, in my case, into an already settled home environment. I was 16 years old. Of course, I knew that since I had gone my entire life without having siblings that it would take some getting used to. My parents had looked at many children and we were under the impression that they would adjust well to our home. We were so naïve. We expected them not to have problems and not to have been abused. We expected that these were basically normal healthy children. These expectations came from what people told us. Social workers, adoption coordinators, the whole group spoon-fed us the idea that these would be normal children with limited needs.

"Though it was a rough four years, I don't think that there will be any permanent scarring for me. I'm just like any other human being on this planet. I will readjust to my normal home life I had before the adoption. My parents seem more disappointed at the failure of this adoption than I am. I suppose I would feel differently being a parent and walking in their shoes. Sometimes I think they think the adoption failure is their fault, which it isn't of course. You just can't change 13 years of abuse, neglect and moving from home to home.

"Four years is a long time. Sometimes I think my parents feel they lost time with me. I disagree. I must say I think I have always been much more independent and responsible than the average child. My independence, I hope, gave my parents more time to try to fix what was wrong with the children they tried to adopt. In the whole scheme of things, it's not a big deal. I'm not going to be petty and jealous just because my parents tried to open their hearts and their home to try to benefit children who were less fortunate than I.

"The two major things that weighed on my mind every day while my sisters were living at home were the loss of the peaceful household we had and the loss of a sense of safety. We lost a peaceful home because there was constant conflict all the time. I think I can count on one hand the number of days we had in the last four years that were not filled with conflict. My sisters antagonized each other, pitted my parents against each other, or just tried to wreak havoc any way that they could. As for a sense of safety, I think that disappeared after the first conflict we had in the home. Before these children came to our home, my bedroom door was never shut, and I never even had a lock to my room. After they came, I had a lock put on my room and my door was shut nearly all the time, so I could block out some of the conflict and bizarre behavior they often exhibited.

"Everything is back to normal with my uncles. While my sisters were living at home, neither would watch my sisters alone without someone from the family being there (i.e., Mom, Dad or me). You would think that three people could successfully watch two teenage girls and there would be no conflicts. You would have thought wrong. I had to stay too. I often did not want to stay because as a 16 to 19 year old, we tend to go out on Friday and Saturday nights. But, I was there helping my uncles watch my sisters."

try adoptions allow only a very brief period for the family and child to become acquainted before the adoption is finalized.

- *Kinship adoptions in which there is continued contact with the birthparents* (pp. 19–20): The continued influence of birthparents is the most common factor for disruption in kinship adoptions. The kin often find it hard to set appropriate boundaries for visitation and other contacts, which lead to unsolicited visits, disturbance and sometimes danger to the child.

Systemic Factors

- *Information received pre-adoption* (pp. 23–24): A lack of full information provided prior to the placement or adoption finalization is clearly a main reason for disruption and dissolution. In light of inadequate information, the child turns out to have more needs than the family anticipated. Parents frequently feel that information was not provided, was only partially given and/or was inaccurate. Caseworkers, on the other hand, report that they feel that they *did* provide information. Obviously, the conclusion to be drawn is that clearer communication needs to occur between social workers and prospective adoptive parents.
- *Caseworker perception of their role* (p. 24): Caseworkers who perceive themselves as advocates for the child leave parents feeling a lack of support and understanding. These families may then expend less effort to make the placement work.
- *Multiple case workers* (pp. 24–25): Several studies have noted that numerous changes in case workers led to the provision of inconsistent information and discontinuity of services to children and parents.
- *Stretching parameters* (p. 22): Parents are often asked to select various behaviors or special needs that they feel unable to accept in a child they will parent. Subsequently, however, parents may be presented children who stretch these preferences. That is, the child possesses qualities the parents had already identified as unacceptable. Such placements may run the risk of greater potential for disruption or dissolution later on.
- *Lack of post-adoption support and services* (p. 22): This occurs for many reasons. As Chapter 1 noted, funding may not be available to support adoptions long-term. The lack of knowledge and training of many workers inhibits their capacity to provide support. Or again, a worker who over-identifies with the prospective adoptee, rather than working with the family as a whole, leaves the family feeling misunderstood.

The Donaldson report did not look at the studies mentioned in Chapter 2, which highlighted that the stability and satisfaction of adoptive placements are impacted by the children—birth and/or previously adopted—residing in the home at the time another child enters the family. These ten research reports conclude that preparing brothers and sisters for their sibling-to-be may be a necessary component to reducing disruption rates as well.

Making the Decision

Most parents make the decision for their son or daughter to leave the family after a continuum of efforts and services have been exhausted (Chapter 10). There are those families who acquire extensive services and make vast efforts to alleviate the adoptee's mental health issues, fears about intimate relationships and/or fantasies of returning to his birthfamily. It is difficult to find fault with situations in which families have run a marathon in their efforts to avoid disruption. However, there are cases in which the option to terminate the placement is implemented too quickly and without prior use of professional help. Let's look at an example of each and then make some points.

> Joan and her sister, Faith, were adopted by Margo and Jay at ages 4 and 1½, respectively. By age 8, Faith was developing well. Joan, on the other hand, by age 11, had been aggressive since her arrival in the family. Joan had suffered two and a half years of physical abuse at the hands of her birthfather. When she arrived in foster care, she was bruised from head to toe, and there was evidence that she had sustained at least one broken bone. This seemed to instill in Joan a pattern of violent behavior that has been irreversible to date.
>
> She has always pushed and shoved to try to get her way. She punched kids time and time again. She broke a neighbor boy's glasses. She hit another child with a stick, and he had to go to the hospital for stitches. She often tried to trip Faith as she came down the stairs. Frequently, Faith was bruised because Joan pinched her and kicked her.
>
> Joan's aggression was not confined to the home. At school, she slammed another girl against the wall. Later that same day, she attempted to stab this youngster with a pair of scissors. Fortunately, an alert teacher intervened and offset what could have been an even more serious situation.
>
> Over her years with Margo and Jay, Joan participated in individual therapy, family therapy, special education services, psychiatric services and two psychiatric hospitalizations. Margo and Jay have seen to it that Joan be assessed by a neurologist, a neuropsychologist and several psychologists. She was moved from a small classroom for children with behavioral problems to a day treatment program. Margo and Jay implemented every type of behavior modification suggested by all professionals with whom they consulted.
>
> Ultimately, the day treatment staff called Margo to report that Joan had run away. They looked all over and could not find her. They had notified the police. At 3:00 a.m., the police brought Joan home. This incident became one in a series of times that Joan would run away. The length of time she was missing increased from a few hours to several days.
>
> The "last straw" happened at day treatment. Joan became angry with another child over the use of the pencil sharpener. In a rage, she stabbed this young man. The school met with Margo and Jay and suggested residential treatment.
>
> Margo and Jay, exhausted and concerned for the safety of Faith and other children, agreed that this seemed like a viable and reasonable option. The local public agency was approached. Due to the vast amount of documentation about Joan's violent behavior, funding for residential treatment was easily secured.
>
> Joan, at age 14½, entered the Christian Youth Home. Joan is now in her second residential treatment placement. The Christian Youth Home found it difficult to manage her aggression, so she was moved to a facility that specializes in the treatment of children with this type of violent tendencies.
>
> This displacement has now lasted two years. Joan is 16½. Margo, Jay and Faith, now age 13, visit Joan frequently. They continue to participate in therapy. They supply clothes and special personal items. Overall, they remain her family, yet it is debatable whether Joan will ever return home. She continues her pattern of assaultive behavior.

> Andrew had been abandoned at birth. He spent his first three years in a Ukrainian orphanage. Cindy and Tim, parents of two birth daughters, Laurie and Tammy, ages 8 and 7 respectively, longed for a son. Upon learning that Andy was available, they selected him and shortly thereafter they were on a plane home to America. Andy was age 3½ when he set foot on U.S. soil. The whole family was so excited!

However, 15 months after the placement, joy had turned to disappointment and frustration. Andy was defiant. He rarely listened, and he certainly didn't enjoy affection. In fact, he pushed away when Cindy or Tim attempted to kiss or hug him. He had been asked to leave two day care facilities. He bit and spit on other children. Cindy was currently staying home to care for Andy, but financially, this situation could not continue without serious repercussions for the family as a whole.

Andy didn't play well. Mostly, he picked up a toy, looked at it, and then moved on to the next toy. He would do this chronically. He pulled everything out of the cupboards and left it strewn about the house. Laurie and Tammy had expected that Andy would be a fun little brother. Instead, they found him "very annoying."

Cindy and Tim contacted their adoption agency and were referred to a therapist. She provided them with books and websites to review. As they read, they realized that Andy's early life in the orphanage had significantly impacted his ability to function in a family. While the therapist was very optimistic, she did explain that it would take a significant investment of time for Andy to develop and to learn how to be a son and a brother.

Six months into therapy, Cindy and Tim reported to the therapist that they had been looking into dissolving their adoption. They had even contacted several families, located via the Internet, who had expressed an interest in Andy. One family could take Andy very soon—two weeks! They had a completed home study and hired an attorney.

When it became clear to her that in these parents' minds the dissolution was past the point of being "negotiable," the therapist offered to prepare Andy and to speak to the "new" family. She also suggested meeting with Laurie and Tammy to help them express their feelings about the loss of their brother. However, Cindy and Tim felt they could handle these matters on their own. They wanted to act before the "new" family got discouraged and perhaps changed their minds.

Andy did move—the following week. Subsequently, his "new" family became his second adoptive family. Andy, now age 7½, is slowly accepting this loss. He occasionally still talks about his "old family" and how they "broke their promise to me." He says, "They said they would keep me forever and then they just gave me away."

Andy's behaviors continued to be troubling in his "new" family. The parents quickly obtained adoption-aware services. Over the past year, Andy has ceased spitting and biting classmates. He can now be managed in a pre-school setting. His parents, Tina and Brian, have learned specific ways to nurture Andy. These interventions should allow Andy to eventually accept their cuddles. Andy's brother, Tommy, age 9, isn't always happy with the way Andy plays, but in his own therapy, he has been educated as to why Andy "can't just play like a regular kid" as he wishes. Tommy, Tina and Brian are backtracking with Andy to his accurate social and emotional age (Chapter 9). Again, with time this technique should move Andy's social skills along. Overall, Andy's "new" family is satisfied with the adoption and they plan to be his "forever" family.

Certainly, Joan's parents accepted a commitment and continue to maintain their parental obligations to Joan. I have provided services to many families like Margo and Jay's who only as a *very last resort* displace, disrupt or dissolve their adoption of a physically or sexually abusive child. They do so with their hearts wrenched. Yet, they also do so knowing that "home" needs to be a place of safety and security for everyone who lives there. Regardless of Joan's past trauma, abuse of family members is unacceptable. Just as an abusive spouse needs to leave the home, so do abusive children.

Yet, I have also been involved in a fair number of cases like Andy's. The adoptee doesn't "fit" in the family. He isn't meeting the expectations of his parents and siblings.

So the family, without attempting to find the resources and do the work required to change the child's problematic behaviors and help him attach, finds another family and a dissolution occurs. Among lay persons this is being referred to as "re-homing" or "re-placement." All disruptions, displacements and dissolutions cause concern in the adoption community, but even more so, dissolutions like Andy's certainly counter the inherent meaning of adoption as a way to find permanent homes for children who need them.

At this time, there are no systems in place to prevent, or to at least attempt to offset, Andy's type of dissolution. There are also no governmentally required formal procedures to oversee the transition of children like Andy or the preparation of the family-to-be. The Internet has made it possible for one set of parents to locate another set of parents and transfer legal custody privately—with little to no guidance for the sending family members or the receiving family members.

Hopefully, policies will be developed or agencies will begin to offer services to these families. Currently, the number of agencies attempting to fill the gap is but a handful.

In the meantime, there are many questions for each member of the adoption community to consider about disruptions, displacements and dissolutions, and the rest of this chapter will address those questions and issues.

Professional and Agency Considerations

Adoption professionals doing both domestic and international adoptions cannot play ostrich—ignoring the fact that disruptions, displacements and dissolutions are a significant risk for many of the children for whom they advocate.

- When will we recognize the need for uniform pre-adoptive training guidelines? Education needs to be carried out regardless of cost and staff time.
- When will we realize that placement is the beginning of our job—not the end? As pointed out under "Disruption Rates," most placements disrupt in the first 12 to 18 months. Enhanced support, immediately post-placement, lends to early identification of problems and thus the potential to offset these difficulties before they reach a crisis level.
- When will we recognize that there *are* children with very serious mental health issues? We need to stop downplaying the severity of the trauma perpetrated against children and the lasting impact of that abuse, neglect and abandonment. We need to develop realistic expectations of the damage to many prospective adoptees, and a family's ability to "cure" the adoptee. Adoptive families may need out-of-home placement options at various points in their adoption. This is not an adoption "failure." Such residential placements ensure safety and help the parents maintain the stamina essential to manage a very difficult child. The typically developing children get needed breaks during which their family is more "normal." They deserve this! In situations like Joan's, in which the child cannot return home, the family is most often still very willing to be the child's "forever" family. They are just doing so from a distance. This is a fine permanency alternative.
- When will we recognize the need to pay social workers salaries commensurate with experience and expertise? Adoption is a specialization. It requires extensive knowledge to place children appropriately and to work well with families.
- When families do approach us with thoughts of a disruption, displacement or dissolution, we need to ask, "Am I the best person to work with this family? Can

I act objectively?" Too frequently, professionals become adversarial with parents. The capacity to carefully and realistically examine the situation becomes muddied. The parents are viewed as the problem. Again, the child's needs are downplayed. Neither the child nor the family receives the appropriate services. Neither the child nor the family is treated with dignity or respect.

- Often, a family seeking displacement (to a therapeutic setting) or dissolution (through the child welfare system) must transfer custody of their child to a public agency. The change in custody allows the agency to tap funding sources for treatment/living options. Custody and some funding streams are governed by federal legislation, so these federal laws must be followed. As part of these regulations, there has to be a domestic relations hearing. This means that the family can be asked for child support. Thus, the family may be penalized financially in these cases. Additionally, they often lose the ability to make decisions about the child they know better than we do. Once again, many children, must rely on a "system" rather than "parents." When will we cease such practices?

Like it or not, in cases like Andy's we must ask the hardest question, "What is the impact on Andy if he stays in a family that doesn't truly want him?" Which is more traumatizing to Andy—attempting to make the placement work, or helping the family dissolve the adoption in a manner that is healthiest for all involved?

Parental Considerations

Prior to the displacement, disruption or dissolution of an adoption, parents need to be encouraged to conduct some serious soul-searching. They need to ask themselves hard questions.

- If my birth child was acting this way, would I move him or her? Why do I view the adoptee differently?
- Have we truly given this child enough time to adequately adjust and integrate into our family?
- Are we certain that this isn't a temporary crisis?
- Are we moving the child because he or she isn't meeting *our* needs?
- Have we fully examined (hopefully with an objective adoption professional) our original and current expectations? Were they and are they realistic?
- Have we truly attempted to attach to this child, even if the child is rejecting?
- Have we sought every possible avenue of formal (therapeutic) and informal (peer) support?
- Have we made efforts to educate ourselves?
- Have we worked to implement a variety of parenting techniques?
- Would altering our lifestyle (for example, moving to a smaller, less expensive home to lower our mortgage and thus provide money for therapeutic services or provide a stay-at-home parent) help our child?
- Are we blaming an agency for our troubled adoption, or are we accepting our role in our current situation?
- Have we given consideration to the aftermath—what will happen with each of us after the child leaves? How will the other children in our home be affected?

This last question is one that agencies, helping professionals, parents—all adults involved in adoption—need to explore.

Kids Talk

John Robert, whom we met earlier, also shares his thoughts on working with various adoption professionals:

"It was like a broken record listening to social workers and adoption coordinators. You'd think adoption was the greatest thing in the world after listening to these people. I mean it was like the integration of abused and neglected kids into your household would be a snap and everyone would just get along all the time with no worries.

"The truth is they lied. And by lied I mean that leaving out information is lying. Downplaying mental health issues was a lie. Not being properly informed of past incidences in previous homes is a lie. To use the words 'some behavioral problems' was the biggest lie of all. They make you think these kids are so great. They'll fit right into your family or any family for that matter. Then, when you get the kids into your home and there was a conflict, the social workers thought we were lying. No one could even fathom what these kids were doing!

"As for classes, my parents had to go to them. I had it easy. I talked to a few social workers and answered the classical questions of, 'What do you think having a sibling in your home will be like?' 'What are your expectations?' 'What are you looking forward to most about adoption?' We had to take time out of our lives for fingerprinting and criminal background checks and it was all for nothing. The children don't even live here anymore.

"There was absolutely nothing that could have been done to assist me prior to adoption. You can never truly be prepared for what is ahead without actually living it. To tell you the truth, things are more than likely going to be worse than people make them sound. Yes, there are probably hundreds of people who have had successful adoption experiences. And maybe I'd feel different if ours was successful too, but I don't. Anyone who has never experienced it can't tell you anything. Although, perhaps first hand experiences would help, sort of like a window into what's to come. Kids could get into groups and share stories. I think having people like yourself to talk to and interact with before and after an adoption is essential in successfully coping with your new home situation.

"I cope by trying to forget the experience. I'm happy to have my life back. The adoption experience will always stick in my mind and haunt me for a very long time. My life is like what it was four years ago only it has a huge chunk missing that I'm trying to forget. I don't like to talk about it. It's a very long drawn out story. It makes me angry to think about what was or should have been.

"I'm very upset. I suppose most of all I'm angry. My sisters don't know how good they had it. In a way, I feel isolated because very rarely did I get to talk to birth children who were in the same shoes as I was."

The Adoptee Leaves the Home: The Impact on Brothers and Sisters

Just as the decision to adopt a child, and that child's arrival and presence, impacted each member of the adoptive family, so will the adoptee's leaving affect parents, brothers and sisters, and the adoptee.

Consider this: the adoptee must deal with being abandoned again. The pain of another rejection stings and re-opens the old wounds of previous losses of birthfamily and possibly other caregivers. He must move on to another family, or he must return to a foster home or a placement in a facility. He gets very little time to mourn before he is expected to form new relationships, go to school and participate in extracurricular activities.

Parents must grieve a child. There are now four places at the dinner table instead of five. A birthday passes with no celebration. A bedroom is empty. Months later, a toy found in the back of a closet is a reminder of the child who once called the parents "Mom and Dad." Anger, sorrow, frustration, guilt, despair, confusion and many other emotions plague these families, often for years after the adoption ends.

Brothers and sisters must cope with the loss of their sibling. Following is an overview of three pertinent issues to keep in mind when a brother or sister experiences the dissolution, displacement or disruption of a sibling. A fourth important issue is facilitating grief. The reader is referred to the section in Chapter 10 which

Kids Talk

Rosie spent birth through age 5 in an Eastern European orphanage. She was then adopted by an American couple, Jill and Peter. After nine months, Jill and Peter opted to place Rosie with another family. In her new family, she has a mom, a dad and a typically developing birth brother, Eban, age 7.

Rosie says, "When I was in the orphanage, I felt sad because the other kids got adopted and I didn't. I thought it was because something was wrong with me.

"When I got adopted, I thought it was going to be fun because in the orphanage it was not fun. When I got adopted, I was afraid of them getting rid of me. I was kind of afraid of learning a new language because I thought people would make fun of me.

"When I met my new parents [Jill and Peter], I was happy and scared because I was wondering if they would keep me and be nice to me. As I said, it was going to be fun but it was not because you had to do chores and manners and in the orphanage they didn't teach you manners.

"You might be wondering if it [living at Jill and Peter's house] was fun. Well, sometimes it was fun. The bad part was that sometimes you will never find out who your birthmom is. The good part was if you found her. My brother Eban found his birthmom. We visit her once every year.

"The hardest part of being a new family member is getting used to all the rules and getting to know people. Don't be shy because if you aren't, they might become your best friend. The other hard part was loving them, because you don't know if they will get rid of you.

"When I found out I was moving to another family, it just broke my heart. I felt sad because I had faith in Jill and Peter. When I met my new family, I felt happy. My biggest challenges in my new home was showing love and giving love.

"I was afraid of this new family because it was really hard letting go of the other family (Jill and Peter) because you thought they loved and cared about you but they didn't. If your child is threatening to do bad stuff, don't call the police, just have them talk about their feelings or take them to a therapist. My mom and dad took me to Arleta's. I did not like her at first, but if you do what is right, you can fix the problem. I will tell you one thing . . . NEVER GIVE UP."

is called "Coming Ashore: Letting Grief Flow" for ways to help the typical children grieve.

Where Is My Sibling Going?

This first question requires that someone explain to the children remaining in the family where the adopted sibling will be living.

When the Sibling Is Going to Residential Treatment

Residential treatment, a group home, a specialized boarding school, a specialized adoption-competent ranch—these are living arrangements unfamiliar to most typically developing children.

Consistent with Chapters 2, 3 and 9, clear and honest explanations about where a sibling is going to be living need to be offered. If some type of residential treatment is

Kids Talk

Bobbie and Amber, currently ages 11 and 14 respectively, were the brother and sister to 9-year-old Sam. Sam arrived at age 5 after spending five years in an Eastern European orphanage. He very recently left the family to join a new adoptive family (dissolution).

Amber writes, "I wanted a girl and expected it to be more like it was with my biological brother. I wanted her to admire me like Bobbie did for a while and help her grow when she became a teenager like I am now. I learned he was a brother when my parents emailed a picture from their hotel abroad.

"Instead, we lost our typical routine and normal lifestyle. We had a decrease in fun activities and *definitely* lost time with our parents.

"We had no preparation. We knew some of the children available had a handicap (medical or physical) but we didn't know anything about the problems Sam had. He painted my bedspread, took food in his closet which grew mold, tried to have sex with my brother, made sexual comments to friends and cousins—which made it difficult to have friends over—stole change, and broke whatever was important to me.

"Our parents divorced after he came. It was so hard to go to visits at my dad's house because Sam would demand all the attention. The visits were ruined. I stopped going. Eventually, he moved to my dad's house until a new family was found for him.

"I am feeling mad, sad, frustrated, confused and guilty. I also wonder if I will ever see him [Sam] again."

Bobbie says, "I also expected another sister—the perfect little sister who would look up to me.

"No, no, no—I got no preparation. I have a list of losses—friends, family, stuff, privacy, time with parents, feeling safe, peace, fun, and on and on.

"I tried to cope by talking to people I trust and when I really needed a break I tuned the world out with music whether it was playing it, listening to it, or writing lyrics. I also wrote in a journal in a poem format because poems help me express my feelings.

"I have a lot of feelings! I feared saying much as I thought he [Sam] would harm me if he knew I was talking about him. I am most disappointed about the fact that I couldn't help my brother to become better than he is or help him learn. I reached out to him over and over. He didn't respond."

the option, information about the facility can be printed from the Internet and shared with the birth and/or previously adopted children. Parents can share their view on what the treatment center has to offer and why they feel it may be helpful for the sibling to live there. Once the troubled adoptee is settled, it is likely that a tour can be arranged. Older children often benefit from meeting the staff. Adolescents can sit in on treatment team meetings or an occasional therapy session.

Recently, in setting up a meeting for a 12-year-old currently residing in a treatment facility due to running away and fire-setting, her 17-year-old sibling asked to participate. This request was met with much resistance from several professionals. Eventually her mother assumed responsibility and invited her daughter to sit down in the meeting. She listened attentively and asked numerous questions. She provided insight about her sister. After the meeting she stated,

> "It was hard to hear all of the things that are wrong with my sister. I mean, I know that they are true. It is still hard to hear. But, I am happy I got to be a part of the meeting. I know there are a lot of nice people really trying to help her. I feel better about this whole situation now."

The same open exchange of information is recommended when discharge of the adoptee is planned. If the adoptee had been unsafe or abusive, the brothers and sisters especially need to know that a safety plan has been developed and what it entails. The typically developing children also need help recognizing that their traumatized sibling is not likely "fixed." These kids ask, "Is she going to be all better?" Hopefully, progress has been made. However, the adoptee, brothers, sisters and parents still have much ground to cover to become a family. Certainly, there are cases in which the troubled adoptee returns home only to resume her previous harmful ways. Subsequently, this child may again depart to a treatment facility or the parents may then decide to terminate the adoption.

When the Adopted Sibling Is Moving to a New Family

If the move is to be permanent, parents should expect immediate queries from siblings such as, "Who is this new family?" "How do we know they are safe?"

Regarding, "Who is this new family?" often the two families meet. This openness quells many fears the children remaining in the family have about their sibling's new family.

> Ben was adopted at age 2 from Guatemala. After years of various therapies, evaluations, special education services, medication, an array of parenting strategies, and much discussion and prayer, Tanner and Erica opted to dissolve the adoption when Ben was 9 years old.
>
> Ben's sexual behaviors had become more than they could deal with. He masturbated incessantly. This sexual stimulation had been present upon his arrival on American soil. As time passed, he attempted to lie on top of other neighborhood children. He talked about wanting to "rape" these kids and his cousins. Many children feared Ben. He could only go outside if an adult was present. He wandered the house at night. Their birth son, Matt, age 12, often awoke to find Ben standing next to his bed. Door alarms had to be installed to curtail this behavior. Matt often stated that he felt like he "lived in a jail."
>
> Overall, Ben required constant supervision. This was exhausting the family. Tanner, Erica and Matt had become scared of Ben. They asked, "If this is what he is like now, what will he be like when he is 13, 14 or 15?"

They contacted an agency offering dissolution services, and eight months later a family was located for Ben. This family had two sons, older than Ben, whom they had also adopted through adoption dissolutions.

The new couple, Audrey and Jack, were adequately informed of Ben's issues and still decided to move forward. A first pre-placement visit was scheduled. The two families opted to meet at a restaurant. Matt was relieved. He was going to get to meet Audrey and Jack. He would see for himself what they were like.

Lunch went well. Audrey and Jack brought many photos of their family. Their home was lovely, and they had a large yard. They loved going to the beach. They had two Irish Setters.

The best part for Matt was when Audrey said, "Our other sons had brothers and sisters too. They still email and call once in a while. In the summer, we arrange a long weekend visit. We'll all talk about this and see what works out for you."

At present, Matt remains in contact with Ben. He is comforted knowing that Ben is safe and is doing okay. Ben is happy that his "old family" hasn't forgotten him and that they "aren't mad at me."

However, in other cases, the adoptee leaves the family and no future contact occurs. The former brothers and sisters (like their parents) are left to wonder, "Where is my sibling?"

Diana and Vic, birth siblings, were adopted at ages 1 and 6. Diana, because she had experienced far less trauma, is developing normally. Unfortunately, Vic suffered years of sexual and physical abuse. As Diana approached age 4, Vic began sexually abusing her. He entered her room at night and forced her to perform various sexual acts. She did not reveal the abuse. Diana's mom, Denise, discovered it one night when she was up sick. She and her husband, Patrick, were horrified!

The family then pursued an array of therapies. Eventually, they requested a placement in a residential treatment facility specializing in treating sexual offenders. The funding required the involvement of the public agency.

Immediately, the situation became adversarial. The family was investigated as the agency was suspicious that they were the root of the sexual abuse. Diana and Vic were both moved to foster care.

Eventually, Vic admitted his actions. Diana was returned home. Vic remained in foster care. He was deemed a safety risk to Diana and so the public agency took custody. However, the family and public agency fought over the best means to treat Vic. The agency believed he could be treated on an out-patient basis. The family continued to press for placement in a facility.

In the meantime, Vic's foster family requested his removal. He moved to a second foster home and then a third. Diana was never able to meet any of these foster families. She had no idea where Vic was living, who he was living with, what he was doing or where he was going to school. She kept wondering, "Is my brother okay?"

Because of the placement instability, Vic received no treatment. Yet, the public agency petitioned the court to return Vic home. The family refused to go along with this plan. They believed that Diana should not have to live with her perpetrator. After much litigation, their parental rights were terminated. To date, they have no idea where Vic is or how he is doing.

Diana's mental health has deteriorated. She wishes she had told about the abuse. Maybe, then, Vic could still be home. She is angry that he abused her. She is sad that he suffered so much at the hands of her birth parents. "Why did they treat him like that?" "Why aren't they in jail?" "Why couldn't he get over it?" "Why didn't he pick to live with me? He is the only person from my birthfamily I could have lived with and now he is gone too."

She is also relieved that her abuse has ceased. However, she would like to see her brother or at least have news about him. She continues to ask, "Where is my brother?" "Why can't I see him?" "Why can't I at least know how he is doing?" The public agency does not respond to phone calls or written requests.

Ongoing contact, as Chapter 6 pointed out, is always an issue to be decided on a case by case basis. In Diana's case she would benefit from a brief, supervised visit with her brother from time to time. For other brothers and sisters, it would be too overwhelming to visit their perpetrator. However, an email or a brief statement every four to six months would at least offset worries and concerns about a sibling that left "home."

Responding to Questions from Others

Matt, Diana, Laurie, Tammy and Faith, the brothers and sisters we have met so far, were all asked many questions as school, and Sunday school classmates, the next door neighbor, the bus driver, the lady at the convenience store, and so on, realized that they hadn't recently seen their adopted sibling.

Parents, brothers and sisters will likely be asked a myriad of questions when a dissolution, displacement or disruption occurs. Parents will need to decide how to tell friends and relatives about their decision to move the adoptee out of the family. The birth and/or previously adopted children will also need some help responding to the queries posed by kids and adults. They will need a "cover story" as will be described in Chapter 9.

In Matt's case, his parents were so grief-stricken after their dissolution that they didn't even think about Matt's schoolmates inquiring about what had happened to Ben.

Matt, a very resourceful young man said, "I just tell them we had to 'unadopt' him because he wasn't working out. He needed a different family and we found him a good one."

According to Matt, his classmates seemed to accept his answer. Quickly, the discussion turned to baseball or the upcoming math test.

In the case of Denise, Patrick, Diana and Vic, the family's neighborhood was comprised of many homes lined along blocks. The kids, from streets away, all knew each other. It had already been noticed that several social workers were visiting their home. Certainly, Diana would be asked many questions after Vic's departure.

Denise and Patrick had to make some decisions. Consumed with their own emotions, they felt professional assistance was best. This mental health guide had experience with adoption dissolution. She was able to help them think clearly.

They first sorted out who was already aware of their decision to dissolve their adoption and who wasn't. Then, they listed those persons that they would see regularly, and as such, would notice and require an explanation. It is helpful to think about how many people may ask questions and in what situations. Parents and kids are better able to respond when they are prepared for what may be coming when they arrive at church, their favorite restaurant, school, a sporting event, the community pool and so on.

The actual explanation was compiled by sifting through what was "private" and what could be shared. Denise and Patrick opted to inform others that,

> Sadly, Vic had behaviors that were not safe for Diana. After much advice from professionals, it was uncertain that his problems could be alleviated. As such, they felt it necessary to ensure Diana's safety. It was a profoundly difficult decision. However, they are at peace with the decision. They have no hard feelings toward Vic. His past was just too great for him to overcome. They will always miss him and they continue to pray for him. He is living with another family at this time."

Diana was offered the choice of simply saying, "I would prefer you ask my Mom and Dad. It's too hard for me to talk about." This deferring to the parents is always an option for the children. Or, she could offer something similar to her parents. Below is what Diana felt comfortable with saying and which maintains confidentiality,

> "My brother had a lot of serious problems. So he went to live with another family who can take care of him. I miss him a lot, but this is safer for our family."

It must be kept in mind that brothers and sisters' responses—cover stories—will most likely be met with shock or with silence. Few of their peers will be able to relate to losing a sibling in this manner. In such instances, parents and professionals should consider connecting these brothers and sisters to other children whose families have experienced a displacement, disruption or dissolution. In Diana's case she continued on in therapy, and she was introduced to another youngster who had experienced a sister leaving the home. The two find each other comforting.

All too frequently, families such as Matt's are left alone to deal with the aftermath of a child leaving home. Busy professionals move on to other cases. The case worker may feel guilty and thus withdraw from their previous relationship with the family. Adversarial relationships cause a "You made the decision so you'll have to deal with it" reaction from some professionals, family members and friends. Or, well-meaning friends and family members stifle grief with comments such as, "Well, it was for the best." "Now you can move on." "She was never right for your family."

Actually, it takes little time and effort to extend some empathy to these parents and children. We need to offer some guidance about managing and coping with the aftermath. No matter what our beliefs about the ethics of their decision, these families are suffering.

Would Mom and Dad Give Me Away?

Nearly all children ages 3 to 5 years old have fears about being abandoned, getting lost, or no longer being loved by their parents (Chapter 8). Loss of a sibling makes these fears seem all too possible for children born to the family. Appropriately developing adopted children, already all too familiar with abandonment, are now watching their parents move a son or daughter out of the family. These children wonder, "Would Mom and Dad give me away?" "What would I have to do to be forced to leave the family?"

Parents may notice that these healthy kids regress or exhibit more fears after an adopted sibling moves. They may also engage in negative behaviors with increased frequency. Sometimes they begin repeating the exact behaviors of the child who is gone. This may especially occur if the siblings are related by birth.

At times, the birthsibling bond is stronger than the parent and child connection. Adopted birth siblings, then, will strive to be reunited. The rationale may be any of the following:

- *Loyalty:* "She is my birth sister. I belong with her."

- *A desire to contribute to the healing process:* "I have to help her. She is my 'real' sister."
- *Fear:* "We have never been separated. I am scared to be without her."
- The two (or more) siblings are connected by a *trauma bond.* The victim child is linked to the exploitive dynamics of the abusive child.

Thus, the adopted birthsibling remaining in the family will begin to spiral out of control. Irrationally, this child believes that his unconstructive actions will cause him to go live with his traumatized birth brother or sister. The behavior of the adopted child who appeared healthy now plummets. His trauma has been triggered by the separation from his birth brother or sister.

It is important that parents be alert to any changes in their typical children. More so, it is critical that parents assure them of their place in the family—repeatedly! Adults must be clear in their explanations: "Vic left the family because he isn't safe." "Joan left the family because she kept hurting people." "You are staying in the family because you are safe. You don't hurt people. In a family, everyone needs to be safe." Seek professional help if necessary. *This may be needed immediately in the case of separations involving birth siblings.*

Conclusions

No one wants a child to leave a family. Yet, adoption practice, parental qualities and a child's age and history of trauma blend to create a living situation that may be unsafe or abusive. In these instances, services and empathy must be extended to the family. When they have taken all steps possible to avoid a disruption, displacement or dissolution, observers and supporters must applaud their outstanding efforts to heal their troubled adoptee. We must not consider the adoption a failure if the family remains connected and involved with the child. In other instances, where the family simply finds the child intolerable because of poor fit or unrealistic expectations, professionals involved must find ways to remind these parents of their commitment, offer intensive services and support, but ultimately keep in mind what is best for the child. Simultaneously, those same professionals must work to improve social work practice in order to prevent these tragic adoptions.

In all cases, we must ensure that our special brothers and sisters are cared for. The loss of a sibling is confusing and painful. It is a loss that occurred through no fault of theirs. When families who displace, disrupt or dissolve adoptions are abandoned, so are typical children. A system that says it serves children should mean *all* children.

Resources

Books

Brodzinsky, David and Jesus Palacious, Eds. *Psychological Issues in Adoption.* (New York: Praeger Publishers, 2005.)

Fahlberg, Vera. *A Child's Journey through Placement.* (Indianapolis: Perspectives Press, Inc., 1994.) (Among much more, this book includes the material in the widely cited, but long out of print, 1979 booklet by Dr. Fahlberg titled, *Helping Children When They Must Move.*)

Gray, Deborah D. *Nurturing Adoptions: Creating Resilience after Trauma and Neglect.* (Indianapolis: Perspectives Press, Inc., 2008.)

Keck, Gregory C. and Regina M. Kupecky. *Adopting the Hurt Child: Hope for Families with Special-Needs Kids: A Guide for Parents and Professionals*. (Colorado Springs: NavPress, 1995.)

McRoy, Ruth. *Special Needs Adoption: Practice Issues*. (New York: Garland Publishing, 1999.)

Smith, Susan and Jeanne Howard. *Promoting Successful Adoptions: Practice with Troubled Families*. (Thousand Oaks, CA: Sage Publications, 1999.)

Articles

Ashe, Nancy. "What to Do When Your Adoption Is Failing." Adoption.com. online at http://library.adoption.com/Failed-Placement/What-to-do-When-Your-Adoption-is-Failing-A-Parents-Guide-to-Adoption-Disruption-Dissolution/article/5178/1.html

Child Welfare Information Gateway. "Adoption Disruption and Dissolution: Numbers and Trends." (2004.) Online at http://www.childwelfare.gov/pubs/s_disrup.cfm

Department of Health and Human Services, Administration for Children and Families. "Report to Congress on Adoption and Other Permanency Outcomes for Children in Foster Care: Focus on Older Children." http://www.acf.hhs.gov/programs/cb/pubs/congress_adopt/index.htm

Evan B. Donaldson Institute. "Adoptive Parent Preparation Project Phase I: Meeting the Mental Health and Developmental Needs of Adopted Children." (2008.) http://www.adoptioninstitute.org/publications/2008_02_Parent_Preparation.pdf

Fahlberg, Vera. "Post-Adoption Services." http://www.perspectivespress.com/vfpostadopt.html

Mason, Mary Martin. "Getting Past the Hurt of Adoption Disruption." *Family Voices* newsletter. Minnesota ASAP. Online at http://www.mnasap.org/Newsletter.aspx?view=3-26-2008(2).pdf

McRoy, Ruth. "Barriers and Success Factors in Adoptions from Foster Care: Perspectives of Family and Staff." AdoptUsKids. http://www.adoptuskids.org/images/resourcecenter/barriersuccessfactors.pdf.

Nickman, Steven and Robert Lewis. "Adoptive Families and Professionals: When the Experts Make Things Worse." http://www.nysccc.org/Post%20Adoption%20Services/Experts worse.htm

Palacios, Jesus; Yolanda Sanchez-Sandoval, and Esperanza Leon. "Intercountry Adoption Disruptions in Spain." *Adoption Quarterly*, Vol 9. 2005, pp 35–55. Research summary written by Stephanie Townsend available online at http://www.informedadoptions.com/index.php?option=com_content&task=view&id=173&Itemid=31

Riggs, Diane. "Plan, Prepare, and Support to Prevent Disruptions." http://www.nacac.org/adoptalk/planpreparesupport.html

Riggs, Diane and Mary Boo. "Disruption Support is Critical." http://www.nacac.org/adoptalk/disruptionsupport.html

Riggs, Diane and Joe Kroll. "Families Need the Whole Truth." http://www.nacac.org/adoptalk/wholetruth.html

Schooler, Jayne. "When Siblings Are Separated: What Parents Need to Know." http://www.nysccc.org/Siblings/adopfamsibs.htm

Seelye, Katharine Q. "Specialists Report Rise in Adoptions that Fail." *New York Times*. 3/24/1998. Online at http://query.nytimes.com/gst/fullpage.html?res=9A03E3DF1038F937A15750C0A96E958260&sec=&spon=&pagewanted=all

Siskeski, Janice. "Adoption Disruption: When Love Isn't Enough." Rainbowkids.com 2/1/2007. Online at http://www.rainbowkids.com/ArticleDetails.aspx?id=456

Sturgeon, Virginia. "Thoughtful Visitation Practices Prevent Disruption." http://www.nacac.org/adoptalk/visitation.html

Williams, Wendy and Pat Johnston, "Losing a Sibling: Helping Your Child Cope with an Adoption Reversal." http://www.perspectivespress.com/siblingloss.html

Websites

Adoption Policy Resource Center
www.fpsol.com/adoption/whoadv.html

This website is a service of Adoption Subsidy Advocates. It covers the guidelines necessary to negotiate a subsidy agreement for those families adopting from the child welfare system. In addition, families may obtain consultation regarding subsidy matters. The website is operated by Tim O'Hanlon. Subsidy may play a crucial role in funding for out-of-home treatment. Families want to know their entitlements and rights in cases involving displacement and dissolution.

Ranch for Kids
www.ranchforkids.org

The "Ranch For Kids Project" is a registered nonprofit corporation in the states of Wyoming, Montana and Maryland with 501(c)(3) status. This project has established a Christian home for "at risk" Russian and other adoptees who may be experiencing difficulties in their new families in the U.S. This program was developed through joint cooperation with agencies and child welfare organizations where troubled children adopted from Russia and other countries could come for respite care and/or referral to licensed agencies for placement into a new adoptive home.

CHAPTER EIGHT

Post-placement: The Family Becomes Immobilized

The pre-placement phase has ended and the child has come home! The optimism and excitement ignited during the pre-placement visits continue. Many families—even families who did not experience "love at first sight"—believe that "things will get better" or that he or she will "settle down" and "everything will work out." Unfortunately, for many families, the arrival of a child with a traumatic past will disturb the equilibrium of the family for quite some time to come. In fact, these families will struggle long-term to recover the calm and peaceful household that existed prior to the adoption. This imbalance can result with a child of any age, including infant adoptees. These youngest of children who have a history of drug or alcohol exposure, neglect, deprivation and multiple moves, or who have been abused, may not escape the long-term effects of these traumas. This chapter will look at what happens in this group of adoptive families by building on some of the things we have learned in earlier chapters.

We must especially keep in mind that the complex trauma we learned about in Chapter 2 provides an excellent systematic *description* of the ways in which the adoptee has been affected by his traumatic experiences, yet Chapter 5 called to attention that the actual *classification* of the outcome of trauma includes various mental health diagnoses. Mental health disorders involve impaired ability to function in developmentally appropriate ways. So adoption often means the addition of a child who suffers mental health issues and developmental delays. This combination of mental illness and developmental delays can dramatically impact the enlarged family. This impact can be very similar to the way that a serious medical condition would shock and distress parents, siblings and the patient.

Next up for explanation are the dynamics that occur in *adoptive* families in which a child with mental health and developmental issues resides. Why is *adoptive* in italics? *Adoptive* is emphasized because the adoption-built component of your family adds additional layers and stressors to the day-to-day experiences of each member of an adoptive family.

Now, I don't want anyone to get discouraged! Many children with mental health issues can grow up to lead productive lives, provided that they receive appropriate treatment and support. The support is you—the adoptive family! Let's also keep in mind that we are almost to Chapters 9 and 10—our solution chapters. Chapters 9 and 10 offer a continuum of ideas so that all families, whether impacted mildly or severely, can enhance their family's interactions.

This chapter also includes "Siblings Talk" boxes. The content of these boxes comes from brothers and sisters living with adoptees with mental health issues. Their honesty helps us to understand how their lives have been affected by the addition of a sibling with "issues." The featured siblings range in age from 8 to 23. Their families adopted children ages infant through age 12.

Post-placement: Development of the Adoptive Family

A child learns to crawl before he takes his first steps. He learns words that eventually he puts together to form sentences. He uses diapers before the potty; he drinks from a bottle before a Sippy cup. Human development proceeds in a predictable manner. Adoptive families develop in a similarly predictable fashion. Parents, siblings and adoptees pass through various stages as the new child is integrated into the family system.

The Honeymoon

The arrival of the child post-placement signifies the end of the pre-placement or *dating* period. Most families then enter a *honeymoon* stage (Pinderhughes and Rosenberg, 1990). This period may be brief or it may last for months. This is a good period; everyone is getting along well. The social worker arrives for a post-placement visit and the parents state, "I can't believe we had to go through all that training. Sally has no problems. We're really looking forward to finalizing the adoption and moving on."

Actually, there are likely some negative behaviors or issues that are being displayed during the honeymoon phase. However, parents typically tend to minimize or overlook these matters. The resident children are encouraged to do the same. There is a certainty that these things will resolve shortly. This early period is also characterized by ongoing welcoming activities—decorating the new child's bedroom, introducing the child to extended family and neighborhood peers, and purchasing new clothes and school supplies. In reality, the adoptee is able to function well, early in a placement, as the emotional depth of relationships with family members is still superficial. The demands for intimacy and full participation as a brother, sister, son or daughter are limited. However, as the adoptee begins to comprehend that the placement is permanent and there is to be an attachment to the adoptive family members, a stage of *ambivalence* (Pinderhughes and Rosenberg, 1990) emerges.

Ambivalence

The ambivalence period is a time when the adoptee's behavior deteriorates. Parents are challenged to manage the adoptee's behavior. Traditional parenting techniques—time-outs, removal of privileges, lectures, rewards, grounding, being sent to a bedroom—seem to have no impact derailing unwanted or unsafe behaviors. The child's delays become apparent. The typically developing children in the household and the

> *Sibling Talk*
>
> I mean it wasn't like he was some wild maniac. He was just—it wasn't something that my family was used to like lying and stealing. He was just the worst liar in the world. You could be like "Is it nighttime?" He would be like, "No it's daytime. I swear it's daytime."

child's peers struggle to play with the adoptee. Parents are likely to hear such statements as

> "Why does he have to come with me? I want to play with my friends without him."
>
> "He won't play fair."
>
> "He's breaking all my toys."
>
> "I'm trying to play in my room. He won't leave me alone."
>
> "He's yelling because I don't want to play what he wants to play."

It is often recognized that the child is off-track academically. Homework is a struggle. The adoptee becomes frustrated by the amount or difficulty level of the homework so he refuses to complete assignments. Evenings are consumed with homework battles. The harder parents work to help the adoptee learn math, reading, spelling and social studies, the more the adoptee resists. Arguments become routine.

The turmoil of the ambivalent stage causes parents, siblings and the adoptee to grapple with various issues.

The Ambivalence of the Adoptee

Remember the irrational beliefs of the child who experienced trauma as listed in Chapter 2? As the adoptee begins to realize that he is to blend into his new family, he begins to have thoughts about his past experiences with adults and families. The adoptee is thinking:

> "I wonder if I can trust this family to keep me. No one else has kept me."
>
> "I wonder if they will abuse me. Others have."
>
> "I want to return to my birthmom. I love her."
>
> "I should be with my birthmom. I am old enough to help her now."
>
> "What would my birthmom think if I love my adoptive family? Maybe she would be angry with me."
>
> "How can my adoptive family love me after everything that happened to me?"
>
> "I didn't stop the abuse. I couldn't make my own birthfamily love me. I am damaged and unlovable."
>
> "I think my birthmom may be looking for me. What if she returns to the orphanage [or the county agency] and I'm not there? How will she find me?"
>
> "If I get adopted, I will never live with my birthsiblings. I want to live with them."

In essence, the move to the adoptive family causes the adoptee to think about his or her past. She longs for her birthfamily, previous caregivers or birth or foster brothers and sisters. Permanency in an adoptive family means that she must let go of her hopes of living with her birthfamily (or perhaps a loved foster family or favorite orphanage caregiver) again. She recalls her abuse in her original home. She is frightened by these memories. She doubts whether she can trust the adoptive family. She is uncertain as to her own self-worth and how a family can even think of loving her.

Social and Emotional Age versus Chronological Age

The adoptee's irrational thought process inhibits his integration into the family. So do his developmental limitations. There is often a difference between the adoptee's chronological age and his social and emotional age. A child age 10 may actually exhibit the emotional skills of a child age 2—do you remember the terrible twos? Can you

Sibling Talk

If people are thinking of adopting, they need to get as much background information on the child before they make a final decision just so that they know exactly what they're going to be dealing with. And, I know sometimes they won't get that information. Go to classes to be prepared, so that you would know the child could be disruptive and you know how you would handle it, and the child could not be disruptive and then you will have a nice family. I would also tell them that they should adopt if they really want to because every kid deserves a home.

imagine going through them with a child the physical size of a 10 year old? A 12 year old may still play like a preschool age child—*beside* another child rather than *with* another child. This is parallel play, and developmentally it occurs after solitary play or onlooker play but before cooperative play in which children engage in more complex social interactions (Parten, 1932). The adoptee may not have the capacity to engage in a board game with two or three other people. Despite her chronological age, she has not yet learned this more intricate level of play. Inadequate care giving and abuse interrupt development. Chapter 2 provided many examples of the types of delays parents may anticipate. To summarize them, the cognitive, emotional and social areas commonly affected negatively by trauma include

- cause-and-effect thinking
- problem-solving skills
- abstract thinking
- moral development
- delayed gratification
- accepting responsibility
- sense of future
- initiative/interest in environment
- play and social skills
- reciprocity
- identifying, expressing and regulating emotions

These delays may be confounded by the child's intellectual capacities. The child may be perceived as "smart," and often this is a correct assessment. This leads to thinking, "He is smart. He could act right if he wanted to." Alleviating issues is believed to be within the adoptee's control. It is thought that the adoptee is "on purpose" or "intentionally" having temper tantrums, breaking rules or ruining family fun. Parental responses can include, "Act your age!" "Grow up!" "Quit talking like a baby!" "You know better!" "You need to play with kids your own age!" "Play with your own toys. Those toys belong to your little sister!" "You could totally stop this behavior if you wanted to!" "Why do you want to be 'bad'?"

In reality, an adoptee in this position is crippled developmentally. He cannot simply "act his age" because he does not have the skills to do so. He is unable to assume his chronological place in the family, neighborhood, school, Sunday school and extracurricular activities. The pressure to perform in the same ways as his close-in-age siblings or peers creates stress for the adoptee. It further heightens his negative thoughts and feelings about himself, and asking him to be something he is not magnifies his issues with rejection. He becomes more ambivalent; he acts out to a greater extent. Parents and siblings ask, "Why is he doing this to our family?"

The adoptee's inability to socially interact in a manner consistent with his chronological age becomes a great source of conflict and despair within the adoptive family. It is heart wrenching to know that your child is the only one in his class not invited to a birthday party. It is difficult to be the parents of the child no one in the neighborhood wants to play with—not even his own brothers and sisters! Chapter 9 will offer numerous ideas about how to narrow the gap between the adoptee's social and emotional age and his chronological age.

The Ambivalence of Parents

Ambivalent parents may respond in a variety of ways. Parents may call their agency and report problems. Some agencies will respond with support. They will meet with the family and help "normalize" the current experience of the family. They will call on the family to look at other times in their life when they encountered ambivalence—starting a new job, getting married, having a first child by birth. The social worker will help the family review skills utilized to successfully pass through these previous hesitant times. The worker may opt to review the Prediction Path (Chapter 5) with the family. This allows the family to see that they had expected the difficulties that are occurring. As the Prediction Path contains solutions, the family has interventions they can immediately implement to stabilize their home. The parents then feel a sense of relief and they feel "in charge" of their family again. The ambivalence is effectively alleviated.

Other agencies may encourage the family to "hang in there" until the adoption is legalized. There is an inaccurate systemic belief that the adoption finalization will signal to the child that his place in the family is permanent. The child will then "settle down" and become a part of the family. Parents told this, believing their social worker an authority, move on to complete their adoption in spite of their ambivalence. In fact, such advice should be approached with caution. One court experience cannot erase past trauma, nor can it wipe away developmental delays. In fact, many children decline in functioning after legalization. The finalization ceremony is a concrete event. The child can "see" the adoption happening. The adoptee then becomes very aware that the court proceedings preclude his return to his birthparents. The adoptee's grief can emerge intensely.

Parents may respond to ambivalence with panic. Intercountry adoptions may already be legalized at this point. The family feels trapped, thinking

"What have we done to our family?"

"We can't handle this!"

"This isn't fair to our other children."

"Why didn't anybody tell us it was going to be like this?"

"What are we going to do?"

Frantic, these parents call their agency.

Norma and Elwin adopted 7-year-old Christopher from Belarus. Already present in their family was their son, Elwin Jr., age 9, also adopted. Elwin, Jr. had been diagnosed with Attention-Deficit/Hyperactivity Disorder upon entering first grade. Medication and behavioral interventions managed this mental health issue quite well. Christopher, on the other hand, presented significant difficulties very shortly upon arrival in the family. He bit and spit on his parents when something wasn't to his liking. He stole food from his brother's plate at all meals. He broke any toy he touched. He was very impulsive. He darted out into the street or busy parking lots. Riding in the car was a hazard. He kicked the back of the seat, refused to wear a seatbelt and threw anything he could get his hands on at the driver. The family had tried various types of parenting approaches to offset Christopher's issues. A year into the adoption, Christopher had not improved. Norma called the international adoption agency. The social worker's response was, "Really? None of our other families are reporting any problems like yours."

This sentiment flustered Elwin and Norma. They had already been receiving criticism from their extended family and friends.

"You're too hard on him!"

"You're not strict enough. If he were my child, I'd make him listen."

"You need to love him more."

"All boys act like that."

The agency's response only compounded their sense of failure. They now began thinking, "Why are we the only ones having problems? Is there something wrong with our parenting? Are Christopher's problems our fault?"

An ambivalent parent may respond by being silent. Some fear that complaints may result in the removal of the child. They perceive they will be deemed inadequate parents. Thus, they will lose the child currently placed in their home, and they believe that they will not be considered for other children. Some parents seem prone to deny the level of commitment involved in legalizing an adoption. It is not uncommon that several years after the family has finalized an adoption, one parent continues to believe that if the child gets to be "too much" they will simply call the county agency and return the child.

Greg and Judy arrived for a mental health assessment for their twin sons, Alan and Andrew. Five-year-old Al and Drew had experienced five foster placements prior to being adopted by Greg and Judy three years before. They had been exposed to alcohol in utero. The birth home had been explosive with domestic violence. The children exhibited delayed development, learning disabilities and attachment difficulties.

Throughout the evaluation, Greg repeatedly stated, "I think it is time to give them back. I never really wanted to adopt anyway. She wanted kids. But these kids are just too much of a hassle. I really think we should give them back."

Judy said, "Honey, we went to court and adopted them. We can't just give them back. They are ours." The interviewer confirmed that Judy was correct. Greg was stunned! He said, "I really thought they could go back if this didn't work out."

Once an adoption has been finalized, the child has the same legal status as a child by birth. Adoption is a legal commitment to parent the child. There are circumstances under which the family can end their parental obligations as Chapter 7 noted. However, also as was explained in Chapter 7, adoption dissolution is complex and emotionally painful for all involved. It can be lengthy and arduous. Obviously, dissolution defeats the purpose of adoption—a child being provided with a permanent home. If you really do not want to adopt, speak up before you go to court and say "I do" or "forever hold your peace."

Yet, other parents remain silent due to marital issues. I have worked with many couples in which one partner, subtly or directly, pressures the other into adoption. A message is generated that the relationship will end or change if an adoption does not occur. As such, one partner usually squelches his or her ambivalence and proceeds to finalization. Rhonda and Pete's situation is an example.

Sibling Talk

I would say there is practically no way to prepare.

Eight-year-old Angela had been living with Pete and Rhonda for nine months. Pete had fallen in love with Angela the day he saw her photo. He was convinced that all of her difficulties could be overcome. Rhonda, on the other hand, felt unsure that she could mother a child who was so rejecting. Anytime Rhonda attempted to give Angela affection, Angela would burp in her face or fart. Pete stated, "I don't know if I can live with you if we don't adopt Angela."

Rhonda was devastated by the words and the tone used to deliver the message. She wondered, "How can I choose between my husband and a child? Either way, I lose."

I certainly encourage couples to ponder issues like this in advance. In a two-parent family, the child deserves two parents who want him or her. The child deserves two parents who are equally invested in helping him attain his best level of functioning. Conversations need to occur, pre-legalization, as to what the couple will do if both parents are not in agreement that the prospective adoptee is the "right" child for the family.

In Chapters 1 and 4, the child's capacity to "split" parents was discussed. Splitting occurs in heterosexual and homosexual homes. In families in which splitting occurs, the mother figure is viewed as the problem. She resolves her ambivalence by believing that if she tries harder the situation will improve. Thus, she convinces herself that there is no need for her ambivalence, and she proceeds to the court house where she agrees to become an adoptive parent.

Ambivalence is also rationalized via hope and optimism. "Okay, we're having a difficult adjustment period. He'll come to see that we love him and everything will be all right."

The Ambivalence of Siblings

The siblings are often the first to realize that their new brother or sister presents problems. Children are less consumed with responsibilities than are parents. They have more time to observe family members and they are often spending a significant amount of time with the adoptee. They relay their concerns to their parents. Frequently, the parental response is, "Give hir some time. She hasn't had the same opportunities as you. You need to be more patient. I had the same problems with my brothers and sisters growing up."

Subsequently, as the adoptee's issues begin to challenge the parents, the siblings observe an increase in parental conflict. Further, this may be the first time a typically developing child has witnessed his parents being unable to resolve family difficulties.

The sibling's ambivalence generates an explosion of thoughts, such as

"I would never get away with the things she does. Why are my parents letting her act like that?"

"They spend more time with her. Do they love her more?"

"This kid is too much trouble. They need to send him back."

"I'll try harder to help him. Maybe that will make things better."

"I'll play the games she wants and by her rules. She won't have so many fits."

"I won't tell on him so much. That will quiet things down."

"I don't like to see my parents fighting. I'll find ways to help them. I don't want them to get a divorce."

"I'll act like him. I'll get more attention."

"She treats my family poorly. She should appreciate my family more. Why doesn't she?"

"She is too hard to play with. I'm giving up."

"What is going to become of my family?"

"Did Mom and Dad make a mistake?"

"What were Mom and Dad thinking when they decided to adopt? I thought our family was fine. Wasn't I enough?"

As we learned in Chapter 2, the children in the family prior to the adoption often keep their thoughts to themselves. Parents, struggling with their own ambivalence, may fail to notice that their resident children are grappling with the changes in the family. In other cases, when the siblings do voice their concerns, the parents must weigh the siblings' perspective in making their decision to finalize. Ultimately, parents do determine how many children the family will include. In intercountry adoption, the adoption is already finalized. Brothers, sisters, parents and the adoptee must come to terms with their ambivalence.

Expectations and Reality Begin to Clash

Remember the expectations from Chapter 1? Ambivalence is a time period in which expectations and reality begin to clash—for each member of the family. One parenting partner may be reacting with a lack of support. The other may perceive that their partner simply cannot parent the adoptee effectively. One parent may resent their partner's eagerness to move forward with the adoption when he or she is overwhelmed by the thought of proceeding to legalization. The adoptee seems to be pushing away from the family rather than joining the family. The children already being parented are questioning their parents' parenting abilities and the decisions they are making about the family. These kids are disappointed, angry and resentful that their new brother or sister is not the pal and confidante they anticipated. None of this is what was expected!

Losses occur whenever there is a major change, perhaps unwelcome, in an individual's life which causes one to relinquish expectations about the world and self (Bruce and Schultz, 2001). Loss involves grief. Stress, as we learned in Chapter 3, also builds. Stress further exacerbates the feelings already flowing as a result of grief. Yet, most families will rationalize these feelings; optimism will prevail and the union of the child and family will proceed. The finalization of the adoption will occur. The family will be hopeful, "We've adopted him now. He'll see we really love him." His place established in the family, he will "calm down" and the family will get back on track.

Hoping and Learning: The Family Decides to "Fix" the Problem

Time passes and the adoptee continues to present challenges. She continues to steal and lie. Her bedwetting persists. She is argumentative. Her bedroom is constantly full of clutter. The pantry is raided of snacks day in and day out. Her friends come and go. She can play with siblings only a short time before a fight ensues.

"Mom, she isn't playing fair!"

"Dad, he keeps changing the rules!"

"Mom, she's in my room again!"

"She keeps standing in front of the television!"

"We're trying to watch a movie and he won't be quiet!"

School performance fluctuates. The teacher calls. Or, if younger, day care may call. The parents are asked to move the child to another child care facility. Parents engage in conflict over the best ways to manage the adoptee. Gradually, the balance in the home begins to tip in a negative direction—conflict increases, pleasure diminishes.

Or, one event occurs which the family considers a crisis.

> Seth and Betty parent three birth children and one child they adopted. Paula, currently age 13, was adopted when she was 3 years old. She has a long history of difficult behavior. She urinates in her bedroom closet. She hoards food. She "finds" things everywhere she goes. Pencils, pens, clothing, jewelry, pocket change, CDs and so on appear in her backpack regularly. Recently, the family realized that she had shoplifted lipstick from the super market. Paula's parents, brothers and sister were shocked! No one in their family had ever stolen from a store!
>
> When confronted, Paula lied. Seth and Betty were even more outraged. They were also sad and fearful. Their daughter's future would be jeopardized if changes did not occur. They decided, "Something must be done!" Paula and the rest of the family could not go on living like this any longer.

Motivated by diminishing pleasures or a crisis, parents determine the problem—the adoptee—must be "fixed." Then, they think, the family will return to the state of peace enjoyed prior to the arrival of the child with a traumatic past.

The family enters the stage of *hoping and learning*. This phase in the developmental process of the adoptive family includes extensive efforts to mend the adoptee. Parents set out to solve what they believe will be a limited and curable problem (Karp, 2001).

Therapy, medication, reading books, surfing the Internet, and networking with other families prevails. The family enters mental health services. A diagnosis is received. This offers relief. There is a name for the problem and there is a course of treatment. Learning, specific to the condition (AD/HD, ODD, PTSD, Bi-Polar Disorder) is now pursued. Parents are hopeful that the right combination of love, care, medication and counseling will heal the adoptee. Initially, or sporadically, there is improvement. Yet, permanent positive changes elude the family. The family obtains new services or adds other types of interventions. The cycle repeats; lasting changes are minimal or remain elusive.

Additionally, the parents are often blamed for the adoptee's problems:

> Seth and Betty had tried various parenting strategies to alleviate Paula's habit of acquiring items that did not belong to her. They had removed television for a week. Then they removed access to all electronic devices for a month. She wrote a hundred times, "I will not steal." She wrote 500 times, "I will not steal." She had returned the items. She returned the items with letters of apology. She carried out a few extra chores to pay for the items. She completed chores for entire days. She spent an hour in her bedroom. She spent the whole weekend in her room.

Sibling Talk

Actually, both of my adopted brothers can be extremely annoying in public. The younger one (age 9) is usually worse. It's worse in the locker room at the rec center. He acts like a total idiot. He thinks it's funny seeing guys walking around on the way to the shower. He'll say, "Hey, you see that guy's thingee!" This is in the middle of the locker room! He just acts so weird!

Betty then read a post on a listserv from a mom who had removed everything from her adopted son's bedroom except for his mattress. His possessions would be returned only when he proved he had changed. He had to "earn" his clothes, dresser, desk, lamp, etc.

When Seth and Betty entered therapy, Paula was in the same position. The therapist, unfamiliar with the dynamics of adoption-built families, concluded that the problem was Seth and Betty's parenting skills. Paula's stealing was the result of the fact that she had no "stuff" and no privileges. He stated to Seth and Betty that he "felt Paula would be fine if they returned her possessions." Seth and Betty were devastated. They wondered, "How did we become the problem? Why can't the therapist see how hard we are working to help Paula? What will happen to Paula? Where will we go for help now? What has happened to our family?"

Overall, the therapist was correct in part. Seth and Betty do need to cease such harsh parenting strategies. Yet, he missed the family dynamics which created this situation. He didn't really listen when they attempted to explain their ten year struggle with Paula. He didn't hear all of the efforts they had made, many of which were good and normal parenting interventions. He totally lacked understanding of the impact of Paula's trauma on Paula, Seth, Betty and their three birth children.

Immobilization

The answer to Seth and Betty's last question, "What has happened to our family?" is that they are a family becoming immobilized. *Immobilization* is extensively prolonged hoping and learning. The family remains consumed with their efforts to "fix" the identified problem—the adoptee. Life continues to revolve around the premise that once the traumatized child is "better," we will be a happy and peaceful family again. The immobilized family is simply unable to accept or believe that the adoptee cannot attain the goals desired by parents and siblings. The family desperately wants to be the family they were prior to the adoption. It is as if family life goes *on hold* like planes circling an airport.

"We'll go on vacation when John is better."

"We'll have family game night again when Joan can participate."

"We'll visit Grandma more when Billy can handle it better."

Individual leisure interests, activities enjoyed as a couple, outings with the typically developing children are set aside for some day when the adopted child can participate in the manner yearned for. The quality of family life deteriorates. Parents, brothers, sisters and the adoptee miss many opportunities.

Sadly, many families remain in immobilization for years! Let's look at the dynamics that underlie this state of immobilization.

The Dynamics of Immobilization

The following dynamics are apparent in many adoptive families. Families experience these dynamics to varying degrees, and not all families experience all of the dynamics. Certainly, there are families that will have unique dynamics. These factors and feelings perpetuate the immobilization stage:

- a continuing clash of expectations and reality
- cognitive dissonance
- the consumption and depletion of coping skills
- the emotional roller-coaster

> **Sibling Talk**
>
> The way he grew up, he had to learn to pass it off as, "If I sit down and cross my legs like her then I'll fit in." He was good at reading how to behave in certain social situations.

- isolation
- afloat on a sea of grief.

A Continuing Clash of Expectations and Reality

The ambivalent period generated a clash between expectations and the day-to-day family life that falls out of living with a child with mental health issues. The immobilization period causes an even more violent collision of expectations and daily reality.

In immobilization, "We need to fix the adoptee" continues to be the paramount expectation. Fixing the adoptee allows fulfillment of the expectations presented in Chapter 1:

"He will love us."

"He will appreciate us."

"She will fill the void in our lives."

"All of our children will have more fun."

"The children will teach each other; they will learn from each other."

"We will have satisfied our duty to contribute to our community and to society at large."

"I will have a fun brother or sister."

"I will have a positive attitude about my sibling."

Fixing the adoptee will also let the family return to a state of harmony and unity. Thus, in immobilization, family life persists in organized efforts to heal the adoptee—to make him "normal." Trips to mental health service providers dominate a significant portion of the family's time. School meetings occur to implement special education services. The child changes schools. The child is removed from school and home schooling is initiated. Medications are utilized. Medications are changed. Dosages are increased. Diet is monitored. Sugar is removed. White flour is removed. Caffeine is eliminated. The child is enrolled in sports. (The camaraderie of team mates will improve his ability to interact.) A pet is provided. (Fido will help teach responsibility.) The list goes on and on.

All of these efforts are certainly worthy. It is likely that many of these interventions do enhance the traumatized child's capacity to function in more appropriate ways. However, as we learned previously in this book, the adoptee moves into the family with expectations also, such as

"I think you will abuse me."

"I think I am moving somewhere else."

"I think you are another orphanage."

"I am unlovable."

Unless interventions are designed to alleviate these expectations, the adoptee does not make the types of changes needed to integrate into the adoptive family system. So the adoptee is not "fixed." He is not achieving the family's or society's definition of "normal." Overall, the family's expectations are unfulfilled.

Sibling Talk

I think that they [prospective families] should get as much background information as they possibly can. They have to know that you have to take the bad with the good.

In reality, the problem is that the family's primary expectation is faulty. There needs to be a shift from "fixing" to "acceptance."

Acceptance is not quitting. Acceptance, or *mobilization*, is more along the lines of the abbreviated version of "The Serenity Prayer" by Reinhold Niebuhr that we all know so well.

> God grant me the serenity
> to accept the things I cannot change;
> courage to change the things I can;
> and wisdom to know the difference.

A primary means of achieving acceptance is the revising of expectations. The means to adjust expectations will be addressed in Chapter 9. At this time, however, we want to identify the additional layers of expectations that contribute to immobilization. In Chapter 1, I suggested that you jot down your expectations as you read this book. You may want to consider expanding your list as you read the following. This will help prepare you for Chapter 9's section, "Taking Stock: Identifying Expectations."

"I expect my partner to support me."

Chapter 4 explained and exemplified partners' expectations of each other. The stories and content helped to understand how spousal or partner expectations create marital conflict and strain. Marital tension persists in adoptive families because time constraints inhibit the ability of the couple to sit down and resolve this discord. Certainly, this marital strife affects all of the children in the family.

Chapter 4 provided the example of the couple, Jill and Mitchell. Mitchell withdrew from his family by working long hours. Jill felt alone and lacking support in her efforts to heal their traumatized children, Ivan and Svetelina. Below are additional husbands' and wives' comments about how a marriage may be impacted.

Jay and his wife, Doreen, are adoptive parents to two children. Their daughter is age 9 and came to their home at age 6 after her first adoption dissolved. She has moderate mental health issues. Their son, age 7, was adopted as an infant and is developing "normally."

Jay says,

> "Marriage, this is a tough one. I do feel our home has become more rigid and colder. I feel warmth and passion have diminished, though we may still feel these things towards one another. I feel we are shorter with each other at times and I witness more sarcasm. I still love my wife very much, and I'm in fact very impressed with her ability to cope and handle this situation. I've credited her more than once with being better prepared for this than I was."

Doreen states,

> "We love each other still and have been together for nearly 18 years. We like to kiss on one another in front of the kids and hold hands when we're walking somewhere. We think it's important that they see that. In fact, our daughter questioned the hand-holding when we first got her. She thought hand-holding was only to keep someone under control. We

told her that it's one way people can show their love for one another. But honestly, after facing a day's fighting and challenges with our daughter and meeting our son's needs, it doesn't leave one feeling too romantic."

Ellie and her husband, Roger (see Chapter 4), are parents by birth and adoption. Their birth (and oldest) son, Vince, is 8 years old. He was age 2 when Ray arrived at 8 months of age. Ray is currently age 6. Ellie writes,

"Our marriage has been deeply affected by our adoption. The havoc our adopted son's behavior has caused in our home has caused our relationship to be filled with tension and fighting, causing everyone lots of stress. Having a young child scream at you, smear his peanut butter across your walls, kick and hit you at various times has caused each of us a great deal of anguish. In addition, the financial strain that his therapies have cost has had a significant impact on our lifestyle."

Robert is the father to two sons by birth and a daughter, Joy, by adoption. His sons are now ages 21 and 17, while Joy is 12. She joined the family at age 3.

"Marriage-wise, I do believe in the past few years that has suffered. I believe that we were so caught up in arguing with Joy that I harbored much resentment against Joy and my wife because it was my wife who wanted to adopt. I never expressed this to my wife until recently. Our lives were a constant fight and I resented the fact that even when I was not involved with the issues my workday was interrupted with phone calls about what Joy was doing at school or home."

"I expect parenting to resolve past issues."

Expectations manifest from parents' family-of-origin experiences.

Margaret's mother passed away after a lengthy illness when Margaret was an adolescent. As the oldest of five female siblings, she assumed the care giving tasks. Her sibling relationships were altered as a result. To this day, her sisters rely on Margaret for motherly advice and support. They perceive her as a parent rather than their older sister. Margaret felt robbed of her roles as daughter and sister. When Margaret and her husband adopted Sheila from the foster care system, Margaret hoped that she could finally fulfill one truly female role. She would be a mother to her own daughter.

Sheila, age 6, wanted nothing to do with a mother. As far as she was concerned, she had a mother—her birthmother. She did not need an adoptive mother. Margaret patiently continued to arrange lovely birthday parties and holiday gatherings. She planned trips to museums and the ballet. She enrolled Sheila in gymnastics, horse-back riding, and an array of other activities. Margaret provided Sheila all of the things that Margaret had wished she had had with her own mother. Sheila remained distant. She preferred her aunts' company to that of Margaret. She perpetually asked, "When will Daddy be home?" Sheila did everything she could to resist any connection to Margaret.

Margaret was devastated. She felt her opportunity to be a mother was sabotaged by a birthmother Sheila barely knew. She became angry with Sheila. She had expected that Sheila would reciprocate her mothering efforts by forming a close and loving relationship with her.

Margaret's case is one example of how a family-of-origin issue carries over to an adult's expectation of her relationship with her child. Numerous other stories to illustrate the same point have been incorporated throughout this book.

Routinely, parents want their nuclear family to be improved over that which they experienced in their childhood. Mothers and fathers are urged to examine such expectations and ask themselves, "Is it appropriate to think that my child can satisfy such expectations?"

"I expect my faith to remain strong."

Expectations emerge from spiritual beliefs. Sadly, many devout individuals will actually find themselves questioning their religious convictions upon adopting a child with mental health issues.

Betty and Rob parent adopted siblings. Their two sons were adopted at ages 6 and 7. They are currently older adolescents. While their older son is slowly starting to recover from his abuse and neglect, their younger son continues to struggle to resolve the trauma he experienced prior to his adoption. Betty was asked to speak at a retreat held by a religious organization. Following are some excerpts from her presentation. These snippets provide a sampling of the types of issues that challenge those with strong religious convictions:

> "I can't tell you how difficult taking the children to therapy and hearing about the abuse and neglect that occurred in two precious lives was for me and my husband. How many nights I heaped sorrow upon sorrow on God. I threw so many arrows at Him. I pounded on His chest and asked how such things could happen. Where was He? Didn't He have compassion? Why did I feel so abandoned?
>
> "Often my sorrowful soul has wondered what God expected of me. Does God truly not give you more than you can handle when you are relying on him? I have even asked God to leave me alone, and then quickly regretted it, because if this is what life looks like with Him, what would it be without Him?
>
> "It's difficult for me to share my story with you. I would much rather talk about something other than my own private life and struggles. But God has asked me to be obedient and to trust Him once again. This issue of obedience has become paramount in my life. I once heard that a reporter commented to Mother Teresa, 'You've spent your whole life helping the poor in India and yet millions of people are still poor.' Mother Teresa replied, 'God asked for my obedience, not my success.'
>
> "You see, I want to tell you—we want to tell each other—that everything will be okay. But God didn't promise me that if I loved the children He gave me they would love me back. He didn't say that just because I chose them as children, they would choose me as their mom. God says that He loved this world and sent his son into the world to seek and save those that are lost. God loves His children, and yet, every day He is rejected by His sons and daughters. They do not choose Him to be their Father, even though He always will be."

Betty, a faithful servant to God, expected that, in return for her service, God would reward her with children—loving children. First she was denied the opportunity to parent children by birth. Then, adoption brought a son so damaged by his abuse that he is unable to reciprocate her affection. She began questioning God and God's plan. She was shocked by her faltering faith. It had been strong since early childhood. She asked, "Why did God allow abuse to occur to my children? Why has God denied me the opportunity to parent loving children? What is it about me that God thought I could handle this? What does being obedient to God really mean? Is God truly loving and compassionate?" Ultimately, Betty was able to restore her faith in God. She accomplished this by re-defining *success* and *obedience*. She realized that God's own relationship as a parent is fraught with the same disappointments and complexities as is her relationship

Sibling Talk

Whenever we're talking to each other it seems like we lose our tempers more easily. Because it's not like we're talking to each other just for fun anymore—it seems like we are always mad at each other.

with her son. God really has not asked Betty to do anything with which God Himself is unfamiliar.

"I expect my extended family and friends to be supportive."

Deciding on a career, purchasing a home, committing to a partner, adding children to our family—these are all endeavors in which we seek and expect the support and approval of our friends, parents, aunts, uncles, grandparents and cousins. Unfortunately, adoptive families frequently find that their friends' and relatives' reactions are contrary to these expectations.

Lena was adopted as an infant. In her late adolescence, her parents adopted a sibling group of two sisters ages 1½ and 5. The older of these two siblings has serious mental health issues. The younger sibling exhibits social and emotional delays, and she also receives treatment for Posttraumatic Stress Disorder. Lena relays the following about her friends' comments.

> "Out in public, sometimes they act fine. Sometimes they'll be disruptive. But, it's not a major scale disruption like at home where they'll throw a complete tantrum. I would be talking to my friends and they would ask, "How are your sisters doing?" I would try to explain the behaviors but they never caught on. They would say, "They can't be that bad. They're only children." I would be like, "No, these are worse problems than what normal children cause." My friends thought I should look at things differently and that I was exaggerating. They thought I was the one who needed to change my views and to understand that these are children and this is what children do."

Lena's friends view Lena as the problem. Their statements imply that Lena needs to change her perceptions of younger siblings.

Lena recalls a therapy session.

> "We had a therapy session where my extended family—aunts, uncles, grandma, grandpa—came. We talked about how our family couldn't handle it all the time and that we needed help from them. They were like, 'Yeah, you guys need help. We'll call and take the kids out to lunch.'
>
> "But then a couple of my family members said, 'Why don't you just give the kids back? You shouldn't even have them because they're horrible for your family. We don't want you to live with this.' It made me feel like, 'I'm adopted. Do you want to give me back?' I think that every child should have a chance to be with a family. It hurt—'just give them back.' There was no thought of them at all.
>
> "The conclusion of this experience was that my extended family never does anything. They don't call unless we call them. Nothing ever gets done. They don't want to come to holidays. Basically, when they call all they talk about is, 'Are you going to give the kids back?'"

Lena and her parents were devastated by the outcome of this meeting. They simply could not believe that their own family would assume they would just give their children away. The subsequent lack of action demonstrated by their relatives was shocking.

Sibling Talk

I knew it was a mistake. I mean you have to figure we already had kids. We had two girls and two boys. We didn't need another person and we didn't have room for another person. You're dealing with a person whose ways are different. You're dealing with a teenager who's basically set in their ways. They have different values than you and your family. So you're trying to put them in a new system and they're used to doing what they want to do. I didn't expect anything. I just didn't want him to come. I didn't care if he was going to be difficult or great. I had a brother and two sisters. What else do you need?

Other adoptive families report a constant stream of advice flowing from their extended family. Many of these suggestions imply parenting flaws. I have worked numerous cases in which extended family members have gone so far as to write the adoptive family a letter outlining their concerns, predominant among which is that the adoptee's problems are the result of insufficient parental love. The devastation of this abandonment is overwhelming to parents and their children. It is not something that is easily, if ever, overcome.

"I expect to be supported by professionals."

Adoptive parents expect that professional assistance will validate their experiences, that professionals will understand the needs of their family, and that professional support will be ample and effective. In reality, as has been stated previously in this book, this may not be the case. The Casey Family Services White Paper, "Strengthening Families and Communities: An Approach to Post-Adoption Services" is an outcome of the 2000 National Post-Adoption Services Conference. The paper summarized concerns in the field of adoption. Below is a selected section of this paper.

"Adoptive families consistently report that they face difficulties obtaining services from professionals who are sensitive to adoption issues and skilled in assisting adoptive families. The need for professional expertise with regard to adoption issues is particularly great in the fields of mental health and education. In neither of these areas do professionals routinely receive education about adoption issues.

"Repeatedly, adoptive parents focused on the problems they had encountered in finding mental health professionals who understood the issues with which they and their children were dealing. Those issues often related to adoption and its impact on children, families and parenting. Adoptive parents often are frustrated by repeatedly spending entire sessions explaining to their therapist the differences between parenting a biological child and an adopted child and then being required to leave a check "on the way out."

"In other cases, therapists do not appear to understand the impact of children's pre-adoption experiences on their current intellectual and social functioning, capacity to attach and form intimate relationships, and their overall development, including the developmental effects of prenatal alcohol or drug exposure, earlier experiences of abuse or neglect, and multiple foster care or institutional placements. Adoptive parents often find that the only recommendation they receive is that their children be placed on medication—an intervention which many parents feel is not appropriate and which does not address their needs for a better understanding of their children's problems. Similarly, adoptive parents all too often find that their children's problematic behaviors are attributed to hyperactivity and treated with medication, rather than first exploring past or present experiences.

> "Educators with whom adoptive parents interact also may have little understanding of or sensitivity to adoption and the issues which adoptive families face. Some adoptive parents report that educators attempt to avoid becoming involved with these issues, responding to the stresses on adoptive families with statements such as, 'You made the choice and adopted him, he's your problem.' In other cases, educators may simply view adoption with 'rose-colored glasses.' They may see adoption as having only positive outcomes and have no real understanding of children's losses or the impact of pre-adoption experiences on their current behavior and adjustment."[1]

The Casey paper concludes by stating that professionals who work with adoptive families and their children must appreciate the role of the birthfamily and the adoptive family in the child's life. They must also view the needs of children and their adoptive families from a strengths-based, as opposed to a pathological, perspective; provide services in a supportive manner, as opposed to "blaming" adoptive families for the needs of their children; and recognize and respect the strengths and culture of children and families, providing services in a culturally competent manner.[2]

Further, studies regarding adult brothers and sisters providing care to a sibling whose mental health issues are continuing into adulthood conclude the following:

> "Involved siblings tended to feel patronized or marginalized in their interactions with professionals, or that information was simply withheld, purportedly for reasons of confidentiality. They described receiving mixed messages from professionals, which they described as a combination of subtle blaming combined with assurances that the mental illness was biologically determined. Siblings also described being excluded from care planning and treatment efforts, on one hand, while at the same time receiving direct requests for crisis placement and financial assistance, on the other" (Lukens, Thorning, Lohrer, 2002; Friedrich, Lively, Rubenstein, 2008).

Even child welfare and adoption professionals contribute to the development of the adoptive family's expectations. Systemic beliefs operate as dichotomies. There is a discernable difference between what we teach families to expect pre-adoption and what we think of families post-adoption.

- We tell parents prior to the adoption to expect problems. After the adoption, we question why the child is still stealing, lying, shouting, making poor grades, etc. years after being placed in their home. The conclusion formed is that there must be something wrong with the parents.
- The adoptive family is held to a high standard, almost that of super family. They will heal all of the child's hurts. When this does not happen, we again conclude the parents are inadequate.
- We tell parents that services will be necessary. Yet, we often make them return to the public agency in order to obtain funding for services. We trusted the parents with the child. Yet, we don't always allow them to make decisions as to what their family needs. We, at times, deny services to families in desperate need. We do so because we believe the family is the problem.
- We claim to operate "in the best interests of the child" yet we become contentious when parents request funding or subsidy increases. We do so because we deny

1. Lutz, Lorrie. "Strengthening Families and Communities: An Approach to Post-Adoption Services." [2000]. *Casey Center for Effective Child Welfare Practice*. Casey Family Services. Online at http://www.caseyfamilyservices.org/p_ccenter_publications.html, pages 20–21.
2. Ibid.

the pathology of the child. We view these requests as if we are giving money to the parent. Actually, when we offer monies, we are supporting the family in their efforts to support the adoptee. Isn't this what we set out to accomplish in the first place?

The child welfare system needs to examine policies regarding adoptive families. We approved them to adopt. If there is something "wrong" with so many adoptive families, perhaps we need to re-evaluate the manner in which we conduct home studies and parent preparation. Better yet, maybe we need to heed our own warnings: these children will frequently have problems due to their past trauma. There are children for whom their pre-adoptive experiences leave long-term or life-long scars. Many adoptive families will require support throughout the adoptee's childhood and adolescence. Many adoptees will continue to need services well into adulthood.

"I expect to be supported by society at large."

The expectation that society at large will want to help improve the functioning of a troubled child makes much sense. After all, a child's future is at stake. However, just in my lifetime, society has undergone many changes pertaining to the "best ways" to raise children. When I was in grade school, any trouble caused by a child was quickly made known to her parents who, in turn, relayed it to every other parent on the block Upon the child's arrival home from school, multiple parents made it clear to the child that the trouble needed to cease. This "shared parenting/it takes a village" concept has given way to the following opinions:

"Parents should be able to manage their children's behaviors. When they can't, they must be bad parents."

"Children should do well in school and be involved in sports, music, dance, church groups and so on. When they don't and aren't, they must have parents who don't care."

"Children should attend college, get good jobs, buy a home and have a family of their own—on a particular time table. When they don't, they weren't raised well. Their parents have failed them."

As stated previously, adoptive family members must adjust their expectations in order to move through the period of immobilization. This is a complex task given the layers of existing expectations. The task is further complicated when the family's support system fades away, and when the family is blamed for the child's difficulties. This undertaking also involves comprehending the concept of cognitive dissonance.

Cognitive Dissonance

Cognitive dissonance is defined as inconsistencies between expectations and experiences. As humans, we do not like inconsistency (Festinger 1957 and Cooper, 2007):

> Imagine that you prepared at great length for a dinner party at your home. You constructed the guest list, sent out the invitations and prepared the menu. Nothing was too much effort for your party; you went to the store, prepared the ingredients and cooked for hours, all in anticipation of how pleasant the conversation and the people would be. Except they weren't. The guests arrived late; the conversations were forced; and the food was slightly overcooked by the time all of the guests arrived. The anticipation and expectation of the great time you were going to have are discordant with your observation of the evening. The pieces do not fit. You're upset, partly because the evening did not go well, but also because of the inconsistency between your expectation and your experience. You are suffering from the uncomfortable, unpleasant state of cognitive dissonance (Cooper, 2007).

Sibling Talk

I would tell other kids not to assume anything. That's what I did, and it was totally the opposite.

Now that we have the gist of this concept, let's look at an example of an adoptive parent experiencing cognitive dissonance.

> Marsha is a single parent to her adolescent birth daughter, Julia, and her 9-year-old daughter, Amy, whom she adopted. Amy joined the family at age 4 after experiencing profound trauma and multiple foster care placements. Amy presented with many behavioral issues. She frequently hit, kicked or punched Marsha and Julia. She was plagued with anxiety and this made it impossible for her to sleep in her own bedroom. Each night, she would crawl into bed with Marsha or Julia. Frequently, she would then wet the bed. This certainly made sleeping difficult for her mother and sister. She refused to do her homework. Her table manners were repulsive. Food fell out of her mouth and onto her plate, the table and the floor. She ate with her hands and used her shirt as a napkin. She chattered incessantly, shouting rather than talking. Shopping was problematic. Amy was demanding, and when she did not get items she requested, she would become loud, refusing to continue moving through the store. She often knocked items off of shelves as the family passed through stores. Marsha stated, "Adopting a hurt child presented many unexpected challenges. The reality is that adopting a hurt child is a difficult journey and is often fraught with many struggles. I viewed myself as a mom with much love to give and share with someone who had had a bad beginning. Being the mother of my birth daughter gave me such joy and positive feedback from others who saw me as patient and caring. As the mother of my adopted daughter, I felt lost, confused and sometimes I felt as if I was abusive to her—not at all the image I had of myself or wanted to have. I learned that Amy had the knack of putting me in touch with my "dark side" and I witnessed not only my own distress at having it revealed, but saw the impact on others as well. The parent I believed myself to be was not visible to Amy, who referred to me as Mrs. Hennigan from the musical *Annie*. I had to learn to forgive myself when I did not live up to my vision of myself as a loving person.
>
> "It's surprising how much powerful emotion can be stirred up by a child. This called for a re-evaluation of myself and my beliefs. At present, I am grateful that Amy has attached and is becoming a loving and kind person. I don't think that could have happened without three years and counting of therapy. I even catch glimpses of the mom I once was, and that's nice."

The cognitive dissonance for Marsha resulted from the development of conflicting beliefs about herself as a parent and person. Going into the adoption, she viewed herself as "patient and caring" and "a mom with much love to give and share." Marsha's parenting of Julia led to positive feedback from friends and family members, thus her image of herself as a good parent was validated. Post-adoption, her self-image shifted to "confused," being put in touch with her "dark side" and being referred to as "Mrs. Hennigan." Marsha's patient nature disappeared under the constant barrage of Amy's behavior. She found herself doling out consequence after consequence. Hence, she began to feel as if all she did was punish Amy. This level of discipline felt "abusive." This punitive aspect was a side of herself that she did not know existed. There was a discrepancy—dissonance—between the type of parent she believed herself to be pre-adoption and the

Summary about Marsha

Expectation

I am a patient, caring parent with much love to give and share.

Experience

I dole out consequences constantly. I am overwhelmed by negative emotions.

Dissonance

I feel abusive (i.e., punitive), confused, lost, being put in touch with my dark side. I am compared to Mrs. Hennigan.

Consonance

Once again, with professional assistance, I am able to "catch glimpses of the mom I used to be." I learned through therapy that I do not have to consequence every behavior. I learned that my strong emotional reaction to Amy is common among parents adopting a child with mental health issues. I have become skilled in ways to manage my emotional reactions. At times, when I regress, I forgive myself and move on. I have come to understand that healing Amy is a long-term venture."

parent she had become post-placement. Her expectation of the parent she thought she would be to Amy was inconsistent with her actual experience of mothering Amy.

Marsha, and many other adoptive mothers and fathers, experience this type of cognitive dissonance—their expectations of themselves as parents become inconsistent with the type of parenting applied to the child with a history of trauma. Can you imagine the anguish caused by feeling abusive, confused, impatient, uncaring and unloving? In essence, cognitive dissonance creates a state of distress. This angst upsets parents, and it drives them into action to reduce the inconsistency. The greater the inconsistency, the more agitated parents will be and the more motivated they will be to reduce it (Festinger, 1957 and Cooper, 2007). Parents will seek to attain a state of consistency—cognitive consonance. They will strive to achieve a fit between their expectations and their experiences.

Marsha sought counseling to alleviate her cognitive dissonance. She resided in a community rich in adoption-competent mental health services. Three years later, her family is achieving a nice state of harmony. The family is healing. Marsha is re-gaining a sense of the parent she was prior to her adoption.

Perhaps the greatest source of cognitive dissonance for adoptive families is the *invisible* quality of mental illness. Let's return to Lena, whom we met earlier in this chapter, to help us with this issue. We learned that Lena's friends thought she was exaggerating when she would talk about the behaviors presented by her younger siblings. Lena's peers felt that she simply did not understand her younger siblings. Lena's extended family repeatedly suggested that Lena's family "give the kids back." They offered little assistance even though Lena's family has requested their help. Lena's family is excluded from holiday meals.

The reaction of Lena's friends and family members has caused Lena to have several questions:

> "Why aren't my relatives more helpful? I spent so much time with them growing up. What happened?"
>
> "I am adopted. If I had problems what would they have told my parents? Did they really ever accept me?"
>
> "Why do my friends think I am exaggerating? They have known me since grade school. Do they think I would make things up?"
>
> "Everyone is questioning my parents' decision to adopt. Why can't they see that my sisters have problems?"

All of Lena's questions are poignant. Her last question, in particular, is a question that almost every parent and sibling of a child with mental illness asks, "Why can't anyone see his or her problems?" As noted in Chapter 1, the adoptee's negative behavior may be more apparent in the home than at school, church, stores, family gatherings and so on. Friends, relatives, teachers, neighbors, mental health professionals and child welfare professionals do not *see* the traumatized child accurately. They do not *see* the behaviors the child exhibits in the home. If a family is parenting a child in a wheelchair, or a child who has mental retardation or Down Syndrome, the child's disability is obvious. However, children with mental health diagnoses "look normal," so parents and siblings hear

> "My siblings acted like that too!"
>
> "My brother and I fought all the time. All siblings do that."
>
> "He is so cute."
>
> "She is so bright."
>
> "Maybe you should try some different parenting techniques."
>
> "My son did that too. He'll grow out of it. Just give it time."
>
> "Give him to me for a week. I'll straighten him out."
>
> "If you would show him more love, he would do better."
>
> "Why do you let your kid walk all over you? You need to toughen up!"

The parents are viewed as having a problem or disability rather than the child. In light of this, many parents go about attempting to achieve consonance by educating everyone involved with their child. There is a drive to make others understand that, "It's him, not us, that has the problem." They explain the child's difficulties. They provide books, articles and Internet links. They ask their adoption-competent therapist to call their child's educators, coaches and child care provider in order to validate that the adoptee does indeed have mental health issues.

The outcome of these efforts is often that the family looks unhealthy. Friends, relatives and professionals silently think, "What is wrong with this mom? Her son is a great kid. He acts fine here at school. Why does she want him to have problems?" A vicious cycle is produced. The more information the family provides, the *crazier* the parents appear. Parents regularly report, "I feel like I am crazy. No one understands. No one listens to me. Why does everyone blame us? Why can't anyone understand that parenting Johnny is a struggle?"

Education is never a waste of time. However, attempting to inform those who do not see the problem (because they do not experience it) can be futile—a venture that actually increases distress. In Chapter 9, we will explore *family energy*. Each family has only so much energy. Each family must decide the most productive ways to use this energy. Chapter 10 will offer ideas for creating a support system of parents and professionals who do understand.

Thus far in this book, we have looked at a multitude of expectations held by parents, resident children, newly placed children and outsiders. Obviously, we can see that cognitive dissonance occurs in numerous areas of an adoptive family's life. Revising expectations actually means moving from dissonance to consonance as Marsha did. Parents, adoptees and siblings have expectations. Helping the family pass through the immobilization stage means helping each member of the family—parents, birth and/or previously adopted children, and the adoptee—attain cognitive consonance.

The question must be raised, however, "How do typically developing siblings achieve consonance after a new child joins the family?" They are not in a position to educate their peers. There are few resources designed to help them navigate the changes in their family. Rarely are they invited to participate in any family therapy or support groups as are parents and adoptees. Within the family, they are not the decision makers. So they have little input regarding the day-to-day operation of the family. Busy and exhausted parents are not always accessible to respond to these normally behaving children's concerns. Frequently, they are left to struggle on their own to make sense of the impact of the adoptee on their family.

As it has been pointed out before, many immobilized families remain so because they pursue fulfilling—rather than adjusting—their expectations. The family persists in trying to "fix" the adoptee as well as hanging on to the expectations presented in Chapter 1 and earlier in this chapter. They believe that achieving these expectations will restore the family to a state of peace and happiness—the consonance they so desire. After all, families desperately want a "normal" life for themselves and all of their children—who wouldn't? However, families also lack the right tools for achieving that normalcy. Just as we wouldn't use a hammer to unclog the kitchen sink, we often can't use traditional parenting tools to heal a family which includes a child with mental health issues. Without the right tools, the family members—mothers, fathers, sisters, brothers and the adoptee—fall into dysfunctional patterns of interactions. The family remains in these negative coping styles until they are provided a new array of tools.

In Chapters 9 and 10, we will offer a large selection of new tools among which are ways that each member of the family can go about revising his or her expectations. Meanwhile, refer back to Chapter 1 which described expectations, and subsequent to each expectation, note its consonant counterpart. Chapter 1 then can be used as a first tool to help adjust expectations. The more each member of the family alters his or her expectations, the more the family can move from immobilization to mobilization. Mobilization is a much happier place to be! To get ready to acquire and use new tools, however, we need to recognize the faulty tools used in immobilized families, so we will first turn our attention to a discussion of the coping styles of the immobilized family.

The Consumption and Depletion of Coping Skills

> "Nothing works! We've tried it all! He won't sit in time out. He won't stay in his room. He doesn't miss his Game Boy or anything else for that matter. He earns a reward but two days later he lies again. Right before he earns the reward, he blows the whole system. We've told him 1000 times to brush his teeth, get his backpack and turn in his homework. Every day we tell him the same things over and over. I tell him, again and again, 'you won't have friends until you stop being so bossy.' Five minutes later he's back outside demanding that the other kids play what he wants to play."

These sentiments are expressed by adoptive family after adoptive family in adoption support groups, in online chat groups and in therapy. Parenting methods that worked well with the children already in the family often have little to no impact on the new child with a traumatized past. Adoptive parents repeat relevant advice to their adoptee, but their guidance falls on deaf ears. The mental illness renders traditional parenting strategies ineffective.

Stymied as the years pass and the hurt child continues to exhibit the same patterns of behavior, as well as his own unsuccessful solutions, parents run out of steam. They have consumed all of the coping skills they know. Then like Seth and Betty, whom we met earlier in this chapter, they become entrenched and embroiled in ineffective styles of coping. Seth and Betty, for example, became punitive.

Ineffective Parental Coping Styles

Punitive Parents

Punitive parents attempt to punish the adoptee into being good (Keck and Kupecky, 2002). Every transgression carries a consequence. When a reasonable consequence does not correct the offense, the consequence is made larger and larger. Soon, consequences dominate the family time. Before long, the consequences decrease family fun. "We can't go to the zoo on Saturday because Paula is grounded to her room all weekend. If I send her to my mother's she'll have fun. Grandma won't carry out any of the consequences." Paula's grounding is causing the whole family to be in a state of confinement.

Implementation of consequences often leads to conflict between the partners. For example, one father assigned his son chores in order to pay for the supplies needed to repair a hole the child had kicked in a wall. The father provided a list of chores and informed his son that they were to be done upon his arrival home from work. With that, he promptly left to go to his job. This left the mom to oversee the completion of the chores. The mother was angry. She had planned to run several hours of errands. One of the stops was new clothes for her daughter. She was now left to either re-arrange her plans or override her husband's disciplinary actions. In effect, she could disappoint her daughter or risk upsetting her husband. There was nothing wrong with the father's way of handling the repair of the damage incurred to the family's home. His lack of communication with his spouse was certainly problematic, however.

In Chapters 9 and 10, we are going to explore this area of dispensing consequences as well as the other ineffective coping skills that follow. We will make a case that successful adoptive parenting is about the way family members *react* to the adoptee rather than the types of punishment assigned to the child with a traumatic past. In the meantime, a good question to ponder is, "What child wants to form a relationship with a parent who is always doling out a consequence?"

Accommodating Parents

Accommodating is another pattern that adoptive families often fall into. In a recent therapy session, a family admitted that they had purchased their child whom they adopted twice as many Christmas presents as their other children. They were hop-

> ### *Sibling Talk*
>
> One time I was babysitting her and she didn't want to dry her hair before bed. It's a rule in our house that you have to dry your hair so you don't go to bed with your hair wet. So I told her she had to go dry it. She told me, "No." So I said, "Okay, I'll dry it for you." I put her in the bathroom and I took the dryer to dry her hair, and then she just went into a complete tantrum. She started kicking and biting. She got herself down on the floor and tried to kick me. There has been lots of violence and hitting and destroying things in the house.

ing that he would acknowledge their generosity and thus "behave" on Christmas day. Another family explained that in order to offset temper tantrums in restaurants and doctors' offices, they would take their daughter to a dollar store. There, she selects numerous new toys. They, in effect, "purchase" good behavior during outings and through appointments.

Can you imagine being the typically developing children in these families? Accommodating parents are utilizing irrational methods to obtain "good" behavior. This sets a poor example for the brothers and sisters, and it gives the adoptee an irrational perception of the world. As adults, we typically receive rewards because we have been responsible. No one hands us a house and a car in order to bribe us to come to work. We must first, and regularly, punch the time clock in order to attain rewards.

"I Give In" Parents

> Daughter: "Mom, can I have a snack?"
>
> Adoptive mom: "No, it's almost time for dinner."
>
> Two minutes later:
>
> Daughter: "Mom, can I have a snack?"
>
> Adoptive mom: "No, it's almost time for dinner."
>
> Another two minutes later, the conversation starts again, only this time Mom angrily says, "Go ahead. Have a snack! I get so tired of arguing with you! Every day, it's the same thing. I say 'no' and you nag and nag."

Likely, scenarios such as this one occur in all families. In immobilized adoptive families, however, they occur more days than not.

Weary parents simply stop trying to set limits with their child, because getting the child who has experienced trauma to accept "no" can be an arduous task. It is often an undertaking that results in a conflict.

> Barbara is 13 years old. She was adopted three years ago. Her parent, Patty, is beside herself. Anytime she tells Barbara "no," the situation escalates into a full blown battle. Barbara throws things, shouts obscenities, spits, and takes on an intimidating posture—puffing out her chest and shaking her fists. This type of scene may go on for several hours. Many times, Patty eventually gives in and lets Barbara do as she pleases. Patty knows she is perpetuating this pattern of behavior, yet every type of parenting strategy she has implemented fails to stop these fits. Frank, Patty's son from her first marriage, contemplates going to live with his father. Frank has stated, "I want to live where there is peace and quiet. But I don't want to leave my mom alone with Barbara. I'm afraid she may hurt my mom."

Making-Extraordinary-Efforts Parents

A parent caught in this style of coping is absolutely consumed with restoring the family to the pre-adoptive status. This parent tries every type of therapy, extracurricular activity, medical testing and parenting technique that exists. Often, *numerous* interventions occur simultaneously, and life revolves around appointments. Or, this mom or dad hops from one form of treatment to the next. Little time is given for any therapy to have an impact.

Needless to say, the adoptee is overwhelmed by what it is anticipated he will accomplish. Additionally, as his drive is so overpowering, those around him tend to retreat. So the extraordinary effort parent may wind up discouraged in the long-run. This parent feels, "No one is helping me. I am working very hard and I get no support." This mother or father often feels a sense of failure when multiple interventions "fail" to accomplish the healing of the adoptee.

Sibling Talk

I'm the type of person if there is a problem I want to fix it 'cause then I don't got to worry about it anymore. You know in that case, it wasn't my problem. I don't want to be like, it's my parent's problem but it really was my parent's problem. I didn't want to go to them and be like, why do you have this demon living with me because they probably already feel bad enough. So I didn't feel the need to come down on my folks for that and in coping with the problem, I just left it alone. It wasn't my problem. I played video games, went swimming and we have a lot of woods behind our house so I would go walking. When you do stuff that you like to do you're not worried about what this idiot is over here doing. So it is easy to get away when you have stuff around you that you have had all of your life.

The extraordinary means parent must be helped to slow down and to prioritize. Chapter 9 will offer a system that parents can use to help determine what is most important for themselves, their traumatized adoptee and the appropriately developing siblings.

Emotionally Withdrawn Parents

"Every time we have a good time, we pay the next day. His behavior is horrible!"

This is another statement made by countless adoptive parents. Many children approach the parent in a warm and caring manner at some times and then shift to avoidance because they are scared to invest in intimate relationships (Chapter 10). Avoidance is difficult to tolerate. It is experienced as a rejection. Think of a time when you were rejected. Most of us have had experiences of being passed over for selection in a school play, being turned down for a date, receiving a letter denying us entry into a college, a divorce, etc. Unpleasant feelings are likely elicited just in recalling such situations. Adoptive parents get rejected frequently—daily or weekly. After three years, five years or eight years, though, the parents' capacity to withstand the adoptee's rejection is depleted. As a result, the parent emotionally withdraws from the child rather than risk being hurt again. The parent begins to operate on auto-pilot, just going through the motions of providing food, clothing and a place to sleep. Beyond that, little is offered to the traumatized child. The adoptee and the family co-exist. This scenario is then an alternative manner of "fixing" the adoptee.

Larry and Brenda adopted three children. Wendy and Bruce were adopted as toddlers. Connie was adopted as a pre-schooler. Wendy, now age 6, and Bruce, age 7, are developing well. Due to severe neglect in her past, however, Connie struggles. Chronologically, she is now 10 years old. However, socially and emotionally she resembles a 2-year-old. She urinates in her bedroom. She refuses to brush her teeth or shower. She prefers to sleep in her clothes rather than pajamas.

She declines to come to the dinner table. Yet, she will eat during the night. Frequently, she makes sandwiches. She leaves the cold cuts and mayonnaise on the kitchen counter. Upon entering the kitchen in the morning, Brenda is instantly aggravated. An argument ensues.

When Connie arrives home from school, she enters the house without uttering a word. Brenda asks, "Where is your back pack?" Connie replies, "I don't know." Brenda then says, "How can you not know where your back pack is? How will you get your home work done?" A heated discussion ensues. Eventually, Brenda sends Connie to her room, where she remains for most of the evening.

Brenda has withdrawn from Connie emotionally and has become comfortable with this situation. When Wendy and Bruce ask if Connie can be included in a board game, Brenda says, "Maybe another day." If Wendy and Bruce want to include Connie in watching a movie, Brenda states, "Oh, next time." Wendy and Bruce feel guilty that they have so much fun. They wonder, "Why do Mommy and Connie fight all of the time? What happened to make Mommy not love Connie?"

Parents who cope through emotional withdrawal must be helped to see that the child's actions are not a personal attack on the parent. The child, whose previous experience is of adults abandoning her, is attempting to protect herself from further perceived emotional pain. He or she believes, "I need to reject you before you reject me." Inadvertently, this coping style leaves brothers and sisters wondering, "Would Mom or Dad withdraw from me?"

"Yes, but . . ." Parents

Greg and Dawn arrived at therapy with their 11-year-old daughter, Lori, whom they adopted. Greg and Dawn also parent two birth sons, Kevin and Ronald, ages 14 and 15 respectively. The parents relayed to the therapist a lengthy list of Lori's negative behaviors. Topping the list was Lori's desire to dress like a boy. Lori preferred to wear her brothers' shirts and sweatshirts. She would go into their rooms and take their clothing from the closet. If Dawn took Lori shopping, Lori immediately located the boys' section. She would demand that Dawn purchase clothing she selected from this department.

The therapist suggested that Greg and Dawn could cease buying clothing that was unacceptable to them. Greg immediately replied, "Yes, but Lori will get angry and who knows what she will do then!"

The therapist suggested that Greg and Dawn could gradually replace the boys clothing with girls clothing. Greg stated, "Yes, but how will we get her dressed when she realizes that she only has girls clothes to wear?"

The therapist then proposed that Greg and Dawn could give Lori a choice. She could wear boy's clothing as long as she purchased it with her own money. If she wanted to use Mom and Dad's money, then she would need to select clothes that were acceptable to Mom and Dad. Greg's reply was, "Yes, but she only gets money on her birthday and holidays. She doesn't have enough money to make that work."

The therapist offered that Lori could earn money by completing extra chores. Greg said, "Yes, but we are busy, and we really don't have time for that."

The therapist explained that Lori's behavior was actually a means to create distance. She feared intimacy and so she used the clothing as a means to generate conflict. Lori felt that anger prevented a relationship from forming. If Dawn and Greg stopped making the clothing an issue, Lori would also discontinue it as a means to prevent attaching to the family. Greg instantly replied, "Yes, but won't we be giving in?"

The "yes, but . . ." parent wants change, but can't decide how to move forward to cause alterations. In some instances, this is a parent who is uncomfortable with conflict. He fears that he cannot manage the conflict, or he simply wants to avoid conflict because he does not like to feel the distress that accompanies a dispute. In other cases, the parents are so worn down that it seems overwhelming to think about implementing parenting interventions. These parents are hoping that therapeutic intervention alone will bring about the changes they are seeking.

An immobilized family, who sees the adoptee as the problem, often feels it is only the adoptee who needs to change. ***In reality, if the adoptee is to heal, the entire family system will have to make changes.*** Please do not misinterpret this statement. This is not blaming parents. Nor is it meant to imply that the family system is inherently dysfunctional. Most families I see at the Attachment and Bonding Center of Ohio were quite healthy prior to an adoption. ***The current state of the family is a response to the challenges involved in parenting a child with mental illness.*** However, children with mental health issues need to be parented in different ways than do typically developing children. Just as a child with juvenile diabetes has special dietary needs, the child with mental illness has unique parenting needs. Chapters 9 and 10 will help parents identify these distinctive parenting tools.

Split Parents

Splitting, described earlier in this chapter and in Chapter 1, is an important phenomenon and one that needs to be reiterated. Splitting leads to extensive marital tension. The core of the marital strain is that one parent, usually the father, receives less of the adoptee's negative behavior than does the other, usually the mother. Because he does not *see* the behavior, one parent perceives the other to be the problem. Criticism then follows.

"You are too hard on him."

"Why don't you lighten up?"

"If you would just leave him alone more, he'd be better."

This criticism is translated by the wife as, "You don't believe me. I have been your wife for twelve years. Since he came to live with us, you think I'm lying and that I can't parent." The damage to the marital relationship is obvious. Marital discord is like an oil spill. It spreads out, affecting everyone in its path—the children!

Derrick is in his early twenties. His parents, Ellen and Roger, adopted their two nieces, Jill and Joyce, when Derrick was 11 years old. Jill and Joyce are now also in their early twenties. Joyce has a job and she attends college part-time. Jill lives on her own.

Jill, Ellen and Roger engaged in conflict from the day Jill moved in until the day she unexpectedly announced that she had rented her own apartment. Derrick stated, "Family meals have always been important to my parents. No matter what, we sat down to dinner as a family. Then, along came Jill. Mom would get on her about eating with her mouth open and not using a fork. Dad would yell at Mom to stop picking on her. The next thing, Mom and Dad were fighting. Mom felt Dad didn't support her. Eventually, I would take my plate to my room and turn on my television. I'm not even sure they noticed that I was gone to my room most of the time. Even now that Jill is gone, they fight about why she left. Dad blames Mom, and Mom blames Dad. I just wish they would stop fighting."

Sibling Talk

Nobody wants to adopt a 15-year-old kid, because maybe this kid might have problems. But, you can get a problem child at any age, so as much background information as you can get is still not enough. You can have a child and still not know until it is born that it's got Down Syndrome. So I think it is the same thing with adoption. I wouldn't say it's a gamble but it's definitely a risk, just like having a baby.

Sibling Talk

Keep communication open with the parents. I would also tell kids not to have expectations of how this kid is going to act because they don't know. Along through the adoption they should continue to talk to their parents and tell them how they are feeling because a lot of times kids won't say anything and then the parents don't know so the parents don't focus on them because they are so focused on the disruptive child and so they need to let their parents know at all times what's going on and if they have any questions they always need to talk to their parents about it.

Ineffective Coping Styles of Typically Developing Children

The Withdrawn Child

Derrick, in the previous vignette, reminds us that not just parents, but also the resident children often respond with irrational patterns of coping of their own. In Derrick's case, he began withdrawing from the family.

Certainly all children enjoy spending time in their bedrooms, being with their friends or participating in extracurricular activities. Subsequent to an adoption, the family's birth and/or previously adopted children may increase the time spent away from the family. In fact, like Derrick, they may avoid almost all family interactions. They begin eating dinner separately, requesting to go to friends' homes weekend after weekend and joining activities they never before expressed any interest in.

This situation may be a reflection of the sadness felt regarding the changes in the family. This may be an effort to escape the growing level of conflict. Whatever the reason, though, the child's withdrawal often generates guilt. The resident child feels at fault for not making more efforts to help the parents heal the hurting child. Lena, who we met earlier in this chapter under the heading, "I expect my extended family and friends to be supportive," stated,

> "I would try to help out as much as I could. But, I also got involved in a lot of activities so that I wouldn't have to be around the disruption. I got involved in so many things. When I went to college, my freshman year I was a commuter and there were two girls I made friends with. I would stay over with them as much as I possibly could. I got involved in volleyball and I had never played volleyball before in my entire life. But, then the next year I became a Resident Assistant because I didn't want to stay at home. So since this paid for my housing, I was like, this is awesome I don't have to live at home! I got involved in theater. I got involved in the dance team and student government. I worked 20 hours per week on campus which is the maximum you're allowed to work. On the weekend I went out places so that I didn't have to go home, even though I wanted to go home because I felt guilty not being involved with home life as much as I should. I would think, 'Well, my parents have to deal with it.' I wanted to help, but I didn't want to have to be around the conflict."

The Self-Sacrificing Child

This child carries out all parental requests, completes extra chores, makes wonderful grades, and may be very involved in and excel at sports, student government and church activities. Parents may find themselves making such comments as, "She never gives us any problems." or "He does so much to help out. We never have to ask him to do his chores." As parents are so grateful to have this cooperation, the self-sacrificing coping pattern often goes unrecognized. This child is attempting to "make up" for the difficulties caused by the child who joined the family via adoption. This child perceives the parents as being under so much stress that he or she does not want to add additional strain.

The Acting-Out Child

Pent up anger and resentment may be expressed through negative behaviors. The typically developing child becomes disrespectful, violates rules, begins to demonstrate poor academic performance and/or changes her peer group. He or she may believe that the way to obtain parental attention is to replicate the negative behaviors displayed by his or her traumatized brother or sister.

> Jeremy is 6 years old. His brother, Cody, was adopted when Jeremy was 3 years old. Cody is now 8 years old. Jeremy stated, "When Mom and Dad tell Cody that he can't have something, look out! There will be big fight! Cody will throw things and call my mom names." Jeremy could be talking about himself as well since he mimics Cody's behavior. He is quite clear that Mom and Dad "have to pay more attention when me or Cody acts bad."

The Regressed Child

This coping style is common among toddlers, pre-school age children and children in grade school. Younger children who are under stress frequently regress to earlier developmental stages. For example, behaviors such as temper tantrums, thumb sucking or bedwetting re-appear in otherwise healthy children when a troubled child joins the family.

The "I'll Cover for You" Child

Resident children may conceal or cover up the negative behavior of their adopted brother or sister. Parents kept in the dark in this manner lack understanding of the depth of the adoptee's problems, so precious time is lost before obtaining services. This can re-victimize the child with a traumatic past. While brothers and sisters may be attempting to decrease the anger level in the family, the new child is likely to be confused about the difference between *sympathy* and *empathy*. The resident child may "feel sorry" for her adopted sibling. "My life was so much better than yours. I'll keep quiet. I don't want you to have any more problems." The more helpful, empathic response would be, "I'm so sad you destroyed my CD player. I will be telling Mom and Dad. I do hope you learn to make better choices."

> Helen, a 15-year-old, resides in her family of origin with her adopted brother and sister—Willie, age 12 and April, age 10. Helen and April get along well. April loves it when Helen helps her with her homework or teaches her how to sew. Willie, on the other hand, is quite difficult. He waits for the girls at the top of the steps and then jumps out and punches them in the stomach. At night, he enters April's room. He stands at the side of her bed. She is often startled awake by his presence. April and Helen are afraid of Willie.
>
> April and Helen also feel sorry for Willie. He has no friends and he is often "in trouble" with Mom and Dad. Mom and Dad are so stressed the girls don't want to add another layer to their burdens. So they have kept Willie's aggression and nighttime escapades a secret since it started several years ago. Willie's parents and his therapist have no idea that Willie exhibits these inappropriate behaviors. His therapeutic goals revolve around an increase in responsibility such as completing chores and homework. Certainly, violence and scaring his sister are matters that should take precedence over whether Willie takes the garbage out on Tuesday mornings.

The Victim Child

This coping style results because the adoptee is abusing one or more of the appropriately developing children—emotionally, physically or sexually. While some children are very quick to bring abuse to their parents' attention, other children, like April and Helen, keep the abuse a secret due to fear of the perpetrator or fear of the parent's reaction. These resident children are at risk for developing a victim mentality. Victims tend to see the control and responsibility for their situations as someone else's fault. A victim blames others for their circumstances. Victims accept little responsibility for their actions. Their sense of self is diminished or destroyed. They expect things will go wrong, thinking, "Bad things always happen to me." Victims develop a sense of entitlement—"The world owes me." They become disappointed and/or angry when they are not treated in a manner that supports their belief system.

Immediate treatment is suggested for any family that learns about child-to-child abuse.

Ineffective Coping Styles: Repeating the Patterns

Examining the irrational coping patterns a bit more closely, we see various themes. For example, in *withdrawal* someone is "out" of the family or someone is "alone." *Conflict* and *anger* are apparent in all of the coping styles. Blame and misplaced responsibility for the problems—a *victim's perspective*—are common occurrences. *Secrecy* or failure to address issues occurs as well. *Split parents* threaten to leave the marriage if the situation does not change, or one parent goes so far as to pack his or her bags. In effect, these are many of the same dynamics that are present in families that are prone to abuse, abandonment, neglect and drug use. These are also many of the same issues that adoptees experienced while in residence with their birth families or in institutional settings.

Do you remember, at some point in your life, vowing, "When I have children, I'll never say that to my own kids?" Then one day you shout,

> "No dessert until you clean your plate!"
>
> "Turn off the lights. Money doesn't grow on trees!"
>
> "Close the door! Were you born in a barn?"

You think, "Oh my goodness, I have become my mother!" "I sound just like my father!"

We all repeat the patterns from our families of origin. Children who have experienced trauma alter the dynamics of the adoptive family in a manner that causes a repetition of their abandonment, abuse, neglect, deprivation or life with a drug addict. Their trauma is reenacted, albeit on a smaller scale, within the adoptive home.

This compulsive repetition or trauma reenactment is unconscious. The child who is compulsively repeating his traumatic experience needs the presence of strong attachment figures—adoptive parents—so that he may explore his pre-adoptive abuse, neglect and abandonment. Once he looks at his trauma, he can learn to interrupt the repetitive patterns. He can begin to live in the present (van der Kolk, 1989). He can function in more healthy ways in his interactions with his brothers, sisters and parents.

Parents and siblings need new coping skills in order to resist playing parts in the traumatic reenactment. Specifically, mothers, fathers, sisters and brothers need to learn

> *Sibling Talk*
>
> You have to have patience. It sometimes takes a long time.

to change the ways in which they *react* to the adoptee—Chapters 9 and 10 will cover this topic in depth. Parents, very much so, also need to look at the styles of attachment within their family. As we will learn in Chapter 10, ineffective styles of coping are reflective of insecure patterns of attachment. Enhancing attachment—forging strong, intimate relationships—among all members of an adoptive family is essential for the short- and long-term well-being of parents and all of the children. Chapters 9 and 10 will make clear that nurture and consistent reactions are a powerful duo in the healing of an adoptive family.

The Emotional Roller-Coaster

"I have never been so angry. I didn't even know that I could get this angry—especially at a child!"

"I am now on anti-depressants."

"I am taking medication for anxiety."

"I have high blood pressure now."

"At times, I have to walk away. Otherwise, I fear I would hurt my daughter. I feel crazy for having these thoughts. What kind of a parent feels like they could physically hurt their own child?"

"He pushes my buttons! He knows the things that make me angry and he does them on purpose to make me mad! Why is he doing this to me?"

Such statements are frequently made by parents of traumatized children. One mom who parents two school-age international adoptees said,

> "The effects these children have on your life are completely devastating. From the moment they came home, nothing was the same. What I hate most is how they changed me. I used to wake up happy and full of energy, usually having a plan for the day. I was full of life and always ready to go do something. Looking back, I can honestly say that before the adoption I never felt rage about anything in my life. NOTHING I felt before compares to the anger and rage I feel now. I hate that I feel this! I hate that I feel so sad. It's so intense, it's very isolating, and I feel so hopeless to change it."

Another mom, who parents seven children by birth and adoption, the two oldest of which (currently ages 17 and 18; arrival ages 9 and 10) have histories of complex trauma, writes,

> "I have uglier feelings from dealing with these children than I even thought I could possibly have. Then I feel guilty for my feelings. For example, I wonder if I had to do this all over again, would I? Then, I feel badly for thinking how much easier my life could have been. I love the girls, they deserve a home, a good family and unconditional love, just like everyone else. As hard as I've tried, they don't always reciprocate, which not only makes me feel unappreciated but also that I haven't done a good enough job—that I'm not a good enough mom."

The section of Chapter 3 called "Stress Management: Maintaining a Healthy Emotional Climate" introduced the concept of a *negative emotional climate*. This concept bears review and expansion as it is a central difficulty within immobilized adoptive families. In essence, the adoptee enters the adoptive family with unresolved emotions from his traumatic experiences. The child with the traumatic history begins to transfer these emotions, by acting out behaviorally, to the adoptive parents and siblings. The adoptee's overall goal with this behavior is to watch and see how the family members handle feelings. The manner in which his mom, dad, brothers and sisters express their

Sibling Talk

In public, he acts the same as at home. When we have friends over, he likes to show off to them. Our friends think it's funny. But they don't know what it feels like to have him all the time.

emotions becomes his template for resolving his own feelings. But the intensity of the adoptee's emotions can be overwhelming to family members. Thus, family members find themselves depressed, angry, anxious and frustrated—daily! The stress level in the family rises!

It is important that parents and siblings understand this concept so that they can learn to avoid it. It is equally imperative that professionals working with adoptive families familiarize themselves with this dynamic. Adoptive families in the midst of this phenomenon appear unhealthy. Parents who enter therapy and make statements to the effect of having thoughts of hurting their child or being so angry that they need to put themselves in a "time-out" look as if they are poor parents or parents with issues. Parents who are depressed or anxious seem like they need help in order to be better parents. Consequently, the child's problems are seen as being caused by the distress of the parents who are actually in the middle of a negative emotional climate driven by the new child's chronic testing. This phenomenon often leads both inexperienced professionals and outsiders such as family and friends to blame parents for the child's problems.

In fact, a negative emotional climate is an indicator of an adoption that can be successful! A negative emotional climate is reflective of the adoptee's desire to connect to her family. It means that the adoptee is reaching out to the family for help. It means that the adoptee trusts the family enough to assist her to resolve her past hurts. Parents who understand this are able to react to the adoptee in a calmer, more rational manner. Thus, the vigilant adoptee learns to model this positive behavior. Professionals who comprehend this concept are able to effectively assist parents in responding to the adoptee with empathy and nurture rather than with fury, exasperation and resentment. While these negative emotions feel terrible to the parents, brothers, sisters and adoptee, once channeled in more productive ways, the entire family can actually achieve an enhanced level of functioning.

Mothers, fathers, brothers and sisters must learn to recognize this so that they will not tend to conceal the strong feelings they have in response to the adoptee's behavior. These feelings are grief-related, resultant from unmet expectations, and due to negative reactions received from formal and informal support systems. With virtually no one to vent to, the emotions are unleashed on nuclear family members. Thus, the negative emotional climate becomes self-perpetuating.

The stress and the negative emotional climate can be intensified by the additional tasks involved in parenting a child with a history of trauma. The chart on the next page demonstrates the additional layers of responsibilities adoptive families must recognize and learn to manage.

The list of everyday jobs is more than doubled in adoptive families. The weight of balancing all of these responsibilities produces tension. Parents, galloping to therapy, work, soccer games, the grocery store, the doctor, the school and so on, find their patience running short over time. Tired, overwrought parents are prone to angry outbursts. Each member of the adoptive family suffers as a result. Again, the negative emotional climate prevails. Chapters 9 and 10 will provide solutions to help families create and maintain a more positive emotional climate.

PARENTAL RESPONSIBILITIES: A COMPARISON	
ALL **families with children**	**Adoptive families parenting traumatized children**
Money management Time management General parenting tasks and responsibilities Household chores and tasks and repairs Jobs Child care Dealing with the schools Illnesses, deaths in the family Social endeavors for the family—vacations, general "fun" Social endeavors for the children—leisure activities, extracurricular activities, maintaining friendships Social endeavors for the parents—leisure activities, maintaining friendships, volunteering Holidays and vacations Intra-family conflict (extended family)	**Everything in the left column, plus . . .** Infertility, step-family relationships and/or other family building issues. "Uneven" motivation between partners about adopting Lack of informed support—formal and informal—for adoption from family, friends, professionals Lack of information about new child's history Adoptee's mental health issues and developmental delays Conflict between birth and/or typically developing adopted children and adopted children with special needs and issues Managing openness in adoption (sibling visits, foster parent or birthparent visits) Locating adequate child care, summer camps for children with "issues" School issues related to special education—negotiating IEPs, phone calls about misconduct, inadequate school performance Learning how to talk to adopted children about birth histories Understanding and dealing with triggers for adoption-related issues Understanding and dealing with triggers for trauma- or neglect-related issues Social conflicts outside the immediate family resulting from hurt child's behavior problems
Based on but expanded from: Ginther, Norma; Betsy Keefer, and Nan Beeler. *Keeping Your Adult Relationship Healthy in Adoption* (Columbus: Institute for Human Services for the Ohio Child Welfare Training Program) (2003)	

Isolation

The conversation below took place between two adoptive mothers at an adoptive parent support group:

> Marge said, "I think the intimacy we had in our marriage is gone. I certainly hope that we can rebuild it. I am thankful that we have had a strong marriage, because I certainly think that the addition of our adopted daughters could have destroyed our marriage. I eat under stress. I've gained 40 pounds. And, I tell myself that I'm going to lose the 40 pounds, for

> health reasons, and then something happens with our daughter and I go eat something else just to feel better.
>
> "Things I used to do in the house have changed—I don't have a regular cleaning day anymore because something always seems to come up," she continued. "I feel bad that I don't call my mom like I used to. She's in her 70s. Weeks and weeks will go by and I'll say, 'Oh, my gosh, I don't remember the last time I talked to my mom.' "
>
> "I understand!" replied Berta. "There's no time. There's no time with trying to do everything with the adoptee. People don't understand why you can't get this or that done. You break your own doctor's appointments because you are at the school. You have to be where the adopted child is. You and your husband are supposed to go to dinner on Friday night and the other kids are all calling on the phone saying, 'You can't! You and Dad can't go because you aren't going to leave us with him!'
>
> "Everything really shuts down. Friends and family don't understand. Of course, they think you are crazy in the first place. 'Well, you're a nut! Why did you do this? You had wonderful kids and then you're going to go get some more! It's your issue.' Friends and family just don't understand. It's like you're on an island all by yourself."

The isolation expressed by these two women ranges from a lack of intimate relations in a marriage to feeling alone on an island. Isolation, like the other dynamics, is comprised of multiple layers.

Strained couple relations due to splitting, exhaustion, working overtime to cover the additional expenses incurred by the adoption, time constraints, unmet expectations, etc. inhibit the couple's sexual relations as well as partners' abilities to satisfy each other's emotional needs.

Siblings retreat to their bedrooms or keep themselves on the go in order to cope with the changes and conflict in the family. Services may also isolate siblings.

> Leslie was adopted at age 7. Now age 11 she is thriving. She has friends, she makes good grades and she has many interests. She openly lets people know how happy she is to have been adopted. She is quite clear that her birthparents "couldn't get themselves together and that was their problem." Three other adopted siblings in her family, on the other hand, all struggle with various mental health issues as well as delays in speech and fine motor skills. They go to mental health therapy, a psychiatrist, speech therapy and occupational therapy. These services take a lot of time. Frequently, Leslie must stay with her aunt while her parents and siblings participate in their therapies. Recently, Leslie asked her mom, "Can I go to therapy so I can spend more time with you?" Leslie's mom was stunned.

Leslie feels left out because she perceives therapy as an activity that allows time with a parent. Siblings are often excluded from information about their brother's or sister's mental illness. Siblings, unlike parents and adoptees, are rarely invited to participate in treatment planning, nor are they invited to services to express their own feelings and concerns. Overall, warm, friendly, in-depth interactions become few and far between—family members become isolated from one another. Family fun diminishes.

In Chapter 3, we introduced Gabe's family. Gabe's father commented,

> We used to take a lot of home movies, especially when a child came into the family from China. Then, we would put Christmas on that same video and a few things like that. We recently played back one of the movies before Gabe came home. I think everybody was just stunned watching the movie! Is this the way our house used to be? We just sat around and had fun.

Gabe's mother further noted:

> "We used to eat out Friday nights and Sunday after church. This has ceased since Gabe's arrival. He often threw food on those dining around us. When his meal arrived, he would scream—loudly—that it was 'yucky.' He would push it aside and pout while everyone else ate."

Like Gabe, many previously traumatized or neglected children struggle to participate in fun, entertaining, enjoyable activities. The amount of sensory stimulation at an amusement park or a crowded zoo may overwhelm a child with Sensory Integration Dysfunction. She becomes agitated and irritable. Underdeveloped social skills render playing board games unpleasant. Cheating, poor sportsmanship, barking directions at the other players certainly dampens the pleasure that should be derived from a game. Family fun shuts down. Again, a lack of time spent together isolates mothers, fathers and siblings from each other.

> Rick, a 15-year-old typically developing adolescent, offers us another aspect of lost fun and isolation. Rick's home had always been the favorite place to hang out. The basement was complete with a pool table and up-to-date video game equipment. Rick's mom always kept an ample array of snacks on hand. Rick's friends came over after school and on weekends.
>
> Four years ago, Rick's parents adopted Lydia and everything changed. Lydia, currently age 9, suffered sexual abuse in her birth home. Rick says, "Lydia is great and I do love her. But, around my friends it has been really hard. She wouldn't leave them alone. She tried to sit on their laps. She hugged them and sometimes she tried to kiss them. It was so embarrassing! My friends didn't know what to do around her or what to say to her. On their own, some of my friends stopped coming over. But, others, I stopped inviting. I started making excuses about having other things to do. I can't go to their houses because I watch Lydia until Mom or Dad gets home from work."

The socially unacceptable behaviors of the mentally ill brother or sister often result in a sense of shame and embarrassment on the part of well siblings. Siblings such as Rick often stop bringing their friends home, and they may avoid public appearances with their troubled brother or sister (Judge, 1994).

Support gradually fades. Friends, extended family members and professionals misplace blame and offer little helpful advice. Time limits the capacity to participate in social engagements. Relationships wither away or become less fulfilling. Initially, this process of becoming isolated from others is involuntary. It is not necessarily the adoptive family's choice to shrink the size of their support system. However, over time, adoptive families voluntarily begin to restrict interactions.

Predicting how others will respond to the adoptive family is difficult. We have learned that traumatized children fear intimate relationships because they have experienced so much rejection. We have also learned that adoptive families experience much rejection—criticism, blame, being misunderstood, being perceived as bad parents, etc. It becomes easier to keep to oneself.

Sibling Talk

In social settings they act normal. So out with other people no one would guess how they act at home. They are a different color so people can guess they are adopted. But it doesn't seem like they are disruptive at all.

Sibling Talk

He would lie about anything for no reason—about something you wouldn't even get in trouble for, he would just lie. He would steal stuff and lie. He stole from the house. I got him a job. He stole from work. Why are we even having this conversation? You know he stole it! Why are you asking me where your ring is? Where do you think it is? He stole it. Anything that we can't find, he stole.

It is hard to commit to relationships, community endeavors, a gym membership, a book club, a girls' night out, a bowling league, etc. Children with mental health issues are unpredictable. Clinton, the adoptive father of 10-year-old Andy said,

> "He would flip from being completely normal to completely going off the wall—throwing things and screaming. You know, a half an hour of screaming can be pretty trying on you."

Such erratic behavioral shifts perpetuate chaos. Chaos disrupts the organization needed to participate in leisure pursuits that require regular attendance or consistent participation. Additionally, after listening to 30 minutes of screaming, many parents do not have the energy to go bowling or run on a treadmill.

Many families report a fear of child abuse allegations as a reason for voluntary isolation. Some adoptees become confused regarding the perpetrator of their abuse. As a result, they may make statements that would suggest that the current family is committing abuse. Other children with a traumatized past have a way of implying that their family is "mean" or not meeting their basic needs.

> Pam and Paul adopted two sons from El Salvador. Several years later, they unexpectedly had another son by birth.
>
> Mark, the oldest son, is age 15. Daily, Pam packs him a lunch to take to school. Unbeknownst to Pam and Paul, Mark throws his lunch out the bus window. At lunch time, he asks other kids for food or tries to get a free hot lunch. He states to the cafeteria employees, "I don't have a lunch." The implication is, "My parents don't give me lunch." Concerns among school staff mounted over time. Ultimately, they called the local public agency and reported that Mark was regularly without food.
>
> Pam and Paul were shocked and outraged when a social worker arrived at their home to investigate the allegations. Why hadn't the school discussed this with them? They could have rectified the situation by placing money in Mark's school account. He could have purchased hot lunch. Would the worker believe them? What if she didn't? Would she take their children? How long would the investigation take? How long would they have to live wondering what would happen? Why had Mark acted in this way?

Fortunately for Pam and Paul, their other sons confirmed that food was always available. The social worker was clearly able to see for herself that their cupboards were well-stocked. This positive resolution, however, did not offset the fact that the family had to go through this unpleasant and frightening experience. Families fear the removal of their children when the adoptee states or insinuates that he is subject to inadequate or abusive parenting. Parents perceive that the way to reduce the chances of a false abuse allegation is to limit interactions outside of the home. Parents may find alternative solutions in the book *Adopting and Advocating for the Special Needs Child* by L. Anne Babb and Rita Laws. Articles by Rita Laws, PhD regarding protecting yourself from false abuse allegations, appear on various websites. Dr. Laws' explanations about why false allegations occur, and her suggested precautions parents can take are thorough. This is wonderful information for adoptive parents.

Difficulties in Breaking Free of Isolation

A lack of child care contributes to both voluntary and involuntary isolation. Let's examine the causes of this issue.

Siblings as Child Care Resources

Older brothers and sisters are very often a main source of child care within a family. *Involuntary* reasons for not utilizing siblings to provide child care in an adoptive family include the following:

- The typically developing children in an adoption-expanded family may not feel capable of supervising their sibling. Their concerns may be correct, depending on the challenges the adoptee presents.
- Typically, oldest children assume care-taking duties of younger children. Adoptive families may find that this does not work if the older children are the adopted children. The adoptee's social and emotional delays render him immature and lacking a full sense of responsibility. Leaving him in charge of younger children presents safety issues.
- Hiring the teen living down the street to watch younger, healthy children will work well. However, the adolescent adoptee will have difficulty accepting that a peer is to take care of him.
- Parents often feel as if the brothers and sisters are already making enough sacrifices. Asking them to look after a troubled sibling so that the parents may pursue a pleasurable activity seems too great to request.

Extended Family, Friends and Professional Respite Resources

Grandpa, Grandma, aunts, uncles or friends—depending on health, geographic location, level of support—are a traditional source of family babysitters. Childcare facilities and families who provide respite are other resources. A respite family is a home in which the parents are familiar with the special needs of adoptive children. They may be foster or adoptive parents. A respite provider could be a retired school teacher or a social worker who has become a stay-at-home mom.

The *involuntary* issues associated with these potential child care providers include the following concerns:

- Some behavioral difficulties are unwelcome in child care settings, in respite families or in the homes of extended family members and friends.
- The child's older age makes finding child care difficult. Respite families, relatives, friends and professional child care facilities question why a child age 13, 14 or older needs a babysitter.
- Child care centers are licensed to care for children of certain ages. A facility can only accommodate youth that meet this criteria. Thus, a local establishment may not be able to meet a family's needs.

> *Sibling Talk*
>
> He acts badly in public. I'm embarrassed to be seen with him. I hate taking him places with us. I want to leave him home. I don't want to be seen with him.

- Parents are concerned that the level of supervision will be inadequate.

Voluntarily, parents may resist child care for the following reasons:

- Parents feel guilty asking others to manage the child given the behavioral difficulties.
- Children with mental health issues often act nicely to adults who are not their parents. Parents are upset when their child's behavior is better for the respite family than for them. This scenario makes adoptive parents feel as if the child's difficulties are the result of their parenting.
- Parents frequently want respite to be unpleasant. They perceive that such a scenario will help the child appreciate the family. Therefore, the child will be inclined to make improvements upon returning home. Fortunately, as Chapter 10 will describe in more detail, this type of respite is mostly unavailable.
- The child often acts poorly upon returning from respite. Parents determine it is easier to simply keep plugging away rather than deal with yet another bout of negative behavior.

These "roadblocks" to reducing isolation will be addressed in Chapter 10 because the lack of adequate child care or the choice not to utilize safe, reliable babysitters plays a role in all facets of isolation. For example, partners can rarely go out as a couple. Further, mothers and fathers have a hard time simultaneously attending sporting events, school concerts, school plays and awards ceremonies in which their previously adopted and/or birth children participate or are getting acknowledged. The child misses being praised, complimented and cheered for by both parents. One parent is isolated from observing his or her child's accomplishments and offering enthusiastic approval.

Parents who say no to the intermittent use of adequate child care for voluntary reasons need to re-think this issue by asking themselves these questions:

What am I missing with my typically developing children?

What are they missing with me?

Do these missed opportunities with my appropriately developing children cause hard feelings?

What happens to these feelings? Do they get unleashed onto my already hurting child? My spouse? My other children?

Would I consider taking an employment position that had a no vacation policy? What would be the impact of such a policy on me, and my family's emotional well-being?

Again, we are going to explore this area of respite more in-depth in Chapter 10. Creative solutions to the family's child care needs, as well as ideas to restore family fun, return to regular dates with your partner, spend more time with your typically developing children and much more await the reader.

Afloat on a Sea of Grief

Throughout this book, multiple examples of the losses experienced by each member of the adoptive family have been mentioned. Overall, the point has clearly been

> *Sibling Talk*
>
> He acted like a total idiot—anything from yelling things out the window at people driving by to yelling things at my parents.

> **Sibling Talk**
>
> He will go into my room. He will take stuff from my room. He hides it in his room and I won't find it for like three weeks. He just really frustrates me. He's just like uncontrollable pretty much.

made that losses abound in adoptive families. Losses are amplified and made more complex for those adoptive families which include one or more children with mental health issues. This is not to minimize the experience of any adoptive family. It is to state that mental illness adds additional losses. In fact, mental illness needs to be recognized as a major loss. When it comes to the experience of loss, the primary distinction between death and mental illness is that mental illness is not broadly and publicly recognized as a significant loss, when in fact, loss may be the primary trauma for family members during the course of mental illness (Johnson, 1994).

Loss and grief—the emotional response to loss—is perhaps the most significant dynamic to develop within the adoptive family parenting a child with mental health issues. Doesn't this make sense when we think about all of the losses incurred by each member of the adoptive family? Doesn't this make sense when we think back to the statement, "It's like you're on an island all by yourself!" This sentiment certainly conjures up an image of profound loss. The grief involved with this level of loss is intense and overwhelming.

It should make even more sense when we realize that at the core of all of the losses experienced by the complex adoptive family, there is one central loss. That is, the loss of the person that their adopted son, daughter, brother or sister could have been. Complex trauma often robs the adoptee of the opportunity to fully participate in all aspects of life. Parents and siblings must mourn the loss of the person that the child may never become because of the damage suffered prior to the adoption. This is an arduous and grueling task. It is a chronic—persistent and lasting—process. Unlike death, there are no formal rituals to assist in this process. There is little outside validation of the loss—others are not standing in line to offer condolences. The family is afloat on a sea of grief with no life rafts or oars—and no end in sight.

Additionally, in families with persons with serious mental health illness, there is *no difference* between parents and siblings in their level of grief (Miller, Dworkin, Ward, and Barone, 1990). Children are more able to cope with grief when there is at least one available adult. We have learned throughout this book that parental time and attention decreases after an adoption, making the parent less available. As has also been confirmed, the adoptee is the focus of mental health services. Siblings are the most excluded member of the treatment team.

Myths about Children and Grief

Sibling grief is further compounded by myths surrounding children and grief. These myths or roadblocks (Chapter 10) also inhibit the adoptee's grieving process.

One common myth is that children don't grieve (Trozzi and Massimini, 1999). There is a desire to deny that children experience loss. Adults prefer to believe that children will simply overcome unpleasant life events and that the adoptee will just move beyond or forget about being raped, abandoned, beaten, abused or left in an orphanage. Adults want to believe that typically developing children will adjust to lost parental time, a family engulfed in conflict or despair, the decrease in family outings, and the changes in relationships with friends and family. Parents and other adults want children to be

> *Sibling Talk*
>
> I used to just walk away and stuff and pretend like it never happened or I used to get real mad or I used to watch TV or do my homework. Now, I just get tired of it and pretend like I can't hear it and stuff.

happy. In efforts to facilitate children's happiness, children are frequently disallowed their need to grieve.

Another common misperception is that children need to be helped to "get over" their grief and move on. Actually, children will experience parts of their pain for the rest of their lives. In Chapter 2, we discussed that children's needs for information vary according to their developmental stage. Grief is also developmental, as the next sections describe.

Grief in Infants and Toddlers

Infants and toddlers recognize significant changes in their environment as well as the loss of a loved one they were used to being with. They will communicate their grief via crying, changes in eating, and sleeping and body language. They are visibly distressed. They may be difficult to console. A change in primary caregiver or the amount of time spent with a caregiver can cause grief for these young children. Older toddlers often have knowledge of physical race and skin color differences. Young children know names of specific groups. They do not comprehend the real meaning of these labels, and may be puzzled by the use of colors to describe both people and objects. Yet, the stage is set for the losses surrounding culture to occur.

Grief in 3- to 5-Year-Olds

Children age 3 to 5 have fears about being abandoned, getting lost or no longer being loved by their parents. They notice that parents do not have control of everything that happens to them. This threatens their sense of security. Children of this age blame themselves for the loss. They feel that a loss occurred as a result of something they did or because they are inherently "bad."

The adoptee has been abandoned. He is grieving this loss while worrying about future abandonment. He feels sad and angry that he is so unlovable he causes people to abuse him and then go away. He wonders if he has been kidnapped by his adoptive parents, or if his birthparents lost him.

Preschoolers can usually identify their own racial or ethnic groups and may place a positive or negative value on their own and other groups. Children notice their own racial and cultural differences from their parents and may express a desire to be the same race or culture as their parents. Some children may act on this desire:

> Five-year-old Aidan was adopted as an infant. He is Hispanic while his parents and siblings are Caucasian. One day, Ian, his dad, found Aidan in the laundry room dousing himself with Clorox®. He grabbed the Clorox® and asked, "What are you doing?"
>
> Aidan said, "I wanted to look like you." Ian found his heart breaking in response to his son's statements and actions.

The appropriately developing child may feel grief as a result of these fears as well, thinking:

> "I wasn't enough for Mom and Dad. They had to adopt another child."
>
> "Mom and Dad spend more time with my new brother. They must not love me anymore."

"Mom and Dad can't make Jimmy stop hitting us."

"Jimmy is bad because of me."

Grief in 6- to 10-Year-Olds

Children age six to ten begin to comprehend that loss is permanent. This can bring about a multitude of feelings at the time of other significant changes in a child's life. For example, this is the time children enter school. So as they are mastering new tasks, they are struggling to come to terms with past and current losses. Kindergarten or first grade is often a time when adoptees gain a depth of awareness about being adopted because they have vast contact with peers. They realize that other children were born to their parents and that they reside with these parents their entire life. School projects—a timeline, bringing in a baby picture, family tree—accentuate the adoptive status throughout these school years. Grief flows as a result. The other children in the family also gain in their understanding of the impact of the adoption on their lives.

"Janet's sister is so nice. Why didn't I get a sister like that?"

"I love going to Janet's house. Her family is so happy. Why couldn't our family be like that?"

Grief in 7- to 11-Year-Olds

Children ages 7 through 11, school-age children and pre-adolescents, develop a firmer understanding of biological versus adopted. The implications of being adopted sink in more deeply. Brothers and sisters begin to realize the full extent of the trauma experienced by their adopted sibling. This may generate initial feelings of survivor's guilt.

This age group usually has a firmer understanding of their own cultural identity and—given the opportunity—will explore what it means to be a member of this group. The transracial or transcultural adoptee will question why her birthparents did not parent her. Internationally adopted children will also question why their country did not figure out a way for them to remain there. Most children are comfortable with their transcultural status during these ages, particularly if parents have provided open communication regarding adoption, race and related issues. These children are usually accepted by their dominant culture peers with whom they want to fit in—the importance of peer relationships has its root in pre-adolescence. Some assume a sort of celebrity status, especially if he or she is the one-and-only child of a particular race or culture.

However, as Chapter 3 pointed out, not all transcultural adoption experiences will be positive. By the age of 6, children notice that most of their peers are of the same race as at least one parent and that most of their playmates are not adopted. Peers question the birth/previously adopted and newly adopted children about the cultural composition of their family.

"Is that your sister?"

"Who is that with your mom?"

"What is adoption?"

Sibling Talk

Usually when I get mad, I go and do something else and come back later and start talking about it again. Go out and shoot hoops or take a jog or walk. And then I come back and talk with my parents about it.

"Why did your family adopt?"

"China? Where's that?"

Publically, the entire family receives stares and gets asked insensitive questions such as

"Where'd you get that one?"

"How much did she cost?"

"What happened to her real mother?"

"What color is your dad?"

"Well, she looks like she could be yours."

The adoptee's loss of culture, and the family's cultural discontinuity with families around them, cause different-ness and being "different" results in grief. This public scrutiny, and the racism and discrimination that comes with it, continue through grade school and sometimes well into adulthood.

Grief in Pre-Adolescents

Pre-adolescents ages 11 to 13 are faced with puberty, and increased academic and peer pressures. When loss is added, they become more vulnerable and insecure. A capacity to think abstractly occurs at this time. They begin to explore the spiritual and socio-political aspects of their life and the lives of others. Adoptees, brothers and sisters will explore various questions:

"Why does God let bad things happen?"

"Why did my sister get abused?"

"Why has my life been so good?"

"Why did her parents give her away?"

"Why can't we stop drug use?"

"Why did my sister get born to her family and have a good life from the start? I didn't."

"Why does she get to grow up with her siblings? I don't."

Children come to discover that life is not fair. There are harsh realities in life. Typically developing siblings may develop a survivor's guilt. "How do I live a normal life when my sibling suffers so much?"

Grief in Adolescence

Adolescents ages 13 to 18 have an adult understanding of loss. However, they have not had as many experiences with loss as have most adults, so they lack the coping skills to deal with grief. Developmental issues of independence and separation from parents can interfere with the ability to receive support from adults. This situation also causes a need to hide feelings of grief. Otherwise, they appear as if they are not in control of themselves. This contradicts the image of autonomy they desire in adolescence.

> *Sibling Talk*
>
> It was a crazy time. I don't too much remember 10th grade pretty much. It just was. We used to go to school. I don't remember what we used to do there. I don't know what classes we took. I used to play basketball. That's what I would do. We all lost a big chunk of time.

Sibling Talk

I think there are a couple losses. I think the kids lose their innocence, like S., he lost his innocence but way before he came to our house, so he had already learned to rob and steal and lie to get by. So when you come to a good home all you know is how to protect yourself. You don't know how to operate in a family unit. But, as far as I'm concerned, if I want to be selfish about it, I lost time. You lose trust in people. One bad experience and my brother will never adopt kids because of this experience. When you adopt kids, you don't know what you are going to get. You lose everything, man. The whole way you're used to living you lose. You gotta rebuild and start over and patch everything up when everything was just peaches and cream before.

Adolescents also rely more heavily on peers for support with everything in their lives! Typically developing teens, who may have lost friendships throughout the adoption process or whose friends cannot understand their losses, lose this developmentally appropriate manner of coping with their grief. The adoptee who is socially inept lacks peer relationships. He often has few, if any, friendships in which he can confide his feelings for his many losses. Knowledge of sex and sexuality are often advanced in the traumatized teen. This understanding of sexual relationships causes adoptees to once again explore, "Why am I adopted?" "Who am I?"

As we have previously learned, the identity process for adopted adolescents is complicated. The identity process for brothers and sisters in adoptive families with mental illness is also difficult. The crisis of identity is intensified when one's environment includes both sibling and family distress (Balk, 1990; Hogan and Greenfield, 1991). Siblings serve as points of reference for each other in the development of identity (Bank and Kahn, 1997). Siblings look at themselves in relation to their brothers and sisters to determine who they are. Yet now the task of determining a personal identity must occur in the context of a distressed, and sometimes even deteriorating, reference point—one's brother or sister with mental illness (Judge, 1994).

Adolescence is a time of exploration, including determining the significance of race and culture, and examining how these apply to the individual as the adolescent attempts to form a personal identity. An adolescent's past experiences with his or her racial or cultural group are important as they determine whether the adolescent's identity will be positive, negative or in transition. Adolescents who have had little or no contact with members of their own group may model themselves after media images, which may be exaggerated and negative. Some teens form same race or culture friendships, while others may experience rejection from dominant culture peers who were previously friends. This may particularly occur with respect to dating. Some teens who are adopted may meet others of the same racial or cultural group for the first time in school, and may not be accepted by these individuals as they do not "act their race or culture."

I hope that the above information makes clear that children—adoptees, brothers and sisters—experience loss and grief at all ages, and at each developmental stage. Myths pertaining to "children are too young to understand what happened" and "children will get over loss quickly" are falsehoods that need to be discarded. Our discussion of the developmental nature of grief and loss also clarifies that loss occurs as a result of experiences. So myths related to "shielding children from loss and grief" are also unfounded. Further, we do children a great disservice when we think, "It would hurt her too much to talk about it." Children who are not provided opportunities to grieve are at risk for

- decreased social, emotional and cognitive developmental growth
- regression to earlier stages of development for an extended period of time
- inability to concentrate—impaired academic progress
- physical difficulties—fatigue, stomach aches, appetite changes, headaches, tightness in chest, shortness of breath, low energy, difficulty sleeping, etc.
- depression
- anxiety
- risk-taking behaviors
- withdrawal from friends or extracurricular activities.

Stages of Grief

In Chapter 2, it was briefly mentioned that grief includes five stages—shock/denial, bargaining, anger, depression, and ultimately acceptance (Kübler-Ross, 1969; Kübler-Ross and Kessler, 2005). Children and adults fluctuate among these stages rather than pass through them in an orderly progression.

- Shock/Denial—The individual can't believe or refuses to believe what is happening. ("I really can't be moving! My birthparent must be coming back!" "My son really can't have these problems! I can't believe that love isn't curing the problems!" "I can't believe that my sibling acts this way!")
- Bargaining—This stage is an attempt to make a promise or bargain in order to achieve an improved situation. ("God, if you help our family, I'll make sure to live a good life and go to church every Sunday.") Although, for the adoptee or the children who were already in the family, the bargaining may include internal irrational thoughts. ("If I act bad, I'll get back to my birthfamily." "If I had been a better kid, I would still be with my birthfamily." "If I was a better brother, my adopted sister would act okay.") Children often manifest this stage of grief behaviorally. Parents feel as though they are always making a deal to get compliance. ("Honey, will you pick up your dirty clothes?" "I'll pick up my clothes if I can have a cookie.")
- Anger—("I get so mad when he steals." "Why didn't the agency tell us adoption would be like this!" "I do everything for him and he wants his birthparents!" "How could his birthparents abuse him!" "Why did the agency send him back to his birthparents—all it did was make more issues for us to clean up!" "I resent the time he takes up!" "I would never get away with the things he does!" "I hate the way he treats my family!" "I hate my birthparents for leaving me!")

Anger varies in intensity from mild irritation to intense fury and rage. Chronic anger contributes to heart disease, heart attack, prolonged stress, diabetes, more frequent colds, and a host of other health problems. Anger is more pronounced in situations in which the person feels he has no control over what is causing the anger.

Sibling Talk

I've lost money [Author's note: It was stolen by his adopted brother] and time with my parents. We can't do things anymore because we just don't have time. I mean we just don't have family time to, like, watch movies because he is always having tantrums. I don't trust him at all. As far as I'm concerned I really won't have anything to do with him once I'm on my own.

- Depression—This is a period of great sadness. There may be decreased interest or pleasure in activities or hobbies. There can be a loss of energy or feeling tired. Many experience a change in appetite with significant weight gain or weight loss. Sleep patterns may be interrupted—sleeping too much or too little. Making decisions or concentrating is difficult. Feelings of hopelessness, guilt and worthlessness prevail as does irritability—a main symptom of depressed children.
- Acceptance—This stage may also be referred to as integration or reorganization. There may not be total happiness in this stage, yet there is peace, movement forward, understanding of what has happened and coming to terms with what may not change. Anger and depression dissipate—periods of accepting the loss last longer than the periods of sorrow and rage. There is a resumption of taking care of one's own needs. Acceptance has many of the qualities of *mobilization*—the developmental stage that we want to help adoptive families attain.

Factors which affect the capacity of the individual to move through the grieving process include the nature of the loss. A sudden, unexpected loss is believed more difficult to grieve. The level of significance of the loss is also important. The loss of a child or parent is considered among the hardest losses to grieve. The willingness to experience the feelings associated with the loss is another critical factor in the process, as is the quality of support systems.

The Role of Triggers in Grief

You are driving in the car and a song plays on the radio. Suddenly, you are reminded of your first love—you smile.

You stop at a bakery. The smell of fresh baked chocolate chip cookies permeates the air. Fond memories of your deceased grandmother come to mind—you feel sad.

The song and the cookies are triggers—identifiable situations or events that can create emotional upheaval.

Each member of the adoptive family experiences triggers.

Paulette, a 9-year-old adoptee, her brother and her dad went shopping for the perfect Mother's Day gift. The three had a great time at the mall. On Mother's Day, however, Paulette wouldn't get out of bed. This made the family late for church. After the service, she became angry because she didn't like the chosen restaurant. She spilled her pop and "accidentally" dropped her hamburger and fries on the floor. The intended-to-be happy day quickly eroded into a "bad day." Paulette's father was quite confounded, "She was so happy shopping for the gift. She seemed to be looking forward to Mother's Day." Paulette's mom felt rejected. "She doesn't want me for a mother." Paulette's brother wondered why Paulette "ruined" every holiday.

Mother's Day triggered Paulette to think about her birthmother. After the trip to the mall, she couldn't stop thinking about why her birthmother "gave me away." All of her feelings about her abandonment flooded her. She expressed her emotions on Mother's Day with her negative behavior.

Sibling Talk

He calls me a jerk face. Sometimes I get mad. I just can't help it. One time, I just like pushed him on the couch.

Sibling Talk

Sometimes he doesn't bother me. Sometimes I get really mad and start yelling at him and getting in his face.

George, a typically developing 12-year-old, was waiting at the baseball field. His mother was late again! Ever since the family adopted Vikki, his mother was always late. George became angry. "Why did my parents adopt her? She is nothing but trouble. I want my 'old' family back."

When his mother did arrive, George got in the car and slammed the door. He sat in the back seat with his arms folded and his head down. He didn't utter a word the entire drive home. His mother wondered. "Why is he so mad? I am only a few minutes late."

George's mother being late is a trigger for the loss of the way the family was prior to the adoption of Vikki. Some of the emotions are about the waiting. More so, his anger is for the loss of the calm, peaceful and punctual family that existed before Vikki.

Peter is the father of two children—one by birth, Daisy, age 6, and one by adoption, Lee, age 8. Lee had gone into a particularly difficult period since Christmas. Temper outbursts, throwing things and swearing had become daily events. Several weeks into this period, Peter called Lee's therapist to see if she could offer any solutions. Peter anxiously said, "We are under siege! Lee won't stop screaming. My wife just left with Daisy to stay at her sister's for a few days. What should we do about Lee?" Peter had flown in combat during the Gulf War. Flashbacks of his time in the Persian Gulf occurred each time Lee became enraged.

Some triggers can be anticipated—Mother's Day, Father's Day, birthdays, holidays, the anniversary of the adoption, the anniversary of the day the adoptee was removed from her birthparents, airplane rides, visits with birthsiblings, birth of a child, adoption of a child, kindergarten or first grade, the beginning and end of each school year, puberty, questions and comments made by strangers, hospitalization of adoptive parents, and school-related projects or classes such as genetics or biology. Other triggers are not as obvious, as George and Peter's examples illustrate.

Triggers can wreak havoc in adoptive families. In Peter's case, Lee's emotional outbursts led to increased anxiety in Peter. Peter's ability to manage the outbursts was undermined by his excess anxiety. His wife and daughter, in essence, fled the situation. The whole family followed Lee into his state of crisis! An entire family in crisis is often the end result of a trigger.

In Chapter 10, we will return to grief and triggers. Only this time, we will look at ways to facilitate grieving and manage triggers—we'll anchor the family to solid emotional ground.

A Model of Care for Adoptive Families

Trauma, by definition, is a single experience or an enduring or repeating event or events, which completely overwhelm the individual's ability to cope—*consumption and depletion of coping skills*. There is frequently a violation of the person's familiar ideas—*expectations*—about the world, and the person is put in a state of confusion and insecurity—*cognitive dissonance*. This is also seen when people or institutions depended on violate or betray the person in some unforeseen way—*isolation*. It usually involves a feeling of complete helplessness in the face of a real or subjective threat to one's life or to that of a loved one's life, integrity and sanity—*losses*. There is also an inability to integrate the emotions—*grief and negative emotional climate*—involved with the traumatic experience.

In Chapter 2, we used complex trauma as a means to understand the needs of the child about to enter the family. In this chapter, we are also using a model of trauma to help parents and professionals understand the needs of the family into which we placed a traumatized child. We can now conclude that

- The adoptive family parenting a child with mental health issues becomes traumatized. The cost of caring for a child with a history of abuse and neglect comes at great expense to each member of the adoptive family.
- The trauma of the adoptive family—the dynamics of *immobilization*—develops in response to efforts to integrate the adoptee into the family. The family is made unhealthy *after* the adoption; the family, in most instances, was not pathological *prior* to the placement of the child with a history of trauma.
- Models of care which center on individual treatment for the adoptee are inadequate. The successful integration of an adoptee into a family requires addressing and alleviating the trauma of all members of the adoptive family—mothers, fathers, sisters, brothers and the adoptee. A parent-centered and child-focused approach more effectively meets the needs of the adoptive family (Keck and Kupecky, 2002).
- The parent-centered and child-focused model of care demonstrates dignity and respect. Parents are asked to make changes because parenting a child with mental health issues requires a distinctive set of tools. The parents are not blamed for the child's problems.
- The parent-centered model is critical to productive work with the adoptive family because
    - Parents know their family best—the adoptee, the brothers and sisters, and themselves. The healing process is expedited when we listen to parents and design interventions that include their input.
    - Parents are ultimately responsible for the well-being of their family. Parents want to and should be in charge in this manner. When guided to develop and implement the correct interventions, most parents can more than adequately meet their needs as well as the needs of all of their children.
    - Parents set the tone for the family. A healthy, happy caregiver infects their children with their good mood. Vice versa—an angry, overwrought, tired parent transfers this distress to their children. A parent-focus provides ongoing support to parents so they can maintain as assured and optimistic an attitude as is possible. In turn, when we support parents in this manner we positively impact the entire family.
- Child-focused service means that professionals are supporting parents in their efforts to support their children. The family is the client.
- Child-focused also includes that services are extended to each member of the family as needed.

Sibling Talk

I don't think everybody's experience will be bad just because ours was bad.

A continuum of solutions is part of a parent-centered and child-focused model of care. Next in this book, families with mild to severe needs will be offered ways to improve their situation. Solutions offer hope. People with hope have a greater sense of energy. Despite their obstacles, their mood is likely to be more up than down. Hope sustains struggling families.

Chapters 9 and 10 will present parent-centered and child-focused solutions in keeping with our model of care—there will be ideas for each member of the family, but with emphasis on parental self-care. Again, parents set the tone in the family. Children follow the parents' lead. In fact, typically developing children tend to be exact replicas of their parents. Adoptees arrive in the family mirroring many qualities in common with their birthparents. They must learn to internalize and exhibit the characteristics of their adoptive parents. Before you read Chapters 9 and 10, ask yourself these questions:

"What am I currently reflecting?"

"What type of parent have I become throughout the adoption process?"

"What type of parent do I want to be?"

Children Learn What They Live[3]

by Dorothy Law Nolte

If a child lives with criticism, he learns to condemn.
If a child lives with hostility, he learns to fight.
If a child lives with fear, he learns to be apprehensive.
If a child lives with pity, he learns to feel sorry for himself.
If a child lives with ridicule, he learns to be shy.
If a child lives with jealousy, he learns what envy is.
If a child lives with shame, he learns to feel guilty.
If a child lives with encouragement, he learns to be confident.
If a child lives with tolerance, he learns to be patient.
If a child lives with praise, he learns to appreciate.
If a child lives with acceptance, he learns to love.
If a child lives with approval, he learns to like himself.
If a child lives with recognition, he learns that it is good to have a goal.
If a child lives with honesty and fairness, he learns what truth and justice are.
If a child lives with security, he learns to have faith in himself and those around him.
If a child lives with friendliness, he learns that the world is a nice place in which to live.
If you live with serenity, your child will live with peace of mind.
What is your child living?

Resources

These resources are four-fold. They focus on all aspects of coping, and they expand on content related to children's developmental stages throughout the adoption process. A section of personal accounts of adoptive parents, adopted adults, adults who experienced foster care, etc. is offered—these are quite inspirational. Lastly, there is a list of books for clinical professionals.

3. Dorothy Nolte, this poem's author, is deceased. We have made repeated contacts to her publisher's permissions department sincerely seeking to obtain formal permission to reprint this widely reprinted poem, but have yet to receive any response. We are still working on this.

Coping

Books

Amen, Daniel. *Change Your Brain, Change Your Life: The Breakthrough Program for Conquering Anxiety, Depression, Obsessiveness, Anger and Impulsiveness.* (New York: Three Rivers Press, 1998.)

Babb, L. Anne and Rita Laws. *Adopting and Advocating for the Special Needs Child.* (Westport: Bergin and Garvey, 1997.)

Canfield, Jack; Mark Victor Hansen and Heather McNamara. *Chicken Soup for the Unsinkable Soul: 101 Stories.* (Deerfield Beach: Health Communications, Inc., 1999.)

Dodd, Pamela and Doug Sundheim. *The 25 Best Time Management Tools and Techniques: How to get More Done without Driving Yourself Crazy.* (Omaha: Peak Performance Press, 2005.)

Donoghue, Paul and Mary Siegel. *Are You Really Listening?: Keys to Successful Communication.* (Notre Dame: Ave Maria Press, 2005.)

Foli, Karen and John Thomson. *Post-Adoption Blues: Overcoming the Unforeseen Challenges of Adoption.* (Emmaus: Rodale Books, 2004.)

Gottman, John and Nan Silver. *The Seven Principles for Making Marriage Work.* (London: Orion, 2004.)

Gottman, John. *The Relationship Cure: A 5 Step Guide to Strengthening Your Marriage, Family and Friendships.* (New York: Three Rivers Press, 2001.)

Grillo Linda; Dee Meaney and Christine Rich. *In Their Own Words: Reflections on Parenting Children with Mental Health Issues.* (Boston: Adoptive Families Together, 2003.)

Gyoerkoe, Kevin and Pamela Wiegartz. *10 Simple Solutions to Worry: How to Calm Your Mind, Relax Your Body and Reclaim Your Life.* (Oakland: New Harbinger Publications, 2006.)

Jarratt, Claudia Jewett. *Helping Children Cope with Separation and Loss.* (Boston: Harvard Common Press, 1994.)

Klein, Art and Brook Noel. *The Single Parent Resource.* (Naperville: Sourcebooks, Inc., 2005.)

Kübler-Ross, Elisabeth and David Kessler. *On Grief and Grieving: Finding the Meaning of Grief through the Five Stages of Loss.* (New York: Scribner, 2005.)

Leyden-Rubenstein, Lori. *The Stress Management Handbook: Strategies for Health and Inner Peace.* (New Canaan: Keats Publishing, 1998.)

Maultsby, Maxie. *Coping Better, Anytime, Anywhere. The New Handbook of Rational Self Counseling.* (Bloomington: Rational Self-Help Books, 1986.)

McKay, Gary and Don Dinkmeyer. *How You Feel is Up to You: The Power of Emotional Choice.* (Atascadero: Impact Publishers, 2002.)

Robinson, Duke. *Too Nice for Your Own Good: How to Stop Making 9 Self-Sabotaging Mistakes.* (New York: Warner Books, 1997.)

Schweibert Pat; Chuck DeKlyen and Taylor Bills. *Tear Soup.* (Portland: Grief Watch, 2005.)

Siegel, Daniel. *The Mindful Brain: Reflection and Attunement in the Cultivation of Well-Being.* (New York: W.W. Norton and Co., 2007.)

Smith, Manuel. *When I Say No, I Feel Guilty.* (New York: Bantam Books, 1975.)

Sparks, Nicholas and Micah Sparks. *Three Weeks with My Brother.* (New York: Warner Books, 2004.) This is an autobiographical story of two brothers spending three weeks together traveling. It is actually a wonderful tale of their journey and of grief.

Trozzi, Maria and Kathy Massimini. *Talking with Children about Loss: Words, Strategies and Wisdom to Help Children Cope with Death, Divorce and Other Difficult Times.* (New York: Berkley Publishing Group, 1999.)

Wesselmann, Debra. *The Whole Parent: How to Become a Terrific Parent Even if You Didn't Have One.* (Cambridge: De Capo Press, 1998.)

Wheeler, Claire Michaels. *10 Simple Solutions to Stress: How to Tame Tension and Start Enjoying Your Life.* (Oakland: New Harbinger Publications, 2007.)

Whitten, Kathleen. *Labor of the Heart: A Parent's Guide to the Decisions and Emotions in Adoption.* (New York: M. Evans and Company, 2008.)

Websites

Grief Watch
www.griefwatch.com

The Grief Watch offers spiritual, emotional and other support to persons who are grieving. This website contains a large number of articles about grief of children, teens and adults. There is an extensive array of links related to infertility support. Grief Watch and its companion program, Perinatal Loss, also publish books, videotapes, audiotapes and other helpful resources aimed at persons who have suffered loss.

The Gottman Institute
www.gottman.com

The Gottman Institute provides practical, research-based tools to strengthen and repair marriages and relationships. Also, in-home training packages are available for any clinicians interested in honing the skills necessary to work with couples.

HelpGuide
www.helpguide.org

Helpguide was created in 1999 by the Rotary Club of Santa Monica with active participation by Rotarians Robert and Jeanne Segal following the tragic suicide of their daughter, Morgan. Since then, a dedicated team of talented people have collaborated to create a free, non-commercial resource for people in need. Topics include improving relationships, grief and loss resolution, living healthy, stress management, raising emotional intelligence, increasing humor and laughter and much, much more! This is a wonderful website to help any family restore harmony and balance.

MindTools
www.mindtools.com

MindTools covers information pertaining to problem-solving skills, time management, communication skills and stress management. Adults who need to fine tune skills in any of these areas will find cutting edge information and solutions.

Prevention
www.prevention.com/

Many readers are aware that *Prevention* is the #1 healthy lifestyle magazine. We look to this magazine to improve our physical well-being. Additionally, the Prevention website has a large segment regarding enhancing caregiver roles, as well as adult and parent-child relationships. *Prevention* is able to assist with improving any aspect of family life.

Single Parent Adoption Network (SPAN)
members.aol.com/Onemomfor2

SPAN is a group of single adoptive parents who have joined together to provide support, recreation and friendship for single adoptive parents and children of single adoptive parents. SPAN encourages single persons involved in (or considering) the pre-adoption process to contact their group for support and information regarding adoption. The website is designed to provide access to information and resources that will assist single adoptive parents and parents-to-be in parenting their children.

Developmental Issues

Books

Brodzinsky, David; Marshall Schecter and Robin Marantz Henig. *Being Adopted: The Lifelong Search for Self*. (New York: Anchor Books, 1993.)

Canfield, Jack; Mark Victor Hansen and Kimberly Kirberger. *Chicken Soup for the Teenage Soul on Tough Stuff: Stories of Tough Times and Lessons Learned.* (Deerfield Beach: Health Communications, Inc., 2001.)

Eldridge, Sherrie. *Twenty Life Transforming Choices Adoptees Need to Make*. (Colorado Springs: NavPress, 2003.)

Eldridge, Sherrie. *Twenty Things Adopted Kids Wish Their Adoptive Parents Knew*. (Colorado Springs: NavPress, 1999.)

Keck, Gregory. *Parenting Adopted Adolescents: Understanding and Appreciating their Journey*. (Colorado Springs: NavPress, 2009.)

Lifton, Betty Jean. *Journey of the Adopted Self: A Quest for Wholeness*. (New York: Basic Books, 1994.)

Pavao, Joyce Maguire. *The Family of Adoption*. (Boston: Beacon Press, 2005.)

Riley, Debbie and John Meeks. *Beneath the Mask: Understanding Adopted Teens*. (Silver Spring: C.A.S.E., 2005.)

Schooler, Jayne E. and Thomas C. Atwood. *Whole Life Adoption Book*. (Colorado Springs: NavPress, 1993, revised 2008.)

Websites

New York State Citizens' Coalition for Children
www.nysccc.org/

Incorporated in 1975, the Coalition is an advocacy organization of concerned citizens, and nearly 140 volunteer adoptive and foster parent groups in every region of New York State. The Coalition is concerned primarily with system-change advocacy, and individuals taking responsibility for influencing and changing the systems affecting their lives and the lives of their children. This organization sponsors an excellent annual conference. The website is packed with articles about all aspects of adoption, including the developmental stages covered in this chapter.

Inspirational Personal Accounts

Baker, Randall. *Adopting Eldar: Joy, Tragedy and Red Tape: A Unique International Adoption*. (Bloomington: AuthorHouse, 2005.)

Berlin, Peter. *A Personal Touch On . . . Adoption*. (Los Angeles: A Personal Touch Publishing, 2005.)

Canfield, Jack; Mark Victor Hansen and LeAnn Thieman. *Chicken Soup for the Adopted Soul: Stories Celebrating Adoptive Families*. (Deerfield Beach: Health Communications, 2008.)

Cooke, Janis. *The Russian Word for Snow: A True Story of Adoption*. (New York: St. Martin's Press, 2001.)

Desetta, Al (editor) and Youth Communications. *The Heart Knows Something Different: Teenage Voices from the Foster Care System*. (New York: Persea Books, 1996.)

Dorow, Sara. *I Wish for You A Beautiful Life: Letters from Korean Birthmothers of Ae Ran Won to their Children*. (St. Paul: Yeong and Yeong Book Company, 1999.)

Fisher, Antwone, Q. and Mim E. Rivas. *Finding Fish: A Memoir*. (New York: Harper Torch, 2002.)

Harrison, Kathy. *Another Place at the Table*. (New York: Jeremy P. Tarcher/Putnam, 2003.)

Harrison, Kathy. *One Small Boat: The Story of a Little Girl, Lost then Found*. (New York: Jeremy P. Tarcher/Putnam, 2006.)

Hochstetler, John. *Journey of Hope: Stories Written by Parents Who have Traveled the Way of Adoption*. (Freedom, Indiana: Nathan Lehman, 2006.)

Jackson, Janet Alston. *A Cry for Light: A Journey into Love*. (Los Angeles: Self-Awareness Trainings, 2005.)

Laws, Rita. *This Explains a Lot: A Family's Funny Profile*. (Hackensack: Presbyopian Press, 2008.)

Loux, Ann Kimble. *The Limits of Hope: An Adoptive Mother's Story*. (Charlottsville: The University Press of Virgina, 1997.)

Maskew, Trish. *Our Own: Adopting and Parenting the Older Child*. (Morton Grove: Snowcap Press, 2003.)

McLain, Paula. *Like Family: Growing up in Other People's Houses, a Memoir*. (New York: Back Bay Books, 2004.)

Miniter, Richard. *The Things I Wanted Most: The Extraordinary Story of a Boy's Journey to a Family of His Own*. (New York: Bantam Books, 1998.)

Parent, Marc. *Turning Stones: My Days and Nights with Children at Risk: A Caseworker's Story*. (New York: Ballantine Books, 1998.)

Rhodes-Courter, Ashley. *Three Little Words*. (New York: Simon and Schuster, 2008.)

Roche, Nancy McGuire. *Adoption is Another Word for Love*. (White Plains: Peter Pauper Press, 2000.)

Silber, Kathleen and Phylis Speedling. *Dear Birthmother*. (San Antonio: Corona Publishing, 1982.)

Clinical Books for Professionals

Blum, Deborah. *Love at Goon Park: Harry Harlow and the Science of Affection*. (Cambridge: Perseus Publishing, 2002.)

Briere, John and Catherine Scott. *Principles of Trauma Therapy: A Guide to Symptoms, Evaluation and Treatment*. (Thousand Oaks: Sage Publications, 2006.)

Cicirelli, Victor. *Sibling Relationships Across the Life Span*. (New York, Plenum Press, 1995).

Fosha, Diana. *The Transforming Power of Affect: A Model for Accelerated Change*. (New York: Basic Books, 2000.)

Herman, Judith Lewis. *Trauma and Recovery: From Domestic Abuse to Political Terror*. (London: Pandora, 2001.)

Hughes, Daniel. *Attachment-Focused Family Therapy*. (New York: W.W. Norton and Co., 2007.)

Karen, Robert. *Becoming Attached: First Relationships and How They Shape Our Capacity to Love*. (New York: Oxford University Press, 1994.)

Lefley, Harriet and Mona Wasow. *Helping Families Cope with Mental Illness*. (Chur, Switzerland: Harwood Academic Publishers, 1994.)

Malchiodi, Cathy. *Creative Interventions with Traumatized Children*. (New York: The Guilford Press, 2008.)

Scaer, Robert. *The Trauma Spectrum: Hidden Wounds and Human Resiliency*. (New York: W.W. Norton and Co., 2005.)

van der Kolk, Bessel; Alexander McFarlane and Lars Weisaeth. *Traumatic Stress: The Effects of Overwhelming Experience on Mind, Body and Society*. (Editors) (New York: Guilford Press, 2007.)

CHAPTER NINE

Mobilization: Becoming a "New and Different" Family—Part I

We have finally reached the first of two chapters that will offer ways for the family to move into the stage of *mobilization*—the state of finding a balance between meeting the unique needs of all members of the family: the adoptee with mental health issues, the brothers and sisters, and yourselves—the parents. Mobilization follows the Honeymoon, Ambivalence, Hoping and Learning, and Immobilization stages described in Chapter 8.

Mobilization requires alleviating the dynamics we learned about in Chapter 8. In so doing, we will repair to the extent possible the impact of trauma experienced by each member of the adoptive family—parents, the birth and/or previously adopted children, and the adoptee. Families with mild to severe issues will find solutions for navigating relationships within their family systems.

The solutions are divided into seven parts. Six of these sections cover the healthy counterparts to those unhealthy dynamics identified in Chapter 8. The seventh section discusses positives. Reflecting on the positives is hard some days. Yet, being able to see positives contributes to mobilization.

So in this chapter, Chapter 9, we will cover

- Developing Realistic Expectations: Achieving Cognitive Consonance
- Acquiring New and Effective Coping Skills
- Weathering the Storm: Creating and Maintaining a Healthy Emotional Climate
- Setting Priorities: A Plan Emerges

Chapter 10 will include the topics

- Coming Ashore: Letting Grief Flow
- Finding Oases: Creating Support
- On a Positive Note: (Yes, There Are Positives!)

Both solution chapters will also respond to the most commonly asked question by adoptive families who parent both typically developing and mentally ill children, "What can we do to promote the well-being of all of our children?" Along our journey, thoughts will be provided regarding other commonly asked questions as well.

- Will I love my adoptive child as much as a birth child?
- How do we prioritize all of the needs in our family?
- What is success?

Throughout this chapter and Chapter 10, we'll see examples of the skills Chapter 3 covered at work—effecting positive changes in the family's well-being. We'll revisit some of the families we've met along the way and we'll meet some new folks. These veteran family guides will help plot the route to mobilization. Success stories will rejuvenate and inspire weary travelers as does beautiful scenery.

The end of the trip will be a re-construction of the family dynamics—mobilization—a "new and different" family. "New and different" isn't "bad" and it doesn't mean that we are "quitting." *It does, however, mean that change will occur.* Change is often difficult. As humans we prefer routine. *Yet, change is essential in mobilization and in order to help children change, parents must take the first steps.*

As pointed out in the closing to Chapter 8, parents set the tone in their family. Children will follow the parents' lead. This is our parent-centered and child-focused approach. Parents are the most important people in the family. Taking care of parents is the best means of rebuilding the entire family and keeping it healthy. Thus, this chapter is laid out with parents first and foremost in mind. Certainly, there are specific tools provided to help each child in the family too. However, if parents are worn out, grief stricken, engaging in continuous conflict and lacking support, they will not be in a position to use the suggestions effectively. So, please take the ideas given to parents to care for themselves under serious consideration.

As we get started, let's keep the following things in mind regarding solutions:

- There are no "one size fits all families" solutions. Each adoptive family is unique. Parents must think carefully about proposed solutions, and implement those that make sense and that are safe for their particular family. Frequently, it takes more than one intervention to achieve success in a selected area. We must try different approaches to accomplish mobilization.
- There is no one "magic moment." There is no one solution that will transform the adoptee and so cause a change large enough to restore the family to "normal." There must be a gradual shedding of the family that existed prior to the adoption, so that a new and different family will emerge.
- There are sometimes no ideal solutions. Often, we must break a goal into parts, and then work, piece by piece, until we reach our goal. Review the solutions presented in this chapter carefully. Don't leave the rest stop with no ice cream because they didn't have butter pecan—settle for chocolate or vanilla fudge if it will help to make a positive change.
- The road to mobilization is usually not smooth. There will be bumps, speed traps, potholes, roadblocks and falling rocks! Overall, mobilization means taking four step 3 forward and then three steps back, then another several steps forward and a few steps back. The long-term picture is that good periods become longer, and negative periods or times of crisis are shorter and occur less frequently.
- Solutions often require making lifestyle changes. If you want to lose weight and keep it off permanently, you must alter the amount and types of food you eat and the exercise you are getting from this point forward, throughout your lifetime. Healing an adoptive family requires a similar approach. This chapter will ask you to make enduring changes in the way you view and carry out discipline and family fun. You will be challenged to alter your perceptions and expectations about success, love, fun, time-management, discipline, commitment, support and so on—on an ongoing basis.
- The road to mobilization may not be short. Solutions require prioritizing. Altering one or two things at a time is more effective than attempting sudden sweeping changes. This takes us back to a point made earlier in this book about New Year's resolutions. It is usually hard to carry out one single resolution. ("I will exercise more." "I will visit my relatives more frequently." "I will join a book club.") This being so, failure is almost guaranteed when we attempt several areas of change

simultaneously. ("I will diet, exercise, read one book per month and spend more time with friends.") It is the rare individual who is able to change two, three, four or more areas of her life from January to December!

- Mobilization operates the same way as does the New Year's resolution. We want to target the one or two areas that cause the greatest source of difficulties for the family and then gradually make the changes necessary in these areas to navigate improved relationships between parents, brothers and sisters, and the adoptee.
- Then, we can move on to other areas of concern. Depending on the state of your family at the time you begin implementing changes, arriving at mobilization may be a process that takes several years. Even after the initial recovery, maintaining mobilization may require tune-ups at regular intervals. However, as with anything, the sooner we get started, the sooner we will reach our destination.

Mirror, Mirror on the Wall

Let's start out on our journey to mobilization with a positive example of a family well into their trip. The mother and son writings below will inspire, give hope and generate some momentum. The writings will exemplify the very important point of how parents influence their children's perceptions of the family. In essence, there is a mirroring of the mother's (Gail's) and son's (George's) perspectives. However, also notice Gail's references to her husband, Don. This is a couple who work together—complement each other—in order to navigate healthy relationships in their family. A discussion follows their entries.

Gail, the adoptive mother, writes . . .

"Our daughter, Betty, was adopted at 11 months of age. She is now 7 years old. We involved our three birth sons, then 11, 8 and 5, and now 18, 15 and 11, in all of the phases of the planning, from meeting with the social worker for our home study to buying clothing and supplies for the little one. We talked a lot about our new addition, including the possibility that she would need extra time and attention. I expected my sons to accept her just as they accepted each other when the younger ones were born. They did accept her and allowed her to slip right into our family as if she had been there since birth. Because she was so young, I think it was easy for her to assimilate into the family. Her 'issues' became more apparent as she got older.

"I think that having adopted a child who has special needs, attachment difficulties, Post-traumatic Stress Disorder, and difficulties with attention and impulsivity has allowed me to truly appreciate my healthy children. Perhaps in the past I took for granted how easily things came to them—everything from relationships to sports to academics. Now, watching my daughter struggle in so many areas of her life, I have a new appreciation for things that my healthy children do so effortlessly. They have always been polite, well-behaved, and obedient children and I did not appreciate that until I encountered the absolute opposite with Betty. I am thankful every day that they are blessed with these gifts.

"No amount of reading or research can prepare you for the experience of adopting a child whose special needs are extreme. I read numerous books, was a member of various on line listserves, and still felt unprepared as our daughter's issues began to emerge [*There is a difference between education and experience as Chapter 1 pointed out.*]. Bringing a child such as this into a household of typical, healthy children is especially challenging. There is a constant struggle to maintain a balance between normal family life and succumbing to Betty's needs. In our family, this balance (or lack of balance at times) plagues me. I wrestle daily with the needs of the traumatized child versus the needs of the typical children. I want very badly for my healthy children to have a 'normal' childhood without the burdens of the special needs child. And yet, I know that this is not entirely possible. And so, we compromise. There are times in our family when we include Betty in outings when she has not earned the privilege to go, or when we know it will prove over-stimulating for her, simply because it is good for the rest of the family.

"In many ways, I know that our sons' childhoods would have been less complicated without the strain of Betty. It is difficult to make plans with extended family members or friends who don't 'get it.' It is difficult to have friends come to the house. Often, if our typical children invite friends to the house I make sure that our daughter is not allowed anywhere near them and their friends. We avoid some of these situations by getting together with friends at the movies, a bowling alley or a restaurant, rather than inviting friends to our home. In these situations, one parent takes the typical children out to meet friends while the other stays home with our daughter.

"On the other hand, I think my healthy children have benefited from having a special needs sibling. They are far more tolerant and compassionate towards others with difficulties than I believe they would have been without this experience. They are more likely to speak up kindly on behalf of a person with special needs. They are incredibly patient and they are our daughter's greatest cheerleaders and coaches. In many ways, this experience has been a positive influence on their morals and values. The two oldest, who are teenagers, volunteered their time at a camp for children with special needs last summer. And our oldest son, who will graduate from high school this year, is planning a career as a child psychiatrist or pediatric neurologist so that he can help children like his sister. I think, too, that they all have a greater appreciation for their own gifts and abilities after watching her work so hard to do what many of us take for granted.

"There is most definitely a sense of loneliness and frustration that can accompany raising a child with mental health issues. Few people (even family members) really 'get it.' They try to tell us that 'Our Johnny threw tantrums when he was small, and look at him now. He's a freshman at Harvard.' Well, I'm betting that little Johnny did not tantrum for two hours at a time. Or, scratch and kick his parents as though they were the enemy. In addition, we have family members who don't understand why our daughter cannot accompany us to all family functions. They will tell us that we HAVE to bring her because it just won't be Christmas without her. 'She'll be fine,' they insist. They don't understand the stress that it places on her and the negative behavior that may result. In addition, they don't understand the stress that this places on the parents. It is no fun to attend a family function if you are constantly wondering how long it will be until your little darling lashes out at a younger cousin or breaks something valuable. Family members need to be aware that it is better for her and for us if she doesn't attend. No one wins if she shows up and makes a scene. When family members insist that 'She's fine.' or, 'She'll be fine,' it makes me angry. It feels as if they are minimizing how difficult she is. As a result of their lack of understanding, we spend less time with them. In the end, I have chosen to do what is best for my daughter and have decided that if they cannot accept that not all of us will attend family functions, then they will see less of all of us.

"Sacrifice—there's a lot of it involved in dealing with a child with special needs. Over the course of the nearly six years that our Betty has been home, many of my friends have fallen by the wayside. They don't understand the restrictions that having a child like our daughter can place on a family. I am fortunate to have a few friends who understand my daughter's issues and accept us as we are. Certainly I don't have as many friends as I once had, but the ones who have stuck with me are true blessings. In deciding to home school our daughter, I sacrificed my free time. I would have had time without her when I might have exercised, volunteered at one of my sons' schools, read a book, gotten something done around the house, worked at a part-time job, or enjoyed a hobby. The decision to home school her has been the right one, but it did come at a price.

"Having a child with emotional and behavioral issues can cause one to question one's ability to parent. I often find myself wondering what I'm doing wrong and what else I should be doing to help her to heal. I feel fortunate to have three healthy children who are well-behaved, great students, and genuinely nice young people. I can look at them and see that Don and I are raising some pretty good kids. It reassures me that I am, in fact, a good parent and that it's not me who has the problem! I have often thought that it would be far more difficult to parent my daughter if I did not have my healthy children to remind me that I am a good parent.

"There is no one on this earth who has managed to make me as angry as Betty can make me. There are times when I actually need to put myself in 'time out' and take a break from her so that I don't let her see how much she has angered me. I know that if she realizes that she has angered me, she will 'win.' So often her goal is just to upset me. If she knows that she has succeeded, then she has the upper hand and I appear weak to her. This is when I get my book of Sudoku puzzles and retreat to a comfortable chair for a few minutes.

"She also elicits feelings of great protectiveness in me. I am upset when other children make fun of her or other parents ignore her. She had a difficult start in this life and I feel as if I need to protect her from further harm.

"I often feel frustrated that Betty can't just love us and accept us. I want her to 'get it.' While it is heartwarming to know that I am making a difference in the life of a child, there are days when she drives me crazy.

"Some strategies we use to cope:

- Don usually takes over our daughter for a couple of hours in the evening so that I can get a break from her.
- Don and I alternate Friday nights out with our healthy children—sometimes a sports event, sometimes just out for pizza.
- On rare occasions, we ask one of our teenage sons to watch our daughter so that my husband and I can get out for dinner or a movie or to go together to one of the boys' school events. We try not to ask them to watch her for extended periods as she is so challenging, but they do well for short periods. We also try not to over-burden them with watching her and we always pay them for outings such as these.
- We encourage our healthy children to participate in things that they enjoy—sports, music, etc. and then do everything that we can to support them in those activities. Sometimes this means that our daughter spends a great deal of time riding with her brothers to soccer practices and games, but that's our way of achieving balance for them.
- We encourage the boys to get away from her when she's making them crazy. We are fortunate to have a rather large house, so it is possible for them to physically get away. At those times, I will not allow her to bother them when they retreat to the game room to play video games or watch a football game on TV. They need their space, and my husband and I do our best to provide it.

"Don and I worry about what the future holds for our daughter. Will she be able to live independently? Will she have secure relationships as an adult? Will she even graduate from high school and be able to hold down a job? If something would happen to us, we fear that responsibility for her would fall to our sons. We feel very blessed to have close friends who have said that if something happens to my husband and me that they would raise our daughter. They are a couple with three adopted children of their own, two of whom have some mild special needs. This has lifted a great burden, as we know that our sons will not be left with primary responsibility if we both die.

"It is interesting to note that my friends with biological special needs children often feel over-whelmed, frustrated, and as though people don't understand. They also say that nothing could have prepared them for this life. I can relate, and yet, I think I also have an added element of guilt on top of these feelings. As an adoptive parent, I chose to bring this child into our family, knowing that there could be issues and difficulties. There is often some sense of having brought some incredible burden into the lives of my healthy children with this choice. There are thoughts of 'what if?' And yet, always, as I watch the positives unfold, I think that, in spite of the difficulties, we did the right thing."

George is the oldest of Gail and Don's birth sons. George was 11 when Betty joined the family. He is now age 18.

"Our family has definitely been forced to make changes since our sister was adopted. Things certainly changed for me personally, in both positive and negative ways. Betty has forced me to become far more patient and compassionate than I ever would have been without her. Her struggles make witnessing her triumphs even more rewarding than those of a typical child. It is both encouraging and scary to think of where my sister would be if we had not adopted her. Obviously, there are personal difficulties that arise. My parents have to devote much more time and effort into caring for my sister, and consequently, there is less time to spend with my brothers and me. The household hasn't been peaceful in years, but you get used to it. Clearly my sister's behavioral issues do not permit us to participate in many activities in public, but, once again, you tend to forget what life was like before your sibling and learn to accept the way things must be. All of these changes are entirely understandable, and do not detract from the quality of my life or the relationships between members of my family.

"What I did not realize going into the adoption process was what a profound effect my soon-to-be sister would have on my extended family. We are able to visit with my aunts, uncles and grandparents far less than we used to because of my sister. This is not because they are put off by her behavior; they consistently voice their support and stress that they wish to see her. The problem is that as a family, we feel it is unreasonable to subject our relatives to her. They are not prepared to deal with Betty, and do not understand the magnitude of her problems, nor do they appreciate her ability to destroy a perfectly enjoyable family gathering. It is not fair to ask our family to undergo this torment for the sake of politeness. While this isolation is self-inflicted, it is the reality of life with a child with mental health issues.

"I don't think there was anything that could have prepared me or my family for Betty and her needs. It's the kind of thing that is very hard to understand until you see it, and the only way to really learn how to deal with my sister is to live with her day in and day out. Dealing with a child with mental health disorders is a lot like many things; you can read about it all you want, but the real, hands-on experience is the only way you can learn to care for one of these children. No speech or reading can prepare you for the rage, manipulation and defiance these children put up as a guard, and the constant anxiety they experience dealing with everyday situations.

"Betty is a masterful irritator, and she demands to make her presence felt by interrupting whatever you are trying to do. The only way to cope with this is to escape; to read a book or watch TV in another room for awhile. Her presence is always much more enjoyable after you haven't seen her for a while. Unfortunately, these breaks are few and far between for my mom!"

GAIL AND GEORGE'S LIFE WITH BETTY

Healthy Family Dynamics	Gail	George
Developing Realistic Expectations: Achieving Cognitive Consonance	• The family felt prepared prior to Betty's adoption. Post-adoption they decided, "No amount of reading or research can prepare you for the experience of adopting a child whose special needs are extreme." • This family has come to accept that their family is now different as a result of Betty's needs and so they have learned to "compromise." • Gail and her husband acknowledge that "balance" is a struggle, yet they have found many ways to work toward healing Betty while simultaneously meeting the needs of their other children. They also work to find ways to meet some of their own needs as individuals and as a couple.	• "I don't think there is anything that could have prepared me or my family for my sister and her needs. • "You get used to it." • "You tend to forget what life was like before your sibling and learn to accept the way things must be." • "All of these changes are entirely understandable."
New and Effective Coping Skills	• "We encourage the boys to get away from her when she's making them crazy. We are fortunate to have a rather large house, so it is possible for them to physically get away. At those times, I will not allow her to bother them. They need their space, and my husband and I do our best to provide it." • "We encourage our healthy children to participate in things that they enjoy." • "Don usually takes over our daughter for a couple of hours in the evening so that I can get a break from her." • "My husband and I alternate Friday nights out with our healthy children—sometimes a sports event, sometimes just out for pizza." • "On rare occasions, we ask one of our teenage sons to watch our daughter so that my husband and I can get out for dinner or a movie or to go together to one of the boys' school events."	• Read. • Watch television. • Go in another room for awhile.

GAIL AND GEORGE'S LIFE WITH BETTY *(Continued)*

Healthy Family Dynamics	Gail	George
Weathering the Storm: Creating and Maintaining a Positive Emotional Climate	• Anger—"There is no one on this earth who has managed to make me as angry as my daughter can make me." Recognizes when these feelings are intense and then takes a break—"I put myself in 'time-out.'" • Works to maintain a positive emotional climate.	• "Escapes" when irritated and then returns (rather than remaining withdrawn) to "enjoy" his sister. Like his mother, he recognizes when his feelings are overwhelming. He takes breaks. This contributes to a positive emotional climate within the family.
Finding Oases: Creating Support	• Support comes from within the family. Gail and husband alternate care giving of Betty. Gail and Don alternate outings with their sons. This couple works together. • This family has identified a guardian for Betty in the event this is necessary. • Gail notes that she does have a "few friends."	• "Breaks for my mom are few and far between." George demonstrates empathy and compassion—support—for the responsibilities of his mother. • Parents support his friendships and extracurricular activities to a high degree.
Coming Ashore: Letting Grief Flow This includes acknowledging losses and feelings.	*Acknowledges losses:* • Extended family and friends—"few people really get it." • Time with her sons. • Free time for herself. • Inviting sons' friends over to the house as frequently as the family would like. • Outings as an entire family. • "Normal" childhood for her sons.	*Acknowledges losses:* • Extended family—"We are able to visit with my aunts, uncles and grandparents far less than we used to because of my sister." • "My parents have to devote much more time and effort into caring for my sister. There is less time to spend with my brothers and me."

GAIL AND GEORGE'S LIFE WITH BETTY *(Continued)*

Healthy Family Dynamics	Gail	George
	• The person Betty could become—"I want her to 'get it' (accept our love)." *Acknowledges feelings:* • Anger—"There is no one on this earth who has managed to make me as angry as my daughter can make me." • Feelings of great protectiveness—"I am upset when other children make fun of her or other parents ignore her." • Joy—"I am thankful every day that they (sons) are blessed with their gifts." Joy for her sons' accomplishments. • "There is most definitely a sense of *loneliness and frustration* that can accompany raising a child with special needs." • Sadness for losses. • "My husband and I *worry* about what the future holds for our daughter." • "I think I have an added element of *guilt* on top of these feelings. I chose to bring this child into our family, knowing that there could be issues."	• "My sister's behavioral issues do not permit us to participate in many activities in public." • "The household hasn't been as peaceful in years." *Acknowledges feelings:* • Anger/frustration/irritation—"My sister is a master manipulator, and she demands to make her presence felt by interrupting whatever you are trying to do." • Sadness for losses. • George feels free to express his feelings.
On a Positive Note	• Instilled patience, tolerance and compassion in her sons. • Influenced her sons' values and morals. • George is currently making plans to enter college. His goal is to become a neurologist or a child psychiatrist. He wants to help other families that include children with special needs. • "I think that, in spite of the difficulties, we did the right thing."	• Patience. • Tolerance. • Volunteered at a camp for children with special needs—compassion and a desire to help others. • Influenced career choice. • "It is both encouraging and scary to think of where my sister would be if we had not adopted her."

Comparing Gail's and George's accounts of life with Betty reveals that they mirror each other in numerous ways. We also see that this family has mobilized in each of the healthy dynamics we will be looking at in this chapter and in Chapter 10.

Certainly, this family still has struggles, and Betty's special needs are not all healed. Yet, Gail and Don have created an atmosphere within their family that is positive, allows free expression, is empathic, reflects well-thought out priorities, values communication, and demonstrates commitment to and on the part of each family member. George and his brothers have followed suit. They have internalized their parents' attitudes toward having a family member with mental health issues. They have followed their parents' lead in coping, adjusting expectations, acknowledging their losses and expressing their feelings for the changes Betty has brought to the family. As such, Gail, Don, George and his brothers, and Betty are each able to live in a manner that is enriching and allows for enjoyment. Each member of this family can experience growth and movement forward. Your family can too!

Now that we are encouraged by one family's success, let's take each healthy family dynamic in turn and learn how your family can get mobilized!

The Road to Mobilization: Navigating the Route to Healthy Family Relationships

Developing Realistic Expectations: Achieving Cognitive Consonance

We have examined expectations throughout this book. We have looked at the individual expectations of parents, the children already in the family at the time of the adoption and the adoptee. We have learned about other layers of expectations as well—involving partners, extended family, friends, professionals, the community at large, family of origin issues, spiritual concerns, etc. We have concluded that expectations abound.

We have also learned that expectations and reality clash and create cognitive dissonance. Resolving the cognitive dissonance—achieving cognitive consonance—helps the adoptive family move from being stuck in a pattern of *fixing* the adoptee so that he or she may fit into the existing family system in the manner desired to *accepting* that the addition of the adoptee has altered the family.

In order to accept the new and different family created by being a family built by adoption, each member of the family—parents, brothers and sisters and the adoptee—must be helped to develop realistic expectations.

Taking Stock: What Are the Expectations?

A first step in revising expectations is to identify the expectations already operating. In essence there needs to be a "taking stock" of what parents, siblings and the adoptee expect of themselves, each other and those around them. In Chapters 1 and 8, it was suggested that you make a list of your expectations as you read this book. If you didn't do this, take some time and think about your expectations now. Read Chapters 1 and 8 again if you need to. Sit with your typically developing children and list their expectations as well. Children as young as 5 can talk about their expectations with help from a parent.

Now that you have compiled your expectations and those of your birth and/or previously adopted children, let's revisit parents Luke and Molly from Chapter 3.

Molly stated (*expected*), "I thought once we had children he (Luke) would be home." Molly spoke about this in reference to the fact that Luke's career change to the ministry required that he work three evenings per week. Her expectation of a family is two parents home in the evening helping children with homework, attending sporting events, playing games, watching movies, etc. This expectation developed as a result of her family of origin's dysfunction. Molly's father was an alcoholic. Molly spent much of her childhood in her bedroom, listening to her parents fight about her father's alcoholism. Confined to her room as a child, she imagined that when she became a parent and wife, her own family would be more enjoyable, close, peaceful, happy, and so on. When Molly felt that Luke was not helping her fulfill this expectation, Molly began to threaten that she would leave their marriage.

On top of this, Molly is fearful that their son Brett will lose such control of himself that she will not be able to prevent him from injuring his siblings, Katelyn and Derrick, or herself. Her original expectations about parenting did not include having to deal with a son who is aggressive, screams and uses profanity. When she exhausted the parenting interventions she knew and Brett's behavior continued, she began feeling as if she was a failure as a parent. Her self-confidence as a parent and a person were undermined to the point that she wasn't even sure she could manage her children alone. She blamed herself for Brett's lack of progress. She also felt, "If I was a better parent, Derrick, Brett and Katelyn could get along better." The parent she expected to be contradicted the parent she believed herself to be.

Identifying Molly's expectations based on what we know about Molly, we can list these:

Molly expected a partner to be home each evening co-parenting—she expected a fully united and cohesive parenting team.

Molly expected a "happy and peaceful" home full of fun. She had created an ideal image of a family due to her childhood experiences. Molly expected to have the family she didn't have as a child. She expected a partner who would help her develop the family she desired.

Molly expects home to be a place of safety. Brett's aggression, in particular, confounds this expectation totally. Most parents are quite taken aback by a child who hits and kicks them. Such behavior is not expected. Likely, the majority of us never even considered hitting our parents.

Molly expected that parenting interventions effective with appropriately-developing children would heal Brett—a child with a history of complex trauma.

Molly expected that her children would develop close and positive relationships.

Obviously, in spending more time with Molly, this list would expand—significantly. Again, expectations abound. Identifying expectations, as Molly exemplifies, requires a thorough review of one's childhood and current experiences. It is a process which takes time. It is a process that can be emotionally painful—so give yourself time.

Molly's expectations are taking a toll on her marriage and herself. Rather than leaving her marriage or continuing to feel like a bad parent, Molly can change her expectations.

Evaluating: Are the Expectations Realistic?

Key Point—Developing realistic expectations is an effective means for each member of the family to navigate closer relationships. Parents, brothers and sisters, and the adoptee must identify and evaluate their expectations of themselves, each other and those around them. Appropriate expectations may be facilitated by reflection, recognizing accomplishments, education, family meetings, and the lifebook.

Once the family members' expectations are identified, each must be evaluated. Again, as we learned, our experiences collide with expectations, creating a dissonance between what we *see* happening and what we *believe* should be happening. Experiences must be reviewed in relation to expectations. Then we must ask if our expectations are realistic, accurate, truthful, reasonable, can be fulfilled and so forth—we must draw conclusions.

> Continuing with Molly as our example, her experience of herself as a parent is that she feels incapable of managing her children alone. This assessment is based on the fact that Brett continues to have temper outbursts in spite of the parents' utilizing an array of consequences. Molly must examine her parenting experiences and ask herself,
>
> "Are my perceptions accurate?"
>
> "Am I actually powerless to manage my own children?"

In fact, there is nothing wrong with Molly's parenting. It is Brett's mental health issues that render her parenting strategies ineffective. In Chapter 8, we acknowledged that parenting children with mental health issues requires a new toolbox of techniques.

A useful format for examining expectations follows, using Molly's family's situation as an example.

Expectation: Molly thinks, "I am a capable parent able to manage my children. I know how to utilize a variety of parenting techniques to correct negative behaviors."

Experience: Brett's temper tantrums persist in spite of an extensive array of parenting interventions. Brett's behavior creates chaos. Family fun is diminished because there is no predicting when Brett might be calm and when he might be screaming and throwing things.

Dissonance: Molly thinks, "I am unable to manage my own child. Brett isn't getting better. I must be doing something wrong."

Consonance: Molly recognizes, "Brett 'isn't getting better' because his psychological issues render my parenting techniques ineffective. There is nothing wrong with my parenting—Katelyn is doing very well. Derrick has mild mental health issues resultant from his pre-adoptive trauma. I can look at him and see slow, steady progress. Overall, I can look at them and realize that I am a good parent."

Conclusion: Molly realizes, "My expectation that I am a good and capable parent is an accurate expectation. However, I need new tools in order to help Brett heal from his past trauma."

Molly must process each of her expectations about Luke, family life and sibling relationships in the same manner as above. Luke must do the same. Molly and Luke also need to work with Derrick and Brett to revise their expectations. Katelyn is age 3 at present. She is too young at this time to participate in this process.

Let's complete two more examples of Molly's self-exploration and then make some points about coming to conclusions.

Example 1:

Expectation: "I expect a happy and peaceful family dominated by fun. Home is a place of safety."

Experience: "My family is almost nothing like I envisioned. I feel alone and scared a lot of the time. My husband is unavailable. Brett calls me names, swears at me and breaks things that have meaning to me. I think he will hurt me, Derrick or Katelyn."

Dissonance: "My family doesn't feel very happy. My home is not a refuge or safe haven."

Consonance: "The family I have includes a child with mental health issues. This means that I may never have the calm and contented family I want. I can have a family with some of the elements I need and wish for. Additionally, my current family cannot make up for past hurts nor is it their job to erase my unpleasant childhood family experiences."

Conclusion: "I need to grieve the loss of the family I thought I would have now, and the loss of the family I wanted as a child. I also need to recognize that Brett may not achieve all that I want—I will most likely need to grieve the loss of the person he could have become. I can certainly still hope and pursue therapies. At the same time, I need to reflect on his abilities and be realistic that he functions much differently than other children his age."

Molly does have a right, however, to expect that Brett will also make changes. He must work toward learning that the use of violence is not acceptable in a family or society. Brett needs to learn new ways to express his anger. So, a part of Molly's expectation is valid—home should be a "safe haven."

Example 2:

Expectation: "Luke should be home evenings with me parenting our children."

Experience: "Luke is at work three evenings per week."

Dissonance: "Luke is not invested in our family. Luke is not helping me create the family I desire."

Consonance: "Luke's position requires evening work. We knew this when he accepted the position. His employment responsibilities remain constant—our family has changed, not his job."

Conclusion: The expectation is faulty. The expectation must change.

In evaluating expectations and experiences, our goal is to draw conclusions. We must decide

- which expectations need to change because they have no rational basis
- which expectations have created losses that need to be grieved
- which expectations need to change because they cannot be fulfilled
- which expectations are valid and can be fulfilled

In Molly's case, her conclusions included that she needed to change her expectation about Luke's availability. This was a result of his job rather than a lack of interest in being with his family. She identified several losses she must grieve—the family she wants now, the family she wanted as a child, the son she expected Brett to be, and the types of sibling relationships she desires between Brett, Derrick and Katelyn. She also discovered that she is a good parent—but that she needs new tools. Brett also needs to make changes. He needs to develop the skills necessary to live in the family in a more peaceful manner.

These conclusions helped Molly improve her entire view of her family. She no longer wanted to leave her marriage. She gained more hope that Brett could change. She located and obtained the services needed to help him. Over time, she and Luke learned new ways to manage Brett. While he continues to have difficulties, the family is not as bogged down by his problems as in the past. Slowly, this family is recovering. "Home" is gradually becoming a safer and happier place!

Molly, as all parents and brothers and sisters, can use several means to carry out the process of developing realistic expectations.

The Means: Developing Realistic Expectations

Reflection

Molly was able to develop realistic expectations simply via having an adoption-competent professional point out her expectations. Many parents and brothers and sisters are able to form new expectations through discussion and reflection. Talk with your spouse and your children, dialogue with an adoption-competent professional or chat with veteran adoptive families—these conversations will help refine expectations, outlook.

Education

Education is a wonderful way to help adjust expectations. The more parents understand their adoptee's mental health issues, the more realistic they can be about their impact on the family. In turn, the better able parents are to help their children accept their traumatized sibling. In Chapter 2, under the heading, "Information Dissemination: Influence on Adjustment," we concluded that how parents handle the dissemination of information about the complex trauma issues of the adoptive child will greatly influence the adjustment of the children already in the family at the time of the adoption. This content also covered ideas about providing information based on the age of the appropriately-developing brother or sister as well as determining the types of information these healthy siblings need.

Penny and Frank, another of our Chapter 3 families, had this to say,

> "We started talking to Scott prior to the adoption about what Marcus and Celeste had been through. We had a very short honeymoon period. Scott was having a hard time understanding why their behaviors were just so off the wall. We reviewed everything we knew about Marcus and Celeste again. He is responsible, and we knew having information would help him in the long run, and it has—he has really benefited from these talks. We explained the types of abuse, physical and sexual, the children had experienced. We helped him understand why this abuse caused them to act so differently. We went into detail. It was a lot for a kid to handle. However, we kept working on it.
>
> "Eventually, Scott figured out that Marcus often tries to agitate him to get his attention because he hasn't learned how to ask for what he needs or wants. The lying and their control issues are about their need to protect themselves. Marcus and Celeste don't trust us yet, so they don't believe we can take care of them and keep them safe. From all of our talks with Scott, he has learned to ignore a lot of their behavior. Often, we hear him say to Marcus, "You don't have to throw things at me to get my attention. You could just ask me if I have time to play with you."
>
> "There are also other things that 'normal' kids do with their siblings. Scott would say to Marcus, "Kiss my butt" and Marcus would have a total meltdown. Scott would feel bad thinking he had done something to so upset his brother like this. Actually, Scott's remark triggered Marcus' anger about his sexual abuse. The temper tantrum was because of the sexual abuse. It was helpful for Scott to know this. We have learned to watch what we say, but this isn't possible or practical all of the time. Marcus has to live in the real world. Marcus has to learn to deal with his sexual abuse. He can't get angry every time somebody says

> something that reminds him of his sexual abuse. Marcus really struggles with this abuse—it is the core of his problems."

Frank and Penny educated themselves and then educated Scott. Scott has been able to understand why his new brother and sister act the way they do, and he has learned to cope effectively with his siblings. The way in which Scott has learned to cope contributes to helping his brother Marcus and his sister Celeste heal. Overall, the manner in which Frank and Penny handle information dissemination has helped their entire family.

A last point that needs to be made regarding education is the issue of privacy. Sharing the adoptee's history with the adoptee or the typically developing children requires helping them realize that the information is private—it should stay in the family. This is not because there should be embarrassment about what happened to the child who experienced trauma, and this is not because there is something "wrong" with or "bad" about the adoptee because of his or her pre-adoptive experiences. It is because the adoptee's history is a private family matter—this is especially true within peer relationships.

> Eric and his sister Rhonda, who we met in Chapter 5, were adopted by Dolores and Rob when they were 10 and 9 respectively. The family acquired therapy shortly after the adoption was finalized and during this course of therapy, Rhonda revealed much sexual abuse. As this abuse was processed, both Eric and Rhonda began to make significant gains in functioning. Rhonda made friends for the first time in her life.
>
> At a sleepover, she told the other girls about the sexual abuse—in detail. These 12-year-old peers had no idea how to react to this news. Some changed the subject and some decided to go to bed early. Rhonda was perplexed. As Rhonda and Dolores were driving home from the sleepover, she told Dolores what had happened. Dolores helped her understand that her friends were only beginning to learn about sexual matters and so they lacked the knowledge to respond to her. She encouraged Rhonda to keep her past private. This talk helped Rhonda rebound from the events of the sleepover quickly.
>
> However, on Monday morning when school resumed, some of her friends were polite but distant. It took several weeks for them to move beyond Rhonda's disclosures and resume their friendship with her. Worse yet, Rhonda's friends shared the information with other friends. In short order, one of Eric's peers started referring to Eric as "gay." Eric's sexual abuse included that his birthmother let men have anal intercourse with Eric in return for payment. Eric was devastated. Over the next few months, his behavior deteriorated. One day in therapy he stated, "Every time I walk down the hall at school, I wonder who knows what happened to me and what they think about me. Every day I see the memories of the sexual abuse in my head. I can't stop thinking about what happened to me now. I feel different from all of the other kids. I don't belong anymore."

Privacy contains an element of control over the information. Privacy allows that children are protected from rude and hurtful remarks, lack of understanding or the pity of others. In Eric's case, this control was lost. Eric was profoundly affected.

We need to help all of the children in the family understand which parts of the adoption story they can share and which should remain private. This is referred to as developing a *cover story*. Parents and children can put together a story that covers the need to provide some information without revealing facts that could prove to hurt the adoptee. Children also need to know that if they are asked questions they don't know how to answer, or that they don't want to answer, they are free to say, "You'll have to ask my mom or dad about that."

Parents may want to check out the *W.I.S.E. Up Powerbook* (see Resources). Designed primarily for kids ages 6 to 12, this book provides children with the tools to handle comments and questions about adoption. *W.I.S.E. Up* gives children, teens and parents the power to choose how to talk about adoption with others.

Review Accomplishments

Reflecting on accomplishments is another means to keep expectations in perspective. Review successes in all spheres of life—education, work, marriage, spirituality, friendships, volunteer activities, hobbies and family—especially note the accomplishments of your resident children who are doing well because of your parenting. Make a list and post it where you will see it frequently. This will help you to maintain a positive, confident sense of self, which is essential when parenting an adoptee who doesn't always respond with affection and respect.

Louise, a parent of five children, two by birth and three by adoption, says,

> "I think a part of the coping is actually knowing that you really are a good person. And if you're not feeling good about that inside, and sometimes the kids can make you not feel so good about that, sit back and think, 'I'm a good person and out of that I'm a good parent too.' And, once you know you are a good person, you can stop second guessing your decisions. The second guessing is what makes you feel like you are out of control and that you can't parent a child with problems, and that the adoption will never work."

It is also important to point out that this issue is applicable to the typically developing children as well. For example, a mom once said to me, "My older healthy daughter has won numerous awards for academic excellence, athletic achievements and community service. They sit on my desk collecting dust. I just can't seem to find the time to hang them up." Shortly after this conversation, she was helped to find respite services for her two adoptees, both of whom had serious mental health issues. This gave her the opportunity to spend time with her daughter framing her awards. A celebratory dinner topped off this mother and daughter day.

In a different scenario, a healthy brother once told me that he felt bad because his brother wasn't getting better. He said, "I have tried so hard to help him, but he just isn't getting better. I just don't know what else I should be doing. I feel like such a bad brother." His parents, shocked, obtained professional assistance to help educate this young man about his brother's issues. His education and subsequent open communication corrected these misperceptions.

We will talk more about positively acknowledging each member of the family in Chapter 10.

Family Meetings

Lena, who we met in Chapter 8, encourages brothers and sisters like this:

> "Keep communication open with your parents. Along through the adoption kids should continue to talk to their parents and tell them how they are feeling, because a lot of times kids won't say anything—then the parents don't know. The parents don't focus on them because they are so focused on the disruptive child, and so kids need to let their parents know at all times what's going on and if they have any questions they always need to talk to their parents about it."

Gabe's parents, Cole and Becky, who we also met in Chapter 3, carry out Lena's advice to "keep communication open" by holding family meetings.

"Before Gabe's adoption we had been told that he had been a failure to thrive baby. At that time, we talked to our daughters, Jennifer, Jessica and Mary, about what he looked like and what it might be like to have a younger brother. However, when we got to Guatemala there was much, much more involved than this failure to thrive. So, in him coming home, we anticipated, because we had previously adopted Mary as a special needs child, that whatever the need was, we could overcome that need. Little did we know that it was a lot of mental health issues that were lying ahead, and that he wasn't going to assume the same role as the other kids did in the family—he wasn't going to blend and adjust as quickly or maybe not at all.

Since the adoption, as we have identified his needs we've had many family meetings about why he eats up so much of our time. Jennifer, Jessica and Mary are well-informed about his diagnoses. We really believe in sitting the kids down and sharing information. We keep telling them that our goal is win-win, and that you're part of this too because you are in the family."

Cole and Becky conduct regular family meetings on the last Wednesday of the month. Gabe goes to his grandmother's for dinner while the rest of the family reviews the month. Topics include feelings, education, progress, ongoing problems, possible solutions as well as a lot of talk about *fairness*!

Jennifer, Jessica and Mary, like most typically developing kids, *expect* their parents to implement discipline fairly.

Expectation: "We expect our parents to consequence each child for the same kinds of behaviors."

Experience: "Gabe seems to get away with a lot more than we do. He lies, steals, won't wear his seatbelt, interrupts conversations, throws fits, calls us names, shouts instead of talks and has terrible table manners. It seems he almost never gets consequences. Mom and Dad would never let us get away with the things Gabe does. Why don't they give him more consequences?"

Dissonance: The previously adopted and/or birth children often think a number of dissonant things regarding this area of discipline:

- "Mom and Dad love him more."
- "Mom and Dad feel sorry for him."
- "Mom and Dad can't manage him."
- "He acts the way he does because Mom and Dad don't do more to stop it."
- "I wish Mom and Dad would send him back."

Consonance: The thinking that needs to be established is that with traumatized children, who exhibit a lengthy list of behavioral difficulties, parents must select only a few behaviors to change at any one time.

Frequently, parents are correcting the adoptee with negative behaviors all day. The end result of this is constant conflict. This situation doesn't benefit anyone, and it meets the adoptee's unconscious need to create distance. Remember that one of his *expectations* is that he will be returning to his birthfamily. In essence, he unconsciously thinks, "If I create a negative emotional climate, I won't attach to you. That way, when I leave I won't be too sad." He is protecting his heart from further emotional pain.

Another of his *expectations* may be, "I am bad and unlovable. My role in the family is to be the 'bad' child." So, when the family argues with him to pick up his clothes, brush his teeth, take a shower, eat with his mouth closed, finish his homework, clean his room, and on and on—day in and day out—in his mind he says, "See, I am bad. I'm always in trouble." The family inadvertently validates the adoptee's expectations when they engage in trying to change too many behaviors at the same time.

Selecting too many behaviors to change at one time is a common *parenting roadblock*. Many more of these roadblocks will be included in this chapter. Parents must prioritize ending a few negative behaviors at a time. This will mean living with various rule violations. To some degree, the adoptee will be "getting away" with behaviors for which the resident children would receive consequences. This is a difficult concept for parents, as well as for brothers and sisters, to accept. Communication and education can help brothers and sisters understand that what is unfair is actually going to contribute to healing their sibling. In the long run, everyone will benefit. This is a good place to reiterate that solutions aren't always ideal.

Further, as we will learn in "Weathering the Storm," the less parents and siblings react to the adoptee's negative behavior, the faster the behavior will cease. Selecting which of those behaviors to end and which to let go (for now) can be a challenge, however. Keep these concepets in mind:

- Behaviors that jeopardize the safety of the adoptee, brothers and sisters, and parents are always selected first to extinguish. Violence is a good example of a behavior in this category.
- Behaviors that lend to long-term impaired functioning of the adoptee are second. Stealing, for example, may lead to incarceration. So, stealing should be a priority.
- After the above two categories are covered, any behavior can be selected, keeping in mind that there are some battles you cannot win. You can most likely ask a child to go to his bedroom. You can't make him sleep. You can make a child do his homework. You cannot make him turn it in. So, in deciding which behaviors to change, have realistic expectations of what you as a parent can and cannot change.

Key Point—Parenting a combination of children with mental health issues and typical development will require parenting each type of child *differently*. Different won't always be fair. If the child had autism, mental challenges or blindness we would make accommodations. We need to do the same for children with mental health issues. In the long run, parenting differently will lend to the overall healing of the adoptee and the entire family will realize an improved atmosphere. So, actually, everybody will win in the long-term picture. The family meeting offers the forum to explain this to the healthy children. Most healthy children do well with this concept as long as they are kept informed.

Key Point—"That's not fair" is a problem in all families. Learning that life isn't always fair is a valuable lesson. However, in adoptive families the inequities are often staggering. Mobilizing an adoptive family means offering solutions that level the inequities to the degree possible. Otherwise, we stand the chance of damaging the emotional well-being of the typically developing siblings. There is no need to damage one child in order to "fix" another.

Colette is the adoptive mother of three children. She and her husband parent Dawn, age 10, and Blake, age 9, who both arrived as infants, and Dennis, age 5, who joined the family at age 3.

> "We have three adopted children. We adopted our first two as 'healthy infants' and our third came to us when he was 3 years old. Our third was identified by his caseworkers as 'only' having some speech delays. In reality, he came to us very traumatized by his early experiences and with serious attachment issues. Our daughter, despite being identified as a healthy infant, has been diagnosed with Fetal Alcohol Syndrome. She has many significant

needs that will last her lifetime. We identify our middle son, Blake, as our healthy child. But, I know that if he had typical siblings to compare him to, he could be identified as having special needs. His diagnoses include Asthma, Reflux, AD/HD and Specific Learning Disabilities. But, in our family, he is the 'normal' one.

"We do parent each child differently and we have very different expectations for each child. This isn't stressful to us. It would be very hard to parent them all the same. Placing the same expectations or rules on each of them would set them all up for failure. We have always parented them according to their individual needs so this is what they expect and they don't complain about it."

Later in the chapter, in the sections "New and Effective Coping Skills" and "Weathering the Storm," and in Chapter 10 in "Finding Oases," we will suggest some ways to offset inequities that occur in adoptive families. These ideas will smooth out the unfairness bumps blocking the route to relationships in the adoptive family.

The Lifebook: Constructing the Adoptee's Narrative

The Benefits of a Narrative

Chapter 2 covered the types of irrational thoughts—expectations—traumatized children develop about themselves, families and the world in general. The lifebook is one of the best ways to help an adoptee recognize and adjust her expectations. The lifebook offers other benefits as well:

- It helps the adoptee make sense of her experiences. Reflecting on experiences and expectations lends to positive changes as we have demonstrated in this chapter.
- It separates fact from fantasy. Facts allow the child to heal. Fantasy perpetuates the adoptee's psychological connection to the birthfamily.
- It enhances attachment. The child psychologically separates from previous caregivers. Thus, she can give herself permission to join her adoptive family.
- It integrates the past, present and future, lending to self-esteem and identity development.
- It brings about behavioral changes. As Chapter 2 explained, behavior is perpetuated by irrational thinking. The narrative alters thoughts and thereby negative behaviors diminish. This point will be exemplified below.
- If facilitates grief for the loss of birthfamily, siblings, foster families, familiar surroundings and items, and traumatic experiences. Grieving allows cognitive, emotional and social development to move forward.
- It identifies positives and negatives about the birthfamily.

The benefits of the lifebook are largely the result of the fact that it contains the child's "story"—a truthful, chronological accounting of the events that led to the need for the child to be adopted. The *story* is also referred to as a *narrative*.

Step one in creating the lifebook is the parent preparing himself or herself to explore painful information with the child The section in Chapter 3 called "Dealing Openly with the Adoptee's Past" offered parents the opportunity to explore questions that, once answered, lend to this parent preparation.

Step two is gathering information. Chapter 6 provided advice regarding collecting photos, written reports, foster family reports, school records, blessings, etc. to ensure that the lifebook can include as much of the child's history as is possible.

Constructing the Narrative

Guiding Principles

Step three is actually writing the child's narrative. This requires having some writing rules—guiding principles—and it requires anticipating questions. Let's take a look at some narratives and then cover the principles necessary to create your child's lifebook.

Below is the story of Isabelle. Isabelle was always a child who had a difficult time accepting a compliment. For example, if anyone commented about her pretty hair, she would immediately undo the braids and take out the bows. This behavior was a result of her thoughts about her abandonment, "There was something wrong with me and that is why my birthmother left me (see Chapter 2)." Therefore, "I am not pretty and I don't deserve compliments." She always had much anxiety. She was unusually fearful when her mother was out or when her mother went to visit family members who lived in another state. Her prior abandonment caused her to be uncertain about her stability with her adoptive mother. The additions of Isabelle's birth brothers to her adoptive family caused Isabelle's anxiety to increase. She asked many questions about her birthparents. She wondered, "Why did I leave first?" "Why does my birthmom keep having babies if she doesn't want them?" "Can we leave this family?" "Are there other birth brothers or sisters?"

Isabelle wrote this narrative at age 9, after about one year of services, during which her parents and her therapist reviewed her story with her verbally and via written reports provided by the public agency.

> "Vera brought me to the hospital and they took me out of her belly. Edward, my birth dad, tried to get Vera to give me up to adoption right away, but she refused to. She brought me to her house and put me on the floor and she left me there a lot. She even let Edward kick me in the head. Everyone offered her help and she never showed up to take the help. They even offered her free food. One day she decided I was sick and she took me to the doctor. The doctor said she couldn't keep me because I was starving. He kept me at the hospital for two weeks or three, then I went to a foster home and a lady rocked me for two and a half months. Then they called my mom and dad and they said they wanted me and they gave me to them and they took care of me.
>
> "Then Brad [foster child] came to live with us, and we thought we were going to adopt him and he would be my brother, but a relative came and adopted him. Then, I was by myself again. Then, my older birth brother got removed from Vera and he came to live with us. When I was 5, Vera had another baby, and he came to live with us too. We all got adopted by the same mom and dad. Mom and Dad are keeping all of us!"

Through her narrative, Isabelle was able to compare her birthfamily to her adoptive family. She came to realize that Mom and Dad didn't leave her lying on the floor, they always fed her, and no one in the family kicked anybody in the head. She concluded that Mom and Dad were safe, and they were "keeping all of us." She also determined that her birthmother could have kept her but chose not to take the help necessary to do so. Isabelle had done nothing to make her birthmother go away. Recording and recognizing these facts, Isabelle's fears diminished, and she began to see herself as lovable. Isabelle was able to change her expectations—beliefs about herself and parents.

Rose was adopted from Russia. Below is the narrative written jointly by Rose, her parents and their therapist. Rose was age 10 at the time this narrative was written.

> "I was born in Russia. I lived with my birthmom until I was 8 months old. Then, she took me to the orphanage. She told the orphanage she couldn't take care of me anymore. I don't know much about her except that her name was Olga and she grew up in the same orphanage she gave me to. She had me when she was 16 years old. I don't know anything about

my birthfather. When I was almost 3, Mom and Dad came to the orphanage and adopted me. The orphanage people told Mom and Dad that Olga had had another baby, a boy, who was also living at the orphanage. Olga didn't visit me when she brought my brother to the orphanage. He wasn't allowed to be adopted. I don't know why. I don't know anything about him or if he is still there or if he got adopted."

Rose added this to her narrative after additional therapy:

"Some feelings I have about the orphanage are mad, sad, glad and scared. I will tell you about mad first. For one, they don't pay attention to you. They don't care about you. They would not help you if you needed help with something. There was not much food. Now, I will tell you about sad. The reasons I would have been sad would be no one there loves you. The orphanage workers don't have time to provide for your needs. You don't have anything to play with. Some feelings of scared would be you would not know if someone might hurt you. The other kids steal your food. You would not know how to trust. The orphanage workers don't take much time to give you attention. The good [glad] part is that my birthmom gave me to the orphanage instead of possibly throwing me in a dumpster or something dangerous. Instead, she made sure that I was safe. Some more good things are that the orphanage workers did take care of me a little and another thing is that my birthmom did not have an abortion. And, that I was adopted!"

As you can see, Rose is advancing to processing her emotions and her experiences. She is beginning to grieve her losses. The benefits of resolving her grief will enhance her attachment to her parents, and her development will move forward. Actually, there have already been gains in her academic performance and her peer relationships.

Now that we have two sample narratives let's look at some guiding principles for writing the narrative. Please note that these tenets promote sharing accurate information—a philosophy encouraged throughout this book when working with any child.

- Tell the child the truth as Chapter 3 recommended. Each of our sample narratives contains the facts as they are known. Both Rose and Isabelle are able to process the facts and come to conclusions that are allowing them to move forward. Children can and must grapple with the truth in order to heal.
- Place the events in chronological order—any story goes from the beginning to the end. Can you imagine watching a movie that started in the middle, skipped to the end, and then went to the beginning? Yet, it is not uncommon to see lifebooks that skip all over the child's life. In order for the child to make sense of her life, the child needs the story organized from her birth through her adoption and the present time in her family life.
- Say, "I don't know" when necessary. Adoptees will have many "I don't knows." It is best to state "I don't know" rather than to attempt to fill in the blanks with opinion, conjecture or untruths. A particular question that often requires an "I don't know" is the question, "Did my birthparents love me?" A way to reply is to say, "I didn't know your birthmom, so I can't answer that." In cases in which the adoptive parents did meet the birthmother, the reply may be, "What do you think?" Too often we rush to tell children, "Of course they loved you!" This is a statement that we need to think about, as it certainly has the capacity to confuse the child. Kathy's narrative will help us understand this point.

Kathy was adopted at age 2. She entered therapy at 6 due to frequent public masturbation, inserting toys in her vagina, daytime enuresis, lying, poor hygiene, inability to sleep, and an overall lack of compliance. This narrative was constructed with Kathy when she was 6 and 7 years old. Much of the language was selected based on terms and words she was able to understand. Concepts such as "sexual abuse" and "physical abuse" were explained to her. In her actual lifebook, her narrative is accompanied by much clip art, actual photos and Kathy's drawings. This combination of pictures and facts has facilitated Kathy's ability to understand her story.

> "You were born and you lived with your birthparents until you were 11 months old. You have two older sisters, Paula and Vikki. You were all taken away from your birthparents at the same time. You and Paula went to live in the Smith foster home. Vikki went to live with the Warren family. She was adopted by the Warren family and you get to visit her.
>
> "You were taken away from your birthparents because they used drugs. These were not drugs the doctor gives you when you are sick. These were drugs that you aren't supposed to take. When they took these drugs they got very angry. They had big fights. They hit each other and they hit your sisters. They made bruises and this is a crime. It is called *physical abuse*. Your birthfather also sexually abused you and your sisters. He touched your vagina and this is why you do this now. You learned it from him. Sexual abuse is also a crime. It is never the fault of the child. It is always the fault of the adult. You couldn't stop him because you were just a baby. Your sisters couldn't stop him either, as they were little, 3 and 4. Your birthmom was supposed to stop him, but she didn't.
>
> "Your birth home was also filthy. This means that it was very, very dirty. This is different than when your mom now says, 'The house is filthy' and 'we need to have a cleaning day.' Instead, this means that there were bugs crawling around, the dogs 'did their business' on the carpet and no one cleaned it up. They didn't always have food or water coming from the faucets. Your diaper didn't get changed very often. You had a very bad rash on your bottom when you got to Mr. and Mrs. Smith's house.
>
> "Your birthfather went to jail for sexually abusing you and your sisters. So, you couldn't live with him. A social worker tried to help your birthmom learn to be a good mom, but this didn't work out. So, there was a court hearing, and a judge said that you couldn't go and live with her again. She wasn't going to keep you safe, and all kids need to be safe.
>
> "Mr. and Mrs. Warren decided not to adopt you because they were older. They wanted you to have younger parents. However, you still see them, and they are like an extra set of grandparents. A social worker put your picture on the computer. Mom and Dad saw it, and they decided to adopt you and your sister. *Adoption* means that you get to live with Mom and Dad until you are all grown up."

Is *love* sexually abusing a child? Is *love* physically abusing and neglecting children? Telling adoptees from such backgrounds that their birth parents loved them equates love with acts of violence or absence—neglect. A better way to respond to children's questions about birthparent love is to let them decide, for themselves, who they want to love. We can simply say, "You can love them if you want to or you don't have to. It is up to you. You can love as many moms and dads as you want." Follow up a discussion like this with *A Place in My Heart* (see Resources, Chapter 5). This is an excellent story that depicts the concept of loving your adoptive family and your birthfamily by demonstrating, through a heart drawing, how many people can fit into one's heart.

Some additional guiding principles for building a narrative include these:

- Construct the story in a developmentally appropriate manner. Kathy's narrative allowed for her young age. Over time, we have expanded Kathy's narrative to include more of the abuse that happened to her siblings. Her oldest sister, now age 15, is faring poorly. The abuse she sustained has impaired her ability to function in any environment. Kathy's growing depth of knowledge helps her to accept her sibling for who she is. She has been able to grieve the loss of the sister she wants her to be.

- Omit value judgments. The three narratives above are free of values—no judgments were passed on the behaviors' of the birthparents. This writing style lets the child draw her own conclusions. However, responsibility was placed on the perpetrators. This approach is useful with children who are concrete thinkers and/or magical thinkers developmentally. As Chapter 2 pointed out, concrete thinkers see the world as black and white—good and bad. In magical thinking, the child views herself as responsible for her abuse and abandonment. So, it is important to place responsibility for the pre-adoptive traumas onto whom it belongs. This permits the child to determine that her past experiences did not happen because of something she did or something "bad" about her. The result is improved self-concept and identity.
- The narratives are comprised of accurate, respectful adoption language—*birthmom*, *birthdad*, *birthfamily*, *birthsiblings*. The adoptive family is *Mom* and *Dad*. Frequently, adoptees and adoptive parents refer to the birthmom as "Mom" years after the adoption has been completed. There are also adoptees who call their adoptive parents by their first names, and they refer to their birth parents as Mom and Dad! Using inaccurate language like this contributes to perpetuating reunification fantasies. If you are parenting the child, *you* are the mom and the dad!
- Repeat, repeat and repeat some more! Children learn best by repetition. This point has been made several times in this book. Narratives, whether long or short, contain a lot of emotionally charged material. The adoptee needs to review the content *many times* before she can internalize the story and express her painful emotions for her losses.

Anticipate Questions

Remember *empathy* from Chapter 5? If not, the discussion of empathy concludes that chapter, and you may want to go back to it. Empathy is the ability to put yourself in another person's shoes. Empathy allows parents and therapists to anticipate the types of questions children may ask as we help them create their narrative. Take some time as you gather all of your child's history together to review it. Think about the questions that might be asked as you make the lifebook. Give some thought to how you want to respond to these questions. Some may require saying, "I don't know." Some, though, you will have the answers to. Others may require obtaining new information. The lifebook is an ongoing process. Keep in mind that the only wrong answers to questions children pose are untruths or not providing any response. Have confidence in yourself as a parent to talk honestly and openly with your adoptee about her early experiences.

Among common questions children ask are these.

"Why did my birthparents use drugs?"

"Do you think my birthmom thinks about me?"

"What do you think my birthmom is doing now?"

"Do you think she is in jail?"

"Does she have any more children?"

"If they get better, can I go live with them again?"

"Are my birthparents sorry for what they did?"

"Why did I move so much in foster care?"

"Why didn't anyone in my country want me?"

"Why didn't the orphanage ladies take me home?"

"Do you think my orphanage friends got adopted?"

"Are my birthparents alive?"

"Are my siblings safe?"

"Do you think my siblings think about me?"

"How did you find me?"

"Why did you pick me?"

"What would you have done if I had been your baby?"

Here are a few final guidelines about lifebooks.

- Construct the lifebook over time. The sample narratives were all put together over a period of one year or longer. Pace yourself and the child.
- Don't be afraid to become emotional with or in front of the child as you make the lifebook. Traumatized children have great difficulty expressing their feelings. Seeing the parent *modeling* deep feelings, is a great way to help children understand that crying or saying, "I'm mad" are acceptable ways to release emotions. Besides, the child's experiences *are* sad and infuriating. Parental grief is to be expected. Chapter 10's section "Coming Ashore: Letting Grief Flow" will discuss grief and grieving in more detail. Parents will learn ways to resolve their grief as well as the grief of their children.
- Make a copy of the entire lifebook. Give the child the copy. An adoptee in the anger stage of grief may decide to express her anger by destroying her lifebook. Keeping a "spare" insures against this and other potential losses of the document.
- Consider using a three-ring binder. This lets you easily place new information in chronological order.
- Place the child's copy of the lifebook where he has access to it, yet identify parameters about to whom he may show the lifebook. Again, take privacy into account, as was explained earlier in this chapter. Birth children are usually privy to photos of family vacations, school pictures, etc. Birth children grow up learning their story. If they have questions, they can go right to the source of their family history—their parents. For adoptees, their lifebook is the readily available source of their birthfamily history.

In addition, please expand your knowledge of making a lifebook by reading *Filling in the Blanks: A Guided Look at Growing Up Adopted*, *Lifebooks: Creating a Treasure for the Adopted Child* and *Telling the Truth to Your Adopted or Foster Child: Making Sense of the Past*. All of these titles are fully referenced in the Resources at the end of this chapter.

Acquiring New and Effective Coping Skills

As we learned in Chapter 8, parents, the children already in the family at the time of the adoption, and the newly adopted child often become entrenched and embroiled in ineffective styles of coping. Parents frequently fall into the categories of *Punitive*, *Accommodating*, *"I give in," Making Extraordinary Efforts*, *Emotionally Withdrawn*, *"Yes, but . . ."* and *Split*.

The typically developing children organize around their parents, falling into categories of *Withdrawn*, *Self-sacrificing*, *Acting-out*, *Regressed*, *"I'll cover for you"* and *The Victim*. Within each coping scenario, the adoptee carries out a trauma re-enactment.

That is, the adoptive family dynamics have been altered so that they seem to resemble his birthfamily—on a smaller scale.

Contributing to the development of these ineffective coping styles are faulty expectations on the part of parents and siblings. For example, the punitive parent believes that, "If I just give him enough consequences, he will 'get it'; he will realize that his behavior needs to change, and so he will stop his behavior and become a part of the family." The emotionally withdrawn parent thinks, "She will readily accept me as a parent." Instead, the child with a history of trauma rejects the parent. The parent withdraws in order to feel less emotional pain. The self-sacrificing child thinks, "I'll be good. I'll 'make up' for all the trouble my brother causes." In reality, the healthy child cannot make up for the loss of the adoptive child the family expected.

As we have also already learned in this chapter, developing realistic expectations lends to improving relationships within the adoptive family. This point is reiterated here because altering expectations is a part of creating any new and effective coping skills. So, one way to develop positive coping skills is to continue with the process of adjusting expectations.

Also perpetuating the use of negative coping methods is the fact that traditional parenting techniques such as time-out, removal of privileges, lecture, grounding, writing sentences, offering incentives, etc. often do little to end the adoptee's unpleasant negative behaviors. The behaviors cause conflict, and the conflict soon diminishes family fun.

Thus, creating new and effective coping skills requires new parenting strategies to reduce negative behavior, and families need the means to restore family fun. But before we can head out into new parenting strategies, we must identify several more parenting roadblocks to be avoided.

Avoiding Parenting Roadblocks

Overall, parenting roadblocks fall out of ineffective coping skills. They perpetuate problems rather than reducing difficulties, so they contribute to the family's immobilization. Moving to mobilization requires removing these barriers. The roadblocks in this segment have something in common—depriving the traumatized child of the ability to learn to think for himself. They are:

- *Remind, remind, remind!* "Pick up your coat." "Brush your teeth." "Do your homework." "Clean your room." All day, the adoptee is reminded of his responsibilities. Actually, in many homes, this carries over to the typically developing children as well. All of this reminding only accomplishes that the adults are doing the child's thinking. There is no need for the child to internalize the daily routine—his parent will always be available to tell him what to do next.
- *Lecture, lecture, lecture!* "If I've told him once, I've told him 1000 times . . .!" Likely, 1001 won't matter either. Children who have experienced trauma have difficulty paying attention. A couple of minutes into a lecture, you've lost him. He has tuned you out.
- *Warnings.* "The next time you forget your homework, I'm not driving to the school." What would be wrong with not doing it this twentieth time? Parents deliver warnings—chronically! Usually, little action is taken. The child perceives that his parents don't mean what they say. Why would he make changes?
- *"I'll do it myself."* Yes, it is often easier to do things yourself. However, what lesson does this teach the child? Will his boss be doing his job for him someday?

Do you recognize yourself above? Worse yet, do you recognize your typically developing children? Older appropriately-developing children often fall into these roadblocks as well. Recently, a family with five children was leaving our office. The oldest sister grabbed her younger brother's coat, another grabbed his backpack and a third said, "Bob, don't forget your water." Bob isn't making changes because he doesn't have to—he has six family members handling all of his responsibilities. This is a good issue to bring up at your next family meeting.

A first step to removing these obstacles is to recognize the particular coping styles in the family and the roadblocks operating there. Take a few moments right now to identify your family's roadblocks and irrational ways of coping. Then read on.

Learning to Let the Adoptee Think for Himself

Enhancing Cause-and-Effect Thinking

Mary Lou, adoptive mom to 10-year-old, Margaret who arrived in the family at age 4, makes clear the challenge of living with a child with underdeveloped cause-and-effect thinking.

> "I feel beside myself repeating the same thing for almost three years. I guess I just can't understand how someone can continue to make the same mistakes, over and over, for so long despite discipline of every typical sort. I don't know if I'd call it anger or just frustration, but either way, it does make you want to stand on the roof and scream sometimes!"

Chapters 2 and 8 discussed the various cognitive delays that result from experiencing trauma. In particular, a traumatic history impairs cause-and-effect thinking. In turn, a lack of cause-and-effect thinking means that the adoptee often does not connect his actions to the consequences of the actions. Often he can repeat the words describing what will happen if he doesn't do his homework or take out the trash. Yet, in the moment, his disorganized brain processes prevent him from implementing the correct choice. Consequently, he makes the same mistakes over and over.

This faulty logic is what renders many "normal" parenting tools ineffective. For example, most children placed in time-out sit quietly on their time-out step or chair. They mull over the behavior that got them there. They decide they don't like to sit in time-out, so they decide to stop the behavior that got them placed there.

The traumatized child sits on the time-out step (well, actually, he might be lying on the step, on the floor in front of the step, screaming on the step, etc.) wondering what sitting on a step has to do with hitting his sister. He can't figure this out and so he doesn't make the same connections as do the healthy children. Further, as we will learn in "Weathering the Storm," he may like sitting on the step. Again, he has an unconscious need to create distance between himself and family members. A time-out is a break from attaching to the family.

As a second example, cause-and-effect thinking is necessary as well in order to understand removal of privileges. The child must connect the privilege to the negative behavior. For example, parents often remove television, computer time or Game Boy as a "consequence" for such rule infractions as lying, breaking toys and ignoring chores. In reality, lying and television don't go together. From a trauma perspective, what is happening here is that you are trying to deprive a child who, early in life, was deprived to a degree that many of us can't even imagine (Keck and Kupecky, 2002). He lived without food, clothes, heat, water, etc. He can live without his Game Boy. Further, children who have attachment difficulties are not connected in a meaningful manner to people or to things. Parents can remove item after item and privilege after privilege—the illogical, poorly attached and formerly deprived child won't "get it."

Implementing Logical Consequences

Different parenting tools must be acquired. Among these new tools is learning about and implementing *natural and logical consequences* (Cline and Fay, 2006). If the child doesn't brush his teeth, the natural and logical consequence is that his snack becomes fruit instead of a cookie. The parent can empathically state, "I would like for you to have a cookie. However, I need to take care of your teeth until you learn how to."

A similarly logical consequence is that a thief must pay for the item stolen. Payment can be money, chores or the next time you are in the store you can be sad for the child as you say, "Well, I'd like to buy you that shirt. However, I'm putting that money toward the CD player you took from your sister." Once home, hand the child who has stolen the CD player the money and have him give it to his sister. He is thinking concretely; he needs to "see" the exchange of money. Then, be done—move on! Don't say, "See, how do *you* like it?" "How does that feel?" This is anger talking, and as we will learn later in this chapter, anger is a typhoon occurring along our journey to mobilization. Anger renders the natural and logical consequence ineffective.

Natural and logical consequences connect actions to outcome. Eventually, the child's brain will form new pathways and he will begin to make better decisions. Thus, natural and logical consequences enhance problem-solving skills too. The child sees or feels the result of his actions—this type of discipline accommodates the concrete thinker. Natural and logical consequences are free of lecture, warnings and reminders—an action simply occurs. Roadblocks are avoided, as is conflict. The family atmosphere becomes more calm and relaxed. This produces an environment in which relationships can form. Natural and logical consequences allow the child to experience the outcome of his actions and this, over time, contributes to the development of logical functioning. Delivered with empathy, natural and logical consequences make for a powerful parenting tool.

Parenting with Love and Logic (and other books, CDs and tapes in the Love and Logic series) by Foster Cline and Jim Fay covers natural and logical consequences in great detail. Check out their website (see Resources) to review the entire line of Love and Logic products. It makes sense and it is fun parenting once you understand it. Having more fun is the best gift you can give any of your children and yourself!

Key Point—All children, especially those with disorganized thought processes, need to learn to think for themselves. Work to rid yourself of reminders and warnings. Stop doing things yourself even when it would be easier. Step back and let consequences occur. Success results from these stumbles. Many of the parenting tools put forth in this book require paradigm shifts. You will stumble. Then, you will try again. Eventually you will succeed. This is a wonderful tone to set, and from it your children learn to navigate relationships and their way in the world.

Facilitating Moral Development

Chapter 2 stated that moral development is the capacity to control one's own behavior internally. Developing this internalized set of morals and values requires logical thinking and the ability to feel a wide range of emotions—empathy, sympathy, anxiety, admiration, self-esteem, anger, outrage, shame and guilt. Natural and logical consequences promote some of the qualities needed to help the child who has experienced trauma move from the pre-conventional to the conventional and post-conventional stages of moral development (Chapter 2). Negative behaviors dissipate when the child can think logically and make decisions based on a universal sense of right and wrong, rather than acting on what feels good in the moment.

Restitution

Parents can use restitution to help the child develop morals and values. Restitution has two parts. The first part is saying, "I'm sorry." Notice, the "I'm." Troubled adoptees tend to say, "Sorry." The "I'm" is necessary because it means "I am taking responsibility for my action." The second part is, "How can I make it up to you?" Now, don't get carried away with this second part. A very simple chore or a hug is more than enough to make the point to children of all ages. The important component is that the "make up" activity is connected to the unpleasant act.

Grace, age 7, came to live with her adoptive family when she was 5 years old. The family was comprised of her parents, Jenna and Stephanie, and her two older sisters, Ella and Zoe, ages 10 and 12 respectively. Grace had the most annoying habit of taking sips from anyone's drink. If a can of pop was sitting on a coffee table, Grace would make it a point to pick it up and drink from it. If her teacher had a beverage on her desk, Grace did the same. This just seemed disgusting to Grace's older sisters, her parents and her teacher.

Jenna and Stephanie decided that this was a behavior they would like to see Grace give up. So, each time she drank from an open drink, she had to apologize and "make up" by buying a new beverage. She had some options as far as purchasing new beverages. She could have water when the family dined out. The purchase price of the beverage she would have ordered was deposited in her "beverage bank," which Jenna kept in her possession. Or she could carry out a simple chore to earn 50 cents—the fee she owed for a contaminated drink. Simple chores included carrying a laundry basket, helping to fold towels, helping to make a bed, helping to clear the table, etc. It didn't take Grace long to decide that contaminating other peoples' drinks wasn't worth the price.

Parents are not always the only ones who initiate the need for restitution.

Angelo is a 14-year-old adopted by Kimberly and Nelson. He was prone to angry outbursts. After he had time to cool off, he would, without prodding, clean up the kitchen, vacuum the living room or carry out some other chore that needed to be done. He would do something nice in order to "make up" for his behavior. Kim and Nelson found this upsetting. They looked at it as his way of "controlling his consequences."

Kim and Nelson are not the only parents who think this way. After spousal arguments, it is common that the wife cooks her husband's favorite dinner or that the husband finally decides to fix the light hanging over the dining room table—adult restitution. This is a perfectly acceptable means of "making up." Children who "make up" in this manner have at least recognized that they did something wrong and that there is a need to correct the situation. Is more really necessary? No. Is this dysfunctional? No. Is this a situation we can simply let go of? Yes.

Restoring Family Fun

Moral development is included in our social domain of development. As many families who live with traumatized children know, their moral development isn't the only social skill lagging well behind those of peers. The child with mental health issues has all around underdeveloped social skills. The inability to play and enjoy family fun creates havoc in adoptive family relationships. Let's look now at some ways we can restore family fun.

Facilitating the Development of Social Skills

Nothing facilitates attachment between family members like laughing, joking, teasing and playing with one another. Yet, in families with a child with mental health issues, giggles and chuckles don't always come easily. This is disappointing to everyone, but especially for the typically developing children who expected that their new sibling would be a playmate. Chapter 1 made clear that this is one of the primary expectations the birth and/or previously adopted children have when a new kid joins the family. Many subsequent chapters have provided numerous examples of the ways in which fun is impeded because of the complexity of the adoptee's inability to play. Chapter 2's section called "Social Development" made clear the lifelong risks of inadequate social skills.

Facilitating the adoptee's development of social skills is important for his long-term functioning, and it is a way to restore family fun. Just as we use natural and logical consequences and restitution to advance cause-and-effect thinking and moral development, we can help the adoptee expand her social skills.

Identifying the Child's Social and Emotional Age

A first step in improving the traumatized adoptee's social skills is to evaluate his social and emotional age in relation to his chronological age. Do you remember the *Social and Emotional Age vs. Chronological Age* discussion from Chapter 8? If not, refresh your memory and then continue reading.

A good starting place for identifying your troubled child's actual social and emotional age is to read a good book on "normal" child development such as *Your Baby and Child: From Birth to Age Five*, or *Ages and Stages: A Parent's Guide to Normal Child Development* (see Resources). There are also online sources of child development such as the sites of Zero to Three, the Child Development Institute, and the Centers for Disease Control and Prevention (see Resources) to name a few reliable websites.

Compare the skills for children ages infant on up to your traumatized child's chronological age. Yes, I said, "Infant on up!" Traumatized children frequently lack the skills of even very small children. They may have a hard time imitating faces, or playing peek-a-boo. They can't stack, mold, build, sort, string beads, sing nursery rhymes, and the list goes on. Using your knowledge of your adoptee, identify the areas he has mastered and those which are underdeveloped.

For example, can your child take turns? Follow the rules of a game? Greet people—say "Hello," "How are you?" Can your child sit and play for any period of time, or does he flit from toy to toy? If so, this must change. Does he initiate any play, or will he just sit and sit and sit? Such a child is like a toddler who has yet to learn to explore his environment.

You can also observe your child in social situations. Visit the park and compare your child to peers. What are they able to do in comparison to your adoptee? Visit the playground at school. What is causing his difficulties on the playground?

If you have parented typically developing children, you have personal knowledge of child development that you can apply to this process as well.

Lastly, you can carry out formal developmental testing via a psychologist, neuropsychologist, a developmental pediatrician, social worker, counselor or pediatric nurse (depending on state licensing policies). An adoption medical clinic, the school, your family physician or your health insurance company can help you locate professionals who conduct this type of testing.

Basic Social Skills

- taking turns
- making conversation
- formulating and communicating opinions
- greeting
- maintaining appropriate personal space
- being able to read faces and tone of voice
- giving and receiving compliments
- really listening to what others are saying
- developing a sense of humor
- sharing
- making eye contact
- negotiating and compromising
- being able to enter a group to join a discussion or an activity
- demonstrating problem-solving skills
- following directions

Once you have all of your information gathered, identify the earliest skills the child is missing. Some children will exhibit a scatter of skills. A child age 9 may exhibit some 3-year-old skills, some 5-year-old abilities, some 7-year-old development, etc. In this case, we would place the social and emotional age at 3—the earliest age for which we noticed deficits.

Let's use Gabe, chronologically age 6, as an example.

> Gabe was given all of the toys of interest to a 6 year old. Quickly, they were broken or cast aside. Other than toy airplanes that made noise, Gabe had little interest in any toys. Even with his planes, he preferred to listen to the noise rather than actually play with the airplane. Mostly, he flitted from toy to toy. He would pick up a toy, look at it, drop it and move on to the next toy. Further, Gabe had significant difficulties with attention and impulsivity. He had little capacity to sit still for more than a few minutes.

Gabe, like many children who experienced abuse and neglect, never learned how to play. In his infancy, his foster mother had not taken the time to play face games or give him bathtub toys. He wasn't provided a stacking ring, shape sorter, nesting cups, cloth or board books, mirrors or rattles. Play occurs in stages—toys are designed to facilitate various skills at various ages. Infant toys build the skills needed to move on to toddler toys and then pre-school age toys, etc. Children who don't progress through this series of age-appropriate toys are often unable to play with toys that are designed for their chronological age.

Backtrack to Begin Building New Skills

There is a common belief that the ability to play and develop social skills will simply happen if we place children in activities comprised of same-age peers. This will work with some children who have experienced trauma. Certainly, if the adoptee can play baseball, enjoy gymnastics and sing in the church choir, do continue their participation in these extracurricular activities. Always keep what is working. However, if you have tried several different endeavors and there has been limited or no social movement forward, it is time to try a new approach.

Play and social skills have their root in parent-child interactions (Chapter 2). Children gain their social skills foundation through interaction with their parents. Siblings influence social development as well. Most parents teach their children to play without really thinking about it. For example, a young toddler is sitting in the living room with some blocks. Mom or Dad, passing by, stops for a few minutes and stacks the blocks. Soon, the toddler is stacking his blocks on his own. The skill of building has been learned. By age 4 or 5, the child is with friends building with Legos™. The skill has transferred to peer relationships.

Thus, placing the traumatized child in a group activity may not advance his social skills because it places the cart before the horse. We are attempting peer play prior to the child having learned to play with parents, and we are attempting complex group play before the child has mastered solitary and parallel play. In these instances, parents may want to consider backtracking to the child's social and emotional age.

Let's continue to use Gabe, whose social and emotional age was determined to be that of an infant, as our example.

> First, Cole and Becky elicited the assistance of Gabe's three sisters, Jennifer, Jessica and Mary, ages 8, 11 and 14. They decided to *assign them a way to be helpful*. They held a family meeting and asked each child to sit with Gabe for five to ten minutes, two days per week—each sister, then, would spend 20 minutes with Gabe per week. The purpose of this was to teach Gabe how to play. Becky then stopped at the local thrift store, where she purchased a set of stacking rings, large blocks, a shape sorter, some small plastic containers and a mirror. She also obtained a CD of nursery rhymes and a few bathtub toys.
>
> Jennifer went first. She spread a blanket on the floor. She gathered Gabe and the shape-sorter. She sat with Gabe, demonstrating what she wanted him to do. He kept moving off the blanket. She would wait a few seconds and then gently guide him back to the blanket and the shape sorter. Mary worked in the same manner with the blocks and Jessica opted to teach Gabe to sing nursery rhymes.
>
> Gabe was shifted from an evening shower to a bath. Cole has many memories of getting quite wet during his efforts to help Gabe dump water from one plastic container to another. Becky spent much time playing face games and peek-a-boo which absolutely delighted Gabe.
>
> Eventually, the days turned into months and the months became almost one year. The family's successes included that Gabe had learned to sit and play by himself for periods lasting about 15 minutes! The family had small windows of calmness! Gabe graduated from the large blocks to large Legos™. Becky expanded his toys as he made progress. He had peg puzzles, Play-Doh™, a toddler age xylophone, a Little People™ car and garage set, a Fisher Price The Farmer Says™ and many more toys designed for kids ages 12 to 24 months. Gabe is currently moving on to learn Candy Land™ and Chutes and Ladders™.
>
> A year of consistently working with Gabe has paid off. Gabe is developing social skills critical to his ability to function at school and eventually in the world. Mary, the child who had been withdrawing, became engaged once again. Jessica, the self-sacrificing child, was channeled into a specific way to be helpful. This guided and validated her desire to be helpful, yet simultaneously reduced the time she had been spending carrying out responsibilities. She was given more free time for her own need to play. She needed this time for her own development to move forward.

Let's further exemplify the idea that siblings need time for their own development.

Adam and Laurel adopted twins, Reanna and Hal, age 6 at arrival, presently 9. The twins had experienced pre-natal drug exposure, neglect, physical abuse, and they had moved through seven foster homes before being placed with Adam and Laurel. Reanna had the social and emotional age of a 14-month old while Hal exhibited social skills similar to a 2-year-old.

Alyson, their infant birth sister, arrived one year later. Now age 3, her development is typical. Socially, then, she is surpassing her siblings. She is moving on to using her imagination. She loves her play telephone and her medical kit. She likes to dress up and take care of her baby dolls. She tries to engage Reanna and Hal, however their delays don't allow them to participate in a reciprocal manner. They can do only what Alyson tells them to do.

Certainly, this is good interaction for Reanna and Hal. However, Alyson needs the company of healthy peers in order to ensure that her development progresses as it should. Laurel makes sure that Alyson has play dates, and she is enrolled in pre-school three mornings per week. Laurel monitors her skills to make sure she is doing all of the things a 3-year-old should do.

Brothers and sisters influence each other's development. In cases like that of Alyson, Reanna and Hal, we must ensure that each child is able to grow and develop. This means that the appropriately developing children need ample opportunities to play with developmentally equal peers in order that their development proceeds along normal lines.

Developing children's social skills can be accomplished directly and indirectly. Choose which method is best for your "little" adoptee.

Parenting at the Social and Emotional Age

Gabe and his family demonstrate that backtracking is an effective way to move skills forward. We must keep in mind that the child who previously resided in an orphanage or a neglectful and abusive birth home had little opportunity to play, and most likely he had access to few toys. Yet many parents have a difficult time allowing such children to act like "little" kids. Daily they are told, "Grow up!" "Act your age!" "Those are the baby's toys. Leave them alone!" The next time you find yourself making any of these statements, stop! If your 11-year-old son wants to play with your 3-year-old daughter's toy kitchen set, let him. If you find your 14-year-old digging in your toddler's sandbox, join in. If your 9-year-old is baby talking, this is a sign that he needs a hug and some lap time just as you would give a toddler. If your 12-year-old plays with the younger kids in the neighborhood safely, this is fine as well. The more you allow the child to be "little," the more the child will actually "grow up." This is called *parenting the child at the social and emotional age.*

Parenting the child at his actual social and emotional age is important when facilitating developmental growth. It can also be important in other ways. For example, would you expect a 2- or 3-year-old to be able to clean her room? Most likely, you would jointly work with the young child to clean her room. If you have a 12-year-old who is actually 3 in social and emotional age, assisting him in picking up his clothes, vacuuming the carpet and making his bed will most likely reduce the power struggles that frequently accompany trying to get him to carry out chores on his own. As he matures socially and emotionally, he will be able to clean his room and do lots of other things appropriate for children of his chronological age.

Key Point—Parenting at the child's social and emotional age is a concept worth understanding and using. When you can see your adoptee for the

More Backtracking to the Social and Emotional Age

Gabe offers an example of a child who was very accepting of a direct approach to advancing his social age. Many children will respond like Gabe. However, other children, especially older children, may find the thought of playing with "baby toys" embarrassing. In these cases, creativity is called for.

Colleen lived in an abusive birthfamily for five years and then a South American orphanage for the next five years. Adopted by Sue and Howard, at age 10, she exhibited a social and emotional age of a 2-year-old.

Sue, Howard and Colleen belonged to a church with a large congregation and so there were many Sunday school classes. They made arrangements for Colleen to be a "helper" in the classes with children ranging in age from toddler through pre-school. They simply presented the idea to Colleen in terms of the teachers needing some assistance. Colleen received the benefit of playing with children who helped her social skills mature, and the Sunday school teachers appreciated having a reliable assistant. Colleen was proud of her contributions to the church. Over this past year, Colleen has mastered many social tasks and so, has now moved on to be the volunteer helper in classes for five-and six-year olds.

Adrianne and Craig adopted Jeremy from a Bulgarian orphanage as an infant. Now, at age 13, his social skills continue to be delayed. He remains stuck in solitary play. He has not advanced to parallel or group play in spite of years of social skills training programs, sports participation, scouting, etc.

Adrianne's sister has four young children—a daughter, Eliza, age 2, and a new set of triplets. Adrianne, her mother, her sisters and sisters-in-laws have been taking turns helping out with the new babies.

Adrianne decided to take Jeremy along. She asked him if he could please play with Eliza because she needed some attention—the babies were taking up a lot of time!

Jeremy did well in this role. He sat with Eliza for hours. He giggled as much as Eliza over her Laugh and Learn™ 2-in-1 Learning Kitchen™ and Eliza was very happy to have a playmate. As the babies grow, Jeremy has been asked to help them learn how to play. Jeremy takes pride in his role as the "fun Uncle."

As these youngsters develop, so have Jeremy's social skills. He has moved on to board games, and for the first time, this summer he actually joined in with kids who were playing water tag at the community pool.

"little" child he or she actually is, healing will occur. You won't be so frustrated by his behaviors or his lack of abilities. He won't stop trying to succeed because of standards that are impossible for him to achieve.

Practice Social Skills

Children "practice" the piano, catching a ball, shooting hoops, math facts and so on. Children can also practice social skills. Eye contact can be improved by having staring contests—brothers and sisters can help with this.

Conversation can be improved by asking open-ended questions. A common close-ended conversation with a child who has experienced trauma goes like this:

Parent: "How was school today?"

Adoptee: "Good."
Parent: "How did you do on your math test?"
Adoptee: "Not good."

Or, there is the opposite: the adoptee who chatters incessantly about things that have very little meaning.

Either way, getting some of these kids to converse can be difficult. Their inability to communicate makes forming relationships, in the family and outside of the family, difficult. Alter the questions you ask.

"What was your favorite part of school today?"
"What is it about that you like?"
"Who did you play with today?"
"Tell me about those kids."

Ask questions that require an answer longer than one word. If you did something special over the weekend, ask your child to re-cap the event. Mention that he could share that with his classmates on Monday—give some specific ideas about the words he can actually use.

Usually, the first response to a child who is talking on and on is to say, "How many times have I told you to quit interrupting?" This is a roadblock—avoid it! Re-direct the child. "Mary, your brother is talking about his baseball game. It's your turn to listen. Then, you can have a turn talking." Practicing, modeling, suggesting and helping children find the words to talk are all ways to practice the art of making conversation.

Look over the list of social skills provided in the sidebar on page 374 and think about what *practice* activities will improve relationships inside and outside of your home.

Parties, Play Dates, Vacations and More

A trip to the zoo, a vacation to Florida, going next door to play with the neighbors, family game night, birthday parties and holidays are all events that can present challenges when a family includes a child with mental health issues. Often, the adoptee struggles to handle such situations. The child with a history of trauma views himself as "bad." He thinks, "I don't deserve fun and special presents." He may enjoy the company of his family during outings. Subsequently, the family becomes the brunt of poor behavior since he is scared of connecting and feels he must go into rejection mode. Family fun may trigger the lack of pleasure in his birthfamily or his few good memories of his birthfamily or orphanage mates. His grief surfaces. Unable to express his emotions, the feelings are manifested though negative behaviors.

In response to such behavior, the family may scale down or stop having fun. Instead, let's look at some options to enhance the outcomes of family fun times.

Practice can be helpful. Traumatized children may need you to practice—review—what will be happening at the birthday party. How many kids are coming? What games will be played? Yes, your brother will get presents. How does this make you feel? How long will the party be? Children, given an idea of what to expect, can often make it through an event better.

Parenting at the child's actual social and emotional age is another consideration. What would you expect of a 3-, 4- or 5-year-old at a museum? In Disney World? At holiday gatherings? If your 13-year-old is really socially and emotionally 4, expect that he may become overwhelmed when there is a flurry of activity. Expect the child with Sensory Dysfunction Disorder to become over-stimulated at sporting events. Build in breaks just as you would with a younger child. One parent may have to sit on a bench with the adoptee, while the other family members move on to the lion and tiger display.

Have an ice cream while you are resting—this isn't a punishment. Later, you can meet back up at the rain forest and proceed on your way.

Set the Timer

Patty and Rich, ages 7 and 8, are a birth child and a child who was adopted. They were able to play well for only about 15 minutes. After that, shouting, bickering and a cry of "Mom, he won't play fair!" ruined the fun.

Joyce, their mom, eventually decided to set a timer for 15 minutes. At that point, she would casually call one of the children to the kitchen to help her "for a minute" or she would arrive in the play area with a candy kiss. She provided enough of an interruption to offset the argument that was certain to occur. Patty and Rich continued playing for another 15 minutes. By that time, dinner was ready.

Joyce gives us a nice way to promote a positive ending to a situation that could easily conclude in an ugly manner. Families can also use this idea when the family sits down to play a card or board game. Announce at the start, "I have 15 minutes; let's play Trouble." When time is up, the parent concludes, "Wow! That was fun! I have to go do the laundry." This style of play also offsets having a winner and a loser. You are playing for 15 or 20 minutes rather than until the game is over. Traumatized children may be "poor losers." So, playing for fun, instead of playing until there is a winner, can end a game on a positive note. Isn't this the way it's supposed to be anyway?

No Batteries Needed

As you can see, many of the suggestions regarding restoring family fun require re-thinking family fun a bit. Until the adoptee is able to play for a longer period of time, family game night may consist of one short game. Or family fun may require returning to a "no batteries needed" approach. A few minutes of collecting lightening bugs or blowing bubbles, or playing hide and seek, musical chairs, ring-around-the-rosie or other such "old-fashioned" games keeps fun shorter and less complicated. These types of activities are great for the child who has problems with attention, impulsivity, planning and decision making.

Overall, parents of a family which includes a socially or emotionally delayed child may need to think about fun in terms of short, frequent increments instead of in terms of day-long or longer outings.

Family fun may also mean re-thinking electronic devices altogether. Computer games, hand-held video games, game systems and television promote interacting with machines. If you want to improve relationships in your family, you actually need to interact! Certainly, there are times when a hand held video game makes a long trip in the car more pleasant, or gives a parent at the end of her rope a break. In these situations, do what is necessary. On a regular basis, however, turn off the television and put away the game system. Everyone will benefit!

Evan and Ethan, twin 13-year-olds adopted from Eastern Europe, spent two or three hours a day playing video games. Yet, they had no friends. In the six years they lived with Kevin and Eve, they didn't develop any enduring interests in sports, art, music or any other type of leisure pursuits. And worst of all they never wanted to play with Russ, the 5-year-old born to the family. They preferred the company of a machine to that of people.

Concerned, Kevin and Eve obtained professional help. The therapist recommended packing up the game system and putting it away. This idea made Kevin and Eve nervous. What would Ethan and Evan do with all of their time? However, while the boys were at school the next day, these good parents took the game system to Kevin's sister's house. Eve went to the store and purchased some board games, a deck of cards, some arts and crafts supplies and kits, paint by numbers, and word puzzle books. She placed them on the dining room table.

Evan and Ethan came home and of course they immediately asked, "What happened to our game system?"

Kevin said, "We're trying some new things for a while." He pointed to the dining room table and he walked away. He didn't engage in any discussion or arguing. He avoided all of the roadblocks.

For about three months, the boys struggled. Often, they would just sit on the couch staring at the space the game system had occupied. At times, Eve would invite them to play a game or make a Christmas ornament. Eventually, they started joining her. A few more months passed and Evan asked if he could learn to play the guitar. This request was immediately granted. In fact, it was met very enthusiastically by parents who weren't used

The Importance of Play

- Play is a simple joy that is supposed to be a cherished part of childhood.
- Play allows children to use their creativity while developing their imagination, dexterity, and physical, cognitive and emotional strength.
- Play is important for healthy brain development.
- It is through play that children at a very early age engage and interact in the world around them.
- Play allows children to create and explore a world they can master, conquering their fears while practicing adult roles. As they master their world, play helps children develop new competencies that lead to enhanced confidence and the resiliency they will need to meet future challenges.
- Undirected play allows children to learn how to work in groups, to share, to negotiate, to resolve conflicts and to learn self-advocacy skills.
- When play is allowed to be child-driven, children practice decision-making skills, move at their own pace, discover their own areas of interest and ultimately engage fully in the passions they wish to pursue.
- Encouraging unstructured play may be an exceptional way to increase physical activity in the resolution of the obesity epidemic.
- Parents who play with their children learn to communicate more effectively with their children and are given another setting in which to offer gentle, nurturing guidance.
- Play is integral to the academic environment. It ensures that the school setting attends to the social and emotional development of children as well as their cognitive development.
- Play has been shown to help children adjust to the school setting, and even to enhance school readiness, learning behaviors and problem-solving skills.
- Play and unscheduled time that allows for peer interactions are important components of social-emotional learning.

Source: Ginsburg, Kenneth, R., "The Importance of Play in Promoting Healthy Child Development and Maintaining Strong Parent-Child Bonds". *Pediatrics 2007* (ISSN Numbers: 0031-4005). American Academy of Pediatrics. Online at http://www.aap.org/pressroom/playFINAL.pdf

to either of their older children wanting to do anything! One year later, Evan is sticking with guitar and Ethan has made a Christmas ornament for each extended family member.

Better yet, Eve's attention was captured by the sound of three voices laughing in the living room. She moved toward the noise to find Ethan, Evan and Russ playing a card game together. Ethan and Evan were actually playing with Russ! She was so excited that she called Kevin at work to tell him!

In therapy, the therapist asked the boys what they used to do with all of their time. Neither could recall the hours they spent playing video games. Two years have now passed. Evan has successfully completed an entire baseball season and recently signed up for another season. Kevin and Eve enjoy listening to him play the guitar. Ethan has joined the school service club. Kevin and Eve can give many examples of their three sons playing together.

Stop reading for a few minutes and think about this. What short activities can you think of that your whole family might like? What did you play as a child that was enjoyable? Which of these activities can you incorporate for a few minutes a couple of days per week to increase the level of fun in your family?

To Go or Not To Go

Liv and Bill parent two children by birth, Peggy and Martha, ages 10 and 11. They also parent their son, Roger, age 12 whom they adopted. The family was to go to a science center on Saturday. Liv and Bill knew this outing could be difficult. Roger would grumble, lag behind and want to see different displays than the rest of the family. Peggy and Martha were already asking, "Why does he have to go?"

Hmmm. How does the parent respond? Sometimes with, "He has to go because he is part of the family, and he needs to learn to enjoy family fun." However, there are instances in which he doesn't need to go. Below, an adoptive father illustrates this point.

"If the situation warrants it, consider taking your family vacation without the child with mental health issues. One year we were to take our vacation in a place where the kids could easily get away from us and get lost. That same year, our troubled son, age 9, had run away from us at Wal-Mart two or three times and my wife had recently had surgery so she was in no condition to chase after anyone. We decided that the only way we and our other two children would enjoy ourselves was to leave our troubled son at his grandparents' for the week. He wasn't being punished. He had a great time with his grandparents, and we called him every day. Everyone had a good time that week."

Gail and Don, who we met early in this chapter, include Betty in some outings and exclude her from others. They do some things just with Betty. They do other things just with one son or with all of their sons together. As a couple, they sometimes go out together. Other times they go out individually.

In Gabe's family, Cole often takes Gabe out while Jennifer, Jessica and Mary have friends over. At other times, he stays home and interacts freely with all of the kids at the house. If Mary goes to the neighbor's house to play, sometimes he goes along. Other times he stays home. During birthday parties or special events, he participates for about an hour—the time period he can handle. Then he gets a break. This may mean that Cole or Becky drive him to the babysitter until the party is over. He may go for a walk with one of the adults attending the party. He may go sit in the kitchen with Becky for a few minutes at regular intervals. He goes in and out of the party. This approach keeps him from getting over-stimulated.

The answer to the question of whether to go or not actually hinges on how the family carries out activities as a whole. If you are always only excluding the child with mental health issues—this isn't acceptable. If you are excluding the child with mental health issues as a punishment—this isn't acceptable. If you carry this out with an attitude of, "In this family, each child gets special time with mom and dad, each child gets time with mom alone and dad alone, and there are times the whole family is together"—this is acceptable. Again, it is all about the tone set. The latter sets the tone that each family member gets what he or she needs from the family.

Fun Is the Parents' Decision

Key Point—Fun is the best way to attach, to navigate new relationships. Carry out your plans regardless of behavior or consequences. The child with mental health issues needs to learn to enjoy life. As for the typically developing children, when they are adults, what do you want them to remember about their family—conflict or joy? Parents have the choice to set either tone in their family.

Key Point—Be the parent you want to be. Expect that your efforts may not be received as you intend. However, you need to do things to feel like a "good" parent. Typically, the children will notice and again ("mirror, mirror") they will follow your lead.

Frequently, the child with difficulties winds up in charge of the family fun (Keck and Kupecky, 2002). It goes like this. The parent says, "If you are good all week, Saturday we'll go to the mall." Faithfully, by Friday evening some rule violation has occurred and the trip to the mall is taken away. Or, because punitive consequences have piled up all week, the family decides to stay home so Billy can wash the kitchen floor, rake the leaves, vacuum and carry out all kinds of other chores. The troubled child has determined the family's weekend plans.

Who does this benefit? A now angry family is stuck at home together. Or, the typical kids go off to their friends' homes. The family is separated. If you want to go to the mall on Saturday then go! Chores can wait. "Good" isn't likely going to happen for a long time. "Good" won't happen if parents and brothers and sisters are always angry at their sibling. Fun is the best way to navigate new relationships.

Chapter 8 closed with the question, "What type of parent do you want to be?" Likely, many of you listed fun as part of your answer. What are you waiting for? Go and be merry! You are allowed to be the parent you want to be rather than the parent you think you have to be. Expect that the parenting you provide may not always be received the way you intended the delivery. This doesn't mean you stop. This means you continue. Children follow the parent's lead—some sooner than others and some more easily than others. But, they can't follow at all if you aren't leading.

Weathering the Storm: Creating and Maintaining a Healthy Emotional Climate

This topic is comprised of two sections: "Reactions" and "Energy." Together, they are a super highway to navigating relationships in the adoptive family.

Reactions: Changing Direction to Avoid the Approaching Storm

Chapter 2 taught us that a traumatized child's brain is similar to that of a deer. It is always wary of a threat in its environment. It can go into fight or flight mode—hyperarousal or dissociation—even when there is no visible threat. Chapters 3 and 8 covered the *negative emotional environment* that occurs because adoptees who have experienced trauma transfer feelings to parents, brothers and sisters. Together these two phenomena generate storms of conflict among members of complex adoptive families.

Parents who learn to change directions in the face of such storms will accelerate their family to mobilization.

> Tara and Danny parent their birth daughter, Mary Ellen, and their son, Chris, whom they adopted, and who are ages 13 and 9 respectively. Chris is obsessed with food. He hoards food in his room. A trail of wrappers from candy, granola bars and cupcakes can be found in his locker, in his desk, under his mattress, in his backpack and in his closet. He constantly asks, "When will dinner be ready?" "Can I have a snack?" If told, "No, it isn't time for a snack" or "You just had a snack," he whines, shouts and cries.
>
> While vacuuming, Tara found numerous wrappers and several empty yogurt containers behind the couch. She placed this trash on the kitchen counter. She stewed the entire afternoon. She was angry that Chris kept stealing food. "Why does he do this? We provide plenty of food. He gets plenty of snacks," she wondered. She was also mad that he wouldn't put the packaging in the trash can.
>
> As soon as Chris entered the house from school, Tara confronted him. "Did you put this garbage behind the couch? Did you steal this food?"
>
> Chris said, "No, Mom. Really, I don't know how those got behind the couch."
>
> Tara responded, "You're lying."
>
> Chris again said, "No, Mom really, I don't know where they came from."
>
> The argument carried on for about twenty more minutes. Chris was sent to his room "until your father comes home."
>
> Danny arrived home about an hour later to find Tara still upset. He went to Danny's room and informed him that there would be no snacks for a month. He had previously tried no snacks for a week and then two weeks. Danny again began to argue, "But, I didn't do it."
>
> The end result was Danny asking Chris, "Do I need to get the paddle?" At this point, Chris had a complete meltdown. Danny then kept adding on swats—"If you don't calm down you'll get three swats. Okay, now it's four. Well, five then."
>
> In the midst of this downpour, Mary Ellen decided to go to a friend's house for dinner.

Chris' behavior had drenched the family in anger. He transferred his feelings of anger about his orphanage trauma to each member of his family. When faced with a spanking—a perceived threat—he entered hyperarousal. His emotions swirled out of control.

Stories such as this are common in families parenting children with mental health issues. Parents must learn to bypass these types of interactions. They're unhealthy for everyone!

Parenting Roadblocks

Let's examine a few roadblocks at work here and then we'll look at changing directions to avoid these storms. These roadblocks increase the intensity of angry conflicts.

- *Threats.* "If you don't get out of bed, I'm going to drag you out!" Threats are an attempt to manage negative behaviors with fear. Many traumatized children respond poorly to threats. Threats trigger their fear, activating memories of frightening incidents from the past. Once scared, the child dissociates—stares or seems as if in a fog—or enters hyperarousal, as did Chris. Heightened emotional states decrease the brain's capacity to access logical thought processes. The child is not capable of thinking clearly when in this state of emotional upheaval, which is often referred to as dysregulation. He cannot calm himself down in order to receive fewer swats. A co-worker of mine, Regina Kupecky, often says to parents, "During these times, it is as if you are trying to reason with a person who is intoxicated. It doesn't work." This is a good analogy and one with which many are familiar.

Fathers often utilize threats. Dads seem to want to be the authority figure in their homes. They want their children to listen and obey quickly. This level of obedience will not occur with children with moderate to severe mental health issues. Further, is this the way you really want to manage your children? Do you want them complying because of fear, or because they trust and respect your decisions?

Lastly, many threats are hollow. The threat can't be carried out or the parent has threatened something that wouldn't make sense to carry out. For example, frustrated parents often draw lines in the sand. "If you don't change, you are going back to the public agency." "If you lie one more time, you're out of here." The public agency won't simply take the child back. You adopted and agreed to raise the adoptee as if he were born to you. Unless the adoptee is presenting serious safety issues, he is staying in your home. Punitive parents threaten lengthy periods of deprivation—no snacks for a month or no television for a month. Is this reasonable? Can you carry this out? If you parent a child who has the capacity to leave a trail of wrappers around your house, likely he will find ways to have his cake and ice cream. If you are having a family movie night, what good does it do to leave out the family member having the hardest time learning to join the family?

- *Corporal Punishment is a no-win situation.* The traumatized child already believes that he has caused his birthmother or birthfather to abuse him. "I made them mad, so they beat me." Spanking is frequently perceived in the same way. "I made Dad mad, so he spanked me." The adoptee feels in control of the spanking. The intended learning experience expected to be inherent in the spanking went by the roadside. As stated previously in this chapter, abused and neglected children are already confused about love and trust. Corporal punishment implies the confounding message, "If you love me, you will hit me." Adoptive parents become comparable to birth parents who could not be trusted. Lastly, spanking and lying, stealing, breaking things, bedwetting, etc. don't go together. Spanking is not the natural and logical consequence for any behavior.
- *"Why?"* This is a word sure to generate a response that can anger a parent. "Why did you lie?" "Why did you break this?" "Why didn't you turn in your homework?" Responses include, "I don't know." "It wasn't me." Some children give no response. The infuriated parent pursues an answer. A lengthy argument results. During the conflict, the "why" was never answered, and the child most likely lied numerous additional times. A negative emotional climate was generated. The family became caught in a typhoon of destructive interactions.

The traumatized adoptee is often unable to explain why. In large part, this inability to determine behavioral motivations stems from the memory mechanisms of the brain.

Declarative or *explicit memory* refers to events we can recall. We have a conscious ability to retrieve the memory and state the facts and events. "On our trip to Florida, we went whale watching." "In first grade, I'll never forget Jean Marie wetting her pants in class."

Nondeclarative or *implicit memory* operates very differently. Implicit memory systems store emotions, sensory experiences, and expectations and assumptions about relationships based on prior experiences. Implicit memories form early in life prior to the individual having language. They cannot be recalled but they can be triggered (Briere and Scott, 2006). Chris dysregulates when he is told, "No, you can't have a snack." A current situation triggers his implicit memory of having little to eat in the orphanage. Lying in his crib, hungry, his brain absorbed the emotions associated with this experience, and his brain learned to expect that caregivers are people who do not meet your needs.

Mapping a Different Route

Key Point—Anger is a tornado hurling obstructions in the path to forming healthy relationships in adoptive families—anger intensifies negative behaviors. Anger creates an unhealthy environment for all members of the adoptive family—the adoptee, the birth and /or previously adopted children, and the parents. Parents must learn to bypass angry interactions. Modeling calmer, more nurturing responses improves the adoptee's emotional skills. Babies learn emotional regulation as a result of such calm interactions with a mom and dad. A fussy baby is held until his crying ceases. Eventually, his brain learns to calm down as needed. Abused and neglected children did not have this type of care giving. They must learn emotional regulation at later ages and with a traumatized brain. This is no small task. The sooner parents learn to interact in a calmer and less verbose manner, the sooner the whole family will enjoy a brighter, optimistic family atmosphere.

Learning to bypass angry interactions takes a conscious effort on the part of parents and the birth and/or previously adopted children. However, if parents and brothers and sisters pave the way to less angry exchanges, the adoptee will follow.

Education

Obviously, education is a main theme of this book. Understanding the transfer of emotions and comprehending that the traumatized brain works differently than does a brain exposed to a healthy environment is a key to reducing lengthy arguments. Once parents realize that the adoptee's early experiences, as well as their own coping styles and roadblocks, contribute to perpetuating their child's mental health issues, they are able to change direction. Education allows the opportunity to see their child differently. He isn't a kid who just likes to "piss me off." She isn't a child who could "stop if she wanted to." She or he is profoundly affected by early experiences—explicitly and implicitly. It will take repetitive calm, nurturing and empathic exchanges to repair the damage. Chapter 10's section "Finding Oases," will explore the use of nurturing in healing the adoptee. Nurture, as we will learn, is the ring that holds all of the keys.

Expect the Behavior

Many parents put a note next to their bed, "I live with a liar." "I live with someone who rejects my hugs." "I live with someone who won't do his homework." "I live with someone who wets the bed." "I live with someone who smears his poop." Each day the note serves as a reminder to deal with the particular behavior more calmly or to let the behavior go totally. The note could also read, "I am teaching Billy to be honest." "I am teaching Sally to be more careful with her things." Notes with this type of message *reframe* the behavior. The behavior isn't intentional—it is a skill the child is learning.

Awareness

Parents can identify those behaviors that are likely to "push their buttons." In essence, some negative behaviors cause stronger reactions than do others and which behaviors are perceived as worse varies from individual to individual. Parents need to examine the root of their reactions. Often, the behavior triggers the parent's own past issues.

For example, in the case of Tara, Danny and Chris, Tara's father had an affair that ultimately ended her parents' marriage. Her father's lie destroyed Tara's family. When Chris lies, it triggers Tara's anger about her father's unsavory actions. Chris receives this stored anger as well as the anger for the chronic lying he commits in relation to his food issues. Once Tara was helped to see this, she realized that she needed to work at moving beyond her father's affair. In the meantime, she was able to manage her reaction to Chris better because she understood why his behavior so enraged her.

Chapters 3 and 8 initiated the discussion of triggers. In Chapter 10's section "Coming Ashore: Letting Grief Flow," a trigger-management plan will be provided.

Step Back

Learn to step back and ask yourself, "Is this behavior worth tackling?" "Can I let it go?" "How can I challenge this situation calmly?" "Do I need to take a time-out?" "Do I need to wait until later in the day when my son or daughter is calm?" "What is the outcome I really want?"

In the case of Tara, Danny and Chris, what did Chris learn during his interactions with Tara and Danny? What did we want Chris to learn? Tara and Danny want Chris to understand that he doesn't need to sneak food. At the very least, when he does sneak food, he could put the garbage in the garbage can.

So, the storm could be averted by saying, "I'll be happy to help you with your homework as soon as you help me pick up the trash behind the couch." Chris will most likely reply, "But, I didn't make that mess." Tara can say, "I didn't say you made the mess. I said I need you to help me clean it up." The natural and logical consequence of making a mess is cleaning it up—no additional consequence is necessary. Further, working together—"I'll help you and you help me"—teaches reciprocity. The rubbish has been taken care of with no conflict.

Tara and Danny could decide to alter their language a bit. Instead of saying "No," either could state, "Yes, you may have a snack after dinner" (Cline and Fay, 2006). "No" is frequently a trigger of implicit and explicit memories. "No, I'm not coming back to be your mom. You'll live in the orphanage." "No, we're not adopting you. You will be moving to a new home." "No, you won't be living with your siblings." Chris hears "No" and nothing after "No." His brain is already moving along the path of his experiences of past rejection—his brain is mapped to follow a specific route. Once it reaches its destination, the tempest begins. All of his feelings about his past losses rumble and roar. Parents who can rid themselves of "No" bypass the storm.

Meet the Need

Tara and Danny also have the choice to meet Chris' perceived need. Early deprivation, especially in the area of food, leaves children consumed with food—overeating, hoarding, sneaking, stealing and so on. For other children, this plays out by collecting pens, pencils, string, cardboard, paper—all sorts of things!

Such issues can be reduced by meeting these needs. For example, Chris and Tara can fill 50 or so baggies with snacks—five M and M's in one bag, five goldfish crackers in another, five cheerios in a bag, etc. The bags would be placed in a basket and Chris could help himself to snacks anytime he feels he needs a snack (Keck and Kupecky, 2002). Chris "sees" a lot of food, but each bag actually holds little, and many of the bags have been filled with nutritious items. Yes, Chris may eat *many* bags over the first few weeks—perhaps as long as 10 to 12 weeks—as will the other children in the home. However, a few weeks later, all the kids, including Chris, will taper off. Chris will realize there is always food in the home. The other kids will have learned their parents were right—too many snacks ruin dinner!

As another example:

> Lisa, age 11, was adopted from the foster care system at age 3. She was removed from her birthparents as a result of severe neglect. She has always "collected" household items. As a pre-schooler, this included shoe boxes, little pieces of fabric and bottle caps. Once she entered kindergarten, pencils became her object of choice. She would arrive home with five, six or more pencils. Fellow students were always looking for their pencils! This has continued through each grade. Her fifth grade teacher, Mrs. Baily, a wise woman, purchased an array of pencils after a consultation with Lisa's mom. Each day, she gave Lisa several pencils throughout the day. The pencils were different colors, some were fat, some were skinny, some had animal shaped erasers and some had writing on them like, "great job." Lisa loved these pencils. She looked forward to getting to school to see what pencils she would receive from Mrs. Baily. This very economical solution ended the disappearance of class mates' pencils. After several months, Lisa, on her own, said, "No thanks, Mrs. Baily. I think I have enough pencils now." Lisa's need for pencils had been met!

Listen to the Behavior

Key Point—Many behaviors have their roots deep within the brain. Processing the implicit memories is called for so that the adoptee learns to differentiate past from present caregivers. Through this process his thinking normalizes, and he is taught how to express emotions. He no longer has a need to transfer emotions or to fear intimate relationships. Children who enter the family via adoption benefit from being told the truth, and in fact, the whole family gains. As the adoptee makes sense of his past, he is able to form deeper attachments to parents, brothers and sisters.

Key Point—Behavioral change is about much more than doling out contrived consequences or earning rewards. Each parenting intervention offered is designed to facilitate developmental growth—cause-and-effect thinking, moral development, reciprocity, emotional regulation, emotional expression, problem-solving skills, social skills and so on. Once your "little" child develops cognitively, emotionally and socially, he will grow and mature into a respectful, responsible family member who is fun to be with (Cline and Faye, 2006).

As we have established, children who have experienced neglect and abuse use their behavior to tell us their feelings. Their behavior also tells us much about the past experiences they find troublesome. For example, stealing is often reflective of, "I feel stolen." Certainly, removing a child from an orphanage and flying a long distance to a strange new environment could appear to the child as "being stolen." Traumatized children sometimes lose possessions right and left. This may mean, "I feel lost." I think many of us would feel lost if we moved from foster home to foster home and our needs were overseen by the complex maze called the child welfare system.

We can use these messages to restructure implicit and explicit memories. We do so through the narrative. Continuing with Chris, he would benefit from understanding that he whines and cries when denied food now because his brain remembers the time when he was hungry. The narrative written for his lifebook needs to contain the information that will explain his behavior.

> "You might have been hungry in the orphanage because there wasn't enough food. You might have been hungry because you dropped your bottle. You were too little to pick it up, so you went hungry. This was very scary when you were a baby. Now, when Mom and Dad tell you 'No' your brain remembers this and you think you will go hungry. Mom and Dad never run out of food. Mom and Dad tell you 'No' because they want you to eat healthy. Too many snacks make it so that you won't have room for the good dinners your mom cooks."

Eventually, with repetition, Chris' brain will integrate the new message and his preoccupation with food will decrease. Thus, the storm will pass over permanently.

Sleep difficulties and problematic car behaviors often have their origins in the implicit memory. Nighttime can be scary in an orphanage or a dysfunctional birthfamily. This is a time when abuse is likely to occur. Or, a youngster awakens to find she is alone, which is frightening to young children. The car can be a reminder of leaving the orphanage. The car can be a trigger for moving from foster home to foster home. The car may be reminiscent of the reunification visits conducted after the child is in foster care.

> Brandy is age 5. She was removed from her birth home at 14 months due to severe neglect that actually required a three week hospital stay before she could go to a foster home. Subsequently, she was transported to visit her birthmother every Wednesday. As time went on, Brandy physically fought the foster mom and social worker on Wednesday mornings. She would scream, hit, kick, head butt and bite. The two women had to physically restrain her to get her into her car seat. Even after she was buckled in, she continued screaming all the way to the visitation center. These visits upset her greatly. Because she could not talk, she used her behavior to demonstrate her anxiety about what was now occurring in her life.
>
> Nine months passed, and Brandy was returned to her birthmother's care. The foster mother was assigned the task of driving Brandy to the birthmom's home and handing Brandy and her belongings back to the birthmom. Within a few days, the birthmother called the foster mother to come take her for the day. The "day" soon became a pattern—the foster mom had Brandy many days and some weekends. The foster mother provided this child care as she was afraid the birthmother would leave Brandy alone if she didn't take her. In Brandy's implicit memory this translated into, "My good mom keeps giving me back to the mom who doesn't take care of me. Neither of these moms seems to want me. I must be a bad baby. Sometimes I get good food and my diaper gets changed, and sometimes I am dirty and hungry—moms can't be trusted."
>
> Ultimately, Brandy was again removed from her birthmother and parental rights were terminated. The foster family adopted Brandy. To this day, the car presents various problems. Brandy won't stay buckled in. She screams and cries in her car seat. She throws objects if she can. She kicks the back of the driver or passenger seats. Brandy's implicit memory system remembers and reacts to her early experiences. Obviously, the entire adoptive family is disrupted by these behaviors.

Consequencing such behaviors or being angry about such difficulties is pointless, because the obstacle—the implicit memories—must be removed. These memories lie along the path, like fallen rocks, impeding the family's journey to improved relationships.

Sibling Rivalry

Sibling relationships are also affected by a transfer of emotions and the adoptee's trigger-susceptible brain. Adoption may mean a change in birth order. Transitioning to a new position within the family constellation will likely generate some unpleasant or uncomfortable situations until children reconfigure their place in the family. Throw unmet expectations into the mix, and sibling rivalry becomes a gale wind. Conflict erupts with every gust.

Sibling conflict is unavoidable. Certainly, the positive side is that it can be a valuable experience. It teaches negotiating, compromising and listening to another's point of view. Sibling disagreements better prepare children for relationships outside of the family—with peers, co-workers, college roommates, boyfriends and girlfriends, and so on.

In complex adoptive families, sibling rivalry will share some elements in common with families built by birth such as, "Mom, she's using my makeup again." "Dad, make him come inside. I want to play basketball with my friends." Yet, other aspects of sibling conflict which are due to grief, jealousy and possible abuse may lead to fierce sibling rivalry and very inappropriate sibling interactions. In Chapter 3, information and recommendations were made regarding siblings and sexual abuse. Below, aggression and emotional abuse will be discussed.

Grief-related thoughts and feelings often underlie sibling rivalry in adoption-built families.

The chart on the previous page depicts thinking that contributes to sibling conflicts. The statements each contain losses and feelings. As examples:

- "You're adopted and I'm not." Anger motivates a typical sibling to shout this at her adopted brother. The anger could be rooted in the changes that have occurred in the family. Or the resident child may be angry that her adopted brother was in her room for the hundredth time! The negative behavior is a reminder that, "I had more privacy before you came." The feelings of being robbed are compounded by the loss of the family as it was.
- "Can you really want me as a brother or sister?" Just as the adoptee wonders how his adoptive parents can want him when his own birth parents didn't, he perceives he is unlovable to his new brothers and sisters.
- "They are so lucky to live together." The adoptee's grief for the birth siblings living elsewhere is triggered by observing brothers and sisters in the adoptive family.
- "I asked for a brother or sister." It is my fault that Mom and Dad aren't as happy as they used to be.
- "You look different. You're not even from America." I look at you and "see" that our family is different. I long for the old family. I am tired of people looking at us when we are out in public. I hate it when people ask me, "Is that your sister?"

Can you identify the hidden issues in the other thoughts and comments listed in the table? Can you identify any thoughts specific to your typically developing children? What losses are at the bottom of their thoughts? What feelings result from these losses?

Siblings with unresolved grief collide. Day-to-day situations trigger feelings about the losses experienced due to integrating the adoptee into the family system. The rivalry is intensified because the grief is unleashed—along with the anger, frustration, resentment, sadness and jealousy about the current situation, which could result in a negative behavior or another unpleasant family outing.

A first step in reducing sibling rivalry is to identify the losses felt by both the already resident children and the adoptee. Then find ways for all of the brothers and sisters to resolve their grief. Chapter 10's "Letting Grief Flow" will offer ways to facilitate grief. In the meantime, here are some other points to keep in mind when helping resident and new kids form relationships:

- Stress increases sibling rivalry. Monitor the amount of stress each child is experiencing in all areas of his life—physical, cognitive, emotional and social. Reduce stress whenever and wherever possible.
- Parents influence their children's sibling relationships by the general emotional climate created within the family. Generally, family conflict breeds sibling conflict. Again, children follow the parents' lead.
- The way parents resolve their own conflicts sets a strong example for kids. So, how do you resolve conflict? Is it the way in which you want your children to resolve conflict?
- Sibling rivalry conjures up parents' own memories of their relationships with their siblings. Here again, parents need to gain awareness of how past experiences contribute to their reactions to their children's individual actions as well as to sibling interactions.

THOUGHTS CONTRIBUTING TO SIBLING CONFLICTS IN COMPLEX FAMILIES

Typically Developing Siblings	Adoptee
I want to "unadopt" him. He is so hard to play with. I wanted to teach her things. I'm the one that wanted a brother or sister. You're adopted and I'm not. You look different. You're not even from America. If I'm not good will I have to move? I hate being told that I have to set the example. I am tired of babysitting. Why wasn't I enough for Mom and Dad?	Can you really want me as a brother or sister? I wish my brothers and sisters would play with me the way they play with each other. My brothers and sisters are so lucky to live together. I want to live with my birth siblings. I look different from everybody in my family. They are having friends over again. They are going out with their friends again. They act so "perfect." Mom and Dad love them more because they were born to them. My brothers and sisters get more, and get to do more, than I do.

"When parents are aware of how much old memories can influence their reactions to their children, they may find they are better able to choose their response" (Sparrow, 2005).

- Families that don't have enjoyable times will have more conflict. One adoptive mom recently stated, "On a really bad day when we're all on each other's nerves, I order pizza and pick out a movie. A good mood arrives along with the pizza!"
- Eliminate battles when possible. Shannon, a single mom, provides an example:

> Shannon adopted Peggy when she was 8 years old. Peggy is now 11. A few months ago, Shannon received a foster care placement, Justin and Joey, 6 and 7 years old. Peggy was instantly jealous of any time or attention Shannon provided the young boys. Arrival home from school was particularly challenging. Shannon would put out cookies and milk for the boys. Peggy usually got her own snack and a drink. However, complaints of, "Why do you get them their snack?" and "I want what they're having," prompted Shannon to put out three plates of cookies and three glasses of milk. This fight was resolved.
>
> Brenda, the adoptive mom of seven children ranging in age from toddler to older adolescents, with the two oldest children, ages 16 and 17, having the most mental health issues, states, "The natural family formation calls for children becoming more independent from their parents as they get older, but we have found just the opposite works in our family. Also, especially one of our adopted daughters, now age 16, is so immature; she spends a lot of time fighting or picking on the younger ones. She is admittedly jealous of them and has often said that she wishes they weren't here. When she gets upset with us and starts throwing a tantrum, even when it does not involve the younger children in any way whatsoever, she starts talking about how all we care about is our 'precious little baby brats' or other choice words that hurt feelings.
>
> "I don't feel freedom to leave the older girls at home alone for any extended period of time, so I usually have to take them with me everywhere, which in turn is difficult. They compete with the younger children for attention, fighting over who is pushing the cart, who is opening the automatic door and other unimportant things.
>
> "There is an age where being the one who turns off the TV is reason for pride, but instead of having a few children take turns turning it off, I have to include a 16 and sometimes the 17-year-old in the rotation. So much energy is spent on those kinds of things that hardly any of it is left over for what really should matter. It is exhausting."

The green-eyed monster darts across the highway, causing havoc time and again. Traumatized children can be very jealous of any parental time and attention given to the other children in the family. Avoid jealousy-generating situations when possible. Humor may also diffuse the situation. In therapy, complaints of, "My brother got a new truck" or "My sister just got new clothes" are responded to with, "Okay, the next time Mom gets a new bra she'll get one for everyone." Immediately, the child replies, "I don't need a bra!" "The mortgage needs to be paid. Go get your piggy bank." Again the child replies, "I don't want to spend my money on that." They precisely draw the correct conclusions—everyone in the family gets what they need and sometimes they get what Mom and Dad feel like buying.

The way in which parents respond to sibling conflicts and aggressive actions is an important factor in the look of further conflicts and their outcome—neither punitive actions nor a total "hands off" approach is effective (Cicirelli, 1995). Jean and Matt parent four children, two by birth and two by adoption. Jean said,

> "Talk about sibling rivalry! My kids fight a lot! And, I do mean fight—push, shove, punch, etc. My adopted son's first reaction is to hit. I used to feel like I was a referee. Then, I decided to take a different approach. I sat the fighting children at the table with some cookies and milk, when the fight was over a larger issue, and made them come up with solutions. I sat with them or listened while I cleaned the kitchen. I made suggestions as I felt necessary. I have a lot less fighting now and a lot more free time."

Jean felt like a referee until she altered the manner in which she handled the siblings' rivalry. Her approach is actually between the two polar opposites noted above. The cookies and milk disarmed the children. Once calm, they were more open to resolving their dispute. Often, one of the kids needed to cool off in his room before he would come to the table. Jean also decided which disagreements warranted her help and which didn't. She didn't involve herself if the matter was minor. Jean's method would work in any family, but it is an essential tool when one of the children has mental health issues. Children who have experienced trauma have difficulty coming up with solutions. They may need a parent nearby to interject ideas. They will need some help to resolve conflicts. She also had "no favorites" and "no comparisons" policies.

However, when sibling conflict escalates into frequent violent interactions, or the physical or mental abuse of a weaker sibling is caused by a stronger sibling this can be harmful (Cicirelli, 1995). There are also cases in which one child repeatedly exposes the other sibling's vulnerabilities in an intentional effort to humiliate that child (Sparrow, 2005). In such instances where there is a clear imbalance of power, the parent will need to step in. Joseph Sparrow, author of *Understanding Sibling Rivalry* (Cambridge: Da Capo Press, 2005) says,

> "When it is necessary for a parent to intervene, it will be important to keep from giving the older or stronger child more to be angry about, more fuel for her fights. Talk with that child about herself, not the other child: 'When you get out of control like this, I'll have to help you.' And to the victim: 'You are going to need to learn to protect yourself. You may have to learn to get away from her for now. But you're going to learn ways to protect yourself.'"

Overall, evacuating the area of conflict is often a good interim solution. Many children, even toddlers, can learn to go to a "safe spot" if an adult or older sibling is not available to remove them from the destructive sibling's path of fury. The safe spot is complete with a safe spot bag that contains snacks and a few new inexpensive toys.

However, the more important point to understand is that when there is an aggressive child in the family, she becomes the focus. She receives the bulk of the consequences and the majority of the attention—anger—while the victim receives sympathy. Actually, the victim is engaging in just as poor of a pattern of behavior as the aggressor, and so the victim needs to change as well.

Further, the parent described above is responding calmly. Keep in mind that aggressive sibling interactions are a good way to elicit parental anger—a negative emotional climate occurs. Parents who react with anger will intensify the sibling rivalry. Brothers and sisters who chronically engage in angry interactions with their mentally ill sibling perpetuate the violence. Much negative sibling behavior will decrease when anger is reduced.

Jill and Mitchell, whom we have met in several chapters, offer this concluding advice about protecting infants from aggressive siblings. Since we last checked in with them, they have adopted again—a beautiful infant daughter from Viet Nam.

"Adopting our infant daughter, Jessica, with two unhealthy children already in residence has been a bit challenging. I take special precautions to keep her safe. We just can't trust Ivan and Svetelina to ever be alone with the baby, or the dog for that matter. When I shower, the baby comes with me. I put her in the stroller and push her into the bathroom where I know she'll be safe. Her crib is in our room, and I never leave her out of my sight. I have a child-proof door knob cover on the outside of our door as a double precaution. If she's napping they cannot get in, and I do keep an eye on them at all times. They've always needed constant monitoring, even before the baby. I've never left them unsupervised so this is really nothing new. Now that the baby is older she wants to play with them and they do seem to like her. I still keep a very close watch; there's no way I'm taking any chances.

"Svetelina really loves the baby. I think Jessica's presence has helped her to develop more nurturing feelings. Watching me with the baby has caused Svetelina to think about when she was a baby. She's been able to talk about it and ask questions with an ease that she didn't have before. She also loves helping out. She'll get me diapers, pick up things when Jessica throws them off the high chair, and she's also very playful with her. If Jessica is crying she talks to her and tries to comfort her. I think it's helped her to understand that moms love their babies and take care of them. She's expressed that she is sad that her Russian mom didn't do those things for her. I think she's finally starting to realize that she's my baby, just like Jessica is and I'm always going to love her and take care of her too. I think she's more affectionate toward me now and is beginning to attach."

Overall, the best solution regarding abusive sibling interactions is to end the violence or emotional torment and the victim mentality. Parents are encouraged to seek professional assistance when these types of interactions persist.

The section in Chapter 10, "Finding Oases," will promote nurture as a way to decrease aggression and inappropriate sexual behaviors. "Good" touch often facilitates decreases in "bad" touch.

Energy

Each person has only so much energy. Energy is comparable to a tank of gas. There is a continuum from full to empty. Parents who top off their tanks frequently are better able to handle the day-to-day challenges of balancing their responsibilities than are parents who wait until the "almost empty" light comes on to tank up.

Keeping up energy requires that parents keep their tanks full. There are no benefits to any family member when parents are worn out, exhausted, frustrated, over-worked, stressed out, rushing from one place to the next, distraught, nervous and in general just run down.

Tick, Tock: Making Time

This heading probably has you saying, "Yeah right! How does she expect me to do that?" Not easily—that's for sure!

Everyday life seems to have become a whirlwind of activity from dawn to dusk. Is this really necessary? Isn't there *anyone* else who can drive the kids to soccer or ballet? Is "no" *really* that hard to say? Does the house *really* need to be cleaned today? Do you actually *need* to answer the phone every time the school calls? Do you need to be in-person for *every* school meeting?

In Chapter 3, you were given the option of completing the pie graph that represented a 24-hour period. You were supposed to use different colors to fill in the amount of time you devote to sleep, exercise/sports, work, school-related matters, personal care/grooming, transportation, meal preparation/eating/clean-up, relaxation, socializing, family commitments and medical appointments. If you haven't done that yet, take a few minutes and complete this now. If your family has expanded since you read Chapter 3, you'll likely need to re-do the graph, as your time usage will have changed since the arrival of the new child.

Now, go back to the skill of reflection we learned earlier in the chapter. Begin to identify the activities that dominate your time. Are there tasks within these areas that could be accomplished more efficiently or in a different way? Some veteran parents are going to help us out with ideas as to how they have been able to enhance their time management for themselves and for their children. These ideas also contribute to leveling out the inequities experienced by the birth and/or previously adopted children that we talked about earlier.

Carol, a parent of four—three by birth and one by adoption

"This past Christmas I asked my family—my siblings, my parents, my aunts and cousins—to pool all of the money they would have spent buying gifts for myself, my husband and my children. Instead of buying the traditional clothes, CDs and coloring books, I asked for a cleaning service. A few of my own siblings thought this was a bit different. But, I really don't care. It's what I needed. I would do the same for them if they asked me. It totaled enough to have the house cleaned, from top to bottom, six times!"

Carol is a great example of someone who can *ask for what she needs*. All too often there seems to be an attitude of "I have to do it myself." Actually, you don't and most likely, you can't without exhausting yourself. In passing this suggestion on to other families, another mom asked her family for gift certificates to restaurants, especially those with a delivery service—no traffic and no waiting in line. She now spends less time in the kitchen. She uses the free time for herself. No, she doesn't use it to get something done. She relaxes!

You can also turn this idea into *ask my spouse what he or she needs*, and *ask my typically developing children what they need*. Often, one spouse *expects* that the other knows what is needed. Well, unless mind-reading is a specialty, it is likely the need will remain unmet. How many arguments does this scenario create?

Frequently, parents think they are meeting the needs of their resident children. Or, worse yet, in the process of trying to "fix" the adoptee, parents believe that because these children are healthy they can meet many of their own needs. Many parents have expressed, "Our daughter is so patient. She understands that we can't do as much for her until Billy is okay." If you are thinking along these lines, think again! All of your children have needs, and all of your children need you. There is no guarantee that you can meet all of their needs, but likely some can be met. Commonly expressed needs by brothers and sisters include being on time for their practices or special events, spending focused time with their parents, one birthday party that goes well, or some extra privacy or alone time.

Diane and Dave parent six children—four by birth and two by adoption

Dave said, "The two adoptees steal and they have no boundaries. We got each child a foot locker. Anything important gets locked in the foot locker. We also had a small room we used as a junk room. We got rid of the junk, gave it a fresh coat of paint and some furniture. This is now a space for anyone who wants to spend some time alone."

Valerie and Peter parent five children—three by birth and two by adoption

"Our one adopted son caused many problems at school. This was an embarrassment to our other children. Eventually we made the decision to place him in a small private school. It means that we had to cut expenses in other areas. But, it has been worth it! Our kids can go to school and not worry about what he will do and who will say something to them about what he did. It has cut down on the conflicts between our kids. Now, we have time to talk about their day rather than talking to them about their brother's day at school and how they were affected by their brother's actions."

Michelle and Mark parent one child by birth and one child by adoption

"We home school both children. Our adopted son throws fits on and off all day, every day. The stress of his screaming affected me and my daughter. One day per week, he goes to a child care center. He is able to do well outside of the home in relationships that aren't as intimate. He enjoys going, and my daughter and I enjoy some nice time together. I am considering sending him to public school for a year. I think my daughter could use an extended break. It has been six years of these fits."

Louise and Ray parent three birth sons and one adopted daughter

Ray states, "Our daughter had various negative behaviors at school. She threw things at teachers, stole school supplies, walked out of classes, etc. When the principal confronted her, she would often become highly argumentative with him. He would call me at work—sometimes I had to leave work and go calm her down. Other times they wanted me to take her home. In these instances, I would have to go to work early the next day or stay late to get my work done. I was losing a lot of time with my boys. Finally, Louise and I sat down with the school and explained that we couldn't do this anymore. Eventually, they moved our daughter to a special education classroom. While I don't think this is ideal, it has improved our home life. I can make it to all the boys' games now. Overall, we don't know how well our daughter is going to get. So, her education isn't as much of a priority as is time with our sons and her mental health services."

Lorraine and Peter, the parents of seven adopted children

Lorraine and Peter have adopted seven children, all of whom have varying degrees of mental health issues. They use a *divide and conquer* approach. She handles three of the children's academic needs while he handles the other four.

"The teachers are informed which parent is assigned to which child. We do their IEP meetings via telephone. The nice thing about cell phones is the speaker phone option. We can participate in a meeting from anywhere. We go once each year, for each child, in person, so the teachers can meet us and we can meet the teachers. After that, everything is by phone. This saves a lot of travel and a lot of time off from work. We also limit the calls from the school to those involving actual emergencies. If we see their number on the caller ID, we know it is important and we need to answer. Otherwise, a note home will do. We also require that all permission slips, requests for cupcakes, anything the kids need to bring in for a project, etc. be mailed directly to us. That way, we don't find something in a backpack that requires we change our routine or plans at the last minute."

Vivian and Frank are a family home schooling a resident child and two newly adopted children

> Vivian says, "I provide instruction to my two sons. My daughter gets her lessons online. Her control issues are too great for her to take directions from me. The whole day is calmer since we made this choice. We are able to have some enjoyable time during the day."

The education environment presents various challenges for adoptive families. The five families above offer us numerous great solutions for school-related problems.

Lorraine and Peter from above provide a good example of setting limits in order to make time for the family. Really, you don't have to go to every meeting in person. *Setting limits* and learning to *say "no"* are two important skills when it comes to time management. They also divide and conquer—they complement each other as parents, which exemplifies discussion in Chapter 4.

Tom, an adoptive father of three children with a range of mental health issues

> "Before the kids, I used to go to the gym every day. I enjoyed this immensely and felt good about myself. Once the kids came, this went by the wayside. I began getting depressed. I decided I needed to exercise, but I couldn't work out getting to the gym. So, I bought a treadmill. In the long run, it is cheaper than paying the annual gym fees. I feel good again. When I get angry with the kids, it's a great way to release my frustration."

Bob, a father of five—three children by adoption and two by birth

> "We lived in a house with a large yard and a lot of landscaping needing lots of maintenance. We moved. We now have a large detached condo. I enjoy sitting on the deck watching the landscapers mow the yard and trim the shrubs. My wife and kids enjoy the clubhouse. The pool is open year round."

Over time, I have known many families that have made the decision to move. Some of the moves occurred due to the cultural composition of their family or to locate to a better school district. But other moves have occurred for reasons such as Bob described. Still other families have moved to lessen their mortgage payments. This means that Dad can stop working a 60-hour week and spend more time with his family.

Nina, a single parent of two adopted children—one typically developing and one with mental health issues

> "Fortunately, my mentally unhealthy daughter doesn't mind going to her room. So, in the evening, she goes to her room 30 minutes earlier than my healthy daughter. She doesn't have to go to sleep. She just needs to play in her room. This is my special time each day to be with my typical daughter. Sometimes we play a game, sometimes we talk, and sometimes we just watch a television show. Twice a month, they both go to their rooms an hour early. I use this time for me."

Robert, a stay-at-home dad, and parent of two children by birth and one by adoption

> "I use the Crock Pot™ a lot more. It is quick. It has definitely cut down on how much fast food we eat. Two nights per week, we use paper plates—no dishes and no arguments about who's going to do the dishes!"

Tony and Maude, parents of three children—two by birth and one by adoption

"We live close to our jobs and our kids' school. We often surprise the kids by showing up to take them out to lunch. Sometimes, we even 'kidnap' our two birth children. We take them out of school for the afternoon, and we go do something special. While we value education, we value our time alone with our kids too. Our adopted child has many needs and this makes it difficult for us to go out as a family, or to go out without him, on weekends or evenings. Given the choice between social studies or time with the children, we choose time with the kids."

Heather and Ray parent four children—three by birth and one by adoption

Heather says, "I used to organize some events at school like the spelling bee, bake sales, etc. Then, when Sam came I thought I needed that time to be with him. Now I realize there is a compromise. Instead of organizing the event, I volunteer. It is a lot less time but still fulfilling."

Notice the word *compromise*. Too often, parents just stop doing pleasurable activities totally. Heather found the middle ground. Can you?

Denise and her husband parent five children—two step-children and three adopted

"The transportation to and from appointments, errands and extracurricular activities was just a nightmare. I finally decided to ask two of my neighbors for help. They are retired. They were delighted to help out. I think it makes them feel good. I have free time now. I have returned to cooking some homemade meals. I have always enjoyed cooking. My parents live out of town, so the neighbors are also like having another set of grandparents. I make sure to give them a gas gift card here and there. The kids help them shovel their walk and driveway in the winter—these things go along with riding in their car, and it saves them the money of paying someone to do it. I wish I had asked sooner."

Transportation is a time-consuming task. It is as if life is all conducted in the car these days. Time in the car does allow for conversation, and many kids seem to get their homework done in the car. However, there is the unproductive flip side of being on the cell phone (which is also very dangerous!), popping a movie in the DVD player and of course playing hand-held electronic games. Think about your car time. Is interaction occurring, or are you all together but everyone is actually doing his own thing? How can you change this?

If I Only Had More Time

When we begin working with families at our office, we always ask the parents, "What did you do before you adopted?" There is usually quite a pause. Then, finally, husbands and wives begin to recall the leisure pursuits they used to enjoy. Now that you are going to make having some extra time to fill up your energy tank a top priority, decide what you might want to do. List a few quick and easy things such as sitting on the porch for a few minutes of quiet time, enjoying a cup of tea, having a bubble bath, reading a magazine article and so on, and then list more substantial interests—playing cards with the boys twice per month, joining a book club, making models, volunteering, taking a class, enjoying a weekend away with your spouse, etc. Starting with the quick things, make a commitment to carry out a few within the next couple of weeks.

Too often we wait until we have a block of time—an entire morning or evening, a whole day or a weekend. Then, something comes up and the pit stop gets put off—your tank becomes dangerously low on energy. Remember that we talked about re-thinking family fun? Well, now we also need to re-think time. Just as with family fun, think about making time in terms of small and frequent increments at first. Work toward larger time periods. Mobilization is a more successful process when we start small and make gradual increases over time.

In Chapter 10, "Finding Oases," we'll look at some additional ways to build support. This content will help free up more time that will allow parents to meet their individual needs and their marital needs. A strong couple relationship contributes to the well-being of all of the children in the family.

Do you remember the section, "Start a Habit" from Chapter 6? Have you scheduled time for the children already in the family prior to the adoption? If not, put this book down and go pick up your date book.

From early bedtime, to moving, to gift cards, to making an alone room, there *are* ways to free up time. Yet, it takes planning, creativity, asking for help, making needs clear, saying "no," setting limits, compromising and establishing priorities for this to be successful.

Priorities: Whose Needs First?

Deciding whose needs take priority is often like trying to see the road through a dense fog. In the day-to-day challenges of complex adoptive families, priorities frequently seem elusive or become muddied. Here we present a framework to guide decision making and goal setting—skills we identified in Chapter 3—in this area of prioritizing. Keep in mind that each family has unique characteristics. Alterations may be needed to apply this information to a specific family.

Clyde and Lillian, whom we met in Chapter 3, parent four birth daughters, currently ages 15–22, and one daughter whom they adopted. Tami arrived when she was 16 months old. She is now age 8. Tami presents various difficulties due to the complex trauma she sustained when she resided with her birthmother. Her current issues include

- behavioral problems
- learning difficulties
- a desire to return to her birthmother
- delayed social skills
- problems with focus and attention.

In response to Tami, Leann, age 17, has withdrawn from the family and Betsy, age 15, has developed depression. This family also continues to foster.

Where should we start? What takes priority?

In our parent-centered and child-focused model, we go in order of parents first and then children. Overall, we divide the family into three main areas:

Family

Parents

Children

⇩

Medical

Mental Health

Education

⇩

Physical

Cognitive

Social

Emotional

Then, within each section—medical, mental health and education—we look at physical, cognitive, emotional and social needs. In Chapter 5, we covered adoptees' medical/physical issues. When complex trauma was discussed in Chapter 2, we utilized a cognitive, emotional and social model. In those chapters, we applied the four spheres to the individual traumatized child. Here we are going to look at these areas in terms of the impact on the entire family. Thus, we are expanding on information presented earlier. It is important to note that these four areas operate like a set of gears. When one isn't working well, it affects how the others operate.

Medical Priorities

Physical Needs

In examining medical priorities, we are basically looking at the proper medical care and overall physical well-being of each family member. Proper medical care is essential for each member of the family. Adoptive parents tend to be very good about making sure their children visit the doctor regularly. However, they often neglect their own physical well-being. They don't schedule routine medical appointments for themselves, or they cancel appointments because they feel they need to be at a school meeting or a therapy appointment. Remember, you need to keep your tank full—keep your own doctor appointment and re-schedule other meetings.

This category also requires answering questions that lend to overall medical/physical health.

Is the family eating a healthy diet?

Is the family eating regular meals?

Is everyone getting enough physical activity?

How much sleep are parents and children getting?

Is there enough rest and relaxation to maintain good physical health?

Is each family member getting routine check-ups?

Is everyone taking medications as prescribed?

As parents, do you work when you are sick?

Physical well-being is a key to mobilization. For example, parents who are rested are less likely to become irritable. Children's behavior is affected by their sleep patterns as well. Certainly, the media has made us all aware of the benefits of exercise for our physical, emotional, cognitive and social well-being. Exercise is a good example of how the "gears" work together. Physical activity contributes positively to all aspects of our lives. Regular meals—shared together—have many documented benefits. Adults and children who share meals are less likely to snack and are more likely to eat fruits, vegetables and whole grains. Kids who are given time to connect with their family members are less likely to smoke, drink alcohol and use drugs.[1] Again, meeting physical needs contributes to meeting cognitive, emotional and social needs.

This physical domain also includes fine and gross motor skills, speech, and sensory development (see Chapter 10.) Children who experience trauma often have deficits in all of these areas. Chapter 5 covered various types of speech and language issues and pointed out that underdeveloped muscles result when children lie in orphanage cribs for extended periods of time, or when children reside in neglectful birth families.

Regarding sensory development, Sensory Integration Dysfunction (SI) is caused by the brain's inability to accurately process information coming in through the senses—eyes, ears, skin and nose. In Chapter 5, it was suggested that parents surf the Internet in order to understand SI. If you didn't do that, the next time you're online, make it a priority. The Chapter 5 Resources section listed two books on SI as well. Neglect, and prenatal drug and alcohol exposure are two culprits in causing SI.

In conclusion, exploring the physical domain requires routine medical exams, carrying out any necessary medical treatment/procedures; evaluating sensory, speech and motor skills development; and monitoring your family's diet, physical activity, sleep and relaxation patterns. The professionals needed to carry out these services include physician/pediatrician, adoption medical clinic staff and speech, physical, and occupational therapists (Chapter 10).

> In our example family, Betsy first visited her pediatrician to rule out any physical causes for her depression. Tami's pediatrician referred her for mental health services. Medical conditions had already been ruled out in her case. Tami was referred for a speech evaluation. She was also referred for an SI evaluation because of her complex trauma, and some of her behavioral issues are associated with SI. The remaining family members reported that they were in "good" health. There were no serious medical concerns impairing their ability to carry out their parenting responsibilities.
>
> Tami was diagnosed with moderate SI. These services were implemented immediately. Her speech evaluation concluded that she also needed services in this area. These services were available through the school. When the school is a viable option for services, it saves the family time and co-pays.
>
> Tami also visited a psychiatrist (Chapter 10). Tami began taking medication to help with mood instability and impulsivity. In Tami's case, the medication did reduce the intensity of her temper outbursts. Medication was also suggested for Betsy. However, therapy was opted for first. Medication would be re-visited if therapy alone didn't resolve Betsy's depression.

1. Gavin, Mary. "Family Meals." http://kidshealth.org/parent/food/general/family_meals.html

Mental Health and Academic Priorities

Here is where the fog begins to get dense. Let's let Betsy, Leann and Tami help us find the road.

> Betsy presents with mild impairment to her mental health. Academically, she is able to perform well simultaneous to resolving her depression. Socially, she has withdrawn from leisure pursuits. However, her social skills are well-developed. Leann is fine medically and educationally, and actually her mental health is good. She stopped communicating with her family because she felt they were under so much pressure dealing with Tami.
>
> Tami, on the other hand, was assessed to have moderate mental health issues. Her mental health issues negatively influence her academic performance, her emotional well-being, and her peer and family relationships.

In cases like Tami's, we aren't exactly in an "either/or" situation regarding which to prioritize first—mental health or academic needs. However, we do have to make some choices. This point will become clear shortly.

Cognitive Needs

Cognitive needs include intellectual development—thinking, reasoning, problem-solving, abstract thinking and language development.

> Tami struggled to learn to read. The school's recommendations for improving Tami's reading skills were for Tami to attend a three-week summer school program as well as a Saturday reading program to be conducted over six Saturdays. Six Saturdays and a three-week summer program would seriously impair the family's summer plans for vacation and other fun.
>
> Leann had irrational thoughts about her importance (or lack of it) in the family. She withdrew because of these thoughts.
>
> Lillian and Clyde were totally befuddled by the state of their family. This confusion inhibited their capacity to reason through their situation. Certainly, at this point in the book, we can clearly see how this has occurred.

Issues to consider in assessing cognitive needs may include

- Are we adjusting expectations?
- Are we reflecting as often as we need to so as to keep our priorities straight?
- Are we engaging in new learning experiences? This contributes to enhanced intellectual functioning and the education it takes to manage an adoptive family successfully.
- Are we communicating effectively? Do we all actually listen to one another? These queries contribute to solving problems, conflict resolution and improved reasoning skills.
- Do we receive feedback or seek out feedback? Do we get any validation for our parenting efforts? Do we make sure to celebrate all of our children's successes? Does my spouse give me compliments? Are we respected at work, among friends and so on?
- Are we maintaining focus?

Exploring the cognitive domain requires clarifying academic needs and placing these needs in their proper place in the priority model, adjusting expectations, learning new areas of information, giving and receiving feedback, reflection, communicating our thoughts to others effectively and listening.

Adoption-competent mental health professionals, teachers, principals and guidance counselors are professionals who can offer directions in the cognitive sphere of family development.

Emotional Needs

This area includes self-concept, reciprocity and the ability to identify, express, and regulate emotions. We're going to look briefly at this need here as we already explored emotional needs in depth under the heading, "Reactions: Changing Direction to Avoid the Approaching Storm."

We learned in Chapter 5 that children who are plagued with anxieties about their past are prone to learning problems. Regarding Tami's reading problems we need to ask, "Is it that Tami can't learn to read, or are Tami's reading difficulties because of her trauma?" If the latter, then resolving her trauma will lead to gains in reading as well as other educational endeavors.

As mentioned earlier in this chapter, there is the option of obtaining psychological or neuropsychological testing to determine the manner in which Tami's brain processes information, and whether any learning disabilities exist. An adoption medical clinic, the school, your family physician or your health insurance company can help you locate professionals who conduct this type of testing. Additionally, psychological testing is available through the school, at no cost, per IDEA (see Chapter 5).

Tami's mental health therapist felt that Tami was already under a lot of stress. She was going to school, speech therapy, SI therapy, mental health therapy and participating in two extracurricular activities, all while she was struggling to figure out why she wasn't with her birthmother. Summer vacation would be a nice break for Tami, and with fewer distractions, she could concentrate on her abandonment issues.

Tami's case calls to light the questions, "How much is an 8-year-old supposed to manage?" and, "What is really *most* important for Tami at this time?" Each family must ask these questions in relation to all of their children. Like Leann, Betsy and Tami, children from very young through adolescence are under enormous pressure to succeed in multiple areas. What is really necessary for success?

In Chapter 2, in the section called "Emotional Development," we learned that children who have experienced complex trauma are significantly impacted by stress. In Chapter 3 we learned that we are all affected by stress. Stress is a big consideration when prioritizing Tami's needs as well as the needs of the rest of the family. The more stress Tami is under, the more she has aggressive outbursts. In turn, this increases the stress of each member of the family.

Tami's behavior is also driven due to her inability to express her emotions. Betsy shares this lack of emotional expression. It is what perpetuates her depression. She reported, "I am so sad about all of the conflict and chaos. I just want to be alone." Being alone isn't going to make her sad go away. Talking about it is what will help.

As we'll learn in Chapter 10's section, "Coming Ashore: Letting Grief Flow," each member of this family has unresolved grief for all of their losses. All of these emotions need to flow in order for the family to get back on solid ground.

Questions we want to consider in the emotional needs category include the following:

What time do we make to meet emotional needs in our family?

Are we expressing emotions in our family?

Are we expressing affection (nurture) in our family?

How often are we expressing affection (nurture)?

How is the family managing stress?

MOBILIZATION INVENTORY

Compiling all of the questions from the discussion regarding physical, cognitive, emotional and social spheres of life gives us a make-shift tool to monitor the well-being of each member of the family. The more questions to which your family can respond positively, the more your family is speeding down the mobilization highway.

Physical

Is the family eating a healthy diet?

Is the family eating regular meals?

Is everyone getting enough physical activity?

Are parents and children getting enough sleep?

Is there enough rest and relaxation to maintain good physical health?

Is each family member getting regular medical check-ups?

Is everyone taking medications as prescribed?

As parents, are you working when you are sick?

Cognitive

Are we adjusting expectations?

Are we reflecting as often as we need to so as to keep our priorities straight?

Are we engaging in new learning experiences? This contributes to enhanced intellectual functioning and the education it takes to manage an adoptive family successfully.

Are we communicating effectively? Do we all actually listen to one another? These queries contribute to solving problems, conflict resolution and improved reasoning skills.

Do we receive feedback or seek out feedback? Do we get any validation for our parenting efforts? Do we make sure to celebrate all of our children's successes? Does my spouse give me compliments? Are we respected at work, among friends and so on?

Are we maintaining focus?

Emotional

What time do we make to meet emotional needs in our family?

Are we expressing emotions in our family?

Are we expressing affection in our family?

How often are we expressing affection?

How is the family managing stress?

How do we respond to losses?

Are we facilitating grieving in our family?

Again, how well are we communicating?

MOBILIZATION INVENTORY (*Continued*)

Social

Have husband and wife gone out on a date recently?

Has each spouse had time for themselves recently?

Have parents and typically developing children spent time together lately? How about the adoptee?

Has the entire family been out? Recently?

Are family members looking and dressing in a manner that makes them feel good about themselves?

How are spiritual matters going? Does the family get to pray, attend church, engage in devotions, finding meaning in life as often as they would like?

How are cultural matters going? What has the family been able to do to facilitate the cultural identity development of their family (see Chapters 3 and 5)?

When was the last time the parents spent time with friends? How about the children?

How often has the family visited or talked with your extended family lately?

Is the family connected with a veteran family? This includes that the resident children know another brother or sister they can talk with. Adoptees benefit from knowing other adoptees as well.

Has there been time for hobbies?

Has there been time to attend events important to your typical children?

Are family members laughing?

Are family members hopeful?

How is the family inspired to keep going?

How do we respond to losses?
Are we facilitating grieving in our family?
Again, how well are we communicating?

Enhancing the emotional sphere of life requires reducing stress, expressing feelings and showing affection. Predominantly, our guides to good emotional health are mental health professionals or perhaps our religious leaders.

Social Needs

This area includes our relationships with other people—our attachments. It also includes moral development, as we learned earlier in this chapter.

Socially, Tami has never advanced beyond solitary play. This is the play of infants and young toddlers. As we also learned in Chapter 2, children need to develop minimal social competence by age 6. Tami is 8. The single best predictor of adult adaptation is not school grades or classroom behavior but the child's adequacy within relationships.

Tami lags well behind her peers in moral development, as is demonstrated by her violence toward family members.

> Tami has not psychologically separated from her birthmother. She has not solidified an attachment to Clyde, Lillian and her sisters. Overall, because the family became immobilized, the strength of the attachments between Leann, Betsy and their parents were stressed. Rather than using each other as a secure base to weather their storm, they moved away from each other.

Meeting social needs also includes that everyone gets time to have their needs met as we discussed earlier in this chapter. The questions we might want to ask to evaluate social needs include

- Have husband and wife gone out on a date recently?
- Has each spouse had time for him or her self recently?
- Have parents and typically developing children spent time together lately? How about the adoptee?
- Has the entire family been out? Recently?
- Are family members looking and dressing in a manner that makes each feel good about himself?
- How are spiritual matters going? Does the family get to pray, attend religious services, engage in devotions, find meaning in life as often as they would like?
- How are cultural matters going? What has the family been able to do to facilitate the cultural identity development of their family (see Chapters 3 and 5)?
- When was the last time the parents spent time with friends? How about the children?
- How often has the family visited or talked with extended family lately?
- Is the family connected with a veteran family (Chapter 10)? This includes that the resident children know another brother or sister they can talk with. Adoptees benefit from knowing other adoptees as well.
- Has there been time for hobbies?
- Has the family been able to attend events important to the typically developing children?
- Are family members laughing?
- Are family members hopeful?
- How is the family inspired to keep going?

Formal support in the social realm may come from your church leader, coaches and mental health provider.

As has been stressed in this chapter, the social domain is essential to the functioning of the family. Having fun and spending time with those you care about are what make any journey fun and worthwhile.

Setting Priorities: A Plan Emerges

Now let's pull this all together. So far

1. We have taken the entire family into account—medical, mental health and education.
2. We have obtained medical and other evaluations to clarify difficulties.
3. We have looked at physical, cognitive, emotional and social issues.
4. We have taken stress into account.

5. We have looked at and weighed all professional recommendations.
6. We have obtained additional information as needed. We asked questions, talked with veteran families, read books, surfed the internet and so on.

Below are the priorities Clyde and Lillian established for their family:

> The family had grown distant. Family dinners became a requirement and Leann stopped withdrawing so much. Betsy, Lillian and Leann began walking several days per week. Betsy's depression alleviated, not to mention the fact that Lillian felt better. Leann realized her needs were important to her parents. In addition
>
> - Tami would continue her participation in SI therapy and speech therapy.
> - Tami would continue with her psychiatric medication.
> - Lillian, Clyde, Betsy and Leann entered therapy along with Tami. These "family meetings" covered issues such as education, communication skills, adjusting expectations, new parenting tools, improved capacity to verbalize emotions—all essential for short- and long-term relief. These interventions contributed to the cognitive, emotional and social needs of the family. Tami additionally received therapeutic help with her irrational thoughts and with making a lifebook.
> - Tami's sisters, as did Gabe's, took turns backtracking with regards to Tami's social skills. One of Tami's extra curricular activities was dropped to make the time necessary for this process of advancing social skills. This increased time with Tami helped them see her more positively. The additional one-on-one time helped Tami manage her behavior better. She had a sister or a parent to help her de-escalate on a more frequent basis. Her temper outbursts decreased and she commented proudly, "Wow! I haven't had a fit for a while." Her self-concept was beginning to improve.
> - The family's mental health provider offered a support group and some special social events. The family took advantage of these opportunities. (Chapter 10 will cover the benefits of these informal support systems in more detail.)
> - Tami's family consulted with a reading specialist. As a family they were able to implement this professional's recommendations at home. They touched base with this professional on a regular basis to revise the interventions as needed. Summer fun was able to continue as planned.
> - The family will take a break from fostering children.
>
> Clyde and Lillian covered medical, mental health and education, as well as their priorities, as they worked to mobilize their family. This will allow for growth to occur in the physical, cognitive, emotional and social spheres of their lives.
>
> Their adoption-competent mental health professional kept all of this organized as any good adoption-focused therapist should. He helped them re-prioritize and form new goals as progress allowed.
>
> Their process to mobilization and to carry out their priorities spanned two years. They saw some progress in the first six months, more in twelve months and yet more at the almost two-year mark.

If you notice, Clyde and Lillian's priorities are more focused on mental health, social skills and increased family time. They opted not to pursue the summer school and the Saturday reading program. There are likely many readers who may struggle with the choices this family made. Again, re-thinking is called for. Certainly, education is valuable and there is no intent to dismiss the value of a good education. However, mental health issues seriously impair the ability to form relationships. Straight As are wonderful. However, if the child obtaining the good grades can't interact with people, will he be able to use his education? Or, there is the flip side. There is the child who has so many mental health issues she can barely learn. Parents battle the school for accommodations, often taking a school district to court if necessary. These extraordinary efforts, as with good grades, are only important if *an equal amount of effort* is being put into improving the mental health issues. Some families pursue mental health services tenaciously. However, more often, the mental health issues are scheduled around school and extracurricular activities as if the mental health issues are the lowest of these priorities.

Earlier in this book, I quoted national trauma expert, Bruce Perry. Here are more appropriate words from him and his co-author, Maia Szalavitz. These final paragraphs are also the last *Key Point* presented in this chapter:

> "Our educational system has focused nearly obsessively on cognitive development and almost completely ignored children's emotional and physical needs. Only two decades ago elementary schools had both significant lunch periods and recess times. Homework rarely took more than an hour to complete each night and children were thought to be capable of remembering deadlines and meeting them on their own.
>
> "In our rush to be sure that our children have an environment as 'enriched' as that of the neighbors' children, we are actually emotionally impoverishing them. A child's brain needs love and friendship and the freedom to play and daydream. Knowing this might allow more parents to resist social pressures and begin to push schools back in a more sensible direction" (Perry and Szalavitz, 2006).

Chapter 3 pointed out that building a family by adoption is all about forming relationships—attachments. Chapter 10 will reinforce this sentiment. Attachment puts all development in motion—physical, emotional, cognitive and social. Attachment is our blueprint for all other relationships. If it is strong and healthy, the individual can navigate the world—happy, motivated to succeed, empathic, with a good self-image. The securely attached individual will be able to get married, raise children and pursue the career of choice—the possibilities are endless!

Now, please go try some prioritizing of your family's needs!

Resources

These resources are divided into two categories: parenting and child development, and talking honestly with children.

Parenting and Child Development

Books

Bank, Stephen P. and Michael D. Kahn. *The Sibling Bond.* (New York: Basic Books, 1997.)

Cline, Foster and Jim Fay. *Parenting with Love and Logic.* (Colorado Springs: NavPress, 2006.)

Cline, Foster and Jim Fay. *Parenting Teens with Love and Logic.* (Colorado Springs: NavPress, 2006.)

Crain, William. *Reclaiming Childhood: Letting Children be Children in Our Achievement-Oriented Society.* (New York: Henry Holt and Co., 2003.)

Elkind, David. *The Power of Play: Learning What Comes Naturally*. (Cambridge: De Capo Press, 2007.)

Elkind, David. *The Hurried Child—25th Anniversary Edition*. (Cambridge: De Capo Press, 2007.)

Faber, Adele and Elaine Mazlish. *How to Talk So Kids Will Listen . . . and Listen So Kids Will Talk*. (New York: Avon Books, 1980.)

Faber, Adele and Elaine Mazlish. *How to Talk So Teens will Listen and Listen So Teens will Talk*. (New York: Harper Collins, 2005.)

Fay, Jim and Charles. *Love and Logic Magic for Early Childhood: Practical Parenting from Birth to Six Years*. (Golden: Love and Logic Press, 2002.)

Gurian, Michael. *The Soul of the Child: Nurturing the Divine Identity of Our Children*. (New York: Atria, 2007.)

Leach, Penelope. *Your Baby and Child: From Birth to Age Five*. (New York: Alfred A. Knopf, 1997.)

Panettieri, Gina and Philip Hall. *The Single Mother's Guide to Raising Remarkable Boys*. (Cincinnati: Adams Media, 2008.)

Schaefer, Charles E. and Theresa Foy DiGeronimo. *Ages and Stages: A Parent's Guide to Normal Childhood Development*. (New York: John Wiley and Sons, 2000.)

Sears, William and Martha. *The Baby Book: Everything You Need to Know about Your Baby from Birth to Age Two*. (New York: Little, Brown and Co., 2003.)

Siegel, Daniel and Mary Hartzell. *Parenting from the Inside Out: How a Deeper Self-Understanding Can Help You Raise Children Who Thrive*. (New York: Jeremy P. Tarcher/Penguin, 2003.)

Sparrow, Joshua. *Understanding Sibling Rivalry: The Brazelton Way*. (Cambridge: Da Capo Press, 2005.)

Sunderland, Margot. *The Science of Parenting: How Today's Brain Research Can Help You Raise Happy, Emotionally Balanced Children*. (New York: D.K. Publishing, 2006.)

Websites

Ask Dr. Sears
http://www.askdrsears.com

After raising eight children and practicing pediatric medicine for more than 30 years, the Sears family of physicians puts their knowledge to work for parents on this amazing website. Parents are certain to find information about any aspect of parenting. An A-Z index makes the site easy to use. The Sears have also authored an extensive array of books and articles.

Centers for Disease Control and Prevention (CDC)
www.cdc.gov

The purpose of the CDC is to promote health and quality of life by preventing and controlling disease, injury and disability. It is the nation's premier public health agency—working to ensure healthy people in a healthy world. Click "C" for child development and learn children's skills at various ages as well as what to do if your child exhibits delays.

Child Development Institute (CDI)
www.childevelopmentinfo.com

Child Development Institute was founded by Robert Myers, PhD Dr. Myers is a Clinical Child Psychologist with 25 years of experience working with children, adolescents, families and parents. Realizing the unlimited potential of the Internet to provide useful information to parents, he decided to utilize this method to provide parent education that is current, relevant and easy to attain. This website is packed with information about child development and play. Plan to spend some time reviewing this valuable resource.

Fisher Price®
www.fisher-price.com

All of us are likely familiar with the toys created by Fisher-Price. The website organizes their products according to what age the item is designed for. Once you have identified your adoptee's social and emotional age, you can quickly locate games and toys appropriate for your son or daughter. The website also offers quality information about child development and play skills.

Love and Logic
www.loveandlogic.com

The Love and Logic Institute is dedicated to making parenting and teaching fun and rewarding, instead of stressful and chaotic. They provide practical tools and techniques that help adults achieve respectful, healthy relationships with their children. Love and Logic is a phenomenal parenting approach! Their products are available as books, DVDs and audio tapes. Love and Logic seminars are regularly offered across the country. Visit their website to locate a Love and Logic training near you.

Zero to Three
www.zerotothree.org

Zero to Three's mission is to support the healthy development and well-being of infants, toddlers and their families. This organization advances this mission by informing, educating and supporting adults who influence the lives of infants and toddlers.

Talking to Children about Their Past

Books

Gabel, Susan. *Filling in the Blanks: A Guided Look at Growing Up.* (Indianapolis: Perspectives Press, 1988.)

Lacher, Denise; Todd Nichols and Joanne May. *Connecting with Kids through Stories: Using Narratives to Facilitate Attachment in Adopted Children.* (Philadelphia: Jessica Kingsley Publishers, 2005.)

Morrison, Marjorie. *Talking about Adoption to Your Adopted Child.* (London: British Association for Adoption and Fostering, 2007.)

O'Malley, Beth. *Lifebooks: Creating a Treasure for the Adopted Child.* (Winthrop, Massachusettes: Adoption-Works, 2000.)

Schooler, Jayne E. and Betsy E. Keefer. *Telling the Truth to Your Adopted or Foster Child: Making Sense of the Past.* (Westport: Bergin and Garvey Trade, 2000.)

Websites

Center for Adoption Support and Education (C.A.S.E.)
www.adoptionsupport.org

C.A.S.E. was created in May 1998 to provide post-adoption counseling and educational services to families, educators, child welfare staff and mental health providers in Maryland, Northern Virginia, and Washington, D.C. In addition, C.A.S.E. is a national resource for families and professionals through its training, publications, and consultations. Parents and teachers can locate the *W.I.S.E. Up Powerbook.* and the *S.A.F.E. at School* program here.

CHAPTER TEN

Mobilization: Becoming a "New and Different" Family—Part II

We have now arrived at the second chapter offering solutions that can help families achieve *mobilization*. Mobilization, you will remember, is the stage at which adoptive parents have learned to better balance the needs of each member of their family—themselves, the new adoptee, the brothers and sisters.

In this chapter, we will cover:

- Coming Ashore: Letting Grief Flow
- Finding Oases: Creating Support
- On a Positive Note: Yes, There Are Positives!

As we move through the chapter, keep in mind that each family has unique characteristics. What works for one family may not work for another. If you try a suggestion and it doesn't work, chart a new course—try something different. There is no one solution that will magically restore the family to its pre-adoptive state. Rather, getting to the destination—a "new and different" family—will require using a variety of solutions.

This chapter follows the same format as Chapter 9. Parents are the navigators and pilots for this journey. As a result, their needs must be kept up front and foremost. They are again encouraged to care for themselves in order to more effectively enhance the well-being of their children. Roadblocks and obstacles are identified and replaced with solutions and key points. We'll visit some familiar faces and stop to make some new friends. Success stories appear around each bend. This scenery inspires and offers hope, making the journey more pleasurable.

As I know you are eager to move ahead, we'll travel right along to the next stop on the journey.

Coming Ashore: Letting Grief Flow

No one particularly likes to grieve. However, just as a dam can only hold so much water, a family (parents, brothers, sisters and the newly arrived adoptee) can only contain so many feelings; eventually there will be seepage.

Parental anger explodes and hurtful words pour out. Sadly, there is little interest in things that were once pleasurable. Day-to-day tasks seem overwhelming. Anger or depression lead to impatience, annoyance and irritation, and these eventually morph into intolerance. Little things surge up and become big deals. Guilt sets in and undermines a once solid sense of self. Parents ask,

"Why am I always yelling?"

"Why did I get mad over that?"

"Why can't I snap out of this?"

"Did I make my adopted son the way he is?"

"What have I done to my other children?"

"What kind of parent am I?"

Worries become consuming.

"What is going to happen to our family if things don't change?"

"How can we live like this?"

"What if my son doesn't have a 'normal' life?"

Brothers' and sisters' grief issues have been pointed out throughout this book. They miss time with their parents, privacy, space, friends, relatives, peace, quiet, happy parents, safety (in some instances), a standard of living (in some instances), etc. They miss their "old" family. They have become cheerless, fuming, frustrated, embarrassed, jealous, resentful, lonely, anxious and guilty.

The adoptee arrives in the family filled to the brim with feelings from past losses. Adoption signals that many of his losses are permanent. A new wave of grief flows. He, too, experiences a flood of feelings.

Overall, grief bogs the adoptive family down like cars in a traffic jam or logs in a stream. Each member of the family moves along, but at a slow speed.

So, the goal of this segment is to provide ways to let grief flow—to create a happier pace. As a way of preparing to implement the stream of ideas that follow, parents may want to review the section in Chapter 3 called "Assessing Parent's Capacity to Handle Grief and Loss" and the section in Chapter 8 titled "Myths about Children and Grief." The roadblocks covered in those segments inhibit the grieving process. In Chapters 2 and 9, the segments called "Preparing the Typically Developing Children: Considerations" and "The Lifebook: Constructing the Adoptee's Narrative" refreshed the reader about the advantages of talking honestly with all of the children in the family.

We will also be finishing our discussion of triggers here. In Chapter 8 we learned what a trigger is and how a trigger leads to setting off those emotional storms we want to avoid. In this chapter, our trigger topic will be *trigger management*.

Facilitating the Flow of Feelings

There are several components to successful grieving covered below. The suggestions are designed to help the tsunami of grief recede to low tide. The family members can then wade out of their emotional ocean and come ashore together. Interwoven is a trigger management plan. Six tools will be offered to reduce the impact of triggers on your family.

All Feelings Are Normal

Adoptive family members experience a range of emotions along a continuum of intensity (Chapter 8).

An adoptive mom wrote,

> "When we first met Jason, he was an infant, only 8 months old. From his infancy to about age 3, we had the same love for him as we had toward our birthdaughter. Our love for him, at that time, was no different from the way we loved her. For the first few years, except for the screaming and the crying at bedtime and naptime, he seemed 'normal.' A 'normal' child is very easy to love regardless of the label of 'birth' child or 'adopted' child.

> But, after his behavior problems started to worsen, and as the years unfolded, our love for Jason started to change to anger, bitterness and resentment due to the effect his behavior was having on the rest of the family. We gave unconditional love to him and received what seems to this day to be hatred in return. We pray daily that the Lord will soften our hearts and teach us how to love him again as his heart heals from the pain of his childhood neglect. We have never totally stopped loving him. But it's almost like an obligatory love right now."

Many readers may be saying, "Oh my, a mother who doesn't truly love her son!" Actually, it is grief that you hear in her note—anger, bitterness, and resentment—that has caused love to be besodden by torrents of difficult behaviors and issues with which their new child has flooded the family. As grief is a part of adoptive family life, it is not uncommon for adoptive parents—mothers and fathers—to talk about lost love when the adoptee has mental health issues, "I love him, but I don't like him anymore." "There are days I feel I hate her." "I try to love her. I want to love her. But, it is hard, harder than I ever imagined."

It is difficult to love *anyone* who rejects you and has a very different value system—this includes your own child. Rather than criticize these parents, they need to be provided with a forum for expressing their feelings. They need support and validation. They are already guilt ridden about the fact that they don't feel love for all of their children equally and unconditionally. Frequently, when helped to grieve, feelings of affection resurface.

In the meantime, a sense of obligation drives parental efforts to heal the adoptee from past hurts. Parents often say, "We adopted. We made a commitment. We are going to follow through." I think that commitment is often the "substitute love" of adoptive parents. Commitment drives positive behaviors toward the child. The following comments from another mom capture this sentiment.

> "I don't think love and affection are based solely on a child being biological or adopted. Personalities play into the equation for me. My biological daughter, Kate, is more loved now than are Bob (biological) or Teresa (adopted). Kate puts more effort into our relationship. I didn't always love her more. Her teenage years, middle school thru first year of college, were rough, and loving her was difficult. My adopted daughter, Teresa, has moments of being most loved; moments where I feel she's connected with me and our family dynamics. There are times when I believe that I need to be most loved and all the kids need to take a back seat. I don't spend much time thinking about my love for my children. My love and care hopefully come out in my behavior."

In adoption, love may be about what parents *demonstrate* toward their children rather than about what they *feel* toward the child at any given moment in time.

Here is a sentiment expressed by Craig, a typically developing brother, currently age 15, in a family expanded by the adoption of older children.

> "My parents adopted my cousins, Sam and Kyle, when they were 9 and 11. They are now 21 and 23. At first, I was excited—I would have two more brothers! I already had two so now there would be five of us. Sometimes it was fun. Boy, other times the fights were huge!
>
> "This year, Sam just moved out one day. He didn't tell anybody. He did it when we weren't home. He hardly calls. He almost never returns my calls. Right now, I hate him. I absolutely hate him. We took him in and gave him all kinds of things. Things he would never have had with his own parents. Then, he just turns around and screws us!"

Likely, there are those who would say to this young man, "Don't talk like that! It isn't nice to hate anyone, especially your own brother." Yet, how will he resolve these feelings if he is stifled in such a manner? In adoption, we take for granted that the adoptee has intense feelings and that expressing these feelings is cathartic. The same courtesy must be extended to the siblings and parents if the family is to heal.

A first step in grieving is to realize that all feelings are normal, even those that are intense and negative.

A Time to Grieve

American society is a rather grief-confining society. That is, there is a prevailing perception that grieving should be a rather short process. Most workplaces allow three days of absence for significant deaths such as those of a parent or partner. Then, it's back to the office to "get on with life."

But grieving is individual. How long an adult or child grieves is dependent upon the person, his support system and the type of loss. Overall, there is no definite timeline for grief.

The grief process can't occur at all if it isn't given time, and today, time is hard to come by. The busy pace of life most families keep inhibits the flow of feelings. The family keeps attending the next baseball game, school concert, karate class, birthday party, and so on. Coping with grief is put off for another day. However, parents are encouraged to set aside their own time to grieve, and time to make it possible for children to express their feelings In her book *Helping Someone with Mental Illness* (co-authored with Susan Golant) former first lady Rosalynn Carter says,

> "You may find it useful to list and grieve for the losses you experience. They can be mundane such as the loss of a weekly bridge game to more abstract and all encompassing, such as lost freedom, privacy, companionship. . . . If, after noting all that you and the one you care for have lost, you feel like crying, let the tears flow. You're entitled. . . . Try to carve out some time every day that is yours and yours alone."

Carter and Golant offer two-fold good advice. Set aside time for identify the losses and grieving. Regarding the latter, if you are charting your family members'—kids' and parents'—expectations as was suggested in Chapter 9, many losses are already on that list. Knowing what it is that you're sad or angry about permits those "tears" to flow.

Trigger Management Tool #1—Identify Triggers

As Chapter 8's section "The Role of Triggers in Grief" pointed out, triggers are identifiable situations that carry an emotional meaning. A trigger generates feelings. For example, the birth of a child is a reminder of infertility. Instantly, a wave of sorrow and sadness may emerge.

In adoptive families, triggers exacerbate the emotional response family members receive from and unleash on one another. Knowing your losses is critical to determining underlying triggers which bring the grief about those losses to surface. Certainly, some triggers will always remain obscure. But many can be discovered.

> For example, in Chapter 8 we met 12-year-old George. He became very mad each time his mom was late picking him up from baseball. He slammed the car door and sat in the back seat with arms tightly folded across his chest. He wouldn't utter a word the entire drive home. Once home, he stomped to his bedroom and slammed that door too. This level of anger was out of character for George.

George wasn't just angry about his mom's lateness. The lateness reminded him of the way his family had changed since Vikki had been adopted. The *lateness was the trigger*. The *loss was of the family as it had been*. He was angry about this change in his life. This resentment was vented, behaviorally, each time his mom was delayed in arriving at the ball park.

George's story adds further clarification to the connection between a loss, a trigger and a feeling. In adoptive families

Loss + Trigger + Feelings = Storms!

Delving under the surface of losses a bit can alter the emotional climate of the family. Triggers become visible and so the storms they often spark can be avoided.

Talk about "It"

Grief is so often like that proverbial elephant in the room. Everyone goes on as if "it" isn't there.

Throughout the book, many vignettes and much content has been included to counter the notion that "it" is better left unsaid. Hopefully, by now, the reader is convinced that each member of the family has to talk about "it" in order to recover and move forward.

Resolution of grief may be more appropriately described as "learning to live with the losses" rather than "getting over it." Resolved grief will no longer be daily and consuming. The painful emotions are lessened when grief has been resolved, and the person resumes a full and pleasurable life while acknowledging that life has been forever changed (lost)—life has become "new and different."

Talking is a primary way to facilitate grief.

George's mother could say, "George, I've noticed that you become so angry when I am late. I'm thinking that I am a late a lot since Vikki came to live with us. This didn't used to happen. Is it hard for you since Vikki came?"

This technique is called using *a ripple effect*. The parent puts forth an idea of what the problem might be. Initially, the child may deny the information or simply not want to talk about it. But, a ripple has been created. George now knows that "Vikki" is a safe topic. His mom is open to talking about his thoughts and feelings about Vikki. Enough ripples usually lead to a wave—of grief. Eventually, kids will respond to the safety net the parent has offered. There will be an outpouring of sadness, anger, fear, jealousy and so on. The ripple effect technique works well with adoptees and with partners as well.

Trigger Management Tool #2—Anticipate Triggers.

Triggers offer a great opportunity to generate conversation and feelings. They can be used as a tool to facilitate grief. As Chapter 8 explained, many triggers, such as holidays, are obvious. They can be anticipated.

About two weeks before a holiday, Mom or Dad, using the ripple effect, can say, "Christmas is almost here. Do you think about your birthmom around Christmas? I do. If it weren't for her, I wouldn't be your dad. I know she hurt you and I am sad about that. I am also happy to have you for a son."

The parent has established that the birthmom is a safe topic. He has acknowledged that there is hurt. He has identified a potential feeling and he has expressed feelings of his own. He *modeled* talking about feelings. Kids do learn from their parents!

Chapter 3, "Stress Management: Maintaining a Healthy Emotional Climate" explained that traumatized children's emotions are manifested in negative behaviors.

Correcting this situation requires modeling how to express feelings in acceptable ways. Talking is one such way.

Art, journaling, music, children's books (Chapter 5 Resources) and dance often provide children creative outlets through which feelings flow. Other children and adults vent strong feelings through physical activity, such as organized sports, taking a long walk or a bike ride. Still others prefer to reflect while weeding a garden, sitting quietly on the porch with a cup of tea, watching sad movies, tinkering on the motorcycle in the garage, raking the leaves, and so on.

Many adoptive families create *rituals*, symbolic ways to remember and reflect. Adoption has often been steeped in rituals for celebrations, such as "gotcha day," as well as in rituals to acknowledge loss. A candle may be lit or a helium balloon released to acknowledge the birthmother on Mother's Day. A small box can be decorated and called a birthmother, birthbrother or birthsister box. At times when birthfamily members are missed, the adopted child can draw a picture or write a letter which is added to the contents of the box. The Resources will provide sources for further reading about adoption-related rituals.

Ask yourself, "What ways work best to resolve my grief?" "What works best for each of my children?" Then, go acknowledge "it" and let the feelings flow.

Don't Hide Your Feelings!

Carol arrived at therapy with her adopted 10-year-old-son Walt. Walt had been struggling a bit lately. His negative behaviors were occurring more frequently. Carol had noticed that once again Walt was chewing on his shirt collars, picking at the skin on his arms, tearing off any scabs, mumbling, drawing on his clothing and refusing to shower. The school year was nearing an end. Walt would miss his friends and his teacher, Miss Benson. The approach of summer vacation acted as a trigger for Walt. Thoughts of not seeing his friends every day reminded him of the loss of his birthmom, whom he no longer saw.

The therapist decided to start out by talking with Walt and Carol about ways that Walt could see his school friends over the summer. The three also discussed writing or emailing Miss Benson. After these plans were settled, the therapist asked Walt if maybe he was also thinking about his birthmom. Instantly, tears appeared in his eyes.

Seeing this sadness, Carol welled up also. She began looking about for a tissue and she kept saying, "Oh, I'm so sorry. I didn't mean to start crying."

The therapist put a hand on her shoulder and let her know that it was okay to be sad. With that, the therapist sat back. Carol held Walt and the two cried together for quite some time.

Many parents react to their own grief as did Carol. They become apologetic for a show of feelings! Other parents work to suppress the feelings. Instead, parents should let their feelings flow. First, parents need to grieve in order to make themselves feel better. Second, this is another great way to model the expression of grief. Many traumatized children fear the release of emotions. It is as if they think the tears will never stop. Some of these children have received a message through their abuse that to be sad is to be weak. A crying parent counters their irrational beliefs. The child then becomes free to shed his tears.

Grieving jointly is a powerful way to firm attachments. Connecting to another through pain forges a deep relationship. Early in therapy, parents view the adoptee as a bundle of "bad" behaviors. As therapy proceeds, the child's grief softens these parental perceptions. The child comes to be viewed more positively. Quite often, lost feelings of affection re-surface. Parents come to recognize that the traumatized child isn't just a force wreaking havoc in the family. He or she is a very hurt human being striving to work through great emotional pain.

Chapter 8 pointed out that individual therapy for the adoptee isn't always the best forum to make lasting and enduring changes in the adopted child or in the rest of the family. Carol and Walt's example further validates this belief. Children need to grieve with parents, not with therapists.

So parents, let your grief flow—in front of the kids! Besides, doesn't a good cry make you feel better? Actually, it is supposed to. Stress proteins build up in the body. Crying is nature's way of releasing these hormones. Men tend to release these same hormones via sweat. This is another of those male/female differences we learned about in Chapter 4, and it helps to explain why women tend to emote through talking and crying and men by activity.

Trigger Management Tool #3: Resolve, resolve and resolve!

Once triggers are identified and anticipated, the grief associated with the trigger needs to be resolved. Chapter 8 offered the case of Peter, a Gulf War veteran who felt under siege by his son, Lee's "attacks" of shouting and swearing. Lee's actions triggered unpleasant combat memories for Peter. Once Peter realized this, he was able to resolve the underlying sorrow, fear and resentment associated with his war experience. While Lee's behavior continued to be irritating, Peter was able to respond with much less emotional intensity. The combat feelings *and* the anger for being screamed at were no longer exploding simultaneously.

Resolving trigger-related grief steers the family along more smoothly. Less maneuvering is needed to avoid the squalls or downpours along the journey.

Validate Feelings: No Stifling!

Many readers remember laughing at the old sitcom, "All in the Family" as Archie told Edith to "stifle herself." Frequently, grief is stifled just as overtly in real life. A co-worker returning to work after the death of her mother is met with, "My, you look so good!" rather than, "How are you doing? This must be so hard for you." A grieving widower is encouraged to "start dating again," or to "go out and get on with life."

Children are often similarly stifled.

- "He doesn't need to talk about his abuse. There is no reason to dredge up the past."
- "You're (adoptee) with us (adoptive parents) now. There is no reason to be angry or sad."
- "Daddy and I love you. You can be happy now."
- "Why do you keep going on about your old foster mom? Why aren't I (adoptive parent) enough for you (adoptee)?
- "Those things (abuse) don't happen anymore. You're safe with Mommy and me. You need to stop worrying."
- "Your brother didn't have life as good as you! You need to be more patient with him"
- "Your dad and I are doing the best we can. He (adopted brother) needs more than you (typical child) do."

Stifling grief can easily be changed to *validation* of feelings. Validation is affirming the emotions being expressed. For example, going back to Walt and Carol from above, what made their joint grief session so effective was Carol's innate ability to say, "Yes, it's so sad you're not with your birthmom. Yes, I know you miss her. I know. It was so scary to be left alone." At times, Carol is silent. She just holds Walt while he cries. Carol validates Walt by re-stating the feelings he is having and by providing comfort. In essence, she gives him permission to have his feelings.

The next time you arrive home from work and your partner is grumpy or stressed out, try some validation rather than the "you need to snap out of it" approach. You could say, "Honey, you have had a bad day haven't you?" Then, give a hug. Of course, validation extends to the spouse who had a "bad day at the office" as well.

Trigger Management Tool #4—Permission

It isn't selfish to make grieving time a priority. In fact, it is essential. Grief is responsible for causing angry blow-ups that throw the family off course for days. Often referred to as *adoption-related crises*, most could be avoided by allowing for a cry, or as one mom does,

> "I drive to a place near some woods. I get out and walk into a nice patch of trees. I shout about everything that makes me angry. The trees seem to take it pretty well and I know I feel a whole lot better after venting to them. They don't talk back!"

Give each member of your family permission and validation in this area of grieving. Unpacking all that excess baggage lightens the load. Each passenger will be more content.

Grief Flows: Over and Over

> Recently, I was conducting a workshop. On the break, an adoptive mother came up to me and asked, "I'm looking for some therapy for my son. Is there someplace you would recommend?"
>
> I, of course, responded with the Attachment and Bonding Center of Ohio where I work as a therapist.
>
> The mom replied, "Oh, we already tried that about six years ago."
>
> I said, "Oh my, was the therapy not effective?"
>
> She stated, "Well, we thought it was. For about five years he did pretty well. Then, last fall he changed. He became sullen. He won't come out of his room. He barely speaks to us. So, I think that therapy didn't work."

Grief is developmental as we learned in Chapter 8. Each stage of life brings along a new perspective on the past. This is true for adults and children alike. Issues resolved once may need to be explored and given a new perspective at various stages of our development. Instead of needing a "new" therapy, we may need to shed light on an "old" topic.

Expect to repeat, repeat and repeat some more! (I think I've mentioned this before.) Children learn best by repetition. Grief is resolved in a similar manner. We must periodically, and over time, review the loss issues associated with abandonment, abuse and institutionalization. We must explore with parents and with brothers and sisters the lost expectations associated with the sibling they expected and the changes that adoption has brought to the family. Throughout, we must help process other past experiences that contribute to the pool of grief which can be triggered and create adoption-related crises.

Trigger Management Tool #5—Resolve, Resolve and Resolve Again

Matters once settled tend to crop up again like debris after a storm. You turn into a bay, and there it is! You swerve, struggling to keep your vessel under control. Sometimes grief is churning but there is a lack of awareness. The hole is discovered after the boat begins to leak.

Parents are encouraged to take stock of potential grief issues to prevent these breakdowns. Make this an ongoing process. Make time to think about your behavior and that of your children. Behavior is reflective of pent-up emotions. Rather than letting these feelings throw you off course—causing you to take your anger or sorrow out on your children or spouse—seek to uncover the root cause of your feelings. Resolve it again! Resolve it again! (Oh, I have repeated myself.)

Start the Engine

Certainly, many parents are able to resolve their own loss issues. Parents often say just the right things to a grieving adoptee, brother or sister.

However, some content of a child's or adult's life is quite difficult to wade through. At other times, parenting interventions have been implemented over a year, two years or longer with no success in ending unwanted or unsafe behaviors. These circumstances warrant professional guidance.

Chapters 1 and 5 talked about early intervention, and it is critical to intervene in a timely manner. It is so common during the initial phone call for services for the conversation to flow like this . . .

Parent says, "Well we've been having these problems since he was 4."

Therapist, "How old is he now?"

Distressed parent, "He's 13 now."

If you thought your child had diabetes would you wait nine years to get a diagnosis? Yet, there is a perception that if we "wait it out" the child will "grow out" of the behavior problems. The trauma will fade into a distant memory. Grief will pass and the adoptee will recognize he is "better off." He'll happily join the family.

As the kids would say, "NOT!"

Waiting is a luxury that is not affordable. Waiting allows the adoptee's pathology to sit, becoming more resistant to treatment efforts. Waiting puts brothers and sisters on lay away, waiting for the family to return to "normal" so fun will occur again. Each group of children has its childhood shortchanged. Further, the family who has waited finally arrives at the therapist's door in a crisis state. This makes the journey to mobilization a long one!

Mental health—parents', typically developing children's and the adoptee's—is as vital as is physical health. Stop waiting! Seek help today!

Trigger Management Tool #6—Start Your Engine!

Quit sitting in the calm waiting for the wind to fill your sails and start the boat. Start the backup engine. Stop expecting that everything is just going to get better on its own. Parents need to take action to generate improvements in the family. Later in this chapter we're going to explore a menu of supports available to adoptive families. Select one and get moving. If that support doesn't satisfy your needs, pick something different. Move from port to port until you find a service, a support group, a babysitter, etc. that is to your family's liking.

Key Point—Unresolved grief leads to impairments in development, lack of concentration, physical ailments, depression, anxiety, and so on (Chapter 8). Grief resolution is a necessity. It ensures the emotional well-being of parents, brothers, sisters and the adoptee. Make grieving time a priority in your family.

Key Point—Use the six steps identified throughout this section to decrease the impact of triggers in your family. In review, identify triggers, use triggers as a grief reduction method, resolve underlying feelings connected to the triggers, resolve those feelings as often as necessary, give permission to grieve trigger-related losses and start using these tools today. The tools prevent breakdowns—adoption-related crises—from slowing the pace to mobilization.

Finding Oases: Creating Support

Let's initiate this segment with the wisdom of a dad parenting an adopted daughter and two birth sons. The oasis located and utilized by this family improved all family relationships.

> "My advice to parents of children with issues is to get help early. Look for help everyplace you can go. Go online, to the library and talk to everyone. Knowledge is power and in our case knowing why our daughter acted like she did gave us the power to deal with her. We still don't have all of the answers on dealing with her actions but it is amazing to us, once we found the correct supports, how she started dealing with some of her own issues. Making the right judgment call or talking it out instead of acting it out is a huge step for any child. They are mile long leaps for adopted children. She now has true friends and the arguing is decreasing. Knowing why she acts like she does has made all the difference in the world. It was very hard to abandon my parenting techniques but in the end, the change to new parenting methods has been good.
>
> "Once her problems were identified, life within our family got better, and our daughter now talks to us rather than at us. The boys seem to enjoy having her around a little more. They share things with her, as well as talk to her. Never once have we ever thought of giving up on our family, but there are many days that the decision to adopt has left us both physically and emotionally exhausted. Do not give up on these children! Many have a bright future and their dark past was not their fault. I am proud to think I have made a difference in her life."

Travel is always better when there is a companion along for the journey. Certainly, many of the solutions to problems created by the addition to the family of a child with serious issues provided in this chapter and Chapter 9 require energy and stamina. Support is critical to stamina. It refreshes and re-energizes us—as if we've been to an oasis—to have been around others with whom we can share a hard day at the office, a marital problem, a financial burden and so on.

Adoption literature research reflects the following facts:

- Assurance of the availability of services and supports following adoption has been found to play a critical role in many prospective adoptive parents' decisions to go forward with the adoption of children in foster care—whether children are adopted by their current foster families or new families are recruited for them.
- As the number of internationally adopted children has grown and the impact of early institutional care on children's health and development has come to be better understood, it has become apparent that families who adopt internationally often have the same needs for post-placement services and supports as do families who adopt children with special needs in this country.
- Services and supports for adoptive families following placement and, importantly, following adoption finalization are crucial in promoting the well-being of families

and minimizing the possibility that adoptions will fail, with traumatizing results for both the child and the family.

- There is evidence of a strong relationship between providing supports to adoptive families as a matter of course or in the form of preventive services and positive outcomes in terms of the health, well-being and stability of the family. This relationship has been found to be particularly strong when counseling and mental health services are provided as supports for the adoptive family.[1]

Unfortunately, as we have talked about, many adoptive families lose support during their adoption journey. Isolation occurs. Friends and family members drift away because they don't understand the issues that adoptive parents face. They provide unsolicited advice with an undercurrent that infers that the problems are due to poor parenting. Isolation may occur as the time needed to tend to out-of-family relationships is unavailable. The adoptee's chaotic ways interfere with the capacity to schedule dinner, attend a party or pursue a regular hobby. Partners often drift apart due to stress, conflict, sheer exhaustion, running many directions at what seems like the same time, etc.

Arthur, the adoptive parent of two children, ages 11 and 13, one typical and one with complex trauma issues states,

> "I very much recommend that parents adopting children with this type of background [complex trauma] save their 'parent to parent' talks and advice sessions for support groups with parents in similar circumstances. To put it frankly, 'regular' parents, as well as relatives, do not grasp what you're going through. There will be no shortage of comments like, 'Well, all children do that' followed by some gesture of how 'great you are for giving this child a home.' Nothing stabs at your guilt more than that one comment because you're receiving accolades for something that you're harboring great struggle and some regret for. You're struggling with both your daughter and yourself, but you're being referenced to like you're Florence Nightingale or Mother Theresa."

The typically developing kids share this isolation. As do their parents, these siblings incur the same loss of friends and extended family. Even more so, the time involved in caring for their traumatized sibling separates the brothers and sisters from their parents. The resident children become isolated within their own immediate family.

The adoptee is isolated because he is trapped in a world of irrational thoughts. He fears intimacy. He unconsciously strives to remain distant from his parents and brothers and sisters. His development keeps his interactions limited as well. He lacks peers with whom to talk and play.

This section will be devoted to support. A wide assortment of supports will be presented. We'll be ending with nurture. Nurture is a special kind of support. It enhances the intimacy of relationships. This depth within interpersonal interactions is a support that improves the quality of all aspects of our connections to other humans—children and adults. As we'll see, it is really the ring that holds all of the keys.

So, come on. Let's go find an oasis—support—for your family.

1. Lutz, Lorrie. "Strengthening Families and Communities: An Approach to Post-Adoption Services." Casey Center for Effective Child Welfare Practice White Paper. Casey Family Services, http://www.caseyfamilyservices.org/p_ccenter_publications.html, pp., 6, 8, 11.)

Support Groups

Support groups abound. Perusing the parent group database of the North American Council on Adoptable Children (see Resources) reveals that over 900 local support groups are available. Support groups offer many advantages to adoptive family members.

Advantages of Support Groups

For parents, support groups provide

- a place to vent and share frustrations and grief.
- an opportunity to meet other adults with similar concerns and problems.
- an avenue to meet the family's cultural needs.
- a location to gain information about various mental health disorders, behavioral interventions, or a qualified therapist or medical professional.
- a means to make a friend to call in a crisis or to provide respite.
- a place to celebrate progress.
- a source of hope and inspiration.

For typically developing children support groups provide

- the opportunity to be with others in similar situations and with similar concerns.
- a means to gain information about the issues of their adopted siblings.
- an avenue to enhance skills in the areas of problem-solving, communication, expressing feelings and handling sibling rivalry.
- a place to obtain answers to adoption-related questions asked by curious strangers or classmates.
- a location to explore the facets of life in a transcultural adoptive family.
- a way to make friends to call in difficult times in adoptive family life.

For adoptees with mental health problems, support groups provide

- the opportunity to be among other adoptees. Adoptees learn they are one member of a large community.
- a place to be with others of a similar culture.
- an avenue to find advice on handling school projects like bringing in a baby picture, genetics projects or a family tree.
- a location to learn how to conduct a reunion with a birthfamily member as well as the information to make an informed choice about conducting a search.
- a place to learn skills to engage as a full member of their family.
- a path to walk with others who experienced trauma.

Roadblocks and Obstacles to Using Support Groups and Alternate Routes

Various obstacles and roadblocks prevent adoptive families from making the best possible use of support groups. These barriers are both parent and agency related. So this segment addresses both groups of adoption community members—families and professionals.

For agencies, the biggest support group-related obstacle is funding.

"Our agency doesn't have the staff or the funding to conduct groups."

Funding post-adoption services is challenging, but it is well worth the effort it takes to achieve that funding. Agencies should consider the following about connecting families:

- Parents can call fellow support group members in a crisis, to locate and arrange respite, to obtain referrals, etc. Support groups have the capacity to decrease agency staffs' workload.
- Agencies that recruit prospective adoptive parents can enhance the success of placements in these families. Participation in support groups before placement better prepares these newcomers. After placement, these recently formed families have a ready-made support system.
- Social events entail relatively little expense. For example, a large support group in Northeast Ohio invites families to the local skating rink and city pool. The adoptive parent support group at the Attachment and Bonding Center of Ohio sponsors an annual pot luck picnic at a lovely park complete with a pond for fishing, basketball and tennis courts, a skate board area and lots of grass for baseball, Frisbee and much more. These events cost agencies little staff time. Advertising such events requires only a flyer. Connecting families can occur with relative ease and virtually no funding. Social events have the advantage of including parents, adoptees and brothers and sisters.
- Consider a time frame of hosting meetings every two months or quarterly. Several agencies and practices can partner. Meetings can alternate among the cooperating organizations. These strategies reduce costs and time to agencies. Longer intervals between meetings may actually lead to greater participation for adoptive families whose datebooks are often overflowing with appointments and transportation responsibilities.
- Agency involvement is not necessarily required over the long term. Review the related box for the advantages of a Parent-Run and Agency-Supported group. These points were created by Diane Martin-Hushman, Parent Group Coordinator, North American Council on Adoptable Children. In essence, agencies can assist in launching an adoptive parent group. Once the group solidifies, agencies can transfer the reigns to the parents.

Funding sources do actually exist for various types of post-adoption services. The Resource section provides links to several websites containing information about these monies as well as descriptions of post-adoption services provided in numerous states. It should also be noted that many families will arrive for services with private health insurance. Most plans contain benefits for participation in groups. When seeking funding, utilize both public monies and private insurance.

Parents, on the other hand, often cite the following four obstacles to using a support group.

"We don't have anyone to watch our adopted child."

Lack of childcare is a valid obstacle to participating in a support group. It usually means that one parent in a two-parent family stays home, while the other, usually the mother, attends the support group. Alternating parental participation is one way to get around this roadblock, although this means that each parent receives less quantity and quality of support than both would, could they attend together. And this solution doesn't work for single parents at all.

Parent-Run and Agency-Supported Groups

Establishing adoptive parent support groups entails making many decisions. One matter is that of whether the group will be parent-run or agency-run. Diane Martin-Hushman, Parent Group Coordinator, North American Council on Adoptable Children offers a middle-ground with the idea of a parent-run and agency-supported support group. This type of group has the following benefits:

- The agency takes on the supportive role, but members control the direction of the group.
- The agency helps with facilitation and may provide guest speakers, but parents have private time to share problems.
- The focus is on parents' needs. The agency is on hand to bring in experts as requested.
- The parents' experience and knowledge are valued and shared; guest speakers and resources are available through the agency.
- Agency involvement is often limited to office hours, but parents are available to each other at all times.
- Experienced parents are role models. Outside speakers can bring in expertise.
- Parents lead the group's advocacy and can dissociate from the agency if the advocacy issues are in conflict with agency policies.
- Parents become close allies. As the group matures, the agency can step back and let the parents lead.

Source: Martin-Hushman, Diane. "Who should Run a Support Group: Agency-Run vs. Parent-Run Support Groups." [online]. http://nacac.org/parentgroups/whoruns.html

When childcare is provided, the kids can come along! Single parents and both parents in dual parent families can then reap the benefits of a support group.

Agencies and peer group leaders may want to consider recruiting interns from local colleges and graduate programs in schools of social work, education, counseling, psychology, pastoral care or some other human service program. Interns in programs like these need to complete hours of community service in order to satisfy degree requirements. Further, very few higher education programs incorporate any adoption-related training into their curriculum. Inviting students into support groups, then, is a great way to expose future professionals to the issues of adoptive families.

Interns can fulfill the staffing needs required to provide child care. Speaking from experience of having used interns to staff many support groups, I believe that they can be a great asset. They are energetic. They can plan activities, gather supplies and come to the meeting ready to organize and occupy the kids.

Contact colleges and universities today!

"We continue to try to educate our pre-existing support system."

Chapter 8 pointed out that parents often attempt to educate the family's support system which was in place at the time of the adoption, expecting this group to continue to be the family's main source of support. They give friends, family and everyone articles, websites, books, etc.

Education is never a wasted endeavor. However, many adults are not receptive to these learning opportunities. Education, with the expectation that others can truly understand the struggles involved in raising a child with mental health issues, requires some re-thinking.

Can we understand what it is actually like to have a kidney transplant from hearing a kidney recipient's explanation? Perhaps we can to a degree, but not fully. We would understand only if we also underwent this procedure.

Adopting a child with mental health issues is similar to this medical analogy. Adoptive parents may want to take steps to move on to meet with those parents living in the same type of a situation. After a support group session it is so common that parents are laughing and smiling. Recently, after a support group one mom was heard congratulating another mom. She said, "Wow! That is such great news that Jimmy stopped peeing in his bedroom. You and your partner are doing such a great job with him!" Now, where else could you get this kind of praise?

Moving on doesn't mean severing old relationships. It may mean making adjustments. Patty, the adoptive mom of two boys and a birth daughter said,

> "I will always be deeply hurt by the fact that my own sister often implies that I am the reason my boys struggle. However, she is my sister, and I do love her. I don't want their adoptions to cut us off. So, I compromise. On really difficult days, I call a friend I made at a support group. But, I attend a book club with my sister. This works for both of us. We spend time together, and we can talk about something we both enjoy."

This solution can work for you too. First, you have to face reality, which is always hard and often painful. Make time to grieve. Then, go ahead. Find a group of adoptive parents near you and cultivate some new companions for the journey.

"Those groups aren't for us"

Some parents attend one support group meeting and don't feel their needs have been met. Rather than trying another group session or even another group, they abandon the whole idea.

Support groups do vary—vastly.

- There are groups that meet for the purpose of venting.
- Others are centered on learning about the culture from which their children were adopted.
- Some are designed for providing information. The members can be contacted for referrals, advice, etc.
- Yet, another group of parents may make advocacy their goal. They recognize gaps in the adoption system or community services that help adoptive families. They may work toward passing a particular piece of legislation. This group is more politically motivated to make systemic changes.

Perhaps a better way to approach choosing and attending a support group is to start by identifying the groups in your area. Then, contact the group leaders. Ask questions,

"How many families attend the group?"

"What topics are addressed?"

"Is it always discussion or are there guest speakers?"

"Are there are also social opportunities?"

"How often does the group meet? What time?"

"Is there childcare?"

In essence, investigate the groups and then select a group that offers what you need.

Some parents may find that attendance at more than one group is beneficial. It is quite common that parents partake in one parent group for cultural advice, and meet with a different group of families for behavioral interventions.

If you follow the above advice and you still can't find a support group that's right for your family, start your own. Visit the North American Council on Adoptable Children's website and download the manual, "Starting and Nurturing Adoptive Parent Groups: A Guide for Leaders." The link is http://nacac.org/parentgroups/starting.pdf.

"The meeting times and locations aren't convenient"

If attendance is blocked because of a busy schedule, then perhaps an online support group is for you. Technology makes it possible to find support 24 hours per day, 7 days per week. With a Google search and a click of the mouse, parents in similar circumstances are connected with one another within minutes. Parents can pick and choose threads of interest or post a new topic relevant to their needs. Parents can do this at their convenience. Some sites schedule live chats or provide the opportunity for parents who happen to be online at the same time to move into a chat room together.

Always keep in mind, however, that online information does not replace the advice of a qualified professional. Check with your adoption-competent mental health guide before implementing suggestions that come by way of technology.

"Where are the groups for kids?"

Families also complain that their children need groups, too!

Groups for adoptees are fewer than groups for parents. Support groups for the typically developing children are even scarcer yet. As was stated earlier, all children who are members of adoptive families benefit from networking with other youths. Below are some ideas about launching groups for children. They are modeled after parent groups. Most require little start up monies and time.

- Interns are cost-effective staff and they offset parental and professional time. Interns can plan and carry out activities, and safely oversee a group of children. Most adoptees, as well as the resident children, would benefit greatly from an evening of learning problem-solving skills, knowing how to approach a busy parent with sensitive questions, learning to navigate peer relationships, improving self-concept or identity development, working on anger management, dealing with anxiety and depression, and so on. If they need some prepared workbooks or games, economical tools are available through ChildsWork-ChildsPlay. See the Resources at the end of this chapter.
- Just as adults participate in book clubs, kids would love the chance to read along with other kids. A list of book titles was provided in the Chapter 5 Resources. Or, the group leader could pop in a movie. *Snow Dogs*, *Elf*, *Babe*, *Anne of Green Gables*, *Pinnochio*, *Finding Nemo*, *Tarzan*, *Riding the Bus with My Sister* are all great movies to use as starting points for discussing adoption or being the brother or sister to an adoptee.
- Ask the dads to organize a softball game, a bowling night or a trip to the zoo. Afterwards, make time for pizza and some networking. A social event conducted every two or three months involves our fathers and helps reduce his and his children's isolation.
- A group with more experienced leaders could host a time-limited, six-part or eight-part group focused on a topic to be explored in-depth. For example, young

sexual abuse victims could greatly benefit by meeting fellow youth who have experienced this terrible trauma. At the Attachment and Bonding Center we use the video, *Scared Silent: Exposing and Ending Child Abuse*[2], hosted by Oprah Winfrey. It acts as an ice breaker. Traumatized children respond to the victims who speak about their own abuse in this video's various segments. They relax and begin to share their own stories. Two other topics for in-depth exploration include understanding mental illness and the Seven Core Issues of Adoption (see Chapter 2).

Key Point—Family members don't have to navigate the adoption journey alone. Support groups provide travel companions and a whole lot more! They are quite an oasis! Parents and professionals can remove the obstacles blocking greater participation for each member of the adoptive family. Adoptees and typically developing children, in particular, need more opportunities—supports—as they make their way through family relationships, and their way to adulthood.

Respite

Respite is defined as an interval of rest or relief. Respite can be a critical pit stop for road weary parents; time without the kids preserves the quality of the marriage. Respite, in the adoption world, is usually thought of as a weekend in length. Most often it is the child with mental health issues who goes to the respite. Respite can also be a difficult support to locate and pay for. Respite is not always used in the most productive of ways for families which include children with mental health issues. Let's get some directions about respite.

Leaving the Home in Times of Crisis

Respite is a common means of managing those adoption-related crises we learned about during our discussion of grief earlier in this chapter. The family, in the midst of a huge storm, calls an agency or a respite provider for help. Swiftly off goes the adoptee for the weekend. The rest of the family stays home.

> Bobby Jo is 15 years old. She was adopted when she was age 3. She has been challenging. Her negative behaviors worsen near the anniversary of her adoption, "gotcha day", as well as at the start of each new school year. August is the month she was removed from her birthfamily. During these trigger times, she becomes mouthy, argumentative and any request is met with, "No, and you can't make me." She is often up in the middle of the night surfing the Internet. Sometimes she leaves the house and wanders the neighborhood until the wee hours of the morning. Then she won't get up to go to school.
>
> These behaviors cause the whole family to skid out of control. The family becomes angry. The end result is that Bobby Jo goes off to respite.

Would you send any other grieving family member away?

Actually, this is a time when Bobby Jo's family needs to hold on tighter. She is grieving her losses. She needs the support of her family. Instead, she is segregated. She is left alone to deal with her intense feelings for her losses. Respite as a crisis management tool

2. *Scared Silent: Exposing and Ending Child Abuse* is available through Discovery Education, Customer Service, P.O. Box 2284, South Burlington, VT, 05407-2284, www.teacherstore.discovery.com.

sends a very powerful negative message to the adoptee, "We want you except when you are really struggling."

Alternatively, regularly scheduled, intermittent use of respite which is not crisis-related would prevent the backlog of negative feelings that put parents, brothers, sisters and the adoptee on this type of collision course. Periodic rest stops let everyone stretch their legs, get some fresh air and get back on the road ready to proceed on with the trip.

What's Really Important about Respite?

Safety

Lynette is 8 years old. Her parents, Doris and Sam, just picked her up from an overnight stay with her respite provider, Dawn. Dawn is a professional child care provider who works for an agency, which has a grant to fund this service. Adoptive parents call the agency to schedule services with Dawn.

Dawn is quite experienced. She has raised two adopted children to adulthood, and she has fostered many children.

Lynette reported that staying at Dawn's was great. She had "lots of fun" and she got to "eat whatever I wanted."

Doris was quite upset by this. When the family arrived home, Doris called Dawn. It turned out that Lynette didn't exactly get to eat "whatever" she "wanted," but, by many parents' standards, Dawn does have lax rules about food. It is one battle she prefers not to take on.

Doris decided that Lynette would never respite at Dawn's house again.

Now, Lynette has some sexual behaviors. She often masturbates, and she runs up to total strangers in an effort to "hump" their legs. Dawn may have less than ideal standards about food, but Dawn understands supervision. Doris needs to know that Dawn can ensure Lynette's safety. In this instance, Dawn kept Lynette close by all weekend so that Lynette had no opportunity to behave sexually with anyone.

Safety is a main criteria in utilizing respite as a support. In the scheme of things, does it really matter if your child stays up a bit past bedtime, watches a little more television than you would like, or has a few too many snacks for a day or two if she is kept safe?

Familiarity

Familiarity is another important criteria in respite. Typically developing children usually don't go stay with people they don't know for the weekend. Their baby-sitter is a familiar face; a person connected to the family. This is "normal." In order to integrate adopted children into their new found families, we need to give them as many "normal" experiences as possible.

Adopted children have already been cared for or moved in with "strangers"—some multiple times. Certainly, it is true that many adoptive families lose their support system post-adoption. It is also true that children like Lynette need a qualified provider who understands the full meaning of the word *supervision*. However, many children can stay with a trusted family friend or relative for a few hours or overnight.

Before we drop them off at some unfamiliar location, let's ensure that this is necessary. First, parents need to explore their support system thoroughly. Perhaps, a friend, neighbor or relative has been overlooked. Perhaps there is a new face from a support group.

Then, examine your motivations for resisting any available options. Many voluntary reasons—identified as roadblocks—for not utilizing available respite were outlined in Chapter 8, "Difficulties in Breaking Free of Isolation." Let's take each one in turn.

Are you worried about how the child will act upon return home? Many children do exhibit more negative behaviors upon returning to the family. Of course, they do! They have no idea how to re-connect. Remember, we are talking about children with poor relationship skills. Coming up in "Nurture: The Ring that Holds all of the Keys," plenty of ways to smooth these bumps will be offered.

Does it bother you that the child often acts better for others than for you? This occurs because the child isn't trying to form the intimate relationship with an uncle or a cousin that he is working on with his parents. The level of closeness of the relationship is the trigger for the challenging behaviors. In conjunction with this, the child care provider won't likely see the problems you deal with daily, so you receive no validation of your struggles. This hurts your feelings. Thus, you choose to carry your burden alone. Re-think this. Consider the impact of this choice on your resident children.

Other parents express such concerns as, "What if he steals something or breaks something?" Well, what if he does? What is the worst thing that can happen? He certainly won't be the first child to shatter a glass or plate. Stealing carries a natural and logical consequence. She'll have to return the item and apologize.

> Devin entered his adoptive family at 8 months of age. Instantly, his parents, Sheila and Lou, fell in love with him, as did his two sisters, Rita and Barbara. But, by age 3, he had developed into a very busy boy!
>
> He whirled around the house at a high rate of speed. Anything in his path was knocked over or stepped on! His high energy level was exhausting. He was on the go from the moment his eyes opened until he fell asleep. He slept so soundly, he usually wet the bed.
>
> Sheila and Lou really wanted a break. Sheila's sister, Aunt Pam, had offered to take Devin on numerous occasions. Sheila and Lou had so many reservations. What if he wet the bed? What if he broke something? He's so busy. How will Pam handle him?
>
> Yet, Rita and Barbara spend much time with Aunt Pam. Her home is situated in a rural area. There is a large backyard.
>
> Exhausted, Sheila finally made arrangements for Devin to spend an afternoon with Aunt Pam. Sheila dropped him off and then went shopping with Rita and Barbara at a nearby mall. She wanted to be close at hand in case of problems.
>
> After about two hours of shopping, the cell phone rang. It was Pam. "Could Devin stay overnight?" she inquired. "He is having such a great time with my sons, I hate to end the fun."
>
> An astonished Sheila gladly agreed. She dropped off a plastic sheet before she, Rita and Barbara drove home. That evening the family enjoyed a *calm* dinner at a favorite restaurant.
>
> The following day, Lou went to Pam's and picked Devin up. Pam offered her services again, "You know, with his energy he needs to play with my sons more. They can wear him down!"
>
> Driving home, Devin said, "I had a really good time at Aunt Pam's. How come I never got to stay there before?"

Devin goes to Aunt Pam's about once every six weeks now. He has a great time, while Lou, Sheila, Rita and Barbara relax. Lou and Sheila wonder why they didn't do this sooner. This is a common reaction the first time parents gain the courage to rely on their support system for respite.

Novel Approaches to Child Care

Here are some examples of the types of respite utilized by other families. If I didn't convince you in the support group information above to go sign up for a group, think about how many ideas in this book have come from adoptive families! Veteran parents are a wealth of resources and creative ideas.

Maggie and Brent parent 9-year year-old Clarissa. Boy, have they gone through baby-sitters! Clarissa is a very anxious child. She becomes fearful when her parents go out. She thinks they won't come back. Her anxiety leads to quite the behavior. Her first child care provider couldn't believe that Clarissa was flushing the cat down the toilet! Another caregiver was locked out of the house as she ran out to retrieve the cell phone she had accidentally left outside. She used the phone to call Maggie and Brent to come home! She had had enough of Clarissa. Yet another reached into her purse only to pull out the spaghetti that had disappeared from the dinner table! Each informed Maggie and Brent that they "needed to get a grip on Clarissa, and please don't ask me to babysit again—ever!"

A tenacious couple, they kept at it. They were determined to go out to dinner or a movie once in a while. One day, while raking leaves, Maggie noticed 17-year-old Mya, a neighbor girl going into her house. Mya had a twin, Ali.

Later, she went over to their house and inquired about the twins' availability to watch Clarissa. She explained some of Clarissa's issues and felt that together, perhaps they could manage Clarissa. She had decided to try a *strength in numbers* approach.

The girls, eager to earn some extra money, came over one Friday evening. Maggie and Brent went to a local restaurant. They planned to be gone no longer than about 90 minutes.

After they left, Mya and Ali braced themselves and held onto the cat. Within short order, Clarissa threw herself on the floor and started having a major meltdown. Mya pulled out her phone and said, "Why don't you call your parents and see what they're having for dinner? Here I'll dial the number."

Brent, expecting the worst, answered the phone. (Maggie was ready to get a to-go box). A crying Clarissa said, "Are you coming home?"

Brent replied, "Of course we're coming back, and I'll bring you a dessert. Here, let me tell you the choices."

The conversation calmed Clarissa down. She sat with Mya and Ali and watched part of a movie. She happily awaited her cherry cheesecake.

Now, calling Mom and Dad while they are out is a ritual. It provides the reassurance Clarissa needs to stay at home with Mya or Ali. That's right. Clarissa no longer needs two baby-sitters.

Many children with anxiety do well when they have a family photo, a special item given to them by a parent to hold onto or if allowed to make a quick call to Mom and Dad. It is a "visible" way to keep their parents with them while parents enjoy a date.

In Chapter 8, we met Lorraine and Peter. They parent seven adopted children all with varying mental health issues. Five of the children have special learning needs. This makes homework time consuming. Arrival home from school means homework, dinner, more homework and then baths and bed. There is little time to simply be a family.

This family resides in a state that has a program through which adoptive families can receive respite monies. The family finds a provider and the state provides the dollars.

In looking at the regulations, there was no mention of "where" the service needed to take place. Lorraine completed an application, clearly explaining her plan. The application was approved.

The next day, her neighbor, Helen, a retired school teacher, came over as the school bus was unloading. Helen took the youngest three and worked with them on homework while Lorraine handled the remaining four. Homework was done in half the time!

This *in-home respite* allowed the family time for games, a movie or some extra snuggles. This is exactly what Peter and Lorrain wanted—more time to respite *with* their kids.

Before we leave Peter and Lorraine, I feel it important to say directly to professionals reading over the shoulders of parents for whom this book was written that if we, as professionals, are going to create large adoptive families, then we need to support these parents and their many children. In-home help could be a great asset to these families. They could have more family time. Isn't that worth the cost?

Josh is a single adoptive dad. His two sons are older adolescents. Josh is a history teacher. But, he is also establishing a martial arts studio. In order to boost his number of students, he started offering "Demonstration Nights." For a $5.00 fee, parents could drop off their children, who would be kept busy watching various accomplished instructors demonstrate their skills. Parents would have three hours all to themselves.

Josh circulated a flyer to all the local adoption agencies and support groups. Soon, his classes were full. He continues to provide these respite demonstration evenings. As an adoptive parent, he knows how hard it can be to get a break.

Annette and her husband, Wayne, parent five children, two by birth and three through adoption. The family is very involved in their church. Annette identified two families in the church that she trusts and whom she feels mirrors much of her and Wayne's thoughts on raising children.

In times of crisis, her birth children go to spend time with these families. This leaves her and Wayne free to deal with their troubled adopted children. The typically developing kids get a nice break. The adopted children with problems get the extra attention they need in their times of adoption-related crisis.

Annette has named this *reverse respite*. It sends a nice message. "In our family, everyone takes breaks, not just the adoptees."

Darlene parents her two birth daughters, Gloria and Michelle, and her adopted siblings, Justin and Judy. She is now a single parent, since her husband moved out. The youngest adoptee, Judy, age 7, is prone to very aggressive outbursts. Gloria is going off to college soon and Michelle is already unsure she can manage Judy alone in the event that Darlene needs to go out.

This family is also strong in their faith. Darlene called their clergy person. She explained her situation. He agreed to give her some time at the next service to address the congregation.

She stood in front of her fellow parishioners and let them know how valuable their generosity had been to many members of the church congregation. They had provided rides to doctor's appointments, casseroles to the ailing, light repair and yard work to the elderly church attendees and so on.

She was now soliciting their assistance. She didn't have a medical problem, she explained, she had a child with a mental health issue. She needed some assistance with child care.

Well, within short order, she had child care. She also had soup, baked goods, and a few young adults mowing the lawn! They don't really understand Judy's needs, but for two years many parishioners have provided support to Darlene and her family with *task respite*.

As a last example, we are again going to hear from Jill and Mitchell, a family very familiar to us at this point in this book. They share their thoughts about respite and they will help us make a final most important point about this support.

> "The best way to cope when dealing with difficult children," says Jill, is to take breaks. Make sure that they are part of your weekly schedule. Otherwise, if you're like me, you won't take the time. After three years of living with children with mental health issues, we've only recently started scheduling respite. It's made a huge difference. I put my son in day care one day a week. I have the entire day to be by myself without the stress of his crazy antics all day. We also scheduled six hours on Saturday for both of our children. We were lucky enough to find a daycare that has evening hours. This gives us time every week to be together with our healthy children. We go out to dinner or shopping or sometimes we'll just relax at home. It's something I really look forward to and it feels so good to just be at peace. I feel totally relaxed like I used to before adoption turned our world completely around.
>
> "Fortunately," adds Mitchell, "our daughter is slowly becoming healthier and we think that she could handle doing more.
>
> "We had been hoping that our son would improve also, but he is not progressing as quickly. For the past three summers, we've put our lives on hold. We were hoping and waiting for him to catch up, because the thought of doing family things without him seems so cruel. Only recently have we faced the facts that he may never be able to do these things.
>
> "It's not fair to Svetelina and Jessica to miss out. They should have a full and enjoyable childhood with things as normal as possible. With the help of our therapists we've come to realize that the family needs to go on.
>
> "They made it sound so simple; why didn't we think of it before? If you have a child who is blind, the entire family doesn't stop going to movies. They make arrangements so everyone can be happy. We need to do the things that families do, like going to the amusement park for the day, something the girls will enjoy. Our son could never handle this right now. That means we'll find a place for Ivan to stay, somewhere safe where he's enjoying the things he can. This is what's best for everyone."

There is a philosophy afloat among some adoptive families that respite should be punitive. As such, the traumatized child will arrive back home with a greater appreciation for his adoptive parents, brothers and sisters. At the Attachment and Bonding Center of Ohio, we feel that this type of respite is quite off track. Jill and Mitchell's approach is a far more proactive path. Ivan goes to respite and "enjoys the things he can" while the other family members go out and have their own fun.

Isn't fun supposed to a part of childhood? Why would we want to deny children who have been abused and neglected enjoyment? What purpose does such punitive thinking serve?

Key Point—Respite doesn't and shouldn't always mean that the adoptee leaves the family. The length of respite can vary. Respite with a safe and familiar face, when possible, conducted at regular, intermittent intervals offsets the storms that triggers blow through the adoptive family. A combination of respite strategies makes clear that in this family, "We all take breaks as a normal part of our family life."

Key Point—The benefits of a healthy marriage are made clear in the accompanying box, "Benefits of a Healthy Marriage." Make scheduling a date with your partner a priority.

BENEFITS OF HEALTHY MARRIAGES

For Children:	For Women:	For Men:	For Communities:
More likely to attend college	More satisfying relationships	Longer-lived	Higher rates of physically healthy citizens
More likely to succeed academically	Emotionally healthier	Physically healthier	Higher rates of emotionally healthy citizens
Physically healthier	Wealthier	Wealthier	Higher rates of educated citizens
Emotionally healthier	Less likely to be victims of domestic violence, sexual assault, or other violent crimes	Increased stability of employment	Lower domestic violence rates
Less likely to attempt or commit suicide	Less likely to attempt or commit suicide	Higher wages	Lower crime statistics
Demonstrate less behavioral problems in school	Decreased risk of drug and alcohol abuse	Emotionally healthier	Lower teen age pregnancy rates
Less likely to be a victim of physical or sexual abuse	Less likely to contract sexually transmitted diseases	Decreased risk of drug and alcohol abuse	Lower rates of juvenile delinquency
Less likely to abuse drugs or alcohol	Less likely to remain or end up in poverty	Better relationships with their children	Higher rates of home ownership
Less likely to commit delinquent behaviors	Better relationships with their children	More satisfying sexual relationship	Higher property values
Better relationships with their mothers and fathers	Physically healthier	Less likely to commit violent crimes	Decreased need for social services
Decreased their chances of divorcing when they get married		Less likely to contract sexually transmitted diseases	
Less likely to become pregnant as a teenager, or impregnate someone		Less likely to attempt or commit suicide	
Less likely to be sexually active as teenagers			
Less likely to contract sexually transmitted diseases			
Less likely to be raised in poverty			

Sources: U.S. Department of Health and Human Services, Administration for Children and Families. "Benefits of a Healthy Marriage." [online]. http://www.acf.hhs.gov/healthymarriage/benefits/index.html, Institute for American Values, Center for Marriage and Families. "Why Marriage Matters, Second Edition: Twenty-Six Conclusions from the Social Sciences." [online]. http://www.americanvalues.org/pdfs/wmmexsumm.pdf

Mental Health Supports: A Continuum of Care

This book has made clear the fact that a majority of adoptive families of children who have experienced neglect or trauma will utilize mental health supports. An overall goal of this book has been to gradually acquaint readers with pertinent aspects of this system of care.

Chapter 1 made clear that pre-adoption is the time to investigate the availability and financial coverage of adoption-competent mental health services.

Chapter 2 described complex trauma in order to help readers understand the impact of abuse, abandonment, neglect and institutional deprivation on the adoptee. In essence, Chapter 2 gave us the "how" and "why" of the development of mental health disorders.

Chapter 3 gave an overview of the parental qualities that lend to offsetting these mental health issues.

Chapter 4 elaborated on the mother and father as a united front in managing their family.

Chapter 5 provided in-depth identification of the types of mental health diagnoses (as well as other special needs) parents may expect to see. This information was offered via content and the Prediction Paths we constructed.

Chapter 6 offered ways to move children less traumatically.

Chapter 8 presented the stages of an adoptive placement, with emphasis on the complex family configuration that can result when a traumatized child enters a healthy family system. Chapter 9 also put forth a "Model of Care" so that parents may more easily identify the adoption-competent professional.

Chapter 9 and the first half of Chapter 10 have offered many practical tips and resources for smoothing the journey of the adoption-built family for adoptees, brothers, sisters and parents alike.

In this chapter, we will provide the concluding pieces of information related to the mental health system. Mental health supports are organized along a continuum from least to most restrictive. This point will become clear as services are described below. More prominent mental health professionals—guides—are identified and described.

Outpatient Services

Outpatient means treated while living at home. The family travels to an office or clinic to receive outpatient services on a regular, usually weekly, basis. Appointment length is typically 45 or 60 minutes. Parents seek outpatient services to tend to the needs of their adoptive child, help their typically developing children cope, and/or to resolve marital or their own personal individual issues. Many outpatient facilities also offer group therapy. A vast assortment of problems can be effectively resolved via outpatient means. This is the least restrictive type of service.

In-Home Services

In-home services, also referred to as *wraparound* or *family-based*, are mental health services provided by mental health professionals coming into the home, school and/or community. Services are conducted multiple hours per week. The goal is to envelope the family in support. A team approach is utilized. Each member of the treatment team carries out specific tasks to improve the well-being of family members. Wraparound services represent a step up the continuum of care as it is a more intensive approach to therapy than is the use of outpatient services.

Day Treatment Programs

Day treatment or *partial hospitalization* programs combine mental health and academic learning. In some instances, the two are carried out at the same location. That is, the child receives schooling and psychological care in the same setting, each day, five days per week. In other instances, the child attends school and then is transported to a community clinic to receive mental health services. Day treatment programs are designed for children with more severe issues and are often utilized with the intention that an out-of-home placement can be avoided.

Psychiatric Hospitalization

This service is short-term, perhaps a few days or weeks, and it is in-patient. The child stays in a psychiatric hospital just as a medically ill person is admitted to a hospital. It is usually reserved for acute crises, such as suicidal attempts. Once admitted, the child or adolescent is observed, participates in treatment, may be prescribed medications or have current medications adjusted. Parents meet with the attending professionals. The child is discharged with out-patient or in-patient treatment recommendations.

Residential Treatment

Unfortunately, there are times when a child's mental health issues will become so great that the child will need to reside (in-patient) in residential treatment. The child lives in a campus setting for an extended period in order to receive intensive psychological and psychiatric care. After 3, 6, 12 months or longer, the child returns home. Often, safety issues prompt admission to residential treatment—ongoing suicidal ideation or suicidal threats, sexual perpetrating, violence, fire setting, eating disorders or substance abuse. Residential treatment is costly and is usually not covered by private health insurance. A family seeking this service may have to rely on community funds or public agency monies. Parents of children adopted from the public system may find it easier to obtain funding for residential treatment than will families of children adopted domestically as newborns or families of children adopted at any age internationally. The bottom line is that funding for residential services requires time and advocacy to obtain. Residential treatment is obviously a most restrictive form of care.

Chapter 7 addressed the issues that occur when children leave the home temporarily or permanently.

Crisis Intervention

Many communities set up and operate phone crisis hotlines. A "live voice" answers and guides the family through their predicament. Other areas rely on 911 to respond to and calm the situation, or to determine the need to travel to the local emergency room in order that a mental health evaluation be conducted for possible psychiatric hospitalization. Frequently, therapists, psychologists, in-home treatment team members, etc. have their own provisions for families to contact them in emergency circumstances via a paging system. Parents are encouraged to know the options available to them in times of crisis. Most often, having someone to talk to during this time alleviates this critical event or helps clarify the best direction in which to proceed.

Key Point—Families need to be aware that the continuum is designed to prevent the out-of-home placement of the troubled child. However, when this out-of-home care is necessary, parents must realize that the continuum must be exhausted prior to moving to in-patient programs. Frequently, parents do not heed the advice to work on issues—over time—before the problems escalate to the point that they are no longer manageable in the home environment. Then, in the midst of a crisis, they contact the public agency requesting residential placement. This isn't going to be available if sufficient documentation doesn't exist to support that less restrictive services have been accessed. Obviously, "home" is believed to be the best place for a child, and all efforts need to be made before placement outside of the home is considered.

Guides to Healing: Types of Mental Health Professionals

Psychiatrist

A psychiatrist is a medical doctor, (MD), who specializes in the treatment of mental health disorders. Child and adolescent psychiatrists predominantly prescribe medication that improves focus, impulsivity, mood stability (anxiety, depression, Bi-Polar Disorder), etc. Some psychiatrists conduct talk therapy as well. Chapter 5 provided a list of questions parents may ask to clarify the benefits and side effects of medications as a component of the care of their son or daughter.

Psychologist

A psychologist has advanced education, a doctorate degree—PhD or PsyD and occasionally EdD—in the study of psychology. Thus, these professionals carry the title of "Dr.," just as an MD does. Psychologists strive to change the way an individual acts, thinks, interacts socially, expresses emotions, manages stress, and so forth. A psychologist may conduct treatment, psychological testing or prepare psychological assessments. There are checklists and questionnaires designed to validate the presence (or absence) of symptoms of various mental health diagnoses, aspects of personality, IQ, etc. The psychologist administers these tests, speaks with the child, parents, previous mental health providers, school teachers and so on. Then, she compiles all of this information into a report—the psychological assessment. The end result of this process provides recommendations for a course of treatment.

Neuropsychologist

A neuropsychologist is a specific type of psychologist who studies the relationship of the brain to behavior. As Chapter 2 described, psychological trauma has an impact on the brain somewhat similar to that of a physical injury. So, in order to understand what a neuropsychologist does, consider an individual who has sustained a head injury. The neuropsychologist would measure the extent of the damage resultant from the injury. He would then offer ways to help the brain operate better. Thus, the neuropsychologist helps to discern issues that are medical in nature. Neuropsychological evaluations are becoming a frequent way to identify traumatic damage. A neuropsychological evaluation may be needed if you feel that your child has difficulty thinking, problems with learning, memory deficits, uncontrollable emotions or behavioral problems.

Therapists

Therapists come from an array of educational backgrounds—social work, pastoral counseling, marriage and family studies, counseling psychology and addictions counseling. Most therapists have earned a Master's degree. Social workers look at individuals and families within the context of their environment. Pastoral counselors include spirituality in the therapeutic process. Relationship issues are a focus of marriage and family trained professionals. Counseling psychology has more of an emphasis on helping the individual function better within his social setting. Families who want to understand or verify the specific qualifications of these professionals may contact their state licensing boards.

Most therapists provide direct, face-to-face service. As Chapter 5 described, they work with the family to establish a treatment plan. Treatment goals are established, and then therapists determine the interventions—the ways—the goals will be achieved.

Key Point—It is important for parents to know that the educational programs that provide general training for the mental health professionals listed exclude substantive information about families created by adoption. The prevailing schools of thought in most therapeutic training teach students to look within the family in order to determine the roots of a child's mental health issues. Adoptive families fall outside of this approach. Rarely is the adoptive family the source of the child's damage. While it might require some extra miles to travel to an adoption-aware professional, the family will find understanding and respect upon arrival. Treatment will encompass the whole family. This professional is certainly an oasis well worth the journey.

Medical Supports

Chapter 5 explained the unique medical issues presented by both internationally and domestically adopted children. The chapter pointed out the advantages of connecting with an Adoption Medical Clinic. Families will want to connect to a local pediatrician with expertise in adoption health care. The American Academy of Pediatrics (see resources Chapter 5) has a searchable database to assist parents in locating the adoption medical clinic nearest to their home.

In addition to an adoption-competent pediatrician, several other medical professionals can contribute to a smoother journey.

Physical Therapist

A physical therapist enhances mobility; they help children move better. Physical therapy may be needed any time a child has difficulty running, jumping, hopping, skipping or moving in any way that impairs daily activities.[3]

The areas of focus in physical therapy include

- muscle control and coordination
- lengthening tight muscles
- range of motion, strength and endurance
- gross motor development throughout the body
- gait (the way a child walks and runs) and mobility training

3. Manternach, Karen. "Physical Therapy." [online]. http://kidshealth.org/parent/system/ill/phy_therapy.html

- balance and coordination
- promotion of healthy, active lifestyle[4]

A pediatrician may recommend the services of a physical therapist for children with developmental delays, pre-natal drug/alcohol exposure, trauma, and an array of medical conditions related to muscular and heart/lung diseases.

Occupational Therapist

A child's occupations are play and learning. So, an occupational therapist enhances the child's performance in these areas. Things like grasping toys, eye-hand coordination, hitting a target, batting a ball, copying from a blackboard, handwriting, or any other fine motor skill can be improved with occupational therapy.

An occupational therapist can also

- help kids with developmental delays learn basic tasks such as getting dressed, bathing, sitting up, rolling over, or feeding themselves.
- help kids with behavioral disorders learn anger-management techniques (i.e., instead of hitting others or acting out, the child would learn positive ways to deal with anger, such as writing about feelings or participating in physical activity).
- work with children who have Sensory Integration Dysfunction (SI) and attentional issues to improve focus and social skills.
- provide parents a wealth of information about child development.[5]

As stated above, occupational therapists can provide the services to treat SI. Those occupational therapists who do assess and treat this disorder have had specialized training above and beyond general training in OT. Families want to inquire about this advanced learning when contacting occupational therapists.

Children who have learning problems, autism, sensory processing problems, developmental delays, mental health or behavioral problems, a history of burns, chronic illnesses (spina bifida, cerebral palsy, juvenile rheumatoid arthritis, brain or spinal cord injuries, orthopedic injuries, traumatic amputations, birth injuries or birth defects, etc.) may benefit from consultation with an occupational therapist.

Speech-Language Pathologist

A speech-language pathologist is more commonly referred to as a *speech therapist*, and these professionals treat speech and language disorders. Speech and language contribute to literacy as we learned in Chapter 5.

According to the American-Speech-Language-Hearing Association ***Language*** includes:

- what words mean (e.g., "star" can refer to a bright object in the night sky or a celebrity)
- how to make new words (e.g., friend, friendly, unfriendly)
- how to put words together (e.g., "Peg walked to the new store" rather than "Peg walk store new")

4. Children's Therapy Corner. "What is Pediatric Physical Therapy." [online]. http://www.childrenstherapycorner.com/whatpt.html

5. Pierson, Kimberly. "Occupational Therapy." [online]. http://kidshealth.org/parent/system/ill/occupational_therapy.html

- what word combinations are best in what situations ("Would you mind moving your foot?" could quickly change to "Get off my foot, please!" if the first request did not produce results)

Speech consists of the following:

- Articulation: How speech sounds are made (e.g., children must learn how to produce the "r" sound in order to say "rabbit" instead of "wabbit").
- Voice: Use of the vocal folds and breathing to produce sound (e.g., the voice can be abused from overuse or misuse and can lead to hoarseness or loss of voice).
- Fluency: The rhythm of speech (e.g., hesitations or stuttering can affect fluency).[6]

Thus, a speech and/or language disorder can occur in any of the above listed areas. Language disorders are either receptive or expressive. *Receptive disorders* refer to difficulties understanding or processing language. *Expressive disorders* include difficulty putting words together or limited vocabulary.

Chapters 5 and 6 pointed out the importance of enhancing a child's speech and language from the moment the child is placed in the adoptive family—especially the internationally adoptee who must learn English.

Any speech or language problem is likely to have a significant impact on the child's social and academic skills and behavior. The earlier a child's speech and language problems are identified and treated, the less likely it is that problems will persist or get worse. Again, as Chapter 2 stated, development is like a set of gears. Each domain—social, cognitive, emotional and physical—impacts the other. Seeking help for your child's speech, language, fine motor skills, gross motor skills, sensory processing skills all lend to facilitating the growth of your adoptee. In turn, the entire family benefits.

A final word about speech therapists is that many are also trained to recognize and treat feeding and swallowing problems. It is not uncommon to see children, with histories of trauma, who can't suck on a straw, practically swallow a slice of pizza in one gulp, cannot breathe and eat simultaneously, refuse to eat various textures, etc. These may be signs of a feeding or swallowing problem. If your child displays signs such as the above or those below, ask your pediatrician for a referral to a speech therapist.

The following are signs and symptoms of feeding and swallowing problems:

- Arching or stiffening of the body during feeding
- Irritability or lack of alertness during feeding
- Refusing food or liquid
- Failure to accept different textures of food (e.g., only pureed foods or crunchy cereals)
- Long feeding times (e.g., more than 30 minutes)
- Difficulty chewing
- Coughing or gagging during meals
- Excessive drooling or food/liquid coming out of the mouth or nose
- difficulty coordinating breathing with eating and drinking
- Increased stuffiness during meals
- Gurgly, hoarse, or breathy voice quality
- Frequent spitting up or vomiting

---

6. American-Speech-Language-Hearing Association. *What is Language? What is speech?* [online]. http://www.asha.org/public/speech/development/language_speech.htm

- Recurring pneumonia or respiratory infections
- Less than normal weight gain or growth[7]

Additional Supports

Neurofeedback

Neurofeedback or *EEG Biofeedback* merits inclusion in this list. Neurofeedback is "training" for the brain. In very simple terms, the brain wants to be in a state of *synchronicity*, a place in which it can regulate all aspects of the individual's functioning effectively. Trauma interrupts this harmony, leaving the brain with the dysregulation we have learned about (Chapters 2, 8 and 9).

In neurofeedback, brain activities—electrical energy that flows in various frequencies—are monitored. Via video games, the brain is trained to change its patterns of operations. Over time, the new patterns become permanent. The brain will have changed the way it works! Neurofeedback is useful to enhance attention, mood (reduce anxiety and depression) and sleep disturbances. Negative behaviors, headaches, migraines and seizures can be reduced or ended also.

The Resource section of this chapter includes the website for EEG Info and EEG Spectrum. Both explain neurofeedback in detail. EEG Info's videos about neurofeedback are quite helpful. EEG Spectrum's article about the use of neurofeedback with children with attachment disorder is quite interesting. Both websites have databases of trained providers. Typically, mental health providers receive neurofeedback training and offer this as a service.

Culture Camps

At *culture camps*, also called *heritage camps*, adoptees have the rare chance to be in the majority. Culture camps seek to familiarize children with culture of origin. They do so by introducing them to the country's music, art, traditions, holidays, clothing, language, food, history, and so on.

The ways culture camps are conducted vary. Some are a weekend in length, others are a week long, and still others are day camps. Many culture camps include the whole family—parents, brothers, sisters and the adoptee—and others are designed for just the adoptee to attend.

Many camps include time for adoption workshops on all aspects of being a culturally diverse family. For example, a camp for families with African American members may learn about hair and skin care. Of course, there is time to informally talk to the other campers about experiences and ways to respond to questions about your family.

For culture camp to be effective, it needs to be extended beyond the camp experience. That is, culture camps should be considered *one* way adoptive parents facilitate the positive identity development of their transcultural adoptee and entire family for that matter. Chapters 3 and 5 offered ways to incorporate culture into the family's lifestyle on a regular basis.

Visit the *Adoptive Families* magazine online listing of culture camps (see Resources) to locate a camp just right for your family. Check out the Resources for articles in which family members' share their experiences of attending culture camp.

---

7. American-Speech-Language-Hearing Association. "Feeding and Swallowing Disorders in Children." [online]. http://www.asha.org/public/speech/swallowing/FeedSwallowChildren.htm

Heritage Tours

Heritage tours, or *homeland tours*, are visits to the child's birth country. The purpose of this trip may be to learn about the country, visit the child's orphanage, and/or to reunite with birthfamily members.

Certainly, planning is essential to ensure that this trip is the best possible experience. There are companies to help with logistics. Whether you belong to an online or in-person support group, talk to families who have completed a homeland tour. What were the benefits? What was negative? What went wrong? What went well?

Planning is more than logistics. Such tours are most valuable to children at specific developmental stages. Preparation needs to include parents being willing and able to answer the types of questions the adoptee may ask as the trip nears and unfolds.

Why did you adopt from a different country?

Why didn't anybody in my country adopt me?

Who took care of me until you got me?

Did they take good care of me?

How did I get to my orphanage or foster home?

What was the orphanage like?

Will anybody there remember me?

Are there other kids there now?

Likely, a heritage tour will generate many questions about the birthfamily as well. Consider your responses. If you need to, return to the discussion of the narrative in Chapter 9 to help prepare answers to your adoptee's potential queries.

Internationally adopted children aren't the only ones who could benefit from a homeland tour. A domestic adoptee moved from one city or state to another may appreciate the chance to explore his beginnings as well.

Searching and Reunion Services

Chapter 1 reported that 50% of all adopted persons search for birth relatives at some point in their lives (Child Welfare Information Gateway, 2004; Muller and Perry, 2001. Adoptees want to locate birthfamily members for many reasons) including the following:

- Medical history
- General Information:

  "I want to see someone who looks like me."

  "I want to know if I have siblings."

  "I want to know about my extended birthfamily."

  "I want to know what they like, what they do, where they live." "Do I have anything in common with them?"

  "Has my birthmom changed?" "If so, can I have a relationship with her now?"

  "Are my birth parents alive?"

  "Are they sorry for the way they treated me?"
- Many adoptees search to answer the question, "Why?" "Why didn't you keep me?" "Why didn't you change to get me back?"

Media reunions are replete with adoptees and birthmothers tearful and joyous to be reunited. However, these portrayals are not reflective of the scope of end results that could occur. Searching requires preparation and thought. Anyone considering a search is advised to read and talk to search veterans. Carefully weigh the pros and cons. Consider carefully whether you or your child is pushing for the search. Most mental health professionals feel that opening an otherwise closed adoption should be left to the adoptee to decide, age-appropriately. Make an educated decision.

Resources have been included to help clarify the emotional issues associated with search and reunion. There are also resources to help locate the information necessary to initiate the search for a birthfamily member.

Conferences

Conferences are a wonderful way to learn about all facets of adoption. There are lots of adoption conferences to attend. Child Welfare Information Gateway's website has a searchable conference database—http://www.childwelfare.gov/calendar/.

I suggest starting with the annual North American Council on Adoptable Children. Information about their conference is posted on their website (see Resources Chapter 3). This conference, one of the two or three best attended adoption conferences on the continent, brings together the top notch professionals in adoption. Attendees include many parents. There is a child care program. Scholarships are available to make this gathering family affordable. You can learn ways to help your family and meet new faces!

National conferences are held in some of the most exciting cities in this country. Many families attend workshops during the day and do some sightseeing on the off hours. A conference can be a part of a family vacation.

If you're not interested in a conference, day-long workshops occur in communities everywhere. Social service agencies, support groups, libraries, hospitals, colleges, and so on—even coalitions of such groups—sponsor seminars on all sorts of topics. Check out your neighborhood today to see what's going on.

Key Point—Support does exist. It may be with a speech therapist, a friend made at a culture camp, a psychologist, or a voice on the other end of a crisis hotline. Along your journey, make as many stops as you can. This way you are certain to find your oasis.

Nurture: The Ring that Holds All the Keys

"Where touching begins, there love and humanity also begin . . ." Ashley Montagu

"Is there anyone for whom the past doesn't shape the present?" (Siegel, 1999.)

Touch is critical to human development (Perry and Szalavitz, 2006). Loving touch leads to healthy attachment, and, as we learned in Chapter 2, attachment is the context in which all development becomes possible. Attachment in family life is also the blueprint for all subsequent close relationships. That's why, as we come to the end of this book, it's important to look at attachment styles—our children's and our own—and how they influence the relationship between us as the family begins to mobilize.

If you have parented an infant, stop for a moment and think about the hours you spent holding, stroking, touching, rocking, caressing, kissing and hugging your baby. As your child grew, touching and holding continued—hugs and kisses before getting on the school bus or while bandaging a boo-boo, snuggling while watching television or reading books, pats on the back for accomplishments, stroking hair as a gesture of affection, and lots of kisses and caresses just out of love!

As a result of consistent and predictable parental nurture and support, this child develops a *secure attachment*. The child trusts his parents to meet his needs, "My parents are always there for me." He feels good about himself, "I am worthwhile." He seeks out his parents when he needs help or comfort, "I can rely on my parents." He has absorbed the skills to navigate life. He can develop solutions, handle stress, regulate emotions, follow directions, complete tasks, and the list goes on.

He demonstrates empathy and remorse, "I have hurt Mom's feelings. I need to make this right." He strives to have fun. He explores his environment. He seeks parental praise for a job well-done, "I want to please my parents." He enjoys intimacy. He seeks out companionship, "I want to be around others." He can do all of these things within relationships with parents, peers, teachers, coaches, neighbors, etc. His blueprint is, "I am safe within relationships." He applies his secure model of attachment to all human interactions.

In adulthood, this secure attachment will allow him to continue to have close interpersonal relationships. He will feel love and give love. He will have a coherent narrative. He will understand his past—emotional baggage will not interfere with his capacity to interact in his marriage, with his children, in his career and so on.

Many adoptees arrive in the family having been deprived of *enormous* amounts of emotional and physical nurturing in the months or years prior to the child's adoption. Or, their sense of touch, love and affection may have become skewed because abuse has taught them that affection is sexual, or being beaten is the way touch is administered from a parent to a child.

Their style of attachment, their ability to navigate relationships, reflects their traumatic experiences and is *insecure*. There are several styles of insecure attachment. They are described below with their adult counterparts.

Avoidant Attachment[8]

This child's model of relationships is that parents or other adults are not all that useful in meeting needs. So, there is no point in seeking parental assistance. Connecting is limited; parents and adoptee remain isolated from engaging in meaningful interactions. There is little willingness to explore the environment or to play. Avoidantly attached children tend to display dissociative symptoms—flight—throughout their lives (Siegel, 1999). The desire— early in life— to have an emotional connection with the caregiver was so frustrating that this child learned to tune out in order to survive the rejecting, neglecting relationship. This pattern of attachment is also associated with a lack of recall of memories, which hinders reconstruction of the narrative (Siegel, 1999). Parents of children with avoidant attachment commonly report,

"He never asks for any help."

"He takes what he wants without asking."

"He stares at me when he wants something. He won't ask."

"He never asks politely. It is always a demand. 'I'm thirsty.'"

"He is always bored. He can never think of anything to do."

"She doesn't play."

"We came home from dinner and he didn't come to greet us. He didn't even act like he noticed we had been gone."

"He can be alone in his room so long that I forget he is there."

"As soon as I start talking, she glazes over."

8. The content pertaining to attachment styles is compiled from the works of John Bowlby, Mary Ainsworth, Cindy Hazen and Phillip Shaver.

"He's always where the family isn't. If we're watching a movie, he's in his room. If we're in the front yard cleaning up, he's behind the house."

"She wanders off when we are shopping or she walks way ahead of us."

The adult version of avoidant attachment is referred to as *dismissive attachment*. A dismissing adult continues to minimize, be uncomfortable in or avoid close intimate relationships. She may instead prefer achievement and activity; ambition and success are important. This adult continues to lack recall of childhood memories and feelings, and so she has no sense of the past in relation to her present actions. Dismissive adults may also side step conflict and prefer to be self-reliant.

Ambivalent Attachment

This attachment style has two subtypes. One is demonstrated by a child who is anxious or "clingy." This child fears the parent may disappear at any moment. These children display considerable distress when separated from parents, although they often aren't comforted when the parent returns. In fact, the returning caregiver may be met with anger and a rejection of their efforts to re-connect with the adoptee.

Parents of these ambivalently attached children may arrive at therapy saying,

"I can barely go to the bathroom. She is at the door wondering if I am in there!"

"We try to go out with friends and he acts so 'bad' the babysitter calls. We have to return home."

"She follows me throughout the house. If I turn around, I practically run into her."

"She can't sleep in her own bed at night. She has to get in bed with us or we find her on the floor next to our bed."

"He won't go to sleep until my husband, who works second shift, gets home from work. He has to know we are both in the house before he will go to bed."

"She can't go to a sleepover."

"She has to be with us at church. She won't stay in the Sunday school class."

A second type of ambivalent attachment is seen in the child who appears to "push" and "pull"—"I want you." "I don't want you." These children had birthparents or caregivers who exhibited inconsistency in responding to the child's needs; sometimes they were unavailable or unresponsive, and at other times they were intrusive. The caregiver misread the child's signals. Thus, internally, this child is uncertain as to his own needs and emotional state. This is a child who may not soothe easily, even when the parent is providing exactly what is necessary to aid in calming the son or daughter.

A parent of this type of ambivalently attached child may state,

"She asks for help with her homework, and when I come to help her she tells me I am doing it wrong. 'That isn't what the teacher said.'"

"When I have bananas, he doesn't want one. If I don't have a banana, look out, there will be a huge fit."

"Getting dressed for school is so difficult. We pick out an outfit and a few minutes later it isn't right. He is screaming and shouting that he can't possibly wear the red shirt!"

"She asks for a hug and when I give it to her, she pinches me or hugs so tight I have to ask her to let go because she is hurting me."

"We have a great time making brownies, and then she won't eat any."

In adulthood, this is known as a *preoccupied* style of attachment. These adults remain tangled up in their childhood experiences. They often, and frequently, interject, in a rambling on manner, events that occurred years ago, with their parents into daily conversation. In essence, they are sometimes present with their children and spouses, and at other times they are psychologically off in their memories of their past; physically present but, emotionally unavailable. They exhibit warmth one moment and then coolness in the next instant. This flip flop back and forth causes them to be unpredictable in intimate relationships.

Disorganized Attachment

Disorganized attachment is a mix of the attachment styles discussed above. These children lacked the ability to be soothed by their birthparents because these early caregivers were a source of fear—abuse. These children must cope with the loss of their birthparents on top of resolving the terrifying events that most likely led to the separation from the birthparents. Children with disorganized attachment have been found to be the most difficult later in life with emotional, social and cognitive impairments (Siegel, 1999).

These parents report many of the themes as pointed out in the ambivalent and avoidant attachment descriptions. Yet, these parents also report, "He can do something that makes me so angry. We have a big fight. Then, five minutes later he asks me what we are having for dinner. It's like nothing happened!" Or, "When I am angry, he smiles. I almost lose control of myself!" Many abused children utilized smiling or hugging the past perpetrator as a defense against further abuse. When triggered, this coping mechanism appears again in the adoptive family.

There is also a corresponding disorganized or *unresolved* adult style of attachment. The abuse and losses sustained in childhood continue to affect all areas of adult functioning. These issues remain unresolved. There is no organized approach to relationships. These people may seek a relationship, but lack the trust and feelings of self-worth to form the connection. They are often selfish, controlling and lack empathy and remorse. These adults are at great risk for mental health disorders, substance abuse and creating families in which there is abuse.

The above descriptions make clear that in common among the insecure styles of attachment is a lack of consistent and predictable care-giving and nurture.

Parental Attachment Style

Do you recognize your adopted child above in the attachment styles? Equally important, do you recognize yourself to any degree? Often, when the adoptive parent had emotionally unavailable parents or experienced abuse himself, the parent, too, has an insecure style of attachment.

> Max and his wife adopted two siblings, Pamela and Katrina, from the child welfare system at ages 3 and 6. Pamela, now age 14, displays an insecure attachment. With therapy she has progressed. She has some memory of her abuse which she is willing to talk about—tearfully. As she started to cry in one session, Max got up and left the therapy session. He went out in the hall and made calls on his cell phone. Yet, in other ways, he has been a very available parent. He coaches her softball team, negotiates her special education services and spends one-on-one time with her shopping, and he enjoys taking her to eat at their favorite rib place.

When this scenario occurred a second time, the therapist knew it had to be addressed. Max reported that Pamela's grief triggered his own unresolved emotions about his mother. She left—inexplicably—when he was 9 years old. He has missed her terribly his entire life.

In effect, Max is displaying a push-pull attachment. He vacillates between begin emotionally hot and cold. "I want you, but, I can't handle your feelings so, I withdraw." Closeness is hard because of his own abandonment. Max's style of attachment contributes to Pamela's mental health issues. She is working to recover with a parent who cannot handle her deepest feelings and her horrifying experiences. She will be hindered in her efforts to heal.

Parents who are adopting troubled children must think about their own style of attachment. Is it secure? Is it preoccupied like Max's? Is it dismissive or unresolved? How it is reflected in your way of coping?

For example, dismissive parents tend to utilize a negative coping style, like being "emotionally withdrawn", "the accommodating parent" or "I give in." Preoccupied parents go to "extraordinary means" or are often "punitive parents (Chapter 8)." These attachment-related coping styles inhibit intimate connections with adoptees, and they also weaken or stress connections to the typically developing children. This statement is exemplified by the negative ways these brothers and sisters learn to respond in complex adoptive families. Their withdrawal, or self-sacrificing, or acting-out, or covering up and/or being victimized (Chapter 8) are reflective of movements away from secure attachments with their parents.

Expectations reflect attachment styles. Again, prior relationships generate our beliefs about how subsequent relationships "should be." Alternatively, a family may be built for the purpose of giving us the intimacy we had hoped for or wanted as children ourselves. We utilize our current family to attain the types of connections desired—expected—from past caregivers. Expectations which are not realistic hinder the formation of secure attachments and leave adoptive families isolated, at cognitive dissonance and grief stricken.

So then, parents must ask, "How does my own attachment style impact the way I parent *all* of my children? Do I need to seek help to alter it?" In essence, adoption is about forming—navigating—close connections. The parent who is secure in intimate relationships models the style of attachment the children need to mirror.

In Chapter 3, the qualities laid out were all identified as those utilized to build close and connective relationships—secure attachments. The unhealthy dynamics laid out in Chapter 8, resulting from the trauma we have learned so much about, prevent family members from making their way to strong attachments. Chapters 9 and 10 are thus a model—the route—to moving (mobilizing) the family toward more intimate relationships. Each solution contributes, piece by piece, to forging solid—secure—ties that bind the family together.

So, this book is really about attachment and forming and maintaining attachments with and among each member of the adoptive family—parents, new adoptees, resident brothers and sisters.

So far, parents have been encouraged to learn to be more consistent. Parents are thus avoiding storms. This contributes to building trust. Parents should have developed more appropriate expectations of others. In so doing, there is less tension in these relationships. Supports that can aid in stress reduction have been identified; a calmer family atmosphere allows intimacy. Mothers and fathers have discovered the means to find the time needed to facilitate closeness, and they have looked at ways to prioritize—to put themselves and their children first.

Now, the benefits and importance of nurture will be explained. In common among the insecure attachment styles, is a lack of emotional connection to a parent. Nurture helps to create the closeness essential in repairing this damage.

In review,

Consistent, nurturing care-giving promotes attachment.

Attachment, in turn, facilitates the manner, in which humans interact with each other.

Attachment contributes to healthy psychological and physiological development.

This is why nurture is the ring that holds all of the keys. Have you ever lost or misplaced your keys? If so, you know that you can't go anywhere until you locate them. Nurture is similar. The adoptee's healing is halted or at least greatly slowed down if we don't find ways to nurture him.

This is no small task. As many examples in this book have made clear, adoptive parents are being asked to hug and caress children who are quite similar to porcupines! Their quills—behaviors—rise up, shoot out and penetrate—reject the parent—frequently!

In sections to follow, we'll look at some ways we can help these fragile creatures quell their fears about intimate relationships. *We'll also see that these ideas are very applicable to the resident children. They need nurture to maintain secure relationships with their parents.*

A Reminder: The "Cycle of Needs"

Chapter 2 described the cycle of needs like this. . . .

> A baby cries. The baby's primary caregiver, Mom or Dad, attends to the baby—a bottle, a clean diaper, comfort, a binky and so on. The baby calms. During this process of going from fussy to feeling safe and secure, there is eye contact. There is talking, "Oh my, what does my baby need?"
>
> "You are such a good baby."
>
> "What a beautiful girl you are!"
>
> And there is warmth—babies get warm when we hold or swaddle them. Feeding and fragrance are also a part of this very sensory cycle—perhaps we put lotion on the baby. Movement occurs—rocking or bouncing the baby on our knees. Touch is involved every step of the way!

So, when we talk about increasing nurture—forming secure attachments—we are really talking about ways to increase the components of the cycle of needs through the child's senses: eye contact, food, smells, movement, talking and touch (Keck and Kupecky, 2002). Throughout this segment, the ideas will all reflect these "key" ingredients. The end result is a recipe for a happier and healthier family!

Finding the Keys: Getting Nurture Going

Another Construction Zone: More Roadblocks

As Chapter 9 stated, roadblocks perpetuate the unhealthy family dynamics described in Chapter 8. Removing these barriers moves the family in the direction of mobilization.

The obstacles described below have in common withdrawal of parental love and affection. Throughout this discussion, we'll lay out possible alternatives—detours around the roadblocks.

Time Out

Time out seems to be one of the most popular forms of discipline today. However, for adopted children it is often ineffective for the reasons listed below:

- Time out occurs in lieu of the use of the more valuable natural and logical consequences.
- Time out frequently becomes a lengthy consequence. The "timer" doesn't start until the child is quiet and seated as the parent prefers. This process can involve a lot of negative interaction.

  "You're supposed to be sitting quietly!"

  "Quit touching the wall!"

  "Why are you laying on the floor? I'm adding another 10 minutes."

  Soon, the time out is 60, 90 or more minutes in length. Remember, you're supposed to be avoiding these storms (Chapter 9's section, "Reactions: Changing Direction to Avoid the Approaching Storm").
- Especially when long and frequent, time outs create disconnects; the adoptee is separated from the parents. Subconsciously, the child achieves his need to avoid nearness. In essence, time out then replicates the child's early experiences of being alone in an orphanage or neglected by his birth parents.

Adopted children need *time-ins*—they need to be *with* their parents (Keck and Kupecky, 2002). Before opting to send the child away from family members, stop and ask, "How can I bring him in closer to me right now ?" What can I do to help her calm down?"

> One great mom of several adopted children says, "Apron strings" to an agitated child. This means, "Come here and let me give you a hug. Let me help you calm yourself. Then we can talk about what has happened and how the problem can be solved."

This mom's approach has numerous advantages. First, traumatized children already know how to rely on themselves. This self-reliance is reinforced when children are separated for the purpose of self-soothing. Instead, when the parent assists the child, the child learns, "I can rely on my parent." This begins to facilitate the development of trust. Second, conflict is avoided.

Responding with nurture diffuses angry interactions. Remember, "You can catch more flies with honey than with vinegar"? This idea works quite well with children with mental health issues.

Lastly, in this mom's apron string technique she jointly works with the child to generate solutions. Traumatized children often have poor problem-solving skills. Helping them find ways to work out their problems teaches them an invaluable life skill.

Certainly, parents are welcome to take a time out themselves when their anger is boiling like an engine overheating. Before steaming with threats or hurtful words, take a few minutes to cool down, and then use the approach described above.

Emotional Gridlock

Withdrawal of affection has been talked about often in this book. To review, the adoptee's actions are perceived as a rejection of the parents' love and affection, so parents stop putting forth the effort to nurture the child. Parents in this situation offer many reasons for this,

"I got so tired of being hurt that I have stopped trying to be affectionate."

"I don't want to get near him at this point in time."

"I can't stand to be in the same room with her."

Yet, there is another dimension to this emotional withdrawal. It is reflected in the following statements commonly made by mothers and fathers,

"He won't let me hug him."

"I'll (parent) change when she (adoptee) changes."

"He needs to show me something first!"

In thinking like this, the onus for providing no affection is placed on the adoptee, "It is her fault that I can't nurture her."

Nurture isn't something the child should have to earn. It is an entitlement for all children!

Families thinking like this are trapped in an emotional gridlock. The types of changes the parents want are not going to happen until nurture is used to make way through the impasse.

A hand on the child's shoulder,
A Hershey's Kiss placed in his mouth,
A love note in a lunch box,
"I love you" written with soap on a mirror,
Painting fingernails,
Styling hair,
Scratching a back,
Rubbing lotion on sore shoulders,
Baking cookies,
Warming mittens in the dryer on a cold school day,
Sprinkling chocolate chips in pancakes, etc.

are all *direct* and *indirect* ways to begin to increase nurture.

Nurture and the Sexually Abused or Aggressive Child

The need for nurture is applicable to all children—even those with histories of sexual abuse. Here is one dad's account of increasing father nurture (Chapter 4) to his four adopted daughters. These siblings all experienced sexual abuse prior to being adopted by this dad and his wife.

> "Parenting daughters who have been sexually abused requires much patience, compassion, creativity and humility. It requires much patience because all four of my daughters had a complete distrust of me. While I've never hugged a rock, I have a very good idea of what it must be like from hugging my daughters for the first three years of our adoption. This would be a slow process.
>
> "The compassion comes from realizing that the two men they should have been able to trust—their birthdad and birthuncle—consistently abused them. It is illogical for them to trust me, when the only messages they received from their birthdad is that it is fine to be a drunk who both abuses his children and allows them to be abused. Obviously, changing such a deep, pervasive concept requires time. Understanding their past allowed me not to take the rejection of my daughters personally.
>
> "I knew from the first that appropriate physical touch was essential for my daughters. If they couldn't learn to accept my touch, they would look for physical touch from someone else. So I decided to make a game of it. Often when I was going up or down the stairs and

> one of my daughters the other way, I'd call out 'cuota'" (toll). (Toll booths are extremely common in the country in which we live.) They would have to give me a kiss on the cheek to continue up or down the stairs. Or I'd reverse it and give them a peck on their cheek. I'd also 'accidentally' plow gently into one of my children in the kitchen, and say jokingly, 'Honey, did you walk into me?', and then hug her. With Carley, my oldest, we'd have pushing contests across the hall floor.
>
> "You want to provide nurture—we have seen incredible changes in trust through non-coercive (not forced) holding. At times, their behavior makes it impossible, or at least seem impossible, to nurture them. Both my wife and I deliberately try to nurture through holding and other ways regardless of their actions.
>
> "Humility comes from realizing (both my wife and I) that we needed professional help, because the problems of our children were so serious. It is amazing how professional counseling helped our daughters in being able to appreciate me and accept appropriate physical touch."

Congratulations to this dad! He painstakingly and creatively worked for three years to revise his daughters' perceptions of love and affection, and it is working!

This dad offers us several important points, among which is that children who cannot accept healthy touch from their parents will seek to have their needs for touch satisfied elsewhere. Parents are often encouraged by social workers and mental health professionals to provide the sexually abused child little to no touch. Their belief is that this violates the child once again, or that such activities will trigger traumatic memories. This school of thought warrants some discussion.

Touch is an essential element of attachment, and thus, of growth and development. Touch is a means of communication—a handshake, a pat on the back, a pinch of the cheek, holding hands—each sends a message. Stress, anxiety and depression reduce with nurturance. Think of any nationally televised disaster like Hurricane Katrina. What did you see people doing? I saw people hugging each other and holding children on their laps. In times of sorrow and stress, humans instinctively reach out—literally—for comfort and to comfort. Touch is a critical component of how we humans relate to each other. Denying children the opportunity to learn how to give and receive "good touch" does them a *serious* disservice.

The aggressive child has learned that the means to fulfill his needs for touch is through hitting, kicking, pushing and shoving. He needs "good touch" to outweigh the seeking of "bad touch." Adoptive parents adding hugs, back rubs, back scratching, and so on will eventually tip the scale in the direction of less violence in their home.

Lastly, I have often wondered how this type of "hands off" philosophy plays out in a home in which there is a combination of traumatized and typically developing children. One or more children are receiving hugs and kisses, and another isn't? What message does this send?

Slowly and non-intrusively, parents must take the driver's seat and find the paths that enable their adoptee to accept and reciprocate physical affection. Of course, keep hugging the brothers and sisters as well! How about your husband, wife, partner or your sister or brother who is a single adoptive parent—did you hug them today? Did you call just to let them know you are thinking about them?

Infant Massage

Who doesn't enjoy a massage? Infant massage is a wonderful way to nurture a child. Before you skip this section because you don't have an infant, you need to know that even depressed or aggressive adolescents show decreases in their negative symptoms after massage (Cozolino, 2006). Many Certified Infant Massage Instructors will work up routines for older children.

Infant massage may be applied to the entire body or to specific areas of the body. For example, if you have a child whose age is beyond the developmental stage of being oral but who continues to chew her tongue, chew or suck on clothing, or who sucks his fingers, puts objects in her mouth, etc. the massage therapist will teach strokes to alleviate such behaviors.

Because of its focused use of touch, infant massage has the following benefits for infants and older children:

- relieving discomfort from gas, colic and constipation
- improving blood circulation
- aid in digestion
- improving quality and amount of sleep
- enhancing development of the nervous system and stimulating neurological development (brain function and brain development)
- increasing alertness/heightened awareness
- reduction stress hormones
- improving immune function
- stimulating the release of oxytocin, the "nurturing hormone"
- relaxing and soothing: nurturing touch is a naturally rewarding way to relieve stress
- deepening bonding: providing essential one-on-one time that will enhance your intimacy, understanding and ability to nurture
- contributing to development: stimulates growth and healthy development of body, mind and spirit[9]

Infant massage is usually taught in a group format, however, individual instruction is available. Visit the International Association of Infant Massage (see Resources) to find a certified instructor near you. Give *all* of the kids a turn. Try it on your spouse. If you are a single parent ask for a gift card to a spa on your next birthday or during the holiday season.

Theraplay®

The developers of this trademarked form of therapy define it as "a structured play therapy for children and their parents. Its goal is to enhance attachment, self-esteem, trust in others and joyful engagement. Because of its focus on attachment and relationship development, Theraplay has been used successfully for many years with adoptive families."

Their web site goes on to say, "Theraplay is organized around four dimensions:

- "*Structure:* The therapist and, once familiarized to the activities the parent, selects and leads the activities. The fact that the adult is in charge is reassuring and helps the child to develop self-control. It is especially useful for children who are overactive, undirected, overstimulated or who want to be in control.
- "*Engagement:* Engaging activities offer pleasant stimulation, variety and a fresh view of life, allowing a child to understand that surprises can be fun and new experiences enjoyable. The child is focused on an intensive way to make a

9. International Association of Infant Massage. "What are the Benefits of Infant Massage?" http://www.iaim.ws/faqs.html

connection. Engagement is especially great for children who are withdrawn, avoidant of contact, or too rigidly structured.

- "*Nurture:* Soothing, calming, quieting, caretaking activities make the world feel safe, predictable, warm and secure. This dimension meets the child's unfulfilled younger needs; helps the child relax and allow herself to be taken care of.
- "*Challenge:* Challenging activities help the child take a mild, age-appropriate risk, and promote feelings of competence and confidence. They stress cooperation rather than competition. Challenging activities are especially useful for withdrawn, timid or rigid children."[10]

Sean was 15 years old. He was adopted at age 3 by Wilma and Andy. He had presented various challenges for 12 years! He especially liked to dismantle things. Anything he could get his hands on was immediately taken apart, because he wanted to "see how it worked." Unfortunately, he lost pieces of items, and so many of his learning projects were ruined. He loved to take batteries. It was difficult to keep a flashlight, the remote control, the other kids' toys and so on operational.

He displayed symptoms of an ambivalent attachment. He hated it when Mom was out of the house or out of sight. He called her on her cell phone constantly. Even if she didn't answer, he kept calling and leaving messages. When she was home, he followed her everywhere. She had had a shadow for 12 years!

Theraplay was selected as one intervention because Sean so resembled a 3-year-old socially and emotionally. He eagerly participated in the activities. He especially enjoyed a cookie game. He laid across his mom's lap and looked into her eyes. She held an animal cracker, and she provided directions. "I want you to bite off the back feet. Good! Now, bite off the head! Great, you are listening so well!" He giggled and giggled and asked for another cookie and another cookie and yet another cookie!

Children, little to big—sometimes very big—love Theraplay! Give it a try. Visit the Theraplay website (see Resources) today to learn more about this fun form of nurturing. Stock up on the cookies—the other kids will want a turn!

Yoga

Prominent trauma experts are now recommending yoga as another tool to help heal traumatized children. Yoga is a practice of physical postures or poses. Combined with exercises to calm the mind. It has many benefits, including

- improved flexibility, strength, balance, muscle tone (also contributes to reduced back pain)
- breath work, important part of yoga, breathwork increases the individual's awareness of their breathing, and then teaches a way to regulate breathing. This is important for calming down.
- taming the Monkey Mind. This is the mind that jumps from thought to thought like a monkey jumps from tree to tree. Emphasis is on being in the present moment. This focus moves aside thoughts about the past and future. Worries are put aside. The mind gains the ability to focus and concentrate.
- stress relief through stretching. Stress-related tension is stored in the body, making a person feel tight, and often causing pain. The intense stretching of yoga

10. The Theraplay Institute. "Theraplay Treatment Protocol." [online]. http://www.theraplay.org/additional/treatment.htm

releases tension from problem areas (hips, shoulders, knees and even the face and jaw).[11]

Many yoga studios have classes for parents and kids to attend together. Spending quality time together is always nurturing. Locate a yoga class near your home. Make it your family's extracurricular activity.

"Music Soothes the Soul"

Isn't this heading true? There is simply nothing like music to connect people to one another, or to raise a down mood. Who doesn't tap a beat on the steering wheel when driving a long distance? Or start singing along with the current top hit or a favorite oldie? Your wedding was accompanied by a special love song. You sing your child to sleep with a favorite lullaby. Even picking up toys is done to the Barney "Clean Up" song. The iPod rage is another indicator of the pleasure millions of Americans receive from music. Did you also know that

- music helps develop brain areas involved in language and reasoning.
- there is a link between music and spatial intelligence—the ability to visually and mentally picture things. This is a type of intelligence used in math and solving problems. For example, researchers found that children given piano lessons significantly improved in their spatial-reasoning scores compared to children who received computer lessons or no piano lessons (Rauscher, Shaw, Levine, Wright, Dennis, and Newcomb, 1997).
- music is part of the arts. Arts promote creativity.
- music provides a means of self-expression.
- performing to an audience in a concert or chorus helps kids conquer fears. They learn that anxiety can be overcome.
- information from the National Education Longitudinal Study showed that music students received more academic honors and awards than non-music students (Ingels, 1992).
- students with coursework or experience in music performance or music appreciation scored higher on the SAT (College Entrance Examination Board, 2001).
- "the musician must make decisions about tempo, tone, style, rhythm, etc. This makes the brain become incredibly good at organizing and conducting numerous activities. This has a great payoff for lifelong attentional skills" (Ratey, 2001).
- singing, chanting and rhythmic play can increase your child's vocabulary, improve coordination, enhance self-esteem, contribute to emotional regulation and reduce stress (Campbell, 2002).
- rhythm is essential. The brain's rhythm-keeping regions, when not functioning properly, are often causes of depression and other psychiatric disorders. These regions are also in charge of regulating sleep, and this is likely why sleep problems are seen in children with mental health issues. Regulating heart rate and the release of stress hormones require the brain to keep proper rhythm as well (Perry and Szalavitz, 2006).

This list could go on to fill volumes!

In therapy, I connect my iPod to a speaker. I find that even the most difficult children will settle down and gaze intently into their parents' eyes during songs about family and adoption. Some of my clients' favorites are from the CD's offered at www.adoption.com (Resources Chapter 6). The CDs include *Do You have a Little Love to Share*, *Adoption . . .*

11. Pizer, Ann. "Benefits of Yoga." [online]. http://yoga.about.com/od/beginningyoga/a/benefits.htm

The Songs You Love, *The Spirit of Adoption* and *Chosen: Songs of Hope Inspired by Adoption*. Also, check out the Resources to learn about Kindermusik and Music Together—sign up for a class.

Let music bring your whole family closer together!

If you want about a hundred more nurture suggestions, then look in *Parenting the Hurt Child: Helping Adoptive Families Heal and Grow* by Gregory C. Keck and Regina Kupecky (see Resources). This book provides list after list of ways to nurture children, and they are applicable to *all* children.

Key Point—All of the above nurturing suggestions contribute to forming strong, secure and healthy attachments. Attachment is essential to human growth and development. With it, humans can navigate their way to endless possibilities. And so, nurture really is the ring that holds all of the keys. Have you nurtured your family today?

On a Positive Note (Yes, There Are Positives!)

Now out of the ocean of emotions and having received nurture, adoptive family members find themselves rejuvenated. There is more energy. Parents, brothers, sisters and the adoptee are eager to pursue rich, full lives. In this atmosphere it is also easier to see the positive aspects adoption has brought to the family. Yes, there are positives!

The Adoptee: A Place to Call "Home"

Adoption means that a child waits no longer for a home. A family wants to care for her and offer her all of life's opportunities. Who can deny the positive aspects of having a family? Certainly it is great to have someone with whom to share excitement about a job promotion, to eat with on holidays, to pet-sit, to make an emergency trip to the doctor, to help choose a first car or to phone when the car breaks down. A parent is available to help out with a new baby, a marital problem or a move to new place. The best part is that this family is available life-long to share the ups and the downs! The adoptee always has a place to call "home."

Below, adoptees, ages 8 to 18, comment on being adopted.

> "I love my family. They get me lots of clothes. They give me lots of toys and they love me. They care about me and go sleigh riding with me. They adopted me and that's the best part in the whole world!"
>
> "Adoption, to me, means being accepted, taken into a new family, receiving things you never had—I receive love and help. Before I was adopted, I was beaten and sexually abused."
>
> "Adoption is joining a new family, the beginning of a new life, comfort, love, safety—no hitting! You don't get rejected. You get fed. You get privileges. You get to learn new things. You don't get hit or abused and you get safety. It was hard leaving my birthmom. It has also been hard forgiving my birthparents. They told me things like, You are dumb! You are fat and ugly! You are not worth anything! I only wish my adoptive family had more of the Mexican dishes I love so much!"
>
> "Adoption isn't really a bad thing. I just thank God that I'm not on the streets somewhere. I think that could've happened if I stayed in the orphanage. The only bad or sad thing is that I am not with my birthmother or birthfather. I always thought my birthmother would

come and get me and take care of me. I think I'm over that now because I got a family now. They love me, feed me and let me get away with things—sometimes! I think I like being adopted."

"Adoption is the willingness of a family to be the kind of parents you need. My parents love me and are always there for me. They give me what I've missed. I got a whole new way of living and freedom to grow up the right way. I learned to speak, think and write in a different language. I can catch up with school.

"Adoption means that you are in an orphanage and a mom and dad come to get you and bring you home. It is good because I get to be with a mom and dad that take care of me the best."

"It has been very hard to learn to trust my adoptive parents. I had to learn that I was going to be safe living with my mom and dad, and that my days of suffering were over. I no longer had to rely on myself I have the opportunity to be a normal teen. I have awesome parents. I am truly blessed by God."

"The positives about being adopted have been numerous. First, I have a permanent family that will always be there for me no matter what. I've been able to do things that I wouldn't have been able to do in foster care such as playing the clarinet, having the ability to make lifelong friends and I've been able to travel. I've been able to trust my family and learn to love them. I stopped having to continually pack my things."

"One of the positives about being adopted is that you have someone that you can ask for help in life. You can count on them to be on your side through good or bad. I was put in one of the best homes I think because my mom loves me for who I am."

"I am staying with my adoptive family forever. It is good to have a lot of siblings (ten). I feel safety and love. I am with a Christian family and don't have to go through fighting every day. We do lots of activities together like games, movies, Bible studies, art projects and go to the library. It is good to have a family you can trust. I miss my bio parents and my one birth sister who still lives with them. I miss my bio grandparents (even though I get to see them sometimes) and other people that were important to me."

"The positives about being adopted are way too numerous to put on paper. I have a family that is all mine. I know that I'm not going anywhere just because I'm not what they were looking for. I know what it means to be loved and in turn to love. I understand that trust is something valuable that I had to give to my parents. I feel safe. I don't have to worry about waking up in the morning and thinking that I'm going to die."

"My foster family told me what was going on. My social workers barely even talked to me. We should have talked more about what was going on when I was going to move to an adoptive family. Maybe I should have started some kind of therapy. I got adopted by a family who cares about me! I'm an only child and I get a lot of attention."

"Adoption means that you want to be part of a family and don't want to move to a lot of homes. And that you want to tell everything about yourself to those new parents of yours.

"A good things about being adopted is that you have a family and you get to do stuff with your family. Another good thing about being adopted is that your new mom and dad can talk to you if you have any troubles about everything and you can also trust them and you can tell them how you feel and stuff that's going at school and other stuff.

"The are bad things about being adopted that I know of are that you get used to moving a lot and you might still have feelings about your old parents. You might be afraid to tell your new parents about them. Trust me, I do sometimes get afraid to tell my feelings!"

Plentiful research supports the positive aspects of adoption expressed by the kids above. Below is a chart comparing foster children who "age out" of the child welfare system between ages 18 to 21 with no permanent family to children who were adopted.

If these are outcomes for American foster children, what must be the end result for children leaving orphanages in less developed countries with fewer social programs?

Economically, it has been demonstrated that, even with subsidy, adoption saves American society billions of dollars each year. Adoption is *far* less expensive than keeping children in foster care long-term (Barth, Kwon, Wildfire, Guo, 2006).

COMPARISON OF FOSTER CHILDREN WHO "AGE OUT" OF THE CHILD WELFARE SYSTEM WITH CHILDREN WHO ARE ADOPTED

Foster Children	Adopted Children
• Poor educational outcomes; more than 1/3 have not completed high school • Considerably, more mental health issues than others in the same age group • Much more likely to have been pregnant and to carry the pregnancy to ter • Within 18 months of discharge from foster care: • More than 1/3 have been physically or sexually victimized, incarcerated or are homeless • One in five has lived in four or more places • Only 61% were employed, earning a median wage of $4.60 per hour	• More likely to complete high school or the equivalent • More likely to attend and complete college • Less likely to become teen parents • Less likely to abuse drugs and alcohol • Less likely to have mental health problems • Less likely to be arrested and incarcerated • More likely to be employed • More likely to have adequate incomes • More likely to have health insurance

Sources:

Courtney, M.E., Dworsky, A., Cusick, G.R., Havlicek, J., Perez, A. and Keller, T. (2007). "Midwest Evaluation of the adult functioning of former foster youth: Outcomes at age 21." Chicago, IL: Chapin Hall Center for Children, University of Chicago.

Courtney, M. E., Piliavin, I., Grogan-Kaylor, A., and Nesmith, A. (2001). "Foster youth transitions to adulthood: A longitudinal view of youth leaving care." *Child Welfare*, 80(6), pp. 685–717.

Freundlich, Madelyn and staff of North American Council on Adoptable Children NACAC): "The Value of Adoption Subsidies: Helping Children Find Permanent Homes." (2008). NACAC. [online]. http://nacac.org/adoptionsubsidy/value of subsidies.pdf

The Typically Developing Children: Sharing "Home"

From very practical sentiments like, "We got a bigger house" or "I didn't have anyone to play with and now I do" to more principled thoughts, brothers and sisters express many positives of sharing "home."

In my clinical experience, the teenage and young adulthood years are the time when these well-developing siblings, most likely as abstract thought and identity development are more advanced, can begin to fully integrate their experience. They see the pros and the cons. They begin to apply the lessons learned from being a brother or sister to an adoptee with "issues" to life.

Overall, six main positives emerge from living within a family raising a combination of children with and without mental health issues. These six positive factors are identified below. Mixed in are the reports of actual brothers and sisters. These birth and/or previously adopted siblings range in age now from 15 to 25. They were between the ages of 7 and 16 at the time their families adopted. Their families adopted children ages 10 months old to 13 years old. The adoptees have now been a part of the family for between six and twelve years.

Compassion

Our typical children develop a compassion for those less fortunate from having lived with a sibling with mental health issues. They are able to realize that adversity strikes many—young and old alike. They listen and strive to see beyond the outside of a person. They acknowledge that there are individuals who require help. Compassion supports the development of tolerance, insight and empathy.

> "As a whole, I believe that our family has had to make numerous sacrifices since my sister's adoption, but we have gained from it. Spending time as a family is more difficult now, and the household is definitely less peaceful. However, I find it much easier to relate to children with differences and the families of those children. Before, when I saw a badly behaved child, it was easy to attribute that to bad parenting. Now I realize that other factors may be involved. Even with a loss of family time, I feel that we have become closer as a family because taking care of my sister brings us together."

Appreciation

There is an understanding of the fact that they are well-off to have been born to (or adopted by) and raised by healthy, loving parents (Smith, Greenberg and Mailick, 2007). On one level, the typical children tend to appreciate fun times and quiet moments. On a different level, they acknowledge that they are fortunate to have escaped the often horrendous long-term effects of neglect, abuse and abandonment.

> "I think a positive experience for me is that this has made me become a stronger person. I look at my brother and see what a horrible past he had with his foster mom (very neglectful). I look at my past and think Wow, I was really lucky to have a foster mom as good as I did. She treated me good and gave me food and all that. My brother grew up in a whole different situation."

Maturity

A maturity develops as a result of the knowledge that life can be unfair, things might not get better, and bad things do not always happen to others (Meyer and Vadasy, 1994).

This maturity produces children who are well-adjusted and more responsible than most same-age peers (Meyer and Vadasy, 1994).

> "I think it's been a positive experience just in the fact that it opened my eyes to other issues that are out there. Like in school, my French teacher would always talk about students who would trash the desks—write on them and stuff—and that it was the parents' fault. The parents didn't care about their children. Bringing in disruptive children, who we have tried to help as much as possible, let me see that, No, that's not always the case. There are parents who actually try to help and do whatever they can. This child, in her own mind, doesn't want to follow it and chooses not to do what the parents want. So, it opened my eyes to the fact that it's not always the parents that are causing the problem. It may be the child herself."

Aware of Consequences

In setting their own life courses, brothers and sisters of children with mental health problems may have a heightened awareness of the consequences of various actions. For example, regarding drinking and pregnancy, they know firsthand how drinking while pregnant can condemn a child to brain damage and a lifetime of challenges (Olesen, 2004).

Making the Best of a Difficult Situation

> "We found a way to occupy our time with making the best out of the situation. You learn how to work with what you got. This is good."

In essence, we all have to learn to "work with what you got." This process helps to develop problem-solving skills. The resident children become quite creative in making life with a sibling with mental health issues work to their advantage. It is not uncommon that they negotiate with parents ways to earn money for comforts like a television, an iPod or CD's. These supplies allow a comfortable escape during major family storms. They learn to be heard when absolutely necessary—demonstrating improved communication skills. Certainly, enhanced problem-solving, communication and negotiating skills, as long as not used maladaptively will serve them well throughout their lives.

Vocational Opportunities

Brothers and sisters whose siblings have mental health issues frequently gravitate toward the helping professions (Meyer and Vadasy, 1994). These young adults are more certain of their own futures and about personal and vocational goals than comparable young adults without similar experiences.

Remember George from Chapter 9? He is entering college with a major in pre-med. Scott, from Chapter 3, is grown now. He is 18 and this fall he will start college. His goal is to become a psychologist.

In closing this segment on how living with a troubled sibling offers positives for our typically developing children, here is a contribution from an adult now in her 50s. Her parents were foster and adoptive parents throughout her childhood, starting when she was age 4. At present, she is the adoptive parent to two children ages 12 and 17.

> "To say that these children disrupted our home life would be an understatement. They had a variety of mental health issues. I will add that I often became the butt of their anger. My imposed siblings would steal and/or destroy my toys, hurt me physically and embarrass me constantly.

"In addition to the chaos and disruption these children brought to our family life, they also robbed me of the time and attention that my parents should have been giving to me. But, even as a child, I was keenly aware that I had a far better life than my foster/adoptive siblings could ever have. I guess I had the ability to put myself in their shoes. Instead of resenting them I was able to empathize with them. And, in retrospect, I have been able to apply what I experienced as a child to enrich my life. Having a bird's eye view of this twisted microcosm of the world during my young life gave me a deep awareness of human nature and the ability to relate to all people in a positive way—in a way that has helped me to continue to grow as a friend, co-worker, leader and, most importantly, as a parent."

The Parents: The Place the Adoptee Calls Home

Parents set out to add a child to their family. Whether you are just starting your journey or in the midst of your travels, you have provided or will provide a child with the place he or she calls home. This experience has different meanings to different parents. Below are some parents' thoughts on the positive aspects of having adopted children with mental health issues. They range from positives for themselves to positives for the adoptee and the children already in the family at the time of the adoption. Their comments expand on as well as confirm the content in the preceding segments.

"I think some of the positive things for us were that we got to keep a sibling group together. That was one of our main goals when we adopted the second time. I didn't have that as a kid, and I thought that was important. It's definitely helped us learn about ourselves—tremendously. I think in the end it will be okay one way or another."

"We opened up a line of communication to a kid who had a disturbed past. He now knows there are some people on this planet who do care about him. The system didn't give him all he needed while he was growing up; he was in a bunch of different foster homes. He finally came to our house as his last actual place. Now he knows there are some people who care for him and people who didn't live the same kind of life that he had [in birthfamily]. We offered him a different kind of life and that opportunity is still open to him and those doors are still open. Since reaching age 18, he has been living on his own. He still calls out of the blue. I would never cut that off. When he decides that he wants to be a part of this family again, he's got somebody to come back to. He's always got a place he can call home."

"I would think that there might be some positives somewhat for the kids even though there were a lot of negatives. They learned something different. Kids look at things as 'It's all about me. I'm the only one. This is how life should be.' But, then, they learned, 'Life ain't always a bowl of cherries. Life is a lot different.' So, even though those experiences for them were negative, in a sense they were positive because now they can go through life with those experiences and know that there are other people out there who need help."

"With our current situation of our adopted daughter in a treatment center, she's getting help now. Although she's still wreaking havoc where she's at, she's making small progress. A big positive is that her younger birthsibling, also adopted by us, has a really good chance of being 'normal' and getting better."

"Really the first positive is that we've given three kids hope in a world that they might have been lost in. And, ultimately it's going to depend on the decisions they make as adults, but clearly we have given them and are giving them a foundation from which to succeed in life, which they might not have otherwise had. That's an incredibly joyful experience."

"I think that one of the main positives is that we've taught our children by what they've seen through our lives—you just persevere. I think, in our society, too many people give up and bag out. Our kids have learned that we're not the type who are ever going to give up, and, hopefully, that will be something that they're going to take on in the real world. I think all of the kids have learned compassion, and that doesn't come naturally to people. So, they've learned because of what's happened at home that there are people who just don't have life as good, and that they can do something at a young age to reach out to others."

"Furthering my faith in God and truly believing that this little guy was sent here to us for a reason has been a benefit for me. And, I also have learned to be a lot more accepting. I like to control everything: control my life, control the issues. Letting go of that and learning to let go and accepting my son for who he is and seeing there's really a neat kid in there if we can get him out has been a positive. And if we can't, what he is will be what he is."

"The positive aspects of adopting far outweigh the negatives from my own perspective. Our birth children have been exposed to a broader view of life through fostering and adoption. If we had not adopted or fostered, our children would have had a very marshmallow life. Things would have been ordinary, easy and pretty predictable. With new children in our family, our girls have learned compassion and understanding for other people that might have developed otherwise, but not in such an intense manner."

Seeing the Positives: Looking Back

Obviously, the parents above have had mixed experiences regarding the outcomes of their adoptions. Yet, even when the adopted child later has little contact with the family or resides outside of the family, the family still identifies positive aspects of adoption.

Most families do describe their adoption as successful or positive in the longrun. Many of these families do so as they have the capacity to look back rather than always looking forward. They can acknowledge the progress instead of chronically worrying about what the future will hold.

I encourage adoptive families to work on developing this skill. As an example, I was recently talking with an adoptive mom about her now young adult adopted daughter, she said,

"I have failed her. She still can't have a 'normal' relationship. She can't reciprocate love and affection. She can't really talk about anything serious. She has to be on the surface."

This mom is correct about her daughter who was adopted eight years ago. Intimate relationships remain a struggle. However, if we "look back" over the past eight years, this same young woman has graduated from high school, has held a job for several years, has not turned to drugs or become a teen mother. She stopped aggressive behavior a number of years ago, and she has learned not to use being flirtatious or sexual to acquire things she wants.

While the mom was comforted by this, she would still have a preference to have a more reciprocal and loving relationship with her daughter. Who can blame her?

Overall, as this book has made clear, many of the adoptees arriving in the family have been damaged through no fault of their own. Some will recover fully. Others will recover in part.

I encourage parents to review progress periodically, noting even the smallest steps. Think to the time the adoptee was placed in your home and ask, "What has changed?" You will see many things. Write them down and look at the list periodically. This method helps parents realize that their efforts have not been in vain. Stamina to continue is

Barriers and Success Factors in Adoptions From Foster Care

The Collaboration to AdoptUsKids, (Ruth McRoy, principal investigator) surveyed 161 adoptive families, a total of 270 parents, and concluded five main factors parents felt made their adoption "successful." The responses are in order from most to least common response.

- Parents were committed to the child and the child's adoption into the family.
- The child was still living in the home and not behaving negatively.
- The child was showing progress in the adoptive home.
- The parent and child bonded with each other.
- Parents were prepared to adopt a child with special needs and had realistic expectations of the child.

This same report also put forth that despite the success of adoption, over half of the families described their child as difficult or very difficult to parent. Children in the study exhibited an average of 10 difficult behaviors in the categories: violating rules of conduct, verbal aggression, physical aggression, stealing and vandalism.

The full report is titled, "Barriers and Success Factors in Adoptions From Foster Care: Perspectives of Family and Staff" and can be viewed online at http://www.adoptuskids.org/images/resourcecenter/barriersuccessfactors.pdf.

renewed. Share the list with the birth and/or previously adopted children who have been developing more typically than their sibling. They need to see that all of the sacrifices are making a difference.

Please also keep in mind the words of this adoptive father,

> "I hope that my other children will learn what their mother and dad can go through to maybe help them when they get older, when they become parents, what it takes to be a family, how far sometimes a mother and dad have to go. Maybe when one of the older kids might have trouble down the road they'll know their mother and dad will go to great lengths to help every member of the family."

This dad's words reflect the biggest positive parents have to offer their troubled children as well as the healthy ones—the value of being a part of a family with a parent or parents to care for and about you. Make this the first item on your list as you look back.

Key Point—The positive aspects of adoption are many. At times, it is difficult to "see the forest through the trees." The day-to-day struggles block a clear view of the distance the journey has really covered. Look back. Acknowledge the ways that adoption has positively influenced each member of the family. Overall, "home"—be it the place called home, the home shared or the home being provided—is a positive with invaluable meaning to those fortunate enough to have a place called "home."

Ava: "Just Look at Me Now!"

We started on our journey to navigate relationships among adoptive family members with the success story of Gail and George and their family. Along our journey, we have witnessed many other families' triumphs. It seems only fitting to close this section with another example of the powerful impact adoption is capable of having on the lives of those it touches.

We met Ava in Chapter 5 and 6. Ava finally found her "forever" family at age 13 after abuse, neglect, a series of foster homes, two residential treatment placements and two psychiatric hospitalizations. Her adoptive family was a single mom. Mom has since married. The marriage was actually the merger of two adoptive families. Now Ava has twelve brothers and sisters—two are birth children and the rest were adopted.

Ava is 20 years old now, and she has grown into a beautiful young woman in all ways possible. She wrote her story for the readers of this book. It is a story that truly captures the essence of adoption in all its facets.

> "Adoption is the hardest thing to define, because it means so very much to me. How do you define being redefined as a person? How can I explain what it means to have a mother who loves me for no reason at all? She didn't give birth to me, and she didn't raise me as a small child and watch me grow into an honest, loving and caring adult.
>
> "She was given a cold, undesirable, manipulative, unruly teen, and she loved me unconditionally. I can say most people would've given up on me because they had all given up on me. She is the greatest person I will ever know, and I am so honored to say she's my mother.
>
> "Adoption, to me, means acceptance—acceptance of peers, acceptance of family, and acceptance of society. The thing that case workers, foster parents and counselors don't understand is that no one accepts a foster child. I can truly say that's how it felt. I felt like an outcast for so long, like no one could really understand me.
>
> "Okay, so even if my foster parents could accept the fact that I wasn't their blood relation, and that I had behavioral problems, they would never understand my secrets. The case workers could explain that I had been sexually abused, or that my birthmother was on drugs and I was beaten, but they couldn't explain how I felt about it. Even after the rape, the abandonment, drugs, neglect and abuse, I still loved my birthmother like any other 9-year-old girl would. I thought the world of her. In fact, when I was 11, and my case worker told me that she wasn't coming back, I wanted to die. I was even hospitalized for attempted suicide. I thought to myself, 'If she didn't want me, who would?' I felt even more isolated. As if this wasn't hard enough, there was something I had to face every day that was much worse—school.
>
> "I must say that school was one of the hardest parts of being a foster child. You know that kid, in school, who had a really runny nose that was so gross? Or, the girl who was just plain fat? Or, the kid in the wheelchair you always felt bad for? I felt as if I was all of them rolled into one. The kids at school were vicious. Because they so badly wanted to fit in, they'd prey on the weak and different. I was all kinds of different. I was so out of the norm that kids that weren't making fun of me or questioning me pitied me. The ironic thing was that as many questions as they had for me, I had for them. What's it like to have the same mom, same school, same house and family your whole life? What's it like to come first in your parents' eyes? These things were all as foreign to me as foster care was to them. With so much emotion running bottled up inside my adolescent mind, school work just wasn't a priority.
>
> "At this point, I had learned to block myself from feeling almost all emotion. I still had anger though. I flew through foster homes until I was placed in residential treatment. Imagine being 11 years old and rooming with 15-year-old girls who had just been released from jail. I learned a lot of new traits, like how to get a male's attention, how to dance, how to fight, and how to play cards. I believe this placement was one of the system's biggest mistakes. I mean, What were they thinking? I was 11! Most of these girls had records and some had children.

"But, in a sense, I felt at home. Sure, it was scary as hell, but everyone was different and had behavioral problems—not just me! It was easier than some of the foster homes, because next to those girls, I looked like an angel.

"My next residential placement was an experience also. Living in a children's home is like having an around-the-clock parent who would never want you as their child. But, at least I knew that up front. No one there wanted me. I knew that the other undesired, unloved, dysfunctional kids and myself were alone.

"Quiet time was the worst. Basically, it was an hour in your room every day with nothing to do. It felt like I was being punished for something I didn't even do. An hour felt like days in my room. Consumed with only my thoughts, I thought I was going crazy. Nights were hard, too. I was somewhat of an insomniac, because in my past, at night when everyone was asleep, was when I was raped, so sleep just didn't seem important to me. Plus, the night shift staff was male, which contributed to my anxiety. Although Mr. Jefferson helped me to trust men a little. He'd sit up with me and talk, laugh, play games on the computer, watch television, and he'd tell me about his family life. He had a wife and two daughters—family, something which I knew nothing about. Nights became easier than the days. And then there were weekends. The weekend staff was bitter. You weren't their child, you were their job. Your enjoyment of life wasn't their concern. They just wanted quiet. I'd sit in my room and cry. I was very lonely. Eventually, they found me a home, but I didn't know that.

"When I first met my mom, she was the same as any other mother I'd ever had—temporary. Little did I know, she wasn't willing to give up on me. It started out the same, the honeymoon. This was short. I was determined to push her away, but she wouldn't budge. I lied, cheated, and did drugs. I must say, she caught me by surprise when she took me to see Arleta.

"Arleta was like no other counselor I'd met. She made me angrier than I thought possible. See, with other counselors, it was easy to play mind games, to persuade them I was sad, when I had actually cut myself off from my feelings. Aside from anger, I was numb. Arleta was a new breed of counselor. I tried everything to show her that I was making an effort, but she saw through it. Unlike me, she let her feelings be known. She just wasn't going to take any of my crap. She wanted me to deal with my pain. It took a long time to get me to open up. I felt as though if I let my feelings out they'd judge me like so many others before them had. It was hard, but I did it. They didn't hate me or judge me! I was vulnerable and they didn't hurt me. I was sure this was a fluke! They couldn't really love me!

"So, I decided to push harder. I yelled louder and stayed out later. I was bad. I got moved back to residential treatment. This time, I was lonelier, because I thought it was going to be my last home. I was shocked when my mom started visiting me again! Was she crazy? I put her through hell! I tried so hard to keep this woman from loving me and to keep myself from loving her. Yet, she still wouldn't give up on me.

"Eventually, I went back to live with her. I was on my best behavior just long enough to get her to adopt me. Then, I broke her heart again. I didn't mean to hurt her. I mean this woman wanted nothing but for me to love her, but instead I put her though a lot of pain.

"I moved to my boyfriend's home. He was 21 and I was 16. He was a real winner: high school dropout, drug dealer, drug user, had no car and no job. He was my birthmother's dream man. I think this was one of the toughest times in my life. I skipped school every day and I partied all the time. I hated myself. I was my birthmother.

"But then one day, I woke up, looked in the mirror and decided I was done. I was going home. I called my mom and asked if I could come home. She was hesitant at first, but even through all the pain, hurt and trouble I had caused, she said, 'Yes.' I started counseling with Arleta again. It was hard. It was knowing I was dealt a shitty hand for no reason. It was picking up and moving forward, gluing back together the pieces of a broken child. One thing I've learned to accept is the fact that I am different, and I always will be. I am strong, but fragile; wise, but still learning, all grown up, but still so young, but most of all I am blessed—I am adopted.

"It's so hard to put into words what it is like to come from the gutter and feel as if this world is a cruel, shallow, evil place. Now, I am a good person. I thrive on the thought of what the world has to offer, when I once shunned any form of compassion. I've worked so hard to get to where I am today and knowing that I have this amazing woman who loves me, no matter what, and who is so proud of me makes every day worth living. I am moved. I have been shaken to the core. I know in my heart that God has watched over me every step of my life.

"There used to be a show on television called 'Touched by an Angel.' It was about these people who were going through tough times. God would send them an angel to help them through their pain. Well that's my life. I was given an angel. She's helped me in so many ways to become the person I am today. You could only be so lucky to meet her. She is everything I hope to be. I am headed off to college now. I have the world ahead of me. I also have a crazy, weird, heaven-sent family, with a saint for a mother and a rock for a father. I am truly blessed."

As you seek to find a child to join your family, please don't overlook the older waiting children. They need families to

Resources

These resources allow for additional reading of the topics covered in this chapter. They are arranged in alphabetical order by topic.

Heritage Camps and Tours

Corley, Colleen. "AF's Complete Guide to Heritage Travel." http://www.adoptivefamilies.com/articles.php?aid=1447

Kizner, Leslie. "A Domestic Heritage Trip." http://www.adoptivefamilies.com/articles.php?aid=1406

Adoptive Families Magazine. "Going Back." http://www.adoptivefamilies.com/articles.php?aid=998

Kitze, Carrie. "6 Questions to Ponder before Making A Homeland Trip." http://www.adoptivefamilies.com/articles.php?aid=1409

Larsen, Elizabeth. "Weekend at Culture Camp." http://www.motherjones.com/news/feature/2007/11/weekend-at-culture-camp.html

Solchany, JoAnne. "Off to Culture Camp?" http://www.adoptivefamilies.com/articles.php?aid=1194

Mikkelson, Katherine. "Camp Days." http://www.adoptivefamilies.com/articles.php?aid=1432

Adoptive Families Magazine. "Should I Send My Child to Culture Camp?" http://www.adoptivefamilies.com/articles.php?aid=831

Adoptive Families Magazine. "Culture and Heritage Events listings." http://www.adoptivefamilies.com/calendar.php?cal=camp

Medical and Mental Health Supports

Please see Chapter 5 for a thorough list of medical and mental health resources.

American Speech-Language-Hearing Association
www.asha.org/

The American Speech-Language-Hearing Association is the professional, scientific and credentialing association for speech-language pathologists, audiologists and speech, language and hearing scientists in the United States and internationally. The website is loaded with articles related to speech and language disorders and information regarding learning a second language. There is also a search function to locate professionals.

EEG Info
www.eeginfo.com

This organization provides information about neurofeedback. They also conduct training for interested professionals. You can read about neurofeedback and watch videos explaining the application of neurofeedback to AD/HD, Autism, Post-traumatic Stress Disorder, and many other mental health and medical issues.

EEG Spectrum
www.eegspecturm.com

This website explains neurofeedback and its applications. There is a provider locator as well as a training schedule for interested providers. The article, "Neurofeedback: A Treatment for Reactive Attachment Disorder" is quite interesting.

KidsHealth
www.kidshealth.org

KidsHealth is the largest and most-visited site on the Web providing doctor-approved health information about children from before birth through adolescence. Created by The Nemours Foundation's Center for Children's Health Media, the award-winning KidsHealth provides families with accurate, up-to-date, and jargon-free health information they can use. KidsHealth has separate areas for kids, teens, and parents—each with its own design, age-appropriate content, and tone. There are literally thousands of in-depth features, articles, animations, games, and resources—all original and all developed by experts in the health of children and teens. This website is simply a wealth of information about everything related medical illnesses, mental health issues, school issues, child development and so on—the topics to just endless!

Nurture and Attachment

Bersma, Danielle; Marjoke Visscher and Alex Kooistra. *Yoga Games for Children: Fun and Fitness with Postures, Movements and Breath.* (Alameda: Hunter House, 2003.)

Campbell, Don. *The Mozart Effect for Children: Awakening Your Child's Mind, Health, and Creativity with Music.* (New York: Black Thistle Press, 2000.)

Chapman, Gary and Ross Campbell. *The Five Love Languages of Children.* (Chicago: Northfield Publishing, 1997.)

Chapman, Gary. *The Five Love Languages of Teenagers.* (Chicago: Northfield Publishing, 2000.)

Eshelman, Lark. *Becoming a Family: Promoting Healthy Attachments with Your Adopted Child.* (Landham: Taylor Trade Publishing, 2005.)

Gray, Deborah D. *Attaching in Adoption.* (Indianapolis: Perspectives Press, Inc., 2002.)

Gray, Deborah D. *Nurturing Adoptions: Creating Resilience after Neglect and Trauma.* (Indianapolis: Perspectives Press, 2007.)

Heath, Alan and Nicki Bainbridge. *Baby Massage: The Calming Power of Touch.* (New York: D. K. Publishing, 2004.)

Hughes, Daniel A. *Facilitating Developmental Attachment.* (Dunmore, Pennsylvania: Jason Aronson/Inghram Book Company, 2000.)

Jernberg, Ann and Phyllis Booth. *Theraplay: Helping Parents and Children Build Better Relationships through Attachment-Based Play.* (San Francisco: Jossey-Bass, 1999.)

Keck, Gregory C. and Regina Kupecky. *Adopting the Hurt Child: Hope for Families with Special-Needs Kids: A Guide for Parents and Professionals*. (Colorado Springs: NavPress, 1995.)

Keck, Gregory and Regina Kupecky. *Parenting the Hurt Child: Helping Adoptive Families Heal and Grow*. (Colorado Springs: NavPress, 2002.)

Mcclure, Vimala Schneider. *Infant Massage: A Handbook for Loving Parents*. (New York: Bantam Books, 2000.)

Montagu, Ashley. *Touching: The Human Significance of the Skin*. (New York: Harper and Row, 1971.)

Munns, Evangeline. *Theraplay: Innovations in Attachment-Enhancing Play Therapy*. (Lanham: Rowman and Littlefield, 2000.)

Wesselmann, Debra. *The Whole Parent: How to Become a Terrific Parent Even if You Didn't Have One*. (Cambridge: De Capo Press, 1998.)

Attachment Disorder Site
www.attachmentdisorder.net/

The Attachment Disorder Site contains a wide variety of attachment-related information. The content is about both adult and child attachment. The site covers every aspect of attachment from home to school to the community. Parents and professionals will find this website valuable.

Children's Music Workshop
www.schoolmusictoday.com/

Children's Music Workshop is a music education company. The website provides a vast assortment of articles, supported by excellent research, as to the benefits of maintaining strong music programs within schools.

International Association of Infant Massage
www.iaim.ws

Aims to promote nurturing touch and communication through training, education and research so that globally parents, caregivers and children are loved, valued and respected throughout the world community. Visit the website to find a Certified Infant Massage Instructor in your area. Or to become a CIMI.

Kindermusik
www.kindermusik.com

Kindermusik is a community of families and educators passionately committed to bringing music to children's lives through developmentally appropriate curricula, CDs, books, instruments, and activities. Kindermusik brings the joy of musical learning to children newborn through 7 years of age. For more than 30 years, it has helped millions of children worldwide explore, express, and discover. Visit their website to find a class near you or to become a Kindermusik instructor.

Music Together
www.musictogether.com

Music together is an internationally recognized childhood music program for babies, preschoolers, kindergartners and the adults who love them. It utilizes a research-based, developmentally appropriate early childhood music curriculum that strongly emphasizes and facilitates adult involvement. Music Together classes recognize that all children can learn to sing in tune, keep a beat, and participate with confidence in the music of our culture. By emphasizing actual music experiences rather than concepts about music, Music Together introduces children to the pleasures of making music instead of passively receiving it from CDs or TV. Visit the Music Together website to review their song collections or to locate a class.

The Theraplay Institute
www.theraplay.org

Theraplay® is a structured play therapy for children and their parents. Its goal is to enhance attachment, self-esteem, trust in others and joyful engagement. The method is fun, physical, personal and interactive and replicates the natural, healthy interaction between parents and young children. Children have been referred for a wide variety of problems including withdrawn or depressed behavior, overactive-aggressive behavior, temper tantrums, phobias, and difficulty socializing and making friends. Children also are referred for various behavior and interpersonal problems resulting from learning disabilities, developmental delays, and pervasive developmental disorders. Because of its focus on attachment and relationship development, Theraplay has been used successfully for many years with foster and adoptive families.

Post-Adoption Service Models and Funding Sources

Smith, Susan and Jeanne Howard. *Promoting Successful Adoptions: Practice with Troubled Families*. (Thousand Oaks: Sage Publications, 1999.)

AdoptUsKids
www.adoptuskids.org

AdoptUsKids offers grants to create respite services. The application form is available on their website.

Casey Family Services
www.caseyfamilyservices.org

Casey Family Services is a fully licensed and accredited non-profit child welfare agency providing a broad range of programs to meet the changing needs of vulnerable children and families. Casey Family Services offers foster care for children, as well as post-adoption, preservation and reunification services for families. In addition, Casey has established a number of specialized and innovative community-based programs to help strengthen families and enable parents to provide the healthy, nurturing environments their children need to grow and thrive. The website contains three wonderful white papers about adoption: "An Approach to Post-Adoption Services," "Creative Strategies to Finance Post-Adoption Services," and "Promising Practices in Adoption-Competent Mental Health Services." It is also recommended to check with Casey to see what types of grants they are offering.

Child Welfare Information Gateway
www.childwelfare.org

Adoption Assistance Database: This provides information about post-adoption services and funding provided by or through state agencies—www.childwelfare.gov/adopt_assistance.
"Post-adoption Services": This article has a list of funding sources—www.childwelfare.gov/pubs/f_postadoptionbulletin/index.cfm.
"Post-adoption Services Bulletin for Professionals": This publication offers some examples of post-adoption programs—http://www.childwelfare.gov/pubs/f_postadoptbulletin/index.cfm
U.S. Department of Health and Human Services, Administration for Children and Families

Healthy Marriage Initiative
http://www.acf.hhs.gov/healthymarriage/index.html

The Healthy Marriage Initiative is designed to help couples, who have chosen marriage for themselves, gain greater access to marriage education services, on a voluntary basis, where they can acquire the skills and knowledge necessary to form and sustain a healthy marriage. This initiative provides grants. These healthy marriage promotion awards must be used for eight specified activities, including marriage education, marriage skills training, public advertising campaigns, high school education on the value of marriage and marriage mentoring programs. There is $50 million designated each year to be used for activities promoting fatherhood, such as counseling, mentoring, marriage education, enhancing relationship skills, parenting, and activities to foster economic stability. Professionals are also encouraged to check with the organizations below, which offer grants. (The national or international website is provided. Local chapters may be located via these main sites.)

100 Black Men of America
http://www.100blackmen.org

The Association of Junior Leagues International (AJLI)
http://www.ajli.org

Kiwanis International
http://www.kiwanis.org

Lions Clubs International
http://www.lionsclubs.org/PO/index.shtml

Rotary International
http://www.rotary.org/en/Pages/ridefault.aspx

Rituals

Bailey, Becky. *I Love You Rituals.* (New York: Harper Collins, 2000.)
Johnston, Patricia Irwin, ed. *Perspectives on a Grafted Tree: Thoughts for those Touched by Adoption.* (Indianapolis: Perspectives Press, 1983.)
Mason, Mary Martin. *Designing Rituals of Adoption: For the Religious and Secular Community.* (Minneapolis: Resources for Adoptive Parents, 1995.)

Search and Memoir

Books

Brooks, Thomas. *A Wealth of Family: An Adopted Son's International Quest for Heritage, Reunions and Enrichment.* (Houston: Alpha Multimedia, 2006.)
Lee, Marie Myung-Ok. *Somebody's Daughter.* (Boston: Beacon Press, 2006.)
Miro, Asha. *Daughter of the Ganges: The Story of One Girl's Adoption and Her Return Journey to India.* (New York: Atria, 2007.)
Rhodes-Courter, Ashley. *Three Little Words: A Memoir.* (New York: Atheneum, 2008.)
Schooler, Jayne and Betsie Norris. *Journeys after Adoption: Understanding Lifelong Issues.* (Westport: Bergin and Garvey, 2002.)
Strauss, Jean A. S. *Birthright: The Guide to Search and Reunion for Adoptees, Birthparents and Adoptive Parents.* (New York: Penguin Books, 1994.)

Websites

The American Adoption Congress
www.americanadoptioncongress.org

The American Adoption Congress is comprised of individuals, families and organizations committed to adoption reform. They represent those whose lives are touched by adoption or other loss of family continuity. They promote honesty, openness and respect for family connections in adoption, foster care and assisted reproduction. They provide education for members and professional communities about the lifelong process of adoption. They advocate legislation that will grant every individual access to information about his or her family and heritage. This organization has a wonderful online Beginner's Search Checklist.

International Social Services
www.iss-usa.org

Among the many things that this organization carries out is assisting American citizens abroad in working with the Immigration and Naturalization Service on aspects of intercountry adoption and specialized adoption services. The latter includes advising internationally adopted persons about locating birth relatives.

U.S. Citizenship and Immigration Services
http://uscis.gov/graphics/index.htm

This government agency includes USCIS Genealogy Program as of August 13, 2008. The Genealogy Program is a fee-for-service program designed to provide family historians and other researchers with timely access to accurate information and good copies of historical immigration and naturalization records. International adoptees can contact the USCIS to obtain copies of immigration papers which might contain leads to birthfamily members.

Support Groups and Respite

Books

Jones, Alanna. *104 Activities that Build: Self-Esteem, Teamwork, Communication, Anger Management, Self-Discovery, Coping Skills*. (Richland: Rec Room Publishing, 1998.)

Schab, Lisa and Andy Myer. *The Coping Skills Workbook*. (Plainview: Bureau for At Risk Youth, 1996.)

Websites

Arch National Respite Network
www.archrespite.org

The mission of the ARCH National Respite Network is to assist and promote the development of quality respite and crisis care programs; to help families locate respite and crisis care services in their communities; and to serve as a strong voice for respite in all forums. The ARCH National Respite Network includes the National Respite Locator Service, a service to help caregivers and professionals locate respite services in their community, and the National Respite Coalition, a service that advocates for preserving and promoting respite in policy and programs at the national, state, and local levels.

ChildsWork/ChildsPlay
www.childswork.com

ChildsWork/ChildsPlay is the leading provider of play therapy resources and training programs in the United States, focusing on therapeutic tools used by counselors and family/child therapists to address the social and emotional needs of children and adolescents. ChildsWork/ChildsPlay offers children's books, workbooks, and games designed to help with social skills, self-esteem, bullying, anger management, impulsivity, anxiety, AD/HD, life Skills, conflict resolution and a whole lot more!

Magination Press
www.maginationpress.com

If you didn't find the children's book you were looking for in the Chapter 5 Resources or you want to carry out a children's book group, visit Magination Press. Magination Press, acquired by the American Psychological Association, was created out of a desire to publish innovative books that would help children deal with the many challenges and problems they face as they grow up. Written for ages 4 through 18, these books deal with topics ranging from the everyday—starting school, shyness, normal fears, and a new baby in the house—to more serious problems, such as divorce, depression, serious injury or illness, autism, trauma, death, and much more. Most of the books are written by mental health professionals or those who work closely with them and with children. The books help children understand their feelings, provide information about the topic or situation, and offer extensive practical coping strategies. A comprehensive Note to Parents is usually included to help guide parents, therapists, social workers, and teachers in using the book.

North American Council on Adoptable Children (NACAC)
www.nacac.org

NACAC promotes and supports permanent families for children and youth in the U.S. and Canada who have been in care—especially those in foster care and those with special needs. Their annual conference, as noted in this chapter, is always exciting and informative. Child care is available at this parent friendly conference. Tapes of conference workshop sessions may be purchased at www.adoptiontapes.com. The NACAC website offers a "parent group" heading. Click on this tab to locate an array of articles about parent support groups, a searchable database to find a support group near your home and the manual, "Starting and Nurturing Adoptive Parent Groups: A Guide for Leaders."

CHAPTER ELEVEN

"We're All Grown Up:" Turning 18 and Beyond

Passing from childhood to adulthood brings with it the expected tasks of leaving home and becoming a productive and independent member of society. Gaining independence includes such social markers as attending college, trade or technical school; service in the armed forces; or getting a job—developing a career or skill. Then there is moving to an apartment and working toward home ownership. Dating, marriage and having children—preferably in this order—are other adult goals to be accomplished. Perhaps there is also a desire to fulfill an element of social responsibility through community involvement in one's neighborhood or society at large.

In healthy families, parents and children look forward to retaining close, intimate ties throughout adulthood. Whether children settle near their parents or far away, parents and siblings want contact via phone, email, visits for special occasions or simply to be with one another. Family members hope to receive support, assistance, encouragement, praise, motivation, congratulations and so on from one another. The family is to be a buttress during bad times and the spot to celebrate joyous events.

The typical young adult, given today's economy, may struggle to separate from the family and attain independence. The young adult with a history of trauma may struggle even more. His entrance and functioning in adulthood will be contingent upon the level to which he has recovered from past abuse and abandonment. The manner in which he transitions into adulthood can impact him as well as his brothers, sisters and parents.

This chapter, then, is included to provide a look at several aspects of adulthood in the adoption-built family which includes children who have experienced abuse or neglect, multiple transitions, institutionalization, etc. in early childhood. It is preparation—or food for thought—about issues that many families, for and about whom this book was written, may wrestle with when their children are "all grown up."

I'm Turning 18!

In the days or months before an 18th birthday, smiling young adults proudly state the fact, "I'm turning 18!" to anyone who will listen. Parents likely tire of hearing, "But I'm almost 18!" This is often a time of great excitement and leads to many new thoughts such as

"I can make my own rules."

"I can do what I want when I want."

"I can spend my money on things I like."

"I can go out when I want."

"I can come home when I want."

Yet, this jubilance about the life that lies ahead also includes anxieties.

"Will I make it through college?"

"Am I choosing the right career?"

"Will I get a 'good' job?"

"Will I have friends?"

"Do I want to marry?"

"How will I know she or he is the 'right one?'"

"Do I want to have children?"

"Will I succeed?"

Young adults who were adopted may experience all of the above normal thoughts and feelings associated with the approach of young adulthood. However, the 18th birthday can also be a trigger, and so the child who has grown up fighting mental health issues may be plagued by insecurities and a resurgence of past issues far more complicated than those of a typically developing child born to or adopted by his family.

> Andrew, age 17, had been adopted from the foster care system when he was 9 years old. His family is comprised of his parents, Joe and Marian, and their two birth children, Rob and Linda, now ages 23 and 16.
>
> Over the years, Andrew has made great progress emotionally, behaviorally, socially and cognitively. At 17, he was a junior in high school. During his years in foster care, he had moved several times. This interrupted his learning, so he had been retained in second grade.
>
> About six months before turning 18, Andrew's grades plummeted—and so did his behavior. He started coming in well after curfew, was quite belligerent, had a different girlfriend each week and started listening to hard rock music. He also blew off shifts at his part-time job. Joe and Marian even questioned whether he was using drugs or alcohol.
>
> In a heated argument late one night, he blurted out, "In a few more months I'll just have to leave anyway!"
>
> Joe and Marian were quite confused. Marian said, "What are you talking about? You don't have to leave. You aren't even finished with high school."
>
> Andrew replied, "Rob left when he was 18."

In this moment, Andrew's parents realized that his current struggle was complex. Rob had indeed left for college shortly after his 18th birthday and has since moved on to attend graduate school. Andrew's learning disabilities made college seem unattainable, so he was steered along a trade path. He continues in high school wherein part of the day he is in a culinary Vo-Tech track. Andrew was feeling inferior to his older brother. Andrew was sad as he felt that his accomplishments paled in comparison to his typically developing brother—his past continued to affect his life.

Additionally, the implied societal ideal that one leaves home on or shortly after eighteen was causing Andrew to believe that he would need to get out into the world and be on his own at that birthday. It was almost as if he thought his days with a family were coming to an end. His behavior was reflective of intense feelings of loss as well as they were an effort to anger his family into rejecting him as in, "It would be easier if you got mad at me and put me out."

Joyce Maguire Pavao nicely sums Andrew's actions in *The Family of Adoption* (Boston: Beacon Press, 1998):

> "At one extreme are the kids who run away, or steal cars, or cause other serious trouble in order to make themselves unwanted and to provoke rejection. Since they sometimes fear

that in a sense they will no longer be adopted after they reach adulthood, they also want to be in control of the rejection by causing it rather than having it happen to them."[1]

At the other end of the spectrum are adoptees who simply don't make any plans to move on.

Russell, "Rusty," adopted at age 3, was now graduated from high school and employed full time. At age 22, he lived at home with his adoptive parents. He was great about going to work, calling home when he would be late and carrying out chores. In all ways, he was a pleasure to be around. The only area in which he was lacking was in having any additional plans for the future. When asked what else he thought he might be interested in doing, he replied, "I don't know" or "I'm happy at my job." Since early adolescence his responses about the future had been vague.

Mom and Dad were getting eager for Rusty to move on. They were looking forward to an "empty nest." Rusty was the youngest of their four children. Their three birth children, 27, 26 and 24, had finished college. Each worked and lived in his or her own apartment. One had married and was expecting the first grandchild!

Rusty's parents had tried leaving the rental ads conspicuously on the kitchen table. They started making him pay rent to live at home. Rather than be annoyed by this or decide that if he had to pay money he could just get his own place, he willingly complied. Each month he promptly gave his father the requested $200.

Ultimately, they had to confront Rusty about the situation. Rusty did his best to avoid the first few of these conversations. Finally, one Saturday morning his dad took him to look at apartments. This brought the matter to a head. Rusty said, "Why don't you want me anymore? Why doesn't anyone want to keep me?"

To Rusty, the thought of leaving home was akin to being abandoned again. Returning to Pavao,

"Many adoptees have been told life-long that they could search for their birthfamily upon turning 18 or 21, and they formed an idea then that this meant there'd be no 'going home' afterward. No one *ever* told them this, but there is this idea or feeling, for many adopted people. They, in reaction, often decide to stay home—often with a vengeance. Because where will they go? Leaving home, to these young adults, means that they won't have an identity."

So for any adoptee, and even more so for those with complex trauma issues, turning 18 may be

- a time of excitement if his mental health and development allow him to move on in accord with peers and siblings.
- a trigger for past issues of abandonment. She may attempt to flee because she believes rejection imminent. She may hold onto the family tightly, unwilling to let go. Independence is overwhelming and frightening. She identifies as a family member instead of a unique person with her own thoughts, feelings, special qualities and abilities.
- another reminder of feeling lesser in comparison to typical siblings and peers. The success of brothers, sisters and friends may contribute further to the lack of self-concept felt by many adoptees.

---

1. Pavao, Joyce Maguire. *The Family of Adoption.* (Boston: Beacon Press, 1998)

- the start of adolescence, in that socially and emotionally, the complex adoptee is finally reaching the time to decide "Who am I?" His quest for identity was delayed due to the trauma and abuse he sustained early in life. He may actually "turn 18" at some point in his 20s.

The adoptee nearing the border of adulthood may benefit from less emphasis on this birthday as a passage from his family to a life on his own. Stress his inclusion (as well as his siblings') in family plans for holidays or vacations beyond age 18 . . .

> "Next summer Dad is planning a fishing trip with you and Rob. Won't that be fun!"
>
> "This fall we'll be painting the downstairs. We're counting on you to help out."
>
> "We'll also be painting your room. It will always be available to you so we'll keep it nice."

In this manner, the young person can recognize that his family membership extends into adulthood. This is also a good time to review his lifebook (see Chapter 9). The lifebook helps put the past in context. The lifebook affirms the differences between the birth and adoptive families. Fears of being re-abandoned can be put to rest.

Adoptive parents may or may not fully understand that the "permanence" of the adoption relationship means that their job won't be complete because of a birthday cake with 18 candles. Certainly, many families celebrate the end of their legal responsibilities. However, psychological and financial support doesn't often conclude for many years to come—for any child! In fact, gaining independence at age 18 is becoming a myth. Adult children, it appears, move in and out of their parents' homes, in their 20s and 30s, for reasons related to finances, change in marital status and more.

It should be noted that otherwise typically developing brothers and sisters can also suffer a delayed entry into adulthood due to the altered family dynamics which have resulted from the adoption of a complicated sibling.

> Pat Ann is 21 years old. When she was 13, her family was expanded by the addition of her two cousins, Peggy and Jeff, then ages 13 and 14. They had been abandoned by their birthmother very early in life. Their birthfather, Pat Ann's paternal uncle, was an alcoholic. He was prone to violent outbursts. Peggy and Jeff had been removed from and returned to his custody several times. However, this cycle ended when he was sentenced to a five-year jail term for assault.
>
> Peggy and Jeff arrived at the home of Pat Ann and her parents within a matter of days. The family was knocked out of kilter for many years. Jeff excelled at sports. The family became very involved in facilitating his success in this area. However, at home, he was defiant, argumentative, non-participative in family outings and chores, and extremely messy. His bedroom looked like a cyclone had gone through it. Clothes, food wrappers, half eaten food, pop bottles full of his urine, papers, cardboard boxes, etc. littered the floor and furniture. He picked the paint off the walls and tore the stuffing out of his mattress. His room was in deplorable shape! No amount of repainting or cleaning seemed to keep it in order.
>
> Peggy had her own issues. While more cooperative, she was severely behind academically. She was held back and still could not keep up with her work. Pat Ann's mother had to invest much time in helping Peggy complete her homework. Pat Ann's needs were chronically overlooked because the family was either in conflict, at a sporting event or helping Peggy catch-up.

When Pat Ann turned 18, she quickly got a full-time job and an apartment. She reveled in the peace and quiet. Her parents, on the other hand, were stunned. They had been certain that she would go on to college. Eventually, she did—at age 24. In the meantime, she enjoyed having friends, shopping, dating and working. Her identity development had been interrupted by the arrival of her two adolescent cousins. Only out of her chaotic home environment could she finally decide who she was and what she wanted to be.

Mindy, a birth child, grew up alongside her sister, Karen, who had been adopted. They became sisters when Mindy was 4 and Karen 2. Mindy's parents wanted her to have "company." Secondary infertility had prevented this from occurring biologically, so the family adopted.

Karen had problems from the beginning. She was withdrawn. She often sat in her room for hours. Mindy's mom would go looking for her and coax her into the family room where she just sat, staring. Eventually, she would return to her bedroom. In school her shyness continued. She developed no friendships. In adolescence, her loneliness became overwhelming. She attempted suicide on more than one occasion. This generated a number of psychiatric hospitalizations and round after round of therapy. At 16, she remained unstable. Past and present, Karen consumes much of the family's time and resources.

Mindy's way of coping was to become the acting-out child (Chapter 8). Her adolescence was fraught with boyfriends, drinking, experimenting with drugs, blowing off school work and, at times, simply blowing off entire days of school. At 18 she was angry! Her anger inhibited relationships and job performance. Higher education was something she was not ready to handle.

Finally, at age 22, after several years of therapy, Mindy is moving forward with career plans. She has let go of her resentment. Her interactions with her parents have improved. This family mobilized too late for Mindy to be on track as she entered adulthood.

Certainly, a majority of brothers and sisters emerge into young adulthood in the fashion most desired by their parents. Yet some, impacted by the adoption-related components of their family, may experience a break before establishing and achieving the goals to move from adolescence to adulthood.

As Chapters 9 and 10 suggested, parents must set priorities, make time, acknowledge accomplishments, facilitate communication and nurture each member of their family. Each child requires parental support to become "all grown up."

Leaving Home

Most parents prefer that their sons or daughters leave home to pursue higher education, a military career, gainful employment or to form a satisfying emotional relationship.

Ava (see vignette in Chapter 10) is an example of a young adult who, after a tumultuous adolescence, realized that she wanted a life similar to that of her adoptive mother. She returned to her family, completed school and obtained a job. She saved enough money for a small place of her own. She enjoyed having her mom and new dad over for dinner. She regularly visits their house as well. Shopping with her younger siblings is something Ava likes to do for fun. Now age 20, she is entering college.

Joel, adopted at age 4, is now 24. He had various behavioral difficulties through the age of 21 which culminated with selling and using cocaine. Sitting in a jail cell at 19, he realized that his life was "going nowhere." Fortunately, he was court ordered to drug rehab. He also received community service and probation. At age 23, he entered college. He successfully completed his freshman year and is looking forward to being a sophomore. He frequently reflects back on the person he "used to be" and appreciates that he "got it" and that his parents remain supportive and available!

David was adopted at age 15 after a 12-year stay in foster care. From birth to age 3, he resided with his birthmother who physically abused and neglected him. Once in foster care, a lengthy family reunification effort finally failed for the final time when he was age 10. Subsequently, he was available for adoption. Many families expressed interest in David, but for no specific reason none proceeded to adopt him. Finally, a family came forward and David found the permanency he had longed for—for many years.

Eager to remain in his "forever" family David made many changes. He curbed his stealing and lying. He worked hard on his homework and graduated from high school at age 20. He obtained work in a factory where he has now been employed for five years, and recently moved to an apartment of his own.

David requires assistance managing his money. His peer relationships are few. Since he lags behind others his age in social skills and interests, friendships are hard to form. However, his older typical brother makes sure to include David in weekend plans, and Mom and Dad are happy to have David accompany them to church and then home for Sunday dinner.

David is a young man who integrated into his adoptive family more easily than many other adoptees with a history of complex trauma. His years in foster care gave him a great desire to have a place to call home.

On the other hand, launching—the process in which youths move into adulthood and exit their family—without cutting off ties completely or fleeing the family totally, may not be smooth nor happen along a contrived timeline for the formerly traumatized child. A successful launch into adulthood will be contingent upon the adoptee's

- level of attachment between himself and the parents, brothers, sisters
- resolution and/or management of mental health issues
- resolution of the seven core adoption issues (Chapter 2)
- possible substance abuse issues
- capacity to seek and maintain a job
- available resources (life skills programs, mental health services, drug rehabilitation programs, Vo-Tech programs, etc.).

Parents often express worries about the launching of the adoptee long before adulthood arrives. Four adoptive moms state their fears below.

"My main worry is that when my daughter, now age 12, is an adult, I won't have the relationship with her like I have with my mother. I also worry that when she hits 18, she's going to be out the door and we won't hear from her again unless she's in trouble. I fear that she'll be wrapped up in her own things as an adult, and we won't hear from her again and she won't keep in touch with our son."

"I worry that my three adopted daughters will go back to their birthfamily and that I really will end up being just someone who raised them for a few years. I didn't go through all these years of pain and stress just to have them go back there."

"I worry about how my daughter, now 15, will conduct herself after she leaves home, and the kind of relationships she will form. She is very easily influenced."

> "As far as the future, I worry that raising them won't have a prize at the end. You know, like they move out and start lives of their own and everyone is happy! I don't so much worry that my unhealthy children will not have a relationship with my healthy children. Instead, I worry about the mutuality of their relationships. I worry that the unhealthy ones will be burdensome—asking for money or to live with their siblings, etc. But I do think that our parent-child relationships will get better when the girls move out. We won't have to see their messes or be around their rude manner. There will be room for an easier relationship. I am looking forward to that."

Unfortunately, many adoptees with traumatic pasts do leave the family in chaotic and destructive ways.

"I want to be with a partner."

Margo, adopted at a young age, became a teen mother at 16. She had an on and off again relationship with Curt, the baby's father, over the next two years. At 18, she decided that she wanted to "make a go of it" with Curt and so the two got a place of their own.

Curt is a rather unsavory character in Margo's parents' eyes. He goes from dead end job to dead end job. Margo often calls home for help to care for her toddler son. Frequently, Margo and Curt fight and Margo returns home. Then Curt apologizes and she goes back to him. This cycle has been occurring for four years.

Her parents and siblings encourage Margo to think more of herself; to believe that she can do better than Curt. At this time, Margo continues to reside with Curt.

April had been a pleasant child from age 2 thru age 14. Her adoption brought her parents great joy. April and her older sister got along famously. Georgia, April's senior by one year, and April were inseparable. They did everything together.

At 14, April began to deteriorate. Her bright smile faded. She withdrew from the band and athletic endeavors. She no longer enjoyed going to the mall with Georgia on the weekends.

Her parents attempted to get to the bottom of the situation. They begged her to talk to them, and they took her to a variety of therapists. Therapy didn't seem to help.

Then April became interested in boys. Boys called the house at all hours of the evening and early morning. April sneaked out her bedroom window. Sometimes she was gone the entire weekend. When she did arrive back home, she refused to discuss her whereabouts. She stomped to her room and slammed the door.

Eventually, at age 17, she began going steady with Darrell. Abruptly, she left the family to move in with Darrell. She has remained in his home, with his family, for several years now. She has refused to talk to her adoptive family or to visit.

Margo's involvement with Curt is due to her poor self-view. Adoptees also suffer in less than satisfying relationships, or flit from one boyfriend or girlfriend to the next due to fear of intimacy or rejection. They think, "I want to leave him before he leaves me." "I need to be in control of breaking up. That way, I won't be hurt as bad." Or, they may be so clingy that others do leave to avoid being smothered. These core adoption issues (see Chapter 2) can affect future parenting styles, friendships and employment positions as well.

April, on the other hand, is known in the adoption therapy community as a *sleeper.* This is a child whose adoption and/or abuse issues are not obvious or go undetected for years. Because the child often functions so well in early childhood and grade school, it is assumed that the child is resilient and her past has had no impact—it is but water off a duck's back. No one sees the need to discuss it or to create a lifebook when there are no "obvious" issues. But then, the adolescent task of identity development triggers the trauma and abandonment. Overwhelmed, the child deteriorates. When this occurs, it is most commonly around the age of 13 or 14, but can also happen in later adolescent years.

"My parents left me."

Timmy was problematic from the day he arrived from a foster home at age 1½. He was inconsolable as a baby. He resisted every effort of affection offered by his parents, Ruth and Leroy. In kindergarten and grade school, he was unable to make friends because he was so "bossy." High school included friendships with kids similar to Timmy. Together, they engaged in a variety of petty thefts and drug use.

When he was home, Tim's parents had little control over his actions. He was demanding. If he didn't get what he wanted, he ripped off the cupboard doors or turned over the furniture. He refused to participate in any therapy. His parents made efforts to move him to residential treatment, but were unable to obtain the funding. Ruth, Leroy, and their younger daughter, Annette, actually feared their son.

Just before his 18th birthday, Timmy was arrested for destruction of property. He was sentenced to one year in prison. His term would begin in a juvenile facility and be completed in an adult jail.

The family moved while he was incarcerated. They left no forwarding address.

Steven, a difficult adoptee, exited the family at age 20, after a huge fight with his father. Refusing to comply with curfew for the "umpteenth" time, his father said, "If you don't like it here, you can move." With that, Steven did. He has opted to have little contact with the family.

Barry's adoptive parents were weary of his behaviors. On his 18th birthday, they presented him with the keys to his own apartment. A financially affluent family, they paid his expenses for most of the next year. He only needed to earn money for food, gas and any extras he desired.

Peter, adopted as an infant, became an adult while living in a residential treatment center. He had been placed there at age 16 because he was physically aggressive toward his mother and younger sister. The facility, in conjunction with community services, transitioned Peter to life in the community. Peter's family refuses to have contact with him.

"I want to return to my birthfamily."

Len, adopted at age 5, left his family the day after his 18th birthday. Unbeknownst to his parents or siblings, Len had located a birth aunt using the local library computer.

His parents arrived home from work to find his belongings gone. Sporadic phone calls over the next few months kept them informed of his moves from his aunt's home to his birth grandmother's home and then to his birthmother's residence. Eventually, he called for bail money. He and his birthmother's paramour had been arrested for theft. The last phone call was again from jail. This arrest was for drug-related offenses. Three years have now passed with no contact from Len.

Although there will be others like Harry.

> Harry was adopted from foster care at age 5. He had many memories of the domestic violence that occurred between his birthmom and her paramours. He carried with him a strong desire to return to her, to help her and protect her. At 19, he fulfilled this desire. He found her and he spent the next few years working and supporting her. He tried and tried to get her to seek help—to no avail.
>
> He realized that he couldn't continue in this lifestyle. He kept hearing his adoptive parents' voices, "You can choose to live your life however you want." "You are very bright. You can be whatever you want." "Our door will always be open for you." Tentatively he called home. After some discussion and meetings with his parents, he moved back home. Harry will graduate from technical school next year. He now enjoys close relations with his mom, dad and brother.

Searching and reunifying with birthfamily members (Chapter 10) can have a vast array of outcomes for the adoptee as well as for the entire adoptive family. It may mean a journey abroad to locate birthfamily members and to continue the process of identity formation as a transcultural adoptee. The search could be for siblings rather than for birth parents. It could result in locating a birth parent recovered from previous addictions. The adoptee may be able to develop positive ties to a birthmother or birthfather who then may need to be integrated into the adoptive family system in some way. The range of outcomes is wide. Leaving home to return to the birthfamily may mean that the adoptee never returns to their adoptive family or that they come home like Harry, saddened, yet more settled and with new direction.

These scenarios demonstrate that the adoption journey doesn't always culminate in the manner expected or desired, or as established by arbitrary societal standards when the child experienced early trauma or neglect. Overall, adult relationships with such young people will likely fall along a continuum from close to severed.

There will be emotional devastation when the adoptee walks away from the family, barely looking back or not keeping in touch at all. These same feelings of guilt, sadness, failure, anger and frustration occur when parents make the choice to move their adopted child on. Either way, the dreams of "happily ever after" are shattered.

Parents may once again review painful issues related to infertility if this was a factor in their decision to adopt, and brothers, sisters and parents experience the loss of a son, daughter or sibling. Dreams of grandchildren, nieces and nephews fade.

Recently, a 25-year-old young adult adoptee, appropriately developed, stated,

> "I watch my parents with their brothers and sisters at Christmas, Thanksgiving and summer barbecues. They laugh and joke. They hug. I love spending time with my cousins. They are among my best friends. I know that I'm not going to have this kind of adult interactions with my sister and brother, and that my children probably aren't going to have fun and relationships with their cousins. It is so disappointing. I was so excited when my parents adopted them. But, I'm coming to realize that they're never going to be normal."

At this time, he is correct. His sister, at 23, has abruptly left the family and his brother, at 17, is already fighting a drug addiction.

Some parents, brothers and sisters find that they can adjust their values, and the yardstick by which they measure success, in order to sustain long-term connections with a troubled adoptee. For example, in the case of Margo described earlier, her parents were not happy with her untimely pregnancy nor her choice of partner. However, they have come to recognize that Margo is an attentive mother. She nurtures her son, and she reaches out for help to make sure that he has what he needs. She far more closely mirrors her adoptive mom and dad as a parent than she does her birthmother. Her parents also want to look out for her son—their grandchild. So they have opted to continue to model positive relationships. They help, yet they don't enable. For example, assistance is offered in the form of diapers or food, or they may pay a bill directly. Assistance is never in the form of cash that Curt may blow on things for himself. Overall, they have found a way to support their daughter and grandson, and enjoy the positive aspects of her personality and lifestyle.

Margo's parents are still raising Margo's three younger siblings, their birth daughters. Margo's lifestyle has caused them to increase their communication about birth control and sexuality, managing finances, and other essential life skills. If the resident children are younger, parents must make extra efforts to encourage them to follow a different path than that of their older, troubled brother or sister. Provided that parents have maintained strong attachments to these children throughout the adoption experience, they will see the consequences of such actions and the younger children will move along a more traditional route.

Overall, in adulthood, family members may need to ask themselves:

Whose value is it that adulthood begins with a particular age?

Whose value is a high school diploma or a college education?

Whose value is marriage and then childbirth?

What is realistic for my adopted child?

What is most important for my adopted child?

What can I do as a parent to continue to help my adoptee be as successful as possible beyond 18?

What are parents,' brothers' and sisters' obligations and responsibilities to adult siblings? How long do family members carry out efforts on behalf of the adoptee? On behalf of any child, brother or sister?

Would family members help arrange drug rehabilitation? Mental health services? Housing?

Would family members assist with legal issues? Visit a sibling, son or daughter who is incarcerated?

Can family members draw boundaries between support and enabling as necessary? Support contributes to gains in development and responsibility. Enabling stymies growth.

In the Resources section of this chapter, a number of books and organizations' websites have been provided that discuss setting boundaries throughout life with a family member with addictions and other mental health disorders.

In closing, Daniel, Kristen, Mary Ann and Ronnie allow the sharing of their story:

> Kristen, now age 37, was adopted at age 10. She was aggressive upon entering her adoptive family which included a single mom (divorced), Mary Ann, and a younger typical brother, Ronnie, age 8. During her teen years, Kristen's violence escalated and as such, at age 14, she was placed in a group home from which she emancipated. At 18, she wanted to be "on her own." She was transitioned from the group home into a small apartment.

Subsequently, she moved through job after job and relationship after relationship. Drugs and alcohol were a part of this lifestyle.

One night, at age 24, in a terrible thunder storm, she found herself with her toddler son, Daniel, taking shelter under a bridge—alone, with no money, no food, no place to live, no car and only the clothes on her back. She called home—collect—and asked if she could return.

Mary Ann came and picked her up. She was pleased to finally meet her grandson and tentative about what life with Kristen would bring. Unexpectedly, over the next two years, Kristen did well. She worked, saved her money, and obtained housing and a car. She proved to be a good parent. She and Ronnie also enjoyed a relationship during this period. Actually, it was really the first time the two ever actually connected. Prior to this Ronnie had stayed clear of her in her adolescence due to fear of being hit, kicked or punched. He infrequently visited her at the group home. She barely spoke to him when he did accompany Mary Ann to the treatment center, so he stopped going except for holidays.

Then, she met Rich. Within a year, she moved in with Rich and began using drugs again. She left Daniel with Mary Ann. Visits with Daniel and Mary Ann were sporadic, as were phone calls. When she did stop by, Mary Ann noticed bruises for which Kristen always had an excuse—"I tripped," "I ran into a door." Mary Ann knew the excuses were lies. She knew the bruises came from Rich. She offered Kristen help from herself and community resources. Kristen refused. She wanted to stay with Rich.

Kristen was hospitalized at age 27 after a particularly violent incident of domestic violence. Mary Ann arrived at the hospital and insisted that Kristen speak with the hospital social worker. Together, these three women made a discharge plan. Kristen would return to Mary Ann's home and utilize counseling and legal assistance should Rich attempt to follow her or harm her, Mary Ann or Daniel.

Kristen waivered about Rich, and actually returned to him a few times. Finally, Daniel created the final turning point. He was now age 7 and he had started to ask Kristen, "When will you be my mom again?" "Why do you keep leaving?" Kristen was reminded of herself asking the same kinds of questions when she was a young child living in foster care. She realized that she did not want Daniel growing up as she did without a connection to his birthmother.

She stopped having contact with Rich, and she obtained a job at a fast food restaurant. She proved to be a reliable and responsible employee. Now, at age 37, she has moved through the ranks to manager of this restaurant. Kristen, Daniel and Mary Ann, who continue to reside together, enjoy spending time with each other. Ronnie, now married, also likes to spend time with Kristen, although this relationship has had its ups and downs. Ronnie has had to overcome much anger for the way Kristen has treated his mother. Kristen has been jealous that Ronnie had a good start in life.

Mary Ann admits that her journey with Kristen has been a huge emotional struggle, but she is certainly glad that she chose to help Kristen every step of the way. Kristen often fondly comments that she isn't sure where she would be without such a "stubborn" mom who "wouldn't give up!"

Resources

Adult Mental Illness/Adult Adoption Issues

Books

Brewster, Susan. *To Be an Anchor in the Storm: A Guide for Families and Friends of Abused Women*, 2nd edition. (Seattle: Seal Press, 2000.)

Brodzinsky, David; Marshall Schecter and Robin Marantz Henig. *Being Adopted: The Lifelong Search for Self.* (New York: Anchor Books, 1993.)

Carter, Rosalynn and Susan Golant. *Helping Someone with Mental Illness.* (New York: Three Rivers Press, 1998.)

Cook, Phillip W. *Abused Men: The Hidden Side of Domestic Violence.* (Westport: Praeger Publishers, 1997.)

Eldridge, Sherrie. *Twenty Life Transforming Choices Adoptees Need to Make.* (Colorado Springs: NavPress, 2003.)

Eldridge, Sherrie. *Twenty Things Adopted Kids Wish Their Adoptive Parents Knew.* (Colorado Springs: NavPress, 1999.)

Johnson, Julie Tallard. *Hidden Victims, Hidden Healers: An Eight-Stage Healing Process for Families and Friends of the Mentally Ill.* (Edina, Minnesota: PEMA Publications, 1994.)

Karp, David. *The Burden of Empathy: How Families Cope with Mental Illness.* (New York: Oxford University Press, 2001.)

Levy, Barrie. *In Love and in Danger: A Teen's Guide to Breaking Free from Abusive Relationships.* (Seattle: Seal Press, 2006, 3rd edition.)

Lifton, Betty Jean. *Journey of the Adopted Self: A Quest for Wholeness.* (New York: Basic Books, 1994.)

Pavao, Joyce Maguire. *The Family of Adoption.* (Boston: Beacon Press, 2005.)

Reitz, Miriam and Kenneth Watson. *Adoption and the Family System.* (New York: The Guilford Press, 1992.)

Schooler, Jayne and Betsie Norris. *Journeys after Adoption: Understanding Lifelong Issues.* (Westport: Bergin and Garvey, 2002.)

Simon, Clea. *Mad House: Growing Up in the Shadow of Mentally Ill Siblings.* (New York: Penguin Books, 1997.)

Woolis, Rebecca. *When Someone You Love Has a Mental Illness: A Handbook for Family, Friends and Caregivers.* (New York: Jeremy P. Tarcher/Penguin, 2003.)

Articles

Child Welfare Information Gateway. "Impact of Adoption on Adopted Persons." http://www.childwelfare.gov/pubs/f_issues.cfm

Evan B. Donaldson Adoption Institute. "The Gathering of the First Generation of Korean Adoptees: Adoptee's Perceptions of International Adoption." http://www.adoptioninstitute.org/proed/korfindings.html

Hillman, Diane. "What Do You Do After She Says 'I'm pregnant'?" http://www.nysccc.org/articles/pregnant.html

Websites

Alcoholics Anonymous (AA)
www.aa.org

Alcoholics Anonymous® is a fellowship of men and women who share their experience, strength and hope with each other that they may solve their common problem and help others to recover from alcoholism. There are links to services for the afflicted family member as well as information for family members.

Al-Anon and Alateen
www.al-anon.org

Al-Anon and Alateen help family members and friends of alcoholics recover from the effects of living with the problem drinking of a relative or friend. Alateen is the recovery program for young people. Alateen groups are sponsored by Al-Anon members. Resources and links to meetings are provided on this website.

Mental Health America
www.nmha.org/

Mental Health America is dedicated to promoting mental health, preventing mental disorders and achieving victory over mental illness through advocacy, education, research and service. The website includes segments such as finding help and making the most of treatment. There are also descriptions of mental health diagnoses and suggestions about funding sources to cover treatment costs.

Narcotics Anonymous (NA)
www.na.org

Narcotics Anonymous sprang from Alcoholics Anonymous and is a nonprofit fellowship, or society, of men and women for whom drugs had become a major problem. Meeting regularly helps the addicted person stay clean. "NA is not interested in what or how much a person used . . . but only in what the person wants to do about the problem and how NA can help." Membership is open to all drug addicts, regardless of the particular drug or combination of drugs used. The site contains an array of publications and meeting locations.

National Alliance on Mental Illness (NAMI)
www.nami.org/

NAMI is the National Alliance on Mental Illness, the nation's largest grassroots organization for people with mental illness and their families. NAMI is dedicated to the eradication of mental illnesses and to the improvement of the quality of life for persons of all ages who are affected by mental illnesses. Visit NAMI for information about all aspects of mental illness or to find a support group near you.

National Coalition Against Domestic Violence (NCADV)
www.ncadv.org/aboutus.php

The mission of the National Coalition Against Domestic Violence (NCADV) is to organize a collective power to advance transformative work, thinking and leadership in communities and individuals who seek to end violence in their lives. NCADV's mission works for major societal changes necessary to eliminate both personal and societal violence against all women and children. This is a very comprehensive website including how to create a safety plan, articles, conference information, a state by state resource listing, information for the battered person, friends and family, and an extensive list of books and websites.

National Institute on Drug Abuse (NIDA)
www.nida.nih.gov/

NIDA's mission is to lead the Nation in bringing the power of science to bear on drug abuse and addiction. NIDA conducts research and disseminates information about all types of drugs and the benefits of treatment for all members of a family.

Acknowledgments

My first thanks go to the many adoptive parents, brothers, sisters and adoptees who contributed to this book. Your lives are busy, yet you eagerly took the time to personally write or to allow me to portray your experiences. You did so out of a strong desire to help those who will read this book. Over time, I have been privileged to learn from you, and now others will reap that same benefit.

Pat Johnston, you initiated this book after attending a workshop I conducted. When your first email arrived about writing a book about brothers and sisters in adoption, I was excited, stunned and overwhelmed all in the same moment. I didn't quite know how to respond. Then I called Greg Keck, with whom I work, and he said, "Well, you better get back to her and let her know you'd be happy to do that." So, between your nudge and his, this book was set in motion. I have not had a moment of regret since being led into this project. I want to thank you for taking a chance on a novice author. Your adoption expertise and your "tweaking," as you call it, has expanded and shaped this book into a work that will finally allow *all* children in adoptive families a voice that might otherwise have gone unheard. I also want to thank you for your long-standing commitment to the field of adoption. I entered the field of adoption almost 15 years ago, and feel I have "grown up" as a professional as a result of many Perspective Press books.

Greg Keck and Tom Collins—my mentors—thank you for the knowledge, patience, guidance and opportunities you have offered me over the past 13 years. You gave me my professional foundation. This work is built from that secure base. It reflects you, and as you look at it, I hope you are pleased with your images.

My human foundation came from my mother and family members. Because of my family, I am able to achieve, thrive and enjoy life. You gave me the gift of a healthy beginning that, in turn, has given me a present and future filled with endless possibilities.

Certainly, I have also been influenced by the work of a significant number of other professionals, foremost among which are Barbara Holtan, Daniel Hughes and Regina Kupecky. Thank you for helping me along my journey through adoption.

Numerous professionals are thanked for allowing me to incorporate their work into this book: Wayne Duehn, Sharon Kaplan-Roszia and Deborah Silverstein, Sharon Glennen, Gabe Chasnoff, Ira Chasnoff, Cheryl Pratt, Gwendolyn Neuberger, Linda Schwartz, Kirsti Adkins, Lisa Aschmann, Karen Taylor-Good as well as Dana Johnson and the University of Minnesota International Adoption Clinic.

Deborah Borchers, Deborah Gray, Daniel Hughes, Greg Keck, Joanne May, Maris Blechner, Barbara Tremitiere and Michael Trout reviewed, commented on and endorsed this book. Thank you for taking the time needed to do so.

Nancy G., no matter where I live or what endeavor I take on, you are always there to help me. In this project, you contributed to the resources. Thank you for being a friend and colleague. Justen and Lee Michael gathered the research incorporated throughout this work. Thank you for tracking down all of those articles!

Erica Marchetti and Jennifer Schuler, you are wonderful proof-readers. Your changes made smooth the rough spots, enhancing the content and the clarity for the reader. Mayapriya Long and the staff at Bookwrights, you lay out the words, boxes and charts in an appealing style and create beautiful covers. Thank you for having the skills to make the book look so nice.

Appendices

Glossary

Ambivalence—This is a stage in the lifecycle of the adoptive family. It occurs after the initial honeymoon stage. The ambivalence period is a time when the adoptee's behavior deteriorates. Parents are challenged to manage the adoptee's behavior. The child's delays become apparent. The typically developing children in the household and the child's peers struggle to play and cope with the adoptee. The adoptive family panics during this stage and questions whether they can maintain the adoptee within the family unit.

Analgesia—An inability to feel physical pain.

Complex Trauma—The term complex trauma describes the dual problem of children's exposure to traumatic events and the impact of this exposure on their immediate and long-term well-being. Complex traumatic exposure refers to children's experiences of multiple traumatic events that occur within the care-giving system—the social environment that is supposed to be the source of safety and stability in a child's life. Typically, complex traumatic exposure involves simultaneous or sequential occurrences of child maltreatment—including emotional abuse and neglect, sexual abuse, physical abuse and witnessing domestic violence—that are chronic and begin in early childhood.

Depersonalization—An alteration in the perception or experience of the self so that one feels *detached* from, and as if one is an *outside* observer of one's mental processes or body. A feeling of watching oneself act, while having no control over a situation. It is as if one's sense of self is unreal.

Derealization—An alteration in the perception or experience of the external world so that it seems strange or unreal. It is as if there is an unreality of the outside world. It is a dissociative symptom of many conditions, such as psychiatric and neurological disorders, and not a stand-alone disorder. It is also a side effect of drug intoxication, sleep deprivation and stress.

Disruption—The termination of the placement of a prospective adoptee with a potential adoptive family prior to the legalization of the intended adoption.

Dissociation—One of a constellation of symptoms experienced by victims of childhood trauma. It includes derealization, depersonalization, anxiety, amnesia regarding the events of the abuse, depression, somatization, low self-esteem, substance abuse, self-mutilation and suicidal ideation/threats. It is a withdrawing from the outside world and focusing on the inner world. A dissociative child is often compliant or may self-stimulate (i.e., rocking, chewing on fingers, playing with hands, etc.). Parents often describe the child who is dissociative as "appearing to be in a fog" or "acting like she just isn't there." Dissociation is often linked to a diagnosis of Post-traumatic Stress Disorder.

Dissolution—The legal termination of adopting parents' parental rights after the finalization of an adoption.

Displacement—The adoptee leaves the family, usually temporarily, in order to receive in-patient treatment. However, there are instances in which displacement becomes a permanent living arrangement. The child may reside in residential treatment until the age of emancipation. In these cases, the family retains legal parental rights and responsibilities—the child still has a family.

Homestudy—The written document covering the legally required screening information necessary for a family to move forward with the actual placement and adoption of a child. The homestudy should also be used by the family and the agency to mutually assess the family's strengths in relation to the needs presented by the waiting children and to prepare them for the specialized way of looking at things and the unique skills that adoption requires. The homestudy should help families answer the pertinent question "Are we a family who has or can develop the skills necessary to parent a child with complex trauma issues?"

Honeymoon—This is the first stage in the adoptive family lifecycle. This period may be brief or it may last for months. This is a good period; everyone is getting along well.

Immobilization—This is another of the stages in the adoptive family lifecycle. The family becomes consumed with their efforts to "fix" the adoptee. Life continues to revolve around the premise that once the traumatized child is "better," we will be a happy and peaceful family again. The immobilized family is simply unable to accept or believe that the adoptee cannot attain the goals desired by parents and siblings. The family desperately wants to be the family they were prior to the adoption. It is as if family life goes *on hold* like planes circling an airport. Families require specialized professional assistance and parenting tools to move out of this stage.

Kinship Care—The term used to describe children being parented by relatives of a birth parent. Kinship care may be arranged *privately*—the arrangements are made among family members with no agency involvement; *voluntarily*—a public agency is involved in placing the child with relatives, but without utilizing the court system to take legal custody of the child; or by *kinship foster care*—a public agency has court-ordered legal custody of the child, and this agency seeks to place the child with a relative.

Mobilization—This is the last stage in the adoptive family lifecycle. In this stage, the family achieves a balance between meeting the unique needs of all members of the family: the adoptee with mental health issues, the brothers and sisters and the parents. There is a gradual shedding of the family that existed pre-adoption, and a "new and different" family emerges. Mobilization follows the Honeymoon, Ambivalence, Hoping and Learning, and Immobilization stages.

Pre-placement—This is the time period prior to the arrival of an adoptee in the adoptive family. During this time, families select an agency, attend pre-adoptive education classes, complete their homestudy, and select the child to join the family. This period should include emphasis on education for each member of the adoptive family.

Post-placement—This period spans the time the adoptee arrives in the family through adulthood.

Somatization—Chronic and persistent complaints of physical symptoms that have no identifiable physical origin. The physical symptoms are believed to be the manifestation of underlying psychological problems.

Transcultural—An adoption is considered to be transcultural when any of the family members are of a different race than the others. This is often referred to as *transracial* or *interracial* adoption. Adoptions are also considered transcultural if older children and their adoptive parents and/or siblings come from different countries but are of the same race. For example, if a white American couple adopts a white toddler from Eastern Europe or an African American family adopts an Ethiopian child, these adoptions are not transracial, but they are transcultural. Nearly all international adoptions are transcultural, then, while it is estimated that about 15% of domestic U.S. adoptions are transcultural because they are transracial.

A Parallel Pre-Adoptive Training Model for Typically Developing Children

This training program was developed by Arleta James, PCC, Attachment and Bonding Center of Ohio, 12608 State Road, Suite 1, Cleveland, OH, 44133, 440-230-1960. This training program was created for the book, *Brothers and Sisters in Adoption: Helping Children Navigate Relationships When New Kids Join the Family* (Indianapolis: Perspectives Press, Inc., 2009).

This model offers training to children, as a group, while parents attend their own simultaneous pre-adoptive education. Session length is contingent on the ages of the children in attendance. Chapter 2's, "Information Dissemination: Based on Age" offers guidelines for presenting information to children of various ages.

Session 1: Overview

This educational period would provide content and group activities that would answer the following questions:

Where is your new brother or sister coming from?

How did he or she get there?

What has to happen before he or she will actually move in?

Who will be helping your family adopt a brother or sister, or a sibling group?

A great activity to supplement such a session was created by Barbara Jordan and is contained in the workbook *Preparing Foster Parents' Own Children for the Fostering Experience.*[1] This "paper plate eco map" includes having children write out names of current family members and pets on strips of paper. The child then organizes these strips of paper in the middle of the paper plate. Subsequently, the child adds strips of paper for the new brother or sister, case workers, therapists, judge, etc. The child must then fit all of these on his or her paper plate. This project allows for a discussion about the changes in time and attention that will be diverted from the typically developing children once the sibling arrives. Subsequently, these children are encouraged to talk about how this might make them feel.

Photos, descriptions and/or videos of the children available for adoption may also be of benefit during such a session. Again, children are concrete thinkers. Visual materials enhance their learning.

Session 2: The Cycle of Needs

A presentation of the Cycle of Needs helps school-age children develop depth as to why children need new families.

1. Jordan, Barbara. *Preparing Foster Parents' Own Children for the Fostering Experience.* (King George, Virginia: American Foster Care Resources, www.afcr.com, 1997.)

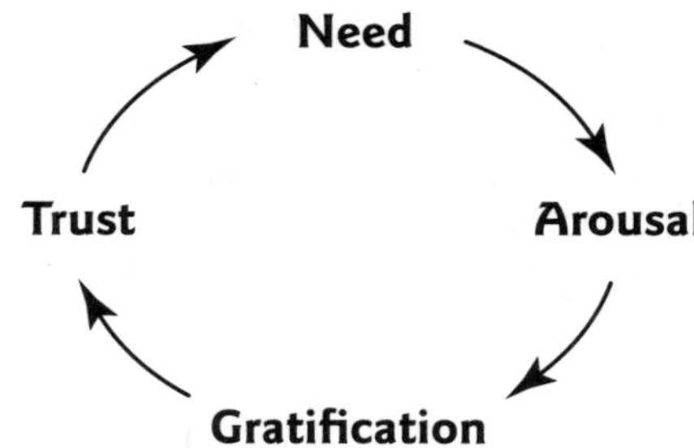

The cycle demonstrates that when the resident child was a baby, his mom and dad met his needs. He cried and Mom or Dad brought him a bottle, changed his diaper or just gave him attention. As a result, he learned the world was safe and that Mom and Dad could be trusted.

A discussion question would be to define a "need" versus a "want." Children can then list the various needs provided by their parents. Children will use this knowledge of needs to compare and contrast their life to the life of the sibling they are anxiously awaiting. The facilitator will provide examples such as, "Children who enter orphanages have not always received such attention. They may have cried and the orphanage caregivers were too busy with other babies to come and feed them, or to pick them up and hold them." Visual aides—video and photos of orphanages—may be obtained from families who have adopted from these settings or from websites related to the orphanages.

If a domestic adoption, the scenario may be: "When your brother or sister cried, his or her birthmother was not home. She left him or her alone while she went out with boyfriends or to buy drugs. So, your new brother or sister will have different ways of thinking and acting than you do because his or her needs were not met. It may take some time before your brother or sister settles into the family."

Great children's books to augment such discussion are *Borya and the Burps* by Joan McNamara (Indianapolis: Perspectives Press, 2005) and *Zachary's New Home: A Story for Foster and Adopted Children* by Geraldine and Paul Blomquist (Washington: Magination Press, 1990).

The cycle can be adapted for various types of issues that cause children to come into out-of-home care. As the above description provides, the cycle can be used to generate much conversation. Children would be encouraged to draw the cycle and review it at home with their parents.

Session 3: Coping Skills

The purpose of this session would be to help children understand what coping skills are and why they are important. Overall, children will need help coping with the new sibling's behavior and social skills, and with questions posed by friends and others.

That is, children need to understand some of the behavior difficulties with which the new child may present—stealing, lying, breaking toys, incessant chatter, temper tantrums, bedwetting, using profanity, etc. Children need help figuring out how they may respond if their new brother or sister steals an item from their room or breaks their favorite toy. They also need specific instructions regarding situations that cause safety issues such as temper tantrums, pushing, shoving, hitting or, again, sexual behavior. Regarding these latter behaviors, a good homework assignment would be to have a conversation with their mom or dad as to what the family policies on these matters would include.

Chapters 9 and 10 of *Brothers and Sisters in Adoption: Helping Children Navigate Relationships When New Kids Join the Family* offer content regarding the immature social skills with which traumatized children may present. These chapters also provide an array of strategies for coping with these situations. Overall, children need to understand that due to the fact that their needs were not met, the new sibling may not have learned to play nicely or fairly.

Questions posed by friends and others occur for a variety of reasons.

> Abigail entered the family at age 9. She and her typically developing sibling, John, attended the same school. One day, Abigail was found eating food off of the bathroom floor. It had apparently been dropped by a preceding student. The news of this behavior passed through the school quickly. At recess, numerous fellow classmates asked John, "What is wrong with your sister?"

> Randy's family adopted Sean when he was 6 years old. Randy and Sean attended the same school. Randy was two years older than Sean. Each day, Sean struggled with emotional regulation. The school's response was to have Randy come to Sean's class to assist in calming him down. This interrupted Randy's education as well as it caused his classmates to wonder what was going on. "Where was Randy going every day?" "What is the problem with his brother?" It wasn't long before questions were posed to Randy about his brother's behavior.

> Tanner was excited with the arrival of his younger sibling from China. Over time, he noticed that everywhere his transcultural family went strangers stared. Some even asked questions such as, "Where did you get that one?" "How much did she cost?" Friends frequently asked, "Why does your sister look different. than the rest of your family?"

In such cases, children need specific guidelines for responding to questions. Children often feel they need to answer questions. They need permission to say, "I would rather not talk about that." "Please ask my mom to explain that." Children also need to know that such issues should be discussed with their parents. At times, parents need to intervene and resolve such situations. So, a coping skill of most importance for children to learn is to rely on parents. Parents will help discern what is acceptable for the child to handle and what matters require parental intervention.

This session could include drawing pictures of situations the child has already encountered in his or her life. Or, the facilitator can utilize examples from the vignettes above and throughout *Brothers and Sisters in Adoption*. The facilitator could also create scenarios for the children from his own experiences with adoptive families. Discussion and identification of coping skills could fall out of the drawings/vignettes. ChildsWork/ ChildsPlay[2] offers *The Coping Skills Workbook* by Lisa Schab and Andy Myer (Plainview: Bureau for At Risk Youth, 1996). This workbook presents nine coping skills: deal with your feelings, adjust your attitude, discover your choices, ask for help, take care of yourself, take one step at a time, give yourself a break, plan ahead and accept things that you cannot change. The workbook provides activities so children may practice each of the skills. The *Less Stress Ball*, also from Childs Work/Childs Play, is covered with slogans children can implement to reduce frustration in difficult situations.

2. ChildsWork/ChildsPlay: www.childswork.com

Session 4: Talking about Feelings

As presented in Chapter 2 of *Brothers and Sisters in Adoption: Helping Children Navigate Relationships When New Kids Join the Family*, the typically developing children avoid discussing their adopted sibling with their parents, as they do not want to burden the family with what they perceive to be additional stress. Some resident children harbor their feelings because they feel guilty for having negative emotions toward their new brother or sister. Children need to know that the expression of feelings is important, and that any feeling they have is acceptable.

The facilitator needs to insure that the children can identify emotions such as sad, mad, glad, scared, embarrassed, frustrated, resentful, jealous, shame and guilt as these are the common emotions that occur during interactions between typically developing siblings and their adopted brothers and sisters. There are a wide array of tools available to facilitators to use in accomplishing this goal: art, scenarios, feeling wheels, feeling charts or feelings games such as *Talk Blocks* or *Feelings Frog Games* (www.childswork.com). Such a group exercise could be created around the experiences of the children attending this pre-adoptive training program as well.

Many materials pertaining to feelings include a component for expressing feelings. Since parents would be available, a great way to end this class would be parent and child role-plays. Overall, children need to understand that sharing feelings is normal and they need concrete ways to express emotions. Talking to their parents is the best means. However, if parents are otherwise occupied, drawing, talking into a tape recorder and journaling offer positive alternatives.

Session 5: Transcultural Adoption

This segment is necessary if the agency makes transcultural placements. It would benefit resident children to have an understanding of the cultural background of their new brother or sister. It may be fun for children to read about various countries or the history of African Americans. For example, the participants may enjoy taking turns bringing in library books regarding the culture of the child their family is planning to adopt.

On a more serious note, however, when parents make the decision to adopt transculturally, the entire family becomes "different" as pointed out in Chapters 1, 3 and 5. Some friends, extended family members, neighbors and strangers will embrace transcultural adoption while others may be more inclined to stare and perhaps make negative comments. Resident children need preparation for this latter situation. They need a working definition of prejudice and discrimination. The facilitator may easily compile this content from Pact, An Adoption Alliance (www.pactadopt.org). Children need some ways to respond to culturally biased remarks about their family and their culturally different sibling. In their book, *Inside Transracial Adoption* (Indianapolis: Perspectives Press, Inc., 2000), Gail Steinberg and Beth Hall suggest that siblings and adoptees be made aware of numerous strategies in order to effectively handle insensitive questions or comments. Their toolbox includes ask a question, disagree, confront, make a joke, whisper in response to a bully, withdraw, talk with a friend, use the power of the family, tell it like it is and code words. These authors explain and exemplify each of these strategies. The Resource section at the end of Chapter 3 of *Brothers and Sisters in Adoption* offers an array of websites and other books related to transcultural adoption.

Unless the family is a transcultural family prior to the adoption, the typically developing children need exposure to what "different" may feel like. This may be accomplished in various ways. For example, the family may begin to attend a religious institution with a diverse population or a congregation comprised of the intended adoptee's culture. The family may participate in community activities or plan trips to places that reflect the cultural heritage of the adoptee. These experiences, if conducted prior to this session, could be discussed as a large group exercise with questions asking for the children's thoughts and feelings relating to what it was like—positive and negative—to be among people "different" from themselves.

Session 6: Panel of Typically Developing Siblings

It is common practice to provide a panel of experienced adoptive parents during pre-adoptive preparation, so it makes sense that a panel of experienced siblings would be beneficial to children in families who are moving toward adoption as a means to add to their family. This could be done separately from the parents, however, there would be obvious advantages to conducting such a group with both parents and children present. Parents and children alike would gain firsthand knowledge about the positive and negative impact of adoption on resident children.

Session 7: Positives, Final Questions and Closure

The video *Supporting Brothers and Sisters: Creating a Family by Birth, Foster Care and Adoption*, created by the Attachment and Bonding Center of Ohio,[3] is centered on five adoptive families discussing the adoption experience. Each family is comprised of adoptees with histories of complex trauma and typically developing children. In total, 13 resident children and ten parents share their experiences of adoption in segment topics called "Expectations," "Behavioral Difficulties," "Loss Issues," "Coping," "Sharing Information Pre- and Post-adoption," "The Kids Offer Advice to Other Kids and Parents," "Peer and Public Interactions" and "Positives." The video concludes with "Bobby and Desera," a segment featuring two adoptees discussing their experience of entering a family in which there were typically developing siblings.

The "Positives" segment and the "Bobby and Desera" segment offer a nice way to conclude a pre-adoptive preparation program for typically developing children. These segments call to light that the experience of adoption may bring struggles, yet there will be positive aspects along the way. Parents will gain from the content of this video as well. Overall, the video could be incorporated into many of the different sessions described above.

Prior to leaving, each participant can be given the "Books for Children and Adolescents" and "Websites for Children and Adolescents" from the Resources that conclude *Brothers and Sisters in Adoption*'s Chapter 5. Books and websites are great for continuing the educational process after the conclusion of this parallel model of pre-adoptive training concludes. Hopefully, the group participants will exchange phone numbers or email addresses so that they can continue to support one another throughout their adoption journeys.

---

3. Arleta James, PCC, Attachment and Bonding Center of Ohio, 12608 State Road, Suite 1, Cleveland, OH, 44133, 440-230-1960.

Sexual Abuse Pre-Placement Activity

Permission to re-print this activity was given by the author, Kirsti Adkins. Ms. Adkins is the now-retired Director of Adoption Services, Lutheran Service Society of Western Pennsylvania.

This training exercise/handout was developed for families who are in training in preparation for placement of children in their homes. Families have a need for both cognitive understanding of the issues involved in parenting these children and specific skills for dealing with situations as they arise in their homes. This exercise takes parents through the recommended steps in the process and gives them specific examples of ways to get their points across. This kind of discussion is often difficult for parents. Discussion with a script in front of them made it more feasible and helped them to prepare for situations which they would almost certainly encounter. The statements following the issues to be addressed are *examples* of what parents might say to get a point across.

A Few Words about Sexual Vocabulary

Although the use of the appropriate sexual vocabulary (*genitals*, *penis*, *vagina*, *breasts*, *anus*, etc.) is recommended, it is important to demonstrate to the child that as an adult you are not shocked by the "street" terms (*dick*, *pussy*, *rod*, *butt*, *boobs*, *tits*, *cock*, etc.), you have heard them before and you are not intimidated by hearing these terms used. In addition, there are many children in care who have not been exposed to appropriate sexual terminology. Later, and when appropriate, the parent will explain to the child that while they are not intimidated by hearing those commonly used sexual terms, and can comfortably say them too, these words are often used to show disrespect for parts of one's own and another person's body, and are often said to exploit, intimidate, groom, victimize, dehumanize and demean another.

For example:

> "Yes, I know what the words *dick*, *cock*, *rod*, and *prick* mean. I've heard them before and at times may have used them myself. But in this family, we will use the appropriate sexual terms when talking about what happened sexually to you and to others. This will let you know that I respect you, I am listening to you, and that I care. The words *dick* or *prick* may be the only words you now know and are most comfortable using. That's OK. I just wanted you to know the reasons why I will use the word *penis*. I want to show you respect and make sure you feel safe."

Verbally Reassure the Child that He Will Not Be Sexually Victimized in His New Home

"Your dad and I want you to understand that we will do everything we can to make sure you won't be sexually abused in this home. In this home, grown-ups aren't sexual with children, children aren't sexual with grown-ups and children aren't sexual with other children."

Assure the Child of Parents' Desire to Protect Him/Her

"We want to keep you safe from harm and sexual abuse in this home. We will do everything we can to make sure that you will not be sexually abused here, and you will not be able to sexually abuse or hurt anyone else. This includes the dog and the cat. We want to keep everyone safe from harm in this family."

Recognize that the Child May Have Initial Difficulty in Accepting that She/He Is Safe:

"You probably don't believe all this and figure you have to find out on your own if what I say is true. If you try to kiss me and lick me on my face, I will tell you to stop and that I don't want you to kiss me that way. And if you touch me in my private areas, I will take your hand away and remind you that in this family children and adults aren't sexual with each other."

Discuss the Family Touch Patterns and What This Means in Order to Alleviate the Child's Anxieties:

"In this family we hug each other sometimes, we kiss each other on the cheek, or we hold hands to feel close to each other. Sometimes we snuggle together on the couch when we are watching a movie."

Discuss the Child's Need for Privacy and How the Family Will Protect This Need:

"Grown-ups have a right to privacy and kids have a right to privacy too. You have private areas on your body, like your vagina (or kitty, penis, dick, butt, boobs, etc.) and no one has the right to touch those parts or put their hands in your pants except you. If anyone does that, it is your responsibility to tell me.

"There are also places in this house where you can have privacy—your bedroom and the bathroom—and when you are in the bedroom with the door closed, people have to knock first to get permission to come in. And if you are in the bathroom peeing or pooping or taking a bath, the door will be closed so that you can do that in private. We won't come in without your permission. And if *you* see a closed door, *you* can't open it without knocking first and asking permission to open that door."

Express Commitment to the Child and Acceptance of the Child:

"We will talk about these things often because it is important to us to know how you feel and to understand what happened to you. Talking about these things will help us to make sure that no one ever hurts you again because you are important to us."

Demonstrate Family Touch Patterns in Different Areas of Your Home:

"Now, if you need a hug or a touch, how can I do that with you? If we are watching TV together on the couch, how can we be close in a way that's OK with you and OK with me?"

"When I put you to bed at night, what kind of a good night do you need to feel safe?"

"Will you remind me if I forget?"

If There Are Other Children in the Home, Discuss Expected Areas of Support and Tension:

"All the children and adults in our family are expected to behave this way and follow these rules about privacy and touch. We need to remind each other about what is OK and not OK. If someone isn't following a rule about privacy or touch, it is your responsibility to come and tell us so we can talk about it."

Clearly State, as Appropriate, How, When and Where Various Family Members Meet their Own Sexual Needs, Especially If There Are Other Children in the Home:

"When Mom and I want to be sexual with each other, we do that in private with each other. Mom and I are a tight sexual unit and there is nothing you can do to interfere with our relationship. We wouldn't even *think* of having sex with a child."

Or, for a single parent, "I take care of my sexual needs in private. I would never think of having sex with a child."

Or, with other children in the home, "If Julia or Tom wants to touch their private areas, they need to do that in private, alone in their own bedrooms, with the door closed."

Break the "Secret Barrier" by Discussing the Past Abuse with the Child:

"Jamie, we know that when you were in the family where you were born, you were sexually abused. Your mom's boyfriend did things to your body that he shouldn't have done. He put his dick into your kitty and that hurt you. We also know that he asked you to touch his dick and put it in your mouth."

"Chris, I know that when you were with your birthmom she did sexual things with you. I know that sometimes she licked your penis and sometimes she wanted you to play with her boobs. I'll bet you did what you were told to do because you didn't know what would happen if you didn't."

Concentrate on Feelings, Acknowledge that the Child May Be Frightened:

"When that was happening you might have been scared or frightened, because you weren't sure you liked the way it felt, and you didn't know what would happen next, or what would happen if you said 'No.' You're probably wondering if it is going to be the same way in this family. And you are scared to even think about it."

Concluding Note: What you say to the child should be *tailor-made* to meet situations you know about in which the child was abused. For example, the child may have been abused in the bedroom or the bathroom, in the basement, after school before a parent came home, or when the other parent went to the grocery store. Try to figure out where/when the abuse occurred so you can address the specific circumstances and concerns of the child.

Adoptive Family Safety Contract

Permission to re-print this contract was provided by the author, Dr. Wayne Deuhn, Professor of Social Work, University of Texas at Arlington, duehn1@airmail.com, or http:www2.uta.edu/ssw/duehn, or 2200 Wilson Drive, Arlington, TX, 76011-32276.

This contract is designed to keep everyone safe in this family. All the children (youth) in this family sign this agreement. It lists the rules for living together safely in this family, for respecting the rights of others, and for ensuring the personal safety for everyone. Your signature on the bottom acknowledges that these rules have been discussed with you, that you understand these rules, that you will abide by them, and that you will help other children in this family to comply with these rules as well.

1. I understand that if I am in another person's bedroom, I must get permission first.
2. I understand that if no one is home to give me permission, I am not to go into that person's bedroom.
3. I understand that when visiting another person's bedroom, the door must be open.
4. I understand that if someone is visiting my bedroom, the door must be open.
5. I understand that undressing is allowed only in my bedroom and in the bathroom with the door closed.
6. I understand that everyone sleeps in their own bed.
7. I understand that there will be no sexual play and sexual touching and that includes playing doctor, nurse, or things like that.
8. I understand there is to be no public masturbation.
9. I understand there is to be no sexual contact or sexual touching between children in this family. The only individuals who have sex together in this home are Mom and Dad and always with the door closed.
10. I understand that there is to be only one person in the bathroom at one time.
11. I will tell an adult if anyone sexually touches me, and I will continue to tell until someone believes me.
12. I will obey these rules of privacy, e.g. no touching of another's private parts, purses, notebooks, private notes, diaries, no opening another's mail, etc.
13. I understand that I am responsible for obeying these rules.
14. I understand that I am responsible if I break these rules.
15. I understand these rules clearly.

Signed: ________________________________ Date ____________

(Adoptive Child)

Witnesses: ________________________________ Date ____________

(Adoptive Parents)

(Siblings) ________________________________ Date ____________

Social Readjustment Rating Scale for Adults

The social readjustment scale was created by Thomas H. Holmes and Richard H. Rahe. It was first published in the *Journal of Psychosomatic Research*, 1967 11, 213–218. It is based on the premise that good and bad life events can increase stress levels and make one more susceptible to illness and mental health problems.

Simply add up the values for all of the listed life events that have occurred to you within the past year. If a particular event has happened to you more than once within the last 12 months, multiply the value by the number of occurrences. Enter your value total at the end of the list.

1. Death of a spouse	100
2. Divorce	73
3. Marital separation	65
4. Jail term	63
5. Death of a close family member	63
6. Personal injury or illness	53
7. Marriage	50
8. Fired from work	47
9. Marital reconciliation	45
10. Retirement	45
11. Change in health of a family member	44
12. Pregnancy	40
13. Sex difficulties	39
14. Gain of a new family member	39
15. Business readjustments	39
16. Change in financial state	38
17. Death of a close friend	37
18. Change to different line of work	36
19. Change in number of arguments with spouse	35
20. Mortgage over $50,000	31
21. Foreclosure of mortgage	30
22. Change in responsibilities at work	29
23. Son or daughter leaving home	29
24. Trouble with in-laws	29
25. Outstanding personal achievements	28
26. Wife begins or stops work	26
27. Begin or end school	26
28. Change in living conditions	25

29. Revision of personal habits	24
30. Trouble with boss	23
31. Change in work hours or conditions	20
32. Change in residence	20
33. Change in school	20
34. Change in recreation	19
35. Change in religious activities	19
36. Change in social activities	18
37. Loan less than $50,000	17
38. Change in sleep habits	16
39. Change in number of family get-togethers	15
40. Change in eating habits	15
41. Vacation	13
42. Holidays	12
43. Minor violation of laws	11

Scoring

Each event should be considered if it has taken place in the last 12 months. Add values to the right of each item to obtain the total score.

Your susceptibility to illness and mental health problems:

Low	<149
Mild	150 to 200
Moderate	200 to 299
Major	>300

Social Readjustment Rating Scale for Non-adults

A modified scale has also been developed for non-adults. Similar to the adult scale, stress points for life events in the past year are added and compared to the rough estimate of how stress affects health.

1. Getting married	101
2. Unwed pregnancy	92
3. Death of parent	87
4. Acquiring a visible deformity	81
5. Divorce of parents	77
6. Fathering an unwed pregnancy	77
7. Becoming involved with drugs or alcohol	76
8. Jail sentence of parent for over one year	75
9. Marital separation of parents	69
10. Death of brother or sister	68
11. Change in acceptance by peers	67
12. Pregnancy of unwed sister	67
13. Discovery of being an adopted child	63
14. Marriage of parent to step-parent	63
15. Death of a close friend	63
16. Having a visible congenital deformity	62
17. Serious illness requiring hospitalization	58
18. Failure of a grade at school	56
19. Not making an extracurricular activity	55
20. Hospitalization of a parent	55
21. Jail sentence of parent for over 30 days	53
22. Breaking up with a boyfriend or girlfriend	53
23. Beginning to date	51
24. Suspension from school	50
25. Birth of a brother or sister	50
26. Increase in arguments between parents	47
27. Loss of job by parent	46
28. Outstanding personal achievement	46
29. Change in parent's financial status	46
30. Accepted at college of choice	43
31. Being a senior in high school	42
32. Hospitalization of a sibling	41
33. Increased absence of parent from home	38
34. Brother or sister leaving home	37

35. Addition of third adult to home	37
36. Becoming a full fledged member of a church	31
37. Decrease in arguments between parents	27
38. Mother or father beginning work	26

Scoring

Score 150 or <	Slight risk of illness
Score of 150 to 299 +	Risk of illness is moderate
Score of 300 +	At risk of illness

"We aren't done yet!" Adopting in Middle Adulthood

This segment was developed specifically as an appendix for *Brothers and Sisters in Adoption: Helping Children Navigate Relationships When New Kids Join the Family* by Arleta James.

It has become increasingly common for adults in their middle years (age 50+) to begin parenting what are often referred to as "another crop" or a "second family" of children. There are several ways that such families are created:

- Sometimes in second marriages, where one or both partners have adult children from prior relationships, the couple wishes to parent "together" and, for a variety of reasons discussed in Chapter 1 of *Brothers and Sisters in Adoption*, may turn to adoption as their family-expansion option.
- Empty nesters may become foster parents out of an overall love for children and parenting, and ultimately decide to adopt some of the children they foster.
- Many "career" foster parents foster children their whole lives. Raising children is what they do! Knowing that moving children impacts children adversely, and feeling the pressure of federal legislation which promotes adoption as a permanency plan preferred to long-term foster care, at age 50 or older some of these parents find themselves committing to raising another child or children to adulthood.

Parents' Expectations about Reactions and Responsibilities of Their Adult Children

Far too often parents beginning a "second family" (the middle adulthood adopters described above) or parents who build very large families over the course of many years hold expectations about the future role of their oldest children with their youngest children. Often, these older children may not have been consulted about these expectations and they do not share them. Sometimes the older children feel taken advantage of, and have no interest in committing to a supportive, mentoring, or emergency caretaking role with children with whom they have not shared a growing-up experience.

My Adult Children Will Be Supportive

The family of Ava, first introduced in Chapter 5 of *Brothers and Sisters in Adoption: Helping Children Navigate Relationships When New Kids Join the Family* and about whom we learned more in Chapter 10, offers an example of a best case scenario in a family with such expectations. Ava's oldest brother, the oldest child in the family, is a wonderful example of an adult son who is supportive of his mother's ongoing care for children. The family is comprised of 13 children ranging in age from 38 to 2. Mom and Dad were each single adoptive parents and parents by birth. They married, in their early 50s, combining their 11 children, and then they adopted two more jointly for a total of 13 children. Here we hear from the oldest brother in this family:

"At 38, I am the oldest brother in this family of 13 children. Eleven were adopted and two joined the family by birth—I am one of the birth children.

"Before Rita was adopted, I was an only child, about age 10. She was a bit younger. I thought a sister would wear bows in her hair and be prissy. She didn't and wasn't. Mom got divorced and I grew up and got married. Then, when I was in my 20s, Mom started adopting again. First came Ava and her birth brother, Forest.

"Prior to Mom adopting Kenny (the third of my mom's adopted kids) I didn't know people lived like his birthfamily, especially in this day and age [Kenny and his three birth sisters, all adopted by this family, lived in horrible neglect and violence]. When I think about how he and his birth siblings live now, I feel sad about what they lived like before.

"I tease the kids and laugh about the silly stuff they do, especially Forest but I really feel like he is my brother. I can't help that Forest and Rosie (adopted tenth and jointly by the parents) are my favorites! I feel I had a big part in Forest and Rosie. The family always says that it seems like Forest has always been a part of our family. We forget he's adopted! I am proud of Ava now. She comes to visit and is part of the family now.

"As they were added to the family, I would have liked more information before on all of the kids' family lives with their birth families as I never know what to expect.

"I know I'll be guardian if something happens to my mom and her second husband. I support them by offering child care and accept the kids and listen to them.

"With my kids, they get jealous of their young aunts and uncles sometimes. My kids are close with many of my mom's kids—my brothers and sisters. I feel that I have played an important part in the family (especially when Mom was single; I was the male figure and had to step in). I don't feel like the adoptive father, but I do feel like the kids have always been 'mine.'

"There are so many positives!"

This son is a stay-at-home parent. His mom and dad work full-time, And his mother often comments that without him she would never have been able to adopt many of her children. His support, child care, role-modeling, empathy, positive attitude, sense of humor and so much more demonstrates that adoptive families can enjoy wonderful interactions no matter what the ages and needs of the children.

Yet, other families have arrived at therapy asking about ways to improve relationships with adult children which have been strained by adoption.

Alice reported, "My adult son's first question, when he learned that my husband and I would be adopting the three siblings we had fostered for over four years was, 'Will they be included in the will? I was counting on an inheritance for my own children!'

"He remains angry, and it has been years since the adoptions were finalized. He and his wife offer us no help, even though they know we are having a hard time managing the children's problems."

Robin states, "My daughter reacted very adversely to our decision to adopt younger children. She claimed, 'You're too old to take on these kids.' While she has softened somewhat, if I mention that there are any issues, she is quick to remind me, 'Told you so.' This is quite disheartening."

Adult children who lack information about the impact of trauma often criticize their parents' style of caring for their younger brothers and sisters in the same manner as do friends, extended family and professionals as described in *Brothers and Sisters in Adoption*'s Chapter 8, "Isolation." Parents have many feelings when their own children—especially those who are successful in their adult lives—turn around and disapprove of the very parenting styles that launched them into a life of opportunity. Carrie, age 23, and one of nine children ages 3 to 25, five by birth and four by adoption offers her perspective on this

"I think I have been most frustrated with the parenting style of my parents with the children that we have adopted. I do believe that even if the children were not adopted but were my biological siblings, I would still have the same complaints. However, since these children have been adopted, my concerns are even stronger, because they require so much more attention, consistency and follow through.

"I have been somewhat annoyed at the noise level at my house since moving home after college. The outbursts and fits are, thankfully, fewer and further between than they once were, but they are exhausting and so incredibly stressful. I do believe that many of the adopted children's behaviors are a result of the time each of the children spent with their birthmothers and their abandonment, however I believe much of it is complicated by the parenting style of my parents.

"When we were talking about adopting my sister Ann, I remember thinking that my mom was not going to have any idea how to parent a child like Ann. I do have to admit that my sisters and I were easy to raise, and I do not believe that my mom understood the depth of Ann's damage. I almost wish that someone had sat my mom and dad down and explained exactly what to expect from her or the possible troubles to come. I think that they may have had better strategies when the problems did arise or not have been so resistant to changing their parenting style.

"I do resent the stress level in my house and I don't think it's good for any of us. I am hoping that my parents recognize their situation. My fears are somewhat rooted in the fact that my parents are older and I believe that eventually my siblings will become my responsibility. I want them to have the solid foundation of love and self-love to be successful, functional adults.

"Still, I do not regret that our family adopted any of my siblings, and our family is more complete because of them. I have learned so much from them and enjoy their company most of the time."

My Adult Children Will Be the Guardians

Mary Ellen's parents adopted four young children through fostering. The older three children, a sibling group, ages 2, 4 and 5, who were ineligible for adoption subsidy, are already exhibiting many behavioral problems and learning delays. Mary Ellen, at age 27, has been away at college and graduate school during most of the time that these children have been in the family. She is the named legal guardian in the event something happens to her parents, a couple in their late 50.

In speaking with Mary Ellen one day, I wondered if she had any idea what assuming responsibility for the children would actually mean. I asked her,

"Do you have any idea about their academic or mental health issues?"

"What financial support has been put in place for you as guardian of these kids? Life insurance? Inheritance?"

"Where would you live as a family?"

"Do you plan to get married? Would you inform your spouse-to-be of your guardianship plans?"

"Would you build a family by giving birth or adopting children of your own? How might they be impacted by your guardianship of these children much older than they, much younger than you?"

"What type of support system do you think you will need?"

"Would your other siblings help out?"

Actually, Mary Ellen had given little thought to this entire matter. Like most of us, she really didn't want to contemplate the thought of her parents becoming ill or passing away. However, guardianship, if it became a reality, would be a life-altering event for her, as well as for her younger siblings.

Both adoptive parents and any older siblings considering agreeing to become guardians for these complicated younger siblings need to understand inheritance laws, subsidy regulations, guardianship rights in their state, etc. Adult children who are willing to assume guardianship need to take the time to understand their younger siblings' needs. Baby-sitting, attending therapy and psychiatric sessions, and IEP meetings at school are a few ways to learn what it will mean to care for adopted youngsters with complex trauma issues.

Parents and adult children also need to recognize that their healthy children's life circumstances may change over time. These children need to be afforded the opportunity to change their minds, and to pursue their dreams inclusive or exclusive of caring for their brothers or sisters.

Grandparenthood for Those Actively Parenting Difficult Children

The birth of a grandchild is joyous occasion. Grandparents can hardly wait to hold their grandchild in their arms. Spoiling is a special privilege reserved for grandparents.

Very often these commonly held expectations of grandparenthood are accurate. But there are a variety of circumstances for all kinds of families, including those expanded by the adoption of children with complex trauma issues, in which they are not.

Not uncommonly, parents of "younger" and "older" families have the expectation that their youngest children will interact with the children of the family's oldest children (technically the adoptees' nieces and nephews) in a special kind of "cousins" relationship. Sometimes this works and grandparents who are also parents to young adopted children from backgrounds like the siblings described in *Brothers and Sisters in Adoption: Helping Children Navigate Relationships When New Kids Join the Family* may indeed find that the long-awaited milestone of grandparent will bring immense delight.

Unexpected challenges and perhaps even heartache, however, are not uncommon outcomes.

For example, below are Peter and Harriet's stories. Peter is the birthfather to three young adult children, Harriet and her two brothers who are ages 26, 25 and 21. They were 21, 19 and 15 when Peter and his wife became foster parents to almost 3 year-old Carl. Carl is now age 8. Harriet married at age 22. She lives with her husband and their two young children.

Peter says,

> "When Carl first came, everyone was excited and happy. We had a good support group with our family. Our older children would watch him and give us some time to ourselves. As time went on and Carl's behavior became more demanding plus his anger, our support group started to pull back. When people came over, we kind of tried to let the care-taking to them so we would have a break. As a result, people saw his true colors. Even one of my

wife's friends, who we went to foster parent classes with, and who has fostered all kinds of kids with problems, said there was something about Carl and how hard he was to control. So, as a result only a very few people would watch Carl for us and only for a short time. Then, when our grandchildren were born and became older, our daughter did not like her children around Carl. Their visits were cut short sometimes or they would just leave in the middle of a visit if things started to get bad, as they most often do. Our oldest son has a big heart and still gives us time to go out on a date while he watches Carl. But, we have gotten phone calls from him in the middle of our date saying he can't take it anymore and is very upset. We would cut our date short and go back home.

"Our middle son, as time went on, does not want anything to do with Carl or so he says. I think he still has a little feeling for him. Most of the time he just stays away from him. But, Carl will do things to get a reaction out of him and then he just leaves the house and goes somewhere else.

"Sometimes, I think our daughter blames Carl for some of the behavior her son is showing at home. He is 2 now and 2-year-olds will do things like this anyway, I think. When the grandkids are over and Carl starts to get out of hand, I will take him down in the basement. Our basement is finished so we sit down there and watch TV or play a game. I try to keep Carl and myself down there usually until they leave. So, I don't get to spend as much time with grandkids as I would like.

"In the end, what used to be about family and friends and other things is just all about Carl. Everything we do is about Carl."

Harriet shares,

"I'll start by saying that when Carl first came to Mom and Dad's house, I was so excited. I always looked forward to seeing him. I played games with him and did a lot of art projects. We had a lot of fun together. Carl was truly a joy to be around.

"After my first son was born, my relationship with Carl changed. Carl was no longer the #1 boy in my life. I never really looked at Carl as a boy with problems until he started interacting with my son.

"When the boys and I spend time at Mom and Dad's house, when Carl is home, it is very stressful. Carl and my son like to run around the house and scream, which seems to be the most stressful thing. I guess Carl is more wound when we are there. Now, I have two birth sons. Mom and I thought it would be best if I would come when Carl is in school. I hate doing that because Dad doesn't get to see my boys that often.

"I thought it would be best if my sons and Carl didn't see each other because of what my oldest son was seeing. The violence in Carl, hitting and biting Mom and Dad, was something that I didn't want my son to see. At times it would get pretty intense and it would scare my son. He has mocked some of Carl's actions, like hitting me and throwing a temper tantrum like Carl. I also feel like I can never let them play alone. Carl, in the past, has wanted to get a toy from my son from under his private parts, and he would ask my son to lie on top of him. That alarmed me and I understand that Carl probably had some sexual things done to him, but it makes me fearful that he may invade my boys in some way. I'll be honest that that action put bitterness in my heart for Carl—and this bitterness showed.

"I thought about it for months and came to the conclusion that the bitterness toward Carl is not going to make him better. I truly want to help Carl. So, I decided to forgive him in my heart and to be a better example. I try not to get stressed at Mom's. I try to do art projects again with him and to tell him that I love him. I'll say it has not been easy.

"One other thing that is hard for me since Carl came is that my mom is not the same mom. She is stressed and bitter. Most of our conversations are about Carl. I don't mind at times, but I want her to be happy and to be able to enjoy her life as it is."

Peter, Harriet and Carl's case contains many unmet expectations and grief issues for each member of this later age adoptive family. Peter misses much priceless time with his grandchildren—a loss for him, Harriet and these little ones. Harriet longs for the happy and calm mom she once used to have. She isn't certain how to help her mother parent Carl and manage to enjoy a satisfying life. Harriet struggled with finding a "fit" with her young brother, Carl. This process was difficult and lengthy. In the meantime, family relations were strained. Time together, as a family, was lost.

And then there are instances such as Sylvia's.

Sylvia and her husband are the parents to nine children they adopted; four came as infants and the last five came as a sibling group through the child welfare system. These siblings currently range in age from 31 to 11. At the time of the adoption of the sibling group of five, however, the children were ages 22 thru 2.

The sibling group has presented many challenges. The greatest of these struggles has come from the oldest brother in the group. It was his violence that led the family through therapy and out-of-home-placement in therapeutic foster care and residential treatment.

In the course of this journey, the family learned that he had sexually abused a young female grandchild, Emily [Whether he has any other victims, inside or outside of the family, is unknown]. The entire family was shocked, distressed, angry, saddened and overwhelmed. As Sylvia stated, "We stood by him in spite of all of our feelings. My daughter—Emily's mother—was of course very much affected by this, and to her credit, she has moved past this and accepted him again as part of the family. A strong religious orientation and Christian counseling allowed her to forgive her brother, but certainly, he is never allowed access to her child or any young child.

"However, our oldest son and his wife allow no contact between our younger children and their children. Prior to this, we had enjoyed the grandchildren coming to our country home and baking cookies, playing with the animals, having cookouts, and generally having good family fun. The younger children and I went to the grandchildren's home almost every week to babysit so my daughter-in-law could have some time to herself.

"Our youngest daughters really miss this time with their nieces and don't understand why they are being punished for their brother's problems. I can't explain it either. I've talked to my son about it, but he and his wife are adamant that they will not allow their children to be around any children who may have been sexually abused. They are unwilling to understand that most children who are sexually abused do not perpetrate other children. Obviously, their stance means the entire family cannot gather together.

"We love all of our children. We cherish them. We do not regret adopting these youngest, but our whole family has suffered greatly for it. I hope that someday our family relationships will be healed. I hope that our oldest son will soften his heart toward our younger kids, at least the three that pose no threat to his children.

"We are proud of our adult children who have accepted the kids as brothers and sisters. Recently, our 15-year-old son attempted suicide. Our second oldest son was very affected by this. He came to the hospital and stood by his brother's bedside. He said, 'I love you. I just want you to know that your big brother is here for you. I had some troubles when I was younger and I want you to know that things will get better.' "

Sylvia also reports, "Despite the nightmares we have been through, I would never give up the blessings of adopting these kids. I love them very much. They are my children."

Overall, it is important that those who have adult children when considering an addition to their family understand that their adult children who are now parents may opt to limit the time grandparents spend with their grandchildren because they view the adoptee as a safety threat or a poor role-model. This is a great loss for grandparents, parents and all of the children.

Facing Realities

Parents considering building a "second family" and their adult children are encouraged to have frank discussions about one another's expectations—hopefully (but unfortunately in real life it happens rarely) before the parents decide to adopt. Chapters 1 and 9 of *Brothers and Sisters in Adoption: Helping Children Navigate Relationships When New Kids Join the Family* suggest some expectations that may be operating and a system to use to form realistic expectations. A mental health professional familiar with families which have included children with complex trauma could be an especially useful mediator for such discussion.

As with any adoptive family, safety issues apply when introducing adoptees with a history of complex trauma to grandchildren. In Chapter 3 of *Brothers and Sisters in Adoption*, the section, "Taking a Proactive Approach to Sex and Sexuality" and the Appendices, "Sexual Abuse Pre-Placement Activity" and "Adoptive Family Safety Contract" help parents and their adult siblings put in place the necessary safety measures. Chapter 9 offers suggestions about managing other types of difficulties that occur due to an adoptee's aggression, stealing, lying and other negative behaviors.

Second families also need to acknowledge that adoption may create great joys, yet also many losses for each member of their family as was pointed out in the cases of Harriet, Peter and Sylvia. Chapter 10 helps families acknowledge and grieve the changes in their family.

A late-age adoption that creates a transcultural family composition may want to review Chapters 3 and 5 for advice regarding preparing their adult children and grandchild for prejudice, discrimination and the types of questions and comments received from extended family members, friends, neighbors and strangers. Certainly, adult children need to reflect on their attitudes about their now transcultural family. Grown children also want to eliminate prejudicial or discriminatory comments, jokes and so on from their interactions with the adoptee, and actually, overall in any of their relationships.

Resources

Articles and Message Boards

The below provide food for thought for older adoptive parents as well as adoption professionals.

Ashe, Nancy. "16 Steps to Older Parent Adoption." http://www.adopting.org/adoptions/16-steps-to-older-parent-adoption.html

Ashe, Nancy. "Older Parent Adoption." http://www.adopting.org/adoptions/older-parent-adoption-2.html

Fisher, Richard. "At Our Age—Older Parents Adopting." http://library.adoption.com/Over-40-Adoption/At-Our-Age-Older-Parents-Adopting/article/213/1.html

Russell, Barbara. "The Foundation for Large Families." http://www.foundationforlargefamilies.com/folder.html

GAARPadopt
groups.yahoo.com/group/GAARPadopt

Gracefully Aging Aware Refined Parents Adopt is an email list for adoptive parents over 40. It was created in 2000 by adoptive mom Cathryn Alpert for older adoptive parents.

Books and Websites

These resources for *Brothers and Sisters in Adoption: Helping Children Navigate Relationships When New Kids Join the Family* describe the types of challenges adoption can bring to families. They offer information for parents and their adult children.

Brodzinsky, David; Marshall Schecter and Robin Marantz Henig. *Being Adopted: The Lifelong Search for Self.* (New York: Anchor Books, 1993.)

Gray, Deborah D. *Attaching in Adoption.* (Indianapolis: Perspectives Press, Inc., 2002.)

Keck, Gregory C. and Regina M. Kupecky. *Adopting the Hurt Child: Hope for Families with Special-Needs Kids: A Guide for Parents and Professionals.* (Colorado Springs: NavPress, 1995.)

Keck, Gregory C. and Regina M. Kupecky. *Parenting the Hurt Child: Helping Adoptive Families Heal and Grow.* (Colorado Springs: NavPress, 2002.)

Schooler, Jayne E. and Thomas C. Atwood. *Whole Life Adoption Book.* (Colorado Springs: NavPress, 1993, revised 2008.)

Steinberg,Gail and Beth Hall. *Inside Transracial Adoption.* (Indianapolis: Perspectives Press, Inc., 2000.)

Register, Cheri. *A Mother Reflects on Raising Internationally Adopted Children.* (St. Paul, MN: Yeong and Yeong Book Co., 2005.)

Wright, Marguerite. *I'm Chocolate, You're Vanilla: Raising Healthy Black and Biracial Children in a Race-Conscious World.* (New York: Jossey-Bass, 1998.)

Websites

Association for Treatment and Training in the Attachment of Children (ATTACh)
www.attach.org

ATTACh is an international coalition of professionals and families dedicated to helping those with attachment difficulties by sharing their knowledge, talents and resources. The ATTACh vision is to be an international leader in creating public awareness and education regarding attachment and the critical role it plays in human development. They provide a quarterly newsletter, an annual conference, membership directory, and other benefits to members and the public. CDs of workshops from their annual conferences are available. The topics cover all aspects of the attachment between child and parent, as well as various aspects of adoptive family life.

Child Welfare Information Gateway
www.childwelfare.gov

The Child Welfare Information Gateway is a comprehensive resource on all aspects of adoption and is a service of the Children's Bureau; Administration for Children and Families; and the Department of Health and Human Services. Services include technical assistance to professionals and policy makers, a library collection, publications, searchable databases on adoption resources, and information on federal and state legislation. This website is packed with articles on all aspects of adoption and trauma. Parents and professionals will find this organization of utmost assistance pre- and post-adoption.

International Adoption Medicine Program, University of Minnesota
www.med.umn.edu/peds/iac/

This clinic was the first clinic in the United States to provide for the health needs of internationally adopted children. Anyone interested in international adoption should review the assortment of articles contained on this website. The articles offer a wealth of information about the medical needs of children adopted inter-country as well as the types of long-term developmental issues parents may expect to face. There are also recommendations for pre- and post-placement evaluations.

The National Organization on Fetal Alcohol Syndrome
www.nofas.org

NOFAS is the leading voice and resource of the Fetal Alcohol Spectrum Disorders (FASD) community. This website provides articles and additional resources for those parenting or working with children with FASD. The "Living with FASD" section offers great strategies for helping children with FASD. The tips are organized according to the child's developmental stage.

National Child Traumatic Stress Network
www.nctsn.org

NCTSN is a unique collaboration of academic and community-based service centers whose mission is to raise the standard of care, and increase access to services for traumatized children and their families across the United States. Combining knowledge of child development, expertise in the full range of child traumatic experiences and attention to cultural perspectives, the NCTSN serves as a national resource for developing and disseminating evidence-based interventions, trauma-informed services, and public and professional education. This website is a must read for parents and professionals. It covers the impact of all types of trauma on the child's development. There are articles and videos viewable online. This website is the home of information related to the complex trauma described in this chapter.

North American Council on Adoptable Children (NACAC)
www.nacac.org

NACAC promotes and supports permanent families for children and youth in the U.S. and Canada who have been in care—especially those in foster care and those with special needs. NACAC offers a quarterly newsletter *Adoptalk* replete with cutting edge articles pertaining to all aspects of adoption. Their annual conference is always exciting and informative. Child care is available at this parent-friendly conference. Tapes of conference workshop sessions may be purchased at (www.adoptiontapes.com). The NACAC website contains articles covering all facets of transcultural adoption. Subsidy information and a nationwide listing of adoptive parent support groups can also be found at NACAC.

Pact—An Adoption Alliance
www.pactadopt.org

Pact is a non-profit organization with a primary mission to serve children of color in need of adoption or who are growing up in adoptive families. In every case, the child is their primary client. They believe that to serve the child we must support and serve his or her adoptive parents by offering the very best resources to help them cope with a world whose attitudes too often reflect "adoptism" and racism. If you are looking for information related to any transcultural adoption issue, you are sure to find it on the Pact website! Pact makes available *Below the Surface*, a self-assessment guide for parents considering transcultural or transracial adoptions. Pact also has an online book store—all books are reviewed by Pact prior to selection for this store.

Magazines for All Families

***Adoption Today* Magazine**
www.adoptinfo.net

This is the only magazine dedicated to international and transracial adoption.

Adoptive Families Magazine
www.adoptivefamilies.com

Adoptive Families magazine is a national, award-winning adoption magazine providing information for families before, during and after adoption. The *Adoptive Families* website offers a *wealth* of adoption related articles!

Fostering Families Today Magazine
www.fosteringfamiliestoday.com

This magazine is packed with honest and poignant articles related to foster care and adoption. This magazine is a must read for anyone involved with children from the child welfare system.

"But will they be *real* brothers and sisters?" Families with Typically developing Siblings by Adoption and/or Birth

This article has been developed specifically for inclusion in *Brothers and Sisters in Adoption* by Patricia Irwin Johnston, author of *Adopting: Sound Choices, Strong Families* and *Adoption Is a Family Affair!*, and adoption educator and mom through adoption to a family of three typically developing children who are now adults. It was adapted from the earlier article, "Sibling Attachment" (see Resources, below).

Research shows that for those who have brothers or sisters, sibling relationships—whether healthy or unhealthy, loving or antagonistic—are the longest-lasting and most constant intimate relationships formed by human beings, lasting longer than most friendships, through the deaths of parents and beyond marriages, extending a shared history and deeply rooted shared experience from early childhood into old age. Many of us who have planned families to include more than one child made this decision partially because we hoped our children would gain from the richness and support of sibling relationships.

As an adoption educator and as a publisher working exclusively in the world of infertility and adoption, among the groups of people I hear from most often are those considering adding to a family already in progress by adopting an infant (sometimes of another race) and those who began a family by adopting and are now pregnant or considering becoming pregnant to add a child by birth. The children already resident in these families are almost always developing in a normal fashion, and because the child who will be added to the family is to be very young and will come from circumstances unlikely to have produced pre-natal or early childhood trauma, the parents' reasonable expectations are that the next child will develop typically as well. Most often those expectations come true.

Still, these parents worry. Even the staunchest adoption advocates can sometimes find that their thinking has been compromised by the adoptism[4] that is rampant in our society. These families' two biggest worries are actually attachment-based:

- "Will we, can we, love a child who is not genetically related to us as much as we could love a child born to us?" Turned another way, this question becomes "Is attachment genetic?"

4. Adoptism defined: Biased cultural beliefs that families formed by adoption are less truly connected than are birth families; that forming a family by birth is superior to forming a family by adoption; that keeping a child with his biological parents is inherently "better" than placing a child for adoption; that for those growing up as adopted people the primary determinant of human traits, characteristics, and behavior is genetics; that differences in family-building structures or methods produce an inherent superiority in family of a particular structure or method. Gail Steinberg and Beth Hall. *Inside Transracial Adoption*. (Indianapolis: Perspectives Press, Inc., 2000.)

- And (most relevant to this article) these parents wonder, "Can children who are not genetically connected to one another forge the same quality of attachment that siblings raised in families formed exclusively by birth do?"

Despite these worries, these parents' desire for their children to have brothers and sisters is strong, because cultural expectations about the value of siblings are also strong. They come to educators and experienced parents like me for answers to these concerns.

The answer to the first question couldn't be easier. The answer for those parenting in pairs is clear: you are already attached to a person not genetically related to you! Attachment between adults follows in the same "cycle of trust" cited several times in this book, as do the attachment relationships between parents and individual children and attachment relationships between siblings.

The bottom line, I tell them, is what follows in this article, and can be summarized like this: ***When typically developing children are raised in a healthy family environment by confident, well-adjusted parents who are treating their children as individuals with unique needs, who respect that the culture of the immediate family they form is one blended by the heritage of each family member, and who bolster the history and the culture of the family as belonging to all family members, sibling relationships can be expected to be "normal" and strong.*** I tell them with confidence that typically developing families like theirs, whether built exclusively by birth, exclusively by adoption, or by a blend of the two, don't need a book of their own. They need general parenting books. Their families are "normal," with an adoption "twist" that must be recognized, but which is adequately covered by books on broader adoption themes.

Brother/Sister Definitions—Child View, Adult View

Fact: Kids think differently than do adults. Those of you who have read the work of Swiss psychiatrist Jean Piaget are already familiar with his theories of the changes in children's cognitive abilities over time. Many of you are no doubt familiar with the related adoption-specific research of Dr. David Brodzinsky. Others have also read the related work of Dr. Anne Bernstein (author of *Flight of the Stork: What Children Think and When about Sex and Family Building*, Perspectives Press, Inc.). If you haven't read these things, you simply must. They should be required reading for all of us—both parents and professionals.

In examining sibling relationships, this research tells us that adults' expectations for their children's sibling relationships reflect many years of personal experience and education, adding to their expectations layers of genetic as well as emotional meaning. But the research also indicates that for young children, family relationships are purely social in nature.

While it is true that we can never have too many people who love us, no matter how adults label other children in their lives—using legal, social, genetic or other ties to create terminology—for young children, the definitions are simpler: brothers and sisters are those children with whom one grows up and shares parents. Young children think in concrete terms. So even in a family that includes adoption, whether open or confidential, whether there are siblings being raised in other families, and however much the adults try to explain, in the young child's mind, it's simple: brothers and sisters are those with whom a child lives. Brother is the guy who *never* shares his stuff. Sister is the person who *never* cleans toothpaste out of the sink and *always* blames me for it. Sister is the person who *always* agrees that Mom and Dad are too strict. Brother is the one who *always* remembers that one time when . . .

That birth brother seen never or infrequently, or that half sister who lives downstate with the weekend-visiting parent in common, will not be experienced by a young child as siblings in the same way as those children with whom he lives his daily life. Good friends? Maybe. Linkages akin to those of close cousins? Perhaps. But not siblings.

Why should this be surprising? Even in the most open adoptions, feelings about birth mother and birthfather are not the same as feelings about mommy and daddy, and do not encompass the societal expectations for those feelings about, and relationships with, mothers and fathers.

It is mostly the limitations of language which create confusion. A brown young child asked about his white housemate—"Is that your brother?"—has no idea why this concept strikes outsiders as odd; after all, this person may be the only brother he has ever known. An older child introduced for the first time to the 6-year-old as "your brother" will not "feel like" brother.

As children mature, they will become better able to make sense of connections that are not just social and will be more interested in the distinctions. We know, for example, that during adolescence, many adopted people begin to feel intensely interested in the concept of genetic connection and what it might mean for them. Genetic relatives might be able to provide some explanation for how one looks, or why one possesses or lacks skills for certain physical or intellectual or artistic endeavors. They might offer some insight into how tall or how shapely one might be as an adult. As adopted people approach adolescence, they are likely to be ready to be interested in, and to understand and appreciate, additional complexities about the existence of, or relationship with, their genetic siblings.

Do sibling relationships differ in adoption-expanded families?

Whether siblings are related by birth or by adoption, a variety of issues colors relationships, including general family culture and closeness, the sex of the children, their relative ages, their position in the family, the size of the family, similarity or disparity of interests and talents, individual children's personality styles, and each person's sense of "psychological fit" within the family system.

Does adoption change this? Yes. No. Maybe.

Even families formed entirely by birth frequently include one or more family members who feel "different" from the others. Certainly, since the children and parents in adoption-expanded families have differing genetic backgrounds, they cannot expect to be as prone to be "alike" physically, intellectually, or emotionally as are people who have a genetic connection. So adoption-expanded families may be more "at risk" for poor matches than are birth-connected siblings and parents.

But parents can do much to work on these issues. Here is a list of ideas to consider:

1. Every child deserves to be wanted, loved and valued for who he is rather than as a stopgap or replacement for a child one dreams of parenting. It is my belief that parents who thoughtfully embrace and consistently practice this principle—treating each child as a unique individual with unique needs—will make decisions for themselves and their children that are truly child-centered. For example, avoid artificial twinning. Many adoptive parents deliberately pursue two adoptions at once. These decisions are nearly always parent-centered. After

struggling so long to become parents, they think it will be great to have two at a time and to get the difficult family-formation period over with. Often parents are not truthful with birth parents or intermediaries about such efforts. Result? Family relationships based on half-truths or outright lies that WILL catch up with you. Two genetically dissimilar kids will nearly always be parented as a pair, and thus are "set up" to be compared by peers, teachers and coaches and on whom the spotlight of being different and being adopted will be obvious throughout their lives.

2. Treat each child as the individual he or she is. For example, life is not fair, so don't base parenting decisions on making all things equal. Just as no two adoptions are alike, and no two sets of birth parents and their circumstances are alike, no two children are alike and so can't be expected to feel the same way about adoption issues in their lives. Some kids wonder, some don't. Some kids enjoy extended family relationships in open adoptions and some don't. Some adopted people who grew up in confidential adoptions search and some don't. What children need more than "fairness" is to know that, as their parent, you are "on their side," ready to help them meet their needs—whatever they may be.
3. Do all that you can to nurture a sense of shared family culture. Carefully cultivating and highlighting religious and holiday traditions, the family's shared mealtime and bedtime rituals, favorite foods and family recipes, books and songs and games, and repeated visits to favorite places all contribute to each child's sense of "us" as a family unit.
4. Watch for and support the ways in which children separated by age or of opposite sexes discover things they enjoy in common—perhaps even more so when you discover that those things shared by your children are not things you yourself enjoy, thus contributing to their sense of conspiratorial generation vs. generation intimacy.
5. Be realistic in your expectations about sibling relationships. Did you always get along with your brother? Did you willingly share friends with your close-in-age sister? It is not uncommon for siblings to be close as very young children, become more distant from or unpleasantly competitive with one another as they grow, and then rediscover one another as adults.

A common store of family-based and sibling-inclusive family experiences enhances the sense of family that each of us takes into adulthood. When parents are gone, it is this we will leave our children: memories and values that root them against the storms of life, and siblings—brothers and sisters—who share these roots.

Resources

Books

Bernstein, Anne C. *Flight of the Stork: What Children Think (and When) about Sex and Family Building*. (Indianapolis: Perspectives Press, Inc., 1994.)

Faber, Adele and Elaine Mazlish. *Siblings without Rivalry*. (New York: HarperCollins, 1987.)

Steinberg, Gail and Beth Hall. *Inside Transracial Adoption: Strength-based, Culture-sensitizing Parenting Strategies for Inter-country or Domestic Adoptive Families That Don't "Match."* (Indianapolis: Perspectives Press, Inc., 2000.)

Articles

Hall, Beth. "Blended Families." *Pact's Point of View, the Newsletter of Pact: An Adoption Alliance.* Online at http://www.pactadopt.org/press/articles/blended-fam.html

Houlihan, Collen. "The Real Daughter." Online at www.pactadopt.org/press/articles/real-daughter.html

Johnston, Patricia Irwin. "Sibling Attachment." *Pact's Point of View, the Newsletter of Pact: An Adoption Alliance.* Online at www.pactadopt.org/press/articles/sib-attach.html and at http://www.rainbowkids.com/ArticleDetails.aspx?id=582

Melina, Lois. "The Sibling Connection." *Adoptive Families Magazine.* Online at http://www.adoptivefamilies.com/articles.php?aid=1182

Meltz, Barbara. "Is That Your Real Sister?" *Adoptive Families Magazine.* Online at www.adoptivefamilies.com/articles.php?aid=1185

Roszia, Sharon Kaplan (interviewed by Beth Hall.) "Adopting Again: Talking to Other Children in the Home." *Pact's Point of View, the Newsletter of Pact: An Adoption Alliance.* Online at www.pactadopt.org/press/articles/again.html

Shore, Amy. "Adopting a Sister." *Adoptive Families Magazine.* Online at www.adoptivefamilies.com/articles.php?aid=1185Glennen, Sharon. (2002.) "Orphanage care and language." http://pages.towson.edu/sglennen/index.htm

Johnson, Dana. (2007). "Medical Issues in International Adoption." *Adoptive Families Magazine*, Jan/Feb, 18–20.

Johnston, Patricia Irwin. (2002). "Sibling attachment." http://www.perspectivespress.com and http://www.pactadopt.org

Judge, Katherine. (1994.) "Serving children, siblings and spouses: Understanding the needs of other family members. In Harriet P. Lefley and Mona Wasow, *Helping Families Cope with Mental Illness.* Chur, Switzerland: Harwood Academic Publishers.

Kaplan, Carol. (1988.) "The biological children of foster parents in the foster family." *Child and Adolescent Social Work*, 5, 281–299.

Kaplan-Rozia and Deborah Silverstein. "Adoptees and the Seven Core Issues of Adoption," developed and presented first in 1988.

Katz, Lilian and Diane McClellan, (1991.) "The teacher's role in the social development of young children." ERIC Clearinghouse on Elementary and Early Childhood Education. Urbana: Illinois.

Van der Kolk, Bessel. (1989.) "The compulsion to repeat the trauma: Re-enactment, revictimization and masochism." *Psychiatric Clinics of North America*, 12 (2), 389–411. References

References

Books

Bank, Stephen, P. and Michael D. Kahn. *The Sibling Bond.* (New York: Basic Books, 1997.)

Belsky, Jay and John Kelly. *The Transition to Parenthood: How a First Child Changes a Marriage.* (New York: Delacorte, 1994.)

Biller, Henry B. and Robert J. Trotter. *The Father Factor.* (New York: Simon and Schuster, 1994.)

Bowlby, John. *Attachment and Loss, Volume III Loss: Sadness and Depression.* (New York: Basic Books, 1980.)

Briere, John, N. and Catherine Scott. *Principles of Trauma Therapy: A Guide to Symptoms, Evaluation and Treatment.* (Thousand Oaks: Sage Publications, 2006.)

Bruce, Elizabeth, J. and Cynthia L. Schultz. *Nonfinite Loss and Grief: A Psychoeducational* Approach. (Baltimore: Paul H. Brooks, 2001.)

Campbell, Don. *The Mozart Effect for Children: Awakening Your Child's Mind, Health, and Creativity with Music.* (New York: Black Thistle Press, 2000.)

Carter, Rosalynn and Susan Golant. *Helping Someone with Mental Illness.* (New York: Three Rivers Press, 1998.)

Chasnoff, Ira, Linda Schwartz, Cheryl Pratt and Gwendolyn Neuberger. *Risk and Promise: A Handbook for Parents Adopting a Child from Cverseas.* (Chicago, NTI Upstream, 2006.)

Cicirelli, Victor, G. *Sibling Relationships across the Life Span.* (New York: Plenum Press, 1995.)

Cline, Foster and Jim Fay. *Parenting with Love and Logic.* (Colorado Springs: NavPress, 2006.)

Cooper, Joel. *Cognitive Dissonance: Fifty Years of a Classic Theory.* (Thousand Oaks: Sage Publications, 2007.)

Courtney, Mark.E., Amy Dworsky, Gretchen Ruth, Tom Keller, Judy Havlicek and Noel Bost. *Midwest Evaluation of the Adult Functioning of Former Foster Youth: Outcomes at Age 21.* (Chicago, IL: Chapin Hall Center for Children, University of Chicago, 2007.)

Colozino, Louis. *The Neuroscience of Human Relationships: Attachment and the Developing Social Brain.* (New York: W.W. Norton & Co., 2006.)

Crumbley, Joseph. *Transracial Adoption and Foster Care: Practice Issues for Professionals.* (Washington, DC: Child Welfare League of America, 1999.)

Fahlberg, Vera. *A Child's Journey through Placement.* (Indianapolis: Perspectives Press, Inc., 1991.)

Festinger, Leon. *A Theory of Cognitive Dissonance.* (Stanford: Stanford University Press, 1957.)

Gilman, Lois. *The Adoption Resource Book.* (New York: Harper Collins Publishers, 1992.)

Ginther, Norma, Betsy Keefer and Nan Beeler. *Keeping Your Adult Relationship Healthy in Adoption.* (Columbus: Institute for Human Services for the Ohio Child Welfare Training Program, 2003.)

Hopkins-Best, Mary. *Toddler Adoption: The Weaver's Craft.* (Indianapolis: Perspectives Press, Inc., 1997.)

Jewett, Claudia. *Adopting the Older Child.* (Boston: The Harvard Common Press, 1978.)

Johnson, Julie Tallard. *Hidden Victims, Hidden Healers: An Eight-Stage Healing Process for Families and Friends of the Mentally Ill.* (Edina, Minnesota: PEMA Publications, 1994.)

Johnston, Patricia Irwin. *Adopting: Sound Choices, Strong Families*. (Indianapolis: Perspectives Press, Inc., 2008.)

Karp, David. *The Burden of Empathy: How Families Cope with Mental Illness*. (New York: Oxford University Press, 2001.)

Keck, Gregory, C., and Regina M. Kupecky. *Adopting the Hurt Child: Hope for Families with Special Needs Kids*. (Colorado Springs: NavPress, 1995.)

Keck, Gregory, C., and Regina M. Kupecky. *Parenting the Hurt Child: Helping Adoptive Families Heal and Grow.* (Colorado Springs: NavPress, 2002.)

Keefer, Betsy and Jayne E. Schooler. *Telling the Truth to Your Adopted or Foster Child: Making Sense of the Past*. (Westport: Bergin & Garvey, 2000.)

Kübler-Ross, Elizabeth. *On Death and Dying: What the Dying Have to Teach Doctors, Nurses, Clergy and their Own Families*. (New York: Scribner, 1969.)

Kübler-Ross, Elizabeth and David. *On Grief and Grieving: Finding the Meaning of Grief through the Fve Stages of Grief.* (New York: Scribner, 2005.)

Lamb, Michael E. (ed.). *The Role of the Father in Child Development* (3rd edition). (New York: John Wiley & Sons, Inc., 1997.)

Lamb, Michael E. *The Role of the Father in Child Development*. (4th edition). (New York: John Wiley & Sons, Inc., 2003.)

Lobato, Debra. *Brothers, Sisters, and Special Needs: Information and Activities for Helping Young Siblings of Children with Chronic Illnesses and Developmental Disabilities*. (Baltimore: Paul Brooks Publishing, 1990.)

Meyer, Donald, J. and Patricia F. Vadasy. *Sibshops: Workshops for Siblings of Children with Special Needs*. (Baltimore: Paul H. Brooks Publishing Co., 1994.)

Montagu, Ashley. *Touching: The Human Significance of the Skin*. (New York: Harper & Row, 1971.)

Pavao, Joyce Maguire.*The Family of Adoption*. (Boston: Beacon Press, 2005.)

Perry, Bruce and Maia Szalavitz. *The Boy Who was Raised as a Dog and Other Stories from a Child Psychiatrist's Notebook: What Traumatized Children can Teach Us about Loss, Love and Healing*. (New York: Basic Books, 2006.)

Powell, Thomas H. and Peggy A. Gallagher. *Brothers and Sisters: A Special Part of Exceptional Families* (2nd edition). (Baltimore: Paul H. Brooks Publishing Co., 1993.)

Pruett, Kyle. T*he Nurturing Father: Journey Toward the Complete Man*. (Clayton, VIC: Warner Books, 1987.)

Pruett, Kyle. *Fatherneed: Why Father Care Is as Essential as Mother Care for Your Child.* (New York: Broadway Books, 2000.)

Ratey, John J., MD. *A User's Guide to the Brain: Perception, Attention and the Four Theaters of the Brain*. (New York: Pantheon Books, 2001.)

Santrock, John, W. *Life-Span Development*. (Dubuque: Wm. C. Brown Communications, Inc., 1995.)

Schooler, Jayne, Betsy Keefer, Denise Goodman, Nan Beeler, and Judith Rycus. (1999.) *Prefinalization Adoption Services*. Columbus: Institute for Human Services for the Ohio Child Welfare Training Program.

Seigel, Daniel, J. *The Developing Mind: How Relationships and the Brain Interact to Shape Who We Are*. (New York: The Guilford Press, 2001.)

Sparrow, Joshua. *Understanding Sibling Rivalry: The Brazelton Way*. (Cambridge: Da Capo Press, 2005.)

Trozzi, Maria and Kathy Massimini. *Talking with Children about Loss: Words, Strategies, and Wisdom to Help Children Cope with Death, Divorce, and other Difficult Times*. (New York: Penguin Putnam, 1999.)

Articles (In Print and Online)

"AFCARS Report #13."Health and Human Services. (Administration for Children and Families, Administration on Children, Youth and Families, Children's Bureau, www.acf.hhs.gov/programs/cb/stats_research/afcars/tar/report13.htm, 2006.)

American Academy of Pediatrics, Committee on Early Childhood, Adoption and Dependent Care. "Health care of young children in foster care." *Pediatrics*, 109 (3), 2002: 536-541.

Balk, David. "The self-concepts of bereaved adolescents: Sibling death and its aftermath." *Journal of Adolescent Research*, 5 (1), 1990: 112-132.

Barbell, Kathy and Madelyn Freundlich. "Foster care today: An examination of foster care at the start of the 21st century." Washington, DC: Casey Family Programs. http://www.casey.org/Resources/Archive/Publications/FosterCareToday.htm, 2001.

Barber, James, G., Paul H. Delfabbro and L.L. Cooper. "The predictors of unsuccessful transition to foster care." *Journal of Child Psychology and Psychiatry*, 42 (6), 2001: 785-790.

Barth, Richard, P.; Chung Kwon Lee, Judith Wildfire and Shenyang Guo. "A comparison of the governmental costs of long-term foster care and adoption." *Social Services Review*, 80 (1), 2006: 127-158.

Belsky, Jay. "The determinants of parenting: A process model." *Child Development*, 55, 1984: 83-96.

Berry, Marianne and Richard Barth. "A study of disrupted adoptive placements of adolescents." *Child Welfare, 69* (3), 1990: 209-225.

Biller, Henry B. and Jon L. Kimpton. "The father and the school-aged child." *The role of the father in child development* (3rd edition). New York: John Wiley & Sons, Inc., 1997.

Briere, John N. and Diana M. Elliott. "Immediate and long-term impacts of child sexual abuse." *The Future of Children*, 4, 1994: 54-69.

Buehler, Cheryl, Katie Rhodes, John Orme and Gary Cuddeback. "The potential for successful family foster care: Conceptualizing competency domains for foster parents." *Child Welfare*, 85, 2006: 523-558.

Casas, Paula. "Toward the ABCs: Building a healthy social and emotional foundation for learning and living." Chicago: Ounce of Prevention, http://www.ounceofprevention.org/downloads/programs/Towards_the_ABCs.pdf, 2001.

Child Welfare Information Gateway. "Kinship caregivers and the child welfare system: Factsheet for families." Washington, DC: U.S. Department of Health and Human Services, http://www.childwelfare.gov/pubs/f_kinshi/f_kinshia.cfm, 2005.

Child Welfare Information Gateway. "Parenting the Sexually Abused Child." Washington, DC: U.S. Department of Health and Human Services, http://www.childwelfare.gov/pubs/f_abused/index.cfm, 1990.

Child Welfare Information Gateway. "Searching for birth relatives: Factsheet for families." Washington, DC: U.S. Department of Health and Human Services, http://www.childwelfare.gov/pubs/f_search.pdf, 2004.

Child Welare Information Gateway. "Selecting and working with an adoption therapist." Washington, DC: U.S. Department of Health and Human Services, http://www.childwelfare.gov/pubs/f_therapist.pdf, 2005.

Child Welfare Information Gateway. "Sibling issues in foster care and adoption: A bulletin for professionals." Washington, DC: U.S. Department of Health and Human Services, http://www.childwelfare.gov/pubs/siblingissues/siblingissues.pdf, 2006.

Child Welfare Information Gateway. "Understanding the effects of maltreatment on early brain development: A bulletin for professionals." Washington, DC: U.S. Department of Health and Human Services, http://www.childwelfare.gov/pubs/focus/earlybrain/earlybrain.pdf, 2001.

Children and Family Research Center. "Multiple placements in foster care: Literature review of correlates and predictors." http://cfrcwww.social.uiuc.edu/LRpdfs/PlacementStability.LR.pdf, 2004.

College Entrance Examination Board. "College-bound seniors national report: Profile of SAT program test takers." Princeton, New Jersey, 2001.

Cook, Alexander, Margaret Blaustein, Joseph Spinazzola and Bessell van der Kolk, Bessell (eds.). "Complex trauma in children and adolescents." National Child Traumatic Stress Network, http://www.NCTSNet.org, 2003.

Cooper, Carolyn.S., Nancy L. Peterson and John H. Meier. "Variables associated with disrupted placement in a select sample of abused and neglected children." *Child Abuse & Neglect*, 11, 1987: 75-86.

Courtney, Mark. E., Irving Piliavin, Andrew Grogan-Kaylor and Ande Nesmith. "Foster youth transitions to adulthood: A longitudinal view of youth leaving care." Child Welfare, 80 (6), 2001: 685-717.

Cummings, E. Mark and Anne Watson O'Reilly. "Fathers in family context: Effects of marital quality on child adjustment." *The Role of the Father in Child Development* (3rd edition). New York: John Wiley & Sons, Inc., 1997.

Cummings, S. T. "The impact of the child's deficiency on the father: A study of fathers of mentally retarded and chronically ill children." *The Role of the Father in Child Development* (3rd edition). New York: John Wiley & Sons, Inc., 1976.

Cowan, Carolyn.P., Phillip A. Cowan, Gertrude Heming, Ellen Garrett, William S. Coysh, Harriet Curtis-Boles and Abner J. Boles, Abner. "Transitions to Parenthood: His, hers and theirs." *Journal of Family Issues*, 6 (4), 1985: 451-481.

Davies, Patrick and Mark Cummings. "Marital conflict and child adjustment: An emotional security hypothesis." *Psychological Bulletin*, 116 (3), 1994: 387-411.

Dore, Martha.M., and Eleanor Eisner. "Child-related dimensions of placement stability in treatment foster care." *Child & Adolescent Social Work Journal*, 10, 1993: 301-317.

Erickson, Marcene. "Talking with fathers of young children with Down Syndrome." *Children Today*, 3, 1974: 22-25.

Evan B. Donaldson Institute. "What's working for children: A policy study of adoption stability and termination." http://www.adoptioninstitute.org/publications/Disruption_Report.pdf, 2004.

Freundlich, Madelyn and North American Council on Adoptable Children (NACAC) staff. "Post-adoption services: Meeting the mental health needs of children adopted from foster care." http://www.nacac.org/adoptalk/postadoptpaper.pdf, 2007.

Friedrich, Rose Marie, Sonja Lively and Linda M. Rubenstein. "Siblings' coping strategies and mental health services: A national study of siblings of persons with schizophrenia." *Psychiatric Services*, 59 (3), 2008: 261-267.

Gill, Margaret. "Adoption of older children: The problems faced." *Social Casework*, May, 1978: 272-278.

Grindis, Boris. "Language development in internationally adopted children." *China Connection* (newsletter for New England Families who have adopted children from China), 10 (2), 2004: 34-37.

Glen, Norval and Charles Weaver. "A multivariate multisurvey study of marital happiness." *Journal of Marriage and The Family*. 40 (May), 1978: 269-282.

Glennen, Sharon. "Orphanage care and language." http://pages.towson.edu/sglennen/index.htm, 2002.

Glennen, Sharon. "Speech and language in children adopted internationally at older age." Perspectives on Communication Disorders and Sciences in Culturally and Linguistically Diverse Populations." *American Speech Language Hearing Association Division 14 Newsletter*, 14 (3), 2007: 17-20.

Goetting, Ann. "The developmental tasks of siblingship over the life cycle." *Journal of Marriage and the Family*, 48 (November), 1986: 703-714.

Hartnett, Mary Ann, Sonya Leathers, Lydia Falconnier and Mark Testa. "Placement stability study." Urbana, IL: Children and Family Research Center, 1999.

Hartup, Willard. "Having friends, making friends, and keeping friends: Relationships as educational contexts." ERIC Digest: ED345854. http://www.eric.ed.gov/, 1992

Hicks, Mary and Marilyn Platt. "Marital happiness and stability: A review of research in the sixties." *Journal of Marriage and the Family*, 32 (November), 1971: 553-573.

Hogan, Nancy and Daryl Greenfield. "Adolescent sibling bereavement symptomatology in a large community sample." *Journal of Adolescent Research*, 6 (1), 1991: 97-112.

Holtan, Barbara, Tim McCarrgher and Arleta James. "Eastern European Adoption Dissolution: An Exploratory Study." Unpublished, 2006.

Hosley, C.A. and R. Montemayor. "Fathers and adolescents." *The Role of the Father in Child Development* (3rd edition.) New York: John Wiley & Sons, Inc., 1997.

Ingels, Steven, J. "National Education Longitudinal Study (NELS): 88 first follow up." ERIC Digest: ED354257, 1992.

Ingersoll, Barbara. D. "Psychiatric disorders among adopted children: A review and commentary." *Adoption Quarterly*, 1, 1997: 57-73.

Iverson, Sandra and Dana Johnson. "Medical concerns for international adoptees: A guide for pediatricians and other health care providers." Report on Intercountry Adoption. Adoption Resource of Connecticut. Glastonbury, CT http://www.med.umn.edu/img/assets/17664/med_concerns_intl_adoptees.pdf, 2005.

Johnson, Dana. "Medical issues in international adoption." http://www.med.umn.edu/img/assets/17664/medical_issues.pdf, 1997.

Johnson, Dana. "Medical and developmental sequelae of early childhood institutionalization in eastern European adoptees." Minnesota Symposia on Child Psychology, 31 (4), 2000: 113-162.

Johnson, Dana. "International adoption: What is fact?, What is fiction?, and What is the future?" *Pediatric Clinics of North America*, 52, 2005: 1221-1246.

Johnson, Dana. "Medical Issues in International Adoption." *Adoptive Families Magazine*, Jan/Feb, 2007: 18-20.

Johnston, Patricia Irwin. "Sibling attachment." http://www.perspectivespress.com and http://www.pactadopt.org, 2002.

Judge, Katherine. "Serving children, siblings and spouses: Understanding the needs of other family members." *Helping Families Cope with Mental Illness*. Chur, Switzerland: Harwood Academic Publishers, 1994.

Kaplan, Carol. "The biological children of foster parents in the foster family." *Child and Adolescent Social Work,* 5, 1988: 281-299.

Kaplan-Rozia and Deborah Silverstein. "Adoptees and the Seven Core Issues of Adoption," developed and presented first in 1988.

Katz, Lilian and Diane McClellan. "The teacher's role in the social development of young children." ERIC Clearinghouse on Elementary and Early Childhood Education. Urbana, Illinois, 1991.

Kaye, Kenneth. "Acknowledgement or rejection of differences?" *The Psychology of Adoption*, New York: Oxford University Press, 1990.

Kendall-Tackett, Kathleen. A., Linda M. Williams and David Finkelhor. "Impact of sexual abuse on children: A review and synthesis of recent empirical studies." *Psychological Bulletin*, 113, 1993: 164-180.

Lamb, Michael E., and Lisa A. Laumann-Billings. "Fathers of children with special needs." *The Role of the Father in Child Development* (3rd edition). New York: John Wiley & Sons, Inc., 1997.

Lemieux, J.D. "The effects of foster placement on the biological children of foster parents: An exploratory investigation." Doctoral dissertation, University of Tennessee. Dissertation Abstracts International, 45, 06 (1984): Sec B.

Lewis, Robert A. and Grahm B. Spanier. "Theorizing about the quality and stability of marriage." *Contemporary Theories about the Family, Vol. I.* New York: Free Press, 1979.

Lindeman, Leslie, Gina Kemp and Jeanne Segal. "Humor, laughter and health: Bringing more humor and laughter into our lives." http://www.helpguide.org/life/humor_laughter_health.htm, 2007.

Lukens, Ellen P., Helle Thorning and Steven P. Lohrer. "How siblings of those with severe mental illness perceive services and support." *Journal of Psychiatric Practice*, 8 (6), 2002: 354-364.

Lutz, Lorrie. "Strengthening Families and Communities: An Approach to Post-Adoption Services." *Casey Center for Effective Child Welfare Practice White Paper*. Casey Family Services, http://www.caseyfamilyservices.org/p_ccenter_publications.html, 2005.

Meyer, Donald. "Fathers of children with mental handicaps." *The Father's Role: Applied Perspectives*. New York: John Wiley & Sons, Inc., 1986.

McClellan, Diane and Lilian Katz. "Young children's social development: A checklist." ERIC Digest: ED356100, 1993.

Miller, Brent, C. "A multivariate developmental model of marital satisfaction." *Journal of Marriage and The Family*, 38 (November), 1976: 643-657.

Miller, F., J. Dworkin, M. Ward, and D. Barone. A preliminary study of unresolved grief in families of seriously mentally ill patients." *Helping Families Cope with Mental Illness*. Chur Switzerland: Harwood Academic Publishers, 1990.

Morgan, Roger. "About Adoption: A Children's Views Report." Office of Children's Rights,http://www.rights4me.org/content/beheardreports/105/about_adoption_report.pdf, 2006.

Müller, Ulrich and Barbara Perry. "Adopted persons' search for and contact with their birth parents I: Who searches and why?" *Adoption Quarterly*, 4 (3), 2001: 5-37.

Mullin, Ellen and LeAnne Johnson. "The role of birth/previously adopted children in families choosing to adopt children with special needs." *Child Welfare*, 78, 1999: 579-591.

Murphy, Henry B.M. "Foster home variables and adult outcomes." *Mental Hygiene*, 48, 1964: 587-599.

National Resource Center for AD/HD, A Program of Children and Adults with Attention-Deficit/Hyperactivity Disorder (CHADD). "Educational Rights for Children with Ad/HD in Public Schools." http://www.help4adhd.org/en/education/rights/WWK4, 2007.

Olesen, Mavis. "How siblings fair in difficult adoptions." *Adoptalk*, Summer, 2004.

Palmer, Sally. "Placement stability and inclusive practice in foster care: An empirical study." *Children and Youth Services Review*, 18 (7), 1996: 589-601.

Pardek, John. "Multiple placements of children in foster family care: An empirical analysis." *Social Work*, 29, 1984: 506-509.

Parten, Mildred, B. "Social participation among preschool children." *Journal of Abnormal Psychology*, 27, 1932: 243-269.

Perry, Bruce. "Incubated in terror: Neurodevelopmental factors in the cycle of violence." *Children, Youth and Violence: The Search for Solutions*. New York: Guilford Press, 1997.

Perry, Bruce. "Maltreatment and the developing child: How early childhood experiences shapes child and culture." http://www.lfcc.on.ca/mccain/perry1.html, 2004.

Peth-Pierce, Robin. "A good beginning: Sending America's children to school with the social and emotional competence they need to succeed." The Child Mental Health Foundations and Agencies Network (FAN), http://www.casel.org/downloads/goodbeginning.pdf, 2001.

Pinderhughes, Ellen. E. and Karen. F Rosenberg. "Family bonding with high risk placements: A therapy model that promotes the process of becoming a family." *Journal of Children in Contemporary Society, 21*, 1990: 204-230.

Poland, Denise and Victor Groze. "Effects of foster care placement on biological children in the home." *Child and Adolescent Social Work Journal*, 10, 1993: 153-164.

Proch, Kathleen and Merlin Taber. "Placement disruption: A review of research." *Children and Youth Services Review*, 7, 1985: 309-320.

Proch, Kathleen and Merlin Taber. "Alienated adolescents in foster care." *Social Work Research & Abstracts*, 23, 1987: 9-13.

Putnam, Frank. "Ten-year research update review: Child sexual abuse." *Journal of the American Academy of Child and Adolescent Psychiatry*, 42 (3), 2003: 269-278

Putnam, Frank. "The impact of trauma on child development." *Juvenile and Family Court Journal*, Winter, 2006: 1-11.

Radin, Norma. "The role of the father in cognitive, academic, and intellectual development." *The Role of the Father in Child Development*. New York: John Wiley & Sons, Inc., 1981.

Radin, Norma. "The influence of fathers on their sons and daughters and the implications for social work." *Social Work in Education*, 8, 1986: 77-91.

Rauscher, Frances H., Gordon L. Shaw, Linda J. Levine, Eric L. Wright, Wendy R. Dennis and Robert L. Newcomb. (1997.) "Music training causes long-term enhancement of preschool children's spatial-temporal reasoning." *Neurological Research*, 19, February, 1997.

Smith, Dana, Elizabeth Stormshack, Patricia Chamberlain and Rachel Whaley. "Placement disruption in treatment foster care." *Journal of Emotional and Behavioral Disorders*, 9 (3), 2001: 200-205.

Smith, Matthew, J., Jan S. Greenberg and Seltzer M. Mailick. "The effect of the quality of sibling relationships on the life satisfaction of adults with schizophrenia." *Psychiatric Services*, 58 (9), 2007: 1222-1224.

Stone, Norman. M. and Susan F. Stone. "The prediction of successful foster placement." *The Journal of Contemporary Social Work*, 1, 1983: 11-17.

Trickett, Penelope.K., Catherin McBride-Chang and Frank W. Putnam. "The classroom performance and behavior of sexually abused females." *Development and Psychopathology*, 6, 1994: 183-194.

Trickett, Penelope.K. and Frank W. Putnam. "Impact of child sexual abuse on females: Toward a developmental, psychobiological integration." *Psychological Science*, 4 (2), 1993: 81-87.

US Department of Health and Human Services. "Child maltreatment 1996: Reports from the states to the national child abuse and neglect data system." Washington, DC: US Government Printing Office, 1998.

US Department of State. "Immigrant visas issued to orphans coming to U.S." http://travel.state.gov/family/adoption/stats/stats_451.html, 2007.

Vadasy, Patricia F., Rebecca A. Fewell, Donald Meyer and Mark T. Greenberg. "Supporting fathers of handicapped young children: Preliminary findings of program effects." *Analysis and Intervention in Developmental Disabilities*, 5, 1985: 151-164.

Van der Kolk, Bessel. "The compulsion to repeat the trauma: Re-enactment, revictimization and masochism." *Psychiatric Clinics of North America*, 12 (2), 1989: 389-411.

Ward, Margaret. "The impact of adoption on the new parents' marriage." *Adoption Quarterly*, 2 (2), 1998: 57-74.

Ward, Margaret and John Lewko. "Adolescents in families adopting older children: Implications for service." *Child Welfare*, 66, 1987: 539-547.

Ward, Margaret and John Lewko. "Problems experienced by adolescents already in families that adopt older children." *Adolescence*, 23 (89), 1998: 221-228.

Wikler, Lynn., Mona Wasow and Elaine Hatfield. "Chronic sorrow revisited: Parent vs. professional depiction of adjustment of parents of mentally retarded children." *American Journal of Orthopsychiatry*, 51, 1981: 63-70.

Wooten, Patty. "Humor: An antidote for stress." *Holistic Nursing Practice*, 10 (2), 1996: 49-55.

Recorded Performances and Presentations

Aschmann, Lisa and Karen Taylor-Good, "The Eleventh Commandment." Nashville Geographic. 4869 Torbay Drive, Nashville, TN, 37211. The Eleventh Commandment was performed by Collin Raye and recorded by SONY/EPIC records.

Duehn, Wayne., and Sherry Anderson (speakers). "Creating Sexual Safety for Adopted Children and Their Parents." North American Council on Adoptable Children 30th Annual Conference, 2004. von Ende Communications 320-589-1092.

Keck, Gregory C., PhD (speaker). "Attachment therapy with adolescents." (Cassette Recording # 13B-9914). Association for the Treatment and Training in the Attachment of Children 11th International Conference on Attachment & Bonding, 1999. Resourceful Recordings 888-673-7732.

Pertman, Adam (speaker). "Attachment in the Media: What They don't Know can Hurt Us." Association for the Treatment and Training in the Attachment of Children. Providence, Rhode Island. (DVD Recording # K1-0739). Association for the Treatment and Training in the Attachment of Children 19th International Conference on Attachment & Bonding, 2007. Resourceful Recordings 888-673-7732.

Trout, Michael. *The Awakening and Growth of the Human, Unit IV: The Newborn, the Family, and the Dance* (VHS or DVD). Champaign: IL, The Infant-Parent Institute, 1986.

Villanueva, Kris (speaker). "Transitions: Moving Children with Sensitivity." North American Council on Adoptable Children 31st Annual Conference, 2005. von Ende Communications 320-589-1092.

Index

About the Publisher

Perspectives Press: The Infertility and Adoption Publisher

www.perspectivespress.com

Since 1982 Perspectives Press, Inc. has focused exclusively on infertility, adoption and related reproductive health and child welfare issues. Our purpose is to educate and support those experiencing these life situations, to educate and sensitize professionals who work in these fields, and to promote understanding of these issues to the public at large. Our titles are never duplicate of, or competitive with, good material already available through other publishers. Instead, we seek to find and fill empty niches.

Currently in-print titles include:

For Adults

Adopting: Sound Choices, Strong Families
Nurturing Adoptions
Having Your Baby through Egg Donation
Adoption Is a Family Affair: What Relatives and Friends Must Know
Attaching in Adoption
Inside Transracial Adoption
PCOS: The Hidden Epidemic
Launching a Baby's Adoption
Toddler Adoption: The Weaver's Craft
Looking Back, Looking Forward
Sweet Grapes: How to Stop Being Infertile and Start Living Again
Taking Charge of Infertility
Flight of the Stork: What Children Think (and When) about Sex and Family Building

A Child's Journey through Placement
Understanding Infertility: Insights for Family and Friends
Perspectives on a Grafted Tree: Thoughts for Those Touched by Adoption

For Children

Borya and the Burps
Sam's Sister
The Mulberry Bird
Filling in the Blanks.

Is there a book for our audience in you?

Our writer's guidelines are on our website at http://www.perspectivespress.com/writerguides.html

About the Author

ARLETA M. JAMES, MS, PCC, has been an adoption professional for a dozen years. She spent several years as a caseworker for the Pennsylvania Statewide Adoption Network placing foster children with adoptive families and then as the statewide Matching Specialist. She now works as a therapist providing services for attachment difficulties, childhood trauma and issues related to adoption. She was the 1999 Pennsylvania Adoption Professional of the Year. She is currently on staff at the Attachment and Bonding Center of Ohio.